1 MONTH OF
FREE
READING

at

www.ForgottenBooks.com

By purchasing this book you are eligible for one month membership to ForgottenBooks.com, giving you unlimited access to our entire collection of over 1,000,000 titles via our web site and mobile apps.

To claim your free month visit:

www.forgottenbooks.com/free556253

ISBN 978-0-483-33419-9
PIBN 10556253

This book is a reproduction of an important historical work. Forgotten Books uses
state-of-the-art technology to digitally reconstruct the work, preserving the original format
whilst repairing imperfections present in the aged copy. In rare cases, an imperfection in
the original, such as a blemish or missing page, may be replicated in our edition. We do,
however, repair the vast majority of imperfections successfully; any imperfections that
remain are intentionally left to preserve the state of such historical works.

FOR

WOMAN.

PUBLISHED BY THE

WOMAN'S BOARDS OF MISSIONS.

1884, Vol. XIV.

———◆———

BOSTON:

our pathway of service, w
with the triumphant powe

With reverent hearts w
this work, that it brings
truly said, that " power to
duty as well as our exalted
with the puissant force oi
workers with himself. In
Him who "pleased not hin
for many."

Some currents flow bac
gifts to foreign shores; but
purely unselfish, more sa
others which are poured ir
is small? Verily it does so

"The daisy, by the
Protects the ling'

Who can trace the lin
notes the sparrow's fall ?
majestic oak; so God may 1
ing of some gracious purp
has thus used us in the pas

Like the colors that floa
purposes are divinely seen
forth in full refulgence w
gather with us around the

We are brought into syn
as we wait for the fruits (
those who sit in darkness.

" The God of all comfor
to the suffering, down-trod

" The God of peace " br
healing over the seething ti
him not. "The Light of
ance the hills and valleys o
corners of the earth, as we
touch, which shall open th
love.

We are brought into sy
God, which will be our ete
tree of life with those wh
shadow of death, and as v
rapturous song, "Blessing
unto him that sitteth upon
and ever."

LIFE AND LIGHT

FOR

WOMAN.

PUBLISHED BY THE

WOMAN'S BOARDS OF MISSIONS.

1885, VOL. XV.

BOSTON:
FRANK WOOD, PRINTER.
1885.

𝔚𝔬𝔪𝔞𝔫'𝔰 𝔅𝔬𝔞𝔯𝔡 𝔬𝔣 𝔐𝔦𝔰𝔰𝔦𝔬𝔫𝔰 𝔬𝔣 𝔱𝔥𝔢 𝔓𝔞𝔠𝔦𝔣𝔦𝔠.

INDEX TO VOLUME XV.

WOMAN'S BOARD OF MISSIONS.

BOARD OF THE INTERIOR.

BOARD OF THE PACIFIC.

I.

O DAY of glory, day of grace,
When Jesus showed his lovely face,
To make the world a holy place
    By his sweet rising!
How shall we tell his precious worth?
How shall we hail his wondrous birth—
This sorrowful and sinful earth—
    With peace surprising?

II.

O Love, all love which overpast!
The Father, in his pity vast,
Out of his secret bosom cast
    This Pearl most holy;
And in the stable it was found,
Where camels stood, their loads unbound,
And meek-eyed cattle gathered round—
    The manger lowly.

III.

The midnight sky is all ablaze
  With sudden light and golden rays
Of angels, watching with amaze
   His opening story:
The blessed virgin mother there,
Bending above her infant fair,
And pondering on that marvel rare —
   ·That undreamt glory !

IV.

And lo ! the echo of a song,
  Which deepens as it rolls along —
The chorus of a countless throng,
   Like a low thunder.
The sacred hills of Palestine
Are flooded with a voice divine;
The shepherds listen to the sign
   With a hushed wonder.

V.

Well might that song of songs be heard !
  Well might the angel host be stirred
To hover o'er the Incarnate Word
   With adoration!
Well might the air with bliss be fraught,
And splendor passing human thought ;
" Glad tidings of great joy " are brought
   To every nation!

VI.

O welcome, then, this happy morn
  On which the Saviour, Christ, was born !
With flowers his infant brow adorn —
   Lilies and roses.
"Glory to God " for his dear Son,
And " peace on earth," through suffering won;
Heaven's hallelujah is begun —
   And never closes.

VII.

Jesus was born this Christmas tide —
　Born that he might be crucified;
The sad-glad tidings, waft them wide
　　Beyond the waters.
In him all nations may be blessed,
In him all weary ones find rest —
Poor wanderers in the farthest West,
　　And India's daughters.

VIII.

Our thanks this day to God we lift
　For his unutterable Gift,
And bid the good news circle swift,
　　On eagle pinion,
Till earth permits " a little child
To lead her " with attraction mild,
And every utmost region wild
　　Owns his dominion !

　　　　Richard Wilton, in " India's Women."

"HAST THOU FAITH?"

BY MRS. W. B. CAPRON.

On the 26th of June, when I went to Pasumalai, to attend to our weekly prayer-meeting, I was anxious to see the Tirumangalam Bible-woman. She had come to a friend's house to be taken care of, for her last days were come. I found her mind very clear, and her voice stronger and more natural than I could have expected. She was glad to see me.

I said to her: "I am very glad to see you once more, S——. You are nearly through with your life on earth; and how does it seem to you as you think over the past, and look into the future?"

She replied: "Jesus is a great Saviour. I believe He has forgiven all my sins."

I then asked, "What verse in the Bible comes oftener than any other into your mind?"

"'The blood of Jesus Christ his Son cleanseth us from all sin.'" Pausing a moment, she added, "I rest upon it."

I then said a few words on praying to have every corner of the heart opened to Him. To this she replied: "There is a verse which I heard from you once which has given me much comfort— 'Fear not: for I have redeemed thee, I have called thee by thy name; thou art mine.' It comes often to my thoughts." So I took its shining parts and went over them, to her evident satisfaction. After some words suited, I hoped, to comfort her, I said:—

S——, would you like a little more Bible-woman's work to do? I can give you some."

With a smile of incredulity and much enthusiasm, she answered: "I should like it very much indeed. Tell me."

I replied that I was afraid that she was too weak to hear so long a story, but that I would stop as soon as I should see that it was more than she could bear. It was most interesting to see this woman's mind take in all that I went on to say, and how it seemed to exhilarate her. This was it:—

"Last Christmas-time I had several calls from a Brahman woman, who was threatened with what I feared would be cancer. I have not seen her since; but on Friday, Saturday, and Sunday my thoughts were so continually reverted to this woman, that I determined to go on Monday evening, after my work in the houses was done, and inquire about her. I had once much relieved her daughter, and the family have always remembered it. When I would call on them I was accustomed to see this woman; but, as a Brahman widow after the strictest sort, she would stand at a distance.

"What was my surprise, on Monday early, to see this daughter driving up to the door. I at once told her how much her mother had been in my thoughts and my intention. To this she replied: 'My mother came down from Trichinopoly on Saturday night. She is a terrible sufferer from cancer, and wrote to us that she wanted to come to Madura to die, and that she wanted you to come and see her, as she knew you would. We wrote to her to come at once; and she would have sent me yesterday, but that it was your special day.'

"I asked, 'Does she know that she cannot get well?'

"'Oh, yes! She knows that; but asks how soon you will come.'

"'To-night,' I answered."

"And did you go?" said the dying Bible-woman.

"Yes; I went. All day long on my mind lay the question, Is that woman come to Madura to be saved? Is it possible?

"I found her in a hopeless condition as to recovery, and I was surprised to have her say that she wanted to be where I could come to see her. I told her that if I was going to give her comfort, it could only be in my way, and not in hers. She smiled brightly, and replied, 'It is your way that I want.' I went again on Wednesday, and I am going again to-morrow. Now, S——," I said, "here is your work. You must pray for her, and beg Jesus, the Saviour, to give her the peace and light that so comfort you. Perhaps you may be in heaven soon, and she may be brought to you, that you may see how gloriously the Lord saves."

"Yes," said the Bible-woman; "I am glad you told me. It will be nice to think about her, and I will pray for her."

She had so much strength, and seemed so mentally bright, that I could not think her end so near. The next morning she again spoke to those about her of the precious verse, "The blood of Jesus Christ his Son cleanseth us from all sin." Then, sometimes seeming to recall the melody, and sometimes repeating the whole hymn, "I Have a Father in the Promised Land," she sank gradually, and breathed her last at half-past two.

Mr. Tracy came from Tirumangalam to conduct the funeral services. His visits had been a pleasure to her, and she had left a sum of money to be used by him as some memorial offering in the station. I did not know this until my return from my visit to my sufferer.

How near to us is the eternal world. I was resting upon her prayers while she was far away. Her great peace and comforting faith in her Saviour were such bright realities that I longed to be, as it were, a heavenly messenger to carry them to my poor Brahman woman.

This was a new experience to me, in a certain way. I have

great faith in the living power of God's Word; and when I know
that there have been opportunities for hearing or reading it, and
especially if some of its precious verses have been stored away in
the memory, my faith seems to lay hold of this; but here was a
case where no such resting-place was to be found. And then to
think of all her accumulated superstitions, and austerities, and
ignorance! Here she was, laying hold of me for comfort in dying,
and I had not faith to believe that the world's Redeemer was
intending to reveal himself as her Saviour!

It was a morning never to be forgotten. It was a severe test
for me, but I could, and did say, "Lord, if it be thou who dost
send me to that house, bid me first come to thee through this sea
of unbelief, for my faith is sinking, and all seems dark and impossible."

There seemed to be no one in the house but the mother and
daughter. I was thinking as I looked at her body, unusually re-
pulsive even for such a disease, how faithful had been her wash-
ings and fastings. She suddenly looked up at me, and said:—

"For years and years I have bathed this body three times a
day, and now look at it!"

"Yes," said the daughter; "and how faithfully she has fasted.
I have often wondered how she endured it."

Said the mother, "It does not seem to have done much good."

Oh! how bitterly she smiled; and then looking with her full,
dark eyes into mine, she asked, "Do you think that God is angry
with me, that he should smite me with this awful disease?"

I replied, "You have been saying all your prayers, and you
have been committing all your fastings and ablutions to your
household *swamy*—I do not know the name. God, my glorious
heavenly Father, has had no part in it all."

With the same bitter smile she waved her hand, saying: "All
for nothing. It does not count anything. You need not think I
set any value on it."

"Do you mean to say," I asked, "that you have no merit to
rest on, after such a long, faithful devotion to all the rites of
your worship?"

"Dust, dust!" was the reply.

The daughter, a beautiful, sympathetic spirit, as I had long
known, with tears running down her cheeks, said, "We do all
these things, and have all these observances, because others do,
and we must go with them; but look at her now."

Heathenism and Brahmanism were laid low. That was evident.
It was, indeed, "Look at her now." The Lord must come, and he
must come now, for the time was short.

" Do you remember anything that I said when I was here last?" I asked.

" You said that Jesus was a better name than Rama or Siva. Did you mean that I must keep saying ' Jesus, Jesus,' instead of ' Rama, Rama ? ' ".

It must be said, in passing, that much merit is attached to long repetitions of these names.

" Oh, no! Jesus does not wish that. He looks beyond the lips, into your heart, and looks all over, to see if he can find any love or trust in him there."

Again those great eyes were lifted to mine. " He sees," she said, " that all my past life has no merit in it, and that it was all the time only dust." This seemed to reveal that she was making Jesus real, or, rather, that the blessed Lord was making himself real to her, and this gave me great hope. So I replied:—

" Cannot you tell Him so? Cannot you trust yourself to him? You cannot think how real all will become to you as soon as you give yourself into his keeping, and his only."

Now the pain and distress came over her like many billows. " Oh!" she cried, " can you tell me how many days I must live? Is God a merciful God?"

When she was soothed, and quiet again, I told her that she had not many such days before her, and that I hoped that God would spare her life until she knew that the Lord Jesus was the Saviour of her never-dying soul. I set before her as clearly as I could his great mission to our world, and the free, gracious pardon to all. I taught her a short prayer, which her soul grasped as it had done nothing that I had said. She repeated it over and over to me. It was touching to see how her daughter would try to make clearer everything that she thought her mother did not quite comprehend. The great love wherewith He loved us seemed around us all; and promising to come in three days, I left.

For three weeks more, three times a week, I went to this house. The next three visits were very trying. I was sure that a Brahman priest was behind a screen, for, although all were polite and kind, the constraint was apparent. Once the dear woman asked me to come in the morning instead of the evening, as there would not be so many people about. So I went in the morning, and was met at the door by the daughter's husband, who said that as she was taking her food it was not a convenient time. I was beginning to feel doubtful as to the wisdom of going again, and asked that the daughter might come to the door.

I told her that I did not wish to intrude, but that her mother was much in my thoughts, and that I much wished to see her.

She replied: "Your words are my mother's great comfort. She is constantly talking to me about what you have said to her, and told me to tell you not to stay away, for she watched for your coming."

Once more I found the mother alone, but the daughter was absent. She was exhausted with suffering, and her mind was less clear. She would follow me intelligently, but said little. I told her that I doubted if I saw her alive again, and asked her if she had anything to say about the Saviour of sinners. I longed for one ray of light.

"You said that Jesus made all holy," was her reply.

"Has he made you holy?" I asked.

"I say it over and over. All the rest is dust."

"This was all that I was to receive. She had spent her whole life in the one great effort for holiness, and at the last found it all a vain thing. In his infinite compassion the Lord Jesus had shown her this, and I could only hope that he had also the blessed purpose to clothe her with his own righteousness. All the anxiety and fear lest I had not done my part are known to him. I tell you all this, dear heart, that you may understand the better what to pray for as you ought when you pray for Madura City. With all that is interesting and inspiring in our work, there remains the fact that the Saviour sought is not the one who saves from the guilt and power of sin, but the one who brings life, light, and immortality.

I went to my poor sufferer one Thursday morning. The daughter's husband came to the carriage. Said he: —

"She sat up on Tuesday, and as she lay down she said, 'I shall never sit up again.' She did not speak after this, though her mind was bright. She breathed her last on Wednesday noon. You have been very kind to come, and she cared more for your visits than for anything else."

There is nothing more to be told; but you, in whose eyes have been tears, will know how much remained to be thought.

WOMAN'S WORK IN THE EASTERN TURKEY MISSION.

To the Woman's Board of Missions: The Eastern Turkey Mission, assembled by representatives in annual meeting at Mardin, sends greeting.

Under an Oriental sky, trains of deliberate camels passing with effortless speed by our windows on the north, while the monotonous, week-long, day-and-night drumming and fifing of an Oriental wedding assail the ear from the south, we remember you in the land of the telephone and the steam-whistle, encouraging ourselves in the thought of your sympathy, and glad that we are not alone in our work.

A condensation of the reports of woman's work in the several fields presented to the annual meeting gives the following items: The girls' school in Mardin has been discontinued this year, owing to Miss Sears's absence in America and Miss Pratt's embracing a long-desired opportunity to labor in Mosul. Ten of the pupils have been teaching school this winter. Ill for five weeks after reaching Mosul, Miss Pratt began in November her work of calling from house to house for prayer and religious conversation. She visited principally at Protestant houses, though going sometimes, by invitation, to those of Jacobites and Papists, who always wished her to read the Bible and pray, and urged her to come often.

One woman, daughter of a Protestant, but the wife of a very wicked man, said to her, "Now I will talk to you just as if you were the father-confessor. I will show you why it is impossible for me to be a Christian." Among the reasons given were the opposition of her husband and the prejudices of the people. These in Mosul are so strong, that even a Protestant's wife and daughter refrained from attending a second service one feast-day because "it was a shame to be seen in the street so often on such a day." This poor woman listened eagerly, and with a look of surprise as the teacher told her how we may feel that Jesus is with us all the time, helping us in everything we do; but Miss Pratt never saw her again, and knows nothing more about her, except that she is one of the very few women of Mosul who are able to read, and have a copy of the Scriptures, "which are able to make us wise unto salvation."

At Van, Misses Johnson and Kimball have been able to take entire charge of classes in the girls' school, Mrs. Reynolds having the care of the domestic department. The school numbers about thirty, of whom one-third are boarders. Two pupils united with the church last year, and two are soon to be examined for church-membership.

At Bitlis there are about thirty-five pupils (all boarders) in the Misses Ely's school. Of these it is believed that nearly all are Christians. It is pleasant to hear of their interest in the weekly "experience meetings," and their zeal in earning money for their society established in aid of girls too poor to provide themselves suitable clothing. Sometimes they earn money by picking over *bulgoor*, a kind of cracked wheat, which forms one of the universal articles of diet here. They agreed together to ask that the money which went to furnish nuts and raisins for their dessert one day in the week, might be given to their society. The Misses Ely discouraged this plan, and supposed it had been abandoned, till one day when two large bags of nuts and raisins were brought them as contributions to the home missionary society.

Besides this boarding-school, there are three day-schools for girls in Bitlis, which are almost entirely self-supporting, only three hundred *piasters* (about fourteen dollars) aid being asked for the three schools.

The work for women in the Erzroom field this year has been encouraging. The girls' school of twenty-five pupils (four of them boarders), under the efficient supervision of Miss Powers, its primary department of fifty pupils, and the four girls' schools in other parts of the field, all report progress. Two of the girl-teachers from the Erzroom boarding-school hold weekly meetings with the women, and to some extent are doing the work of Bible-readers. One has charge of a Sunday-school.

Miss Van Duzee accompanied Mr. Wm. Chambers, last fall, on a tour to Khanoos, stopping on their return to see the work on the Passim plain, and would gladly have joined him on the Russian tour had there been money enough to defray the additional expense.

In the city of Erzroom over eighty calls have been made during the fall and winter, almost always with reading and explanation of Scripture and prayer.

The female department of the college at Harpoot numbers eighteen pupils, the preparatory department sixty-two, the primary ten, giving a total of ninety. The preparatory course of study extends through four years, the same amount of time being required for the college course. All those in the college course are church-members; six only from the preparatory department, though it is hoped that a number of those who are not church-members should be regarded as Christians. Sixteen pupils are now in the field teaching, besides many pastors' wives, who are extending the influence of the school in their several homes.

The school has this year entered the new and commodious building erected under Mr. Wheeler's supervision. A class of three was graduated this summer. Miss Wright having resigned her connection with the school at the Easter vacation, Miss Seymour assumed its temporary charge.

The touring work of Misses Seymour and Bush was reported by the following paper from Miss Seymour's pen:—

WORK FOR WOMEN.

The importance of work for the women of our field has constantly grown this winter in the minds of the workers. Their many burdens, their needs, their influence on the future of the land we are all trying to lift out of its degradation and sin, demand all our energies, and enlist our warmest sympathy and most earnest prayers.

When we see how many times promises to read the Bible daily, and to pray, or to begin a new life, are remembered and kept long after *we* have forgotten them, how quickly and in what numbers the women flock to hear our words, apparently hungry for sympathy and encouragement, we can only wish that the hands to work might be multiplied, and the hearts to feel might receive a new baptism of the Holy Spirit.

One stormy day this winter an old man, scantily clad, but with the air of one assured of a welcome, came to the *konak* [missionary quarters] in Harpoot, and said he had come from his village just to get a primer for his son's wife.

"We had long felt," he said, "that she ought to learn to read, but when you came and talked to us about it we decided we would not wait any longer."

It was the village sexton, whose chief fitness for the office, we all know, is his extreme poverty.

The women in the village are so busy with their field-work, and our city sisters in their preparation of supplies for winter, that they are not very accessible in the early autumn; still, touring was commenced about September 10th, and, with the exception of occasional visits to Harpoot, was continued till the time of the annual meeting (May 19th). Last year nearly every place in our field where there are Protestants was visited. This year the villages in the Arabkir region were left out.

Our plan of working has been to visit the schools for both sexes, to go to the homes of all the Protestant families, and, so far as possible, converse with each woman about her spiritual condition and the performance of her home duties. Not only do we visit Protestant homes, but we go wherever we think the women will receive us; and we seldom meet with a rebuff. When we make a short stay in a village we try, if practicable, to hold daily meetings with the women. We are always sure that the evenings will bring quite a number of the brethren, accompanied by their wives, and try to have the time pass profitably in reading stories or tracts in Armenian, or in translating extracts from our well-filled religious newspapers. Intemperance has become such a trying evil in our field, that the subject is frequently brought into our evening conversations.

In one place that we visited even one of the stronger sex said to the wife of the pastor, "I have tried all the week that these ladies have been here to get an opportunity to talk with them about my religious state, but I have never come without finding them occupied with others."

In some of our larger cities greater numbers than ever before have gathered at our noon-day meetings. In the last tour made, two hundred and fifty women were present at the Sabbath meeting in Choonkoosh, one hundred and fifty at Diarbekir; and Hulakegh always rejoices our hearts with its large gatherings of women, nearly every one a reader, and well instructed in the Bible. We would like to record a similar interest where the pastor's or preacher's wife tries to sustain the weekly meetings; but in some places too little interest is felt in these gatherings.

One little instance gave us encouragement. In a small village, where the wife of the helper was not with him, the wife of the chief Protestant, self-moved, began last fall to hold meetings with the few sisters. This spring, in passing through her village, we stopped at her house to tell her how glad she had made us in our former visit, by her efforts for the women, and asked if she still continued her meetings.

"Yes, teacher; the sisters have come to my house every Sabbath this winter but once, when I went to my mother's home in another village." Six years ago this woman was not a Protestant, and could not read; but becoming the wife of a Protestant brother, and being very bright, she soon learned to read her Bible, and now uses her influence for Christ.

We should like to tell you of the work of the women in their societies, the avails of which have bought vessels for the communion service, carpets for the chapels (the more desirable, since all sit upon the floor), or otherwise aided in improving the appearance of the house of God; have purchased maps for the school-room, and aided in paying the salaries of the female teachers.

These teachers, being old pupils of ours, are always ready to listen to our suggestions for any improvement in discipline or teaching. We should like to have an efficient corps of Bible-readers to constantly stimulate and help the weak and easily-discouraged readers of the Bible, and to give lessons to those who have never learned.

Often the wife of the pastor or preacher is so burdened with family cares as to make it impossible for her to undertake such service, and it is difficult to find one fitted for it. Owing to the difficulty of finding suitable workers, and because of our insisting that a portion of their salary shall be paid by those for whom they labor, the number of such workers in our field is limited.

While work for women has been going on in the out-stations, Harpoot City has not been forgotten. Mrs. Barrows and Mrs. Browne have held meetings in a lower quarter of the city. These meetings are held at the house of a Protestant sister, but the comers are always women from the old church, who are attracted by the spirit of love that seeks to help them. The attendance is from eight to fourteen. We have reason to thank God and take courage as we remember the guidance and help vouchsafed to us the past year. The Lord always prepared our way before us, and often blessed our efforts far beyond our expectations. Though "only women," we have invariably been treated with deference by both men and women. We never left a place without a feeling of sorrow that we must leave so much work undone; and as we gain more and more acquaintance with the field, with individuals, and with the needs of the churches, our daily question is, "Who is sufficient for these things?" while, even when mind and body are most weary, and the soul most oppressed by care and anxiety, comes the comforting answer from above, "My grace is sufficient for thee."

Yours in Christian love,

MARY P. WRIGHT.

Young People's Department.

LETTER FROM MISS HOLBROOK.

DEAR YOUNG LADIES, SHAREHOLDERS IN THE TUNG-CHO DISPENSARY: A few months ago a request was sent to the "central office," asking for funds for a new dispensary, and that message was "telephoned," through LIFE AND LIGHT, to all the "Branch Offices," and the young ladies circles enthusiastically made themselves responsible for $1,500.

Before the answer reached me, even, the land was purchased, and all odd minutes were full of what was to be done "year after next." Certain scraps of paper laying around bore marks suspiciously like house-plans. The whole affair did seem to me a little like an air-castle, sometimes, when I stopped to think about it; but the fever was on, and with me, as you who know me personally can testify, it had to run its course!

The solution of that problem which I have been to work at all my life,— how to get the most out of the least,— this time resulted in a beautiful plan that just fitted into the building-lot, and not a scrap of space left over.

This attack proved contagious, too, or infectious, — we won't quarrel about the term,— for I was hardly convalescent when word came that the money was all collected, and building might begin as soon as practicable. And so you see my "year after next" was changed into "day after to-morrow," and the castle turned out a pretty substantial one, after all.

Before me lay a pile of twenty-one letters from friends, new and old, expressing sympathy, encouragement, and support in this work. One young lady writes: "To read this letter is part of the price you pay for being a missionary." What price *did* I pay? Really it was so small, I've most forgotten. One thing I know: it was a most paying investment — shares way above par, and no watered stock. If reading and writing letters is a part of the price I pay, a wide circle of very dear friends, I know, is a part of the dividend I receive.

In the September number of *The Century* is an appeal by Julia Dorr to the "young women whose school-days are but lately over, and to the memory of every woman who has not forgotten her girlhood," not to "settle down into the inexpressible weariness and depression that comes from a little crocheting, a little embroidering, a little housework, a little music, a little visiting, a little dressing, a little reading, a little of this, that, and the other." She then sets forth a scheme for mutual improvement, whereby we can "choose and hold fast the very best in our individual reach."

But, girls, I think we have found a still better way — we whose motto is not to choose and hold fast all in our reach even of the best, but to give as much, as fast, and as far, as we can of that which is best of all: first to Christ, and then, in his name, to all for whom Christ died. Is not that an individual reach wide enough to satisfy every earnest, ambitious heart? We who, either at home or abroad, have thus given the work of hand, mind, or heart, do not find ourselves "feeding on husks," neither does "life, that seemed to our young imagination so noble, so grand, something to glory in and thank God for, dwindle down to a thing of mere shreds and patches," but rather does the very giving of life and light to those who sit in darkness and death make our own lives broader, deeper, and richer.

And now, dear girls, older and younger, to each and every one who has opened her heart and hand to this good work, in the name of all suffering women and children who, so long as this dispensary stands, shall receive bodily and spiritual healing, in the name of all these, accept my thanks.

Your co-laborer in one and the same work,

MARIANA HOLBROOK.

THE COMING YEAR.

ANOTHER year has closed. It seems but a moment since, as a Board, we stood upon its threshold gazing anxiously into its dim mysteries, wondering what its weeks and months would bring forth of success or failure, joy or sorrow, encouragement or disappointment. At its close we have but one note to sound through all our borders — a note of praise and thanksgiving, "The Lord hath blessed his people!" "Sing unto the Lord a new song, and his praise in the congregation of saints."

We think we may say that in no other year in our history has there been more satisfactory progress than in the one just closed. There have been years when the number of new organizations has been greater, when statistics of all kinds have made a more decided advance; but never, we believe, has the progress in true and permanent strength been greater than in the year of our Lord eighteen hundred and eighty-four. To those who are watching this work among the women in our churches in all the length and breadth of our territory, it is a matter of much thanksgiving, not unmixed, we must confess, with a certain wonder to see how the interest deepens and widens; how the enthusiasm not only continues unabated, but is constantly adding to its swift current, becoming with some almost an absorbing passion; how the various meetings grow in spirituality and power, making them in deed and in truth heavenly places; how the giving grows spontaneous and consecrated;

how the bond that draws the workers grows closer and dearer, creating social enjoyments on a true foundation, and so giving un-alloyed pleasure; above all, to see that the foundation of it all is one that never can be moved—a true love for our Lord, his work, and his kingdom. What gives us the greatest strength, however, is the abiding conviction that our God has set his seal upon our work; that he is beginning the fulfillment of his ancient prophecy that has received a new meaning in the Revised Version, "The Lord gave the word: great was the company of women that published it;" that he means to use the women and children in bringing the world to himself.

We may be sure that these results have not been brought about by accident, neither has there been any miracle. At the begin-ning of the year we asked for four very simple things—more prayer, deeper consecration, greater effort, larger gifts; and we believe it has been through just these means that progress has been made. If the story of all these earnest prayers, new conse-crations, special efforts, and individual thank-offerings could be written out, we believe they would bring to light such heart-search-ings, such spiritual uplifting, such sacrifice of time, and ease, and precious treasures as would fill a volume of intensest interest. Now in the retrospect, do we hear of regrets over these experiences? Does any one say, I am sorry I made this sacrifice, that I gave up that pleasure, that I "abridged a ruffle or subtracted a tuck," that I might make time to attend the missionary meeting? Does any one say, How foolish I was to be led away by my enthusiasm to make such a large thank-offering? I wish I had never made that special consecration, that seemed to lead me to do things I never thought I could do before? Ah no! we never hear such words as these. The tongue would falter and the lips refuse to utter such thoughts. Does not every such recollection the rather send a glow through our hearts and a feeling of satisfaction at every such treasure laid away where it can never be lost nor defiled.

Now, dear friends, are you willing to make equal effort and sacrifice the coming year? What has been done *can* be done again. What cost us much during the past twelve months may, perhaps, be done with ease in the future, but we cannot doubt that other efforts, other sacrifices, no less costly, may be needed for the coming work. With King David we wish to ask, Who is willing to consecrate her service this day unto the Lord afresh? Does the work demand it? Never so much as now; never did our Lord so surely beckon us onward; never were the openings so many and so grand as at the present moment.

The greatest need just now is for men and women for the foreign field. There is positive and immediate call for eleven young women for this work. Before this year is over there are those who will be called upon to give their lives to this work; and there are those who will be called to give that which is dearer than life — a loved daughter, or sister, or friend. May the dear Lord give the strength for this sacrifice to those from whom it shall be required. But this is a call that will come to the few. To most of us comes the infinitely smaller request of a full and hearty support, unstinted sympathy, unceasing, earnest prayers. In dollars and cents, should the eleven young ladies be found, it will cost for outfits and traveling expenses at least ten thousand dollars. The estimates sent us by the American Board for 1885 amount to nine thousand dollars more than ever before. This includes almost no new work; the increase is only the natural growth to which we are pledged. This is a responsibility which we cannot throw aside. We must also plan for requests to come for special emergencies during the year, for new openings that must be seized at the moment, or irreparably lost; so that we are compelled to ask for $125,000 for the absolutely necessary work in the year 1885.

It is not needful for us to go into details as to how this work is to be done. Each one who did her share last year knows how she did it. As she looks over the year, she sees how she might have done more; how this and that opportunity slipped by without improvement; how a word here, or a suggestion there, might have been just the stimulus needed to bring some half-hearted sister into earnest work; how a little more self-denial might have doubled her subscription; how a little more effort might have brightened up a meeting or strengthened the hands of some weary one in the foreign field. Of any who have these thoughts we ask, Will you continue your good works for 1885, and add to these the might-have-dones of 1884? If there are those who have done all they possibly could,— and we believe there are such much-to-be-envied persons,— we wish to beg of them, having done all, to stand. Of those who are half-hearted and indifferent, if any such should chance to read this paragraph, we wish to ask, Will you not, for once, carefully consider whether it may not be your duty to take some active part in woman's work for foreign missions? We do not pretend to say it is your duty; that is a question that can be settled only between your conscience and your Lord. We do not believe that any Christian woman would thoughtfully say that "I'm not interested," or a careless "I don't believe in it" would be a sufficient reason to throw aside any duty. What should we think of a mother who would give "I'm not interested in children," as a

reason for neglect of her little ones? What would we say if a
soldier should say, "I don't believe in it," in excuse for disobey-
ing his leader's commands. We need not multiply illustrations.
We know very well that such excuses would not be received in the
ordinary affairs of life. No one would pretend to offer them. All
we ask is a sincere, prayerful consideration of the whole matter
the condition of women without the gospel what it can do and has
already done for them; whether it is the desire of our Lord that
they should have it; in what way and by whom it should be sent to
them; whether it should be done by a few or by all; who is excused from it, and who is especially called to it; whether it should
be done this year or a hundred years hence; and, finally, whether it
is really a matter that concerns yourself as a Christian woman in
this nineteenth century.

Now, may we say just a word to those who are faint-hearted —
for we believe those with faint hearts are quite as numerous as
the half-hearted or the indifferent. Down deep in their souls they
believe in foreign missions, and in woman's part in them, but they
are easily overcome by obstacles; they shrink from anything that
looks like "fanaticism" or publicity; they wish they could do
more, but they think they can't; they distrust their own powers.
How often do we hear, "If I had as much leisure as Miss C., or a
quantity of money like Mrs. F., I should feel that I could do something;" or, "If I could talk in a meeting as well as Mrs. H., or lead
in prayer like Miss B., or write a fine paper like Mrs. G., I would
be glad to do it, but I have no talent for such things;" and many
like excuses. Suppose these things to be so. Suppose one hasn't
the time, the money, the talent of some one else; is that a
reason she should not use what she has? A few moments seized
from a busy day, or an hour planned for beforehand and obtained
with much effort, has twice as much zest in it as time taken from
a heavy, aimless day; a hundred pennies given with earnestness
and prayer, have much more value than a dollar given carelessly
and without thought; a bright piece of information culled from
a magazine or newspaper may sometimes have as much effect as
an elaborately written paper; two or three petitions from the
heart will reach the throne of grace just as quickly as the most
eloquent prayer. Let us remember that the few loaves and the
small fishes had to be brought to the Master before the multitude
could be fed, and that the little lad was just as important
in the great transaction as the apostles who gave bread to thousands. Let us comfort ourselves that it is in what we have to give,
and in the one who multiplies it, that the power lies — not in ourselves, nor in the way we give it. The greatest boon the human

race has ever known, the Christian religion, was in the beginning intrusted to eleven humble men. They taught its principles to the best of their ability, sending them forth to the world, and they have told upon the fate of empires.

As we start on another year in the life of our Board, remembering the power that lies behind us, let us take heart and press on as never before; let the success of the past year give us courage; let the dire necessities of fifty million of women and children urge us on; let the cries for help from our missionaries inspire us to new zeal; let us one and all "brace ourselves against our God and lift" with all our hearts and all our strength.

--------◄♦►--------

NOVEMBER MEETING.

THE quarterly meeting of the Woman's Board of Missions was held in the Chapel of Park Street Church, on Tuesday, November 4th at 3 P. M. After devotional exercises, conducted by the President, the report of the Home Secretary was presented, showing an encouraging growth in the work both at home and abroad. The statement of the Treasurer showed the receipts since January 1st to be from all sources $86,682.64.

A paper entitled "After Many Days," showing how the patient labors of years, so often seeming to be without results, almost always reap their reward. The subject was illustrated by an account of Mrs. Capron's work in Madura and vicinity, where the first years brought comparatively few results, but where there are now over a thousand women under regular instruction from the workers under her care.

The closing address of the meeting was given by Miss F. M. Washburn, of Marsovan, who gave an interesting account of work in Marsovan among the women in the boarding-school, comparing these labors with those in other parts of Turkey, bringing out the obstacles and encouragements of the one work in the Turkish Empire.

--------◄♦►--------

ANNUAL MEETING.

THE annual meeting of the Woman's Board of Missions will be held in Mt. Vernon Church, Boston, on Wednesday and Thursday, January 14 and 15, 1885.

TO OUR READERS.

WE wish to remind our readers that this number begins a new year in our magazine, and that it is very desirable that subscriptions be paid in advance. We depend largely upon those received in December for the following year to supply the deficiencies of the summer months. At the time of writing, December 13th, these receipts have been very small in comparison with former years. Please send all possible subscriptions for 1885 before the first of January, and save the magazine from debt.

WOMAN'S BOARD OF MISSIONS.

RECEIPTS FROM OCTOBER 18 TO NOVEMBER 18, 1884.

MAINE.

Maine Branch. — Mrs. Woodbury S. Dana, Treas. Calais, Aux., of wh. $25 const. L. M. Jessie Wilson Grant, $35.72; Richmond, Aux., $4.87; Otisfield, Cong. Ch., $6; Bethel, 1st Ch., Aux., $10; Rockland, Aux., $50; Portland, Y. L. M. B., $10, $116 59
Richmond.—A Friend,   2 50

Total, $119 09

VERMONT.

Vermont Branch.— Mrs. T. M. Howard, Treas. Morrisville, Aux., $10; No. Craftsbury, Aux., $20; Dummerston, $1; Bennington, Aux., $27.25; E. Poultney, Aux., $11.42; Enosburg, Aux., $12, Young People's M. C., $40; Swanton, $1; Dorset, Willing Workers, $15; Montpelier, Beth. Ch., Aux., $22.50; Westminster, West, $25; Waterbury, Aux., $14.75; Underhill, Aux., $19; Rutland, Ann. Meeting, for Morning Star, of wh. $75 const. L. M's A Friend, Mrs. Farrar Peacham, Mrs. Layyah Barakat, Syria, $166.70, $385 62
Waitsfield.—Lydia A. Bigelow,   5 00

Total, $390 62

MASSACHUSETTS.

Ashby.—Cong. Ch., $1 00
Barnstable Co. Branch. — Mrs. Bernard Paine, Treas. Yarmouth, Aux., $5.75; Wellfleet, Aux., $4,   9 75
Berkshire Branch. — Mrs. S. N. Russell, Treas. Williamstown, Senior Aux., $213,

Gleaners, $10; Housatonic, Aux., $79; Adams, Aux., $6; Pittsfield, 1st Ch., $2.85, So. Ch., $22.68; Hinsdale, Aux., $56 88, $390 41
Dunstable.—Aux.,   3 00
E. Braintree.—Mrs. E. F. Stetson,   8 00
Essex North Conf. Branch.— Mrs. A. Hammond, Treas. Ipswich, 1st Ch., Aux., $30; Newburyport, No. Ch., M. C., $86; Campbell, M. B., $10; A Friend, $5   131 00
Essex South Conf. Branch.— Miss Sarah W. Clark, Treas. Danvers, Maple St. Ch., $27; Lynn, Chestnut St. Ch., $15, 1st Ch., Aux., $51, Young Ladies' Aux., $25, No. Ch., Aux., $12; Salem, So. Ch., $374; Middleton, Aux., $2; Beverly, Washington St. Ch., Aux., $60, Unity Band, $20; Centreville, M. C., $30; Swampscott, Aux., $44; Ipswich, So. Ch., Ladies, of wh. $25 const. L. M. Miriam Orswell Waters, $31; So. Peabody, Do What We Can, $13,   704 00
Hampshire Co. Branch. — Miss Isabella G. Clarke, Treas. Williamsburg, M. C., $30; Southampton, Bearers of Light, const. L. M. Miss Lilian E. Boyd, $28.87; So. Hadley, Faithful Workers, $8,   66 87
Harvard.--Cong. Ch.,   8 75
Mansfield.—Cong. Ch.,   7 19
Middlesex Branch.—Mrs. E. H. Warren, Treas. Wellesley, Aux., $212.45, Penny Gatherers, $3, Young People's M. C., $22.55; So. Natick, Ann Eliot Soc'y, $10; Natick, Aux., $22, Y. L. M. C., const. L. M. Mrs. Anna Messenger, $25; Hopkinton, Aux., $79.50; Marl-

boro, Aux., of wh. $50 const. L. M's Mrs. S. E. Warren, Mrs.L.G. Stevens, $77.78; Holliston, Aux., $8; Saxonville, Aux., $10; Maynard, Aux., $34.35; So. Framingham, Willing Workers, $33; Lincoln, S. S., Cong. Ch., $25; Southboro, Aux., $10; Northboro, Aux., $10; Dover, Aux., $4, Ann. Meeting, Thank-Off., for Morning Star, $150, $736 63

Old Colony Branch. — Miss F. J. Runnels, Treas. New Bedford, Union Workers, $40; Taunton, Aux., $147.52, Broadway Ch., M. B., $46; Lakeville Precinct, Aux., $100; Attleboro, 2d Cong. Ch., Aux., const. L. M. Mrs. Walter Barton, $100; Attleboro Falls, Aux., $31; Rochester, Aux., $35, Loving Helpers, $5 Dighton, Ladies' M. C., $60; Middleboro, Aux., $20.17, Henrietta Band, $5.83; Somerset, M. C., $36; Rehoboth, Aux., $20, Mizpah Circle $40,   686 52

South Hadley Falls, Cong. Ch. and Soc'y,   30 00

Springfield Branch. — Miss H. T. Buckingham, Treas. Wilbraham, Willing Workers, $40; Chicopee, 3d Ch., Aux., $15, Busy Bees, $18, Earnest Workers, $16; W. Springfield, 1st Ch., Aux., $83.50; Westfield, 1st Ch., Aux., of wh. $25, by Mrs. L. M. Hawley, const. L. M. Miss Annie E. Lockwood, $260, T. T. T. Club, $100, Light-bearers, $40, 2d Ch., Aux., $130.31, Scatter Goods, $79.50, Mitteneaque Gleaners, $20; Palmer, 1st Ch., Thorndike, $16.50, 2d Ch., Aux., $50; Chicopee Falls, Aux., $13.60; Blandford, Aux., $30; Ludlow Centre, Aux., $2; Monson, Aux., $86; Holyoke, 2d Ch., Aux., $96; Agawam, Aux., $42, Fresh Laurels, $18.77; E. Longmeadow, Aux., $45, Young Disciples, $6; Springfield, 1st Ch., Cheerful Workers, $82, Circle No. 2, $4.67, Sandford St. Ch., Aux., $7, So. Ch., Aux., $7.75, Y. L. M. C., $5 54, No. Ch., Aux., $91, Olivet Ch., Aux., $81.12, Hope Ch., Aux., $41, Memorial Ch., Aux., $148.10, S. S., $40, Young Ladies' Guild, $40, Willing Helpers, $30; Indian Orchard, Aux., $19, 1,805 36

Suffolk Branch. — Miss Myra B. Child, Treas. Boston, Berkeley St. Ch., Ladies, $180, S.

S., $38, Mt. Vernon Ch., Aux., const. L. M. Mrs. Laura P. Chapin, Acworth, N. H., $25, Central Ch., Aux., $27.83, Union Ch., $203.76; So. Boston, Phillips Ch., S. S., $59.30; Roxbury, Immanuel Ch., Aux., $15.67, Eliot Ch., M. C's Eliot Star, $2.59, Mayflowers, $2.59; Ferguson, 50 cts.; Anderson, $5; Cambridge, A Friend, $2; Brookline, Harvard Ch., Aux., $18; Brighton, Faneuil Rushlights, $2; Waverly, M. C., $75.50; Newton, Aux., $182.60; Dedham, Asylum Dime Soc'y, $2.20; W. Medway, Aux., $12, $854 54

Ware, E. Cong. Ch., Miss L. A. Tucker's S. S. Cl.,   10 00

Woburn Conf. Branch. — Mrs. N. W. C. Holt, Treas. Winchester, Aux., $55, Seek-and-Save Circle, of wh. $25 const. L. M. Miss Fannie M. Morris, $30; Lexington, Aux., $14; Hancock, S. S., of wh. $25 const. L. M. Miss Minnie C. Thayer, $37.50; Billerica, S. S., $6.25; Reading, M. B., of wh. $100 const. L. M. Mrs. Frank W. B. Pratt, $185; Carlisle, Cong. Ch., Ladies, $6.25. 334 00

Worcester Co. Branch. — Mrs. G. W. Russell, Treas. Whitinsville, Aux., $105; Westboro, Aux., prev. contri. const. L. M. Miss Susan M. Hardy, $35; Lancaster, Aux., of wh. $25 const. L. M. Mrs. D. A. Newton, $35; Grafton, Aux., prev. contri. const. L. M's Mrs. B. A. Robie, Mrs. Jesse Smith, Miss I. H. Dennis, $60; Oxford, M. C., $15; Barre, Thank-Off., $1; Worcester, Woman's Miss'y Asso., Piedmont Ch., $159, Central Ch., prev. contri. const. L. M. Miss Mary R. Greene, $50.13, Plymouth Ch., $85.50, Old South Ch., A Friend, $2; Leicester, Aux., const. L. M. Mrs. Carrie W. Denny, $100; Strawberry Hill, Gleaners, $15; Winchendon, North, Cong. Ch., $60; Gilbertville, Aux., $84; Warren, Aux., $43; Spencer, Aux., $25, Hillside Workers, $16; Paxton, $14; Millbury, 1st Ch., $62; Leominster, Aux., prev. contri. const. L. M. Mrs. P. W. Newell, $15,   981 63

    Total, $6,768 65

LEGACY.

Legacy of Mary Hartshorn, Reading, $500 00

RHODE ISLAND.

Rhode Island Branch. — Miss Anna T. White, Treas. Barrington, Aux., $50, Pettasett M. C, $13.75; Little Compton, $1; E. Providence, $2.25; No. Scituate, 75 cts.; Central Falls, 25 cts.; Tiverton, Aux., $11.50; Providence, Beneficent F. M. C., $10, Our Boys, $10, Cheerful Workers, $10, Friends, $6.50, $116 00

Total, $116 00

CONNECTICUT.

Brooklyn. — From the late Mrs. Mary J. Crosby, $25 00
Hartford Branch. — Miss Anna Morris, Treas. Hartford, Wethersfield Ave. Ch., Aux., $35, Miss J. R. Clarke, $1.40; Simsbury, Pearl Gatherers, $13; Rocky Hill, Fragment Gatherers, $29.50; Plainville, Aux., $73; So. Windsor, Aux., Poquonnock, Mrs. E. H. Marcy, $12,   183 90
New Haven Branch. — Miss Julia Twining, Treas. Bridgeport, South Ch., M. C., $43; Higganum, Shining Stars, $20; Fairhaven, Second Ch., to const. L. M. Mrs. H. E. Hovey, $25; Middlesex Co. Meeting Tithe-Offerings, $98.50; Middletown, First Ch., $31; Milford, Mrs. Clark's S. S. Cl., $20; Norfolk, of wh. $8 fr. Y.L. M. C., $110 fr. Mountain Wide-Awakes and Hillside Gleaners, $118; New Haven, Davenport Ch., S. S., $60; Wilton, a little girl, for Morning Star, 50 cts., Morning Star, 50 cts; Fairfield Co. Meeting Thank-Offerings:— Bethel, $5.50; Darien, $6; Greenwich, $5; North Stamford, $1; Norwalk, $29.30; Sound Beach, $6; Stanwich, M. C., $1.25; Stratford, $10; Stratford, M. C., $8.05; Unknown, $11.50, for a good wife, $10, from prayer-meeting, $4.25. Unknown, $3.27; Easton, $1,   518 62

Total, $727 52

NEW YORK.

New York State Branch. — Mrs. G. H. Norton, Treas. Rochester, Miss'y Friends, $13.50; Millville, $14; New Haven, $20; Napoli, $10;

Westmoreland, $17; Greene, $19.50; Brooklyn, Puritan Ch., $25; Newark Valley, $15; Fairport, $20; Buffalo, W. G. Bancroft M. B., $20, Ann. Meeting Thank-Off, Morning Star, $400, $574 00
Newtonville. — Desert Palm Soc'y,   5 00

Total, $579 00

NEW JERSEY.

Roselle. — Mrs. B. Tenney, $4 40

Total, $4 40

PHILADELPHIA BRANCH.

Mrs. Samuel Wilde, Treas. New Jersey, Plainfield, Aux., $10, Westfield, Aux., $20.30; Orange Valley, Aux., $32, Children's M. B., $1.78; Orange, Grove St. Aux., $43; Proctor, M. C., $80, Trinity Cong. Ch., Aux., $47.70, M. C., $20, Jersey City, Aux., $25.35; Bound Brook, Aux., $25, Beavers, $30; Woodbridge, Aux., $26.50; Paterson, Aux., $12; Vineland, Aux., $35.50; Montclair, Aux., of wh. $100 const. L. M. Mrs. J. H. Cooper, $25 by Mrs. Samuel Wilde, const. L. M. Mrs. M. F. Reading, $132.55, Y. L. M. Soc'y, $190, Benefit Jugs, $2.76; Newark, 1st Cong. Ch., Aux., $44.87, Workers for Jesus, $78.80; Maryland, Baltimore, Aux., $45.80; D. C., Washington, Y. L. M. C., $45; Virginia, Falls Ch., Aux., $9; Herndon, Aux., $13, $970 91

Total, $970 91

FLORIDA.

Daytona. — Aux., $10 00

Total, $10 00

CANADA.

Woman's Board, $166 00

Total, $166 00

Friends, $15 00

General Funds, $9,867 19
Weekly Pledge,   4 26
Leaflets,   26 60
Legacy,   500 00

Total, $10,398 05

MISS EMMA CARRUTH, Treasurer.

In Memoriam.

Entered into the Glory of Heaven.

Mrs. Richard Borden,

of Fall River, Friday, November 14, 1884, in the 87th year of her age.

AFTER three-score and seven years of devoted service in the Church of Christ on earth, Jesus said unto her, "Well done, good and faithful servant; enter thou into the joy of thy Lord." Entering into the celestial city, she joined with her glad alleluias, "kept by the power of God through faith unto salvation." And now she continues her life eternal, so long since begun on earth, in the service and joy of heaven.

In her life this side of heaven we have a beautiful gift of God which stands as a rich legacy to the world; for Mrs. Borden's life was endowed with a large, rich, and full nature, which was in early life consecrated to God, and infused with his light, and grace, and power. She was a woman of great energy of character, firm in purpose, wise in plan, keen in perception, quick in understanding, true to the right, resolute in action, faithful in duty, weighing well that which she was about to do or say before she gave it outward expression. With these traits were mingled grace of manner, gentleness of bearing, loveliness of spirit and sweetness of speech, charity in thought and act, exquisite sensibilities, and an ardent love of nature.

I have watched the engine bringing the freighted vessel, with steady stroke, into port, laying in the waters of gold and crimson circles of action, widening and widening till lost to sight. So this life, springing from God, threw its circles of power in golden light far and wide in the world.

Mrs. Borden joined the First Congregational Church in Fall River in 1817, the year after its formation; and she and her husband were among the founders of the Central Congregational Church in Fall River in 1842. To them is this church largely indebted for its prosperity, its peace, and its power, by reason of their prayers, their wise counsels, and their liberal and constant gifts. Well have her pastors called her, "Mother in Israel," for she nourished and cherished the church much as she did her own family. She loved the courts of the Lord, and often went to the public worship and to the prayer-meeting in spirit after her feebleness detained her in body.

And for the church she continued her active watchcare and co-operation till the end of her life.

The city of her home blessed her for her warm heart and open hand, always ready to minister to the poor. The trees and vines which she planted about the Children's Home will always sing of her tender care for poor and needy children.

For her country's weal she always felt the deepest interest and solicitude, and for it gave her services when required. To this time our spring-time memorial day always finds the Grand Army procession, on their return from the graves, playing "Auld Lang-Syne" before her door, in memory of her honored husband and herself.

For the education of the Freedman and the Indian she was zealously interested.

Christ said, "My field is the world;" and with her Christ she went abroad in her own land and in foreign lands praying for, and sustaining, home and foreign missions.

Almost from the beginning of our Woman's Board of Missions she has been one of its Vice-Presidents, and it was her great delight, while she was able, to sit in the counsels of this Board. Her last contribution, given a week before her departure with great emphasis, was for this cause. And, in the tender love of Christ, she and her husband drew the missionaries into their own home ministries, where they found rest for their weariness and refreshment for their souls. Many have gone from thence to lands far away with their burdens lightened and their faith strengthened by reason of the tender interest and care found under their roof. From the bed of her last illness packages of material comfort went forth to each.

Many of the children of these missionaries, sent back by them to their native land for education, yet strangers and homeless in a peculiar sense, have found in her a mother, and have been cheered and comforted in her home.

Mrs. Walker's home for missionary children, at Auburndale, received her warmest prayers and generous gifts.

Obeying the Bible injunction "given to hospitality" Mr. and Mrs. Borden have given to many of God's ministering servants, and to others, days in their home which have refreshed and strengthened their lives. Thus she still lives in the cherished remembrance of many homes and hearts.

And this activity in the service of Christ kept this good and noble woman young in spirit, even to more than four-score years.

She loved life for the holy work of the Lord in fellowship with him, and her life thus lived was, and is, eternal.

Passing from earth to heaven in perfect confidence and peace, she said, "I shall see Christ, and be like him; and in this I shall be satisfied."

Board of the Interior.

ANNUAL MEETING OF W. B. M. I. AT MINNEAPOLIS.

BY MRS. A. L. MILLER.

THE happy company that started from Chicago to attend the sixteenth annual meeting of the Woman's Board of Missions of the Interior, found they need not wait to set foot in the "City of Waters" before tasting the pleasures of this yearly feast; for even the beginning of the journey was crowned with happy greetings, as we met at the depot the delegates from Michigan and Ohio,— as fresh in spirits as if their hours of travel had been but minutes, and with faces that promised a happy story when their time to report should come. Morning found us more than half way to our destination, and with new recruits from Milwaukee and LaCrosse. Breakfast over, it was suggested that morning service might be observed; and all being assembled in one of the parlor cars, a fortunate stopping-place gave us a chance to hear a short story from St. Paul about one of his missionary journeys, and to join in earnest prayer for the meeting before us, and for the "loved ones left at home." As the train moved on, we joined our voices in "The Lord is my Shepherd," — riding, meantime, through the beautiful hill-pastures and along the clear waters of the upper Mississippi,— and raised above the noise of the wheels the strains of "Coronation." Arrived at Minneapolis, we were welcomed at the depot by a waiting company with white satin badges, whose responsible bearing and cordial greetings gave promise of generous and efficient hospitality, — a promise which each succeeding day most abundantly fulfilled.

Tuesday evening brought the preparatory meeting — "the new feature" of last year, which bids fair to make itself a regular part of our exercises. Plymouth Church was well filled. In the absence of the pastor, Rev. R. G. Hutchins, who had been called away by the death of his father, Rev. J. L. Scudder presided. Prayer was offered by Dr. Sample, of Westminster Presbyterian Church; and then Mr. Scudder gave an address, which took us at once into the very heart of missionary work. Dr. Dana, of St. Paul, followed, speaking in eloquent sentences of "Woman's place in the redemption of the world," and Dr. Greene, of Constantinople, gave a forcible description of the life of women in Turkey, and a feeling tribute to the zeal and wisdom of our workers there, and to the work already accomplished. And then the day closed, as for some of us it had begun, with "All hail the power of Jesus' name."

There was the semblance of a shadow on the full house that gathered Wednesday morning at the opening of our regular session, when Mrs. Leake announced that our beloved President, Mrs. Smith, was prevented by illness from being with us. But the assurance came to our hearts, "Lo, I am with you;" and as we gathered at the Master's feet in our opening prayer, we felt that as our coming together had been "in His name," he would be with and guide our meeting.

Mrs. Baird, having been elected chairman, read Mark v. 25-35 and Matt. ix. 27-29, and gave us as our motto for the day the words, "According to your faith be it unto you."

The Committee on Credentials having been appointed, Mrs. Hutchins offered the greetings of the ladies of Plymouth Church, whom she compared to the porter standing at the gate of the Palace Beautiful, to offer to the coming, weary pilgrims its rest and blessing. The days of preparation to leave home, the perplexities of planning for the journey and the meeting, were our Hill Difficulty; and having safely overcome its trials we were welcomed now to all the sweet hospitalities of this house, built by the Lord of the Hill, and to the refreshment of that chamber looking toward the sunrising called "Peace."

Mrs. Baird replied in a few words of graceful acknowledgment, after which were offered greetings from other missionary organizations. Mrs. Williams, of the Presbyterian Board, referred to their happy meeting in Minneapolis two years since, when hearts and homes were opened to them as now to us, and, "best of all, the Master's heart was opened, and his presence made us glad." She reminded us that the joy and fruitfulness of our mountain-top revelations must depend on the preceding days of humble, prayerful preparation, and that the Mount of Transfiguration must be followed by Gethsemane and Calvary. Mrs. E. H. Miller, of the Methodist Board, spoke of the close fellowship of all Christian workers, being "members together of Him for whom the whole family in heaven and earth is named." Mrs. Barker offered words of kindly encouragement for the Baptist Board, which held its thirteenth annual meeting last April, and finds the work pushing the workers. Letters were read from the Union Missionary Society of New York, the oldest woman's missionary society in the United States, "the mother of us all;" from "our older sister," the Woman's Board of Missions from Boston; and "our youngest sister," the Woman's Board of the Pacific from San Francisco; and from our Secretary, Mrs. Blatchford, dated "Ocean Steamer Adriatic, nearing Queenstown."

After the reading of the minutes of our last annual meet

ing, came the Treasurer's report—"nothing but figures," but listened to with an interest more intense than any other; for is not this the measure of our success? The figures showed a fair advance over the previous year, $48,220.40—but not the sum set for our goal.

The foreign report was then presented by Mrs. G. B. Willcox. With graphic description she led us around the world, stopping at bright spots where the gospel flame is kindled and tended by our faithful workers in the midst of deepest darkness. It is impossible to do justice to this report by any extracts, and we can only advise our readers to secure it for their own study and future reference. It, as well as the Treasurer's report, forms a part of the annual report of our Board, and may be obtained from our rooms by inclosing fifteen cents. The summary of what has been accomplished reads as follows : "Our Board has supported the past year, 42 missionaries, 10 boarding-schools, 47 common, or village schools, and 35 Bible-women, besides native teachers, matrons, stewards, etc."

Mrs. Thomas Gulick stirred our hearts by her eloquent story of the spiritual bondage of the women of Spain; and compared it with their possibilities under the light and freedom of the Gospel.

The devotional hour which closed the morning session was led by Mrs. Magoun, of Iowa, who fed our faith by the thought, "The omnipotent God is the power behind the weakest effort put forth in obedience to his word." Miss Kate Scudder, who is very soon to sail for Japan to join Mrs. Oramel Gulick, at Niigata, was introduced, and all hearts joined in an earnest prayer of consecration, voiced by Mrs. Angell, of Ann Arbor.

With kindness and hospitality that knew no bounds, and with skill and wisdom that awoke constantly new surprise, did our enterprising and wise-hearted sisters of Minneapolis provide every possible comfort for their guests. At noon of both days, all delegates were invited to a most bountiful lunch prepared in the church parlors, and so gracefully offered, that had the fare been the Pilgrim's traditional crust and water, it must have proven amply sweet and refreshing from the very grace of its serving.

Afternoon brought us to the Home report, read by Miss Wingate. From it we glean: "Some changes in our working force have occurred during the year. Miss Hope Martyn, whose presence at our rooms has been valued and helpful, was compelled by ill health to resign her place, which is still vacant. And the Angel of Death has not passed us by. August 3d, Miss Mary E. Greene, for fourteen years an honored Secretary of our Board, was called, after a brief illness, to her reward. The day following, the same summons came to Miss Helen A. Leavitt, State Secretary of Nebraska. What these events mean to us as a Board, words cannot express, but 'He doeth all things well.'" Our publications for the year reach 620,000 pages; besides the *Monthly Mission Studies* with its valuable lessons, and our department in LIFE AND LIGHT with its glimpses of missionary life, and our weekly column in the *Advance*, which takes, through all the Interior, the story of our Friday meetings. The appropriations at the beginning of the year amounted to $37, 319.18, and before its close swelled to $42,388.28. Ten married missionaries already on the field are added to our list; also Miss Eva Swift, of Dallas, Texas, sent to the Madura Mission, and Miss Welch, teacher in Umzumbi Home; a house for Misses Dudley and Brown, at Kobe, and half the expense of our single ladies at Kalgan. We have 87 new senior auxiliaries, 34 junior and 59 juvenile, in all 1,248.

Immediately following this report came words of tender appreciation of Miss Mary E. Greene, whose death, already mentioned, has been felt so deeply by our Board. From all parts of the Interior have come these messages of loving and sorrowing remembrance; and from some of these, extracts were read and listened to with tearful interest, as we realized that we "should see her face no more." "May we follow her even as she followed Christ."

Among the workers from the field whose presence gladdened our hearts and stimulated our resolves, were Miss Pinkerton of South Africa, Miss Ogden, M.D., from India, Miss Barnes from Marash College, Miss Parsons from Bardesag, Turkey, Miss Spencer from Hadjin, and Dr. and Mrs. Greene of Constantinople. Miss Pinkerton spoke with tender, anxious interest of her twenty-eight girls, left, during her enforced absence, in care of Miss Welch, who is herself much in need of rest, having been twelve years at work, and suffering from serious trouble with her eyes. It is pleasant to know that Miss Gillis is already under appointment to this school. Dr. Ogden spoke with enthusiasm of her work in India, and reiterated the appeal which comes so universally from all whose eyes have seen the sufferings of women and children in heathen lands. Dr. Ogden's very presence must carry with it those accessories to all medicine, hope and confidence; and we wait anxiously for that restoration of her strength which will enable her to resume her healing ministrations. Miss Barnes told us of the impetus received by the college at Marash in its new and convenient building; of the satisfactory progress of many of her pupils in the more advanced branches of study; and, best of all, in the knowledge of the "way of life."

Three papers of marked interest and ability were read during the session: one by Miss A. B. Sewell, of Wisconsin, on "Thus saith the Lord;" one by Mrs. Tozer, of Wisconsin; and one by Mrs. Scudder, of Minneapolis, on "Children's Work." We regret that want of space forbids more than mention of these and other valuable papers given during the meeting. We hope that means will be found through our publications of the coming year, or by hektograph copies, to place them within the reach of all our auxiliaries. The ever-interesting theme "Children's Work" was next presented in an animated discussion. Among the thoughts which found expression were these: Children should learn to conduct their own meetings, under leadership. *Should give their own money.* Parents are often enlisted through their children. Let the collection form a part of every meeting. Present not only what has been accomplished on heathen ground, but also the great need still existing, that they may realize there is still a place for workers.

And now it was whispered that the young people were waiting for the older ones to make a place for them; and two rows of seats were cheerfully vacated for a goodly company of "Earnest Workers," who marched in to the music of the piano, bearing their pretty banner, with their name in letters of gold. Their sweet voices united in the song, "Over the Ocean Wave," and they were welcomed with bright, loving words by Mrs. Bradley, of Aurora. Miss Spencer then introduced a little girl dressed in the costumes of the interior of Turkey, and proceeded to enfold and muffle her in the cumbersome wrappings worn by all brides of that country; exhibiting, also, many articles of domestic use, and holding the attention of her young hearers by her winning presence and graphic story.

The evening session found Miss Evans, of Northfield, in the chair. Eloquent addresses were given to a crowded house by Dr. Greene of Constantinople, and President Northfield, of Minnesota State University; and then Mrs. Magoun followed with earnest words respecting, "The place of the Woman's Board among Christian Forces." As she enumerated the "reflex benefits" which return upon all who labor in its service, and step by step led us along the pathway of duty and privilege which stretches before our feet in this blessed work, it seemed to need no Divine command, no sadly echoing voice from out the darkness of heathen lands, where our sisters dwell in their sorrow, to lead us to rise and enter the happy ranks of workers.

THURSDAY.

The morning session opened with prayer by Mrs. Phillips, of

Illinois, and then came the hour devoted to reports of State Branches; an hour full of interest to all who would keep informed of our progress, though to those not acquainted with our organization it may seem to bring much repetition of thought and experience. Travelers pursuing the same road have largely the same story to tell, and our societies find great similarity in theirs. But to those who have an eye for detail, there are distinguishing features in each.

Minnesota opens her story with rejoicing over the privilege of being allowed the annual meeting — a privilege from which they hope to realize new growth and inspiration; and having borne it in their hearts with loving preparation, and in their prayers, for months past, we are sure their hopes will be fulfilled. "An overflowing treasury" is theirs, having one thousand dollars more than their allotted portion. Wisconsin tells of the helpful visits of Capt. Bray and Mr. and Mrs. Logan, and has remembered that "increase of object means doubling, not halving, the dollar." Iowa rejoices in the support of two missionaries more than in previous years, and has given a daughter, Miss Nettie Palmer, of Cedar Rapids, who has this year gone to Micronesia. They tell us of the five P's by whose aid their work goes on: "Pluck, Plan, Patience, Perseverance, and Prayer." Illinois, modestly acknowledging a falling off in its contributions from last year, begs to explain that it has been in the amount given as legacies; the gifts of the living have showed increase. Indiana reports an advance over last year of fifty dollars. Ohio has had her heart and hands filled with special labors within her own borders, having sufferers from floods to care for early in the year, while unusual drouth caused suffering in later months. Still, it brings honorable record. Michigan, pledged to the support of four missionaries, has this year added to the number Miss Searle, of Kobe Home, whose letters have added fuel to their zeal. Missouri has also taken charge of a new worker, Miss Eva Swift, of Dallas, Texas, who went last summer to Madura. They speak of the benefits following the distribution of missionary literature. "Gifts are large in proportion to the Christian intelligence of a people, rather than in proportion to their wealth." Nebraska stands before us in the garb of mourning, having been bereaved of a beloved Secretary, Mrs. H. A. Leavitt, of whom loving mention has already been made in the pages of LIFE AND LIGHT. Kansas has trebled its auxiliaries this year, and gives much credit for its growth to the labors of Miss Hillis, now of India. Colorado still testifies to the power of Miss Shattuck's residence among them last year: when apparently laid aside from service, her earnest love for missions found a way to sow plenteous seed. Dakota has had its annual meeting made glad by the visit of Mrs. Magoun, who brought to them the greetings of the parent Board, and planted truths which will be hopefully watched in their growing there. North Dakota Branch has a large proportion of churches yet in their infancy — promising infants, some of them. One formed its Missionary Society when only two weeks old, and a Mission Band is already at work. God bless this young Branch.

The periodicals and leaflets of the Board formed the subject of some earnest words, introduced by a paper on the subject of their distribution, by Mrs. Kellogg, of St. Louis. The value of these sources of knowledge in awakening interest and building up auxiliaries, receives abundant testimony from every source; and here is a suggestion of possible seed-sowing to some who are cut off from more active efforts. Even the shut-in ones may, by inclosing to a friend a leaflet like Mrs. Pickett's Missionary Box, Thanksgiving Ann, or Aunt Mehitable's Story, start a fountain whose outpouring shall be enriching and permanent. The discussion of where, when, and how shall we so distribute as wisely to "sow beside all waters," brought out such need of careful discrimination, wisdom, good judgment, and persistence as raised this form of service from an ordinary level to a high plane of Christian endeavor.

Then followed the report of the Committee on the Treasurer's report, recommending its adoption, calling attention to the present opportunity for rising above discouragement, and urging that we "try again" for $60,000 the coming year; which report was, with entire unanimity, adopted by vote.

The question of appropriations for 1885 was presented in an able paper by Mrs. Temple, which so clearly presents the relations of need and supply, that we wish all our constituents would give it a careful perusal. Hektograph copies may be had upon application to our rooms. With the burden of heavy responsibility suggested by this topic still upon us, we came to the precious devotional hour. Mrs. Leavitt, of Chicago, read Isaiah xii., and wove together promises of strength from Old and New Testament. From many lips came grateful testimony to the sure foundation of our hope, while letters from Miss Brown, in Japan, and Mrs. Porter, blessed mother of missionaries, showed that to the young laborer in her perplexities and weakness, and to the ripened Christian in her rich experience, the same blessed strength is freely given for the asking.

The ladies to whom had been committed Miss Wingate's story of our Home work, gave, through Mrs. Ide, of Milwaukee, a

bright and cheery review of the same, in which some very practical advice was dexterously interwoven with a most older-sisterly
emphasis, as this: "We should now and forever break up the
careless, needless habit of withholding our gifts till the last days of
the year;" and this message, to be taken by every delegate to her
auxiliary: "It would greatly facilitate the work, and save much
anxiety, if the treasurers would remit to State treasurers monthly,
or, at most, quarterly, that our Board may know how far we can
sustain the progress reported by its missionaries. And a word to
those who wait for the lady of the parsonage to lead in all such
work: "The ministers' wives ought to be willing to *take their
turn with the other ladies of the churches* whenever their peculiar
cares leave them time and strength to do so."

The Young Ladies' hour was occupied by the reading of a most
delightful paper, "Five Years' Review," written by Mrs. Purington.
The closing session was very full, and time fails us to describe all its
good things. Mrs. Greene held us breathless with interest as she
told of her experience during many years among the Turks, and introduced Miss Spencer in the dress of a lady of Constantinople — a
red silk robe, abundant jewelry, and a gauze veil, which only par-
tially concealed the face. Miss Emily Bissell stirred our hearts to
tearful overflow as she stood before us in the garb and character
of a Brahman woman, and told the story of her life — its isolation,
its abundant labors, its bondage to superstitious beliefs; and pictured the mother's agony as she, constrained by dread of greater
evils, consented to offer her darling baby a sacrifice to Gunga.

And now the closing hour had come. The missionaries, and
mothers of missionaries present, gathered on the platform, and
were remembered in special prayer by Mrs. Van Cleve. Our
thanks for the untiring and loving care which had provided us
with every comfort, and enabled our machinery to move so
smoothly, even to providing willing young feet to go noiselessly
back and forth with messages, were woven in happy sentences
by one who never fails to speak aright; — an hour of social cheer,
and our annual meeting was over.

Home Department.

STUDY IN MISSIONARY HISTORY.

THE Lessons of this year will be devoted largely to the study of
the work of the American Board in the Turkish Empire and
Persia. We shall watch with interest the unfolding of God's

beautiful plan, beginning with the explorations of only two men, Fisk and Parsons, in 1820, and extending until the Gospel has leavened more or less the whole empire.

Study first the extent and condition of the Turkish Empire at that time.

Work of the Board from 1820 until 1830.

Explorations of the first two years.

Death of Mr. Parsons.

Re-enforcements. Beginnings of work at Beirût.

Who were the Druses? The Maronites?

Converts. Asaad Shidiak, Pharez Shidiak, Girghis, Asaad Jacob, Wortabel. The biographies of these men will furnish material for a paper of great interest.

Persecutions.

Beginnings of work in Smyrna.

Political agitations of 1828. Interruptions from the war.

Re-enforcements of 1830. Explorations of that year. Return to Beirût.

Thompson's "Land and the Book" will be of great interest in connection with this lesson; also Van Lennep's "Bible Lands," and the "Women of the Arabs," by Dr. Jessup, "Bible Work in Bible Lands," by Rev. I. Bird, and the Ely Volume, are both helpful. The latter contains illustrations of the Seminaries in Beirût and of Smyrna, besides articles on the geography of these places. The Cyclopedias contain helpful articles.

The expansion of the work subsequent to 1830 makes it necessary to subdivide the study under the head of separate missions. *February* will be devoted to the Syrian Mission down to the time when it was transferred to the Presbyterian Board. The lesson for *March* will be a brief glance at the *Nestorian Mission* in Persia.

RECEIPTS OF THE WOMAN'S BOARD OF MISSIONS OF THE INTERIOR.

MRS. J. B. LEAKE, TREASURER.

FROM OCTOBER 15 TO OCTOBER 22, 1884.

ILLINOIS.

ILLINOIS BRANCH. —Mrs. W. A. Talcott, of Rockford, Treas. *Cable,* John J. Higgs, 1.39; *Canton,* 5; *Chicago,* 1st Ch., Y. L. Soc., 94.19, Union Park Y. L. Soc., 52.67, Mission Band, 20.02, New Eng. Ch., Y. L. Soc., 75, Bethany Ch., 8.60, Millard Ave. Ch., 15.87; *Elgin,* Y. L. Soc., 49.02; *Evanston,* Aux., 189.70, Y. L. Soc., 97; *Galesburg,* Philergian Soc., 20, 1st Ch., Mission Band, 20, Knox Sem. Miss. Soc., 12 10; *Geneva,* Y.L. Soc., 10; *Hinsdale,* Aux., of wh.

25 to const. L. M. Mrs. J. A. Porter, 38.18, Y. L. Soc., to const. L. M. Miss Jessie M. Bowles, 25; *Illinois*, 3.50; *Ivanhoe*, 5; *Kewanee*, 15; *Lawn Ridge*, Mission Band, 36.20; *Lyonsville*, 35 cts.; *Lombard*, 16; *Malden*, 10.88; *Marseilles*, 6.50; *Mendon*, 25; *Neponset*, Aux., 5.60, Mission Band, 14.74; *New Windsor*, Mission Band, 7.40; *Oak Park*, Little Sunbeams, 20; *Oswego*, 8.50; *Ottawa*, 85.25; *Pecatonica*, 2.40; *Princeton*, Whatsoever Band, 30, Acorn Band, 10; *Providence*, 14; *Rio*, 10; *Sandwich*, 32.67; *Udina*, 5; *Wilmette*, 20; *Woodstock*, per Dea. Hobart, 3.76, $1,126 64

THANK-OFFERINGS.

Canton, 6.25; *Hinsdale*, 10; *Lyonsville*, 4.65; *Marseilles*, 13.95; *Sandwich*, 11.88   46 73
ADDITIONAL, *Ashton*, M. B. H., 2; *Chicago*, First Ch., L., 10, Leavitt St. Ch., C. B., 25 cts., Lincoln Pk. Ch., Y. L. Soc., 40, New Eng. Ch., 11, Plymouth Ch., Aux., 275.12, Y. L. Soc., 25, Union Pk. Ch., D., 1; *Griggsville*, C. L. B., "stamp act," 2.20,   366 57

        Total, $1,539 94

INDIANA.

INDIANA BRANCH.— Miss E. B. Warren, of Terre Haute, Treas. *Michigan City*, Aux., 2.13, Juniors, Wall Builders, 3, Juveniles, Cheerful Workers, for New Morning Star, 1.51, $6 64

        Total, $6 64

IOWA.

IOWA BRANCH. — Mrs. E. R. Potter, of Grinnell, Treas. *Big Rock*, 10; *Cedar Falls*, Twelve Ladies, 14, Mission Band, 15; *Davenport*, Aux., 45.50, Mrs. Kate Borland, 10; *DeWitt*, Mrs. M. J. Taintor, 5; *Downey*, Mrs. D. O. Goodrich, 5; *Ogden*, 16.05; *Tabor*, Mrs. Dr. Clark, 2, $122 55
For New Morning Star:— *Grinnell*, Mrs. J. B. Grinnell, 1; *Ogden*, Mrs. C. B. Sylvester's S. S. Cl., 1.25,   2 25

        Total, $124 80

CORRECTION. — In June LIFE AND LIGHT, Iowa's total should be $181.15, instead of $118.15.

KANSAS.

KANSAS BRANCH.— Mrs. F. P. Hogbin, of Sabetha, Treas. *Auburn*, 11.93; *Chase*, 1.60; *Diamond Springs*, 6.25; *Blue Rapids*, for New Morning Star, 9, $28 78

        Total, $28 78

MICHIGAN.

MICHIGAN BRANCH.—Mrs. Geo. H. Lathrop, of Jackson, Treas. *Columbus*, 5; *Covert*, 10; *Detroit*, 1st Ch., Aux., 105, Woodward Ave. Ch., Aux., 97, of wh. from Mrs. D. M. Ferry, for L. M.'s of Blanch and Queenie Ferry, 50; *Eaton Rapids*, King's Young Daughters, 12.50; *Grass Lake*, 14.50, S. S., 3.77; *Kalamazoo*, 87.25; *Lansing*, Plymouth Ch., Aux., 57.29; *Owasso*, 44.07; *Port Huron*, Aux., 5, Earnest Workers, 5; *St. Johns*, 23.69; *St. Joseph*, Aux., 17, S. S., 6.52; *Union City*, 7.75; *Waconsta*, 10, $511 34
For New Morning Star:— *East Saginaw*, Wide-Awake Soc., $10 00

        Total, $521 34

MISSOURI BRANCH.

Mrs. J. H. Drew, 3101 Washington Ave., St. Louis, Treas. *Lebanon*, 15; *St. Louis*, Pilgrim Ch., 8, $23 00

        Total, $23 00

NEBRASKA.

NEBRASKA BRANCH.—Mrs. Geo. W. Hall, of Omaha, Treas. *McCook*, Mrs. Dungan, 2; *Omaha*, St. Mary's Ave. Ch. Aux., 17.25, First Ch., Mrs. S. H. H. Clark, const. L. M. Mrs. A. F. Sherrill, 25, Aux., 46, Memorial Fund, 2, Juvenile, 5; *Stanton*, Acorn Band, for New Morning Star, 5.58, $102 83

        Total, $102 83

Omission.— The following statement should have appeared in LIFE AND

LIGHT for May, 1884. The amount was included in the total for the month.

Nebraska Branch:—
Camp Creek, Mrs. G. T. Lee, 2 60
Clay Centre, Chh., 5 00
Columbus, 3 00
Lincoln, Aux., 11.75, Children's Soc., for Star, 2.50, 14 25
Omaha, St. Mary's Ave. Soc., 10 35
Springfield, A few friends, 3 85

Total, 39 05

OHIO.

OHIO BRANCH.—Mrs. Geo. H. Ely, of Elyria, Treas. *Brownhelm*, 6; *Cambridgeboro*, Pa., 5; *Cincinnati*, Walnut Hill Ch., Mrs. Woodbury, to const. L. M. Mrs. H. N. Hollister, of Riverside, Ill., 25; *Cleveland*, First Ch., 45, Miss. Band, 8.14, Dew-Drop Miss. Band, 5; *Cleveland Heights*, 17; *Cuyahoga Falls*, 3.75; *Jefferson*, 21; *Locke*, 3; *Lorain*, 14; *Lyme*, 19.05; *Marysville*, 2; *Nelson*, 4; *No. Monroeville*, 11.55; *Paddy's Run*, W. H., 11; *Painesville*, Aux., 25, Y. L. Soc., 10; *Pittsfield*, 21; *Ridgeville*, Henry Co., 5; *Ruggles*, 10, M. C., 10; *Roolstonn*, 15; *Steubenville*, Y. L. Soc., 18.30, Willing Workers, 9.72; *W. Williamsfield*, 10.50, A friend, 1. Branch total, $336 01
INGATHERING, *Brooklyn*, 17.03; *Cincinnati*, Columbia, 17.50; *Painesville*, 1.50; *Saybrook*, 2; *Springfield*, 15, 53 03

Total, $389 04

ROCKY MOUNTAIN BRANCH.

Mrs. Hiram Jones, of So. Pueblo, Col., Treas. *Cheyenne*, Aux., 100, S. S., 25, S. S., for New Morning Star, 1; *Colorado Springs*, Pike's Peak

FROM OCTOBER 22 TO NOVEMBER 18, 1884.

ILLINOIS.

ILLINOIS BRANCH.—Mrs. W. A. Talcott, of Rockford, Treas. *Aurora*, 1st Ch., 7.20; *Chicago*, Bethany Ch., B. M., 1.32; *Crete*, 8.50; *Galva*, 10; *Greenville*, 1; *Lyonsville*, Seed Sowers, 8.28; *Marseilles*, Helping Hands, 10; *Roseville*,

Miss. Band, 50; *West Denver*, 20, $196 00

Total, $196 00

DAKOTA.

SOUTH DAKOTA BRANCH.—Mrs. K. B. Finley, of Vermillion, Treas. *Vermillion*, const L. M. Mrs. G. S. Bascom, 25, $25 00

Total, $25 00

WISCONSIN.

WISCONSIN BRANCH.—Mrs. R. Coburn, of Whitewater, Treas. *Antigo*, 4; *Baraboo*, Aux., 20, Mrs. A. G. Clark, 5; *Blake's Prairie*, 4.77; *British Hollow*, birthday gift, Mrs. E. L. Davies, 5; *Beloit*, 1st Ch., Y. L. Soc., 37.30; *Bloomington*, 1; *Delavan*, Ingathering, 31; *Fox Lake*, 14; *Green Bay*, 25; *Kilbourn*, 5; *Kenosha*, 43.80; *Lake Mills*, Mrs. A. V. Mills, 1; *Madison*, Aux., 2, Mission Band, 13.07; *Mt. Stirling*, Gay's Mill S. S., 4.16; *New Lisbon*, thank-offering, 5.50; *Oconomowoc*, Y. L. Soc., 25; *Prairie du Chien*, 53; *Platteville*, Y. L. Soc., 15.45; *Pittsville*, 10; *Ripon*, 28; *Racine*, Pansy Soc., 5; *Stoughton*, 1; *Shopiere*, 3; *Sharon*, 14; *Waukesha*, 28, Wisconsin Cong'l Convention, 29.27; *Evansville*, 10; *Milwaukee*, Grand Ave. Ch., Aux., 25, Mrs. Lucy A. Dawes, thank-offering, 1; *Whitewater*, 1; *Ripon*, Do Good Soc., 2; *La Crosse*, 12.80; *New Lisbon*, for New Morning Star, 25 cts. Less expenses, 7.48, $425 42

Total, $425 42

MISCELLANEOUS.

Sale of leaflets, 29.58; envelopes, 5.77; charts, 1.20; cash, 6; income from LIFE AND LIGHT, 491.75, $534 30

Total from Oct. 15 to 20, 1884, $3,917 09
Previously acknowledged, 44,303 31

Total year end. Oct. 22, 1884. $48,220 04

of wh. 85 cts. thank-off., 8.85; *Winnebago*, Y. P. Soc., 2.26, $57 41

Total, $57 41

IOWA.

IOWA BRANCH.— Mrs. E. R. Potter, of Grinnell, Treas. *Algona*, 3; *Cedar Rapids*, Y. L. Soc., 8, Mrs. Louisa B.

Stephens, 88; *Des Moines,* S. S., 7.15; *Grinnell*, 30.80; *Grand View*, 1; *Ottumwa*, First Church, 5, Second Ch., 1.25; *Stacyville*, Children, 16; *Tabor*, Estate of Miss Abigail Cummings, 70; *Winthrop*, 10, $240 20
For Morning Star: —
Miles,   2 25

     Total, $242 45

MICHIGAN.

MICHIGAN BRANCH.—Mrs. Geo. H. Lathrop, of Jackson, Treas. *Armada*, 28; *Cooper*, 13; *Detroit*, 1st Ch., Y. Ladies, 79; *Dowagiac*, 6.45; *East Saginaw*, 58; *Grandville*, Earnest Workers, Sale of Silk Quilt, 41; *Grand Rapids*, Park Ch., Aux., 50, 2d Ch., Aux., 8; *Lexington*, 7.10; *Manistee*, Young Ladies, 12.50; *Port Huron*, .8; *Potterville*, Mrs. Saunders, 2; *Webster*, 12, Coll. taken at meeting of ladies of Olivet Conference, 14.25, $339 30
INGATHERING, *Richmond*,   1 00

     Branch total, $340 30

MINNESOTA.

MINNESOTA BRANCH.— Mrs. E. M. Williams, of Northfield, Treas. *Clearwater*, 6; *Glyndon*, 2.47; *Lake City*, 9; *Mazeppa*, 5; *Medford*, Aux. and Willing Workers, 7; *Minneapolis*, Mayflower Ch., 5.39, A Friend, by Mrs. Hutchins, 10; *Northfield*, 17.29; *Owatonna*, Aux., 44.75, MerryHearts, 25; *Plainview*, 8, $139 90
For New Morning Star: —
Fairmont, 7.50; *Sherburne*, 7; *Westford*, 1.50; *Winona*, add'l, 13.75,   29 75

     Branch Total, $169 65

Minneapolis, Chas. A. Pillsbury, at Annual Meeting, for African Quilt,   100 00

     Total, $269 65

MISSOURI.

MISSOURI BRANCH.—Mrs. J. H. Drew, 3101 Washington Ave., St. Louis, Treas. *St. Louis*, Pilgrim Ch., Aux., 10, thankoffering, 1, Fifth Ch., 10; *St. Joseph*, Juvenile Soc. of Tabernacle Ch., 20, $41 00

     Total, $41 00

NORTH DAKOTA BRANCH.

Mrs. R. C. Cooper, of Cooperstown, Treas. *Cooperstown*, 15; *Wahpeton*, 10, $25 00

     Total, $25 00

OHIO.

OHIO BRANCH.— Mrs. Geo. H. Ely, of Elyria, Treas. *Alexandria*, 2; *Claridon*, 12; *Cleveland*, First Ch., Y. P. M. Soc., 7.12, Jennings Ave. Ch., Y. L. Soc., 7.70; *Columbus*, Eastwood Ch., 5; *Steuben*, 8; *Tallmadge*, Cheerful Workers, 27; *Toledo*, First Ch., 110; *Twinsburg*, 18; *Wellington*, M. W. L., thankoffering, 1, $197 82

     Total, $197 82

TENNESSEE.

Memphis, 2d Ch., Aux., $7 15

     Total, $7 15

WISCONSIN BRANCH.

BRANCH.—Mrs. R. Coburn, of Whitewater, Treas. *Brandon*, 2 65; *Menasha*, Cheerful Workers, 36; *Racine*, 1st Ch., Aux., 37.75, K. Y. Daughters, 4.25, Welch Ch., Y. L. Soc., 5.75; —— A Friend, thankoffering, 4. Less expenses, 1.73, $88 67

     Total, $88 67

NEW HAMPSHIRE.

Northwood Centre, Aux., $5 00

     Total, $5 00

CONNECTICUT.

Stamford, Aux., $12 00

     Total, $12 00

MISCELLANEOUS.

Sale of leaflets, 18; of leaflets, etc., at Annual Meeting, 12.27; of "Life of Coan," donated by Mrs. C., 4; Collection at 16th Annual Meeting, 152.06, $186 33

     Total, $186 33

Receipts from Oct. 22 to Nov. 18, 1884,   Total, $1,472 78

Board of the Pacific.

ELEVENTH ANNUAL REPORT OF THE RECORDING SECRETARY.

THE monthly meetings of the Board have brought the same hours of pleasant fellowship as in the past, with increased opportunities of work for the Master. Our average attendance is about fifty — a slight increase over that of former years. As we take a bird's-eye view of this work, we see the laborers at home and abroad brought nearer to each other each successive year.

When Paul "went through all Asia preaching the Word," and then into Greece, afterward to Rome, by that long, perilous journey, how far distant and inaccessible were those mission stations! Five days from Phillippi to Troas!

Now, one of our own number, in the short space of six months, has, from these "ends of the earth," sped across the ocean and looked with her own eyes upon some of the "seven churches of Asia," and has taken by the hand some of the dear missionaries laboring there, thus linking in a vital way the work at home and abroad. . . .

OUR SOURCES OF INFORMATION.

Firstly and always LIFE AND LIGHT. Its monthly visits send a quickening thrill through our hearts. You who can appreciate literary merit in the interesting, intelligent, bright and cheery letters of our sisters in the strange lands, read our LIFE AND LIGHT.

Young ladies, are you discussing the matter of How and what shall we do? Take, for instance, the March number, and read what the young ladies at the East are doing for a hospital at Tung-cho, in North China, with which a young lady physician,

Miss Holbrook, is connected, and of which Miss Evans of that mission recently told us.

Mothers, whose yearning hearts, like the mother of Samuel J. Mills and of the sainted Augustine, would consecrate their little ones to this divine work, do you want a simple story to convey to them some precious truth? Here you will find it. Do any wish to know of our share in this work? We have here four pages in which to tell it. Mrs. Savage, of Berkeley, is the efficient editress of this our department.

An elderly gentleman in one of our churches, a convert from Judaism, reads and feasts on every word of this little magazine; and as a result of his reading an occasional gold-piece, sometimes a $10, again a $5, finds its way into our treasury. We hope to report this year a large increase in the number of copies taken.

Those of us who are Sunday-school teachers of young ladies, can we not place it in their hands? Its price is but sixty cents. And do any prefer a more systematic and less superficial method of gaining the needful information? Here it is in the *Mission Studies*, so admirably prepared for this purpose by the Board of the Interior? This is a four-leafed paper, monthly, at twenty cents a year. The *Mission Day-Spring*, an illustrated little periodical, published by the Board at Boston for Sunday-schools mainly, is beautiful for this purpose. This also is twenty cents a year. And, lastly, to complete our education in this line, to put the finishing touches, as it were, in these studies, we have our own column in *The Pacific*, edited by Mrs. Jewett. This is the artery that carries the warm pulsations of our hearts to the very extremities, and brings us closer to our sisters throughout this coast.

We would not forget that all these means of quickening are as nothing in comparison with the influence of the Holy Spirit on individual hearts. Great missionary zeal has followed the great revivals which have marked the religious history of our country, and it is to this we must look and pray before our ideal is reached. A new feature has been added to our meetings the past year; viz., that of having "notes from the wide field" gathered up and presented at each meeting. This embraces items of interest connected with the work of other missions besides our own. Mrs. Richardson, of Oakland, was appointed for this work, and she has well fulfilled her task, and given us a comprehensive view of what is being done in the wide field of missionary effort.

OUR MISSIONARIES.

This brings us to the very heart of our work; but as you will hear from our foreign secretary something of each in detail, it will be sufficient for this report simply to give their names, one of which has long been familiar to you, with the appropriations as accepted by us in the fall of 1883.

Zulu Mission, South Africa: —

Salary of Mrs. Carrie Goodenough . . .		$450 00
Broosa, Western Turkey Mission: —		
Female Seminary, ten scholarships .	$374 00	
Teacher	264 00	
Service, fuel, etc.	193 60	
Salary of Mrs. Baldwin . . .	396 00—	1,227 60
Japan, Kioto: —		
Salary of Miss Starkweather		650 00
San Sebastian, Spain: —		
School under the care of Mrs. Alice Gulick . .		500 00
For the running expenses of the Morning Star . .		500 00
Total		$3,327 60

It may be a matter of interest to some to know how our contributions compare with those at the East. First, collectively, the Board at Boston, including all the New England States, with New York, New Jersey, and some others gathered in last year, including legacies, $128,468. The Board of the Interior, includ. ing the great interior States, formerly called the "Western States," $45,564. Our Board of the Pacific, *not* including some gifts sent directly to the Board at Boston, $3,397. This, a collective comparison, is not especially encouraging. Taking it individually, the average contributions for each female member of our churches stand thus: For those connected with the Board at Boston, seventy-six cents each; for those connected with the Board of the Interior, sixty cents each; and for our own Board, ninety-six cents each. How easy it seems in thought to bring up our contributions to at least one dollar for every female member of our churches!

It may, and will, probably, be said that this represents but a small part of our giving. We have the Home Missionary work, besides what comes in the line of our church and local work for the sick and poor. The Home Missionary Society aims at $2 per member for its distinctive work. Can we not ask for one dollar for every female member of our churches? To do this, there must be some systematic effort in the beginning of the year. Statistics will probably give 4,000 as the number in our churches, of female members. Can we report $4,000 for this work?

AUXILIARY SOCIETIES.

The condition of these will be given in the report of the Home

Secretary. We rejoice to be able to add the names of some strong and helpful societies. We have felt this to be an uneventful year, but there has been a bright spot, which we must record and rejoice over together; viz., the delightful communication from Oregon, which you have probably read in the column, asking to be identified with us in this work and through our treasury. This is what we have long desired and labored for. Our sisters at the East look upon us —Washington, Oregon, Arizona, Nevada, and California — as one. And why should we not be? We are geographically more closely allied, as well in history and in material interests, than with any others east of the Rockies; and so, sisters in Oregon, Washington, and Arizona, we clasp your hands in cordial welcome in this fellowship of labor.

One outlook more ere this bird's-eye view is closed. As we take notice of our appropriations to the work of missions, we can but observe the change that years have wrought in the methods employed. Instead of the direct preaching *only* of the Word, the almost undivided efforts of the missionaries are given to schools for the young.

It is a hard task to preach the pure gospel to the untutored mind of an adult, and so Christian women of truly consecrated hearts are sent to take the children and youth, and teach them the sweet "old story," and with it many of the simple industries of our Christian civilization, which do so much in our homes to make them what they are. Thus a new generation will arise thoroughly imbued with Christian principles of heart and life, that will renovate these nations, and hasten the dawning of that glad day for which all eyes are looking.

Another new feature of the missionary work in these our days which goes to our very hearts, is the medical work being done by Christian, educated women for the suffering of our own sex. And we who know the needs and possibility of good in this direction, can rejoice that it has no longer escaped the notice of the Christian world. And what an avenue for good is here! The tender ministrations, the healing, soothing, common-sense remedies, the kindly counsels as to the care of our bodies, these temples of the Holy Ghost, then the quickened hearts led upward to the Great Physician of the soul — what a work is this! Is it not more closely allied to the Master's blessed ministrations while here on earth than any other?

And as in this our annual meeting we are gathered here to concentrate our thoughts on those whose lives are in such sad contrast with ours, we must recall anew our Saviour's words, "Freely ye have received, freely give!"

FOR WOMAN.

VOL. XV. FEBRUARY, 1885. No. 2.

AFRICA.

PIONEER WORK TOWARD UMZILA'S KINGDOM.

BY MRS. M. B. RICHARDS.

WE left Natal last July, and came to Inhambane with Mr. and Mrs. Wilcox, who were returning to their work after a visit to Natal. We are now six hundred miles nearer the equator, which brings us to the edge of the tropics. When we arrived at Inhambane we all went first to Mr. Wilcox's house, which was only a temporary affair, made of reeds and thatch, and was in a somewhat dilapidated condition. Mr. Wilcox and Mr. Richards went to work at once to select a location and put up our two little iron houses, the materials for which they had brought with them from Natal. As soon as there was enough of the material put together so that it could be called a house, we moved in, preferring it to a tent, or to the old house, which was a long distance from the work.

The partitions were up and a floor in our room, but the rest of the house was guiltless of floors, ceilings, or doors. Our table was a large box; our kitchen was all out-doors; our storeroom our boxes, which were yet unpacked. The deep sand which abounds everywhere furnished a carpet, whose softness muffled every footstep, and which possessed the one advantage, at least, of not having to be swept; while the low underbrush, which grows thickly up to our very doors, supplied an abundance of fuel. Gradually these first conveniences for housekeeping have been improved upon, till we feel that we have quite a comfortable little home.

Our home is surrounded by the casne-tree, which bears a great deal of fruit in summer. The house is on the top of a steep hill, and faces Inhambane Bay; and at almost any hour in the day we can see white-sailed boats sailing up and down, while long-legged white birds wade along the shore in search of fish; and once a month we eagerly watch the steamer as she comes in, bringing, as we hope, a large number of home letters.

Our neighbors are mostly native Bitangas, with here and there an Arab trader, or a Portuguese who cannot speak English, who has always lived here, and seems to us to have imbibed a good many native customs. Our native neighbors are very abundant, and we never lack for company, although we cannot understand a word they say to us.

Inhambane is a thickly populated place, especially on the sea-coast, where the natives come for the sake of getting fish, crabs, and oysters to eat. Every day rows of women and girls pass our house with baskets on their heads filled with every imaginable living thing that inhabits the briny deep; at least you would think so if you could see the mass of wriggling, creeping things within their baskets. They take these home, boil them, put in a cocoanut, a little corn-meal, and enough red pepper to make one feel as if he were eating hot coals, and this makes a gravy, of which they are very fond.

Cocoanut-trees are abundant here. In every direction may be seen their tall, slender trunks, and broad, tropical leaves crowning the top. The nuts sell here for a cent apiece. Pineapples and peanuts also grow profusely, and bananas where there is any care taken of them. Though we have these things, which are a luxury to you, we would willingly give them all for some of your common potatoes, apples, and peaches.

It has been winter ever since we have been here; so, though the leaves are green, things in general have a dry, parched appearance, and we can hardly tell what beauties of flowers and foliage, what tempting fruits and garden vegetables, may develop when the rains come.

We have a grant of land from the Governor. On this we are permitted to preach, teach, or do anything we please. Away from this small space, however, we are given to understand that we will not be expected to teach religion in any way. Since this is a Portuguese colony the government is Roman Catholic; so, of course, it would not do to allow Protestants to come in and teach their doctrines, although the people now are not taught any kind of religion. So our plan for the present is to preach within our prescribed limits; to hire as many boys and girls as we can, who are to support themselves by work on the farm, and to form them into a school, to be taught night and morning, hoping for the future that the Government may become more lenient; so that we may get further grants of land; that the people may come to see the advantages of an education, and be anxious to come to us to be taught. If all these hopes fail, there is still the resort of extending our work beyond the Portuguese territory, which only reaches a short distance inland.

Following out this plan, we already have about thirty young men and women, boys and girls, studying night and morning, and working for us out of school-hours. At first we taught in our sitting-room; but now we have a little iron schoolhouse just completed. Every night and morning, at seven o'clock, the bell is rung, and all meet here. First we have prayers. Here we are troubled, because none of the Bible has yet been translated into Bitanga, and we have only one hymn, "Come to Jesus." Mr. Wilcox has translated part of the story of the Gospels. This he reads, and asks questions upon; then we sing either our one hymn, or something in Zulu, as some of our boys understand that language. After prayers each one of us takes a class to his particular corner of the schoolroom, and commences teaching *a*, *b*, *c*, or *b*, *a*, *ba*, as the case may be. This continues for an hour. Probably we shall teach longer as the classes advance. We think the majority of our scholars learn very quickly. Some of those who commenced two weeks ago can now pronounce words of two syllables, and during most of this time they have only studied one hour a day, while others have learned their letters in a week. Our trouble is, lest they get ready to commence reading before we can have anything in their language for them to read. Our work so far has been done by means of charts and cards, which we have printed by hand.

I begin to realize a little what an immense work it is to learn a new language without the aid of books, to reduce it to writing, and get books translated and printed. In this language some of the words, and sometimes the grammatical construction is like the Zulu; but as a rule it is quite different, so that we cannot understand anything that is said to us. Some of the people living here can speak Zulu, which is quite a help, as we can use them as interpreters.

The people here look very much like the people in Natal, but they have a different style of dress and different customs. It does not seem to me they are quite so handsome as the Zulus; but this may be because I have not yet become accustomed to their faces and manners. They cut their hair in many fantastic shapes. Parts of the head are kept shaved, while the rest of the hair is allowed to grow as long as it will, which is often three or four inches. These spots of long hair may be square, round, triangular, or any other shape, according to the taste of the owner or hair-dresser. Often it is made to stand out straight from the head by having each·little separate branch tied around tightly with strings. I have seen curls of this kind reach from the top of the head to the neck. One of our boys has his head closely shaven except a little bunch the size of my finger on the back of his head, and a similar bunch over each ear, which gives him the appearance of having horns. Another has a bunch on the back of his head exactly the shape of an old-fashioned chignon; while another has a bunch low down on his forehead, which, undoubtedly, he thinks is as handsome as any young lady's bang. Their chief ornaments are heavy brass rings. These clasp about the neck until it is impossible to move the head with any degree of comfort. They also wear them about the arms from the wrist to the elbow, and round the leg below the knee. Often there are so many it must be a burden to carry them around. They do not indulge in anything like the number of ornaments that the Zulus wear; but they are pleased if they can find either a string, or a piece of cloth, or of the bark of a tree, to tie around their heads, or a string of animal's teeth, or white buttons, or shells to wear about their necks. They do not wear many beads.

A well-dressed woman will have two colored handkerchiefs tied under the arm-pits, reaching to the waist, and two more from there reaching almost to the knees; this makes quite a respectable dress. It is more usual, however, for them to wear only two handkerchiefs fastened around the waist, leaving the upper part of the body uncovered. Many of the men dress in the same way, with two reaching from the waist to the knees. It is the first time I have ever seen men and women wearing the same dress. As a general thing I do not think the men dress as well as the Zulus; but here every little child has its handkerchief tied about it, while at Natal it was often thought unnecessary to put on any clothing at all until a child was almost grown.

This is called Umzila's mission because many of the people originally belonged to that chief, and I do not know but they consider themselves his subjects yet. In a short time we hope to reach out beyond the narrow limits of the Portuguese territory into Umzila's country proper. As a first step in this plan Mr. Richards is intending, next week, to start on a trip inland to a place called Balene, which was originally Umzila's headquarters, and where he keeps his cattle now. He will go prepared for a month's absence, and the news which he brings back may materially change our plans.

BULGARIA.

THE STORY OF MAREEKA DOSKALORA.

The following touching story is taken from private letters from Miss E. M. Stone, of Philippopolis: —

LET me tell you who Mareeka Doskalora is. When I reached Samokov the first time, she was in the school, a widow, whose husband had been killed in the war. She was still lame, from the effects of the bullet which lodged in her foot as she fled when her husband was killed. She was the one we sent to Palanka, in Macedonia, to teach a school of fifty children; but she proved unequal to the temptation which a Mr. Kristo brought before her, that she should marry him, and proved unfaithful to her trust, left her work without fulfilling her engagement to teach a year, and without notifying us. But how sorely she has suffered in consequence! She believes that she is dying of the remorse that she has suffered since that time.

Mareeka is very low in consumption, but she has had a great desire to have the sister's prayer-meetings in her house while she is still able to attend. A dozen of us gathered, and Mareeka insisted upon sitting on a chair like a well woman, and also spoke to us, warning every one to prepare for death while still in health. She had hoped to lead the meeting herself; but not being strong enough, Mrs. Nicolitza, who is from Mareeka's village, led it for her, as her substitute. Mareeka chose the subject, "Our Heavenly Home," and also selected one of the hymns. It was a sight to be remembered — the weak sufferer sitting in the midst, the bright flush upon her cheek and the brilliancy of the eye telling of the fever that raged within her frail body, while with husky tones and great effort she uttered the solemn words of testimony and of warning. At her knees stood her beautiful child, a tottling thing about fourteen months old. At last nothing would satisfy the small maid but that her mother should take her. She had been coaxing, pulling her mother's dress, looking pitifully into her eyes, and kissing the thin hand which was put down to restrain her; but at last burst out with a wailing which was only stopped when lifted to her mother's knee. Poor little willful, loving, baby girl! How little she knows what is before her!

Last Saturday morning it became plain that it was my duty, as I had for sometime felt that it would be my privilege, to take into my home our weak and suffering sister, Mrs. Mareeka Doskalora and [her family. Her landlady seemed to be beside herself when she learned that Mareeka had consumption. She was sure that she could never again rent her house, or use the furniture which they had hired with the house, and she acted like an insane person. Mareeka's husband could not succeed in finding a place to which to move, and Saturday last came to consult with me. Mr. Locke, of Samokov, was here, and on hearing the state of the case advised that I should take them; so I told Mr. Kristo not to look any farther for a house, but to bring Mareeka at once to me. He hesitated, fearing that I did not apprehend all the commotion which the coming would bring into our home; but the case admitted of no delay, and I hurried him away to tell Mareeka, feeling sure she would be relieved to know that she was to come. After dinner Mr. Locke took my steamer shawl and hood down for Mareeka, and soon a carriage brought her to our gate. Poor tired child! She met me with expressions of thankfulness that she had come to spend her last days with me. Her husband lifted her in his arms and bore her up to my room, where she was soon resting upon my bed, almost exhausted from the short journey. She passed a comfortable night, and in the morning seemed so bright and cheerful that her husband, Mrs. Nicolitza, and Mareeka Nerona went to morning service while I stayed with Mrs. Mareeka.

In the afternoon I was obliged to go to my little people in the Sabbath-school: they now number about thirty, and are now working earnestly for the new Morning Star. Mareeka rested very much during the Sabbath and the following night, and often in her feeble whisper gave expression to the thankfulness of her heart that God had brought her into such a quiet resting-place. Her room is a chamber of peace indeed. What bits of heavenly experience we have by that bedside! To-day I was preparing food for her when Mrs. Nicolitza came, saying, "Mareeka wants you!" How heavy were the eyes, while the cruel hectic burned fiercely in her cheeks! "What is it, Mareeka?" She stretched out her poor weak arms and tiny, emaciated hands, and took me into them as she said, "Pray." In her urgency she repeated the request; and as we together carried her and her needs to the Father, the peace which the blessed Master promised to his own came into all her being, and she rested. Each evening she calls us around her bed for our family prayers, and usually she selects the hymns. To-night it was, "They talk of the heavenly land;"

and it is always of heaven. We are living upon the border-land with her during these days. She will pass over, and be satisfied in the joy of her Lord. The rest of us must return, and labor on until our call comes. Then, what joy! The dear baby girl is here now; also her aunt and little cousin, ostensibly to take care of her.

March 12th. Our dear Mrs. Mareeka is steadily going down into "the valley," and I know not whether she may not cross the river before the morning light; but so I feel every night now, and during the day it sometimes seems as though she were slipping away from us, and she rallies again. To-night I come to you from Mareeka's bedside; she expects me every evening to go to her for a good-night talk. She has been able to say but very little for almost a week past, and to-night she said, "You talk, and I will listen." Her whisper is so very faint that I must put my ear close to her lips in order to hear. So, on my knees at her side, we talk together of going "home"; of her meeting with her Lord, and with the loved ones who are already there; and it seems as if I, too, were almost "home," as is this blessed child. It is a precious hour to me.

March 15th. Yesterday we had our sister's meeting here in my room, and it was a very precious season. We were not many in number, but I am sure we all felt that the Master was with us. Our poor Mareeka was so much distressed that I could hardly bear to leave her for the meeting, but we had great comfort in praying for her; and when the wife of Pastor Tonjoroff went in with me to see her after the meeting, we knew that while we were yet speaking, God had heard and sent her peace and quietness. As she grows weaker she grows more clinging; and it is a tax upon my time which I feel it is right for me to allow, as it comforts her if I am often with her.

The next letter from Miss Stone is dated March 19th — written on the way to Yamboul. She received a sudden call to that place to investigate a matter connected with the Bible-work which needed her special, personal attention. She writes:—

I left my sick one in Mrs. Thomson's care. It was very hard to leave her. I hope to find her living when I return on Saturday; but I know that she felt when I was leaving her this morning that she was bidding me good-bye for the last time. It seemed unquestionably God's call that I should go. I cannot help feeling anxious; yet God will care for her.

On her return she writes.—

Was not God good to me? I found Mareeka still living, but

dying. When the train drew up at the station, I hardly dared ask for her; but, when I ventured, Mr. Thomson thought I might find her living, but very low. I shall always be thankful that I was permitted to get home to her, for she had wanted me. She had suffered terribly during my absence; but now the end was near. "Remember that I die with a sure hope in Christ," was her word to us who stood watching by her bedside. More than once she called upon us to pray that Jesus would come and take her "home." Although so under the influence of powerful opiates (given to relieve her pain) that she could not open her eyes, I think she was perfectly conscious to the last. The burial was at 4 P. M. on Monday.

TURKEY.

NOTICE OF THE CONSTANTINOPLE HOME.

We are indebted to Miss Patrick and Mr. H. O. Dwight for the following translation of an article which appeared in the *Tarik*, an Armenian paper issued in Constantinople. When we remember the adverse articles with reference to the Home that have appeared, from time to time, in the city papers, the favorable tone of this one affords gratifying evidence of the position the institution is gaining in the community.

THE AMERICAN GIRLS' SCHOOL IN SCUTARI.

ALTHOUGH many have observed the handsome buildings erected for the girls' school which the Americans have founded in Scutari, few have seen their interior.

Yesterday, one of our staff had an opportunity to look over this school, and this is what he saw.

Entering the premises, one encounters trees and flowers beautifying a garden that surrounds the buildings. On the right is a wooden building, where the primary classes are taught. The children there were busy with reading, writing, and sewing.

The school itself, which is called *Home* (that is to say, being interpreted, *House*), consists of two elegant stone buildings. As we entered, we saw a pile of books in French, handsomely bound in red and gold, which had just been brought in for the library of the school. A maid invited us into a saloon set apart for visitors. In the room was a lady just brought from America to superintend the household. She was learning Turkish from a professor. This lady received the guests, and word having been sent to the lady Principal, she also came, and showed us into the schoolrooms and recitation-rooms.

On entering the first room the teacher and pupils rose and saluted the guests, and then went on with their recitation. The lesson was in geometry, and three or four girls were at the blackboard, where they drew the figures with skill, and afterward explained the problems in English, in full accord with the text-books. These text-books were printed in America, prepared in such a way as to greatly facilitate the acquirement of the science. They were adorned with the necessary figures, and their paper and delicacy of printing, and even their bindings, were in accord with the rules of elegance.

There was not the slightest noise in the room. Every pupil, cleanly and neatly dressed, sat quietly in her place with her book before her.

In another recitation-room a lesson in geology was going on. The text-books in this class were also printed in America, and supplied with all needed illustrations.

The teacher was explaining about the extinct reptiles found fossilized in the rocks. The ready answers of the girls showed that they had well learned their lesson.

In another room a French recitation was going on. There a lady from Paris was causing the pupils to read a poem, correcting with great care every error in pronunciation. Afterward she had them write on the blackboard, explaining the grammatical relations of the words, and correcting all mistakes in spelling.

As recess then occurred the Principal took her guests over the other building. Over one of the doors a tablet recorded in gilt letters that the building had been put up at the expense of an American named Mr. Barton.* The dormitory, on the upper floor, was a model of neatness. By the bed of every pupil was a closet, for her clothes and other requisites. Each one was ornamented with pictures inside. The dormitory and some other rooms had in the walls or in the floors an instrument made of thick glass, with a brass grating over it, by which they were warmed from a stove burning in the basement or in another room.

One room was set apart for the use of pupils who wished to read outside of school-hours, and there were in this room many books of science and literature in English and French, besides an American Encyclopedia in several volumes.

In another hall was philosophical apparatus. For instance, there was, to illustrate anatomy, a real skull, with the crown arranged to take off, so that the student of this science might see the most delicate parts of the eye, the nose, and the ear.

The dining-hall of the institution was of a neatness entirely in keeping with the rest of the building.

---

* Barton Hall; the gift of Mr. Chapin, Providence, R. I.

In concluding this description of the order and good organization seen in this school, we only pray that thoroughly good schools may hourly increase in our Fatherland.— *From the " Tarik," Nov.* 15, 1884.

GLEANINGS FROM RECENT LETTERS.

Miss Price writes from Inanda, South Africa:—

Another additional work was cutting and making dresses for the outside heathen girls. All around Inanda there are schools under the care of the missionary for these undressed heathen people; but just as soon as they begin to go to school they want clothes. The first step toward civilization is, as I think it should be, a dress. But these have no sort of an idea how to begin to make one. They never sewed a stitch in their lives; so what are they to do? They are mostly little girls, who have no money, and whose fathers do not care anything about having them dressed. They manage to beg corn enough from their fathers to partly pay for some calico, and we give the rest, and the lining, buttons, and thread. Then who is to make them? The missionary, if they are made at all. So to work we go, believing a dress will, or may do, as much good as a sermon. The school-girls, while they were here, helped cut and baste, while the seams were sewed on the machine. After the girls went away we had it all to do ourselves, so dress-making occupied most of our vacation. We have clothed about sixty girls; and Mrs. Edwards, who has charge of these outside schools, has clothed as many more. So over a hundred girls have in the last two months put on a dress for the first time; and you have no idea how intelligent it does make them look to have on a clean, new dress. Dress certainly does a good deal toward making the woman.

Miss Harding writes from Sholapur:—

Oh! how we should thank God for the happy homes Christianity gives us! The more one learns of the wretched child-marriage of this land, the more dark the picture grows, and we who live here know it is not simply a sad romance, with no foundation, like the stories in books, but the living, bitter reality in almost every heathen home. I am reminded here of what Mrs. Bissell saw on one of her tours last winter. If I remember rightly, it was one day when Mrs. Bissell was on her way to speak to the women of a near village. Along the road in front of her she saw what looked like an old woman, bent with age, creeping feebly along, and she wondered why such an one should be alone; but as she overtook her she found, to her great surprise, that it was a young girl not more than ten or twelve years old. On inquiring what caused her pain and weariness, the child began to cry bitterly, and little by little let the story out. She had been married two or three years ago, and, as is the custom, was sent to her mother-in-law's, to learn her ways. The Hindu mother-in-law is noted for her heartlessness, but the course this one took seems almost incredible. Some little thing the child could not help annoyed the woman, and so in a fit of anger she took up a hot coal and burned the child on her back. They know nothing about caring for a burn like this, and so it has grown worse and worse, until the child had reached the crippled state in which Mrs. Bissell found her. Does it not make one's heart ache to hear of such misery?

It is pleasant to turn from such a picture to the happy Christian marriages of many of our girls. And if we can only teach these girls how to make a happy home, and prepare them to be the helpmeets they should be to their husbands, it will be doing a little, will it not, to undermine this great curse?

----◄◆►----

A SILK QUILT SERMON. A Christian woman was laid aside from active usefulness, yet her hands still followed her heart in labors of love. Silk quilts amused and employed her time, shut in as she was not only from out-door life, but the pleasant variety of household duties. One quilt found its way to a distant mission-house in Turkey. Would it not be a comfort to somebody there? By and by it was heard from.

"I assure you," wrote the missionary lady, "your quilt was, is, and will be a joy to our hearts, as well as a very useful article in our house, filling a niche which has been empty for some time. When I reach home Sabbath morning from my large class of men, and a walk of twenty minutes up a steep hill, it is a real luxury to throw myself on the lounge for a few minutes and wrap such a thing of beauty over me; and I do not think it is all imagination that I rest faster because my eyes rest on its pretty colors; but I have a story to tell of good done in another direction. The week it came, permission had just been received from the Government to begin building for the sufferers of the great fire; and as our means are very limited compared with our needs, the pastor felt that, though the brethren, like others, could sincerely say, 'Silver and gold have I none,' yet it was very necessary to stir them to the giving of 'such as they had.' How to do it was the question. When your quilt came we had the answer. It was taken to the church, hung on the black mud wall, and the pastor, with your daughter's letter in his hand, saying that though aged and feeble you had 'done what you could,' urged every man, woman, and child to come and do 'likewise.' Some could bring water; others, stone and mortar; the stronger could handle pick-axe and shovel; while the skilled could assist in building up the walls, or in preparing the timber. The result was not less than a hundred days' labor on the houses so far built, besides the free labor promised on those to be erected. We thank our Father every day for the beautiful quilt, and we know he will give you a hundred-fold joy for your work of love.''

Was not this pastor skilled in object-teaching?   H. C. K.

Young People's Department.

TURKEY.

LETTER FROM MRS. BARNUM.

HARPOOT, TURKEY, Nov. 6, 1884.

DEAR FRIENDS: If the daughter of one of your judges should visit one of your colleges, you would not regard it as a matter of very special importance. But when, a few days ago, the daughter of the Turkish judge, or *cadi*, as he is called here, visited our Girls' School and made an address, we felt that it was quite a remarkable event, and worthy of special notice.

We had heard something about this lady before she came; that she had been educated in Constantinople, and that she felt much interested in the education of her sex, and had written a letter to the Board of Education here asking that a school be opened for Turkish girls, and promising her assistance.

When she arrived at our house, and had taken off her black gauze veil, and thrown back the bright silk sheet which enveloped her figure, we saw a young, pretty girl, very affable and pleasing in her manners.

As she had come from Mezeré, the seat of Government, about an hour distant, and was to return that afternoon, she could make but a brief call at our houses. After refreshments had been served, she asked if she might go to the Girls' School. An Armenian Protestant lady who accompanied her, privately informed us that she had prepared an address, which she would like to read to the girls.

We looked into some of the rooms as we passed along, heard the girls play on the organ, and sing, stayed a few minutes in the room for the little girls,—being a sort of Kindergarten,—and then took our seats on the platform in the large schoolroom, where all the girls were assembled for her to see. The *cadi's* daughter then arose, and gracefully saluting the girls in Oriental style, read the following address in Turkish, of which she gave me the copy:—

"GENTLE GIRLS: Seeing the complete order and arrangement of your school, I am impelled to say a few words to you. I count myself fortunate to be able to congratulate you upon your attainments in different branches of knowledge.

" Of the countless blessings which God has graciously given to mankind, one is mind, the value of which it is impossible to compute. Therefore every girl who is conscious of possessing this priceless gift should strive to outstrip her companions in the pursuit of knowledge and science, putting aside all vain things, because it requires very little observation or experience to distinguish between the learned and the ignorant.

"If girls give their minds earnestly to the acquisition of knowledge, they render a real service to their country, because all the children of the land, for at least seven years, are under the care and training of females.

"I, also, through the favor of His Majesty, our Emperor, having acquired a little education at the Imperial Female Normal School, hold His Majesty always in grateful remembrance in my prayers; and reminding you who are so fortunate as to live under the reign of such an Emperor, who is the zealous friend and patron of learning, of your obligations to him, I beg you, for the love of country, not to spend your time in vain, but to give your best endeavors to your advancement in knowledge.

—NEIME, *daughter of the Judge of Harpoot.*"

When she had finished reading she again made the *salaam*, and sat down.

As all the girls are not very familiar with the Turkish language, the pastor's wife, Mrs. Shimavonian, translated for them, and then they arose, and, thanking the young lady, returned the salutation.

We afterward visited the various rooms and departments of the building — the kitchen, bathroom, sinkroom, office, etc.; and the *cadi's* daughter expressed great delight at everything which she saw.

The girls performed some of their gymnastic exercises; and as they marched past the platform each in turn saluted our guest, which she as politely returned to each one. This was the more noticeable because Turkish women have sometimes visited us and never given the salutation, either on entering the room or on leaving. The more bigoted believe it is a sin to give the *salaam* to Christians. The *cadi's* daughter was quite charming in her manners, and won all our hearts.

It is quite a wonderful thing in this region for a Turkish girl to know how to write, though many of them can read. The reason which has been given for not teaching them to write is, lest they should begin to correspond with young men. Such an example, though so rare, gives us encouragement in the work of promoting female education in this land.

THE BRIGHT-FACED WOMAN WHO LIVES IN THE CHURCH.

BY MISS JULIA A. GULICK.

LAST week I heard the story of the bright-faced woman who lives in the church, and takes care of it. Her home was with her parents, in Murakami, some forty miles to the north of here, just outside of treaty limits, and her husband was an adopted son.

They had lived together a number of years, and had a daughter six or seven years old, who died about the time they heard of Christianity.

The husband became interested, and attended the meetings held in that town, frequently with the consent of his adopted father, and his wife was allowed to attend sometimes, till she also became much interested. Then the idea began to get abroad that these young people were becoming identified with the Jesus religion, and the father, hearing of it from the neighbors, concluded it was time this should be stopped, and told the adopted son that he must give it up, or he would not have him in his house.

But it was too late; the young man had rather give up his house than his new-found treasure. So he was cast out of the family; but his wife, who declared that she was of the same mind as her husband, and wished to go with him, was not allowed to do so. She was taken to the police headquarters, where she was reprimanded for her disobedient spirit, and sent back to her parents. For a year she lived a sort of prisoner at home — not allowed to attend any of the meetings nor to read her Bible at home; and only by stealth did she manage to see some of the Christians occasionally, and through them exchange messages with her husband, who had come to Niigata to earn a living. At the end of a year the parents professed to adopt another husband for her in place of the one who had been sent away. But she declined to accept another husband, though she would make no objection if they chose to adopt a son, who might be as a brother to her.

But they were determined, and gathered all the relatives together to compel her consent. She stood firm, however, in the presence of all the assembled relatives, and said she would do anything else they wished, but she *could not* take another husband. This was the harder because a woman, no matter what her age, is not supposed to have any rights in such a matter which relatives and friends are bound to respect; and concluding that she would be forced to yield if she remained there, she planned her escape. That very night, after the company had dispersed, and at a late hour, when ready to retire, she stepped out the back-door in her night-dress and made her way round to the street, and thence to the house of a Christian doctor, who is now here connected with Dr. Palm's hospital, and our nearest neighbor.

The doctor dared not keep her in his house, lest the parents should come there to look for her; but he gave her advice, and sent her elsewhere to lodge. Early the next morning she started for another town fifteen miles distant, where she was kindly entertained by the Christians two or three days, till she could come and join her husband in this place. Here she kept in the house, and out of sight as much as possible for some time, until the breeze had blown over.

She learned in some way that her parents searched the ponds in the neighborhood, to see whether she had drowned herself. As she left in her night-clothes, and had taken nothing with her, they hardly thought she could have run away. Whether they learned of her whereabouts soon or not, I do not know; but, after a time, they sold all her clothing, for they could not bear the sight of it.

Latterly she has tried to get the register of her name transferred from her parents' home to that of her husband, which is necessary in order to make her legally his wife, but she cannot. Her parents will not give it up, though they are not reconciled enough even to receive a present from their daughter.

She wonders now how she stood so firm when she knew so little of Christ, and had been in the habit of implicit obedience. She thinks the Lord must have helped her in an especial manner; and she thinks he took her child in kindness, as she might not have had courage to escape the snare and leave her child behind. This occurred about five years ago. I have never seen the husband — he is away on business; but the woman is a very bright-faced, happy Christian, though her heart yearns over her parents, whom she seems unable to reach in any way. May there be more such people ready to give up all for Christ.

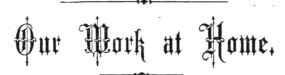

Our Work at Home.

SPECIAL APPEALS IN MISSIONARY WORK.

IN connection with the article on "Special Appropriations," in the December number, we should like to say a few words with reference to contributions for objects outside the regular appropriations of the Board. We are not sure that the method of deciding on these appropriations is fully understood; and for the sake of those not fully informed we will explain it somewhat in detail.

The territory under the care of the American Board is divided into missions — such as the Zulu Mission, the Western, Central, and Eastern Turkey Missions, and others. These are subdivided into stations, as the Inanda station, the Aintab station, etc. Each Mission holds an annual meeting, composed of representatives from each station, to decide upon the needs of its own field. At this meeting every missionary has an opportunity, either personally or by proxy, to present what he or she considers necessary for the work under his or her special care. All matters of interest are discussed; but it is the subject of money that concerns us in the present article.

Each mission receives word from the Prudential Committee of the American Board of the amount of money that can probably be relied upon from the churches for its needs, and requested to bring the estimates within the sum specified. Other items can be adopted as contingents, to be provided if the contributions at home will warrant it. This sounds very simple; but we are assured that it is one of the most perplexing parts of missionary work. The difficulty is, that the funds promised fall so far short of the absolute necessities of the different stations. What part of the work shall be retained, and what shall be given up for want of funds? Each item is scrutinized over and over again; this one and that one is reluctantly taken off the list; till at last what are considered as most vital to the work are retained, and put into the estimates to be sent to this country. These, when adopted by the Prudential Committee, become what are called the regular appropriations of the Board.

The woman's work in these appropriations is taken by the three Woman's Boards, and given out to the branches; and they, in turn, assign it to auxiliaries and mission circles, on whom rests the final responsibility as to whether it shall be provided for or not.

Since the responsibility rests where it does, it becomes important that the money raised by each organization shall be used in the very best way. Since the various missions, by a majority vote, point out the absolutely necessary work, and since it is to this that Boards, branches, auxiliaries, and mission circles are alike pledged, it is reasonable, indeed, it is really a duty, to ask that this shall be provided for first; that the contributions, on which it depends, shall not be diverted to any other purpose, however important it may seem to be.

Now let us suppose a case. Some missionaries — to apply the matter to ourselves, we will say some young ladies — attend the annual meeting of the mission. They are ardent and earnest, and full of plans for the work opening before them. They are teachers in boarding-schools, and are giving themselves heart and soul to the girls under their charge — anxious only for their best interests. One of them is fresh from America, and well versed in all the modern ideas of teaching. She remembers the well-appointed school-rooms,— possibly the delights of her *alma mater*, like Wellesley or Mt. Holyoke, linger with her like a beautiful dream,— with every appliance to make a royal road to learning; and then she contrasts them with a certain school she has begun to love in a dark, dingy room, without charts, or maps, or apparatus of any kind, without even desks, perhaps, where the sleeping-accommodations are cramped and crowded, and she naturally feels that some improvement is absolutely necessary. Another knows of several promising girls whose parents, after a long struggle, have at last consented to have them come to her school if their support can be provided, and she feels she must have a larger appropriation for her school. A third has a graduate, an earnest Christian, who is anxious to go to work as a teacher or Bible-woman in her native village; a matter much to be desired both for the girl and for her village.

These items are presented, and one after another they are voted down. The combined estimates make up a sum much larger than the outside limit given from America, and something must be cut down. What shall it be? Girls *can* learn to read and study the Bible sitting on a floor in a dingy room. The promising girls are young, and if they wait a year they may find some way for their own support, and another year the people in the distant village may feel the need of the services of the young graduate sufficiently to provide her salary. To be sure, there is always the danger that the same opportunities may never occur again: the girls may drift away and lose their interest, and the little spark in the distant village, for want of fanning, may die out altogether. If there were money enough for all, these would be gladly voted; but there are other things more important, where the work of years may be lost or long retarded by the lack of assistance at the opportune moment. There is also another aspect to the case. What is asked may, in the judgment of those of long experience, be a positive injury to the work. Too much luxury in a school might unfit the girls for the dark, dingy homes to which they must go when school-days are over. Of course their ideas of home-life must be elevated, but not beyond a point that will prevent their usefulness and happiness in the work they are preparing to do. It is well known, also, that the attainment of self-support in the schools and village work may be much retarded by giving injudicious assistance. The instances we have mentioned would require only small sums, but the principle would of course apply with greater force to large amounts.

Our missionaries go back to their work sadly disappointed at the failure of their cherished plans. They remember the lavish expenditure in this country; and all they need is the cost of one luxury among thousands. They remember, also, the many kind letters they have received from friends and auxiliaries, with the question, "What can I do for you?" and the temptation is almost irresistible to make a special appeal to some of these sources. This appeal comes to the auxiliary warm and glowing from the heart of the writer, and the response comes spontaneously, and often without much thought. The society has been in the habit of sending its money to the general fund of the Board or Branch, or for some object that has come to it through the ordinary routine; but "this is so much more interesting." It is voted that the funds of the society shall go for this special purpose; and the treasury of the Board lacks just so much for the work to which it is pledged. All money sent in this way goes to the recipient as a "private donation;" it does not go into our treasury, nor appear in our accounts, or published acknowledgments. Our Treasurer merely passes it along, as a matter of convenience.

If such cases occurred only once or twice in the course of the year, the matter would be comparatively simple; but if they were to be multiplied indefinitely, danger would become serious. Within the week from this time of writing, between four and five hundred dollars has been received, specified for work not in the regular appropriations of the Board. There are instances where the response to appeals is an extra effort beyond the regular work of the society, which are not open to the same objections; and with the gifts of individuals we have, of course, nothing whatever to do. By way of caution, however, we wish to say that the experience of many shows that such extra efforts are very liable to re-act, though unintentionally, on the usual contributions.

Since we are on this topic we would like to guard against misunderstandings that may arise in the way of correspondence. When a person writes to the missionary that a certain sum of money has been sent to the treasury of the Board, for some one under her care, it should be stated whether it is for the regular work of the Board, or for her private use, as an extra gift. Instances have occurred where money has been thought to be extra, and the missionary having discovered that it was for the regular work, has been obliged to pay for the new work she has planned through the gift, from her own purse. Care should also be taken in sending private donations to the Branch or Board Treasurer, to state distinctly that it is such, and so prevent mistakes and disappointments.

From what has been said we hope no one will think the officers of the Board do not sympathize in the special need of its missionaries. They feel them very strongly, and strain every nerve to supply them, but it is an absolute duty to be just before they are generous; to fulfill their pledges before undertaking other work; and to be sure the money intrusted to them accomplishes the greatest possible good. The simplest solution of the whole question is, for the regular receipts of the Board to be so increased as to supply all reasonable demands.

ANNUAL MEETING OF THE PHILADELPHIA BOARD.

BRIGHT Indian summer days greeted the delegates as they wended their way to the fourteenth annual meeting of the Philadelphia Branch on November 12th and 13th, while glad faces and banks of glowing chrysanthemums smiled their bright welcome within the church.

Being held this year in Trinity Church, Orange, N. J., within easy access of most of the societies, a larger number of delegates was reported than usual.

Miss A. P. Halsey, the president, conducted the opening half-hour of prayer, giving for the motto of the sessions, "For the love of Christ constraineth us."

After the presentation of the annual report, the Woman's Board was represented by Miss Stanwood in a spirited, earnest address, while letters from the missionaries brought them spiritually near. At the children's service, at four o'clock on Wednesday afternoon, a large number of children and young ladies were present, taking active part in the Bible exercise and singing. One little fellow was so delighted that he asked permission to come again in the evening. Short addresses were made by Miss Stanwood, Mrs. Knapp, and the president.

Rev. R. G. Greene, pastor of the church, conducted the evening service, and a large audience listened with close attention to the rapid utterance of eloquent, prophetic thoughts on "Foreign Missions, and their Relation to and Influence upon Woman," by Rev. Arthur Brooks, of New York City.

On Thursday morning interesting reports were read from each Society, all manifesting growth and zeal — one sending three delegates which for several years has been unrepresented. An increase of nearly $400 was reported by the treasurer over last year's receipts. Mrs. Knapp, from Bitlis, in her address, touched all hearts deeply with the simple story of their life in Turkey.

A bountiful lunch, prepared by the hospitable entertainers, drew the guests together in social converse, thus cementing more strongly the "sweet tie that binds all hearts."

All through the closing session pearls of wisdom and experience dropped from the lips of Miss Gilman, president of the Eastern Connecticut Branch, Miss Foster of the Board of Missions of the Episcopal Church, and Miss Stanwood of Boston, who congratulated the Branch on retaining the services of the new district secretary. Miss A. P. Halsey, as the president of the Branch, with the tender regret of the parting hour, mingled joy in each heart that another year was before us of glad work for Him.

HARRIET C. HINDS.

ANNUAL MEETING OF THE HARTFORD BRANCH.

THE tenth annual meeting of the Hartford Branch of the Woman's Board of Missions was held in the Center Church, October 15th.

The meeting opened with the singing of Coronation. Dr. Thompson then followed, reading the forty-fifth Psalm and offering prayer.

The recording secretary, in speaking of its being the tenth anniversary, said, "Only one has remained in office the whole time — Mrs. Jewell." Mrs. Williams spoke of our beloved missionary, Mrs. Winsor, leaving her only daughter in this country to be educated while she returned to India, to resume her mission work. Ought she not in time of trial to be especially remembered by her co-workers in America. Five mission circles have been added to our number the past year.

The treasurer reported $4,774.75 received during the year; all of which was transmitted to Boston, incidental expenses being provided in other ways.

Cheering reports of Hartford and Tolland Counties followed.

Miss Child brought a pleasant greeting from the Boston Board, encouraging the small auxiliaries by speaking of their great helpfulness.

Mrs. Jewell gave us a bird's-eye view of the ten years just ended. Six missionaries have been supported by the Branch, and $35,000 raised during that time. The auxiliaries number 43, and the mission circles 33.

It was a pleasure to hear Miss Cumings give an account of the beginning of the Huguenot Seminary, in Wellington, South Africa, and to know that already four missionaries had gone out from that school, and that the pupils, interesting themselves in the blacks, had started a Sunday-school and cottage prayer-meetings, which were well attended, and organized a temperance society.

After a few moments spent in devotional exercises, the meeting adjourned till afternoon.

Greetings from the Springfield, New Haven, and New London Branches made us all feel that we were serving under one banner, and for one end — the extension of Christ's kingdom.

Miss Eliza Talcott, from Japan, spoke of the change in that country since she went there fourteen years ago. Then, Bibles were sold at the risk of one's life; now, a store had been opened for their sale, the Governor ignoring its existence. Ten years ago only one church in all Japan; now there were twenty-two in this one station (Kobe), with two thousand members.

The report of mission circles was encouraging, showing the formation of five new ones.

A paper entitled "Missionaries of Hartford County" was read by Mrs. Curtis. The first missionary sailed for the Sandwich Islands in 1822. Much was made in those early days of mission work among the Indians, many choosing that field. Mary Van Lennep, dying at the early age of twenty-three at Smyrna, is familiar through her biography to many of us, and as the daughter of the Rev. Joel Hawes, pastor of the Center Church in this city.

All too soon the closing hour came. Prof. Bissell encouraged us by contrasting our feeble beginnings with our present growth, and the thought of what might be accomplished within ten years.

We sang once more our closing hymn, "Blest be the tie that binds," and bade each other good-bye with the encouraging thoughts uttered through the day stored in our memories, to cheer us through the coming year.   A. A. W.

INTERNATIONAL MISSIONARY UNION.

An assembly entitled "The International Missionary Union," was held at Wesley Park, Niagara Falls, beginning Monday, Aug. 18, 1884, and continuing through the week. This assembly was the result of an attempt made to get missionaries of, all societies together, that they might compare their methods of work, talk over the difficulties met with, and form themselves into an organized body in order to increase their power and influence as workers, both at home and abroad.

A great many were present at the first gathering, and addresses were made by missionaries representing the Methodist, Congregational, Baptist, and Presbyterian societies, both in the United States and Canada. India probably had the most representatives, but there were several from China, others from Japan, Africa, Siam, West Indies, Mexico, and South America. Each meeting was attended by an interested and enthusiastic audience.

One of the features of the gathering was an exhibit of a large number of missionary periodicals published by the several societies in Canada, the United States, Great Britain, India, and Mexico; also of missionary maps, leaflets, books, etc., many specimens being given away to persons in the audience desiring them. At the close of the meetings an organization was formed, to include all foreign missionaries abroad and at home, whether on furlough or retired, and the following officers were elected: —

President, Rev. J. T. Gracey, D.D., American Methodist, India. *Secretary,* Miss F. M. Morris, American Board, Zululand. *Executive Committee,* Rev. S. L. Baldwin, D.D., American Methodist, China; Rev. W. H. Porter, Canada Baptist, West Indies; H. T. Whitney, M.D., American Board, China.

It is requested that all *retired* missionaries who are willing to help in this organization will send name and address to the Secretary, No. 1 Congregational House, Boston, Mass.

WOMAN'S BOARD OF MISSIONS.

RECEIPTS FROM NOVEMBER 18 TO DECEMBER 18, 1884.

MAINE.

Maine Branch. — Mrs. Woodbury S. Dana, Treas. Skowhegan, Aux., $8, M. C., $5; Greenville, Aux., $17; Thomaston, Cong. Ch. and Soc'y, $7, Morning Star Circle, $3; Albany, Mrs. Lovejoy, $5; Farmington, Aux., $8, Mrs.

F. V. Stewart's S. S. Cl., 50 cts.; Yarmouth, 1st Cong. Ch., Aux., $18.49; Limerick, Cong. Ch., Ladies, $6; Calais, Aux., $9.35; Brownville, Gleaners, $25; Brunswick, 1st Parish, Aux., $94.70, $207 04
Wells.—1st Cong. Ch., Ladies,   16 50
                    Total, $223 54

NEW HAMPSHIRE.

Greenville.—Mrs. Alma Scripture, $1 00
Newport.—Mrs. Eliza Comings, 2 55

Total, $3 55

VERMONT.

Vermont Branch.— Mrs. T. M. Howard, Treas. Burlington, Aux., $21, Helping Hands, $40; Cambridge, Aux., $14; Middlebury, Aux., $103.83; Vergennes, S. S., $40; Royalton, Aux., $10; Hartford, Aux., $28; St. Johnsbury, No. Ch., Boys' Miss'y Soc'y, $15, Girls' Benevolent Circle, $30, Redeemed Pledges, $4; Post Mills, 50 cts.; Thetford, Aux., $8, $314 33
Coventry.—Children's M. C., 23 00

Total, $337 33

LEGACY.

Vermont Branch.—Legacy of Miss Mary Hastings, St. Johnsbury, $100 00

MASSACHUSETTS.

Barnstable Co. Branch. — Miss Amelia Snow, Treas. Chatham, Aux., $10; Sandwich, Aux., $2.50; Falmouth, Aux., of wh. $100 const. L. M. Miss Effie L. Fish, $172.35; Harwich, Aux., $20; E. Falmouth, Aux., $16; No. Falmouth, Aux., $20; Orleans, Aux., $5.25, $246 10
Berkshire Branch—Mrs. S. N. Russell, Treas. Pittsfield, 1st Ch., Aux., $10.89; Monterey, $20, 30 89
Essex North Conf. Branch.— Mrs. A. Hammond, Treas. Newburyport, Aux., $68.75; Bradford, Aux., $113.25, Academy, F. M. S., $26.11, · 208 11
Essex South Conf. Branch.— Miss Sarah W. Clark, Treas. Boxford, Earnest Workers, $15; Beverly, Dane St. Ch., Aux., $156; Ipswich, South Ch., $7, 178 00
Franklin Co. Branch.— Miss L. A. Sparhawk, Treas. Ashfield, Aux., $10; Bernardston, Aux., $13.50; Northfield, Aux., $17.80; Greenfield, Aux., $5.25, Sunderland Acorns, $8, 54 55
Freetown.—Cong. Ch., 3 62
Greenwich Village.—Miss L. A. Parker, 1 40

Hampshire Co. Branch.—Miss Isabella G. Clarke, Treas. Southampton, Aux., $25.25; Northampton, Edwards Ch. Div., $33; E. Amherst, $26.90; Hadley, Aux., $43.50, M. C. Rally, add'l, 50 cts, $129 15
Lowell.—Union Aux., 106 00
Norfolk and Pilgrim Branch.—Mrs. Franklin Shaw, Treas. Hanover, Aux., $12; Holbrook, Little Lights, $14; Weymouth and Braintree, Aux., $6.50; Braintree, Aux., $6, 38 50
Old Colony Branch. — Miss F. J. Runnels, Treas. Middleboro, Band of Good-Will, 50 00
Phillipston.—A few Ladies, 4 50
Springfield Branch.—Miss H. T. Buckingham, Treas. Westfield, 2d Ch., Girls' Guild, $40; Springfield, So. Ch., Mrs. C. E. Blake, const. L. M. Mrs. Lucy S. Blake, $25, 65 00
Suffolk Branch.—Miss Myra B. Child, Treas. Boston, Central Ch., Aux., $225, Union Ch., $1; Roxbury, Eliot Ch., Aux., $60, Thompson Circle, 50 cts., Olive Branch, $1, Walnut Ave. Ch., Mrs. C. A. Aldrich, const. L. M. Miss Bell B. Aldrich, $25; W. Roxbury, So. Evan. Ch., Aux., $50; Cambridgeport, Prospect St. Ch., Aux., $20; Cambridge, Aux., No. Ch., $139.12, Shepard Ch., $160.88; Somerville, Franklin St. Ch., const. L. M. Mrs. H. M. Moore, $25; Brookline, Mrs. Lydia Hooper, $2, E. P., $1; Brighton, Fanueil Rushlights, $1; Dedham, Chapel Rays, $30, Asylum Dime Soc'y, $1.54; Waltham, Miss N. S. Bond, $5, 748 04
Templeton.—Aux., 25 00
Wellesley Hills.—Aux., 85 50
Woburn Conf. Branch.— Mrs. N. W. C. Holt, Treas. Billerica, S. S., prev. contri. const. L. M. Miss Nettie R. Bruce, $1.74; Bedford, Pine-Needles, $10.50; Medford, Aux., $100; Woburn, Aux., of wh. $25 by Mrs. M. J. Keyes, const. L. M. Miss Clara M. Ames, $25 by Miss R. M. Leathe, const. L. M. Mrs. W. W. Hill, add'l const. L. M. Mrs. Harriet P. Brown, $110; Woburn Workers, $15; Maplewood, Aux., $12; Winchester, Aux., $77, Eddie's M. C., $10; Malden, Aux., by Mrs. E. A. Stevens, const. L. M. Mrs. C. O. Walker, $25; No. Woburn, Aux., $9, 370 24

64 *LIFE AND LIGHT.*

Worcester Co. Branch.—Mrs. G. W. Russell, Treas. Fitchburg, Rollstone Ch., $108, C. C. Ch., $50.08; Shrewsbury, Aux., of wh, $25 const. L. M. Mrs. F. H. Allen, $32; Athol, Aux., $26; Westminster, Aux., $16; Uxbridge, Aux., $27.50; Gardner, Aux., $20; Winchendon, No. Cong. Ch., prev. contri. const. L. M's Mrs. M. L. Manzer, Mrs. A. M. Royse, Miss Hattie M. Wyman, Miss Addie L. Royse, $45; Upton, Aux., const. L. M. Mrs. Maria E. Bull, $25; Worcester, Miss'y Asso., Salem St. Ch., $15, Union Ch., Thank-Off., $53.75; Royalston, Aux., $50; Auburn, M. C., $7, — $475 33

Total, $2,819 93

CONNECTICUT.

Eastern Conn. Branch.— Miss M. I. Lockwood, Treas. Stonington, 1st Ch., Agreement Hill Soc'y, $9; 2d Ch., $11.26; Groton, S. S., $8.25; Plainfield, Y. P. M. S., $18; Thompson, $13; New London, 1st Ch., $72.98, S. S. Infant Cl., $2.50, Blackball St. Mission, $8, 2d Ch., of wh. $75 const. L. M's Mrs. Robert C. Neff, the Misses Willia Porter, and Caroline W. Butler, $116.87; Norwich, Broadway Ch., Helping Hands, $55; Taftville, Aux., $20.75, M. C., $7.28; Pomfret, Aux., $15, M. C., $3; Ledyard, Newell Soc'y, $8.25, $369 14
Hartford Branch.— Miss Anna Morris, Treas. Bristol, Aux., $82.80; Hebron, Aux., const. L. M. Mrs. S. G. Gilbert, $25; Buckingham, M. C., $10.63; Tolland, Aux., $8; Windsor, Aux., Thank-Off., of wh. $25 by Mrs. William Pierson, const. L. M. Mrs. Mary Welch, $48.50. $174 93
New Haven Branch.—Miss Julia Twining, Treas. Ansonia, Ruby Circle, $10; Bridgeport, of wh. $29 fr. Dew-Drop, $60.35; East Canaan, Yr Ls M. Circle, $45; East Haven, $13.80; Kent, $25; Litchfield, $9.40; New Britain, Centre Ch., $31.35; New Haven, Centre Ch., $366.23, Davenport Ch., $37, Humphrey St. Ch., Y. L. M. Circle, $25, Mr. Dwight Williams, $20; Norfolk, Y. L. M. Band, $100; Norwalk, Senior Circle, $5; Prospect, Gleaners, $35; Redding, Ready Folks, $30;

Sound Beach, $25; Southport, S. S., $30; Stratford, Y. L. M. Circle, $5, $873 13

Total, $1,417 20

LEGACY.

Legacy of Cynthia E. Dayton, North Haven, $1,000 00

NEW YORK.

New York State Branch.—Mrs. G. H. Norton, Treas. New York City, Home Circle, $10; Albany, Morning Star M. C., Thank-Off., $4.26; Lockport, $25; Moravia, $4.50; Crown Point, Willing Hearts, $12.35, 1st Cong. Ch., Young Ladies, $6.50, $62 61
Pekin.—Abigail Peck, 5 00

Total, $67 61

PHILADELPHIA BRANCH.

Mrs. Samuel Wilde, Treas. New Jersey, Orange, Trinity Cong. Ch., Aux., 5; Orange Valley, Cong. Ch. S.S., $15.54; Plainfield, Aux., $10; Washington, D. C., 1st Cong. Ch., $22.70, Y. L. M. Soc'y, $100, Coll. at Annual Meeting, $62.98. Expenses, $18, $198 22

Total, $198 22

OHIO.

Kinsman.—A Friend, $5 00
Pomeroy.—Welsh Cong. Ch., 6 38
Toledo.—Washington St. Cong. S. S., $25 00

Total, $36 38

ILLINOIS.

Elgin.—Mrs. J. H. Wells's S. S. Cl., $7 00

Total, $7 00

KENTUCKY.

Woodbine.—S. S., $1 25

Total, $1 25

CANADA.

Woman's Board, $166 00

Total, $166 00

General Funds, $5,278 01
Weekly Pledge, 8 64
Leaflets, 41 16
Legacies, 1,100 00

Total, $6,427 81

MISS EMMA CARRUTH, Treasurer.

Board of the Interior.

CHINA.

EXTRACTS FROM LETTERS OF MISS HAVEN.

Among the many "rumors of wars" that come from China, it is pleasant to have a glimpse at our own Bridgman School, and to know that there a steadfast and quiet heart is at the helm. Miss Haven writes of the prospect of war, September 2d: —

I LOOK upon it with the exultant excitement with which one watches the clouds piling up for a thunder-storm. Let it come. We shall see some of the grand workings of God in it, even though the instrument used savors of brimstone. The air will be clearer afterward. The scholars are all back — glad to come, in fact, thinking they will be safer with us. Miss Garretson has just received a letter transferring her to Foochow, at her request.

Again, a little later, she writes: —

We live in the quietest style, seeing no one from one day to another. The destinies of the nation may be deciding any time, and we never a bit the wiser. Our life runs on in a quiet current, busy enough in preparations for the winter, as though it were absolutely certain we were to stay here. This is for outside diversion and amusement, this preparation for winter — house-cleaning, stove-blacking, repotting plants, and getting the girls' wadded garments ready. The main work, teaching, is going on steadily all the while, but with rather a small school. One nice girl from Tung-cho appeared in due time, but had not been here five days when her mother came for her again. The neighbors had stirred her up to thinking she would certainly be killed if left at a foreign school.

To friends who expressed solicitude as to her safety, she writes, October 22d: —

We were rather unsettled at one time, uncertain whether we should stay through the winter; but now we are settling down in quiet. We shall probably not be disturbed by the French, as Peking is not easy of access in winter. Here, again, is an instance of a trial proving a blessing. Always before, we have lamented the fact that we live on the outside edge of the world; now it is a very good thing. Our enemies must approach carefully when they run amuck against anything which stands so near to the jumping-off place. China is well guarded as to her northern ports by breastworks of ice. No one would care to fight elements and men when they join their forces for the attack. The overland journey from Shanghai through a hostile country would not be thought of. So we lay in our coal and winter vegetables with heart of grace, but do not make elaborate orders home for spring shipments.

INDIA.

LETTER FROM MISS SWIFT.

MISSION BUNGALOW,
MADURA, Sept. 4, 1884.

DEAR FRIENDS AT CHICAGO: I know you would like to take a peep at us just now; and since you cannot come to us, I will give you a glimpse of what is going on. In the first place it is mission-meeting week, and all the missionaries and helpers, boys and girls from the school and villages, are in from the out-stations, and our compound is like a bee-hive, with the constant passing to and fro. Quite a crowd are snugly ensconced in the Mission House, which, as you know, is my home.

There is Mr. and Mrs. Burnell, with their dear little baby, in the room back of Mr. Jones's office. Mr. and Mrs. Howland and their three children are nicely settled in the large back room. In the center room is Mr. Noyes, whose wife did not feel equal to the long trip from the Hills, so we have not the pleasure of her company. Mr. and Mrs. Hazen have one of the upstairs rooms, and Mr. and Mrs. Jones have the other, and your little missionary is very comfortable in a corner room downstairs. Now you see us in the house, come with me and take a peep at the compound itself. Over there in the corner is a very large tent, occupied by Mr. and Mrs. Gutterson and four children. Not very far off is seen Mrs. Capron's bungalow; and if we were to go in, we would find dear father and mother Chandler and Gertrude. Then, every day, the Pasumalai Chandlers and Mr. and Mrs. Tracy come in to Madura; and when we are all together we are as happy as can be. And such times we do have, visiting, and talking, and going to meetings, and getting acquainted with the new missionaries! There! I knew I had left some one out of the list. There is Dr. and Mrs. Chester, whom I didn't mention at all, and I can assure you they are by no means unimportant.

I wish you could all be here during the meeting. I am sure

you would enjoy it immensely. By Tuesday morning all the
missionaries had arrived, and all who were not too much
wearied by their long, and in some cases tedious, journey, went
out to Pasumalai, where the business meeting was held. Wednesday morning the meeting with the helpers began, and I enjoyed
very much being there and seeing them all together, though I
could understand very little of what was said. The concert was
exceedingly interesting. The church was filled to overflowing,
and the windows were blocked even by the crowds of people from
the city. The performers were the boys and girls from the different boarding-schools of the mission. They were all seated in the
center of the church on the floor around the two organs, which,
with a violin and any number of cymbals and triangles, accompanied the singers. It took nearly two hours to go through with
the programme, and I believe we all enjoyed it very much, in
spite of the stifling air. The girls looked so pretty in their little
red jackets, white clothes, and with their black, glossy hair decorated with white jasmine, the exquisite fragrance of which filled
the air! Dr. Chester treated us to a couple of pieces on the cornet,
accompanied by Mr. Jones on the organ.

A great deal of attention is now being paid to singing in the
schools, and the voices of the children are gradually becoming
softer and sweeter, and it is a real pleasure to hear them sing.
They enjoy learning English songs, and last night we heard "Joy
to the world," "Heavenly Father, bless me now," and "Over
There," sung sweetly. Think of hearing these songs in these
far distant lands! Often these songs are taken by the boys and
girls back to their homes, and sometimes heathen women are
heard singing them to their children. I cannot but believe that
all these things will bear fruit and glory for our Master. There
are nearly seventy girls, all of whom are bright and intelligent.
There are now four teachers in the school — two masters and two
mistresses. My "munchi" also takes classes in the school for a
couple of hours each day. The school is so large that it is
necessary to have a matron and a cook-woman. The dormitory
arrangements are very simple indeed. Each girl has a mat, and
during the cool season a counterpane, and every morning these
are rolled up and put away.

Their food is rice and curry, varied with meat twice a week,
and buttermilk three times; and on Sunday, after church, they
are treated to plantains. Though I use very little Tamil as yet,
I find there is much I can do to help. Mrs. Jones is not well, and
I am very glad to be able to relieve her of some of the school-
work. Each girl has a certain duty to perform every morning,

to help with the work. They are arranged in circles, as they are called, and I have taken the supervision of three of the circles. With Mrs. Jones's permission and help I expect soon to reorganize these circles, and get them upon a different footing. I think it would do them good to have things a little changed, because when things go on too long' in the same way the girls are apt to become negligent. I have taken charge of the Sunday meeting with them several times, using the head master as interpreter. I have been trying to spend four hours a day in study, two of which are spent with my "munchi." After the meeting is over I expect to go on with real hard study.

ONLY AN APPLE-CORE AND ITS SEEDS.

BY CARRIE L. POST.

ROSY, and golden, and juicy the apple, and crisp was the spicy pulp, and eagerly devoured, till only the core, with its pretty brown seeds, remained. This a young maiden held with graceful poise, aiming at the stove-door into which she designed to cast the worthless thing, thoughtlessly so considered, when up spoke her little sister, moved by economic impulse: " You wasteful creature! you could save that apple-core for our pet pig, or the old hen and her chickens; and the seeds we could plant, and have an orchard all our own, from which in a few years bushels of golden, rosy-cheeked apples could be gathered for apple-hungry boys and girls, who could give all the cores to their pigs and chickens.after they had planted the seeds; and then — and then — oh! think of all the baskets and bins that could be filled, and all the thousands of boys, girls, pigs, and chickens that would be benefited by that one little core that you are going to burn up!"

The little speech was uttered with such earnestness and impetuosity, that the fingers tightened their grip around the core as if it had suddenly grown valuable: the stove-door was closed, the precious germs folded away in the pretty brown seeds were not consumed by the flames; and years after, stately trees cast their shadows, and shook sweet incense from their rosy bloom, and the flowing sap held rich fruitage for harvest.

It is from such little incidents in our everyday life that we sometimes draw our choicest lessons — little words rightly spoken, little acts carefully directed, little mites prayerfully consecrated to the cause of the Master, how great and manifold the results!

Perhaps missionary workers more than any others feel obliged to save, plan, invent, and seek direction from the Lord. He it is who suggests ways, quickens the perceptions, and enables them to secure their offerings for this Christly work.

However straitened or perplexed a church organization may be, let the young girls in that church once make up their minds to organize a missionary society, choosing some definite object to maintain, and they will soon learn to be thinkers, planners, workers. Pennies and dimes will be earned and saved until they multiply into dollars; and, like the little brown apple-seeds, send forth fruit which shall make glad the nations of the world.

That straitened and perplexed church will receive a new baptism of God's Spirit; a new fountain of sweet, life-giving water will gush from hearts that may have been rock-hard. The elder, as well as younger, members will feel themselves drawn nearer to their Saviour when once they begin to do something for his needy ones, who are calling to us in pleading tones, " Help, oh, help, ere we perish in our blindness!"

Even the very little ones in our churches to-day are putting their tender shoulders to the gospel wheels; and their youthful zeal, in united effort, is a strong force helping on the good work.

The testimony of those who have watched the reflex influence of missionary work on the character of the young people, is this: they become earnest, working Christians earlier in life than others, and are found more ready to take hold of all other beneficent work. Said a mother to one who superintended a young girls' missionary society: " My little seven-year-old girl torments me nearly to death by teasing every month to go to the missionary society with her other sister. What shall I do? Will you allow her to come? I fear she will annoy you."

Remembering that Christ withheld not his hearty welcome from the little ones, permission was granted, and her name was duly enrolled with those of the working members of the society; and a zealous little member she has been for three years. The wee fingers cannot accomplish much, but they are so willing to be pricked in learning to sew for a good cause, that older ones are sometimes moved by her example to greater industry. Her dime is just as large and valuable, and as faithfully remembered at each succeeding meeting, as those of the older girls, and neither heat nor cold, ice nor snow, keeps her away.

The children's dimes, like the seeds in the core of the apple, are truly valuable; and how happy are they when led to feel that they can do something for Jesus! How ready to earn their monthly mites, that they may have something to give away to others!

Our future missionaries are among the children. Do the

mothers remember this? The isles are waiting for them: the heathen are stretching out beckoning hands and calling, "Oh send your sweet daughters and your brave, gifted sons with the life-giving crumbs which fall from your table, that our little ones may eat and live!"

That valuable seed which was planted by those young men nearly one hundred years ago, when they kneeled by the hay-stack in Williamstown and consecrated themselves to missionary work among the heathen, may be even now sending its vital forces through the brain and soul of your beloved offspring, O mother!

Hinder not its course, but let proper training, and culture, and judicious pruning be your work; for among your sons and daughters may be a prophet or prophetess of the Lord, who may respond to the God-given call, and, rising up in self-con-secration, exclaim, "Here, Lord, am I: send me to teach, or preach, or heal the sick in regions of spiritual darkness and ignorance." What greater honor can your heavenly Father bestow upon you?

SPAIN.

LETTER FROM MISS SUSIE F. RICHARDS.

AVENIDA 40, SAN SABASTIAN, Oct. 21, 1884.

One of the piers of our Bridge rests at San Sabastian, just across the border from France; a city beautiful for situation at the foot of the Pyr-enees, on the Bay of Biscay. The Seminary occupies two flats of a four-story building. It is the only school of the kind in Northern Spain. A sec-retary of a Young Ladies' Society, rightly feeling herself privileged to open correspondence with any of the missionaries connected with the Bridge, addressed a friendly letter to Miss Richards, and was rewarded by the following, which she generously shares with us:—

MY DEAR MISS ———: It is not often I get a letter telling me not to hurry about the answer. It is quite a pleasant experience, on the whole, and makes unnecessary any apology for tardiness or procrastination. In the first place, I want to thank you and the society whom you represent for your kind interest in our work here. It is very comforting to have our daily labors accom-panied by prayers from the home-land, even while the prayer-givers are often entire strangers to us personally.

You ask about our school, and whether it is for boarders or day-scholars. In the beginning it was a boarding-school, but it now partakes of a double character. The boarders number about twenty, and for the most part have lessons quite distinct from the other — a primary department.

We have one girl of twenty-two, but most are under seventeen. The new-comers this year are quite young, under twelve; and we should be glad if all could come at an age before bad habits of study or deportment are firmly established. The school is especially for girls, but two little nephews of one of the teachers live with us. Both boys and girls come to the day-school. Their studies include the common branches,— arithmetic, grammar, geography, history, domestic economy, and literature,— taught in the native language, besides English, French, and music, both vocal and instrumental. The more advanced class in English read and understand our language very readily: of course they have more difficulty in speaking it. They are reading that beautiful book, "Stepping Heavenward," at present, outside of lessons, and understand it very well without a dictionary. They love the book almost as much as we do, though until they know every word, they cannot see all its beauty. Our principal reason for teaching them English and French, is because Spanish literature is very poor in Protestant religious books.

Needle-work forms a very important part of a Spanish girl's education, and a large part of each afternoon is devoted to that. They learn all kinds of sewing, including fine embroidery and fancy work.

Their hours are as regular as the clock itself, and each girl has some share of the housework to perform. After morning prayers and breakfast, and the subsequent dish-washing, comes school, from nine until twelve; then dinner; and after dinner an hour's walk with one of the teachers. The afternoon is devoted to needlework and organ practicing, as well as the lesson in singing, with an hour of freedom just before tea. The evening time for study for the older ones is from 7.15 to 9 P. M.; the younger ones retire at eight. We follow the American custom of having Saturday a holiday. There is some little increase of household duties on that day, but the lessons are discontinued from Friday until Monday.

Our school-year begins in September and ends the last week of July. Other years we have had four weeks' vacation in the summer; but this year we had six, and did not begin school until the middle of September.

Our summer was beautiful and bright, and not too warm. We did not any of us care to leave home; rather, found quite enough rest and diversion in frequent little walking excursions or picnics. You are very kind in your offer of advertising-cards: they are very little used in Spain, and would give great pleasure to many of our pupils, even those who are not kindergarteners.

THERE is no tie that binds a church to the work of foreign missions like that which arises from sending from its own members the "messengers of peace" to tell the glad tidings of God's wonderful love to sinners. Plymouth Church, of Chicago, has just bound itself, by such a cord of twofold strength, to the mission in Japan. A large company of friends assembled in the church parlors, on the evening of December 12th, to give a parting "Godspeed" to young Dr. Scudder and his sister, ere they sailed for their distant field of service.

The cordial and loving greetings, the voice of prayer and singing, the few words of parting salutation, with the social repast that followed, will ever linger as a tender memory in the hearts of all who were present.

Would God that every church in our land might this coming year send, at least, *one* missionary to the eight hundred million of heathen souls. "The harvest truly is great." Where are the laborers ?   E.

Young Ladies' Department.

FOURTH ANNUAL UNION MEETING OF THE YOUNG LADIES' SOCIETIES OF CHICAGO.

DEC. 12, 1884.

DEAR GIRLS OF THE INTERIOR: When I, who long ago ceased to stand

> "With reluctant feet,
> Where the brook and river meet,"

received an invitation to attend the fourth annual union meeting of the Young Ladies' Societies of this city and vicinity, to note points of interest for you, who were unable to be present, it gave me much gratification.

When I found myself in the hospitable parlor of Union Park Church, among the eager, enthusiastic girls, I said to myself, "Such good times, and I (in spite of whitening locks), still in them!"

Mrs. Lyman Baird, Chairman of the Committee on Young Ladies' Work, presided.

Mrs. George M. Clark, who has this year been added to this committee, led the devotional meeting.

She said it had seemed to her, for a long time, that if she could choose her work, it would be something in connection with the young ladies' efforts; and so it was especially fitting that her first service should be to lead them in the devotional half-hour. In thinking of the meeting, these words of Mrs. Browning, in the "Rhyme of the Duchess May," remained in her mind, until she felt that they held the thought which she was to bring to them:—

> "And I smiled to think God's greatness
> Rolled around our incompleteness—
> Round our restlessness, his rest."

Unless their girlhood was very different from her own, they were often filled with unrest—with an uncertainty as to whether they were making the most of their powers of body and mind; but if they would bring to God their restlessness and incompleteness, they would find in him perfect rest. She then read Prov. i. 33, Col. iii. 3, Rev. i. 14, and Ex. xxxiii. 14–16.

Delegates from nearly all the societies in and around Chicago were present. Their reports showed a steady, healthful increase, both in interest and contributions, and give much promise for the coming year.

A discussion, "How to make our missionary meetings interesting," was opened by Miss Hess, of Evanston, who said: "We feel sure that idle lives are not happy ones, that of all the work in the world, Christian work is the most satisfying; of all Christian work, perhaps the highest is that for those separated from us by continents and ocean, whose thanks may never reach us."

From this paper and several others which followed, I noted these hints for you:—

A spirit of consecration; individual responsibility, not leaving the burden to the leader, but responding quickly to requests for aid; preparation for the meetings, by thought and study of the topic assigned; much prayer, and keeping in mind these words of St. Paul, "Lord, what wilt thou have me to do?"

Not much, you see, dear girls, was said of fairs and fancy-work, but a great deal of personal consecration, of prayer, of building on the sure foundation, which is Christ Jesus, our Lord.

The paper, "Our Encouragements," which was the last on the afternoon's programme, was of greater interest. I will only give you these figures; but are they not eloquent?

The societies have grown in numbers the past three years, from twenty to two hundred and seventeen, with a membership of perhaps four thousand. In 1881, the collections amounted to seven hundred dollars; during the past year it has received seven thou- sand dollars.

Three missionaries were present — Mrs. Greene of Constantino- ple, Miss Spencer of Hadjin, and Miss Barnes of Marash.

Mrs. Greene and Miss Spencer gave us two minutes each; we wished it had been two hours. Miss Spencer told us of the way she and her girls collected stones for building the walls of their school — going out to the hillside, after lessons were over, and bringing them to their inclosure with their own hands!

After a pleasant social hour and a bountiful tea we felt quite refreshed, and ready for the evening feast.

The *pièce de résistance* was Mrs. Baird's paper, "Statement of Work for 1885." This will soon be in print for your perusal, and I am confident that the watchword she has given you, "The Bridge," will be taken up by you with enthusiasm, and that her desire that you may make "its foundations your prayers, its piers your contributions, its arches faith and works, its keystone Christ," will be realized.

That you all may grow "unto the measure of the stature of the fullness of Christ," shall be my prayer.　　　　　E. M. B.

Home Department.

STUDIES IN MISSIONARY HISTORY.

1885.

SYRIAN MISSION.
1830–1870.

Political Events of this Period. Conquest by Ibrahim Pasha. Bombardment of Beirût, 1840. Restoration of the power of the Sultan, 1841. Civil war between the Druses and the Maronites. What was the effect of these commotions on the missionary work?

How long was the *station at Jerusalem* continued? Character of the work there.

Religious Excitement among the Druses, 1839.

Religious Movement at Hasbeiya. What persecutions followed?

Civil War of 1845. What effect on the work at Hasbeiya? Fate of the Maronite patriarch who martyred Asaad Shidiak.

Stations of Abeih; Sidon; Tripoli; Aleppo. What churches organized at these places?

Anarchy in region of Hasbeiya, 1851–52.

Native Converts. Their work and character. Native missionary societies.

Village Work. These two topics will furnish abundant material for interesting papers.

Massacres of 1860.

Death of the Sultan as affecting missionary work.

Persecutions, 1862.

Work of the Press for the Arabic-speaking people. An interesting summary of this may be found in the "Ely Volume."

Education. Seminary at Abeih. Protestant College at Beirût. Girls' Seminary at Beirût. (See "Ely Volume.") Village Schools.

In studying this lesson, note especially the growth of sentiment in favor of *Religious Liberty* during the half century of work by the American Board, before the mission was transferred to the Presbyterian Board.

Present State of the Work. Send to Secretary of Woman's Presbyterian Board of Missions, 48 McCormick Block, Chicago, for statistics.

Helps. Dr. Anderson's "Missions to the Oriental Churches," "Reports of the American Board," and files of *Missionary Herald.* Dr. Goodell's "Forty Years in the Turkish Empire." Dr. Jessup's "Women of the Arabs and Syrian Home Life."

RECEIPTS OF THE WOMAN'S BOARD OF MISSIONS OF THE INTERIOR.

MRS. J. B. LEAKE, TREASURER.

FROM NOVEMBER 18 TO DECEMBER 18, 1884.

ILLINOIS.

ILLINOIS BRANCH. — Mrs. W. A. Talcott, of Rockford, Treas. *Amboy*, of wh. 4.09 from S. S., 9.64; *Cambridge*, 10; *Champaign*, Coral Workers, 23; *Chicago*, Coll. at Young Ladies' Union Meeting, 40.25, Y. W. M. Soc., 1st Ch., of wh. 29.35 thank-offering, 74.88, New Eng. Ch., 33.37; *Lawn Ridge*, Mrs. G. R. Ransom, 5, S. S., 7.50; *Ontario*, Aux., 10, Willing Workers, 20; *Peoria*, Aux. and Y. L. Soc., Feast of Ingathering, 57.15; *Providence*, Workers and Gleaners, 50.75; *Rockford*, 1st Ch., Y. L. Soc., to const. L. M. Mary Penfield Shelden, 25.81, 2d Ch., Aux., 9, Girls' Mission Band, 90; *Roseville*, Girls' Mission Band, 16; *Springfield*, Little Helen's pennies, memorial,

3.65; *Stillman Valley*, Merry
Gleaners, 30; *Summer Hill*,
14; *Udina*, King's Young
Daughters and their Broth-
ers, 29.57, $559 57
                              ─────────
            Total, $559 57

CORRECTION. — In November
LIFE AND LIGHT, Tamazoa
should read Tamaroa.

IOWA.

IOWA BRANCH.— Mrs. E. R.
Potter, of Grinnell, Treas.
Council Bluffs, 34.88; *Charles
City*, 10; *Le Mars*, 23.70; *Mus-
catine*, 75; *Quaqueston*,
thank-offering, 7; *Sioux
Rapids*, Children's Soc., 4.99;
Toledo, Mrs. E. N. Barker,
25, . $180 57
For Morning Star:—
Mt. Pleasant, S. S.,   9 27
                              ─────────
            Total, $189 84

KANSAS.

KANSAS BRANCH.— Mrs. A. L.
Slosson, of Leavenworth,
Treas. *Atchison*, Aux., 8.10;
Bethel, 25 cts.; *Emporia*, 5;
Garfield, 2; *Kimeo*, Little
Sunbeam Band, 40 cts.;
Pleasant Prairie, 4.25;
Ridgeway, 1, Telephone
Fund, 25 cts. Less expenses,
15.15, $6 10
For Morning Star:—
Blue Rapids, Acorn
Band.   5 00
Smith Centre, No-Surren-
der Band,   5 00— 10 00
                              ─────────
            Total, $16 10

MICHIGAN.

MICHIGAN BRANCH.—Mrs. Geo.
H. Lathrop, of Jackson, Treas.
Alpine and *Walker*, 10. *Ann
Arbor*, 26.59; *Hilliards*, Mrs.
Pomeroy, 1; *Nashville*, 5; *Ro-
meo*, 50; *Three Oaks*, Young
Ladies' Circle, 10, $102 59
For New Morning Star:—
Detroit, Miss. Gleaners, bal-
ance of pledge,   5 75
                              ─────────
       Branch Total, $108 34

MINNESOTA.

MINNESOTA BRANCH.— Mrs. E.
M. Williams, of Northfield,
Treas. *Minneapolis*, 2d Ch.,
10.68; *Northfield*, 8.65, $19.33

For Morning Star:—
Lake City, S. S., $21 15
Minneapolis, Vine Ch.,
S. S.,   2 00— 23 15
                              ─────────
       Branch total, $42 48

MISSOURI BRANCH.

Mrs. J. H. Drew, 3101 Wash-
ington Ave., St. Louis, Treas.
Brookfield, Ladies' Soc., 14,
Young Ladies' Soc., 22, Will-
ing Workers, 141; *Kansas
City*, 1st Cong. Ch., 12.57;
Lebanon, 3.75, $53 73
                              ─────────
            Total, $53 73

NORTH DAKOTA BRANCH.

Mrs. R. C. Cooper, of Cooperstown, Treas. *Fargo*, 13.37;
Harwood, 15.05, $28 42
                              ─────────
            Total, $28 42

OHIO.

OHIO BRANCH.—Mrs. Geo. H.
Ely, of Elyria, Treas. *Brook-
lyn*, Waste Not Soc., 7.60;
Gambier, 5; *Hampden*, S. S.,
1; *Huntsburg*, 7; *Lodi*, 7.90;
Mansfield, 50; *Oberlin*, 52, $130 50
                              ─────────
            Total, $130 50

WISCONSIN.

WISCONSIN BRANCH.—Mrs. R.
Coburn, of Whitewater, Treas.
Arena, Aux., 11.27, Young
Ladies, for Bridge, 2.57, Wil-
ling Workers, Morning Star,
1.55; *Beloit*, First Ch., Young
Ladies, for Bridge, 11.26;
Baraboo, proceeds of Miss
Bissel's Lecture 11; *Ft. At-
kinson*, 4.25; *Sparta*, 5.52;
Shopiere, Little Travellers,
15. Less expenses, 11.24, $51 18
                              ─────────
            Total, $51 18

MISCELLANEOUS.

Sale of articles donated 8.60;
of leaflets, 32.51; of envelopes, 5.80; of the Home Missionary quarter, 25 cts.;
cash, 15 cts., $47 31
                              ─────────
            Total, $47 31

Receipts for month, $1,232 47
Previously acknowledged,   1,472 78
                              ─────────
Total since Oct. 22, 1884, $2,705 25

Board of the Pacific.

HOME SECRETARY'S REPORT.

THE year just closed began with hope and courage, inspired by the tenth anniversary meeting at Santa Cruz. In view of the results of its ten years' work, our Woman's Board of Missions could not fail to see that the Master had set the seal of his blessing on the efforts it had put forth in his name and for his glory.

Thankful for the past, we were encouraged to devise more liberal things, and to strive more earnestly for growth in all that could increase our efficiency as a Board of Missions.

The year has flown on very swift wings, and now that the end has come we anxiously ask, Has it brought with it the fulfillment of our plans, the realization of our hopes? Has the missionary spirit, which is pre-eminently the Christian spirit, the spirit of Christ, increased in our churches, bringing under cultivation new fields, and reaping larger harvests in the old?

The work of the Home Secretaries during the year has had comparatively little to do with existing societies, but has been chiefly one of extension — an effort to secure friends and helpers in new places, to awaken an interest in the work of foreign missions, and to incite to organized effort in its behalf.

It is with gratitude to God that we are able to report a larger addition to our list of senior societies than for several previous years; and also the realization of our long-cherished wish to be allied in this work with our sisters of Oregon and Washington Territory. The secretary of this new branch of our Board modestly calls it a "tiny bud," leafless as yet, there being, so far as is known, but one Woman's Foreign Missionary Society in Oregon and Eastern Washington Territory [in Western Washington Territory we have had two auxiliaries for several years]. She adds, "God willing, there will be more than one ere another twelve months rolls around."

The Woman's Board of the Pacific warmly welcomes this "tiny bud," and gladly grafts it upon the parent vine, realizing what possibilities it infolds.

These new societies, as well as the old, ask for equipment and arms for the warfare upon which they have entered. We have regretted our inability to adequately help equip them for service.

(77)

Some copies of letters from missionaries have been sent, and more would have been had not nearly all received been published in the Woman's Column in *The Pacific.* This column, so faithfully and ably edited by our Foreign Secretary, Mrs. Jewett, is relied upon as our channel of communication — our telephone to the auxiliaries. We assume that *The Pacific* is taken wherever there is a missionary society. But matter in the form of leaflets, which can be scattered broadcast, is much needed.

Leaflets with such titles as "Do Foreign Missions Pay?" "For Christ's Sake," "The Mute Appeal," "Individual Responsibility," "Somebody is Shirking," "Thanksgiving Ann," etc., have been used by the Board of the Interior with excellent results. We have heretofore appropriated little or no money to the cultivation of the home field, but the need for more missionary literature for gratuitous distribution is so great as to suggest the wisdom of investing some money in that way.

From a few places have come donations to our treasury made doubly precious by the encouraging words accompanying them. In due time we shall hear of missionary societies in those places; for as leaven hidden in a measure of meal will leaven the whole lump, so is the influence of an earnest Christian woman with the burden of foreign missions on her heart.

Not a few of our churches are carrying very heavy burdens in the support of the gospel at home. When this is hindered and is suffering for lack of money, can we wonder if the appeal for foreign missions is unheeded, or the response delayed? But there is danger of the near eclipsing the remote, of our heeding only the obligations that lie nearest, and of growing narrow and selfish in our ideas of Christian duty, forgetting that "the light that shines farthest shines brightest on those near by." The poorest of us cannot afford to turn a deaf ear to the piteous cry for help from those whose needs are immeasurably greater than our own. That is a dwarfed Christian life which is not world-embracing in its sympathy and love.

The condition and methods of work of our auxiliaries during the year we learn from their own reports, and the financial results from the Treasurer's report. We have reason to believe that most of them are in working order, and that their zeal has suffered no abatement.

From some of the auxiliaries no word has come to the Secretaries during the entire year; and we learn that in some, regular meetings have not been maintained. We know how difficult it is for women burdened with many cares and duties, and perhaps living at long distances apart, to gather together statedly, and make a missionary meeting attractive and profitable. There is a dearth of fresh information concerning missionary work, and little comes to them to awaken enthusiasm. We who live in San Francisco and Oakland know how much we owe to the occasional presence of living missionaries. How their story thrills our hearts, and makes us feel the awful realities they portray. As we listen we seem to breathe the polluted air of heathenism; to hear the cry of murdered babes, the wailing of child-wives and outcast widows. We see hopeless women "grinding in the prison-house of superstition." And from all this we know that the religion of Christ alone can rescue them. We cannot hear these things from the lips of living witnesses, whose testimony we know is true, and not receive a fresh impulse to send more swiftly the means of rescue. We wish all our auxiliaries might sometimes hear the inspiring voice of the living missionary; but, lacking this, they must find other means of keeping abreast of the times in knowledge and sympathy with these apostles of to-day.

Missionary societies are organized not alone to gather money, but to promote a missionary spirit by united prayer to the Great Head of the Church, and by the use of means for diffusing missionary intelligence. This is a sure way, and the only way, to overcome indifference toward foreign missions. Depend upon it, indifference is born of ignorance; and so we urge our auxiliaries to systematic study, and to the zealous use of all available means for the increase of missionary knowledge. In some of our young ladies' societies there has been most praiseworthy activity and zeal, notably in that of the Bethany Gleaners, of Bethany Church, San Francisco; and we are happy to know that elsewhere in our State are young people whose work shows that they have been animated by the same spirit as these dear Bethany Gleaners.

If on the part of some there has been, as we fear, less interest than formerly, it is surely a matter for anxious solicitude. We cannot possibly exaggerate the importance of enlisting our young people in this line of Christian service, and so training and educating them that they will be equal to its demands in the future, when all will be committed to their hands. The hope of the world is in them. We feel strongly that this department of our home-field requires more careful cultivation than it has yet received.

And now let us consider what is the mark toward which we aim in our home-field. In the words of the constitution, it is to secure an auxiliary in each of our churches, and the practice of systematic giving by every woman in our congregations. There are in this State, Arizona, and Nevada some one hundred and six

Churches, with a female membership of perhaps four thousand. The Woman's Board has thirty-five senior auxiliaries, twenty-five junior or juvenile societies, and probably about one thousand contributors to its treasury. The mark aimed at calls for aggressive work from each and all of us.

Obedience to the Divine command, "Go, teach all nations," means toil and self-denial to those who send, as well as to those who are sent. Said a lady missionary from China to the Woman's Board of the Interior, lately: "I realize as never before how hard you work here. I am glad that I am at the other end of the work." At this end there is no more difficult work than breaking down the wall of heedless indifference, behind which so many Christians intrench themselves. In this work we earnestly solicit the co-operation of the pastors of our Churches. We believe Paul would say to them, "Help those women." It is not in churches where the pulpit echoes the command, "Go, preach the gospel to every creature," and in the missionary concert, where the needs of the nations sitting in darkness are considered and prayed over, that we hear women saying, "I am not interested in foreign missions; there is enough for me to do at home."

How to awaken our sisters up and down this coast to a realization of their duty at this time, when "the day breaketh," and there is an open door for the gospel in every land, is a question for earnest consideration and prayer. As it was said to Esther, raised up to be the deliverer of her people, so may it be said with added force or emphasis to the Christian women of this favored land: "Who knoweth but ye are come to the kingdom for such a time as this."

Millions of wretched heathen women stretch out to us, of this generation, appealing hands. Those who come after us cannot help them. It will be too late; they will have passed away. The heathen of to-day are our special trust. If we fail to discern this opportunity to testify our love to Him who loves them as he loves us, and who, "though he was rich, yet for our sakes became poor, that we through his poverty, might be made rich," shall we not have been weighed in the balance and found wanting?

May the Lord Jesus help us all to rise to the high plane of our privilege, and press on this precious work of woman for woman in heathen lands; and, sure as the promises of God, she shall emerge from gloom and darkness, and arise and shine, the glory of the Lord being risen upon her.   E. A. WARREN.

FOR WOMAN.

VOL. XV.   MARCH, 1885.   No. 3.

CHINA.

CHEMNA'S STORY.

BY MRS. S. B. GOODRICH.

"COME, Chemna, "I said to my sewing-woman one day, "tell me the story of your life. What led you to become a Christian, and to have anything to do with foreigners."

"If Mrs. Goodrich would like to hear, I shall be glad to tell about myself," she replied. "My father is a school-teacher. I was married, when a girl, to a wealthy family in the country. There were over twenty of us — three or four brides besides myself (all the sons' wives are called brides), with their children, and one sister who never married, because húmp-backed from a fall. My father-in-law owned over one hundred and sixty acres, — a large farm in China, — horses, cattle, and sheep. My mother-in-law would never give to the villagers, and so they hated us. One day we heard the soldiers had come to meet a foreign army marching in that direction. Oh, how frightened we were! We heard that foreigners ate little children for food, because their flesh was tender, and did all sorts of dreadful things. Suddenly the Chinese soldiers burst open our gate, and entered our court. They took our sheep, and killed them before our eyes, laying hands on anything they wanted. Then we found our neighbors had fled before, and had not told us, because they disliked us so. You know how it is — the poor people in China are very imperious. They must have their share of everything, and in the country they are very lawless; but still it was a punishment, because my mother-in-law, especially, had a very covetous heart, and could not bear to part with anything. We began to prepare to leave. We bound cloth about our little feet, to make them look large, and donned large shoes, because we heard that the foreigners would not kill the large-footed women. We buried our little shoes, our jewels, and our best clothes in the ground. We put our little babies and our little children inside our garments, to make believe we had none, and started toward Peking, to a relative. And when we came there we found we had come just to the scene of the conflict. While they fought we spent our days and nights in wailing. One day I saw a foreigner looking in at the window. I covered up my face and screamed. I thought I had been bewitched. After all the fighting was over we still remained, fearing to go home; but at the end of three months my father-in-law said we must start. We went home. Oh, what a scene met our eyes! A large number of our buildings were in ruins. The foreign soldiers had pulled them down, to get the beams for firewood — you know foreigners use so much fuel in cooking. Not an animal was left, not a tool for farming; and when we searched for our buried treasures, not one could be found; all had been stolen. We had a few buildings, our land, and nothing else.''

[Just here let me state that no small amount of work has been done in Tung-cho and in the villages about us, but very little fruit has been reaped. We have sometimes felt that Tung-cho and vicinity has borne less fruit for the work done than that of any other field. The reason, we think, must be because the scene of this war, in 1860, with the French and English, when Peking was opened to diplomats, was in this vicinity. The mass of the Chinese know not the why and the wherefore of these wars. They only know when their crops are destroyed, their houses pulled down, their cattle taken and slaughtered, when they flee for their lives and return to find no homes, no cattle, no implements for work, everything gone, that the foreigners caused all this. They say, "We never trouble them. Why need they come to us, and not only destroy our homes, but force opium, that soul-destroying as well as life-debasing weed upon us, when we said we did not want it. These prejudices are slowly beginning to give way, but so very slowly that it is almost imperceptible.]

" And after the war famine followed; due to the evil influences the foreigners left behind them, our people said. We pawned our land, first to buy horses and tools, and then to buy food. My mother-in-law, shocked to find such an amount of much-loved treasure gone, sickened and died. She wanted a fine burial; and her sons, to show their filial piety, bought her splendid silken robes, and buried her with great pomp. She feared if not dressed well she would be kept in hades, and never pass to the realms above; if without ornaments, she would have nothing to bribe the keeper of that lower gate with. It was a year of great distress. Her grave was opened, and all her gold and silver ornaments and silken robes were stolen from the coffin. One sorrow after another followed. One sister died, then our father-in-law; and it was decided to divide the property left, and the brothers live in separate households. The crops were bad; and finally one brother played false, and cheated us out of our rent, and my husband, in a fit of anger, threw his land away. And now you know he has nothing, but picks up the manure on the streets for argol. Not a single member of my husband's family now own anything. I suppose it is largely in judgment. My husband was given by his mother to the priesthood. When a little child he was very ill, and she vowed, if he recovered, to consecrate him to the life of a priest; but when he was better she did not fulfill her vow. Again and again when he has abused me and the children, people said it was because he had a priest's heart, and had no love for family. In one year I all but died of anger three times. I frothed at the mouth, and became insensible. Since I have become a Christian, God has helped me. Oh! how I have prayed for help to overcome my temper; and it is a long time now since I have been angry."

"How did you happen to become a Christian?" I asked her.

"Oh, that is a long story; but if you would like, I will tell you. The husband of Tsua-nai-nai, the Bible-woman, lives near my father's home, where we were then living. He made arrangements with my husband to betroth our oldest daughter to his son, who was then studying to be a helper. When I heard of it, I said, 'No; never shall my daughter go where those dreadful foreigners are.' My husband beat me to make me give my consent. He broke the few dishes we had; he locked me up for three days without food. Still I said, No.

"Why were you so afraid?" I asked.

"Why, such dreadful stories as they told about the foreigners here in Tung-cho! One story was, that every one who entered the Court was made to first wash their eyes, and then everything looked perfectly right; but one day one man on the sly only washed one eye. With one eye everything looked as it should; but when he looked with the unwashed eye he saw them eating uncooked meat and the manure of donkeys; and they made the Chinese eat it, too. Finally a brother came to me, and said: 'Sister, it is fate. If you don't give your daughter up something worse will happen to her. It's too bad; but it's fate.' [Yes, it was fate, or the good hand of God, under the unlovely name of fate, leading them on.]

"And so with tears I consented; and after a few months my husband and others took our daughter to Tung-cho, where she was married. They came home and said the foreigners had some performances we could not understand, but they were not half married; they never worshiped heaven and earth, nor their ancestors, nor anything at all; and the girl looked frightened to death. 'They'll treat her dreadfully,' some one said. I heard they were going to take all her ornaments away the next day, and not let her do up her hair, but make her a slave and a wife to them all. How I screamed when I heard this. I said to my husband, 'See what you've done! Aren't you glad? Aren't you happy?' He walked away, and for days and days never came near us. One day I could stand it no longer, thinking over my daughter's trials, and I walked over to Chas-nai-nai's village; for I heard she went every seven days to Tung-cho to the foreigner's to worship, because she believed their doctrine. I told her I must see my daughter. Would she go with me some day? 'Come with me, to-morrow,' she said. 'It's Sunday, and I'm going to church.' 'Oh, but it's too soon after the wedding. It would not be polite to go so soon.' 'Not the slightest difference,' Chas-nai-nai replied. 'They will be glad to see you any time. They will treat your daughter splendidly. Don't you fear.' I went home, took the only good garment in the house, pawned it to buy some cakes to present, and the next morning went with Chas-nai-nai to Tungcho. Tremblingly I came with her into the compound fearing every moment something might befall me. After service my daughter took me to her room. She seemed well and happy; and when I came to leave, her mother-in-law said: 'Come whenever you can, but don't try to bring us cakes. We shall always be glad to see you.' My daughter took me aside and said: 'They could not treat me better. Don't worry over me, mother'; and so my heart was comforted. It seemed after that as if I always went on Sundays. Gradually I began to love the Gospel story. I commenced praying and keeping the Sabbath. Soon the neighbors noticed my frequent visits, and would call out whenever I went along the street, 'Going to the foreign devils?' They would taunt my children with it, and often and often is the time my little ones have cried, and begged me not to go to church. They disliked to go and buy a little oil even at the village store, for some one would ask them about the 'devils.' And now you know the rest of my story — how I joined the church; how part of my children are in school;

and I firmly believe that some day my relatives will be brought to the Saviour. My own father is a school-teacher, highly esteemed, as are all of my family relatives. For years my younger brother would not speak to me or own me as a sister, because I am a Christian; but last summer he spoke to me. Yes; I am sure their hearts are being touched. I can't love my husband, he treats me so, but I pray for him."

TURKEY.

OCTOBER IN THE COUNTRY.

BY MISS H. G. POWERS, OF ERZROOM.

To the New England mind "October in the country" conveys suggestions most charming: the cool, restful days of cheerful but not blinding sunshine; the purple haze of the mountains and the gorgeous colors of the woods; the sweet, autumn fragrance of changing — we will not say dying — vegetation. Then when daylight fades into starlight, the cozy evenings about the open fire, and the long nights of wholesome sleep in the bracing, frost-touched atmosphere — ah, yes! such an October fortnight is a thing — no, fourteen things to be thankful for! But in this wretched land, with no "home," no "country," only villages, no beautiful, brilliant forests — what is one to say here? We must remember, however, that everything is relative after being shut up for months in one of these cities. There is a delightful sense of space and purity in the wide and silent reaches of rolling hill and plain; of dignity and endurance in the wild majesty of the mountains — Nature's sphinxes.

But when we come to the villages — huts half hidden under ground, huddled together, about the low doors of which are hanging strings of red peppers, giving the only touch of beauty to the heaps of earth and stone that grovel abjectly before us; when we make acquaintance with the squalor — which means poverty and filth, does it not? — of the interiors and occupants, — then, what of a trip to the country?. Yet these same hut-dwellers are Eve's sons and daughters, and although I have not shaded the picture too darkly for the majority, I must not overlook the minority implied in that very word; indeed, I shall try to keep in the foreground those whom it is easy to call brothers and sisters. Now and then you find a true, warm heart, a keen mind, a neat and wholesome household — all the more attractive for their surroundings. . . . . .

It was in the middle of October that Mr. Chambers and I started for Khunmoos, taking with us Esther, one of the girls from the boarding-school who is to teach this winter. We had fine, warm weather,— a blessing which was duly appreciated. Esther managed to tumble from her perch between the bags of bedding and other luggage once or twice, but no harm was done except to my sunshade, which she was carrying. The first day we had to climb the mountain called the Saddle-emptier, which lies to the South of Erzroom; then, after various ups and downs, we descended a long, rocky defile. The sun had just set, and the hills opening out before us lay in a soft dream-light — the reflection of a reflection! On we went till the weird twilight faded into dark. ness, and at last the silence was broken by voices — both human and canine — which indicated our arrival at the village.

As usual, we entered a stable; and turning to the left ascended a step or two to the left, to the *oda* or room where two sides toward the stable are open above the dais, so as to furnish grateful warmth (?) to the chilled traveler. After supper was eaten, and the traveling-cots and curtains put up, Mr. Chambers opened his Armenian Testament, and immediately a buffalo calf came up and stuck his nose out over the dais, and with his big flaps of ears open and fixed, remained a most attentive listener to the end. Do you remember Dr. Watts's "Where the horned oxen fed" ? . . . .

The weather was not settled, but several of the nine days of our stay were fine. Every morning at dawn the silence was broken by the voice of one calling,— not to repentance, but the Gregorian Church. Now near, and now dying away in the distance, as the crier went up and down among the houses, resounded the call, "Come to church! Blessed be God, and may he have mercy on your parents!" thus summoning all good Armenians to begin the day with an act of filial piety in putting up a prayer for their dead.

It was difficult to get the women together,— fall work not being out of the way,— but at six different points, three to nine miles away, we had eight meetings, with from twelve to sixteen at each one. I was greatly assisted by Pompeesh Kohar, a most faithful and efficient Bible-woman. When I was weary she would take charge, and always relieved my eyes of reading. She has a strong voice, and sings quite accurately, which was also a great help. Our first meeting was the day after our arrival. Several came in and sat down in a dull, stolid way; then followed a former pupil of the Erzroom School, with her three pretty little girls, far too bright to be quiet. The pastor's baby broke into a fit of indignant crying when strapped into a cradle,— so that he could move neither hand nor foot,— and we waited some minutes for him to quiet down and for others to come in. Soon after we began, the patience of one of the little girls gave way, and she commenced skirmishing with her sister, who, nothing loath, retaliated with great vivacity, till their mother stopped them, and sent one of them to sit by Pompeesh Kohar. After a slight interval the pastor's youngest daughter, about four years old, tumbled off the seat, and we had to wait till her wails subsided.

I had selected Exodus iv. 1-19, and had just warmed up to the subject,— Moses' weakness made strength by the grace of God,— when several passed through the room to go to another village for the afternoon service. This helped to arouse one or two who had settled down for a nap. Ten minutes later, one of the men came in to say that the horses were waiting and we were to go. "No!" I said, with more decision, I fear, than sweetness. "When we are ready we will let you know." But I was by this time utterly depressed, and closed as soon as possible. One untaught by experience can have no idea of the distraction to a mother, or the leader of a woman's meeting, by the presence of little children.

We mounted and went to Chevermeh, a village where we three times essayed to hold a meeting, and failed twice; but on both occasions we crossed the stream to a little hamlet, and had most pleasant meetings at the house of a good Protestant. Two years ago we were invited to dine there, and sat in the *oda* when an old white horse amused himself by flicking my face with his tail. But to return to the present. As we entered the *doon* — kitchen, dining, and bedroom for four married couples and their children,— my attention was attracted by the three cradles, and still more by the unusual silence of the occupants. It seemed that the three young mothers, all wishing to go to the meeting at Chevermeh, had simultaneously washed and fed their babies and strapped them into their cradles, depending on sleep to prevent the mother-want for a time. We had a very pleasant and well-attended meeting, and I told them they could not know how much good their active interest had done me, weary and discouraged as I was.

We returned to the preaching service at Chevermeh, and had notice given of the woman's meeting another day before the lighting of the *sundoors* (ovens). Yet when we arrived, at the appointed time, no one had come,— their time was so much more precious than ours they could not run the risk of waiting for us,— but at last they began to drop in. After meeting I spoke to a poor woman standing near, and heard, as often before and since, not "What must I do to be saved?" but, "How fortunate you, and unfortunate me!"

"How lucky you are," she said, "with nothing to do but travel about and amuse yourself!"

"Ah, no!" I answered. "I should have been far more comfortable at home than roughing it here at this season."

I tried to turn her thoughts to spiritual things; but how difficult this is for all of us at times!

"I am poor, and hungry, and naked! I have seven children to care for day and night: what time have I to think of such things? You who have nothing else to do can of course be pious."

"My dear sister," I responded, "if, as you say, you are so burdened with troubles, if your cares and trials are so much greater than mine, then your need of Christ is far greater than mine, and he is far more ready to help you than to help me."

In the meantime another had been examining my back hair, and calling attention to its being "wet." "No; it is cold, not wet," I said; and then returning to my subject tried to point them all to the Saviour of whom they are in such bitter need,— a need of which they themselves are conscious in a dim, groping kind of way. "O Lord!" was the cry of my heart, "open thou these blind eyes and unstop these deaf ears! Bring these 'blind by a way which they know not,' O, thou most merciful!"

At Boornaz there are, I believe, three Protestant men. One is a good man with a bad wife, and another a bad man with a good wife,— a fair division, you see, insuring some good to each household. When we dismounted we stepped into a narrow, dark passage, from which we passed into a *doon*—not a "Bonnie Doon." By the dim light from the hole in the roof — we ourselves obscured the door — we saw a baby in a tub of water, being conscientiously scrubbed by its mother, regardless of its cries. We were at once invited into the parlor, or rather *oda*, opening into the stable. A large piece of heavy felt was spread down in lieu of a carpet, and we were invited to seat ourselves upon it. Soon the baby was brought in, all dripping; the mother sopped it up a little with her apron, and strapping it into a cradle proceeded to rock it violently over the uneven floor, the little head rolling and bobbing on the pillow like an apple fastened only by its stem. Women and girls came and went, lingering only long enough to gratify their curiosity, for the ovens were lighted, and it was time for them to bake their bread — a business which seems to occupy the female portion of the family most of the day. After our tea, served in native style, our colporteur tried to sell some Bibles, but was not successful.

We spent a day at Pert. We went directly to the house of Pompeesh Kohar's friends. The house was a new one, had no suggestion of a stable in it, and seemed quite palatial compared with the dark, dingy places to which my visits generally led me.

On another occasion we visited several homes, and were pleasantly received by the people, who seemed more comfortable and civilized than at the other places, and I was glad to see the women so much attached to Pompeesh Kohar.

Soon after our arrival our host came in from his shop, greeted us warmly, and ordered coffee. The coffee was of course taken first to Mr. Chambers, who equally, of course, sent it to me. When I had taken my cup the servant returned to Mr. Chambers; but he begged to be excused, as he did not wish it. Then our host ordered tea; and supposing the coffee had been sent to me simply because it was not desired, sent the first cup of tea to Mr. Chambers, who again sent it to me. This time the lesson was learned; and when tea was again served, the first cup came to me — a triumph of courtesy doing honor to both gentlemen. At dinner-time the servant brought in the stool on which to set the large, round tray which was used as a table, and our host being out, he put it in front of Mr. Chambers. According to their ideas the man must have the corner seat, the best cushions, and must not be disturbed; any inconvenience or discomfort belongs to the woman. Again Mr. Chambers asserted his rights as a gentleman, and had it placed by me. As a representative woman, I was exceedingly grateful for these attentions which civilization has made common, and which help to raise the position of women in the minds of those who have despised her for ages. I cannot tell you how proud I am of the manly gentleness and deference toward woman of our American men: their influence wherever felt, has already accomplished a great, though quiet, revolution. But we women have laid upon us the heavier task of making our sisters worthy of respect and honor.

While the men were out two women callers came in. In the course of conversation one of them said, "Oh, I'm going to hell, I know." I tried to show her, that far from there being any necessity for this, Father, Son, and Holy Spirit were utterly unwilling that any should perish, and they had opened a way to salvation and happiness. When the men returned, Mr. Chambers and the pastor were occupied for several hours discussing measures for putting the work on a permanent basis. Every evening we returned to the pastor's house at Hervamig, where we were made most comfortable in every way. As soon as the family could be gotten together after dinner we had prayers. One after another of the men and women would drop in, till the room was quite full. We all sang at prayers, and sometimes we had as many parts as any orchestra — only our score was never written.

Sometimes the talk turned on theological problems and ecclesiastical history. On one occasion "The Wandering Jew" and "Uncle Tom's Cabin" were discussed; and strange enough it seemed to hear Legree, Cassy, and St. Clair spoken of familiarly by Armenians in this little village — yes, and humiliating to hear the comparisons between free Canada and the slave-holding United States. At another time the population of Madagascar and the width of the Isthmus of Panama were required of us. "Dear me!" I exclaimed to myself, "how much one has to know!" I ought to say that these people were, perhaps, the most intelligent in the whole district. . . . .

We decided to make the journey home in two days. We arrived just at the time of the Persian Mooharem— the annual lamentation over the untimely fate of Hassan and Hussim. We spurred up and dashed through the crowd of spectators, reaching our door just a little in advance of the long line of scimitar-armed and blood-stained men who, by wounding themselves, show their grief for the wounding and death of these young heroes of a dozen centuries and more ago. They weep not tears but blood-drops — a ghastly yet suggestive spectacle!

Young People's Department.

THE BOARDING-SCHOOL IN SMYRNA.

We give below an account of our School in Smyrna, as a specimen of what is being accomplished by our schools in Turkey — a work for which we hope to receive the special help of our young ladies during the coming year, both as individuals and societies. The article is composed of extracts from letters from Miss Page, who went to Smyrna, in 1882, in company with Mr. and Mrs. Bowen, under whose care the school had been started the latter part of the year 1881. In February, 1883, Miss Page writes:—

THE majority of scholars in our school are Armenians: there are a few Greeks and a few English. The primary department, numbering over thirty boys and girls, day-scholars only, are from five to eight years old. We have just passed them over into the hands of an Armenian teacher, who, with his wife, will take charge of them. The Board pay one-half of his salary, and he is to get the rest from the tuition. He has been employed as teacher in the Mission for some time; he is a faithful Protestant, and we are very glad that he is willing to undertake the school, as it seems to be a step in the direction of self-support. There are left then about forty scholars — girls — directly under our charge. I should have said that the primary scholars are all Armenians. The mixture is in the upper school. The oldest are fifteen and sixteen years of age, the youngest nine or ten — the average number between the extremes. Of these, eleven are boarders, the rest day-scholars. These all pay tuition, as a rule, though there are a few who are unable, for whom special provision is made.

The majority of our girls belong to the middle class in society. Their parents send them to us because, apparently, they value a good education, and in many cases they really seem to appreciate the effect of Protestant teaching upon the character and morals of individuals. It is thought that there are a large number of Armenians and Greeks here who at heart agree fully with Protestant views.

In the following autumn Miss Page writes: —

I wish you could see our school now! Our large schoolroom is very full when all come in for devotional exercises in the morning. I am wondering where I am to put the next applicants. They have been coming steadily — new scholars — ever since the term began. If you were here I would have them sing to you "I love to tell the story." They sing with a will that makes the schoolroom ring. Some of them have learned our familiar hymns, "My faith looks up to Thee"; "Almost Persuaded", "Saviour, breathe an evening blessing," and others. If it would seem strange to you to hear our own tunes in a foreign tongue how much stranger would it seem if you could walk in and hear Greeks and Armenians, of whose language you could not understand one word, singing, "God is the refuge of his saints," in good English. We call this the earthquake hymn; and in this city, which has been destroyed by earthquakes, and is liable to be shaken at any time, it seems specially appropriate that they should say,—

"Let mountains from their seats be hurled,
Our faith shall never yield to fear."

Can you see us, in imagination, as we go about our duties — as we go about them from day to day? We begin at half-past eight, and close at half-past four, with an hour and a half for rest at noon. Our most advanced class of Armenians are trying this year to take their studies in English. Reading, spelling, and something of grammar they have had already. Now, in addition,

they take geography and arithmetic. The latter they have studied
with an Armenian teacher, going as far as "Pieces," she told me;
she meant fractions. I have special delight in one of my arithmetic classes, for it has been said that girls in the East cannot master mathematics. This class of girls is a living witness against
the truth of this statement. The very brightest of them all — and
I have some English girls — is a little Armenian about ten years
old, who has to stand on tiptoe to reach the blackboard. She will
take a stiff dose of fractions without wincing, and is now learning
the mysteries of decimals. Monday afternoon we devote to sewing. The little ones have patchwork, and all but the more advanced have plain sewing an hour and a half; then fancy-work
the rest of the afternoon. Mrs. Bowen is teaching them the Kensington stitch, and giving them some lovely things to do which
she brought from England.

In August, 1884, Miss Page writes: —

The resignation of Mr. and Mrs. Bowen has been a very great
sorrow to us. Notwithstanding our trials, we have had many
blessings this year. We feel that all our sixteen boarders have
become Christians. Our three Greek girls from Cyprus were the
first to take a stand. They came to us from Mrs. Fluhart's
school. One of them was almost a Christian, I think, before she
came; the others were not. However, they became very much
interested in Mr. Constantine's prayer-meetings, and in the spring
they came out openly, and said they would live for Christ. From
that time there seemed to be a quiet interest among all the house-
girls.

I began a little prayer-meeting in my room, asking at first only
the three girls to pray for the others. Afterward I invited those
who seemed interested, until finally they all came. There are
three little girls, considerably younger than the others: those I
did not ask, thinking they did not appreciate the feelings of the
rest; but one night they begged that they might come, too, and
never failed afterward. Such delightful little meetings! We had
them every Thursday evening at half-past seven. This is in addition to the regular church prayer-meeting, which they always
attended.

I gave them a subject beforehand, and they learned texts of
Scripture upon it, repeating them in whichever language they
chose, but the majority in English. Then we knelt in prayer;
every one was voluntary, and there was rarely ever a pause. Such
earnest, heartfelt prayers they were, each in their own language
(they never pray in English), that I am sure you would have been

interested in them if you could not understand a word. We began
with fifteen-minute meetings, but they lengthened out to half and
three-quarters of an hour. Besides that, I found they were getting
together by themselves on evenings when there was no other meeting, going into a recitation-room, reading the Bible, and praying
without any teacher at all. Then the Armenian theological student from Adana came to Smyrna, and seemed to bring some of
the freshness of the revival with him. He had several meetings
with the girls, until one Sunday evening, after a faithful talk, he
asked all those who wished to serve God to lead in prayer for
themselves. They knelt, and every girl prayed, some of them
with tears. It seemed as if the Spirit of the Lord was there. The
next morning one of them came to me and said, "Last night I
asked God to forgive my sins. Now I will say to all the teachers,
Excuse me for all my bad things: from this day I will be God's
child." That was Verkinia, who is supported by the young ladies
of Dana Hall, Wellesley. She was always a sweet child, but after
that she tried doubly hard to do right. Sometimes on going to
my room at night I would find her waiting to ask me to pray with
her for God's help. There are several others who we think decided
for Christ that Sabbath evening. One by one the others came;
until near the close of the term, one Sunday night, they all
declared they were trying to be God's children. I think they
were in earnest. We have watched them carefully, and they all
try to do their very best, because it will please God.

One Sunday some of the girls came to Miss Lord, and asked her to
talk with them and give them some advice, to tell them what they
should do, as Christians, in particular cases. They wished it to be
in Turkish, as they could understand it better. So they all gathered about her in the garden, and listened with the greatest attention for over an hour. It is very hard for many of them when they
go home for vacation. Their parents wish them to do things which
they consider harmless, but which the girls feel to be wrong, like
visiting and going on excursions on the Sabbath. One of them
said, the first Sunday she was at home this vacation, her uncle
asked her to go out sailing on the Bay. Her mother told her she
might do as she pleased. She wished to go at first. She said, "I
thought about it an hour; then I said, 'No, I will not go; it is not
right.'" She came to church instead, and her uncle with her, much
to her surprise. On the last Sunday night of the term, when we
met to repeat texts and sing hymns, as usual, it was suggested that
the girls should choose a hymn which we would all sing every Sunday evening during vacation, in our separate homes. They chose
"I gave My life for thee" and "What a Friend we have in Jesus;"

so we sing them both. "What a Friend we have in Jesus" seems to be the general favorite in school. They are all such sweet girls! There does not seem to be a really naughty one among them. They clung to us that Sabbath evening, feeling badly at the thought of going away. Some of them have not very pleasant homes. "How can we bear to be separated from you so long?" they said. They promised to read the Bible faithfully every day. As we said good-bye to one of them going to a family who hated Protestants, and had no interest in religion, I said, "You will not forget what you have learned here, will you?" She answered, "Shall I throw away a pearl after I have found it?" Two of the Cyprus girls remain in Smyrna at the house during the summer, their parents not being able to pay their expenses back and forth. One of them has just been through a very severe operation : she had her eye taken out. She lost the sight of it years ago by an accident, and we found it was injuring the other, and she would in time be blind. We found a good occulist, and it was done at the house. She bore it beautifully, but did not have sufficient chloroform to make her perfectly unconscious. She cried out in her agony, "Dear Lord, save me! I do love you! Have mercy on me!" When she was fully conscious, she told us she had thought she was dying, but she said, "The Lord let me live." She is one of the sweetest girls I ever saw,— very gentle and refined, and a beautiful scholar. We hope in two years to have a graduating class, of which she will be one if she continues in school.

TO THE YOUNG LADIES.

WE wish to express our thanks to our young lady friends for the earnestness and zeal with which they took up the work proposed for the past year. The heartiness and enthusiasm with which it was done embolden us to ask for a similar work for 1885. We wish to propose that they shall erect a building for another center for woman's work in Japan. The Secretaries of the American Board have called for four young ladies for Japan, and they must have an abiding-place — a cheerful, comfortable home, as a refuge from their wearying toil, the bewildering sights and sounds of a foreign city, and the wearing contact with heathenism. It will also be a center for gospel work, and possibly for medical assistance for the women of Japan. Such a building will cost from three to four thousand dollars, and we propose to give out the amount in shares of ten dollars each, to be taken by individuals or societies.

For the sake of the women of Japan, who will feel the elevating influence and learn many a practical lesson from a well-ordered Christian home, for the sake of our young lady missionaries, for the sake of Him who gave to woman her elevated place, and needs her co-operation in bringing the world to himself, we ask for a cordial response to our proposition from all the young ladies in our churches. We believe we shall have it.

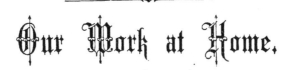

Our Work at Home.

ANNUAL MEETING.

BY MRS. S. BRAINARD PRATT.

ON the morning of the 14th of January there was an increased stir on Beacon Hill, where little groups of ladies, by twos and threes, seemed all converging toward a common center —the quiet stone church in Ashburton Place.

Some hastened with unerring footsteps straight to the goal. These were natives of Boston, accustomed to turn aside unto their crooked ways. Others hesitated at corners, watched street-signs, and looked doubtfully at the narrow cross-cuts; while some, under the very shadow of Mt. Vernon Church, insisted that this street could not be Ashburton Place, because it had *two ends!* Great is Boston, of Massachusetts, O stranger friends of ours! and she has *four ends* to her places, if so it seem wise unto her.

All uncertainty vanished, however, when once the vestibule was passed, for friendly hands, and eyes, and lips all gave a welcome "in His name."

The platform was tastefully decorated, as usual, with plants, and vines, and flowers; while behind the pulpit three richly illuminated banners bore a verse from Psalm lxviii., given according to the Revised Version, "The Lord gave the Word. great was the company of women that published it."

This was also the psalm selected by the President, Mrs. Albert Bowker, for her Scripture-reading in opening the meeting. She reviewed briefly some of the women who had published the Word, from Bible-times to our own, giving thanks that the multitude of them was so great, and that we were privileged to unite with them in the service.

Mrs. Taylor, of Providence, led in the opening prayer, and the annual report was given by Mrs. S. Brainard Pratt.

The report of the Treasurer, Miss Emma Carruth, showed the total receipts of the year, 1884, to have been $117,658.65.

Miss Myra Proctor, of the Central Turkey Mission, gave an interesting address on the village-schools, which are so important a factor in evangelical work in that country. Miss Proctor was present at the first annual meeting of the Board to speak of the work of ten years in Turkey, and now, sixteen years later, she had a still more wonderful story to tell of the way in which the country was becoming honey-combed with these light-giving schools, preparing the way for a triumph of pure Christianity in the Turkish Empire. The address was full of interesting incidents drawn from her long experience in the work.

Several of the branches gave reports of their work for the year. Instead of beginning, as usual, with the oldest of this band of twenty-two sisters, the order was reversed, and the younger members of the family spoke first.

The reports were all of marked excellence, and an abstract of each will be given in the next number of LIFE AND LIGHT.

WEDNESDAY AFTERNOON.

After the noon collation, served in the rooms below, and of which a large company partook, the meeting was called to order at 2 o'clock, and opened by singing the hymn "Mortals, awake! with angels join."

Mrs. Horace Fairbanks, of Vermont, chairman of the nominating committee appointed in the forenoon, presented the list of officers for the coming year; and after their election, Mrs. Leeds, of Hanover, N. H., led in prayer.

Five more branches presented their annual reports, after which Miss Talcott, for eleven years a missionary in Japan, gave an interesting account of the work in that country. Twelve years ago the difficulty was for the ladies to gain access to the homes; now, it is to select from the many which are open. There were not many Bible-women hired in Japan, because Christian women entered so largely upon this work, voluntarily giving themselves to the uplifting of their sisters.

The school-life is much the same in routine as school-life at home, only that Christian teaching is made more prominent, and the Bible furnishes the key-note to all the training. "Our ways," said Miss Talcott, "are as foreign to the Japanese as are theirs to us. One gentleman of Kobe said to me, 'Well, it seems strange to us that you hang yourselves on a chair when you want to sit down, or lay yourselves on a shelf when you want to go to sleep; but I suppose our ways are as strange to you.'"

Mrs. Leeds, of Hanover, read a very graphic account, written by Mrs. Goodrich, of Tung-cho, of the conversion of a Chinese woman, given in this number.

More branch reports followed, and Miss Halsey, secretary of the branch office in New York, said a few words of the work as it is opening there.

A solo, "Let Thy hand help me," was beautifully given by Miss Sarah Fisher. Mrs. A. C. Thompson led in the concluding prayer, and the afternoon session closed with singing.

THE EVENING SESSION

opened at 7.30 with a very full house, the galleries, and even the aisles, being filled. Dr. Herrick welcomed the Board, and introduced his friend and classmate, Dr. Judson Smith, the new Secretary of the American Board. The latter spoke of the greeting which the older organization, a veteran of seventy-four, gave the other, now a blushing maiden of seventeen. They were amazed at what she intended to do, but jubilant over what she had done. He then spoke of what had been accomplished in aiding the American Board in disseminating missionary intelligence at home; and in training children to interest and participation in the work.

Dr. Herrick then introduced Mrs. Layyah Barakat, a young Syrian woman, whose romantic history is well known to those who are familiar with missionary affairs. The address was a story of Layyah's life, conversion to Christianity, and subsequent adventures, closing with an appeal to Christian women to give the gospel to "other Layyahs." Not even a verbatim report could do justice to this address; for though the eloquent words might be given, they would lack the fire and earnestness of her manner, and the charm of her broken English. Smiles and tears succeeded each other on the faces of her audience as she spoke, and at the close she was greeted with a burst of hearty applause.

THURSDAY MORNING.

Fair and welcome as the sunshine of Wednesday had been, it seemed more natural to meet a lowering sky on Thursday morning; and when later in the day the snow fell briskly, changing in the afternoon to a steady downpour of rain, there seemed at last nothing wanting to complete the homelike character of the meeting. Neither lowering skies, nor snow, nor rain, abated the crowd who filled the church.

The devotional meeting in the vestry at 9.30 o'clock, to-day as yesterday, made a fitting introduction to the more public service in the church.

At 10 o'clock the meeting was again called to order by the President; and after singing the hymn, " One in Christ, and not as strangers," a part of the seventeenth chapter of John was read and commented upon. Mrs. Palmer, president of the Springfield Branch, led in prayer.

Greetings from other societies followed. The Methodist Board gave a Godspeed through its secretary, Mrs. Alderman. Mrs. Train, editress of *The Helping Hand*, brought greetings from the Baptist Board; and letters were read from the sister Boards of the Interior and the Pacific.

Miss E. H. Stanwood, Secretary of the Bureau of Exchange, read an able paper entitled, " Through Darkness to Light." It was a *resumé* of the progress of Christianity through the centuries — showing that through persecutions and seeming defeats, God is bringing forth victory, and that now, as always, " The blood of the martyrs is the seed of the Church."

Mrs. Williams, of the Constantinople Home, drew a very marked contrasting picture between Boston with its privileges, its educational and benevolent institutions, and Constantinople with its sore lack of all these. She gave a graphic account of the Home, with its many nationalities represented among the pupils, and traced the lives and work of some of the scholars since leaving the Home. All the graduates have been earnest Christian girls, and in the various spheres of life to which they have been called have honored the training received in the school.

Miss Chapin, of the North China Mission, followed with an address, in which she spoke of the medical labors of Miss Holbrook, of Tung-cho, of the work among the women, showing that some of them when converted are making pure, Christian homes, with all that the word implies. She spoke, too, of the schools, and particularly of the Bridgman School in Peking.

The interest of the meetings was largely increased during all the sessions by the solos so feelingly rendered by Miss Anna Spear, Miss Fannie Massie, Miss Nellie B. Obison, Miss Laine, Miss Sarah Fisher, and by Miss Rhea, daughter of Rev. Samuel Rhea, of the mission to Persia.

Thursday afternoon was specially devoted to young ladies; and notwithstanding the storm, large numbers of them gathered with wide-awake faces, which boded well for the Board of the future.

A very interesting story, called " The Beginning of It," written for the occasion by Miss Alice M. Eddy, formerly of Detroit, Mich., was read by Miss Anna Duryea. It was a very quaint and charming story of the way some earnest women interested some young girls in missionary work, and the results that followed.

Miss Morris, of the Zulu Mission, followed with an address, speaking particularly of the medical work abroad, and giving personal incidents in her own missionary life, showing the close connection often between physical and spiritual healing.

"A Legend of the Maizeen," written by Miss Child, touched all hearts by its pathos as read by Miss Sarah Forsythe.

Miss Chapin, of North China, gave great pleasure to the audience by singing in Chinese, "The morning light is breaking."

Miss Clarkson, from Kobe, spoke to the young ladies of the work in Japan, and the wide field opening there, urging them to greater interest in missionary work.

Mrs. A. C. Thompson presented a paper on "The Relation of Prayer to Missionary Work." She spoke of prayer as the foundation of all evangelical labor, and of the danger of forgetting its importance in these days, when we are tempted to rely so much on science.

Mrs. G. C. Knapp, from Bitlis, Turkey, spoke pleasantly of the benefit missionaries derive from occasionally revisiting the homeland. They go back with fresh zeal to their work.

By special request, Mrs. Layyah Barakat spoke for a few moments, being received with applause.

Miss Gilman, of Norwich, Conn., moved a vote of hearty thanks to the trustees of Mount Vernon Church, for permitting us once more to convene here; to the ladies who have decorated the building so tastefully; to the sweet singers who have contributed to our pleasure and have led in our service of song; to Mrs. Barakat and our missionary sisters who have told us of their work, and stimulated us to a new consecration to our Lord and Master; to those who have cheerfully given themselves to serving at tables, and patiently and faithfully have been "doorkeepers in the house of the Lord;" and to all whose generous hospitality has again welcomed us, and made us feel that we are all one in the Lord. After the unanimous passing of these resolutions, Miss Child announced that the Board had accepted an invitation to hold the next annual meeting in Providence, R. I. After prayer by Mrs. Durant, and the singing of the Doxology, the meeting was adjourned.

THE CHILDREN'S MORNING STAR MISSION.

AT the delegates' meeting, in connection with the annual meeting, it was voted that the Board assume $3,000 of the expense of the Children's Morning Star Mission. We therefore appeal to leaders of mission circles, and to ladies who have the charge of raising money among the children, to bear their part in the fulfillment of this pledge. If these leaders are in earnest, we believe it

FAC-SIMILE OF CERTIFICATE FOR CHILDREN'S MORNING STAR.

Woman's Board of Missions.

This Certifies, that

*is owner of*_____*Share, in*

✦ THE CHILDREN'S MORNING STAR MISSION ✦

FOR THE YEAR

Emma Carruth,
Treasurer.

1885,

*Attest,*_____

ROOM I, CONGREGATIONAL HOUSE, 1 SOMERSET ST., BOSTON.

TO BE SIGNED BY TEACHER OR SECRETARY OF MISSION CIRCLE.

REVERSE SIDE.

will be an easy matter to continue the interest already awakened in the Morning Star, and secure offerings from the children for our treasury. This enterprise, as may be known, includes the whole of the Micronesian Mission, and we trust that the offerings of money will be accompanied, so far as possible, with systematic teaching adapted to children as to the condition of the people, their needs, and the progress of the gospel among them. We hope, also, that the contributions for this object will not disturb work already pledged in the mission circle, but will be an extra — or rather an increased — offering for the year.

The whole amount is to be divided into ten-cent shares, for which we have certificates printed on tinted cards, the two sides of which are given on the opposite page, the ship being an exact representation of the New Morning Star. To fulfill the pledge will require thirty thousand shares — a number that will not be secured without great effort and vigilance on the part of friends of the Board. We believe this is a great opportunity to enlist the children in missionary work in a permanent way, and to lay an absolutely necessary foundation for the future of our Board. May we not have your hearty co-operation, dear friends, though it may cost you labor and self-denial?

WOMAN'S BOARD OF MISSIONS.

RECEIPTS FROM DECEMBER 18 TO DECEMBER 31, 1884.

MAINE.

Biddeford.—Pavilion Soc'y, $26 00

Total, $26 00

NEW HAMPSHIRE.

Goffstown.—A Friend, $3 00

Total, $3 00

MASSACHUSETTS.

Acton.—Cong. Soc'y, $18 25
Andover.—Aux.,   127 20
Essex South Conf. Branch.— Miss Sarah W. Clark, Treas. Gloucester, Aux., of wh. $25 const. L. M. Mrs. J. S. Eldridge, $77; Peabody, Mrs. L. W. Thatcher, const. L. M. Miss Augusta Proctor, $25,   102 00
Hampshire Co. Branch.—Miss Isabella G. Clarke, Treas. Northampton, Aux., 1st Ch. Div., $100, Edwards Ch., Mrs. W. H. Stoddard's S. S. Cl., $20, Jun. Aux., $10; Williamsburg, Mrs. Helen E. James, const. L. M. Mrs. Abby Everett, $25,   155 00
Lowell.—1st Cong. Ch., $91.27, Buds of Promise, $18.46,   109 73

Mansfield.—Aux., $10 00
Mayn rd.—Mrs. E. Smith, in mem. little Amy,   2 00
Middlesex Branch.—Mrs. E. H. Warren, Treas. Lincoln, Cheerful Givers,   5 90
Old Colony Branch. — Miss F. J. Runnels, Treas. Taunton, M. B.,   9 00
Springfield Branch.— Miss H. T. Buckingham, Treas. Chicopee, 3d Ch., Busy Bees, $32, 1st Ch., $20.25,   52 25
Suffolk Branch.—Miss Myra B. Child, Treas. Boston, Central Ch., Aux., $50, Berkeley St. Ch., Y. L. Aux., $8; Roxbury, Eliot Ch., Aux., of wh. $25 by Mrs. Martha A. Curtis, const. self L. M., $74; Dorchester, 2d Ch., $255.80; Brookline, Mrs. Charles E. Miles, prev. contri. const. L. M. Mrs. Mary C. Tucker, $5; Charlestown, Winthrop Ch., Aux., $113.50; Chelsea, 1st Ch., Aux., $290; Somerville, Broadway Ch., $12.66; Cambridgeport, Pilgrim Ch., Y. L. Aux., $28.65; Brighton, Aux., of wh. $25 const. L. M. Mrs. S. N. Dickerman, $95; Newton, Eliot Ch., Aux.,

$104.55; Hyde Park, Aux., $164.75; D e d h a m , Aux., $190.60, $1,392 51
Woburn Conf. Branch.—Mrs. N. W. C. Holt, Treas. Burlington, Aux., $12; Maplewood, Aux., 50 cts.; Malden, Aux., of wh. $25 const. L. M. Mrs. Abby Brooks, $48; Melrose Highlands, Aux., $20, Bates M. C., $6.25; Wakefield, Aux., $81; West Medford, Aux., $10; Winchester, Aux., $10; No. Woburn, Aux., $3; Woburn, Aux., $15, 205 75

Total, $2,188 69

LEGACIES.

Legacy of Sarah Hale Stickney, Lowell, $603 25
Essex So. Conf. Branch.—Legacy ot Miss Caroline Nash, Gloucester, 100 00

CONNECTICUT.

Columbia.—Aux., $12 00
Tariffville.—A Friend, 4 40

Total, $16 40

NEW YORK.
Coxsackie.—Union S. S., $1 60
Gouverneur.—Mrs. J. P. Crane, 3 20

Total, 4 80

NEW JERSEY.
Jersey City Heights.—Mrs. Caroline L. Ames, $5 00
Princeton.—Mary C. Vinton, 3 20

Total, $8 20

FLORIDA.
Hawthorn.—M. A. Bell, $5 00

Total, $5 00

FOREIGN LANDS.
Turkey.—C o n s t a n t i n o p l e , Miss'y Soc'y of Turkey and Bulgaria, $13 44

Total, $13 44

General Funds, $2,265 53
Morning Star, 21 10
Weekly Pledge, 15
Leaflets, 5 97
Legacies, 703 25

Total, $2,996 00

RECEIPTS FROM JANUARY 1 TO JANUARY 18, 1885.

MAINE.

Maine Branch. — Mrs. Woodbury S. Dana, Treas. Bethel, 1st Ch., Aux., prev. contri. const. L. M. Mrs. E.W. Woodbury, $5; No. Bridgton, Ladies, $10; Bangor, Aux., $48; Acton, Aux., $10.50; Auburn, Aux., High St. Ch., $126.88; Waldoboro, Ladies' M i s s ' y Soc'y, $16.25: Bath, Central Ch. and Soc'y, $31.1u; Portland, Aux., State St. Ch., $75, 2d Parish Ch., $93.66, Williston Ch., $37.72; Waterville, Aux., $16.68, S. S., $8.32, $479 11
Dennysville.—Y. L. M. C., 10 00

Total, $489 11

NEW HAMPSHIRE.

New Hampshire Branch.—Miss Abby E. McIntire, Treas. Acworth, Aux., $8; Alton, Cong. Ch., S. S., $3; Bath, Aux., $10; Brookline, Aux., prev. contri. const. L. M. Mrs. Lewis M. Emery, $4; Campton, Aux., const. L. M. Mrs. Sarah Cutter, $27.20; Centre Harbor, Aux., $10.25; Concord, Aux., $10, Wheeler Cir., $83; Durham, Miss Su-

sie Mathes, $5; Exeter, Aux., of wh. $25 const. L. M. Miss Charlotte M. Kelly, $42, Lily Band, $5; Hanover, Aux., $6; Hollis, Aux., $33.05, Pansies, $34; Keene, 1st Ch., Aux., $7; Littleton, Aux., $17.20; Nashua, Mrs. Alvah Kimball, const. L. M's Mrs. Levi M. Flint, Mrs. John B. Tillotson, $50, Aux., of wh. $25 const. L. M. Miss Susan W. Pearson, $120.50, Union M. C., of wh. $50 const. L. M's Miss Lizzie M. Bancroft, Miss Hattie M. Gordon, $100; New Boston, Aux., $6; New Ipswich, Aux., $19, Hillside Gleaners, prev. contri. const. L. M. Miss Dora B a i l e y , $15.75; Piermont, Aux., $15; Portsmouth, Mizpah Cir., $5; Rochester, Aux., $30; Webster, Aux., prev. contri. const. L. M. Mrs. Mattie B. Little, $14; W. Lebanon, Aux., $16. Ex., $62.65, $633 30
Monroe.—Ch. and Soc'y, 7 00

Total, $640 30

VERMONT.

Vermont Branch.— Mrs. T. M. Howard, Treas. Bridport,

Aux., $14; Jamaica, Sunbeam Band, $20; Springfield, Aux., of wh. $25 Thank-Off., $37.53; St. Johnsbury Centre, Aux., $5.50; B a k e r s f i e l d, Aux., $9; Lunenberg, Aux., $9.50; W. Brattleboro, prev. contri. const. L. M. Mrs. Laura B. Merrill, $5; E. Corinth, Chain of Daisies, prev. contri. const. L. M., $11; E. Berkshire, Aux., $12; Windham, Aux., of wh. $25 const. L. M. Mrs. S. C. Woodburn, $30; Chelsea, Children's M. C., $20; Georgia, Aux., $18; Salisbury, Aux., $10; Westford, Aux., $12, Redeemed Pledge, $5, $218 53

Total, $218 53

MASSACHUSETTS.

Berkshire Branch—Mrs. S. N. Russell, Treas. Gt. Barrington, Aux., of wh. $25 by Mrs. M. E. P. Beckwith, const. L. M. Miss Alice Beckwith, $95; Lee, Jun. Aux., $123.06; Hinsdale, Aux., $21.51;. Housatonic, Berkshire Workers, $52.50; Dalton, Aux., $24; Sheffield, Aux., $16, $332 07
Dunstable.—Mrs. Mary B. Taylor,   25 00
Essex North Conf. Branch.— Mrs. A. Hammond, Treas. Georgetown, 1st Ch., Happy Workers, $10; B r a d f o r d, Aux., $4,   14 00
Gloucester.—Evan. Cong. Soc'y,   5 20
Hampshire Co. Branch. — Miss Isabella G. Clarke, Treas. Williamsburg, Mrs. Helen E. James, const. L. M. Mrs. Sarah Rice,   25 00
Lowell.—Kirk St. Ch., Aux.,   120 00
Middlesex Branch.—Mrs. E. H. W a r r e n, Treas. Natick, Aux., $23.50; Framingham, Plymouth Ch., S. S., $15,   38 50
Nahant.—Mrs Walter Johnson,   1 00
Norfolk and Pilgrim Branch. —Mrs. Franklin Shaw, Treas. Quincy, Aux., $30, Girls' M. C., $10; Weymouth and Braintree, Aux., $18, Morning Star, 85 cts.   58 85
Norwood.—Aux.,   10 00
Saugus.—Miss A. F. Newhall's S. S Cl ,   5 00
So. Attleboro. — Miss Ellen J. Harris, $2, Cong. Soc'y, $3 96, S. S., $15.   20 96
So. Abington. — Miss Caroline H. Whitman, const. self L. M.,   50 00
So Chelmsford.—Aux.,   5 00
Springfield Branch.— Miss H.

T. Buckingham, T r e a s. Springfield, South Ch , of wh. $25 by Mrs. L. M. Pierce, const. L. M. Miss L. May Pierce, $152.81, Y. L. M. C., $25.90, $178 71
Suffolk Branch.—Miss Myra B. Child, Treas. Boston, Charles Nichols, $10, Old South Ch., Mrs. Alpheus Hardy, const. L. M's Mrs. Catherine Gordon, Aberdeen, Scotland, Miss F. F. Phelps, So. Africa, Miss Hannah C. Woodhull, Miss Kate C. Woodhull, China, $100, Bartlett Band, $33, Mt. Vernon Ch., Aux., Mrs. E. K. Alden, const. L. M. Miss Maria Hyde Palmer, E. Saginaw, Mich., $25; So. Boston, Phillips Ch. S. S., $88.75, E. St. Ch., Dayspring M. C., $20; Roxbury, Eliot Ch., Mayflowers, $5.50; Brookline, Harvard Ch. M. C., $5; Dorchester, 2d Ch., Aux., $25, Village Ch., Aux., $12; Chelsea, 3d Ch., Aux., $32; Somerville, Prospect Hill Ch., Aux., $37; E. Somerville, A. L. M., $50; Cambridgeport, Prospect St. Ch., Aux., $103.08; B r i g h t o n; Cong. Ch. and S. S., $30; Newton Centre, Aux., $1, Maria B. Furber Miss'y Soc'y, by May Belle, Martha and Paul Ward, $2.50; Auburndale, Miss L. L. Mitchell, $6, Aux., $10.90; Hyde Park, Aux., $6; Dedham, Asylum Dime, $2.05; Arlington, Mrs. L. A. Randall, $1; Walpole, Aux., $52,   657 78
Tewksbury.—C. L. Fisher,   10 60
Webster.—1st Cong. Ch.,   24 70
Worcester Co. Branch.—Mrs. G. W. Russell, Treas. Fitchburg, Rollstone Ch., Y. L. M. S., $60; Southbridge, Aux., $20; Blackstone, Aux., $5; Spencer, Aux., $57, Riverside Helpeis, $10; No. Brookfield, Aux., $20.49; Ware, Aux., of wh. $100 const. L. M's Mrs. H. M. Corey, Mrs. D. W. Miner, Mrs. E. W. Hall, Miss E. Sturtevant, $119.60; Charlton, Aux., $10; Millbury, 1st Ch., Aux., $4; Upton, $25; Worcester, Woman's Miss'y Soc'y, Plymouth Ch., $52.65; Union Ch., Aux., $56.41,   440 15

Total, $2,021 82

LEGACY.

Legacy of Honora A. Clark, East Cambridge,   100 00

RHODE ISLAND.

Rhode Island Branch. — Miss Anna T. White, Treas. Providence, Plymouth Ch., $3; E. Providence, Aux., $3; Barrington, Bayside Gleaners, $50, ... $56 25

Total, $56 25

CONNECTICUT.

Bantam Falls. — Mrs. H. M. Bartholomew, $1 00
Bloomfield.—A Friend,   40
Eastern Conn. Branch.—Miss M. I. Lockwood, Treas. Norwich. 2d Ch.,   214 48
Hartford Branch.— Miss Anna Morris, Treas. Hartford, South Ch., Aux., of wh. $25 const. L. M. Mrs. F. R. Foster, $72, S. S. $30, Centre Ch., Aux., of wh. $25, by Miss Louise K. Root, const. L. M. Miss Mary Shipman, $398.30, Asylum Hill Ch., Aux., $336.52, Mrs. E. C. Bissell, const. L. M. Julia Maria Birkenmeyer, $25; Ellington, Earnest Workers, $25; Windsor Locks, Aux., $50; Vernon, Aux., $22; Hebron, A Friend, $1; W. Hartford, Aux., $105; So. Coventry, Aux., $30; Berlin, Aux., of wh. $25 by Mrs. Clarissa H. Wilcox, const. L. M. Mrs. Elizabeth A. Northrop, $101.75,   1,196 57
New Haven Branch.—Miss Julia Twining, Treas. Bethlehem, $32; Bridgewater, $50; Brookfield Centre, 4; Darien, $27.60, Busy Bees, $6.48; Greenwich, $40; Madison, $110; Middletown, 1st Ch., A Friend, const. L. M's Miss Elizabeth F. Patton, Miss Addie A. Russell, Mrs. Kate P. Hale, $75; Morris, $25; New Britain, South Ch., $52, Standard Bearers, $12.12; New Hartford, $10.18; New Haven, Centre Ch., $5, United Ch., Y. L. M. C., $70; Northford, $31; Norwalk, $100, Sunbeams, $10, 1st Ch., S. S., $10; Salisbury, $28; Sherman, $24.20; Wallingford, $30.07; Waterbury, 1st Ch., $53.70; Woodbridge, $20, A Friend, $40, $66 35
Plantsville.—Cong. S. S.,   30 00
Wapping.—Cong. Ch.,   1 00

Total, $2,309 80

NEW YORK.

New York State Branch.— Mrs. G. H. Norton, Treas.

Binghamton, Mrs. Sykes's S. S. Cl., $2; Homer, Mrs. B. W. Payne, $5; Smyrna, $40; Rochester, Plymouth Ch., $28; Brooklyn, Tompkins Ave. Ch., prev. contri. const. L. M. Mrs. Theo. R. Davis, Mrs. Geo. C. Stebbins, Mrs. Wheaton Welsh, Mrs. Harriett B. Salisbury, $25; Newark Valley, $24; Perry Centre, $40; Antwerp, $30; Orient, $40, $234 00
Brockport.—Mrs. Mary J. Holmes,   50 00
Fredonia.—Martha L. Stevens, $5, Friends, $1.80,   6 80
Newtonville.—Desert Palm,   20 00

Total, $310 80

PHILADELPHIA BRANCH.

Mrs. Samuel Wilde, Treas. Neath, Pa., Aux., $14 00

Total, $14 00

MARYLAND.

Baltimore.— Miss Alice Gilman, $10 00

Total, $10 00

OHIO.

Milan.—Aux., $20 40
Ruggles.—Mrs. S. L. Gault,   1 00
Windham.—Y. L. M. B.,   21 00

Total, $42 40

MICHIGAN.

Adrian.—A Friend, $ 40
Grand Rapids.—A Friend,   50
Hancock.—M. B.,   9 00

Total, $9 90

CALIFORNIA.

Santa Barbara. — Mrs. M. E. Cummings, $5 00

Total, $5 00

DAKOTA.

Sanborn.—Mrs. J. W. Donaldson, $1 00

Total, $1 00

General Funds, $6,129 01
Morning Star,   44 10
Weekly Pledge,   4 85
Leaflets,   27 64
Legacy,   100 00

Total, $6,305 60

MISS EMMA CARRUTH, Treasurer.

Board of the Interior.

MICRONESIA.

LETTER FROM MISS FLETCHER.

PONAPE, Sept. 30, 1884.

LONG ere this the mail sent by Capt. Garland has doubtless reached you. Your letter to me came to hand September 3d. I was very glad to hear from you once more. Many, many thanks for the appropriation you send us. How much good it will do these poor girls, and what a heavy care it takes from me to know they are provided for, you will never know until you learn it in a better world than ours. May the dear Saviour make each offering bring forth an hundred-fold.

The vessel which brought to us our mail was sighted early on the morning of September 3d, but it was almost noon before anything came on shore. Having waited so many long months for word from home, I felt no little anxiety when my letters were handed me to learn the contents. I untied the package, and the first envelope on which my eyes rested bore the token of bereavement. I then knew that some dear one had passed away. With nervous hands I broke the seal, to learn that I was motherless. My dear mother had gone home! I read the letter again and again; for it did not seem possible that she was dead, and yet she had been in the "golden city," eight months ere news of her death reached me. I wrote her letter after letter long after she had gone. It is hard to part with our friends at home, even when we can stand beside them and see them go; but no tongue can tell, no pen write, what it is to hear of it in this far-off land. I know it was the dear Father's will to have her go, and I know that it is well; but the thought will come, if I could only have stood beside her; if I could only have heard one parting word. But it is well; it is well. Whatever mysteries wrap His providence, we know it is for the best; but earth seems blank enough when I think of her not being here. It seems so strange to prepare mail and no letter addressed to her; but it ought to be a comfort to know that where she now is she needs no letters to tell her how and where I am, for she knows far better than I could tell her.

The vessel which brought us our mail this year is expected to return in a few days. I cannot prepare my mail so as to send it all by her, but will send a little now. We always have an opportunity of sending by the whalers in January and February, and the rest I will send by them

(105)

The girls' Home is all finished, and we moved into it in April. At that time, however, it was not completed, so we had to wait some weeks before the dedication. It was dedicated on the 28th of May, and on the following Monday school opened regularly.

The arrival of the "Jennie Walker" found our school numbering fourteen. I could not take the other six till I heard from the Board, as I did not know if the support would come or not. The work is opening up beautifully, and if we only had another teacher we could move on rapidly. Miss Palmer, as you will learn from herself, has remained at Strong's Island : in this we are very much disappointed, for the work is needing her so badly. She writes stating she will come at the close of the year. Mr. Doane has tried to persuade me not to take in the other six girls till she comes ; but I cannot tell them, when they wish to lead a better life, to wait one long year. Moreover, that future is not ours — and when that time comes, it may be too late for some of them. A year on the life of a native girl is a great deal. If my health remains as it is now, I feel sure I can take care of the twenty, though it does require much strength, health, and care to keep them as they should be, and you cannot imagine how rejoiced I shall be when another teacher comes. I have tried to teach the girls what heavy burdens the dear ladies in America are bearing for them, and I think they in a measure appreciate it. In the beautiful home which you have given them they have a constant reminder of the "Board of the Interior." Your names have become a household word, and in language unknown to you they are each morning borne upward in prayer. On their maps they have learned to perfection the location of Chicago. I wish you could look on this Home which you have erected, and be with these girls some morning when we are all assembled in the schoolroom for morning worship. If you could hear their clear but mild voices as they sing,—

> "   me kaul me jeri jota?
> Jijoj jaik mat kin isail?

English : —

> "Who shall sing it if not the children ?
> Did not Jesus die for them ? "

you would feel certain that all our efforts for Micronesia were not made in vain. The girls do all the housework (we have nothing in the way of servants), and some of them are becoming quite good cooks. We use the native food for them with some rice. Their principal food is the yam, a vegetable similar to our potato, and prepared in much the same way. All this work they can do quite well, providing I can watch them in order to prevent all waste.. We are in hopes they will soon be able to do, in a measure, without so much watching. Their beds are native mats: their quilts are similar to ours, only smaller.

They learn sewing quite quickly. Several of them can now cut and make their own clothing. We try to keep constantly before them the fact that, if it be the Lord's will, we expect them in future to go as teachers to the Islands west of us; and our object is to teach them everything that will tend to fit them for this life, ever making the salvation of the soul the one thing around which all others cluster. If all is well, you will hear from us again in a few months.

Mrs. Rand was on the Star when she was wrecked at Kusaie, and had no opportunity of returning till the Jennie Walker brought her. During eight months I never saw a white lady; so you may be sure I was rejoiced to see Mrs. Logan and Mrs. Rand.

CHINA.

LETTER FROM MISS DIAMENT.

Though delayed in its publication, the following letter will be welcome to all Miss Diament's friends who have been looking for the fulfillment of her heart's desire in the establishment of a girls' school at Kalgan.

KALGAN, Aug. 4, 1884.

MY DEAR FRIEND: I am spending my vacation a guest in my own rooms. The Mission decided that I should teach in Peking the coming year, to assist Miss Haven, during Miss Chapin's absence. I return to Peking in two weeks. We have had a very pleasant vacation, Mr. Sheffield and family and Mr. and Mrs. Beach having been with us. We have tried to make the most of our opportunities in every way. Dr. Murdock has taken a vacation, which she has spent at Tientsin and Tung-cho. Miss Garretson remained with Miss Haven after the annual meeting, and will return to Kalgan when I go down. The change has done her good. It seems like old times to be back in my old rooms, where everything remains much as I left it. I have been able to do some work in the little girls' school. There were seven girls when I came up, but two have left. Their parents moved away. They are very bright little girls, and very attractive. They are taught by a helper and his wife. She is a very nice woman to have charge of them, quiet and lady-like; she keeps them in perfect order. The school is in a good court a little distance from us. I go every day to hear them recite. I have a young lady reading with me every day in my room,—a very interesting girl. We are studying Acts, and enjoy it very much.

We have had a warm summer, but have all kept pretty well. Our fears of cholera have not been realized. We have heard of only one case. The war-cloud makes us feel disinclined to build houses just now. We thank the Board for their kind consideration of our needs, and shall make our plans and build as soon as it is expedient.

------------------◆------------------

EXTRACTS FROM LETTERS.

A word from our "happy missionary," Miss Shattuck, comes to inspire with new courage some of the home workers who are bearing heavy burdens. She writes from Marash, Turkey, Dec. 1, 1884: —

I AM just brimful of joy in this delightful work that so fully occupies my time. Miss Childs joined us November 1st. She is a lovely young lady, a graduate of Wellesley College, sent to our mission in 1880, to take my place with Miss Proctor, *loaned* to Constantinople Home last year, and now returned to be my assistant. Do you know I am planning a thirty years' work here in Turkey? Our girls number thirty-four in the school and twenty-six in the family — all doing well.

Our Missionary Society is awake, and earnest in prayer and effort for needy ones beyond their horizon. Quite a number have been earning money the past two weeks by using English exclusively at meal-times. They are each promised two *metaliks* (two and a quarter cents) a week, if perfect.

From Adana, Turkey, we have received a long letter from Miss Tucker, so full of interest, we hope all our auxiliaries will send to 75 Madison Street, Chicago, for copies and read the whole. As an inducement, we give the following extract: —

When school opened last year our girls were very few in number, so I introduced fancy-work, and spent an hour in teaching it. Before the close of the first month a very large class of girls, under thirteen years of age, were eagerly digging at arithmetic, language, and Bible-lessons, for the sake of spending an hour at the close of school in the afternoon on fancy-work. When the eight months of school were over we had crochetted shawls, jackets, tidies, mats, hoods, fancy mittens, scarfs, slippers, and lounge pillowcases on hand. What must be done with them? A member of the School Board suggested a sale.

At last examination-day came, and all our guests were delighted with the Bible lessons. Those who could appreciate it were pleased with the knowledge of history the girls had gained in connection with these. The arithmetic lesson went very well, and the singing, too, to my great surprise. Three hundred childish voices filled the room, and the listeners, about one thousand in number, including Islams, Armenians, Greeks, and Protestants, were well pleased. Then came the "sale." The expenditures for materials had been twenty-two dollars; we received ninety, netting seventy dollars, which sum we are going to use toward putting windows in our new schoolroom. The three girls' schools have been under the church in one room as large as the whole building. The room had neither windows, doors, nor partitions. As for seats, they were quite out of the question.

We expected, when the cold winter rains came on, to dismiss school; but the girls were too much engaged with the novelty of their work to give up entirely. Only one or two days were quite intolerable, though the wind often blew the rain clear across the room. In spite of all that, our school-work has been all we could expect. Our seventy dollars will put windows in the north side and east end of the house; and if prosperity reigns in the community I hope they will finish off the rooms. They are going to support their own schools from this time.

One of the teachers at the Umzumbi Home, South Africa, sends us the following account of the exercises at the close of the school-term: —

The term which has just closed has been a very pleasant one, with the exception of the death of Lucy, and a little sickness among the other girls. Martha has done very well in teaching, and been helpful in many other ways.

Examination commenced at 9 A. M., and lasted till 1.30 P. M. In the evening we had a little entertainment; the girls read essays, and recited poetry, and sang. Prizes were given by Mr. Bridgman, and Mahuda (the native pastor) and Joseph made speeches; after which came the gathering of the promiscuous and varied fruits of the girls' industry, from a goodly sized tree which stood in the corner. You can imagine what a happy crowd left the schoolroom when all was over, and a benediction had been given by Mr. Wilder.

The girls had a prayer-meeting almost every evening nearly all the term—the big girls in one room and the little girls in another; and on the last Sabbath of the term seven boys and girls united with the church,—four boys and three girls, Martha, Alice, and Ella. A good many more wanted to come in; but when the test came to consent to the new rules as laid down by the church, they went back, as did Christ's disciples of old, saying, "This is a hard thing; who can bear it?" That Sunday was a day that will not be forgotten. I felt so overcome as I recalled the long years of work and weary waiting in behalf of these girls, Martha and Alice, their trying obstinacy and utter indifference, and then to see them standing there humbly acknowledging Christ as their Saviour, and giving, themselves up to him, the tears would flow, and my heart was full of thanksgiving and praise. May He whose they are keep them, that the world may not cause them to soil their garments, which Christ has made white with his blood.

STUDIES IN MISSIONARY HISTORY.

1885.

MISSION TO PERSIA — 1835–1848.

The Country. A helpful chapter on this most interesting land may be found in the "Ely Volume."

History.

Ancient Religion.

Government. A sketch published by the Presbyterian Woman's Board at Philadelphia, which may be had for ten cents, will give needed information on these three topics.

The Nestorians. Their Missions. Their Social Condition. Customs. See Chapter XXI. of the "Tennesseean in Persia."

Ooroomiah.

Beginnings of the Mission Work. Influence upon the native clergy.

Work of Mrs. Grant.

Dr. Grant's Mountain Journeys. His Death.

Subjugation of the Nestorians.

Growth of Boys' Seminary. The Girls' Seminary.

First Revival. Influence in the Seminaries. Interest at Geog Tapa. Fruits.

Work of Translation.

Change in Mar Shimon toward the Mission.

Death of the King.

Fate of Bader Khan Bey; of Nûrûllah, Bey ; Suleiman Bey.

Helps. Dr. Anderson's "Missions to the Oriental Churches"; "Faith Working by Love," a memoir of Fidelia Fisk; "Woman and Her Saviour in Persia"; "Life Scenes Among the Mountains of Ararat," Rev. M. P. Parmelee; "Missionary Life in Persia," Dr. Perkins; "Nestorian Biography." The *Foreign Missionary* for October, 1884, contains several brief, bright articles on Persia.

AN AUXILIARY TO THE W. B. M. I.: WHAT IS IT?

BY MRS. GEORGE H. IDE.

"AUXILIARY—a helper, a confederate," says a world-renowned scholar. If your little society be but a handful it must be helpful, in order to be an auxiliary in the true sense. It must seek to increase by offerings not only of the gold and silver, "which is mine, saith the Lord," but offerings of time, ease, culture, the voice, the pen, the will, and possibly the children. If your organization be ten handfuls, a goodly number, then to be an auxiliary you must be a powerful confederate in the action of our parent Board

But a missionary auxiliary is not worthy of the name unless each sister is doing helpful work. The minister's wife is not an auxiliary to the Woman's Board of Missions of the Interior, though she should be a significant figure, if possessed of a sound mind in a sound body. The most popular and gifted woman in the church is not an auxiliary. A faithful secretary or an accurate treasurer is not an auxiliary. One hundred dollars raised, no matter how, and sent to 75 Madison Street, is not an auxiliary. A constitution is not an auxiliary. Yet all these are factors of the common multiple. What, then, is it? Why, a company of women who shall collect money (money set apart: 1 Cor. XVI. 2), and seek the cultivation of a missionary spirit among its members. See Article II., cover of LIFE AND LIGHT, if you take that little magazine; if you don't, and ever expect to have life "abundant" and light proportionate to a Christian of the last quarter of the nineteenth century, subscribe at once.

There is need of coming forward into the daylight of responsible, concerted action; of studying at home and at the missionary meeting; of praying at home and at the prayer meeting; of talking about missions at home and at the quarterly meeting.

An auxiliary to the Woman's Board of Missions means active, earnest effort, systematic and persevering enough to engage the attention of the most fashionable, the most scholarly, or the most modest and retiring who sit at our church communion-table. *

ESTIMATES FOR 1885.

THE estimates for 1885 are in the hands of our State secretaries: the special work of each auxiliary is, we believe, planned and entered upon. A question sometimes asked at our rooms we would like to propound to our auxiliaries: "How many of our 75,000

---

* Extract from a paper written for the annual meeting of the W. B. M. I., the whole of which is hectographed, and can be obtained at 75 Madison Street, Chicago.

women in the Interior will give $1.00 each this year?" Another
question is akin to this: "How many of the 75,000 are *able* to give
$1.00 each?" We believe they all are. Remembering a certain
pastor's wife in Connecticut who, in a little church of about one
hundred members, male and female,—farmers' families in moderate
circumstances,— collected $60 for the Woman's Board of Missions
the first year after an auxiliary was formed, we believe the pastor's wife or the auxiliary secretary can secure the $1.00 per
female member in every church. And we appeal to you, pastors'
wives, though you already bear many burdens, to make this special
effort, that your one pillar in the temple into which shall enter
every kindred and tongue, and people and nation, may not be
wanting. We appeal to you, State secretaries, to make it your aim
to secure from each church in your field an average of one dollar
for every woman connected therewith. Dear pastors' wives, and
secretaries, do we ask too hard a service? You will have to seek
out and persuade many individuals and churches whose one talent
is now hidden in a napkin. Some will have to give more than their
share to make up for others who cannot be reached. The women
of a few of our city churches now give more than one dollar each,
by securing pledges of $25, $15, $10, and smaller sums. Even there
the burden upon individuals is not equalized. But we shall come
nearer to equalizing the burden resting on the whole when all
churches do as well. When every church is reached, and each
assumes for itself the responsibility of contributing not less than
an average of one dollar per member, we shall see a great advance
in our work. We ask for a special effort to secure this end before
our next annual meeting. The estimates of work recommended to
the several States are given below, with the number of women in
the churches, in the hope that these figures may help. Colorado
is the only State where we have dared to ask more than one dollar
per member. Past experience warrants it: —

	No. of Women in Cong'l Ch's.	Estimates Recommended.
Colorado	918	$1,000
Dakota and N. Dakota	1,533	800
Illinois	16,090	18,000
Indiana	1,236	800
Iowa	10,994	5,000
Kansas	4,461	1,000
Michigan	11,997	8,000
Minnesota	5,204	4,200
Missouri	3,151	2,800
Nebraska	2,784	1,000
Ohio	15,961	8,500
Wisconsin	8,520	5,200

BROIDERY WORK.

BY ALICE M. GUERNSEY.

And so the "willing-hearted," with many a precious gem,
Or gold for solemn chiming upon the ephod's hem,
Or for the holy symbol, the priestly diadem,

Responsive to the summons,— glad that the Lord of all
Had need of woman's service, although so weak and small,—
Come with their eager tribute, in answer to the call.

And when the Eastern morning brake over Sinai's plain,
Before they ground the wheaten flour from out the perfect grain
To offer, as oblation, with the flesh of victims slain,—

Before the fiery pillar became a cloud of grey,
While yet the hush of slumber upon the valley lay,—
Before the crowding duties and questions of the day,

With spindle and with distaff wise-hearted women spun,
Or wrought in broidery pattern the colors one by one,
And gladly brought at eventide the work which they had done.

Some twined with dainty fingers the ephod's lace of blue,
Or wove with slender fibers the goat's-cloth, smooth and true;
Or wrought pomegranates on the robe, in triple-varied hue.

And some, whose life of toiling had left the marks of care
On hands that ached with longing the blessed work to share,
Sewed patiently the badger-skins, or dyed the ram-skins there.

And some, the gay and haughty, forgot their pride and mirth,
And holy thoughts and wishes within their souls had birth,
As toiled they for the dwelling of the Lord of all the earth.

And others learned the lesson that e'en the trembling mite,
From hearts all warm and loving, is precious in His sight
Who clothes the lilies royally, and notes the sparrow's flight.

At last, one sultry eventide, a weary mother bore
The folds of snowy linen for Bezaleel's store;
And, turning, said with anxious voice, "I cannot broider more.

"The home cares press upon me, the claims of nearer things;
My eager children must I feed, mend broken sandal-strings;
The nights are overburdened with the calls each morning brings.

"The stately Prince of Judah, my husband, thou shalt tell
To bring the fitting offering of a Prince of Israel;
Be mine the hearthstone duties — be mine to do them well."

Out spake another mother: "O, my sister, say it not;
The meed the Master giveth hast thou so soon forgot?
For *him* to toil, doth lighten and brighten every lot.

"Thy mother-mission holy, and thy cares, are gifts from him:
But if thy love be centered there, its light will soon be dim:
Thy soul-life will be bounded by the tent's contracted rim."

The days went on; no mother there evinced a tenderer care,
Or kept the home-hearth brighter than Judah's matron fair;
And the sick upon their beds of pain thanked God that she was there.

But angels knew the fairest of all the treasures brought:
The veil before the mercy-seat, by loving fingers wrought,
Was woven 'mid repentant tears for an earth-born, doubting thought.
— Heathen Woman's Friend.

SAXTON'S RIVER, VT.

PUBLICATIONS.

MEMORIAL OF REV. TITUS COAN. By Mrs. Lydia Bingham Coan.

Two extracts from the words of this remarkable man, who, "being dead, yet speaketh," must incite the reader to greater humility and zeal. Just as he was buckling on the armor, he wrote, "My good works need covering; my prayers need praying for; my repentance needs to be repented of"— so humble was his estimate of himself.

After years of labor in the Sandwich Islands, he says: "I climb mountains and precipices, cross deep and dangerous ravines, swim or ford rapid rivers, travel in drenching rain or under a tropical sun, preaching four, five, or eight times a day for weeks,— but at night my sleep is sweet, my meditation joyous, my heart peaceful."

The word-pictures of those wonderful volcanoes, Mauna Loa and Kilauea, and the account of that greater wonder of grace, which ended with the baptism of 1,700 in one day, would alone make the book worthy of a place in our household literature.

Mrs. Coan has kindly left a supply of these at 75 Madison Street, to be sold at $1.00 each, all the proceeds of which will go into the treasury of the W. B. M. I.

We have also for sale "Mrs. Pickett's Missionary Box," by Miss Alice Eddy, which we hope will introduce a box for thank-offerings into every household in our land. 2 cts. each, 15 cts. per doz.

"A Story of the Bees" and "For His Sake": two leaflets by Dr. Humphrey that must interest every one, and tell upon our treasury. 2 cts. each, $1.00 per 100.

"Aunt Mehitable," by Miss Pollock, which we cannot read too often. 10 cts.

"Mothers and Homes in Africa," by Mrs. Hull: a vivid picture of woman's degradation there, 2 cts. each, and the following:—

	Each.	Doz.
Aunt Mehitable's Account of the Annual Meeting. Miss Sarah Pollock: 10 cts. each; 75 cts. per doz.; $5 per hundred.		
Daughters of the Orient and of the Occident. Mrs. L. C. Purington	$ .10	$ .75
Literature of Missions. Mrs. L. C. Purington	.05	.50
Young Ladies' Manual for Foreign Mission Work	.05	.50

	Each.	Doz.
Another Message to the Coral Workers from Miss Sarah Pollock,	.05	.50
Helps for Leaders of Juvenile Mission Bands	.05	.55
Tamil Women. Mrs. H. K. Palmer	.03	.30
Birthright of the King's Children. Miss H. A Hillis	.03	.30
Responsibility of Christian Women Respecting Culture. Mrs. M. D. Newcomb	.02	.15
"Come Jewel" and "Glory." Miss Ada Haven	.02	.15
How to Manage a Missionary Society. Mrs. S. J. Rhea	.02	.15
Mrs. Purdy's "Parquisites." Mrs. S. E. Henshaw	.02	.15
For Christ's Sake. Mrs. E. E. Humphrey	.02	.15
The School at Hadjin and its Teachers. Mrs. A. W. Wood	.02	.15
The Scriptural Significance of Thank-offerings. Mrs. I. L. Hauser,	.02	.15
Experiences in Real Life. Mrs. N. Slaght	.03	.25
Brother Ox. Miss Ada Haven	.02	.15
Life Membership: What does it Mean? Mrs. W. H. Rice	.01	
Annual Report W. B. M. I.	.15	
Pamphlets of Missionary Maps (Published by A. B. C. F. M.)	.10	

---◄•►---

RECEIPTS OF THE WOMAN'S BOARD OF MISSIONS OF THE INTERIOR.

MRS. J. B. LEAKE, TREASURER.

FROM DECEMBER 18, 1884 TO JANUARY 18, 1885.

COLORADO.

Denver.—First Ch., Aux., $165 00

Total, $165 00

ILLINOIS.

ILLINOIS BRANCH.—Mrs. W. A. Talcott, of Rockford, Treas. *Alton*, Ch. of Redeemer, 5.80; *Ashkum*, 2.85; *Blue Island*, 15.50; *Canton*, 23.40; *Champaign*, 10; *Chicago*, First Ch., 62, New England Ch., 38.70, South Ch., 16.91, Western Av. Ch., 20; *DeKalb*, 3.20; *Delavan*, Mrs. B. H. Reed, 2.50; *Downer's Grove*, 6.86; *Earlville*, Ross Grove Soc., 6.72; *Galesburg*. First Ch., Aux., 37.50; *Highland*, 5; *Kewanee*, for Marash, 10; *Lisbon*, 8; *Moline*, 25; *New Milford*, 6.25; *Oak Park*, 20.95; *Ottawa*, 35; *Plymouth*, 10; *Rockford*, 2d Ch., 4.50; *Sycamore*, 10; *Waverly*, 12, $398 64

JUNIOR SOCIETIES: *Chicago*, Lincoln Park Ch., 21.75, South Ch., thank-offering, 7.75, Union Park Ch., 74.15, Western Ave. Ch., Star Soc., 10; *DeKalb*, Miss. Band, 1.80; *Geneseo*, Busy Workers, const. L. M. Mrs. G. F. Wait, 25; *Geneva*, Y. L. M. Band, 25; *Port Byron*, Y. L. Soc., 4,   169 45

JUVENILE SOCIETIES: *Chicago*, Oakley Miss. Industrial Sch. of Union Park Ch., 4.50; *Geneseo*, Miss'y Rill, 1; *Payson*,

IOWA.

Cheerful Workers, 55 cts.; *Providence*, Children's Band, 20, $26 05

Total, $594 14

IOWA.

IOWA BRANCH. — Mrs E. R. Potter, of Grinnell, Treas. *Atlantic*, 8, *Anamosa*, 5; *Cedar Rapids*, 7.70; *Farragut*, 15; *Montour*, 10.40; *Monticello*, 15.30; *New Hampton*, 4.24; *Pilgrim*, 10; *Red Oak*, 6; *Seneca*, 5; *Webster City*, 5.50, $92 14

JUNIOR SOCIETIES: *Creston* 40; *Clay*, 5; *Dubuque*, 15; *Stacyville*, 35; *Ottumwa*, 11,   106 00

JUVENILE SOCIETIES; *Cromwell*. Busy Bees, 1.50; *Manchester*, Rainbow Band, 10.   11 50

SABBATH SCHOOLS:*Des Moines*, 7.86,   7 86

Total, $217 50

KANSAS.

KANSAS BRANCH.—Mrs. A. L. Slosson, of Leavenworth. Treas. *Dial*, Miss E. Newman, 3; *Exeter*, Mt. Vernon Aux., 5.75; *Manhattan*, Mrs. Mary Parker, 10; *Parsons*, 1.30; *Sabetha*, 6.35; *White City*, 6.20, $32 60

JUVENILE SOCIETIES; *Sabetha*, Rushlight Mission Band, 10,   10 00

Total, $42 60

MICHIGAN.

MICHIGAN BRANCH.—Mrs. Geo. H. Lathrop, of Jackson, Treas. *Almont*, 19; *Cheboygan*, A Friend, 1; *Detroit*, 1st Ch., Aux., 54.50; *East Saginaw*, 38; *Grand Rapids*, Park Ch., Aux., 87; *Kalamazoo*, 12.75; *Lake Linden*, 12.25; *Morenci*, 16.85; *Olivet*, 17.60; *Sandstone*, 5; *South Haven*, 8; *Union City*, 10; *Vermontville*, 12,　　　　$293 95
YOUNG PEOPLE'S CIRCLES: *East Saginaw*, Young Ladies, 50; *Greenville*, Young Ladies, 18.01; *Jackson*, Young People, 40,　　　　108 01
CHILDREN'S BANDS: *Flint*, S. S. scholars, 3.75; *Greenville*, Cheerful Toilers (girls) and Morning Star Band (boys), 31; *Jackson*, Sunbeam Band, 12; *South Haven*, S. S. Mission Band, 6.90,　　　　53 65

Branch Total,　　　　$455 61

MINNESOTA.

MINNESOTA BRANCH.— Mrs. E. M. Williams, of Northfield, Treas. *Austin*, 10.15; *Minneapolis*, Second Ch., 5.82, Plymouth Ch., 159.30, Mrs. Borey, 15; *Northfield*, 55.71; *Zumbrota*, 14.71,　　　　$260 69
JUNIORS: *Austin*, Scatter-Good Soc., 14; *Minneapolis*, Plymouth Ch., Y. L. Soc., 31.25; *Northfield*, C. College, Aux., 43.88; *Medford*, Mrs. Abbott's S. S. Class, 5　　　　94 13
For Morning Star:—
Plainview, Busy Bees,　3 00—　3 00

Branch total,　　　　$357 82

MISSOURI BRANCH.

Mrs. J. H. Drew, 3101 Washington Ave., St. Louis, Treas. *St. Louis*, Pilgrim Ch., Y. L. Soc., 56.25, 5th Cong. Ch., Aux., 20.05, Coral Workers, 36.29, Hyde Park Gleaners, 4.00; *Kansas City*, Cheerful Givers of Clyde Cong. Ch., 2.50; *Amity*, Jewels, 45.41,　$164 50

Total,　　　　$164 50

OHIO.

OHIO BRANCH.—Mrs. Geo. H. Ely, of Elyria, Treas. *Atwater*, 20; *Chagrin Falls*, 10; *Cincinnati*, Vine St., Miss J. W. Carpenter, M.D., 25; *Cleveland*, Euclid Ave., 20; *Elyria*, 55.32; *Hudson*, 12;

Painesville, 50; *Springfield*, 25.50; *Tallmadge*, 32.39,　$250 21
JUNIOR: *Marietta*, Y. L. M. S.,　75 00
JUVENILE; *Bristolville*, S. S., 2.7 ; *Elyria*, Little Helpers, 3,　　　　5 75
Less expenses, 31.03.

Total,　　　　$299 93

SOUTH DAKOTA BRANCH.

Mrs. K. B. Finley, of Vermillion, Treas.
JUNIOR SOCIETIES; *Yankton*, Y. P. M. Band, 18.55; *Vermillion*, Ready Hands, 2.73; *Meckling*, for Star, 73 cts.,　$22 01

Total,　　　　$22 01

WISCONSIN.

WISCONSIN BRANCH. — Mrs. R. Coburn, of Whitewater, Treas. *Alderley*, 3.20; *Burlington*, 10; *Broadhead*, 5; *Bloomer*, 5.02; *Boscobel*, 4; *Beloit*, 2d Ch., 26.06; *Clinton*, 5; *Ft. Atkinson*, thank-offering, 5; *Fon du Lac*, 30; *Milwaukee*, Grand Ave. Ch., 35.75; *New Lisbon*, 1.25; *Rosendale*, 5; *Stoughton*, 3.50; *Shopiere*, 5; *Waukesha*, 9.67; *Whitewater*, 2,　$155 45
JUNIORS: *Burlington*, 10; *Durand*, Willing Workers, 8; *New Lisbon*, 4.50; *Stoughton*, for Morning Star, 1.50,　24 00
JUVENILES: *Brownstown*, for Morning Star, 25 cts.; *Milwaukee*, thank-offering of Mrs. E. D. Holton's grandchildren, for Morning Star, 2; *Pestigo Harbor*, S. S., 4.39; *River Falls*, Mrs. Weld's S. S. Cl., 2.13; *Ripon*, Do Good Soc., 15 cts., S. S., 2.95.　11 87
Less expenses, 13.76.

Total,　　　　$174 46

GEORGIA.

Atlanta, 1st Ch., Aux.,　　$5 00

Total,　　　　$5 00

CHINA.

Peking, Aux., for Star,　　$ 75

MISCELLANEOUS.

Sale of mittens from Keokuk, 1; of "Coan's Life," 4; of bracelets, 16; of leaflets, envelopes, etc., 28.07,　$49 07

Total,　　　　$49 07

Receipts for month,　　$2,548 39
Previously acknowledged,　2,705 25
Total since Oct. 22, 1884,　$5,253 64

Board of the Pacific.

ANNUAL REPORT OF FOREIGN SECRETARY. — VISITS TO EACH OF OUR MISSION STATIONS.

COME with me to Northern Turkey, and to our Broosa school! Reaching Constantinople, we take a Turkish steamer for Mondania, and from there we must go by carriage or on horseback to Broosa. These steamers sail only every other day, and we shall be five hours on board. . . . .

Over in the cotton-fields see the men and women picking the feathery tufts! Let us stop here for some of these luscious grapes! Now we are coming to a Turkish village. How many dogs there are coming out to meet us! See the stork's nest on the roof of that house! Look at the men walking the streets, decked in all the colors of the rainbow, while the women go about with veiled faces — sheeted ghosts. We pass the public khans, which at best will afford but a mat and a shelter to any one who wishes to tarry. The wayside fountains are the center of many picturesque scenes, as the women must wait about them for hours for their turn to fill their water-jugs. As they stand and wait, generally with a baby tied on their backs, they fill up the minutes with coarse knitting or hand-spinning of wool or cotton. When their jars are filled, see them walk off with one in each hand, baby still clinging to their shoulders, or held on by being tied firmly with a strong shawl or broad, homespun girdle! There comes a little company of women, carrying clothes, wood, boiler, and all the appliances for their weekly washing, fully half a mile to running water. At night they will return with them, wet but clean, to be hung in their own courts to dry. Here are

(117)

extensive forests of mulberry-trees.   See them gathering the silk cocoon!

Now we have a sight of Broosa.   Nestling under the verdure-clad and snow-capped Olympus, it presents a picture of perfect beauty. We *might* put up at the "Mt. Olympe," kept by "Loschi," but we have another haven in view.   So we move on, through the narrow but clean streets, past the citadel, rising upon a bold rock in the center of the town, past several fine mosques, till we reach a large building, European in its architecture, surrounded by a lovely garden.   It needs no guide to tell us what *this* building is: photographs and pictures have made us familiar with its exterior.   It has no cupola of emerald green, no exquisite carvings, no dome of silver, no minarets, but it is dearer to our California hearts than *all* the mosques of Turkey.

Five thousand dollars was put into our Broosa School.   Five thousand dollars and more we have paid toward the support of a missionary there and the education of individual Turkish girls.   We have a pride in it — in its location, in its teachers, in its appliances.   Let us take one more look before we enter the building.   In the background rise majestically the cliffs and snowy summits of Olympus.   About us are the domes and minarets of Broosa's two hundred mosques.   In front stretches the beautiful plain, covered with trees and verdure; in the far distance, hills and mountains with their ranging lights and shades. Truly, as we have often heard, but never before realized, the location is ideal in its beauty and picturesqueness.

Having safely landed this large company, and having secured for them a cordial welcome at the hands of our missionary, Mrs. Baldwin, a few facts concerning the *work* of the school during the past year may be of interest.   I read from the official report of 1883-84:—

The whole number of scholars for the school-year is 47.   Our present number is 38, including 18 day-pupils and 20 boarding-scholars. . . . .

During the year ten of our scholars have been received into the church, all of them giving evidence of true Christian life.   Most of these believed they became Christians during the special religious interest we enjoyed a year ago. . . . .

Our work in Africa has been done in Zululand, through the school of which Mr. and Mrs. Goodenough have charge; but reports from there have been very meager, so I pass on to our "Morning Star" work.

We have paid $500 this year toward the running expenses of the "Star," and, of course, have followed her, in thought, with much interest as she has threaded her way in and out of the rocky lagoons of Micronesia, carrying joy and blessing everywhere. Our sorrow at her loss was more than balanced by the thought of the new steamer "Star," in which so many of our Sunday-schools have been interested, and we thank God once more for the business energy and foresight of our grand American Board. So, friends, we have still a work to do for the "Star" — a ship larger, stronger, fleeter than any of her predecessors! Long may she survive the perils of the sea!

We entered upon our new work in Spain "as a Board," last year. To many of us, as individuals, it was not a new field. We had followed Mr. and Mrs. Gulick in the pages of *The Herald* and *Life and Light* ever since they sailed from Boston, in 1876. To have a part in their work was joy indeed!

Through letters from Mrs. Gulick, her assistant, Miss Richards, and their friends in the East, we have learned much about our school even in this one year. To know much of missionary work anywhere is to be interested in it. . . . .

A letter has just been received from Mrs. Gulick, dated August, 1884, giving more graphically than could be given by any one else, the results of the past year's work. Accompanying the letter are the programmes of the closing exercises of the school, and a musical entertainment given by them. On the latter, we notice selections from Herold, Rossini, Mozart, Mendelssohn. On the programme of the closing exercises we notice examinations in sacred history, arithmetic, domestic economy, Spanish grammar, Spanish history, English, political geography, compositions in English and French, and a dialogue in French; also gymnastics and kindergarten exercises. Diplomas were presented to Elisa Ruet and Mercedes Villanueva, both of whom give great promise of future usefulness.

I wish I could command the services of a skilled portrait-painter. I would show you two pictures — the one of a fair, young, lovely face, with bands of dark, wavy hair; the other, the same face, with lines of care and sickness, aged by twenty years in the time of eight. The one was our Miss Starkweather, as she stood before us Feb. 29, 1875, in what was then Dr. Stone's church, and told us of her plan for Christian work in Japan. She was full of courage and zeal, and anxious to be "about her Master's business."

In the girls' school at Kioto she found much to do. The difficult language overcome, she entered with all her soul into the work before her. Nor did she forget our Woman's Board. Letters, full and long, came to us every month from her hand. Others associated with her gave up, and came home for needed rest; but she still kept at her post, ever ready with her loving counsels and generous helpfulness.

But one day there came a letter —"The summer found me far more tired than I had thought; and all through the fall nothing but the kind Father's care, and his promise, 'As thy day, so shall thy strength be,' enabled me to 'hold on,' and carry out my daily duties, as I did after weeks of almost sleepless nights, with a distressing cough."

Under date of April 18, 1883, we have another letter from her, which is not so much of a surprise to us, after all, saying that she is coming home.

We are glad of the opportunity she had to return to her aged mother, to her home-friends, and to us. We rejoice in her joy. We somehow forget the years that have intervened,— "that distressing cough," so incidentally mentioned; the hard work done, both mental and physical,— and look for the same Miss Starkweather who bade us "good-bye" that February afternoon in 1875.

In June, 1883, we assembled to greet her: the same dear face, but how tired, and thin, and pale — the roses all fled, but her smile still as bright and cheerful. In the language of another, I was reminded of Paul's "I count all joy," and of a few words I have read in a good little book, "Better and sweeter than health, or friends, or money, or fame, or ease, or prosperity, is the adorable will of our God," for it was all written on her face and manner. Miss Starkweather is still East, suffering from her cough and from asthma; sent by her physician, first, to absolute rest in the bracing climate of St. Paul, Minn., then to Denver, Col.

Here we must leave her in the tender care of "Him who doeth all things well." Remember her lovingly; pray for her. She has need of all our prayers and sympathy.

Much good work is being done in our school at Kioto during Miss Starkweather's absence, as the following extracts will show:—

The school, numbering forty-three scholars, opened in September, with a revised course of study.

Three girls have graduated this year. Since the special religious interest last spring, fourteen of our girls have been baptized, and joined the church. . . . .

The older pupils take turns in conducting three Sabbath-schools for children. One opened a few months since in the suburbs of the city, numbers sixty scholars in regular attendance.

So our Miss Starkweather's school is like "a light set on a hill" in the great city of Kioto, with its three hundred and seventy-four thousand inhabitants.

Let us see that its flame is steady and clear, for it is shining in upon young Japan — a nation that must be won to Christ.

ALICE D. JEWETT.

An Easter-Offering.

Dear Lord, I find no offering meet
To lay at thy beloved feet:
For lilies fade on Easter morn,
And fairest roses bear a thorn;
The green wood and the flowery
  field .
No living, fadeless garland yield.

Ah! there is yet a place apart,—
The sheltered garden of my heart.
Its thornless rose of love I'll glean;
The lily, Hope, and living green
Of Faith; and in a garland sweet
I'll bind and lay them at thy feet.

           ELLA G. IVES.

INDIA.

IN A STRONG CITY.— No. 1.

BY MRS. W. B. CAPRON.

I SAID to the Bible-women one Friday evening, "How was it that you had so many listeners in the month of January?" There were 2,359, and that is a large number. They all replied at once that it was in that month that I sent them from house to house to read six verses on what God thinks of sin. I remembered it well.

I then proposed that we have a blessed week's work with reading verses on the great love of God in as many houses as we could, without reference to those who are studying with us. We will stand on the doorsteps bearing the rich and wonderful message, and ask to be allowed to carry it in, and the whole city shall hear the sound. May it please God to bless us from heaven. The response was in itself an inspiration.

The first of the selected verses proved more blessed than we had expected, and in a way somewhat different. Many women who read with us accepted them at once as a prayer suited to them, and as a prayer that would be acceptable to God. I could not but think, as each Bible-woman was giving her testimony, that the Lord was thus teaching our weak and timid ones how to pray. These were the words:—

"For thou, Lord, art good and ready to forgive, and plenteous in mercy to all them that call upon thee.

"Give ear, O Lord, unto my prayer, and attend unto the voice of my supplication.

"In the day of my trouble I will call upon thee, for thou wilt answer me."

Said one woman: "In our religion it seems as if the Swamy was always seeing how much he could get out of us. As soon as we are in trouble we are always planning what we must give to get out of it: and who gets it when we have given it?"

Said another: "Every time I hear those verses I think how the Lord seems to be always giving us 'in advance.'" This is a very good point, if we consider the custom of this part of the country. In settling any bargain we are expected to give "advance," be it ever so small a sum, as a sort of security that the contract be faithfully carried out, whether in hiring a conveyance or ordering a piece of furniture.

A Brahman woman said: "These verses make me think of the sandal-wood tapers that we burn so much in our worship. We have to continually relight them. These are fresh and fragrant all the time, and always ready to use."

One of the Bible-women had a great desire to take the brightness and sweetness of God's love into a large house which she had
passed and repassed many times. Finally she caught sight of a
woman just within the doorway, and stepped on to the third of the
flight of five steps, and stood there feeling as if she were indeed
God's messenger. The woman came to the door, and looked her
inquiry as to what was wanted. The Bible-woman said:—

  "I want to come in and tell you of God's love."

"What's that?" said the woman.

"It is because you don't know that I want to come in and tell
you. Do let me tell you just a little."

The woman smiled at her eagerness, and bade her come in.
They sat down, and the Bible-woman read the following:—

"'Oh, how great is Thy goodness which thou hast laid up for
them that fear thee: which thou hast wrought for them which
trust in thee before the sons of men.

"'Thou shalt hide them in the secret of thy presence from the
pride of man: thou shalt keep them secretly in a pavilion from the
strife of tongues. Blessed be the Lord, for he hath showed me his
marvelous kindness in a strong city.'"

The Bible-woman stopped reading. "Does that mean the
strong city of Menachi?" asked the woman; for it must be said in
passing, that this is a common term applied to the city of Madura.

"Yes," said the Bible-woman; "it is Madura, and there are
many women like you who say it."

"What is the marvelous kindness, and how do you get it?"
asked the woman. The verse, "For God so loved the world," was
repeated to her, and one of the most interesting visits of the week
followed.

Many a dear woman of our own would repeat the last verse,
and say how true it was. The expression, "Thou shalt keep them
secretly in a pavilion (in a tent, in the Tamil) from the strife of
tongues," attracted the attention of many, as I expected it would.
The forlorn widows, who have to bear so much contempt, would
be glad to find such refuge. "I am a widow," said the Bible-
woman, "and the Lord has given me his own shelter, and I praise
him all the time."

Thus did these dear women go into hearts and homes, showing
in their faces and in their kind words the love of God shed abroad
in their hearts.

We found that many of our own women were impressed by the
words, "which Thou hast wrought for them that trust in thee
before the sons of men." They felt that they could not claim comfort from this while they were afraid or unready to declare them-

selves on the Lord's side. One was troubled on hearing all these verses read, and asked to have them read again, which was done. She then said to the Bible-woman: "I don't care at all about many customs that are called idol worship; I have given them up; but there is one thing I enjoy so much, I should not know what to do." This was the worship of the evening lamp. These, in all well-to-do houses, are of brass, more or less showy, always kept bright, and standing about two feet high. When first lighted a garland is often put upon it; sometimes a few flowers only are laid before it; and sometimes the halves of a newly broken cocoanut. The housewife folds her hands before it in worship. Sometimes all the household will gather together, and the tiniest child can gleefully worship the evening lamp. It is festive, it is social, and most enjoyable. To give this up would startle the whole household into declaring this woman "one of the Christians."

"So you think it is wrong to worship the evening lamp?" was the question. The Bible-woman replied wisely: "You know very well whether it is wrong or not. You know very well whether you are speaking from your heart to the God of love, or whether you are keeping up a custom which you have not courage enough to give up."

The woman burst into tears. "What shall I do? More than anything else I desire to be at peace with my heavenly Father, and to please him."

The Bible-woman lifted her heart to heaven for a fitting reply. Said she: "When you light the evening lamp, and the bright light shines through the rooms, think of your heavenly home, and how God says to you, 'They need no light of lamp, neither light of the sun, for the Lord God shall give them light.' Then thank him for the bright hope of one day being there. You will soon find this far more precious and satisfying than the old way, for our God is a God who loves us, and knows every struggle in our hearts."

The dear woman, whose heart the Lord had touched, then asked the Bible-woman to go with her to an inner room, and then and there pray with her that God would help her to trust in him before the sons of men.

(*To be continued.*)

MICRONESIA.

EXTRACTS FROM MRS. LOGAN'S JOURNAL.

. . . WE left Honolulu the twenty-third of July, and have been nine days at sea. It has been rather rough weather some of the time, but we have made very good progress, and are now more than half way from Honolulu to Jaluij, in the Marshall Islands, which is our first stopping-place.

The Jennie Walker is not very large, and we are quite heavily loaded. Our little "ten by twelve" house on deck makes us far more comfortable than if we were down in the cabin, but it is rather crowded, with a small table, two bed-lounges, two large trunks, two chairs, and two corner wash-stands. We get along very well, however. . . . We are trying to take quite a number of plants which we hope will grow on Ruk; among them a fine little mandarin orange-tree, which will be of untold value if we can make it grow there. The plants are covered by one of the boats, so that they have escaped a salt-water bath which would kill them at once. Then there is our cow and our two Jersey calves, whose stalls are just forward of our little house. There is a coop with ducks and chickens, and another with doves; and there are some cats — I cannot state with any degree of exactness how many — and a little dog, which some children in Honolulu gave Beulah. The captain and sailors are all very kind, and the cook does fairly well, although our appetites are very capricious. The cook is a Chinaman, as is also the cabin-boy. I am sure they do better than I should if I had to cook for fourteen or more people in a place hardly more than four feet square. . . . Mr. Cooke, of Honolulu, put on board a number of pounds of ice, which lasted us through the worst of our sea-sickness, and was a great comfort.

August 2d. We are a little at a loss just now whether it is to-day or to-morrow, as we are just about where the world's day begins. We shall know this afternoon, when the captain takes his observation. If we have passed over into the eastern hemisphere we shall have no Sunday this week except from four o'clock in the afternoon until midnight; but if not, then Monday will probably be the day to be lost, and that is the captain's birthday.

August 4th. Our Sunday began sometime in the afternoon yesterday. After supper we went up on deck and had a short service, and then went to bed trying to think we had had a Sunday—but feeling a little as though we had been defrauded. It was calm much of the time during the night, and this morning, also. This is our first calm, and oh! I hope it may not last long. The thermometer is at 86 in the cabin to-day; probably not quite so hot in our little house, but it is very hot here.

August 11th. We are not yet at Jaluij, though we are eighteen days from Honolulu, and the captain hoped to reach there in four-teen days; but we had very poor weather much of the time. How natural it seems to be becalmed in the Pacific Ocean! How many weeks of my life have been spent in this way, longing and praying for wind when there is none, fearing it may leave us when we have a good breeze! We are about thirty miles from Mille, the first one of the Marshall Islands that we expect to see.

August 15th. We are still close upon Mille. It is only one hundred and twenty miles from Jaluij, but we have no present hope of getting there, as wind and current are both against us. The sea is almost like glass, and the sun beats down upon us very scorchingly. We try to be patient and cheerful; and it is surely not because we have not prayed for wind that we do not have it. How glad we are that the next missionaries who come to Micronesia will not have so much to endure!

August 16th. Our much desired wind came last night, and at midnight we were really leaving Mille behind. Mr. Logan says we have seen all the sides of Mille except the inside. We are carrying a large square sail, and making at least ten knots an hour. . . . If the wind holds good we may hope to sight Jaluij before dark.

August 28th. We left Jaluij August 19th, and had a fair wind all the way to Kusaie, reaching there on Friday, the twenty-second. The distance is nearly four hundred miles. It was a joy indeed to reach Kusaie. Dr. Pease and Mr. Walkup came on board before we were at anchor, and then we learned the particulars about the wreck of the Morning Star. . . . Dr. and Mrs. Pease are looking much worn, and are needing a change. They were much disappointed that no one had heard their distressed cry for help, and come to their relief. With the Marshall Island training school, with twenty or more scholars, on their hands, it seemed hard to tell what could be done, or what arrangements could be made for them to go to America; but at last Miss Cathcart suggested that Miss Palmer remain with her this year, and they two together hold the fort and let the Peases go to Honolulu by this boat-vessel. Mr. and Mrs. Walkup, with their training-school for the Gilbert Islands, are not far away, so it is not like leaving them all alone. It was no easy matter for Miss Palmer to decide to remain. Her heart is in the girls' training-school at Ponape, but she thought it duty, and cheerfully yielded her own will and desire in the matter. . . . Wednesday morning we left our friends, and went on our little vessel. Our progress has been very slow; much of the time we have been becalmed, with now and then a squall and some head-wind.

September 20th. It is almost a month since I have written in this journal, and we are not yet at Ruk. . . . We drew near to Ponape on Tuesday, and with one or two more hours of daylight we might have gotten safely in, but the next morning we were becalmed. We found the friends at Ponape usually well. . . . It was pleasant to see them all once more, to know how glad they were to have us back, and how sorry we were not to remain here, but to go on to Ruk. There were many of our old friends among the people, and we were warmly welcomed. Of course there were changes: some had passed away; the old house was changed so as to be hardly recognizable in the lower part; and the trees that we planted — limes, mangoes, guavas — were grown large; but the old home feeling soon came back.

Mr. Doane rejoices greatly with us in our new work. He came on board the last morning, as we were about to sail, to bid us God-speed. We sat down together in our little room, and he read a part of Paul's last charge to Timothy; we prayed together, and said good-bye. . . . We were so long in getting into the vicinity of the Mortlocks, the captain was inclined to urge that we should not stop there at all, but push on at once to Ruk. We were very unwilling to do this, and the wind was unfavorable for it, so on Thursday afternoon we were anchored in the great Satoan lagoon. . . . In the little glimpse we have had of the work at the Mortlocks, we see many things to make us sad, and to show that something more must be done for these people. The teachers themselves hardly realize what has been done for them in giving them the New Testament, for they have never had that in their own language; but we hope the value of it will grow upon them. . . . It is an impressive thought that these dear workers who have been missionaries so long, have never before had the privilege of reading what is told us about heaven. It must be that they, too, will get food from the new book, as well as the Mortlock people.

September 29th. Ruk Lagoon. I am sure you will all be glad to know that our voyage is safely over. We had a tolerably quick passage from Mortlock, leaving there Thursday: we came to anchor here yesterday.

[*To be continued.*]

JAPAN.

EXTRACTS FROM RECENT LETTERS.

FROM MISS DAUGHADAY.— The work grows daily more absorbing and satisfying. The strong liking I had at first for the Japanese has not diminished, so far as the Christians are concerned. They are so unfailingly pleasant and courteous that it is more a joy than a duty to go to their homes; while their simple faith, warm love, and earnest zeal are most encouraging. I am becoming more and more deeply impressed with the Oriental character of the Bible. Early in the morning, when I see persons passing with their *futon* thrown across their shoulders, the command, "Take up thy bed and walk," flashes through my mind. Removing the shoes and sandals at the entrance of a house, taking a seat just within the door until invited to "come up higher," or to the more honorable place further within, repeating prayers publicly in the streets, are constant reminders. Occasionally when men are seen with huge fans removing the hulls from the rice, the text "His fan is in his hand" comes with a fresher, deeper meaning. It is not many years since watches and clocks have been in general use. Formerly when a man wished to make a feast, he sent his servants in the morning to invite the guests; and, again, later in the day to say, "Come, for all things are now ready." Yet while their dress and customs are so very different from our own, daily intercourse with them leads me to realize "He hath made of one blood all the nations of the earth." An Aino man of Yezo said to me in the summer, "Although the languages of men are all different their hearts are all the same." At a funeral and at a pastor's farewell meeting lately, when both missionaries and Japanese were affected to tears, it made no difference whether they were wiped away with long, loose sleeves, paper, or linen handkerchiefs; they sprang from the same source.

The revival in the spring was of a more quiet nature in Osaka than either at Kioto or Kobe, as in those cities its work was chiefly felt in the schools. Here there was a quickening of the churches, and a clearer spiritual apprehension of divine things noticeable among the Christians, but there was not any marked or great ingathering. There seems to be a deep, steady work going on all the time. Two of our pastors have told me that during their pastorates, extending over a number of years, there has not been one communion season when they have not received new members; and I understand it is about the same with the other churches. At one service that I attended quite recently eighteen persons were baptized. The willingness to give in order to support men doing evangelistic work, and to prepare others for the ministry at the Kioto Theological School, is certainly increasing.

The priests are alarmed at the great progress Christianity is making here, and are stirring up the people to hold opposition meetings. It has now become a common sight to see a paper pasted on the door of a house announcing, "There will be a lecture against Christianity given here this evening."

In Kioto it is reported that the Herodians and Pharisees are to unite, as the Buddhist and Shinto priests are desirous of forming a

" National Religion Society," to check the progress of the "Jesus way." Yet, with the combined strength of these two great bodies, they must soon learn how futile their efforts must prove. In Tokio, at the beginning of winter, great preaching services, lasting several days, are held annually by the Japanese Christians. During the one just closed, the largest theatre in the city, although refused them last year, was rented for the purpose. There were twelve thousand tickets printed and distributed, and about six thousand persons attended each of the two days; and the building was so densely packed, many others could not gain admission. A secular paper, which has a foreign editor, commenting upon it, said: " The fact that Dr. Hepburn, who was one of the foreign chairmen, had just completed the twenty-fifth year of his labors in Japan, gave the occasion the character of a commemoration of the first quarter of a century of Protestant missions in Japan. The large attendance, the earnest attention, with so little dissent or interruption in so public and free a place, give evidence of a marked advance in public sentiment in favor of Christianity within the space of one short year." Have we not great reason to thank God and take courage?

FROM MRS. JOHN GULICK.—I do not think we in the field fully realize the progress of the work here. We have to stop and think in order to do so; and when we do, we almost hold our breath while we wonder what God has in store for us. Truly this is not man's work: none but God could stir the hearts of this people as this nation is being stirred. Yet he calls on his people to work. If we are idle, we know not but the golden opportunity to save Japan may be lost. We have to learn, too, that our way may not be His way. He shows us by methods that cause many a tear and many a heartache, that those whom we consider most essential to the work, may be the very ones to be laid aside by illness, or taken to the mansions above. I think I have never been so impressed with this truth, since the death of Mrs. Curtis, as during the past week. Last Wednesday the pastor of one of our churches, one whose ringing eloquence had twelve days before stirred the hearts of many hearers; one whose love and burning zeal had endeared him to his own and all the other churches, and to the missionaries; one whose youth and physical vigor gave promise of a long life of service; one who, after long years of preparation was just entering the field into which he had been longing to thrust his sickle, bowed his head at the command of his Lord, and entered into rest. The earthly tabernacle was laid away just three weeks from the day of his wedding; and his young bride, bowing in sweet submission to the will of the Father, gives up all her plans of usefulness as a pastor's wife, and goes home "sorrowing, yet always rejoicing" to her father's house in a neighboring city. The church of which he was pastor seems stunned by the blow. They do not know which way to turn. He was ordained and installed their pastor just before the summer vacation. All the Christians united on the day of his funeral in showing their love and respect for the one who had gone. So many flowers were sent in that the bier was covered, and the procession was so long that the bystanders said to each other, "The king of the 'Jesus way' must have died, and this is his funeral."

FROM MRS. DE FOREST.— Not long ago we heard of a very encouraging item in Nara, which is three or four miles from Koriyama, where a church was formed and pastor ordained the first of the year. A very intelligent gentleman there, formerly connected with the military school in Tokio, had heard a good deal about Christianity, had read the Bible more or less, and entertained any of us missionaries who had been in Nara for work. An adopted son became very much interested, and wanted to be baptized, but the father objected. Several weeks ago this gentleman, Hayashi, was thrown into prison for alleged embezzlement of money of a ward of his. Always delicate in health, the confinement and lack of home comforts brought on an increase of his consumptive tendencies, and he failed so rapidly that he thought he was going to die immediately. Then he began to think about what he had read in the Testament. He had been very angry that he had been put with thieves and less respectable criminals, but he remembered that Christ suffered with thieves. He was angry that his lawyers had not saved him from imprisonment, and then called to mind how Christ felt toward his accusers, and how much more reason he would have had to be angry. The result of his meditations was a determination to follow the Saviour with all his heart, and he was filled with joy, so that he hardly felt that he was imprisoned. One day his wife came to see him, accompanied by the Japanese guard. Instead of inquiring about things at home, he told his wife about his change of feeling, and advised her to study the Bible, and receive all the instruction she could from Mr. Naruse, the Koriyama pastor. During the long talk she sat on her knees, respectfully answering "Heh, heh!" at proper intervals; and when he had finished she surprised him by saying that she, too, had been greatly troubled by his imprisonment, fearing the result on his health, and somehow had taken to reading the Bible, and had made up her mind to be a Christian.

The next day one of the higher officers went to Mr. Hayashi and said, "I hear that you are a Christian." "Yes," he said; "I am." "Well, we have learned that Christians tell the truth, and we are inclined to believe your version about the trouble for which you were sent here. You are now discharged, but must be ready to report to us at any hour." So he went home, and sent for Mr. Naruse to come right over and baptize him. The latter could not come, because it was Sunday, and he had his regular appointments for the day, but he went on Monday. Hayashi said that he might be recalled to prison at any time, or he might die, and he wanted to be baptized first. Naruse had not time to consult the missionaries as to what would be proper, and so he went to the Bible itself, and in reading Acts he found so many cases of immediate baptism that he concluded he could not be wrong. So in a day or two a party of Christians came over to Mr. Hayashi's at Nara, from Koriyama, had supper together, examined him until nine o'clock in the evening, and then he, his wife, and adopted son were baptized. We have had later news of his entire release from prison, and an intended social meeting with the Koriyama Christians.

Young People's Department.

CHINA.

LETTER FROM MISS HOLBROOK.

TUNG-CHO, Dec. 8, 1884.

To the shareholders in the Tung-cho Dispensary: —

WHILE we are waiting for Jack Frost to get over his sulks, and help us build our dispensary, I must tell you of a plan that I have been working out for the past year. Now I can tell you about the "Training-Class for Medical Bible-Women," for, in this country of mother-in-laws to interfere with young women's plans, I didn't want to tell you before what we hoped to do; beside, we need you to help us next year on this, as you helped this year on the dispensary. This class is composed of four young women from the Bridgman

School. Mary, Hannah, Ruth, and Jennie are their school names; though, as they are now all married, they should be called Mrs. Kao, Mrs. Fan, Mrs. Chiian, and Mrs. Hung. But they like their old baptismal names best; and so we will call them by them.

Mary, or Mali, as we call her in Chinese, is the young woman who has helped me in the dispensary since I first came. She has been adopted by the Wide-Awakes, Springfield, Massachusetts. Though she was in the Bridgman School but one year, she learned so rapidly, and has so improved her opportunities since, that now she is able to take up this medical study, though it comes rather harder for her than for the others. Though her husband was a heathen when she married him, nine years ago, yet, by her prayers and influence, he has gradually been brought to the light, and is now a member of the church. He is my chair-bearer, gate-keeper, fire-builder, and factotum generally; but he can read quite well, and promises by and by to be a valuable helper for me.

Jennie is the wife of one of our theological students belonging to our station. She will not probably complete the course now, as her husband graduates this year, and hopes to settle in the country next year. She has been in school twelve years, and has a well-disciplined mind; so I have great hopes that she will be able to accomplish much, even in the short time she can spend here.

Ruth is also the wife of one of the theological students. They belong to the Peking station, and will also go to their work in the country next year. Miss Andrews says it gives her peculiar pleasure to teach Ruth, she seems so recipient of Bible truths. Hannah is also a young bride. She is the wife of a servant of Mr. Goodrich's. He is of a good family, and a member of the church. He also studies every day, Mrs. Goodrich having a class every evening with any men on the place who desire to study. Hannah will probably take the full course, and is, perhaps, the best scholar. Having such a guarantee for co-operation on the part of the husbands, and the mother-in-laws, on the whole, quite manageable, we have great hopes for the future of these young women.

It is our plan to give them a two years' course, that shall be every way practical, but not our hope or desire that they shall become doctors. They are to be Bible-women, using their knowledge of medicine to open their way to the hearts of their people.

Are you interested to know what the course is? The first year takes vegetable and animal biology, anatomy and physiology, chemistry and nursing. The second year takes up surgical anatomy, *materia medica,* with compounding of drugs, and disease as taught in the different branches of general practice. You may wonder why we put in biology in so short a course. They know but little of natural science; the structure and growth of plants is entirely unknown to them; the composition of earth, air, and water is a mystery. Such facts as are contained in Child's Book of Nature must be taught as an introduction to the higher branches. This does not reflect upon their previous education, for science, as such, forms but a small part of our plan of education for girls.

Natural theology is taught in our Bridgman School, and through it the minds of the scholars are awakened to look at nature in a general way — but, of course, to investigate no further than answers the purpose of illustration to religious truth.

Their list in *materia medica* will comprise about one hundred different remedies, and we hope they will gain knowledge and wisdom sufficient to treat the more common diseases, and to let alone those they do not understand. This will give you an idea of the scope of our plan for medical study.

Mrs. Sheffield, at present, is teaching biology, and will follow with physiology. My class for the present is chemistry.

The Biblical department is under Miss Andrews' care and instruction. She teaches them with special reference to presenting these Bible truths, now so familiar to them, to others.

Would you like to know the order of exercises? Morning prayers and Bible lesson from 8 to 9; biology from 1.30 to 2.30; dispensary from 2.30 till all the patients are gone; chemistry, 7 to 8 P. M. This with their housekeeping makes a very full day for them. In order that they may give their time to study, we give each, money enough to buy her food and fuel. This year they have been supported by private funds; but we have asked help of the Board for next year.

At present they are in very crowded quarters, ten people living in three small rooms for in-patients belonging to the dispensary. It is my desire to build rooms for the use of student Bible-women; for now that it has been proved a practicable thing for the theological students to bring their wives here to study, we hope we shall always have those whom we wish to train for Bible-women, even if they do not take the medical course.

I wish you might look into our classes, and see the varying expressions as new truths are opened up to them.

Jennie said the other day, in Mrs. Sheffield's class, when she was teaching them about endogens and exogens: "We have always looked at trees, and thought they were just trees. Who would have thought there was so much that is wonderful about them!"

Mali said to me one day: "There is a cave outside the city, and once an official ordered some men to go in, and see what was in there. It was dark, so they took a candle; but when they came to a certain place the candle went out, though there was no wind. It went out as often as they would relight it and go back to this spot. The men were afraid to go farther, saying a spirit had blown the candle out. I never believed it was a spirit," she said; "and now I *know* it was not. It was just carbonic acid gas." She said this with a very amusing triumph in her manner, as though that question was settled for all time so far as she was concerned.

And so it is that the superstition of this country is to flee away before the life-giving air and sunlight of *all* God's truth.

THE LITTLE CAKE.

BY MRS. G. ANDERSON.

Out from the gates of Zarephath,
  When evening winds blow free,
A widow creeps to gather up
  The driftwood of the sea;
  Wan as a ghost is she.

Gaunt hunger haunts the city streets,
  Fell famine sweeps the land:
The fields upon the fertile plain
  Are barren as the sand —
  All smitten by God's hand

Long years, nor rain nor healing dew
  Has fed the drooping wheat;
Not e'en the shadow of a cloud
  Falling athwart the heat,
  Has cooled the torrid street.

The oil is wasted in the cruse,
  The wolf is at the door;
E'en of the precious meal remains
  A handful and no more,
  Of all the widow's store.

Her only thought is one of pain:
" I faint, yet I must try
To bake me yet one little cake
　To eat before we die,
　　My little son and I."

From the far Jordan comes Elijah,
　Hunted, and hungry, and weary, he,
Here at the gate meeting the widow,
　Cries, " Fetch a morsel of bread to me!"

" As thy soul liveth — God in heaven
　Knows if I lie — I have naught to give.
Wouldst have me snatch my child's last mouthful
　From between his lips, that thou may'st live?"

" Yet," said the prophet of Jehovah,
　" Go, and first bake me a little cake;
Then shalt thou and thy son, in gladness,
　From God's provision your portion take."

" Thus the Lord saith: meal in the barrel
　And oil in the cruse shall never fail
Till, at the sound of rain, the famine
　Shall disappear like a specter pale."

Is here no lesson, O my sisters,
　To our souls, hoarding the oil of grace,
Crying, " We cannot share our morsel,
　Our Bread of Life, with a starving race"?

When the dear Lord says, like Elijah,
　" Go, and *first* bake me a little cake,
Oil of your cruse, meal of your barrel,
　To feed the souls of my brethren take,"

Shall we say, " Nay! we and our children
　Have not enough of this heavenly bread;
Scarce can we spare crumbs from our table;
　Let the dead nations bury their dead"?

*　*　*　*　*　*　*

When the oil of joy is low,
　When the lamp of peace burns dim,
When bread of heaviness we know,
Water of tears, and wine of woe,
　That overflow the brim;

When the voice we knew of yore,
  When the Master cried, " Arise
And open, I am at the door,
Arise and sup," is heard no more,
  Or heard with dull surprise;

Is it not that we forget
  That the first of all is His ?
God loves the cheerful giver yet;
And he who gives as 'twere a debt,
  Is sure to give amiss.

Let us bake our little cake,
  Let us send it far and wide:
The Lord's creating hand will take
Our humble offering, and break
  Till all shall be supplied.

And our share ? O God, how sweet
  Is their share who freely give !
The bread of heaven they shall eat:
Christ's hidden manna is their meat
  Who for his glory live.

                 —*The Helping Hand.*

Our Work at Home.

REPORTS OF BRANCHES AT THE ANNUAL MEETING.

WE give below brief extracts of the reports of branches given at our annual meeting. The almost universal comment with reference to them was, that they were never more interesting, and that the record of work done was never more encouraging; and we think it will be pleasant for our readers to see this record from the branches side by side, in goodly array. The results are briefly told; but the story of the persevering labor and patient effort that has brought them about, would fill a volume. As was stated in the last number, the usual order was reversed; and although observing the time of formation, the youngest organization reported first. This was the Andover Conference Association, which was reported by its president, Mrs. Samuel Bowker, of Ballardvale, who said the Association was in a transition state, owing to its vote to unite with the Woburn Conference Branch. As yet the union had not been fully consummated, but the different auxiliaries and mission circles had been pursuing their way steadily and quietly, with sincere desire for the promotion of the interests of the cause. It is hoped that their new relation will prove the stimulus needed for greater work in the future. The report of the Middlesex Conference Association was given by Mrs. F. D. Sawin, secretary. A new departure in this organization is the holding of an all-day meeting by itself, instead of an hour's session in connection with the conference of churches, as has been done hitherto. The experiment was most successful, the presence of Miss Proctor, of Aintab, adding much to the interest of the occasion. Several auxiliaries that have been connected both with the Association and the Worcester County Branch, have been transferred entirely to the Branch, leaving the present number of organizations only five; but a plan for the visitation of the churches promises an increase of this number.

The Barnstable Branch was represented by its president, Mrs. R. B. Baker, of Dennis. This Branch is in its second year; and the experiment begun in hesitation and uncertainty has become an assured success. The receipts for the year, including a fund for Branch expenses, have been $573.75—being $112.93 more than the previous year. The plan of devoting the pennies saved by the reduction of the postage, brought in $13.50. The Branch supports one missionary — Miss Burrage, of Cesarea,— one Bible-woman, a pupil at Ahmednagar, and a teacher at Constantinople.

The report of the Old Colony Branch was given by its secre tary, Miss M. J. Capron. It now numbers thirteen auxiliaries and nine mission circles; and the receipts for the year were $1810.51. The donations of some of the auxiliaries were quite large in proportion to the numbers, one of nineteen members raising $108. The Branch supports three missionaries, one Bible-woman, two schools, a teacher at Bombay, and five scholarships. Letters from the field have proved very valuable in awakening an interest in the work, and, through the Branch bureau of exchange, have done much to familiarize the work and the workers to the members of the auxiliaries.

The report of the Essex North Branch was presented by Mrs. A. C. Swain, corresponding secretary, for the recording secretary, and was one of good cheer, showing, among the auxiliaries, an increase and hearty interest in the work. One new society has been formed during the year, making fourteen auxiliaries and nine mission circles. More money has been raised than ever before, and specially interesting praise and thank-offering meetings have been held.

The Suffolk Branch was represented by its secretary, Mrs. T.

J. Holmes, who reported quiet progress in several ways. Four new auxiliaries and two mission circles have been formed, making the present number sixty-two auxiliaries and thirty-five mission circles. A system of visitation among the churches has been inaugurated, which, it is hoped, will bring substantial results. The Branch supports fifteen missionaries, seven Bible-women, two teachers, twelve schools, and nineteen scholarships; and the receipts of the year have been $11,963.87.

Miss M. T. Caldwell, secretary, reported for the Essex South Branch, progress in what might be called a subjective work among the auxiliaries — meetings more fully attended, old members more interested, new ones brought in, greater earnestness in prayer, a more thorough education in the missionary work inaugurated. Three new organizations have been formed, making a net gain of one, as two others have disbanded, for unavoidable reasons. The receipts show an increase of about one hundred dollars over the previous year. The principal item of interest during the year was the departure of one of the members to the foreign field — Miss Henrietta West. Before she left the country, she did much to inspire the auxiliaries which she visited, with zeal for missionary work.

Mrs. F. N. Peloubet, of Natick, secretary of the Middlesex Branch, gave a brief review of the work of the Branch since its organization seven years ago. It now has seventeen auxiliaries and sixteen mission circles, an organization in every church, and two in many of them. The last annual meeting was memorable for a thank-offering service, which was one of great spiritual power, and brought a large sum into the treasury.

The report of the Berkshire Branch was given by the corresponding secretary, Miss E. A. Morley. This Branch has held steadily and quietly on its way; has received two new auxiliaries, making in all thirty auxiliaries and ten mission circles; and the contributions have amounted to $2,488.97. A short history of the formation of the Branch was given, showing how one devoted worker, in spite of illness and family cares, started a train of events that are bearing their fruits to-day. The work throughout the county seems full of hope and encouragement.

The Woburn Conference Branch was represented by its secretary, Mrs. W. T. Greenough. It now has fifteen auxiliaries and ten mission circles, having one, two, or three organizations in all but three of the churches in the Conference. Three new ones have been formed during the year, and no shoots of the Branch have been cut off as dead. The contributions amount to $2,309.18—an increase over the previous year. Two missionaries have been supported, also a teacher at Constantinople, four Bible-women, ten schools, and four scholarships, besides other work. During the year the Branch extended an invitation to the Andover Conference Association to unite with it, neither being very large or strong. The invitation was accepted, and the union will soon be consummated. Another year it is hoped that it may be proved that union is strength, and that in dividing the burdens and doubling the joys, the working capacity may be increased a hundred-fold.

The Norfolk and Pilgrim Branch was reported by its secretary, Mrs. F. N. Thayer, of Holbrook, who spoke of continued health and good signs of growth in the Branch. One new auxiliary, two young ladies' circles, and two mission circles have been added during the year, making the present number twenty-five auxiliaries, five young ladies' circles, and eleven mission circles, with an aggregate membership of fourteen hundred and forty-three. Public meetings have increased in interest and attendance, the young ladies have grown more active in the Branch work, and the children's hearts have been greatly drawn toward the Morning Star.

The Hampshire County Branch was represented by Miss Kate E. Tyler, recording secretary, who spoke of large public meetings, and prominent among them a mission circle rally in Amherst in October. The mission circles contribute nearly one-fourth of all the money raised by the Branch. Auxiliaries mention increased interest in mission study and enlarged membership, one, by special effort, having nearly doubled its membership during the year. The societies have suffered much from the removal of officers, but find consolation in the fact that so many go to other fields of usefulness carrying their missionary interest with them.

The report of the Franklin County Branch was read by Miss Jameson. One mission circle has been formed during the year, and the missionary spirit seems to continue unabated. The quarterly meetings have been well attended, and of much interest. The president of the Branch has been removed to a new field of late, and two earnest workers, Mrs. Hazen and Mrs. Crawford, both returned missionaries, have left their work here for the grander sphere beyond.

Mrs. E. W. Clark, secretary, reported for the Worcester County Branch. In 1883 the Branch went through the process of a "kind of moral house-cleaning," a time of reconstruction and re-adjustment, which being passed successfully, the prospect for effective work was never more hopeful. Two new auxiliaries have been formed during the year, making the whole number thirty-nine, while there are counted upon the roll twenty-five young ladies' societies and mission circles. A wider circulation of missionary intelligence has resulted in greater interest, and prayer has become more frequent and earnest. The Branch supports six missionaries, two Bible-women, two schools, and eight scholarships, besides other work, and the receipts have amounted to $3,332. The report closed with the expressed desire that each individual should make the year 1885 one of greater activity and devotion to the Master's service.

Mrs. W. A. Welsh, secretary, brought the greetings of the New York Branch, and reported the year as one of progress. It now has ninety auxiliaries, with a membership of two thousand two hundred and thirty-four mission circles with thirteen hundred and forty-eight members. The receipts of the treasury were $6,611.22, nearly $900 greater than the previous year. A thank-offering service in connection with the annual meeting was one of great interest, bringing $400 into the treasury.

The report of the secretary of the Eastern Connecticut Branch was read by the president, Miss E. S. Gilman, of Norwich. This Branch now numbers over sixty societies, several having been added during the year; the treasury has also made a decided advance. Its pledges cover work in Turkey, Mexico, and Ceylon, and mission schools and Bible-women elsewhere; quite a surplus was also given to the general fund. The quarterly meetings of the Branch have been made attractive by the presence of missionaries, special interest centering on Japan.

The Hartford Branch was represented by its vice-president. Mrs. C. D. Talcott, of Talcottville. She reported forty-four auxiliaries and thirty-three mission circles — an increase of one auxiliary and five mission circles over the previous year. The contributions for the financial year were $4,774.45. The Branch has just celebrated its tenth anniversary, which was a most interesting occasion. The work in the foreign field is the support of four missionaries, seven Bible-women, thirteen schools, and nine scholarships, besides other general work. In some of the hill towns of this Branch the churches are weak and it is difficult to form organizations in them, but it is hoped they may be reached in time. In a mission circle formed in one of these small towns the past year nearly every member, it is believed, has learned to trust in Christ as a personal Saviour.

The report of the Springfield Branch was presented by Mrs. Clara S. Palmer, president. The year has been one of prosperity and increasing usefulness. It has twenty-eight auxiliaries and twenty-four mission circles, two new auxiliaries having been formed during the year. The contributions were larger than ever before, being $4,563.33. It has supported four missionaries, three schools, five scholarships, and a medical assistant, and has contributed to several other objects in the foreign field. Annual and quarterly meetings have been of much interest, and the auxiliaries are increasing in activity and zeal.

The report of the secretary of the New Hampshire Branch was read by Mrs. C. H. Wallace. Special effort had been made to reach a large number of churches in which there is no organization of the Board, and it is confidently expected that several new societies will be reported from them. The present number of organizations is one hundred and sixty-six, with a membership of about thirty-four hundred. There has been increased activity among the young ladies and children, and the Master seems to have set the seal of his approval on their service by bringing a large number from some of their circles into his fold during the year. The receipts for the year were $4,276.17. The annual meeting was one of great power, and gives courage to take up the work of another year with hearts ready to obey the command, "Whatsoever He saith unto you, do it."

The Maine Branch was reported by Miss J. L. Crie, secretary. Six new auxiliaries and three mission circles have been formed during the year, and the receipts were $4,297.76 — a much larger sum than in any previous year. This Branch takes a degree of interest second to that of no other State, in the Morning Star, built of Maine timbers, and launched in her waters. This Branch has a record of eleven years, and only He in whose name and by whose grace they labor knows the work which has been accomplished.

The report of the Rhode Island Branch was given by Mrs. Edward E. Slocum, secretary. The growth of this Branch the past year has manifested itself in the larger attendance at meetings and the more efficient work of its auxiliaries, than in new organizations, the number of which remains the same as the previous year. There has been special progress among the young people and children, more particularly in the way of sewing for missionary families, indicating a spirit of willing service, and forming a loving link between the home and foreign workers. The receipts of the year amount to $3,643.34. It is hoped soon to have the great privilege of sending one of the members of the Branch to the foreign field; and already the inspiration is beginning to be felt which it is earnestly hoped may be the forerunner of a true missionary revival.

The report of the Vermont Branch was given by Mrs. Horace Fairbanks, president. The past year in this Branch has been one of quiet growth, and among the young people, of increased activity. One new auxiliary and thirteen mission circles have been formed, making the present number one hundred and thirteen auxiliaries and ninety-six mission circles. The receipts have exceeded any previous year, being $5,306.01. The Branch supports six missionaries, two native teachers, one Bible-woman, nine day-schools, and nine scholarships, besides pledges to other objects. The annual meeting was one of special uplifting, made memorable by the presence of Mrs. Montgomery, of Marash, Turkey, and Mrs. Layyah Barakat.

The New Haven Branch was reported by Miss S. E. Daggett, vice-president. The special feature of interest during the year has been among mission circles. New ones have been formed, and the work among them is very encouraging; two new auxiliaries have also been added. The various meetings of the Branch have been largely attended, and full of interest. The Branch supports seven missionaries, thirty Bible-women, three native teachers, fourteen schools, and eighty-two scholarships; and the receipts for the year were $11,258.46. Many experiments have been tried as to methods of work, and when the perfect way is discovered it will be reported.

The report of the Philadelphia Branch was presented by its president, Miss A. P. Halsey. The position of this Branch has come to be rather a fixed one, as no large advance can be made from new churches, nor is a great increase of numbers possible in the old organizations. The receipts for the year were $2,566.79. The aim of the Branch is continued, unabated effort, courage to hold firmly what has been gained, more prayerful consecration, and more liberal, systematic giving.

WOMAN'S BOARD OF MISSIONS.

RECEIPTS FROM JANUARY 18 TO FEBRUARY 18, 1885.

MAINE.

Maine Branch.—Mrs. Woodbury S. Dana, Treas. Cornish, Aux., $8, Hillside Gleaners, $3.05; Madison, Aux., $3; Machias, Aux., $14.30; Gorham, Aux., $50; Portland, Aux., State St. Ch., Miss E. L. Libby's S. S. Cl., $10; Norridgewock, Cong. S. S., $20, $108 35

Total, $108 35

NEW HAMPSHIRE.

Atkinson.—Mrs. Priscilla Markham, $1 00

Total, $1 00

VERMONT.

Vermont Branch.—Mrs. T. M. Howard, Treas. Randolph, Aux., $3, S. S., $5; Montpelier, Aux., $8.82; Westminster West, prev. contri.

const. L. M. Miss Laura Stevens, $4; Fairhaven, M. C., $18; St. Johnsbury, South Ch., Aux., $35.80, No. Ch., of wh. $5 Thank-off., S., Nov. 16, $25 by O. W. H., const. L. M. Mrs. Jane K. Burnham, $39.51, Girls' B. C., $13.30; ·Bakersfield, Satie Page's mite-box, 60 cts; Townshend, Aux., const. L. M., Miss Mary J. Holbrook, $25; Lower Waterford, Aux , $5, Maple Wreath, $5; W. Brattleboro, Y. L. M. C, $23; Sudbury, Mrs. J. A. Hawkins, $1; Brattleboro, Center Ch., A jug-breaking, $30.91; Rutland, Aux., $95.67; Fairlee, Aux., const. L.M. Mrs. Louisa G. Stratton, $25; Burlington, Aux., $15; Williamstown, Aux., $6; Ludlow, $1; Johnson, $1; Wells River, Aux., $8; Benson, Aux., $25; Newbury, Aux., $4.10, Beacon Lights, $5.38, 1st Cong. S. S., $4.70. Expenses, $98.96. Bal., $309 83

Granby.—M. C.,   86
Saxton River.—A Friend,   3 00
W. Charlestown. — Mrs. Huggins,   1 40

    Total, $315 09

MASSACHUSETTS.

Barnstable Co. Branch. — Miss Amelia Snow, Treas. Cotuit, Aux., $36; Yarmouth, Aux., $7; Waquoit, Aux., $3; Orleans, Aux., $4, $50 00
Berkshire Branch. — Mrs. S. N. Russell, Treas. Pittsfield, 1st Ch., Aux., prev. contri. const. L. M. Miss Martha Brewster, $34.45; Dalton, Aux., $50; Blackington, Aux., $33.46; Hinsdale, Mountain Rill, $60; W. Stockbridge, Aux., $21.75; 199 66
E. Douglas.—Cong. Ch.,   10 00
Essex North Conf. Branch.— Mrs. A. Hammond, Treas. Ipswich, 1st Ch., Aux., $28; Georgetown, 1st Ch., Aux., $13.71,   41 71
Essex South Conf. Branch.— Miss Sarah W. Clark, Treas. Lynn, 1st Ch., Aux., of wh. $25 by Mrs. Esther S. Cobb, const. L. M. Miss Elizabeth D. Deedman, $30, Central Ch., Aux., const. L. M. Mrs. Hannah O. Trefren, $25, M. C., $10; Middleton, Jun. Aux., $30; Marblehead, Aux., $53,   148 00
Franklin Co. Branch. — Miss L. A. Sparhawk, Treas. Greenfield, Aux.,   22 53

Hampshire Co. Branch.—Miss Isabella G. Clarke, Treas. Williamsburg, Aux., $32.40; Easthampton, Aux., of wh. $100 const. L. M. Miss Sarah E. Wright, $132 20; Amherst, Aux.., of wh. $200 const. L. M's Mrs. Abbie J. Cooper, Mrs. Mary W. Crowell, $244.86, M. C., of wh. $100 const. L. M. Miss Elizabeth H. Grover, $120; So. Hadley, Faithful Workers, $12, $541 46
Haverhill.—1st Ch.,   1 00
Marion.—Cong. Ch., Ladies,   5 00
Methuen.—Aux.,   30 00
Middlesex Branch.—Mrs. E. H. Warren, Treas. Marlboro, Union Ch., M. C., $33.50; Concord, Aux., $34 33, S. S. Miss. Asso., $40, Ashland Gleaners, $10,   117 83
Norfolk and Pilgrim Branch. —Mrs. Franklin Shaw, Treas. No. Weymouth, Pilgrim Ch., Aux., $26; Plymouth, Aux., $90; Hanover, Aux., $5.25; Weymouth and Braintree, Aux., $7,   128 25
Springfield Branch.— Miss H. T. Buckingham, Treas. Springfield, 1st Ch., $65.77; So. Ch., 25 cts.; Longmeadow, Aux., $22; W. Granville, $5,   93 02
Suffolk Branch.—Miss Myra B. Child, Treas. Boston, A Friend, $10, Mrs. Dr. Culver, $1, Miss Wheeler, $25, Miss F. M. Morris, $10, Central Ch., Aux., $5, Union Ch., Aux., of wh. $25 by Mrs. Margaret B. Adams, const. self L. M., $120; So. Boston, Phillips Ch., Aux., of wh. $25 by Miss Lucinda Smith, const. L. M. Mrs. Annie G. Morse, Dedham, $25 by Mrs. Alvah Simonds, const. L. M. Mrs. John Alden Abbott, Taunton, $250; Roxbury, Walnut Ave. Ch., Aux., of wh. $25 by Mrs. H. B. Hooker, const. L. M. Miss Jennie F. Hamlin, Falmouth, $107.40, Highland Ch., Aux., Mrs. S. N. Stockwell, const. L.M. Mrs. Eugene Russell, $25, Immanuel Ch., Aux., of wh. $25 const. L. M. Mrs. Willard White, $46.75; Dorchester, 2d Ch., $25, Village Ch., Band of Faith, $30; Brookline, Harvard Ch., Aux., Mrs. Geo. W. Merritt, $10; Cambridgeport, Ladies' Soc'y, $33, Prospect St. Ch., Aux., $50; Chelsea, 3d Ch., Children's M. C., $5; Somerville, Broadway Ch., Aux., of wh. $25 const. L. M. Mrs. L. V. Price, $29.34; Brighton, Y.

L. M. C., $30; Waltham, Aux., const. L. M's Mrs. Anna M. Baker, Miss Ellen Hastings, $50; Watertown, Aux., of wh. $25 const. L. M. Mrs. L. A. Turner, $40.37; Dedham, Asylum Dime, $2.55; Foxboro, Aux., $40, $945 41
W. Warren.—Mrs. E. G. Carter,   4 40
Woburn Conf. Branch.— Mrs. N. W. C. Holt, Treas. Malden, Aux., A Friend, $10; Reading, Aux., $38.50; Wakefield, Aux., 2; Lexington, Aux., $43.71; Bedford, Aux., $12; Wilmington, Cong. Ch., Ladies, $27.60, Snow-Birds, $12.50; No. Woburn, Aux., $6.50, Prim. S. S. Cl., $1.25,   154 06
Worcester Co. Branch.—Mrs. G. W. Russell, Treas. Ware, Aux., $1.50; Westboro, Aux., $35; W. Boylston, Aux., $14.72; So. Royalston, Aux., $10; Spencer, Aux., $10; Harvard, Aux., $32, M. B., $11,   114 22

Total, $2,606 55

LEGACIES.

Legacy of Mrs. Mary Vinton, Boston, $500 00
Legacy of Mrs. Anna F. Washburn, Worcester,   500 00

RHODE ISLAND.

Rhode Island Branch. — Miss Anna T. White, Treas. Providence, Union Ch., $3.60, Little Pilgrims, $30, Central Ch., $5, A Friend, const. L. M. Miss Eliza C. Root, $25; Central Falls, Aux., $40; Tivoton, S. S., $9.35, $112 95

Total, $112 95

CONNECTICUT.

Eastern Conn. Branch.— Miss M. I. Lockwood, Treas. Wauregan, prev. contri. const. L. M. Miss Carrie L. Fellows, $15; Chaplain, Aux., $24, Happy Workers, $60; Mystic Bridge, Aux., $5.70, Daisy M. B., $4.13; Thompson, M. C., $10, 1st Ch., $6, 2d Ch., Miss Annie L. Smith, const. self L. M., $25; Danielsonville, $16; Old Lyme, $27; New London, A Friend, 40 cts., 1st Ch., of wh. $25 const. L. M. Mrs. Eleanor Avery, $53.16, S. S., $33 81, 2d Ch., $34.85; Greenville, $1, $316 05

Hartford Branch.— Miss Anna Morris, Treas. Granby, Aux., $3; Hartford, Mrs. M. M. Prior, $15, Mrs. C. P. Welles, $1, Miss Lucy A. Brainard, const. L. M., Corinne Brainard, West Chester, $25, Pearl St. Ch., Aux., of wh. $50 const. L. M's Mrs. J. B. Wesley, Mrs. G. L. Stevens, $124.25; Berlin, Golden Ridge, M. C., $52.50; Bolton, Girls' M. C., $3; Rocky Hill, Cong. Ch., $3.40; W. Hartland, Aux., $10; Unionville, Aux., $20; Plainville, Treasure-Seekers, $25; Hebron, M. C., of wh. $25 const. L. M. Miss Jennie E. Learned, $35; So. Coventry, Willing Hands, $20, $337 15
Manchester. — Miss Emily P. Sherman,   5 80
Westport.—Friends,   4 00

Total, $663 00

NEW YORK.

New York State Branch.— Mrs. G. H. Norton, Treas. Brooklyn, Tompkins Ave. Ch., Co-Workers, $28.50, Park Ch., M. C., $25; Rochester, Mt. Hor Miss'y Friends, $18.75; Moravia, $6.25; Flushing, $32.26; Oswego, $40; Ellington, $18.75; Norwich, $17, $186 51
Baiting Hollow, L. I.—Youths' Aid Soc'y,   80
Brooklyn.—Mrs. J. L. Partridge, 10 00
Cherry Creek.—Mrs. A. Morian,   5 00
Miller's Place.—A Friend,   3 80

Total, $206 11

PENNSYLVANIA.

Philadelphia.—Sarah Furber, $1 00

Total, $1 00

OHIO.

Cedarville.—Mrs. MacMillan, $1 95
Edinboro. — Mrs. B. E. Bingham,   3 00

Total, $4 95

General Funds, $4,019 00
Morning Star,   48 40
Weekly Pledge,   66
Leaflets,   29 17
Legacy,   1,000 00

Total, $5,097 23

Miss Emma Carruth, Treasurer.

Board of the Interior.

TURKEY.

A WEEK OF BLESSING.

BY MISS C. D. SPENCER.

You ask me to tell you of the revival in Hadjin, in the spring of 1883, the recording of which has so far been crowded out. That year the opening of the Girls' College called away our best teachers, causing us much perplexity; and some of the pupils who had, we hoped, been converted the summer previous, often showed a very unlovely spirit. Much effort and prayer with them individually and collectively, only more fully impressed us with the sense of our utter inability to reach the root of the difficulty without the special aid and enlightenment of the Holy Spirit. Laboring to impress this upon the minds of teachers and pupils, the Week of Prayer came and went, and we began to hear of the wonderful work of grace in Adana, and to pray that it might spread to us.

We had sixty girls in our school, thirty-one of whom were in our family, and among these latter were three or four large girls (teachers) in for an additional year of study, and members of the church. Calling these, with the two other teachers, we had a long, serious talk with them, one result of which was their quietly gathering in our sitting-room for half an hour of united prayer for the conversion of their mates, and renewed consecration in the church. It was not long before the girls became touched, and gathered in groups to pray for themselves; until frequently during the hour from eight to nine — the play-hour — the sound of prayer would be heard issuing from three or four rooms at once.

It was finally thought best to put into execution a plan which had been before our minds for some time, but for which the time had seemed hardly ripe; i. e., to dismiss school for an all-day prayer-meeting, to be held in our schoolroom, for the conversion of the girls.

Notice was given to the women that all who wished to join us would be cordially welcomed, especially those having daughters or relatives among them. We meanwhile prayed much for guidance and help.

During the week an unusual earnestness had been observed

among the women in their weekly meetings; and numbers, singly
or in small companies, had called for religious conversation, and the
expression of hope from one or two was to us as an earnest of the
harvest to be. The teachers in the boys' school, and the preachers came frequently for help and counsel; another hopeful sign.

Thursday, the day appointed, came, and a much larger number
of women than we had expected were present. The meeting
opened with the text, "Choose ye this day whom ye will serve,"
as its key-note. Leaders appointed for each hour seemed to be
especially led in the choice of texts for presentation, so that
instead of diverting the mind from that previously presented,
they seemed to add to, and mass together, truths in a most over-
whelming and convincing fashion. Truly God's Word was felt to
be "with power," and from the first the house seemed filled with
the presence of the Holy Spirit. Leaders were brief, and most of
the time went to prayer, confessions of sin, and consecration.
Conviction of sin was a marked feature, and several of the girls
rose again and again, to confess something to teachers and some
others after they thought all had been confessed. The women,
come to pray for others, remained to pray for themselves, and to
confess their own sins. The proposal to adjourn for noon met
with no response, and a more complete and general breaking
down is seldom seen. At half-past four it was thought best to
dismiss the meeting, though several were on their feet waiting an
opportunity to speak.

After some time spent in conversing with individuals, we sent
them home. About two-thirds of the girls had given themselves
to Jesus, and for the sake of the remaining ones, and on account
of the deep interest of the women, notice had been given that the
meeting would be continued the following day. The next morning brought a houseful, and the same interest and conviction of
sin was manifest. As on the previous day, we felt that God's wondrous gifts would be even "according to our faith," and were
moved to ask that all in the house might be brought to him. At
the end of the day seventy-three professed to have enrolled themselves under the leadership of Christ. Among these were several
Armenian women, who knew that such a decision would cost
them opposition from husband and friends. Much prayer was
offered and requested in behalf of others.

An interesting case was that of a sweet little girl in our family,
one of the first to yield. Her father, a profane, bad man, came
from a neighboring village to see her; and finding no one at the
house came down to the schoolroom, and creeping into a corner
seat remained for hours an astonished observer. His daughter

saw him, and poured out her heart in simple, earnest prayer that he might love Jesus. As the hours passed, and the time came to close, he still sat silent. She could bear no longer the fear that he might lose his blessing, and in a trembling voice asked all to pray for him, then burst into a sobbing cry to God to soften his heart; "For oh!" she said, "He does not come to thee — he does not come!" and broke completely down. For a few moments there was no sound but that of weeping from all parts of the room, as the silent prayer for the father went up to God.

He seemed to melt at this; and when, after meeting, his daughter went to him with the same plea on her lips and tears in her eyes, he drew her to him, saying, "I will come to Jesus, my lamb — I will come." Since then all who know him witness to his changed life.

That evening the two teachers and the preachers in Middle Hadjin called, with their faces all aglow, and we learned that they, as well as we, had a wonderful tale to tell of the Lord's marvelous doings among us.

It seems that on Thursday both teachers and pupils felt a strange restlessness and inability to apply themselves to the work in hand, and soon the scholars asked if they might have a prayer-meeting. The teachers, finding the desire so unanimous and so in accord with their own feelings, dared not refuse; and the preachers took charge of the large class of young men, while the two teachers, with their school, united in prayer in another room. One of them, after many of the boys had expressed their desire to become Christians, proposed, in order to deepen their sense of personal guilt, that each one on going home should make a list of sins which he himself had committed, remembering that each one was sufficient to insure his condemnation. This was done, and they were gathered a heavy-hearted set of boys. Much feeling and conviction of sin were shown, and a general readiness to accept at once the proffered mercy through Christ.

In the other room the text chosen for the morning was the fifty-first chapter of Isaiah, — "He was wounded for our transgressions," "He was bruised for our iniquities." The work took powerful hold; and those strong young men fell upon their knees, weeping aloud in their agony, and some crying, "Oh, I have crucified Jesus!" and seemed to see him hanging on the cross before them. Presently one of the teachers in the other department, feeling that they were inadequate to meet the needs of their anxious boys, came in to secure the preacher's help, and found him going from one to another in almost greater perplexity than their own. People in the street, attracted by the unusual sounds, came in, and on being told that they were crying for their sins, were convicted by the same invisible power. Time passed rapidly, and before they knew it the day was gone,— but not before the young men and many of the boys had found rest in believing. Many a mother, son, and daughter rejoiced together that night in their new-found Saviour.

Mrs. Coffing had been in the habit of meeting with another class of young men in our schoolhouse every week, and they were invited to bring their young friends with them to their meeting the following evening. Some twenty-five or thirty came, and a most interesting meeting followed, characterized by the same strong feeling of the Spirit being present, and all who had not done so previously, declared themselves for Christ.

The daily noon meetings for the women were well attended, and most interesting.

The work seemed to be confined for the greater part to the women and youth. This may be accounted for in part by the fact that fruits were more abundant where most effort to enlighten had been expended. We believe that the foundation for the interest among the women was laid in their weekly meeting the previous summer, when the plain, simple truth from "Finney's Lectures on Revivals" was given them. Definite results have been hard to get at, on account of the destruction by fire of the church and the homes of a large part of those concerned not long after, and the consequent scattering of the people. But among the women and girls we believe there are very many who, though ignorant, are really born into the kingdom.

We have realized as never before how important and responsible a work is this, of educating new converts in a land where no previous religious instruction has laid foundation on which to build.

In view of this, I ask your earnest prayers for those in foreign fields in this respect; and also for the converts, that they may be strengthened to meet their manifold temptations. It seems due to the Lord and his glory that mention should be made to those who pray for the work in Turkey, of this wonderful manifestation of his power.

A WOMAN'S MISSIONARY MEETING IN TURKEY.

BY MISS C. O. VAN DUZEE.

A MONTH ago, after a woman's prayer-meeting in which I had talked of missions, I proposed a missionary society. That being agreed to, I carried the thing along until we had elected a president, secretary, and treasurer, and were to have a monthly meeting. Yesterday we had the meeting, and there was a good attendance. The president, who is the pastor's wife, talked well; and after the regular meeting was finished, said we must settle on a fee for membership: though some would give more and some less, we must have a fixed amount. I proposed five piasters (twenty cents). The pastor's wife thought half of that would be plenty, for some could not pay so much. "But those who cannot, need not be members." "And what are the privileges of members?" "They can vote. We must vote what to do with the money collected." Several agreed that was unnecessary. "Every one wants the money to go to the Koords. One who has given money, especially *asks* to have it used in that way." They were sure there would be no dissenting voices. One said she should be pained if any one who gave even four cents could not vote. Again I tried to urge the thing, and spoke of the election of officers for the next year. "Oh, we've got those for this year; let next year take care of itself." Meanwhile other things were being discussed. Giving a penny or two a week was spoken of, but one said, "We don't buy things by the pound, as you do in America, so we can't save a penny here and there. We lay in our store by the year." This is more than half true; and then the housekeeping money does not pass through the women's hands, as it does in America, as they cannot go shopping or to market. So, many of them decided that what they gave for the year they must give at once. One woman kept throwing on cold water: "We can't give much. We must ask our husbands for the money. What does our little amount to?" And, again: "We can't do as you do in America. There the women can work, like the men. They are free. We can't do anything. Our husbands won't give us money." I read to them the story of Mrs. Purdy's Parquisites. "There, there," the women said to the doubter, "can't you keep one hen's eggs separate?" It was getting late, so I did not press the matter more, but it was hinted that even officers were unnecessary. They could give their money, and that would be the end of the thing. They all agreed that the Koords were in a sad condition, and needed help. Most of the women give something every year to a collection taken for work among the Koords. The Armenians consider this their mission, and support a preacher, his wife, and a teacher, who are at work among these people. What the end of our society will be I know not; but, as they say, they have officers for this year, and I think most of the sisters will give something.

CHINA.

A WORD FROM MISS EVANS.

TUNG-CHO, Dec. 8, 1884.

YES, I am at home — and had no difficulty in reaching here so far as the war was concerned, although the mouth of the river was well filled with torpedoes. I reached here, "home," October 22d. What a reception they all gave me ! It brought tears. I felt quite a hero as I marched up the city, almost across it, escorted by such a band of Chinese. The people on the route would stop and look, and make comments. It was something they could not understand, to see a woman thus escorted. I left the other foreigners to follow as best they could, and went on with my retinue. I wish you could have been here to see what a large place we hold in the hearts of these people. Why shouldn't we love them when they so love us? . . . As soon as I had unpacked, and put my room in order, I began work, for the others were doing far too much. There was no teacher for the geography in the school, and Mr. S. asked me to take two classes.

Rusty as I was in Chinese, never having even read Mr. Chapin's Chinese geography, it has taken time to make "yah-shi-yah," "ah-pha-lé-chia," with all that grows in those countries,— the people, what they believe and what they don't,— studied in Wen-li, to be understood and recited in "Kun-hua." To make it all plain, first to myself and then to the scholars, is no small task ; but perseverance accomplishes almost everything, and I begin to wonder at myself. . . . I wish some of my Chicago friends could spend a week in our courts, and see all that is being done to prepare native helpers. The young men who finish their theological course next spring are noble, earnest workers, and we look with not a little interest to their beginning of their life-work. I wish you could have heard and understood the sermon one of them gave us yesterday from Ps. cii. 17.

There is a nice class of boys in the school now; most of them large boys, and many of them Christians. Oh for God's Spirit to come to them with great power!

Miss Andrews and I have divided our work for the women: to me fall three prayer-meetings a week at three different places, and a class in Old Testament, with some bright young mothers, whom we hope to employ as Bible-readers when their little families are older. Our Christian women have grown the past year. . . . I cannot tell you all my vacation has been to me. The work is different from what it used to be. "I am with you always" has a new meaning. Pray for me, that His abiding presence may be with me, not for a time, but *always.*

INDIA.

SCENES BY THE WAYSIDE.

BY MISS EVA M. SWIFT.

OCTOBER 17, 1884.

LAST Thursday night, riding in a bullock-bandy from Madura to Mana Madura, a distance of thirty miles, I found so much to be seen on this my first trip by night that I had no desire to sleep. The road was most of the way along the river's edge, and the banks were made beautiful by the groves of cocoanut palms. The fig banyan-trees on either side of the road in many places met above with interlacing boughs, and with the moonlight on the river made an exquisite picture. The river had been "down," or, as we should say in America, "up," only for a few days. Although I have had some experience with rivers of this kind in my Texas home, yet it still seems strange to me to go down to the river's edge and find no water. At the same time one sees crowds of people performing their ablutions, and washwomen on both sides of the river-bed for a long distance washing and drying their clothes. One looks around at the dry sand of the river-bed and wonders where the water is. But if we look a little more closely, we shall see that the people dig into the apparently dry sand for a short distance and find clear, pure water. The river is really flowing along a little below the surface. It seems a remarkable provision of God for a people who do not seem to know how to take care of themselves. All the filth of this great city goes into this river. When it is "down," or full, there is much sickness among the people, since they all use the river-water for bathing, drinking, and cooking purposes. But when the river is low, the sand makes a filter for it, and it is always clean and pure. The people always prefer to have the river low, for their own comfort. But this year every one has been looking anxiously for the rains which bring the river down. There has been much talk of another famine this year. The usual early rains failed, and consequently the dry crops also. If the rainy season did not come on as usual, there would result another famine. It is horrible to think of these countless thousands so poverty stricken that they could not tide over one failure of the crops. The people were so frightened that they were praying to their gods to send rain. Near Madura they got together and prayed the gods to send rain

enough for twelve years, so there would be no more fear of
famine. The priests assured them that on the morrow rain
would begin to fall. Every one waited with most intense
anxiety, but not a drop came. The burning sun was strong
as ever, and the skies just as cloudless. But on the second day the
Lord of all, the Lord who sends rain alike on the just and unjust,
sent the cooling, refreshing shower which foretold the approach
of the latter rains. So night before last the rainy season proper
began with a thunder-storm and a steady, soaking down-pour — a
blessing for which we cannot be too thankful.

--------◄♦►--------

SPAIN.
OUR WORK THERE FOR WOMEN AND GIRLS.
BY MRS. ALICE GORDON GULICK.

SAN SEBASTIAN, Feb. 1, 1885.

WE heard with great joy and rejoicing that the Woman's
Board of Missions of the Interior had voted to help support the
San Sebastian school, but we did not know before reading *your
letter* that you were also interested in the work of the pastors'
wives in Zaragoza and Santander.

In Zaragoza the wife of the pastor is Manuela de Aranjo. She
is not very strong in body, but is a gentle Christian, who has a
good influence upon those about her. She has written to me of
the mothers' meetings she has held as hopeful and helpful. Her
five little ones, Carlitos, Herman, Rosalia, Manuel, and three-
months-old Elisa, while they sometimes keep her at home, open
her heart to other mothers' needs.

Mrs. Henrique de Tienda, of Santander, or Dona Matilde, is a
French lady, who is devoting her life, with her Spanish husband,
to the evangelization of his country-people, and whose heart is in
her work. She is also a mother; and while her two little ones
naturally take much of her time, she is able to visit the sick, hold
mothers' meetings, and engage in general missionary work.

In regard to the school at San Sebastian, I send you by mail
some copies of letters, programmes, etc., which may, perhaps, be
sent to some of the mission circles interested in this school.

We have now twenty-six boarders and nineteen day-scholars,
and have every reason to be encouraged in regard to the future of
the school. This province is somewhat peculiar, in that the people
here speak a distinct language, which they claim to have been the
language spoken by Adam and Eve. They are obliged to learn
Spanish, or they could have very little communication with the

rest of the world. We however come across some, now and then, women especially, who speak only Basque. It is said that Satan himself studied the language for seven years, but was obliged to confess himself overcome by the difficulties. The people are industrious and enterprising; and San Sebastian is probably the best governed and cared for, as it is the most healthy, city of Spain. The people are religious, and are called fanatical, but we have met with no opposition whatever here. We have made many friends among them; and although as yet there is no apparent desire to hear and know the gospel, we do not feel discouraged. We believe that if it is God's will, there will sooner or later be found an open door. I beseech you not to let any one lose interest in this work. We need your prayers and sympathy.

STUDIES IN MISSIONARY HISTORY.
1885.
PERSIAN MISSIONS.—No. 2.

The Work of the Press.
Revivals — 1849, 1850.
Protection and Equal Rights granted to Christians, 1851.
Revivals of 1856; of 1857.
Work of the Concerts in the Villages; in Schools.
Progress in the Mountains.
Missionary Biography. Mrs. Stoddard; Mrs. Rhea; Mr. Rhea; Mr. Crane; Mr. Stoddard; Fidelia Fiske; Dr. Perkins.
Female Seminary at Oroomiah. Revivals among its students; Results in Village Evangelical Work.
Need of Separate Church Organizations. 1869; 1870.
The late semi-centennial celebration of the Persian Mission — Rev. Mr. Shedd's review of fifty year's work.

Helps: "Mission Studies for April;" "Dr. Anderson's Missions of the American Board to the Oriental Churches;" "Woman and her Saviour in Persia;" "The Tennesseean in Persia and Koordistan;" "The Cross and the Crown; or, Life of Fidelia Fiske."

"The Foreign Missionary" for October 1884, and February 1885: "Sketch of Persian Mission," issued by President of the Woman's Board.

Woman's Board of Missions of the Interior.

Work of the Young Ladies' Societies for 1885.

Mexico, Miss Haskins. $600. Micronesia, Miss Fletcher. $300. Japan, Mrs. Gulick. $625. China, Dr. Murdock. $815. India, Schools. $1,239,77. Turkey, Marash & Samokov. $2,739. Spain, School. $1,000. Africa, Miss Gilson. $450. Gen'l Fund $731.23

THE BRIDGE.

$8,500.

Its foundations—our prayers. Its piers—our contributions. Its arches—faith and works. Its key-stone—

Christ.

"Ye are complete in Him which is the head of all.'
"Let the word of Christ dwell in you richly in all wisdom."

Shares may be divided as follows:—Two, $300; Three, $250; Four, $200; Twelve, $100; Fifteen, $75; Twenty-six, $50; Thirty-six, $25; Fifty, $20; Thirty, $15; Thirty, $10.

Chicago, January 1, 1885.

MRS. LYMAN BAIRD,
MRS. GEO. M. CLARK, } *Committee on*
MRS. H. M. HOBART, *Young Ladies' Work.*

The above Plan, with a blank pledge, has been sent to every one of our three hundred young ladies' societies. Each society fills out the Pledge, tears it off and sends it back to our "Committee on Young Ladies' Work." Pledges are coming in fast at our office. The following words on methods of work from Mrs. Baird, chairman of that committee will be helpful to the Bridge-builders.

The work of the junior societies opens encouragingly. During the month of January, the committee reached all existing societies with the pledge, statement of work for 1885, the five years' review, and a personal letter. Now they are planning to enlist new recruits to the already enthusiastic company of Bridge-builders.

An occasional request has come from a society, asking that they might support an individual, instead of contributing to the Bridge; but a few minutes' talk, or an earnest letter from one of the committee, has every time convinced those who thought *one* interest better than several, that they were mistaken.

There is such a thing as being too diffuse; but there is little danger of falling into this error while so much thought is constantly given to the best means of interesting " our girls," and accomplishing the most good, by those who have experience in and love for the work.

We are glad to note a growing tendency among our juniors to discard entertainments as a means of meeting the pledge, and to rely on the safer and surer method of regular giving. When this spirit of self-sacrifice, which cometh only through prayer, pervades our societies, we may confidently expect " more money and more missionaries."   E. M. B.

RECEIPTS OF THE WOMAN'S BOARD OF MISSIONS OF THE INTERIOR.

MRS. J. B. LEAKE, TREASURER.

FROM JANUARY 18, 1885, TO FEBRUARY 18, 1885.

ILLINOIS.

ILLINOIS BRANCH.— Mrs. W. A. Talcott, of Rockford, Treas. *Aurora,* New Eng. Ch., 13.25; *Buda,* 5; *Chicago,* Union Park Ch., of wh. 25 fr. Mrs. Harriet E. Morton, to const. L. M. Mrs. Dora F. Crosette, 25 fr. Mrs. Ralph L. Greenlee, to const. L. M. Mrs. Wm. Brooks, 25 fr. Mrs. H. W. Rice, to const. L. M. Miss Mattie Moore, 25 fr. Mrs. Wm. H. Rice, to const. L. M. Miss Sarah N. Isham, 25 fr. Mrs. I. N. Camp, to const. L. M. Miss Charlotte M. Camp, 248.65; *Dundee,* 9; *Galva,* 1st Ch., 29.50; *Galesburg,* Brick Ch., 19.56; *Garden Prairie,* 5; *Granville,* 9.50; *Geneseo,* of wh. 25 to const. L. M. Mrs. Homer Wolcott, 66.81; *Prospect Park,* 6.50; *Rosemond,* 4.50; *Seward,* 17; *Wauponsie Grove,* 10; *Wilmette,* 12.48, $456 75
JUNIORS: *Canton,* Y. L. Soc., 17; *Chicago,* South Ch., Y. L. Soc., 35, 1st Ch., Y. L. Soc., 66.60; *Geneva,* Y. L. Soc., 25, 143 60
JUVENILE: *Garden Prairie,* Willing Workers, 65

Branch total, $601 00

IOWA.

IOWA BRANCH.— Mrs. E. R. Potter, of Grinnell, Treas. *Burlington,* 5 35; *Corning,* 5; *Corydon,* Mrs. K. M. and C. E. Rew, 10.50; *Davenport,* 23.15; *Des Moines,* Plymouth Ch., 40; *Farragut,* 5; *Grinnell,* 48.70: *Iowa Falls,* 4.95; *Magnolia,* 4.85; *McGregor,* 10.17; *Quaqueston,* 4.15, $161 82
JUNIOR SOCIETIES: *DesMoines,* Plymouth Rock Soc., 16.30; *Keosaqua,* Willing Workers, of wh. 10 is fr. Miss Carrie Taylor, 20, 36 30
JUVENILE SOCIETIES: *Tabor,* Busy Gleaners, 30; *Davenport,* Wide-Awakes (boys),

15.45; *Corydon,* Myra, Jennie, Gertie, and Albert Rew, 2.50, $46 95
SABBATH-SCHOOLS:*Des Moines,* Plymouth Ch., 13 55

Total, $258 62

KANSAS.

KANSAS BRANCH.—Mrs. A. L. Slosson, of Leavenworth, Treas. *Centralia,* 5.50; *Dover,* 9; *Fairview,* 12, $26 50
JUVENILES; *Dover,* Children's Band, 3; *Kimeo,* Little Sunbeams, 40 cts; *Sabetha,* Rushlight Band, 8.50, 11 90

Total, $38 40

MICHIGAN.

MICHIGAN BRANCH.—Mrs. Geo. H.Lathrop, of Jackson, Treas. *Adrian, West,* 5; *Ann Arbor,* of wh. 7 thank-offering, 19.29; *Calumet,* 50; *Charlotte,* 41.24; *Chelsea,* 15; *Detroit,* Woodward Ave. Ch., 60.76; *Dowagiac,* 10; *Flint,* 33.28; *Grand Rapids,* South Ch., 18; *Greenville,* of wh. 25 for L. M. of Mrs. Caroline E. Stevens, 57.10; *Jackson,* 145; *Lansing,* Plymouth Ch., 13.06; *Olivet,* 4.25; *Portland,* 10; *Stanton,* 16.40; *Three Oaks,* of wh. 3.25 is thank-offering, 20.20; *Tawas City,* Mrs. Laura J. Kelly, 10, Mrs. W. B. Kelly, 50 cts., Mrs. Ott, 50 cts., Mrs. Wilson, 54 cts.; *Ypsilante,* 6.50, $536 62
JUNIORS: *Detroit,* Woodward Ave., 63, First Ch., Sunbeam Band and Opportunity Club, 50; *East Saginaw,* Faithful Workers, 100; *Jackson,* Y. P. Circle, 5; *Manistee,* 12.50; *Port Huron,* Y. P. Circle, 10, 240 50
JUVENILES: *Ann Arbor,* Children's Band, 68.92; *Detroit,*

Harper Ave., Gleaners, 10;
Kalamazoo, Children's Band,
3,   **$81 92**

   Branch total,   **$859 04**

MINNESOTA.

MINNESOTA BRANCH.— Mrs. E.
M. Williams, of Northfield,
Treas. *Excelsior*, 3.07; *Medford*, 95 cts.; *Minneapolis*,
First Ch., 40, Pilgrim Ch., 10;
Northfield, A Friend, 65; *St.
Paul*, Plymouth Ch., 30,   **$149 02**
For Morning Star:—
Winona, S. S., add'l,   1 50

   Branch total,   **$150 52**

MISSOURI.

MISSOURI BRANCH.—Mrs. J. H.
Drew, 3101 Washington Ave.,
St. Louis, Treas. *Breckenridge*, Aux., 16, Juvenile Society, 5; *Cameron*, Aux., for
Miss Tucker, 11; *Kidder*, 5,   **$37 00**

   Total,   **$37 00**

NORTH DAKOTA DRANCH.

Mrs. R. C. Cooper, of Cooperstown, Treas. *Hope*,   **$9 00**

   Total,   **$9 00**

SOUTH DAKOTA BRANCH.

Mrs. H. H. Smith, of Yankton,
Treas. *Huron*, 4.51; *Sioux
Falls*, 25. Branch total,   **$29 51**
Lake Preston, Mrs. L. K. Robbins,   7 00
JUVENILE: *Huron*, S. S.,   6 50

   Total,   **$43 01**

OHIO.

OHIO BRANCH.—Mrs. Geo. H.
Ely, of Elyria, Treas. *Cincinnati*, Central Ch., 65; *Lodi*,
6.60; *Lorain*, 4.22; *Salem*,
Mrs. D. A. Allen, 5; *Steuben*,
8; *Wakeman*, bequest of
Mrs. Susan C. Strong, 50, Aux., **$138 82**
Bellevue, Y. P. M. C., Junior,   20 00

   Total,   **$158 82**

PENNSYLVANIA.

Corry,   **$5 00**

   Total,   **$5 00**

ROCKY MOUNTAIN BRANCH.

Mrs. Hiram R. Jones, of So.
Pueblo, Col., Treas. *Coal
Creek*, 1; *Colorado Springs*,
25,   **$26 00**
JUVENILES: *Coal Creek*, S. S.,
1.20; *South Pueblo*, S. S., 50
cts.,   1 70

   Total,   **$27 70**

WISCONSIN.

WISCONSIN BRANCH.—Mrs. R.
Coburn, of Whitewater, Treas.
Delavan, 24.42; *Evansville*,
6; *Ft. Howard*, Cong. Ch., 8;
Lancaster, 6; *Milwaukee*, a
lady, for Bulgarian Bible-reader, 43; *Madison*, 25 of
wh., fr. Mrs. Emma C. Bascom, to const. Mrs. Maria S.
Johnson L. M., 26; *Ripon*, to
const. L. M. Mrs. Amanda
Upham, 25.40; *Racine*, 81.20;
Whitewater, 2,   **$222 02**
JUNIORS: *Evansville*, 6.60;
Green Bay, S. S., for Bridgman Sch., 40; *Janesville*, 25;
Milwaukee, Plymouth Helping Hands, 100; *Ripon*, Do
Good Soc., 1.60,   173 20
JUVENILES: *British Hollow*, 1;
Plymouth, Cheerful Givers,
50 cts.; *Pittsville*, 2; *Racine*,
Presbyterian S. S., 30,   33 50
Less expenses, 18.57,

   Total,   **$410 15**

ALABAMA.

A Friend,   **$2 00**

   Total,   **$2 00**

IDAHO.

Cash,   **$4 40**

   Total,   **$4 40**

CHINA.

Tientsin, Mrs. M. J. Clapp,   **$5 00**

   Total,   **$5 00**

MISCELLANEOUS.

Interest on bond, 30; sale of 2
pair of mittens, from Keokuk, 2; of leaflets, 34.27; envelopes, 5.39; waste-paper,
6.37; charts, 1.10; cash, 22
cts.,   **$79 35**

   Total,   **$79 35**

Receipts for the month,   **$2,430 39**
Previously acknowledged,   5,253 64

Total since Oct. 22, 1884,   **$7,684 03**

Board of the Pacific.

LETTER FROM MRS. SARAH L. HOLBROOK.

We publish this month our first letter from Mrs. Holbrook, our new missionary in Africa, whom we have this year adopted, and who thus introduces herself and her work to us:—

MAPUMULO, NATAL, S. AFRICA, Nov. 19, 1884.

DEAR FRIENDS: A short time since a letter was received from Dr. Alden, stating that you had kindly taken me into your fold of love and prayer. It is a helpful thought that we in our isolated homes are thus tenderly remembered.

"More things are wrought by prayer than this world dreams of," and a great proportion of missionary success may be owing to those in the home-land who so earnestly besiege the throne of grace, and, as it were, hold up the weary hands of the more immediate toilers.

Last December, almost a year ago, we reached Natal, and until April spent our time at the different stations, learning the language, and becoming acquainted with the best methods of work among this people.

In April we reached our home at Mapumulo, which is the most northern point of our Zulu Mission. Umvoti, the next station, is thirty miles south of us, over a rough, mountainous road. There is a station occupied by Norwegian missionaries about five miles to the north, and also a few white settlers located at distant intervals along the way. Thus in our isolation from the outside world, we learn to sympathize with so many of the missionaries in our western home-land.

But you want to know about our work — and when I stop to think, my mind wanders far back in the past to Paul, the tentmaker, and I wonder if he did not often think it more satisfactory

(157)

to be telling the story of Jesus than working on those innumerable holes for the tent-pins? or preaching to multitudes on Mars Hill a nobler occupation than sewing those never-ending seams? I can imagine he did; but he kept at work just the same. In these few months we have found our "tent-work" consumes a great share of time which, it would seem, might be better employed in telling the Gospel story to the heathen about us. But if we are to give them an example of a Christian home, much time must be spent in restoring from decay the long-neglected residence to which we have come. We trust these outside duties will soon take less time and strength.

Still, we feel that something has been accomplished which tells directly for Christ. The temperance work, which has made such strides in some of the stations, has gained a foothold here. Some have taken the pledge who are proving earnest workers, and we are looking for still greater results.

I have spent many hours in the day-school, which was in great need of oversight, and can see a marked progress. Then the Sabbath-school, which could hardly be dignified by that name, is now showing some signs of life, and we hope in time its usefulness may be great.

I have just received news that kind friends at home have sent the needed funds for starting a kraal school, and thus some of the people outside the station may soon have an opportunity to learn to read, which is often a stepping-stone to a desire for Christianity.

You see, there has been only a beginning made in these things, and where the field is so wide and the need of work so great, we are sometimes tempted to discouragement. But the battle is the Lord's, and surely he will not allow heathenism to prevail, if our armor is all right.

I feel that what we need more than all else is the gift of God's Spirit, not only upon ourselves, but on the whole church here. Only so can the power of vile habits and superstition be overcome.

It is a great comfort to feel that you will often remember us in our little corner of God's world, and that those prayers may be heard and answered is my earnest wish.

AFRICA AS A MISSION-FIELD.

BY MISS LUCY M. FAY.

A few words in regard to Africa may inspire us to greater fidelity in prayer and effort, and may give us a fuller realization that we are linked, on this Pacific Coast, with that resistless current of Christian love and zeal that will flow through that dark land till the shadows shall flee away, and the everlasting light shall flood with glory those waiting souls who are unconsciously stretching forth their hands unto God.

We talk of "*foreign* missions," and of sending money far away, but we forget that Africa touches us through her millions who have helped to enrich our land; that she touches us through commercial and scientific interests; that she touches us by the learning of Alexandria, whose vital force will always be felt in the Church, forming a part of that historic splendor of Egypt whose impress will always be felt not only in our country, but throughout the civilized world.

Africa touches us, too, with a tenderer memory as we see one of her dusky sons coming out from obscurity to bear the cross after Jesus, as if to plead by the very act for his brethren whom Christ came to save.

We need not seek further for the many motives that rise at our bidding for mission work in Africa. Let us glance, then, at her needs and at some of the positive accomplishments in this vast field.

The province of Natal, where the work of the American Board was established in 1855, is in Southeastern Africa, and has an area of 18,750 miles. It is separated from the wild Zulu tribes on the north by the Tugela River. The Drackenberg Mountains guard its western border, and send their fertilizing streams through her valleys to the sea.

Some foreigners reside in the province, but the inhabitants are mostly of the Zulu tribe, who have some characteristics of the negroes, but are superior to them in their splendid physique and in their intellectual powers. They live in huts "like huge bee-hives," which are gathered together in kraals or villages. A man here guards his property, which is his cattle, and in women, who are his slaves, though they have the name of wives. The heavy work of the field, wood-cutting, and burden-bearing, are done by women. Daughters are often sold for cattle. Mothers, think of your little girls rejoicing in their fathers' love, and then remember those heathen women whose daughters are thus despised; for mother-love is instinctive even there, rising like a pure stream in those polluted places.

In the harems of the chiefs in Central Africa the head-wife, or queen, rules all the rest. If one displeases her lord she is accused of witchcraft, and poisoned without scruple; and if this method fails, she is shot or drowned. This faith in witchcraft brings untold misery in its train.

Du Chaillu tells a pathetic story of a poor girl, Okondaga, in Central Africa, who was compelled to drink poison for having bewitched a person who had recently died. As she was borne along by her furious accusers, the cry rang in the traveler's ears, "Chally! Chally! do not let me die!" but he was powerless, and could only shed bitter tears. With two other women she was taken in a canoe upon one of their beautiful rivers, and the fatal cup was put to their lips. Soon they reeled and fell, when they were instantly hewn in pieces and were thrown into the water. At night the brother of Okondaga stole to the traveler's house in his distress. He had been forced to join in the curses that were heaped upon his sister. He was compelled to conceal his grief. Du Chaillu tried to give comfort, and spoke to him of God. The poor man cried, "O Chally! when you go back to your far country, America, let them send men to us poor people to teach us from that which you call God's mouth." "And," writes Du Chaillu, "I promised to give the message." Okondaga perished more than twenty years ago, and hundreds like her have been condemned by the witch-doctor, whom the people dare not disobey. Such sufferers the American Board is trying to reach by its mission to the Western border, where our sainted Bagster laid down his life.

Natal is the base of supplies for all this work. From her training-school the native pastors go out, who are the strong towers of the mission. In that training-school we have been interested through the work of Mr. and Mrs. Goodenough; and from our new missionary, Mrs. Holbrook, we shall continue to hear good tidings from this center of education and religious life. Mrs. Edwards' school, at Granada, is lifting girls from degradation, and even now much fruit can be seen from the seed that has there been sown with patience and with tears, yet with joyful hope.

There are peaceful homes where young women preside who owe all they are, and all they have, to the missions of the Church. These wild people can be trained, civilized, and Christianized. We know that the depravity of generations cannot be controlled in a day; but noble native pastors and their devoted wives are leading weak disciples in the path of holiness, and are the living proof that missionary effort in Africa has not been in vain. Revivals have swept with power over these schools and churches. Temperance has more and more prevailed. Kings have come, wondering and questioning, to the brightness of Christ's rising.

> "Hail, O Africa, thy ransom!
> Raise to heaven thy grateful song!
> Last in rank among the nations,
> Thou shalt lead the choral throng;
> Land of promise,
> Thy Redeemer's praise prolong."

—Pacific.

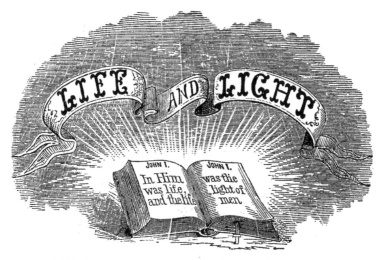

VOL. XV.   MAY, 1885.   No. 5.

INANDA SEMINARY.

BY MISS M. E. PRICE.

As this school has just completed the fifteenth year of its existence, it seems a fitting time to review the past and take a closer
look at the present. Some notice of its early history was given
in the LIFE AND LIGHT of June, 1879, and what was said then
need not be repeated.

At the time when the school was opened, so little interest was
taken by parents in the education of daughters, that it seemed
doubtful whether a school for girls would succeed at all. Nineteen, however, presented themselves the first term, and the number increased during the year to twenty-eight. Nine of these first
pupils remained from four to six years, and one of them has been
a valued helper in the school ever since her graduation. In the
third year there were forty-seven pupils, more than could well be
accommodated, and the overcrowded state of the rooms and the
lack of sufficient help in teaching, made it necessary to send home
an entire class.

This, although fully explained to the parents, caused some dis-
satisfaction, and kept away some in years following. In 1877 the
increasing number was again reduced by enforcing the payment
of board. A few were sent home on this account; others stayed
away; but it was only a temporary reduction, and since 1879 the
rooms have been well filled. The largest number of different

INANDA SEMINARY.

pupils present in one year was fifty-six, in 1880. The whole number connected with the school during the fifteen years, is two hundred and five. Of those who have left the school, thirty-one remained from four to six years, sixty-two from two to four years, and seventy-two less than two years. Day-pupils were connected with the school for several years: these are not included in the numbers given. For a time the station school of Inanda was taught at the school under Mrs. Edwards' supervision: over sixty scholars were in it.

There is a course of study arranged which covers five years. Most of those who come to us have been taught in the station schools, and are expected to read well in Zulu, and to have finished the English Primer and First Reader, and know a little of arithmetic. But many who come are poorly prepared to enter, and, as has been shown already, many are unable or unwilling to remain long in school; so it has been impossible for them to advance very far, as a whole. The instruction is given as far as possible in English, and much time has to be spent in the lower classes in reading and translating. More time is spent on the Bible than on any other book, as it is a daily study through the entire course. "Line upon Line" is used the first year; then the Bible itself is the text-book; the whole of the Old Testament history is taken up, also parts of the prophetical and poetical books, then, "Harmony of the Gospels" and Acts. The stories are read, then written by the pupils, and copied after correction. It is a great pleasure to teach these lessons, it is so easy to interest them, and they often ask a great many questions.

Arithmetic is studied through Interest and Proportion; Language Lessons and Grammar occupy considerable time — Geography, also. Besides these, the course includes a little of English History, Physiology, and Physical Geography.

Although quite a number had completed the course before that time, diplomas were first given to the class of 1881, numbering four. Eight have since graduated, and this year a class of six graduate. Two of last year's class are back for an additional year of study, and we hope future classes will follow their example, as it is very desirable for them to remain longer than the five years, if possible.

As may be supposed, many lessons have to be taught besides those found in books. The attempt must be made to form habits of personal cleanliness and tidiness in dress, as well as of punctuality and order. This requires line upon line and precept upon precept; still there has been progress. Some things are now established,— principles and matters of course,— which have become such only by much care and painstaking in the early years.

INANDA SEMINARY — TEACHERS' HOUSE — FRONT VIEW.

The girls have always been taught to make and mend their own clothes, and the older ones to cut them. This year an afternoon session of an hour and a half is spent in cutting and sewing,— making shirts and dresses for sale. All the work of the institution is done by the girls. The regular work, cooking, washing dishes, care of rooms, etc., is chosen weekly by the girls themselves. The miscellaneous circles are given an hour's work daily.

Then there is the wood to be cut, mealies to be ground, paths to be kept clean, and the grass to be cut in the large yard, which all take part in doing. This work gives them needed exercise, and helps to keep them happy and contented; they very often sing while doing it. With all their work they find some time for play, and enjoy a swing or a game of ball very much.

They are very fond of sewing, and often put a great deal of stitching on their dresses, which are usually of print. Then, if they have any spare time, they like to embroider " dukes " (handkerchiefs for the head) for their friends.

The school is not yet self-supporting, and may not be for a long time yet, but there has been progress. At first dresses were given, and for nine years only £88 were received from the parents. No clothes have been given since the first few years; and during the six years since payment has been required, £736 8s. 4d. have been received — an average of over £122 per year. None are sent away who are too poor to pay, but all who are able are required to pay £4 10s per year. This usually pays for all their food, but there are many other expenses which are met by the Mission and Government grants. The Government gives us £100 a year. The food given them is much the same as they have at home, the staple article being " mealie " (meal), which is made into porridge or mush for the morning and evening meal, and eaten with sugar. They like rice very much, and have it for dinner: they do not have curry. Meat and bread is given them twice a week. Potatoes, pumpkins, or green mealies furnish an occasional variety. They eat at tables, as many of the Christian natives now do in their homes, and have iron plates and spoons. The teachers have usually taken their meals in the same room with the girls, finding that the best way to educate them in table-manners, in which they are naturally quite deficient. In their sleeping-rooms are iron bedsteads, with mattresses and pillows filled with dried grass; sheets, blankets, and spreads. Their rooms are inspected twice a day, and marks given for any untidiness; and for each mark extra work is given on Saturday. Some of the girls who have been in the school have very pleasant homes of their own now,—houses of brick, with neatly furnished rooms. Forty-five of those who have been connected with the school are married, eight have died, fifty-eight have been or are still engaged in teaching, sixty have become members of churches. The Mission has not thought it wise as a rule to encourage young girls to enter the church, so that few of the girls have joined while connected with the school, though a large number have expressed a hope that they were Christians. While there has been much to discourage in the conduct of many after leaving school, and of some of whom better things were expected, encouragement is not wanting; and when we consider what a short remove they are from heathenism, and how many temptations they have to meet, it is not surprising that many have not had strength to rise above their surroundings. Some have done good service as teachers, and have been helpers in good work at their homes.

On Mrs. Edwards' return to the school this year she received a very pleasant letter signed by the missionary ladies of the different stations expressing their appreciation of her work here in the past, and speaking of the help received from the school-girls on their return to their homes.

One of the graduates of 1882 is now at Inhambane, and Mrs. Wilcox writes of her, "She is a true missionary." Mrs. Edwards has just received a long letter from her: she incloses money to pay the board of a younger sister in the school. Two others are teaching in the large station school at Inanda. One has paid the board of three younger sisters in the school, and furnished their clothes. Ten of the girls and women at Inanda Station, who have nearly all been in the school, have joined the Blue-Ribbon Army.

IN A STRONG CITY.— No. 2.

BY MRS. W. B. CAPRON.

ANOTHER of our verses was this: "God willeth that all men should be saved and come to a knowledge of the truth. For there is one God, one mediator, also, between God and man, himself man, Christ Jesus, who gave himself a ransom for all, the testimony to be borne in its own times."

"What is that you are reading?" said a silk-weaver, leaving his loom, and coming nearer the women; "the testimony to be borne in its own times." "I am reading God's proclamation," said the Bible-woman. "Your time and the time for Madura to hear has now come."

"Then read it to me," said the weaver. So she began the verse. He stopped her at almost every word. He questioned her closely on whether she herself had "a knowledge of the truth," and how it was to be had. The word "mediator" seemed to reach his soul. "That's the word for us," he said; "and here is His name given." He seemed greatly interested in hearing how this very same Jesus came down from heaven, the glory shining all around, until this poor world was reached. The Bible-woman told him that knowledge of the truth meant knowing all about this Mediator, until our hearts went out to him as a living, present, personal friend. Her narrative greatly interested us all as she went on to describe this man's eagerness. Her own enthusiasm was enough to rouse any soul.

Another Bible-woman was passing the head of a lane, and heard a voice calling her. She found the mother of one of our pupils standing on the doorstep with a group around her. "Come here," said the woman, "and read what you read yesterday about that Mediator, and how the Swamy gives us all knowledge." The Bible-woman is rather shy, and a survey of the situation disconcerted her. The central figure below the steps was a soothsayer, with his drum. He had intended to frighten that household into banishing the Bible-woman. So, beating away on his horrid drum, he finally, in a slow and solemn tone, said,—

"Your Swamy is very angry at something that is being done in this house."

Beating his drum again in a mysterious sounding thud, he stopped.

"You must give that up, or the Swamy will send a plague upon you."

"No, he won't," said the woman, fearlessly. "He is the Creator, and he wishes to save us, not punish us; and there is a Mediator for us."

The woman was going beyond her depth, when, as she afterward said, "the Lord himself sent the Bible-woman to pass that way." In obedience the Bible was opened, and there, under the clear sky, in that remarkable assembly, these wonderful words were read.

"There, that's it, and I like it," said this fearless woman. "I like that word Mediator; the great Swamy has let us know about him. He is not going to send a plague upon us."

The soothsayer was completely silenced at first; but as he turned away he gave his testimony. Said he: "These women, carrying a book about, are to be found in every street and every lane. There is no end to them. They get inside all the houses, and tell all their things till the women's heads are turned." And away he stalked, with his poor, old, little drum, leaving the Bible-woman with her words of blessing, instead of his words of cursing.

"Blessed be the Lord for he hath showed me his marvelous kindness in a strong city," was the fitting close to this most interesting narrative.

The last verse was this: "Eye hath not seen, nor ear heard, neither have entered into the heart of man, the things which God hath prepared for them that love him."

I have no words to describe how the glory and beauty of this message broke over the groups of women to whom I read it. Whether interpreted as the glory of heaven yet to be revealed, or the unspeakable comfort of peace that environs us when in our distress we turn from all else and cling to One mighty to save, there was a reality that seemed like a seal of blessing from God himself. One woman said—

"Have you been to God's place to see, so that you know?"

A few days after, one of these listeners was herself in suffering, and there was reason for anxiety. She was using the expression, "Oh! Lord Jesus, have mercy on me, body and soul! Some one said to her, "Say, Oh Menachi, save me; don't say that other name."

"No; I will not say Menachi. If I am going to die, I am not going to Menachi. I am going to the Lord Jesus Christ in heaven, and he is the one to whom I am going to call." The Lord heard her, and spared her to give her testimony to her faith in him again. Her husband was taken with cholera in the dead of night. The relatives proposed going to Menachi Temple to break two cocoanuts, and that two cocoanuts should also be broken by the sick man, and Menachi invoked to save. To this, this dear woman quietly replied, "I do not trust Menachi, and I need no cocoanuts." As she told the Bible-woman: "I went into that room and shut the door and raised my hands to heaven, to the Lord Jesus, and told him that my only trust was in him; and then I did everything I could for my husband, and I all the time felt that he would not die." The Bible-woman read our precious verse again to her, to meet her warm response. Those of us who have known her for three years were much rejoiced over her.

A Bible-woman going into a house that seemed to offer no listeners, heard voices in an inner room, and hearing the word Lazarus, stopped to listen. To her surprise and delight she heard the parable of the rich man and Lazarus told with many Oriental touches; but the one fact that God loved the lonely and deserted man, and sent angels to take him to heaven, was dwelt upon with evident comfort. Going into the room she found two women who have always been interested listeners to Bible-readings. One was lying down with her foot badly burned, and the other was kindly endeavoring to divert her. "You see," said she, "our kind of stories are always the same; but your kind are always like new ones, and I thought I would tell this one to cheer her." The Bible-woman read our precious verse, and they both saw how God's love shines through all his word.

I must allow myself but one more incident. Bible-woman Harriet going to one of our pupils whom we think of as a Christian, found that she was prostrated from a recent attack of cholera. This was her account of it: "I was taken at midnight with great severity. I begged my brother to go for you, but he did not think best. I then shut my eyes and thought of the Mission Compound, and the trees, and your face, and the lady's face. Then I thought of heaven and the Lord Jesus, and it was comfort. I said: "O Lord Jesus, if it is thy will that my time to die has come, forgive all my sins and take me to heaven. If it is thy will that I get well, thou wilt help me. Thou knowest that I love all thy verses." She then asked that all these verses might be read to her. She had heard them all before, but she seemed like one with a new experience, who expected a new revelation.

"Though the Lord be high, yet hath he respect unto the lowly."

MICRONESIA.

EXTRACTS FROM MRS. LOGAN'S JOURNAL.

[Concluded.]

RUK LAGOON, Sept 29.

I AM sure you will all be glad to know that our voyage is over, and safely over. We had a tolerably quick passage from Mortlock: leaving there Thursday, we came to anchor here yesterday. It looks very beautiful to us here; and our hearts are full of thankfulness to the dear Father for bringing us safely through all the trials and dangers of the long, long way. We had a little praise service on deck last night, and all joined with full hearts in thanksgiving and praise.

We are just now anchored quite near a little island; and yesterday, after coming to anchor, a canoe or two came off to us. We made them understand that it was our sacred day, and asked them to go away and come again to-morrow. The chief man in the canoe assured us that the cocoanuts at this particular island were the largest, and the people the best: the ship must not move from here, etc. They brought some young cocoanuts, which they wished to sell. Mr. Logan started at about five o'clock this morning to go to Uman, where Moses, the Ponape teacher, lives.

We hope to get our location fixed upon to-day. The natives are beginning to come on board in numbers. Their ear-jewels exceed in number and length those of the Mortlock people, and there is plenty of yellow paint on them. A big native sits at the door of our little room as I write, and says in English, "Good; you savy write; me no savy write." Later, he came to the other door, and said, "You savy much read; smart woman; good feller." Then, feeling, I suppose, that he had paid me the compliments which the occasion required, he took his departure. The cattle ate the last of their hay yesterday.

  October 1. Yesterday was quite an exciting day for us. Moses came early in the morning, and we set off in the boat to find our future home. Mr. Logan had been the day before to the island of Uola, to see a place picked out for us by Mr. Doane and Capt. Bray. He found the people there very anxious to have us come, and ready to do anything in their power for us. The location seemed, in many respects, a desirable one. We would have access there to a large number of people; yet we wanted to feel sure that it was the place for us, before anything was settled. Moses now proposed to take us to the large island of Fefan. Manassa, a Ponape teacher, is located on one side of it; but there are many people, so there would be plenty of room and work for us. Our boat stopped on the beach, and Moses went on shore to see the chief, as he said it would be in accordance with their etiquette that the chief should come out to welcome us before we should go on shore. We waited, what seemed to us, a long time, and were beginning to think it best to go away, when word came from Moses to be patient, as the chief was some distance away at work, and he would soon be here now. Moses had talked with some of the people while he was waiting; and when he asked them if they wanted the missionary to come to live among them, they replied, "Why do you ask? Don't we want all good things?"

  At last the chief came, and, with quite a number of his people, waded out to the boat and gave us a formal welcome. He was a kindly old man, and we were favorably impressed with him. We went inland a little way, and sat down on a stone to rest. Many people — men, women, and children — gathered about us. We were objects of interest and curiosity to them. We found a beautiful spot, with a fine view off at sea; and after inquiry it seemed that the location might be, in every way, a desirable one, if the people wanted us enough to give us a piece of land there. When we first talked to them about putting our house there, they seemed very willing; but when they began to understand that we wanted not merely land enough to build a house on, but enough for large mission premises, so that in case a school should grow up from our work, and we should wish to have scholars from other islands, there would be room enough and land enough, it began to look differently to them. We also told them that we had some cattle to bring on shore. They inquired if they would bite. We assured them that they would not; and, also, that we would not turn them loose to destroy their gardens, but would keep them tied until an inclosure could be made for them. There were some houses which would need to be moved; and the old chief said that though he would be glad to have us come, his people were rather unwilling to give up their claim upon the piece of land which we thought suitable for the mission. We looked about to try to find another place, but could see nothing that would answer; so that place seemed shut up from us. It was now three in the afternoon; and the boat coming for us, we decided that it was best to go to Uola, where Mr. Logan had been the day before. We had dined on shore from warm bread-fruit and a few sea-biscuits, so were ready for a boat-ride of seven or eight miles. I think we both felt a little blue; but we asked the Lord to choose for us, and to make the way very plain. Arriving at Uola, we were at once pleased and interested to see the different spirit manifested by this people, in contrast with those whom we had left at Fefan. Although they have never had a missionary of their own, yet, with Moses' help, they had built a nice little church. The location is not so pleasant or so desirable in many points as that at Fefan, but the chief said: "All this land here is mine. Take as much as you want, and have it for yours; and if you want some of this adjoining, I will see the man to whom it belongs, and you can have it." It did not take us long to choose a place for the house to stand; and we went back to the ship through the moonlight, weary enough, but feeling that the Lord had directed our steps.

October 2. The Fefan chief, with a number of his people, came to the ship to-day to tell us that they were very anxious to have us come and settle with them. They would now gladly give the land if we would come. They seemed much disappointed to find that they were too late, and we could not come. Mr. Logan told them that we would come to see them sometimes, and teach them; and perhaps a teacher would come for them some day. We felt sorry for them. If we could only multiply ourselves by five, there would still be work to spare. Cannot some one come to help us? A number of invitations have come in from people on the different islands since our location was decided. One man came yesterday while Mr. Logan was away, so I talked with him, and asked him *why* he wanted a missionary. He answered, "I am tired of fighting, and I want my people to learn not to fight. I want them to be like the Uman people" (where Moses lives). Surely, here is a longing after better things.

October 4. The ship moved round to Uola yesterday, anchoring off the place which is to be our home, just before dark. Later, we came on shore with a boat-load of things, and have taken up our abode in the church for the present. We have been intensely interested to watch the people. Of course we and our many belongings (as they seem to them) are very wonderful. Nearly every day, thus far, fresh canoe-loads of people have come from a distance to see the strangers who have taken up their abode here. They thought it must be that we had knives and guns in our boxes. What else was worth bringing? The people seem very kind in their rude way. We have seen nothing like distrust or suspicion, and they have worked wonderfully well in getting our boxes up from the shore, and in carrying the lumber for the house; and of course we do not think of paying them for such work.

Young People's Department.

MICRONESIA.

LETTER FROM MRS. RAND.

We know our young friends will be interested in the following account of the wreck of the Morning Star by one who was on board. Although a little late, we trust it will, nevertheless, be interesting.

HAVE so much to write about that I hardly know where to begin. I think I will take you back to last January, when the Morning Star reached us. . . . I cannot begin to tell you what we passed through last autumn waiting for the Star. She ought to have reached us four or five months before she did. We were out of provisions, out of clothing, and, in fact, we were out of almost everything. I do not know what we should have done in case of sickness, with no medicine nor food; but, fortunately, we were kept well. There were nearly seventeen months in our year — that is, in our Morning Star year. We were a whole year with no mail, with the exception of one letter I received in July, which contained the sad news of my father's death, and of my mother's severe illness, which they feared would result iu death. From that time till the Star came, six months, I was in the greatest suspense to know how she was. I sincerely hope I shall never have to pass through another such six months.

The Star came, at last, in January. Soon afterward I went with Mr. Rand to the Mortlock Islands. Then, as the Star had to go east to Pinglap and Mokil, permission was granted us to come to Strong's Island, to see Dr. Pease, and remain here till the Star would be ready to sail for Honolulu, which would be in a week or ten days; and then, as she sailed for home, she could drop us at Ponape. We reached Strong's Island on the morning of February 22d. We had entered the passage, and were smoothly gliding along without a thought of danger, when the kedge which held the line from the ship slipped from its place on the reef, and before anything could be done we were at the mercy of the cruel breakers, that were higher than I have ever seen them before.

I was sitting in the cabin braiding Mabel's hair when the terrible crash came. The jar threw us over to the opposite side of the cabin, where we were obliged to hold on for dear life. Mabel screamed, and said, " Oh, save my doll! " A Kusaiean, who came on board before we struck, endeavored to calm her fears by telling her he would save her; but it was of no use, and her crying continued until we left the wreck. Every crash seemed as if it would break the vessel in pieces. We managed to get to the companion-way, which seemed to be the safest place, while the masts and spars were falling. The foremast broke away, and the mainmast was cut away. Then it was considered safe for us to leave. Mabel and I were picked up from the deck (there were no other ladies on board) and dropped into the arms of a sailor, who stood in the boat ready to catch us; and then, with natives outside to steady the boat, we were pulled safely through the breakers. When I looked back and saw our dear little vessel lying on her side, dead, as it were, my tears fell thick and fast. It is a great relief to us all to think that no blame can be attached to Captain Garland; he was very calm through it all. There were no lives lost, and the cargo was all saved. We feel very grateful that the vessel was wrecked at this island rather than at any of those farther west, where we should probably have suffered for food. Dr. and Mrs. Pease, the Walkups, and Miss Cathcart, gave us a warm welcome, and we were made to feel at home at once.

But what of Miss Fletcher, the only lady on Ponape? I

begged her to come to Strong's Island with me instead of Mr. Rand, for I thought she needed a change; but she did not want to leave this year. At the end of six weeks, during which time Capt. Garland was decking over one of the Star's boats, to make her sea-worthy, he and Mr. Rand, with two foreigners and one sailor, set out for Ponape; and if no ship was found there, the Captain, with one of the foreigners and the sailor, was to keep on to Bonnim's Island, a distance of 1,800 miles, where he would take the steamer to Japan. You can imagine, I know, how I felt about having Mr. Rand leave me to go 300 miles in a boat, supposing it would be months before I could even hear if he got there. He felt from the first that he ought to go, knowing how his work would suffer were he away from it much longer; but I said I would never consent to his going. A few days before the boat left, the Lord made me feel that I was doing wrong to withhold my consent, so I gave it, and this is the way I was rewarded: they left the 7th of April, and in less than two weeks after, we had letters from Ponape that they had arrived there safely. Wasn't it delightful to hear so soon? . . . It is now four months and more since we were wrecked, and I have had no opportunity to go home.

Ponape, October 20, 1884. I still have a letter which I wrote a few months ago. I sent it on board a schooner bound for San Francisco, but it went no farther than the mouth of the harbor. The vessel was wrecked; but the letter came back, so I inclose it. I was still waiting at Kusaie, when the chartered Jennie Walker came, the 24th of July. We reached home the 3d of September. Mr. Rand and I had been separated five months. It does seem good to be at home once more.

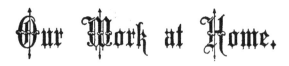

Our Work at Home.

THROUGH DARKNESS TO LIGHT.

BY MISS E. HARRIET STANWOOD.

[A paper read at the Annual Meeting of the Board.]

THE convention is not a modern institution; nor was that the earliest which met twenty-five hundred years ago, in response to the edict of a proud and despotic king, calling for an assembly of princes, governors, captains, judges, treasurers, counsellors, sheriffs, and rulers of provinces. When they had come together they gazed in wonder upon a colossal image which the king had set up, and their eyes were dazzled with its brightness. Then the king's herald proclaimed another decree; and at the sound of the cornet, flute, harp, sackbut, psaltery, and all kinds of music, the people bowed their heads and worshiped this golden image. Had not those three young men whose heads were not bowed, heard the threat which accompanied the decree? Expostulation elicited only this reply: " Be it known unto thee, O king, that we will not serve thy gods, nor worship the golden image which thou hast set up "; and they strengthened their own faith as they declared, " Our God whom we serve is able to deliver us from the burning, fiery furnace, and he will deliver us out of thine hand." The story is familiar to every child born into a Christian home. We have seen the three young men walking unhurt in the midst of the fire; and the form of the fourth was like the Son of God.

Six centuries later, upon a hill a little way out of Jerusalem, a company of men and women bowed their heads, not before a golden image, but before a simple cross, bearing the form of the Lord of life, the Son of man, the Son of God. They had already endured for his sake, and they had witnessed his persecution even unto sentence of death; and now they looked upon the agony of his crucifixion. When he burst the bars of death, and again appeared, to the command, "Go teach all nations," he added the promise, " Lo, I am with you alway, even unto the end of the world."

The obstinate unbelief of the Jews and their bitter hatred of this gospel, although it seemed to culminate in the crucifixion of our Lord, was not satisfied. It made Stephen's name immortal by the flinty missiles which it hurled at him; it executed James the elder, imprisoned Peter and John, and ran wild in its rage against Paul, and in the murder of James the Just. It put to death Symeon, Bishop of Jerusalem, burned Polycarp, and cursed the sect of the Nazarenes.

As soon as this faith appeared under the form of a new religion, the jealousy of government officials, the superstitious fanaticism of the people, and the selfishness of priests, all combined to persecute its adherents. Legislation, violence, and craft would fain have banished it forever. Public calamities were regarded as punishments inflicted by the gods, justly angry at the neglect of their worship. Flood, drought, famine, or pestilence provoked the people to cry, "Away with the atheists!" "To the lions with the Christians!"

Of successive persecutions under different emperors much has been written. All the virtues of Christian heroism were called into activity, and efforts which aimed to exterminate, served only to purify. Christianity won adherents not only from the poor and down-trodden, to whom this religion brought new comfort and hope, but from the higher and educated classes — men whose talent and culture compared favorably with their most learned heathen contemporaries; and at the end 'of the third century the name of Christ was known, revered, and persecuted in every province and town of the Roman Empire. Martyrdom followed persecution, and the moral earnestness of Christians was a strong contrast to the corruption of the age. A star of hope had risen upon the darkness of that night. Tertullian's words have passed into a proverb, "The blood of the martyrs is the seed of the Church."

The recent Luther celebrations have directed our attention to the period of the Reformation, and we have gazed with almost incredulous eyes upon the portraits which have been painted for us of the heroes of the sixteenth century. We have entered into the long and painful struggle against the oppression of the Papal power, and the echo of that battle-cry has sounded in thrilling accents from this desk *; but heroism was not all burned at the stake, and we do not yet know whose head shall wear the crown of the last martyr for the truth.

In the light of the history to which we have barely alluded, is it strange to find early missionary operations encountering opposition?

Pioneers in the work in India were opposed by British authority, lest the preaching of the gospel should excite rebellion, and diminish the Government revenue from the protection of idolatry. The Isle of France holds the sacred dust of Harriet Newell, because that little company were not allowed to remain in Calcutta. For nearly a year Hall and Nott were in suspense, twice receiving definite orders to return to their own country, and being repeatedly told that there was no alternative. Even in 1832 the missionaries were pelted with dirt in the streets of Ahmednagar; and when Vishnupont became a Christian, in 1853, funeral rites were performed by his parents. The number of missionaries who

---

* "Some Heretics of Yesterday." Lectures by Rev. S. E. Herrick, D.D., of Mount Vernon Church, Boston.

might labor in Ceylon, was for years limited by the British Government; but in India and Ceylon the work has been carried on in
spite of discouragements, persecution, and ill-treatment of converts.

Ten years after our first missionaries entered Turkey, we hear
of a plot to expel all Protestants from the land. Long lists of
heretics were prepared, and the reading or possession of missionary books was prohibited by both Greek and Armenian patriarchs. This storm was suddenly stayed by a rebellion in Egypt,
and the demand which it made upon the attention of Government;
and by the death of the Sultan, whose successor granted a charter
of civil protection and religious liberty. In 1843 the beheading of
a young converted Armenian in the streets of Constantinople, ral-
lied the ministers of France, Prussia, and Austria to the support
of the English ambassador, in securing from the Sultan a written
pledge that no longer should any one be persecuted for his religious opinions. Two years afterward this pledge was violated,
and sentence of excommunication was issued against those who
espoused the new doctrines. Enemies, however, had accomplished
what they never intended; they had advertised the missionaries
far and wide, bringing to them many who asked about this new
way; and, after this long abuse, Christians were organized into a
Protestant community. Even the anathemas which had been
printed and sent to the Armenian and Greek churches resolved
themselves into blessings. The missionaries began touring from
village to village, talking with the people, preaching, and distributing religious books; and, wherever they went, a love for the
truth began to appear as the " little leaven." First or last there
was resistance almost everywhere. And this persecution died
slowly. Died? Alas! is it dead, when Protestant schools anywhere within the limits of the empire are suddenly closed? when
work upon a new building for a girls' seminary is suspended by
order of Government? when, even in Constantinople, a copy of
Neander's Church History is held for fifteen months from reaching its destination, and then is released only on condition that it
be sent out of the country? But trial still brings blessing in its
train, even to Turkey. The sweeping conflagration at Marash,
last July, which destroyed all the business portion of the city,
severely crippling the resources of the Protestant community,
burning shops, houses, grain, and merchandise, but sparing
churches and schoolhouses, aroused a surprising spirit of thankfulness for what was left. Words of comfort and tender deeds
abounded. On Sunday, three days after the fire, twelve hundred
people assembled for a prayer-meeting, which lasted two hours,

and was full of grateful recognition of forgotten mercies, and confession of great unworthiness. This was followed by a request from the people that daily meetings should be held in the three churches. Surely the voice of God was in the rushing flame.

The great advance of Christianity in Japan during the last year, makes us almost forget that in 1861 a law was in force which compelled every individual to sign a paper, yearly, declaring that he was not a Christian, and stating to which Buddhist sect he belonged; and that large rewards were then offered to those who informed against Christians. Contrast with this the words of one of the most prominent men in Japan in a recent number of a Japanese paper. From political and economic motives he says: "If it is impossible to impede the rapid diffusion of Christianity in Japan, it would be far better for us resolutely to grant it full toleration for its legitimate propagation, rather than follow the hesitating indecision of leaving it unrecognized either by prohibition or toleration."

What wonder if, when we come to our annual gathering and review the last twelve months, painting a faithful picture whose strong lights rivet our thankful attention, looking a little farther into the shadows, we discern there realities which we must not ignore!

All the way across the Pacific Ocean and our own broad continent have come "war notes" from the Celestial Empire. We rejoiced a year ago that we had been able to send Emily Hartwell back to her native city, to gladden not only her father, but the whole mission at Foochow. We read with eager interest her first letters, giving the account of her long voyage, her entrance to the River Min, her enthusiasm over the beautiful scenery, the light-colored feldspar rocks, the terraced hills and jagged mountains, the islands and little villages; and we were sure she felt at home when she wrote, "And now, from the Golden Gate of the Occident through the Golden Gate of the Orient, I have reached my childhood's and my womanhood's home." Later she told us of her tours into the country, with Miss Newton, up the Ing Hoh River into the Ing Hoh — Eternal Happiness — region, where one family gave them their clay idols, nearly one hundred years old. We longed to find an owner for that "unclaimed letter" from the girls in Foochow Seminary, and we were glad when we knew Miss Newton was to have Miss Garretson as an assistant, even if it did not add a new name to our list of workers in China.

Then the war cloud arose, growing denser and blacker, and we find our young missionary at Sharp's Peak Sanitarium, watching the French gun-boats on their way in, the river all brilliant with

Chinese banners and soldiers. When war was inevitable, she went up to the settlement with her father, to stay until the contest was over. Following her graphic pen, we see the forts and breastworks, the large encampments farther back among the hills, the myriad red and green flags, the 60,000 soldiers in Foochow, 30,000 of whom cannot speak the Foochow dialect. We hear the drum-beats which mark the change of watches. We almost feel the panic among the natives, the impulse to flee somewhere. We see the poor foot-bound women hobbling with their canes, and the little children following with their bundles. In the midst of this excitement, the fidelity of the Christians who guarded the mission property was remarkable, placing duty far above safety, urging that prayer be offered not only for themselves, but for all Foochow. The young missionary at this time was sending them messages such as these: "Who can separate us from the love of God?" and "The trying of your faith is more precious than gold." Although the foreigners were all away from the city during the French attack, service was held in the Mission Church every Sunday, and the people wondered as they heard the roar of the guns and saw the Christians praying. Imagine Miss Newton's need of courage as she was borne through the crowded street in her chair, and heard the first of a company of soldiers whom she met say, "Catch and kill the foreigner." It could not have been altogether easy to look quietly the other way. Surely, in the midst of these trials we may join in the thanksgiving of our workers in China. They have all been kept from harm. Only one chapel has been injured, and Miss Newton, writes: "Opportunities for work are better than before. Sometimes I have almost longed to see persecution, to arouse the people — anything rather than coldness and indifference. God will carry out his plans in his own way." The Misses Woodhull, and others who were to accompany them, were undaunted by the tidings of war, and there is now a stronger force to do valiant service for the King of kings in Foochow.

From the Celestial Empire we turn to the Dark Continent. In North Africa, centuries ago, arose the proverb, "If God does not send rain, lay it to the Christians." Our first missionaries to the Zulus, of South Africa, were kindly received by king and people. Five hundred in the Sunday-schools, and six hundred in a congregation, was an encouraging prospect. King Dingan sent pupils to the missionaries, and said, " If you succeed in teaching my people to read and write, you must come immediately to me, and teach me and my chiefs to read and write; and then I should want schools in all my country." Suddenly he became jealous of the

increasing influence over his subjects, and was bent upon retalia-
tion. The missionaries were obliged to leave the field, and the
work was almost abandoned, when Natal passed under the control
of the British Government, and the missionaries were urged to
return. At the end of ten years one solitary Zulu woman sat
with them at the Lord's table. The jubilee of this mission ap-
proaches, and the review will show that a great work has been
more than begun.

A little more than four years ago we sent our messengers to
the western coast of this same continent; and among their new
acquaintances they very soon introduced to us a royal personage
under the somewhat classic-sounding name of Kwikwi, His Majesty,
the King of Bailundu. They described him as "a savage of
kindly disposition, and far above the average black in common
sense." He received his pale-faced guests in a friendly way, and
said that he was an old man, but they might live in his country a
thousand years, if they liked. His people were spoken of as " a
fine race, intelligent, brave, full of poetry, and worthy to give birth
to a powerful Christian nation by and by." This company was
soon re-enforced; and Mrs. Stover, describing her housekeeping,
showed us far more "Sunnyside" in it than is found in many a
convenient New England kitchen.

While King Kwikwi was busy with his plundering expeditions,
and the missionaries were making a vocabulary and a grammar,
the Portuguese trader was on the alert to poison the kindness of
this dark-skinned king, who reluctantly believed the fabrications
concerning his white children. But when his suspicions were too
much aroused, his love for the promised gain of rum, cloth, and
guns still more so, he sent them away. What stayed his hand
from taking the lives which he might have ended by one word of
command? Was it only instinctive kindness which prompted the
queen, Chepapa, to send her embassy of forty women to say she
was ready to die with the missionaries? What more pathetic
appeal than that of these forty women, sitting in front of the mis-
sion-houses, and saying, "You teach our children; you pay us for
our work; you speak the truth; your little children have been
born among us; we do not want you to leave?" The girl, Naseko,
who carried the baby's food in a tin box upon her head two hundred miles to the coast, only once admitting that she was tired,
deserves to be made a member of the Humane Society; moreover,
she has done something for her people. The four years' work is
not lost. The king has already relented; has kindly received the
missionaries who have returned, is ready to receive the others, and
probably will not again be so easily persuaded to send them away.

Africa is not all dark; and the day will dawn when, unto it across the sea, our favored nation may send the Christian salutation, " Thy light is come, and the glory of the Lord is risen upon thee."

> " After the darkness — light!
> Out of the evil — good!
> From foulest Wrong upriseth Right —
> Sin-cleansed, O Christ, in blood!

> " Though dark the dun clouds roll —
> Though deadly fierce the fray —
> God can the battle-storm control,
> And bid the billows stay!

> " O doubting heart, be still!
> O fainting soul, be brave!
> By devious ways works He his will —
> Omnipotent to save!"

WOMAN'S BOARD OF MISSIONS.

RECEIPTS FROM FEBRUARY 18 TO MARCH 18, 1885.

MAINE.

Maine Branch. — Mrs. Woodbury S. Dana, Treas. Woodford's Cong. Ch., $8.42; Ellsworth, Aux., $23; Calais, Aux., $11.68; Solon, Aux., $6; Bath, Aux., $13.50; Monson, Sunshine Band, $16; Portland, Aux., Williston Ch., $3; Bethel Ch., $13.75, Ocean Pebbles, $20.77, M. B., const. L. M. Mary A. Plummer, $25, **$141 12**
Ellsworth. — S. S. Cl., 30 00
Minot Centre. — A Friend, 20 00
Shapleigh. — L. M. Trussell, 1 00

Total, **$192 12**

Ellis, $5; Mrs. Lucy Ellis, $5, Mrs. R. E. Davis, $1; Exeter, 2d Cong. Ch. S. S., Edward C. Chickering, $1.50; Francestown, Aux., $31; Haverhill, Aux., $38.14, Harvesters, $40; Hinsdale, Aux., $4.25; Newport, Ladies of Cong. Ch., $42.28; Northwood Centre, Mrs. E. E. Wiggin, $34; Plainfield, Ladies of Cong. Ch., const. L. M. Mrs. W. O. Kenyon, $25, **$532 17**
Franconia. — Woman's Aid Soc'y, $5, Cong. S. S., Willing Workers, $6, 11 00

Total, **$543 17**

NEW HAMPSHIRE.

New Hampshire Branch. — Miss Abby E. McIntire, Treas. Amherst, Miss L. F. Bee, $50; Bennington, Mrs. A. M. Holmes, $5; Claremont, Aux., const. L. M. Mrs. Caroline H. Ainsworth, $25; Concord, No. Ch., $60, Aux., $31, Merry Gleaners, $4, Mission Helpers, $100; Derry, 1st Cong. Ch., $30; E. Sullivan, Mrs. N. A.

VERMONT.

Vermont Branch. — Mrs. T. M. Howard, Treas. Wallingford, Aux., $57; Enosburgh, Aux., $26; Jericho Centre, Aux., $15 38; Quechee, Aux., $15; St. Johnsbury, No. Ch., Aux., $28.46, Boys' Miss'y Soc'y, $15, So. Ch., Little Helpers, $11, Boys' Miss'y Jug Soc'y, $20.

Total, **$187 84**

MASSACHUSETTS.

Andover and Woburn Branch. — Miss E. F. Wilder, Treas. Melrose, Aux., $80; Malden, Star Circle, $5; Ballardvale, S. S., $3.60; Andover, So. Ch., $50; Stoneham, Ladies of Cong. Ch., $3.75; Winchester, Aux., of wh. $25 by Mrs. M. A. Herrick const. L. M. Mrs. Elizabeth P. Pressey, $43, Eddie's M. C., $12.50, Seek and Save Cir., $390, $587 85

Berkshire Branch—Mrs. S. N. Russell, Treas. Adams, Aux., $30; Parousia, M. C., $30; Stockbridge, Aux., $39; Hinsdale, Aux., $15.15,   114 15

Essex North Conf. Branch. — Mrs. A. Hammond, Treas. Haverhill, No. Ch. S. S., $100; Centre Ch., Harriet Newell, Aux., of wh. $25 by Mrs. M. F. Ames const. L. M. Miss E. C. Ames, $60; Newburyport, Aux., $68.75, Willing Helpers, $5; Campbell, M. B., $12,   245 75

Fall River. — Mite-Gatherers,   4 00

Hampshire Co. Branch.—Miss Isabella G. Clarke, Treas. No. Amherst, Aux., const. L. M. Miss Martha E. Harrington, $25; Hadley, M. C., $40; Northampton, Aux., Edwards Div., $36.66; Plainfield, Aux., $13.50; Williamsburgh, M. C., $10,   125 16

Middlesex Branch.—Mrs. E. H. Warren, Treas. Holliston, Aux.,   50 00

Norfolk and Pilgrim Branch. —Mrs. Franklin Shaw, Treas. Easton, Aux., $18; Brockton, Aux., $176; Abington, Aux., $19.09; No. Abington, Aux., $5; Y. L. Circle, $6; Cohasset, Aux., $23; Duxbury, Aux., $10; Plympton, Aux., Thankoff.,$11; Rockland, Aux., $50; Bridgewater, Aux., $11; So. Weymouth, Aux.,$53.30; Marden, M. C., $35; No. Weymouth, 1st Ch., $30; Busy Bees, $100; No. Ch., Wide-Awake Workers, $20; Kingston, Aux., $15; Chiltonville, Aux., $20; E. Marshfield, Aux., $6.05; Marshfield, Aux., $8.00; Holbrook, Aux., $25, Torch-Bearers, $40, Little Lights, $5; Braintree, Aux., $8.50, Happy Workers, $14 90; Randolph, Aux., of wh. $25 by Miss Abby Turner const. L. M. Miss Emma H. King, $47; Quincy, Mr. Hardwick's S. S. Cl., $30; Hingham, Willing Hands. $20,   806 84

Suffolk Branch.—Miss Myra B.

Child, Treas. Boston, A Friend, $50. Mrs. M. H. Baldwin, $5, Central Ch., $11, Shawmut Ch., Aux., $125, Mt. Vernon Ch., Y. L. M. C.,$183; Roxbury, Highland Ch.,Aux., $126, Eliot Ch., Aux., $28.50, Anderson Cir., $6, Olive Branch, 50 cts., Thompson Cir., 62 cts., Fergurson Cir., 50 cts., Mayflowers, $2.66, Eliot Star, $2.66, Immanuel Ch., Aux., $34.83; Dorchester, 2d Ch., S. S., $23.81, Life and Light M. C., $5.60; Jamaica Plain, Central Ch., Aux., $80 25, Y. L. M. C., $25; W. Roxbury, Spring St. Ch., Aux., $10; Charlestown, 1st Parish, Aux., $35; Hyde Park, Aux., $22; Dedham, Asylum Dime, $2.35, Chapel Rays, $15, Junior Aux., $10; Newton, Young Ladies'Soc'y, $10, Eliot M. C., $5; Newton Centre, Maria B. Furber Soc'y, $60; Auburndale, Miss M. Davis, $10; Arlington, Young Ladies' Aux., $40, $930 28

Wellesley, College Miss'y Soc'y,   70 00

Worcester Co. Branch.—Mrs. G. W. Russell, Treas. Whitinsville, Aux., of wh. $50 by Mrs. Chas. P. Whitin const. L. M's Miss Amelia D. Halliday, Brooklyn, N. Y., Miss Mary Hamlin, Middlebury, Vt., $75, M. C., $90; Oxford, Woman's Miss'y Soc'y, $40; Leominster, Aux., const. L. M. Miss Flossy Miller, $25,   230 00

       Total, $3,164 03

LEGACIES.

Legacy of Miss Armeda Gibbs, East Boston, $500 00

Legacy of Mrs. Mary P. Eddy, Fall River,   500 00

RHODE ISLAND.

Rhode Island Branch. — Miss Anna T. White, Treas. Providence, Beneficent Ch., $110.-40, S. S., $1; Newport, Aux., $231.73, United Ch., S. S., $268.27; Slatersville, Aux., $8, S. S., $15; Pawtucket, Aux., Mrs. H. N. Blodgett, const. L. M. Miss Edith Carpenter, $25, Mrs. Darius Goff, const. L. M. Miss Jessie L. MacGregor, $25, Mrs. Eunice E. E. Davis, const. self L. M., $25, Mrs. D. L. Goff, const. L. M. Miss Una MacGregor, $25, Mrs. L. B. Goff, const. L. M. Mrs. Geo. M. Thornton, 25, $759 40

       Total, $759 40

CONNECTICUT.

Bethlehem. — Willing Hands, $3 00
Hartford Branch. — Miss Anna Morris, Treas. Rockville, Aux.,$34; Glastonbury,Aux., $176.07; Berlin, Aux., $12.50; Poquonnock, $22; Hartford, Park Ch., Aux., $103.90, Pearl St. S. S., $40, Asylum Hill Ch., M. B., $12.50, 400 97
New Haven Branch.—Miss Julia Twining, Treas. Bethel, Aux., of wh. $25 const. L. M. Mrs. Frank W. Smith, $71, Willing Workers, $5; Bridgeport, of wh. $30 fr. Pearl-Seekers, $50 fr. North Ch. M. C., $30 fr. Park St. Ch. M. C., const. L. M's Mrs. W. Minor Smith, Miss Mary F. Kensett, Miss Mary J. Minor, $166.63; Canaan, $20; Cornwall, $20; Cromwell, of wh. $25 const. L. M. Mrs. Wm. E. Hulbut, $93.05; East Haddam, $25; Greenwich, Bearers of Light, $24.57; Guilford, 1st Ch., $40; Haddam, $17.60; Kent, Y. L. M. C., $35; Killingworth, $25; Litchfield, of wh. $25 by Mrs. Adams, const. L. M. Mrs. F. M. Sandford, $32.91; Meriden, 1st Ch., Y. P. M. S., $40; Middletown, 1st Ch., $10; New Britain, Centre Ch., $120.88; S. S. Prim'y Dep't, $32.32; So. Ch., of wh. $25 by Miss S. M. Hinsdale const. L. M. Mrs. Harriet L. Humphrey, 49 43; New Canaan, $30; New Haven, Centre Ch., $11.52, Ch. of the Redeemer, $105.30, Aurora, $70.10, Davenport Ch., M. C., $40, Dwight Pl. Fairbank M. C., $25; Fair Haven, 1st Ch., $150, Humphrey St. Ch., $19, United Ch., of wh. $25 by Mrs. Eleanor Shepard const. self L. M., $185, Yale College Ch., $125; No. Branford, $30; Orange, $34; Saybrook, $17; Sherman, $10; Stratford, $63.31; Torrington, 3d Ch., $45; Wallingford, M. C., $25; W. Haven, Y. L. M. C., $30; W. Torrington, $30.25; Westville, Y. L. M. C., $90; Wilton, Light-Bearers, $70; Winchester, $2, 2,035 87
Waterbury. — 2d Ch., Sunshine Cir., 5 00

Total, $2,444 84

LEGACY.

New Haven Branch. — Legacy of Mrs. Louisa M. Parker, New Haven, $200 00

NEW YORK.

New York State Branch.—Mrs. G. H. Norton, Treas. Brooklyn, Park Ch. M. C., bequest of Miss Flora Robertson, const. L. M. Miss Mary Robertson, $25; New York City, Pilgrim Ch., $47.73; Suspension Bridge, Aux., $6; Oxford, Mrs. A. Watson, const. L. M's Mrs. Elizabeth E. Lee, Mrs. Susan Sophia Gleason, $50; Albany, Morning Star M. C., $10; Binghamton, Doers of the Word, $25; Sherburne, Aux., $50; Homer, M. C., $20; Walton,Aux.,$10.75; Black Creek, M. C., $5; Lockport, Aux., $10; Little Valley, Aux., $6; Gloversville, Aux., $30; Oswego, Y. L. Miss'y Soc'y, $10; Buffalo, Aux., $20; W. Bloomfield, Aux., of wh. $25 const. L. M. Miss Sarah L. Brown, $30, $355 48
Newtonville. — Desert Palm, prev. contri. const. L. M's Miss S. E. Dowd, Fairport, N. Y., Mrs. C. T. Russ, Hartford, Conn., 35 00
Rochester.—Plymouth Ch., S.S., 3 00

Total, $393 48

PENNSYLVANIA.

Stevensville. — A Friend, $15 00

Total, $15 00

GEORGIA.

Savannah.— Cong. Ch., Ladies' Miss'y Soc'y, $10 31

Total, $10 31

MINNESOTA.

Brainard. — Mrs. C. J. Veon, $1 50
Grove Lake.—Mrs. F. C. Stranahan, 5 40

Total, $6 90

DAKOTA.

Howard, Cong. Ch., Aux., $2 00

Total, $2 00

General Fund, $7,719 09
Weekly Pledge, 2 12
Leaflets, 39 44
Morning Star, 5 20
Legacies, 1,200 00

Total, $8,965 85

In Memoriam.

MRS. WM. J. KING.

ANOTHER of the great army of Christian women has gone to her reward.

For many years Mrs. William J. King had been active in all good works, and when the time came to form the Rhode Island Branch of the Woman's Board of Missions, she was chosen its first president. This burden she took up tremblingly, so far as her own sense of fitness was concerned; hopefully, because she remembered whose the work was, and knew He would give strength equal to her necessity. She was willing to do what she could, and her love for the cause deepened from year to year, as she came to know more and more of the needs of the women who were sitting in darkness, and to whom the light had not yet come.

For several years Mrs. King had a strong desire that there might go out from the churches of Rhode Island at least one foreign missionary. Those who have been associated with her in the ladies' prayer-meeting, know that this has been one of her constant petitions. At the annual meeting of the Woman's Board of Missions in Boston, January 15, 1885, the announcement was made that Miss Bessie Jillson, of the Central Church, Providence, was under appointment by the American Board of Commissioners for Foreign Missions to go as missionary to Smyrna. This intelligence was received by Mrs. King with great satisfaction; and it is a comfort to her friends to remember that this cherished desire was fulfilled while she was yet present with them.

Foreign missions did not absorb Mrs. King's whole thought. The home missionary cause was also dear to her heart; and many laborers have been cheered by her gifts, as well as encouraged by her words of sympathy. During her last illness, the only reading that seemed to really interest her was items from missionary periodicals regarding the work she so loved.

Mrs. King found great delight in the ladies' prayer-meeting, and attended as long as her strength would permit. Those who met her there know her enjoyment of the meetings, and will long remember her prayers and her comments on the subjects discussed, and her rare gift of adaptation in her prayers and remarks.

Mrs. King's interests in foreign and home missions and in the prayer-meetings, were those of which any one might know; but of her care and thoughtfulness toward those who were poor and burdened, who can tell? Her family may know when money was bestowed, and how much, but it is doubtful if even they know all she gave in the way of sympathy, advice, and encouragement. In making her choice of gifts for the needy ones who looked to her for help, she remembered, "Blessed is he that *considereth* the poor," and gave time and thought as well as silver and gold.

After a long and active life, with a few weeks of special weakness, Mrs. King passed suddenly from her earthly home to the heavenly city, February 9, 1885, trusting in Him in whom for so many years she had believed. It seems impossible to realize we shall not see her among us again; but she will not pass away from our thought, and we may look forward to that day when our work shall be finished, and we, too, shall enter into rest. "And so shall we ever be with the Lord."

Board of the Interior.

JAPAN.

EXPLORING NEW FIELDS.

BY MRS. ANNIE E. GULICK.

Our Young Ladies' Societies are doing pioneer work in Japan through their missionary, Mrs. Gulick, and if we do not place her letter in a separate department for them, it is because we fear it might thereby escape the eyes of some of our grown-up auxiliaries; while we believe our enterprising young ladies, in their tireless search for information, will begin at the beginning of LIFE AND LIGHT and read it through.

NIIGATA, Dec. 5, 1884.

TOURING among the towns and villages in this province forms a large part of our work during the warmer months, and I made several tours with my husband during the summer and fall. We visited a second time Murikami and Nakajo, places I wrote of visiting in the spring; and it was very pleasant to see how wide-awake and earnest the Christian band in Murikami were. They were, at their desire, formed into a church, adopting creed and rules, and choosing officers. They have not yet a pastor, but are hoping to secure one, though men to fill that office are scarce. The church now numbers fourteen, about half of whom are women, who meet weekly to study the Bible — one of the women, more intelligent than the others, being the leader.

We visited two villages, later, where there were no Christians, and where the gospel has been preached only once or twice. Quite a number came together at our hotel to hear Mr. Gulick and our helper tell of the way of salvation through Christ, and listened very attentively and quietly, and seemed eager to receive the tracts distributed at the close of the services. These were pretty mountain villages, and one was a place to which many came from the country around to bathe in the medical waters. The bathing-places had only a roof overhead; and long as I have been in Japan, and much as I have known of Japanese life and customs, I was unprepared for the nudity and unblushing immodesty to which it was impossible to shut one's eyes. We might have imagined ourselves in savage Marquesas, rather than in cultivated, polite Japan. We were thankful to hasten away from this pretty mountain nook, first having had a meeting with a company who came to our hotel, some of whom had heard something of Christianity before in other places.

In October we went one hundred miles south of Niigata, to the city of Takada, where no missionary has been before. The first forty miles were easily accomplished in a comfortable river steam-boat. It is small, to be sure, and we sit upon the floor in the little cabin; but it is a pleasant sail to Nagaoka, the large city to which the steamer runs. From Nagaoka we traveled by jinrikishas — drawn sometimes by one man, and sometimes by two, according to the steepness of the road. These little carriages tip over pretty easily, as I found from experience on this trip. A hand-cart loaded with wood, coming rapidly down a side street into our street as we were passing, came plump against my jinrikisha. As the man with the hand-cart held back with all his might, it did not come with great force; but in spite of the efforts of my man to hold it, the jinrikisha went slowly over upon its side, not, however, hurting me at all.

During the journey the rain came down in frequent showers; but, snugly stored away in our covered carriages, we did not get wet. We met quite a number of religious pilgrims, mostly women, walking in the rain. I could but admire their walking-attire, protecting them from the rain, and making walking easy. Their dresses were tucked up so that they reached a little below the knees, and oil-paper waterproofs kept their clothes dry. On their heads were very broad, trimmed, light straw hats, protecting head and shoulders from rain and sun. Tightly fitting, thick blue and white stockings, and straw sandals, completed their attire.

It was harvesting season, and men, women, and older children were all at work in the fields, cutting the grain, tying it up in bundles, carrying it home on their backs, and hanging it up to dry on frames prepared for the purpose. I was surprised to see what heavy loads the women carried; and as I saw them bending under the heavy weight, I did not wonder that so many of the old people we see are bent nearly double. The younger children from five to ten years old were running about the streets with little babies tied on their backs — poor, patient little creatures. I pitied both nurse and babies, though I seldom saw a baby crying.

One chilly evening, as we were riding at dusk through some villages, I judged that the parents were still in the fields — for there was no light in the houses, and the children, with babies on their backs, were gathered in little groups on the streets, quietly waiting. I thought of how babies I had known about were sure to want mamma as night came on, and were rather likely to let their voices be heard if she were not near, and wondered at these patient little creatures, learning to "bear the yoke" in babyhood.

Two days and a half brought us to Takada—a rather uninterest-ing city, so far as business is concerned. On one side, however, are the castle-grounds and former homes of the Samorai, covering quite an extent of country, as this was once a castle town where the Daimio resided. The buildings are gone from the castle grounds, but the broad moat and fine old trees remain, and on two sides are the Samorai houses, almost hid by trees, and surrounded by yards inclosed with neatly-trimmed green hedges, looking very pretty and homelike.

We knew no one in Takada, and as the hotel-keeper did not wish us to hold a meeting at the hotel, we were in doubt as to whether we could have one at all; when, as we were entering our hotel the day after our arrival, two men who had seen us in the street came to us, and asking my husband if he could speak Japanese, desired to learn about Christianity, of which one of them had heard something. We had a long talk with them, and in the afternoon they came again, and escorted us about the Samorai quarters; again in the evening they came with some friends, and after a long talk asked if we were not going to have a public service. On being told the difficulty in the way, they offered to get a room for preaching, and did so. The next evening, Sunday, Mr. Gulick and the helper, who accompanied us, addressed an audience of about a hundred. At the close several asked if we could not stay another day, and hold a meeting the next evening. We consented, and Monday evening there were nearly twice as many present as on the previous evening, who paid quiet, respectful attention to what was said. The men who interested themselves in obtaining the room would not allow us to pay for it, but said they would see to that — a new experience in our missionary work. We could but feel that Takada was a most hopeful work, and that it ought to be occupied by missionaries as soon as possible. But while there are only two families here in Niigata, none can be spared to live in Takada, and our earnest plea to the churches at home is, to send us more men and women for the interesting work to be found on every hand. Are there not among those who compose the young ladies' mission circles, many who are considering the question as to whether the Master calls them to carry the word of life to those who are sitting in heathen darkness?

CHINA.

THE LITTLE GATE SCHOOL.

BY MISS ADA HAVEN.

PEKIN, Jan, 22d.

I HARDLY remember how far I had told you the story of my day school. I think we had moved into the room in the gate-house, but had not made our second move into the coal-house.

That does not sound like a move in the upward direction; but it proved so. Mrs. Ament's class was growing, as well as mine, so one day we had a consultation, and decided to arrange for rooms for both of us. On the other side of the gateway was a little room for keeping the chapel coal. We decided to put new fronts on both these rooms, and throw a partition across the back of one to make a little coalroom, hardly larger than a bin, but making the room in front of it quite large enough for our purposes. The door of the coalbin opens into the gateway, — not into our house, — so we quite forget that we are occupying the former coalroom. The south wall of the room forms part of the wall of the compound, so we cannot have much of a window there; but I felt that we really ought to get some of the southern sunshine into the dreary little den, so I had a small window, shaped like a transom, put under the eaves. This is so high that no one can see in or out without climbing up. We occasionally see a face there, but it is always in friendly curiosity. As the compound adjoining ours is unoccupied, it is but seldom that we receive such notice.

The furniture of the room is simple: a brick platform extending across the back, a broad settle on one side, and a long bench on the other; also a wicker throne for myself. I like this seat, because it defends me from encroachments from all sides but the front. A big, domestic apron covers my defenceless front; for the babies who amuse themselves, while their big sisters are reading, with some greasy, juicy, or sticky substance, alternately eating it and using it as a paint-brush, could not understand me if I did say "Hands off!" I take the big school-bell when the time comes, and, opening the great compound-gate, give two or three taps, standing in the gateway. Then I go and seat myself in state. It is not many seconds before I hear the wooden soles of their shoes rattling through the gateway. They used to come in without any greeting, and so utterly filthy that there was no clean spot on them. Their dirty, ragged clothes they are not to blame for, but they might at least show three clean spots, and their manners certainly could be mended. Exhortations were of no avail. Finally I received a hint from one of the girls that helped me to alter the matter. She noticed the pins with which I fastened up the bib of my apron. (The Chinese do not have pins.) "Oh, Wenku-mang," she said, "won't you give us each a pin Christmas?" I pondered the matter for a moment, and the girls apparently conjectured that I was thinking whether I could afford to give them each a pin, for when I came out with my proposition they seemed surprised and delighted. "I will tell you what I will do," I said. "I will write your names on a slip of paper, and then, underneath each name, I will make one mark for each day that you remember to give me a curtsey when you come and go, and another for each day that you come with face and hands washed and pig-tail properly combed. Then on Christmas Day I will count up the marks, and for every six I will give you a pin.' I hope they will never learn the price of pins!

My school was rather broken up during the summer. I went out to "The Hills" twice, and when I was in town I was house-keeper for the compound, and entertaining guests sometimes made my time for opening the gate a little irregular. I think the war rumors, perhaps, helped to keep some away. Then a family containing four sisters, who had been daily present, moved away; also the hollyhock season was over. (I had given a hollyhock each day for a perfect lesson.) These four reasons were enough to account for a diminished attendance; and soon I found I really ought not to be gone from the school compound so long, while the care of that rested solely on me. So I changed my plan, and instead of staying out in the gate schoolroom, I took any who were ready to come with me through the courts to my own room. Of course I had to leave the compound-gate locked when I was not there to watch it, so I could get only those who happened to be on hand when I opened the gate. This plan proved so unsatisfactory that I gave it up at Christmas, and told the girls they could take a holiday till warm weather; meantime coming only Sundays, to Sunday-school. I shall try it again when the weather becomes warmer.

In another letter, finished January 9th, Miss Haven speaks of the boarding-school (the Bridgman School) as follows: —

Who would have thought it would be just one month after writing the first page before I should take up this letter again. Into that month have been crowded many duties — the hasty preparation of a text-book for a class who kept even pace with me, so that I could never give them any more than the pages just written; then the preparation for Christmas, and the balancing of personal and school accounts at the end of the year, followed by the Week of Prayer. We are still in the Week of Prayer, and the text-book is unfinished yet; but it is so nearly done that I do not have to spend time studying up the subject, and it is Miss Diament's turn to lead the prayer-meeting to-night. So I will pick up dropped stitches.

Though there are no marked conversions to gladden our hearts this Week of Prayer, we are pleased by the spirit among the girls. There is not a girl in school whose influence is positively bad. The only doubtful one is a source of anxiety, simply from her heedlessness. The influence of all the others is positively good. All the older girls are so strong, steady, and reliable, that it is a real support to me. In all this I see the providence of God, giving strength in time of need. In ordinary speech it only *happens* that the troublesome girls are all gone; but we who know better say it was so ordered that the best girls should remain to help us now, and the bad ones should all go. So, though we have no conversions to report, we have much to make us rejoice in the earnest, Christian spirit pervading the school. Yet we always rejoice with fear, and woe to us if we ever venture to glory. But we can be a little thankful with a good conscience.

THE MORNING STAR.

A journal letter from Capt. Bray, the last date of which is January 19th, at Sandy Point, half way through the Straits of Magellan, describes the parting from friends, November 5th, in Boston Harbor, the singing of "Waft, waft ye winds," by the party about to return to the city in the tug, and then tells of the night which followed.

ACROSS the bay we flew, passing several vessels which sailed about the same time, and thereby showing the fast-sailing qualities of the Morning Star, until we left Cape Cod astern, and launched out into the broad Atlantic. How little I realized the night before us! The breeze which the dear ones had invoked to "waft" us on, increased till it blew a terrible gale. One sail after another was taken in, until we were scudding before great high waves that rolled our little bark about and filled her with water, and only one close-reefed topsail remained set. It was a time to prove officers and crew, and I was satisfied that I had brave hearts and ready hands around me. But what shall we do? The lower deck is getting filled with water. It is washing into the cabin, and every state-room is filling. It will soon find its way to the engine-room, and we shall founder, in sight, almost, of our home. It was a fearful thing to bring the ship's head to that sea and try to "heave to;" but it seemed the only hope, and we must try it. "Stand by the fore braces with one watch, and the mizzen halyards with the other!" And now we watch the great sea rolling up behind us to find a moment of comparative quiet. We think we have it, and "Put your helm hard down!" is the order to the man at the wheel. She quickly obeys the helm, and comes up nobly to face the wind and waves, and then falls off again, and lies with her lee rail under water.

We see in a moment that we have more freight (coal) on the main deck than she is able to stand. Each roll makes me fear she will roll over. Dangerous as it is to run before that gale and high sea, it is far safer than "lying to." "Lower down the mizzen and square the headyard!" is the next order given; and, filled with water as she is, she gradually falls off until we are again scudding before the gale under a close-reefed fore-topsail. Never do I remember feeling in so great danger before.

There was but one thing to do, and that was to throw overboard some of the main-deck cargo. So much weight on the upper deck made the Star top-heavy. All night (and a long, long one it seemed), and all the next day, without sleep, and with little time to eat, the officers and crew stood in the washing waters of the flooded deck, and with buckets passed the coal over the side till we had jetsomed ten tons or more, which, although the gale had not abated, made the ship ride the seas more easily, and ship less water. It was Wednesday night, November 12th, just one week after sailing from Boston, before the gale subsided, and I felt it prudent to go to bed, and try to get the first regular sleep. Much of the ship's provisions were spoiled by the salt-water. All our new carpets were saturated and discolored by it. Bedding and curtains were wet, doors and partitions were stove in, our only three turkeys for Thanksgiving drowned, etc.; yet it all seemed as nothing compared with saving the ship and our lives. But it was a wild beginning for this new vessel of peace.

Capt. Bray speaks with appreciation and thanksgiving to God of his officers, especially the first mate, Mr. Garland, who was captain of the old Morning Star on her last trip, and Mr. Snow, engineer, son of the venerated Micronesia missionary. He tells us that Mrs. Bray and Carrie were perfectly calm, and Arthur Logan slept through the first wild night, though the water was washing back and forth in his state-room; and he gives thanks for the Christian hope that makes one ready, either to go into the presence of the Master at a moment's call, or to stay and work longer for him. The next date is Thursday, Nov. 27, 1884.

Thanksgiving.— The experience of the previous pages is a thing of the past. All the fury of the winds seems to have died out with the blasts of the first few days, and we have had very light winds ever since. We are now in a region where we always expect a strong, steady, northeast trade-wind; but we have had none of it. This light weather has brought its satisfaction, however, for it has shown us what a fine sailer the new Star is in light winds. This was a point we particularly studied, for we have so many light winds in Micronesia; and we are pleased, of course, to know that this very desirable point is attained. When there seems scarcely a breath of wind she moves through the water a knot or two, and obeys her helm. The old vessel would have remained stationary.

To-day we are observing Thanksgiving. There is no work going on, and we have all had the best dinner we could get up, but it had to be chicken instead of turkey. We are settling down to the regular sea-life of a long voyage. Everything is going on in ship-shape order, which is quite agreeable to the feelings of an orderly person after the confusion of shore-life. Carpets have been dried, provisions overhauled, etc.; but there is much work to be done. Even so long a voyage will be far too short to get a new ship in perfect order, with "a place for everything and everything in its place." Arthur and Carrie are having their regular studies and music, to which Mrs. Bray devotes each forenoon. We have our regular Chautauqua readings, and our evening worship with all hands is growing more interesting. Some who boasted before sailing (as I have heard) that they would have nothing to do with that part, now come into the cabin regularly, and join in the reading and singing, both at evening worship and Sunday services; but I expected it, for they cannot escape the power of the Spirit which the Lord has promised.

Jan. 8th, 1885.— On Christmas we all had a number of presents that had been given us to open on that day. Arthur and Carrie could scarcely wait for Christmas morning, and were planning to get up very early, when I suggested, much to their delight, that Christmas eve would do as well. The presents were quickly produced and opened. We had a number of charming letters given us by friends before sailing, and it was a perfect delight to read them while so far away.

January 19th.—We are at Sandy Point, and half way through the Straits. We have been very much favored of the Lord, and arrive here to-day in company with a mail steamer that leaves to-night for Valparaiso and Panama; so we are hastily getting off a mail. We can get fresh meat and provision — a great treat after seventy-five days of sea. Will write again from Honolulu.

A later word from Capt. Bray is dated at Honolulu, March 16, 1885:—

I am glad to send you news of the arrival of the Star at this her first port, after a long, long passage. This is not owing to slow sailing qualities, but to extraordinarily light winds, with the exception of the first three days after sailing from Boston, when it seemed as if all the winds blew out at one time. One great object has been attained: the Star is the best sailer in light winds I ever saw, without any exception. With the winds we have had I doubt if any other vessel would have made the same passage in thirty days more. Our time has been one hundred and thirty days. We used steam to pass through the Magellan Straits, and realized the first benefit from it in saving the Cape Horn passage. We were one week in the Straits, lying at anchor over Sunday and two other days at a settlement, where we obtained fresh water, both our tanks having leaked out, keeping us on short allowance all the voyage. There is grand scenery in the Straits — high mountains, and glaciers, and valleys of green.

Very cordially yours,
ISAIAH BRAY.

Home Department.

STUDIES IN MISSIONARY HISTORY.
1885.

MISSION TO THE ARMENIANS — 1831–1842.

WE begin this month the study of the far-reaching work of the American Board among the Armenians, which, beginning with Constantinople as its center, has influenced, more or less, the whole Turkish Empire. The mission properly began with the removal of Dr. Goodell to Constantinople, in 1831; but it will be of interest to note the *work of preparation* that had been going on prior to that date. Notice, especially, the *effect of Dr. King's Farewell Letter, The School of Peshtimaljian,* and his influence on the public mind.

Study of Constantinople and its Surroundings. See "Constantinople," by Edmonds Amicis, published by G. P. Putnam & Sons; LIFE AND LIGHT, 1877, p. 113; "Forty Years in the Turkish Empire," p. 112; "Chambers' Encyclopedia."

The Armenians and Greeks of Constantinople; Beginnings and Aims of the Mission.

Early Obstacles: Fire; Plague; Cholera; War.

Early Converts: Hohannes Sahakian; Senekerim; Sarkis Vartabed; Der Revork; Der Haritun, and Der Vertanes of Nicomedia.

Stations: Smyrna, for descriptions; see "Chamber's Encyclopedia;" Broosa; Trebizond; "Oriental Churches," p. 103.

Persecutions: Opposition of the Patriarchs Stepan and Matteos; of Boghos; Action of the banker of Ras Reny.

Persecution of 1839: Aid of the Sultan secured by the persecutors; Stepan deposed; banishment and imprisonment of converts; God's interposition through the Egyptian war; Death of the Sultan; reaction; Stepan re-elected.

Education: School at Bebek.
Progress: at Adabazar; Native Armenian Mission.
Helps: First and best, if it can be procured, is Dr. Anderson's "Missions to the Oriental Churches." "Forty Years in the Turkish Empire," and "Among the Turks," by Cyrus Hamlin, are both valuable; also "Mission Studies " for May.

QUARTERLY MEETING.

A QUARTERLY meeting of the Woman's Board of Missions of the Interior, was held at Plymouth Church, Chicago, on the afternoon and evening of February 26th, Mrs. Moses Smith in the chair. After devotional exercises, Miss Wingate, in a few potent words, urged the individual responsibility of Christian women, and the Bible argument for missions. Mrs. Greene, of Constantinople, brought good tidings from Miss Patrick, of the Constantinople Home; and Mrs. Stover, lately driven out from Benguela, Africa, told a thrilling story of the help given the missionaries in their flight, by the children they had taught. In the young ladies' hour, Mrs. Baird, chairman of the Young Ladies' Committee, brought favorable reports from their societies. She noted two points of importance in their methods of work: First, that there should be greater consecration to Christ, since now and then we hear of young people who enter into it "just for the fun of the thing;" and, second, that there should be more study — a suggestion prompted by a recent question whether it was a *real bridge* they were building. A story by Miss Baker, of Detroit, one of our young ladies, was read, telling how in a recent public meeting they did build (or furnish the wherewithal for) a real bridge. It was to arch over a ragged ravine Miss Spencer and Mrs. Coffing have to cross every time they go to the village.

Mrs. Gilbert, chairman of the Children's Committee, urged patient continuance on the part of their leaders. She said the work could not be all done at a great mass-meeting, however much the children may be there aroused and interested. They must have "line upon line." The old couplet about planting corn may be in place. It was: —

"One for the worm, and one for the crow,
And another one to sprout and grow."

A social tea added greatly to the interest of the day. In the evening Mrs. Stover moved the audience to tears with her stories of her dark-skinned pupils. One of them, watching her baby playing on the floor with a rubber doll one day, showed his dawning conscientiousness by asking Mrs. S., "Ungana Stover, does not Sukp's book say you shall not make images?" Dr. Scudder closed the evening with one of his rousing addresses, as unreportable as chain lightning, and perhaps as startling to some who think life is worth living only for home enjoyment.

The helpful words of our president added greatly to the pleasure of the meeting. It was a rest in the "Interpreter's house," very refreshing and long to be remembered.

THE statement in our last issue that we have 300 Young Ladies' Societies was an error. Two hundred and seventeen were reported at our last annual meeting.

In Memoriam.

Miss Minnie Brown.

WE who knew Miss Brown as one of our own youngest missionaries, would bear loving testimony to her great natural gifts, her many attainments, her energy, tact, and enthusiasm—all consecrated to the help of the needy in Turkey. We would tell of the interest she awakened in the churches of Missouri before sailing; of her hopeful beginnings in a foreign land; of the cheerful spirit with which she bore the disappointment of her plan for life; and of the patient devotion with which she labored for foreign missions here, always expecting to return to Turkey. We would sympathize with the father and mother, called to say a second and longer good-bye to their idolized first-born; and with the young associate, Miss Tucker, who, though she went out leaning upon this friend, has learned to work bravely on alone. But Miss Brown's young friends at home have sent their tribute, and we gladly give place to their words of loving remembrance.

Died, at her home in North Springfield, Missouri, on the morning of February 26th, Miss Minnie Brown. She was born at South Kingston, R. I., in 1859, and became a Christian while yet a child. In 1878 she graduated from Drury College, and two years later began work as a missionary in Central Turkey — first at Hadjin, and afterward at Adana. But in 1883, after two years of work, her ill-health compelled her to return to her home for a short rest. Up to the beginning of her last illness, it was her plan to go back to her work when she became stronger. During this last two years she devoted herself untiringly to church and home duties. She was president of the "King's Messengers," our missionary society; and we who knew and loved her, then saw, and now often speak, of her never-failing earnestness in her work with us. To all whom she met she was the same bright, sweet-natured, lovable Christian. Words seem meaningless when we try to tell those who have not known her, of what she was and *is* to all who knew her.

> " For she has gone to join
> . . . the choir invisible
> Of those immortal dead who l:ve again
> In minds made better by their presence: live
> In pulses stirred to generosity,
> In deeds of daring rectitude, in scorn,
> For miserable aims that end with self."

HATTIE J. BALLARD.
For the " King's Messengers."

SPRINGFIELD, MO., March 14.

RECEIPTS OF THE WOMAN'S BOARD OF MISSIONS OF THE INTERIOR.

MRS. J. B. LEAKE, TREASURER.

FROM FEBRUARY 18, 1885, TO MARCH 18, 1885.

ILLINOIS.

ILLINOIS BRANCH.— Mrs. W. A. Talcott, of Rockford, Treas. *Amboy*, 9.92; *Batavia*, 6; *Bowensburg*, 7.50; *Canton*, 13; *Chicago*, New Eng. Ch., Mr. and Mrs. E. W. B., 100, Aux., 19, Union Park Ch., a lady, thank-offering, for L. M'ship, 1, Plymouth Ch., 250; *St. Charles*, 10; *Creston*, 2.75; *Downers Grove*, 4.19; *Elgin*, 19.21; *Genoa Junction*, 7.71; *Huntley*, 6.30; *I v a n h o e*, 20; *Jacksonville*, 28; *La Harpe*, 4.15; *La Moille*, 5.50; *Lockport*, 10; *Lyonsville*, 9.50; *Ottawa*, 34.50; *Peoria*, 1st Ch., 42.85; *Princeton*, 29.60; *Rockford*, 2d Ch., 76.75; *Ross Grove*, 11.50; *Sycamore*, 8.76; *Waverly*, 5; *Wayne*, 3.38; *Wheaton*, 7, ... $753 07

JUNIORS: *Bartlett*, Lit. and Miss. Soc., 8.18; *Batavia*, Y. L. Soc., 6; *Chicago*, Union Park Ch., Y. L. Soc., 33.26; *Elgin*, Y. L. Soc., 13; *Huntley*, Harvesters, 7.06; *Ravenswood*, Y. P. M. Soc., 10; *Richmond*, Y. L. M. Soc., 3.85; *Springfield*, Jennie Chapin Helpers, 10, ... 91 35

JUVENILE: *Bartlett*, S. S. Miss. Band., 16.94; *Chicago*, New Eng. Ch., Steady Streams, 26.18, Lincoln Park Ch., Lamplighters, 13; *St. Charles*, Miss. Band, 10; *Huntley*, Acorn Band, 3.50; *Waukegan*, Miss. Band, 4.36; *Wayne*, Busy Builders, 16.27, ... 90 25

Total, ... $934 67

INDIANA.

INDIANA BRANCH.— Miss E. B. W a r r e n, of Terre Haute, Treas. *Elkhart*, 5; *Indianapolis*, Mayflower Aux., 9; ... $14 00

JUNIOR: *Indianapolis*, May-flower Y. L. Soc., ... 10 00

Total, ... $24 00

IOWA.

IOWA BRANCH.— Mrs. E. R. Potter, of Grinnell, Treas. *A l g o n a*, 1.55; *Clinton*, 10; *Central City*, 18; *Chester Centre*, 15; *Garden Prairie*, 2; *Kenebech*, 11; *Lyons*, 34.65, $92 20

JUNIORS: *Des Moines*, Plymouth Rock Soc., for The Bridge, ... 17 50

JUVENILES: *Decorah*, Children's Miss. Soc., ... 6 00

SABBATH-SCHOOLS: *DesMoines*, 8 00

Total, ... $123 70

KANSAS.

KANSAS BRANCH.— Mrs. A. L. Slosson, of Leavenworth, Treas. *Dial*, 2.53; *Ottawa*, 1; *Sedgwick*, 2, ... $5 53

Total, ... $5 53

MICHIGAN.

MICHIGAN BRANCH.— Mrs. Geo. H. Lathrop, of Jackson, Treas. *Augusta*, 3.20; *Bedford*, 5; *Bridgeport*, A u x., 1.40, Monthly Concert, 1.70; *Charlotte*, 4.12; *Galesburg*, 25; *Grand Blanc*, 18.44; *Laingsburg*, 5; *Litchfield*, 12; *Manistee*, 25; *Newaygo*, 5.26; *North Dorr*, Mrs. Gilbert, 2; *Port Huron*, 20; *Raisinville*, 3; *Richmond*, 4.10; *Summit*, 5.29; *Walton*, 3.89, ... $144 40

JUNIOR SOCIETIES: *Augusta*, Y. L. Bible-class, 50 cts.; *Jackson*, Y. P. Circle, 30, ... 30 50

JUVENILE BANDS: *Augusta*, Look Up Legion, 8.30; *Memphis*, Cheerful Workers, 3, ... 11 30

Branch Total, ... $186 20

MINNESOTA.

MINNESOTA BRANCH.— Mrs. E. M. Williams, of Northfield,

Treas. *Brownton,* 3; *Duluth,* of wh. 25 const. L. M. Mrs. E. M. Noyes, 42; *Glyndon,* 13.50; *Mankato,* 3; *Minneapolis,* special gifts at union meeting, Mrs. Taylor, 1, Mrs. Bell and Mrs. Woods, 18.80, Mrs. Horr, 5.50; *Northfield,* 14.39; *Owatonna,* 24.19, $125 38

Total, $125 38

MISSOURI BRANCH.

Mrs. J. H. Drew, 3101 Washington Ave., St. Louis, Treas. *Carthage,* 25; *Hannibal,* 12; *St. Louis,* Pilgrim Ch., 361, of wh. 150 fr. Mrs. Rebecca Webb, to const. Mrs. C. W. S. Cobb, Mrs. C. D. De Staebles, Mrs. W. E. Barnhart, Miss Jennie Carman, Miss Katie P. Fisher, Miss Blanche L. Morgan L. M's, 25 fr. Mrs. S. M. Edgell, to const. Miss Ada Bartlett, of Springfield, Mo., L. M., Hyde Park Gleaners, for The Bridge, 6, $404 00

Total, $404 00

NEBRASKA.

NEBRASKA BRANCH. — Mrs. Geo. W. Hall, of Omaha, Treas. *Clarke,* 2.50; *Omaha,* 1st Ch., Aux., 9.65, St. Mary's Ave. Aux., 12.35; *Sutton,* 3; *Syracuse,* 10, $37 50
JUVENILE: *Crete,* S. S., birthday offering, 3.13; *Omaha,* Mountain Rills (girls), 5.20, Steady Streams (boys), 3.10; *Stanton,* Acorn Band, 5.58,   17 01

Total, $54 51

OHIO.

OHIO BRANCH.—Mrs. Geo. H. Ely, of Elyria, Treas. *Claridon,* Miss Stebbins, 3; *Cleveland,* Plymouth Ch, 25; *Columbus,* 1st Ch., 25; *Madison,* Mrs. H. B. Fraser, to const. L. M. Grace Selina Fraser, 25; *Marysville,* 20; *Medina,* 10; *Mt. Vernon,* 34; *Oberlin,* 100, $242 00
JUNIORS: *Berea,* Girls' Miss. Band, 5; *Cincinnati,* Central Ch., Y. L. Soc., 125; *Painesville,* Lake Erie Sem. Miss. Soc., 50,   180 00

JUVENILES: *Cincinnati,* Columbia Ch., Willing Workers, 5; *Ironton,* Girls'-Work-for-Girls' Sec. 6.75; *Springfield,* Ruby Band, 5, $16 75

Total, $438 75

PENNSYLVANIA.

Allegheny, Plymouth Ch., Aux., $6 00

Total, $6 00

SOUTH DAKOTA BRANCH.

Mrs. H. H. Smith, of Yankton, Treas. *Faulkton,* 1.55; *Sioux Falls,* 25; *Yankton,* 12.75, $39 30
JUVENILE: *Faulkton,* Prim. Cl., 2; *Valley Springs,* Miss. Band, 2,   4 00

Total, $43 30

TENNESSEE.

Memphis, 2d Ch., Aux., $12 50

Total, $12 50

WISCONSIN.

WISCONSIN BRANCH. — Mrs. R. Coburn, of Whitewater, Treas. *Arena,* 2.78; *Brandon,* 4.50; *Bristol* and *Paris,* 20; *Darlington,* 5; *Durand,* 10; *Eau Claire,* 20; *Koshkonong,* 7.07; *Milwaukee,* Grand Ave. Ch., 25.68; *Oshkosh,* friends, 2; *Ripon,* Mrs. A. E. Smith, 30.75; *Sparta,* 5.50; *Spring Green,* 3.65; *Union Grove,* 6.90; *Waupun,* 5, $153 83
JUNIORS: *Evansville,* 3.40; *Milwaukee,* Grand Ave.; 25,   28 40
FOR MORNING STAR: *Arena,* Mrs. E. R. Bovee,   5 69
Less expenses, 13.42.

Total, $174 50

MISCELLANEOUS.

Sale of "Coan's Life," 7; of leaflets, 55.76; of envelopes, 4.57; of chart, 60 cts., $67 93

Total, $67 93

Receipts for the month, $2,574 75
Previously acknowledged,   7,684 03

Total since Oct. 22, 1884, $10,258 78

Board of the Pacific.

A few months ago we had the pleasure of having with us at one of the meetings of our Board in San Francisco, Miss Evans, for twelve years a missionary in Tung-cho, China. Her familiar talk on matters connected with her life there was full of interest, and from a report of her address we make the following extracts : —

MISS EVANS described a visit made to one of the villages adjoining Tung-cho. In the first place, ladies rarely make any such visits unless invited to do so: it would not be proper.

A CHINESE AUDIENCE.

On reaching the village the news of their arrival spreads very quickly, and the house selected for service is filled before they reach it with an eager, curious throng of women and children. The houses are all on one floor, built of unburnt brick, and generally consist of two rooms. In the outer room the household goods are kept and the cooking is done; the inner room is where the family live. In the center is the bed — simply a raised platform of brick, which in the daytime takes the place of chairs and table. Seating themselves upon this bed, the lady missionaries invite the women to sit down, that they may talk with them. All stand aloof, a dirty, ragged throng — the jabbering of the women and the cries of the children making the scene a noisy one. Miss Evans said that sometimes, in looking upon such a company as this, and realizing how dark their minds were, she had asked herself, Have these creatures souls? But the thought that Christ died for all, " that these souls are precious in his sight as my own," has been most assuring. As, one by one, the women venture nearer, they ply the ladies with ques-

(197)

tions, such as, "Have you combed your hair to-day?" (a reflection upon Miss Evans's curls),— and others equally annoying, but which must be answered civilly — "What is your honorable name?" "How many children have you?" This last is a leading question, and its answer awakens suspicion ; the looks of distrust go round from one to another, for there are no respectable single women in China. They think there must be something wrong. But they have heard of Mr. and Mrs. Chapin, and when Miss Evans tells them Mrs. Chapin is her sister, and she makes her home in Mr. Chapin's family, the look of distrust gives place to one of relief. They examine her dress; they tell her it is very different from theirs. Now comes her opportunity: "Yes," she says, "we are different — different in dress, in language, and in religion. We have one God, who sees all things, who knows all things." From this starting-point it is easy to go on to the wonderful truths of the gospel, only they must be very slowly and gradually unfolded to be understood. Those of us who saw and heard Miss Evans, will follow her work with special interest. May she see the fruit of her labors even to the hundred-fold!

AN HOUR IN A CHINESE WOMAN'S BIBLE-HOUSE.

[Extracts from letters from Rev. C. R. Hagar to the *Pacific*.]

IT is a Sunday afternoon at the Canton hospital. Three Bible-services have already been held during the early part of the day, to which many of the patients and attendants have resorted; but this is the hour for Mrs. Dr. Kerr to instruct the women. I obtain permission to attend the service, so that I may see for myself how Bible-work among women is performed. I am to be a silent listener and a careful observer. The teacher's first object is to collect her scholars, and so she dispatches different ones to various parts of the hospital in quest of every woman. Some of them are a little loth to come, but she says they must come. She will not take no for an answer. One woman is just passing out, and about to leave the hospital; but she is stopped on the way, and compelled to attend Bible-class. To all this marshaling of the class I am a silent observer, and as they are brought around the teacher I cannot help but think that this is "compelling them to come in," and I recall the parable of the Saviour, of the man who made a great supper, and sent out his servants into the streets, lanes, highways, and hedges to compel the poor, the maimed, the halt, and the blind to come. Surely this scene is very much similar to that, for before me I see the aged, the lame, the halt, and blind, and if they have not been gathered directly from the highways and hedges, still they have come to this hospital from many a humble home, where poverty reigns, and where very often they have not enough to satiate their hunger. I do not wonder at the teacher's earnestness to have all present, for she knows not but that to some it may be the last opportunity to hear the gospel.

But at last we are all seated, and ready to begin. In all the company of forty or fifty women there are but few that can read, and these have been taught by the missionaries. There is no book in the hand of the. teacher; much less does she read from the sacred page. To the question previously asked, what chapter she would read, she replied: "I never read from the Bible to them, for they are too ignorant to understand what is read. Even the colloquial Gospels are incomprehensible to them. I can only tell them the story, and then very few comprehend what is said." And so the lesson is commenced, perhaps, by a very simple question of who made them, and who is the ruler of them all. Very many things are brought up that might seem to a Bible student irrelevant to the subject, but these poor women have only a few ideas. Money, food, and clothing are about the extent of a Chinese woman's knowledge, and with these few ideas many a Chinese woman lives and dies. Beyond this she knows little or nothing. No wonder that the teacher uses such simple language, and strives with all the ingenuity that she possesses to impress some truth upon them.

Even then she seems to fail. "How many souls have you?" she asks one whom she has brought very close to her; and what do you think the answer was ? "Seven souls." Oh, what a sense of oppression I felt in my heart as I heard that answer, and knew that it came from a heart that was as dark as night! Poor woman! and yet she is a representative of the Chinese women who are just so ignorant. But the teacher proceeds, trying to fasten some thought in their hearts here and there, and yet how difficult the task. Some of them can scarcely understand that this gospel is for them. From the creation to the cross the teacher goes step by step, and tries to enlighten them, and as a closing appeal she asks them all to tell the story to their friends. They promise, but perhaps they will not remember it until to-morrow.

A few picture-cards are distributed at the close for the little children who may be present with their mothers; but the mothers themselves are anxious to get them, even more so than they were to receive the gospel. Aye, a little card seems in their estimation to be of more value than the "pearl of great price." As I stand in the doorway to leave that sick-room I realize the greatness of the Chinese work, and especially that connected with the women. The picture of that hour is still in my memory, and I shall carry it to the grave. On the one hand I see the maimed bodies, the sightless eyes; on the other, souls clothed in the garments of the grossest superstition and of the blackest darkness. Their bodies are diseased, but their souls are far worse affected than the human frame, which soon must waste away. O light that has illuminated so many darkened lands, come to this vast empire, where woman is still a slave, and infanticide of the female sex is no secret!

A CHILD BAPTIZED.

One of the Christians, once a faithful helper in Sacramento, wished me to baptize his young son, not yet quite a month old. The mother is still a heathen, although her husband says she does not worship. "But," said I, "do not all your relatives still worship images?" "Yes; but my child is going to be a Christian." "I fear you do not understand the nature of infant baptism: it is a solemn thing for a parent to offer a child to God in baptism. I am afraid I cannot baptize your child while his mother is a heathen." "If I do not have my child baptized, my relatives will teach him to worship idols." "But what assurance have you that when you have returned to California they will not compel him to kneel to Buddah? You know it would be an awful thing if he should become an idolator after being baptized in Jesus' name." "I realize all this," said he; "but if my child is baptized, all the rest of my relatives will look upon him as being a Christian, and will not require him to worship the idols for them." And so, upon the solemn promise that he would bring up his child in the fear of the Lord, I consented to administer the rite. It was rather a mixed company that gathered in a small room in a newly-erected house. A few heathen men, with quite a number of children, were curious enough to see what was going to be done. A short prayer, a few words from the Bible read by all present, and then the administration of the sacred ordinance. "Do you promise that you will not permit this child to worship idols, images, or ancestors?" Slowly I uttered the words, waiting for the answer; and in a firm and unfaltering voice he said, "I promise." The other questions were equally as well answered, and so I baptized Lam Ch' eung Fat's little son. During the same time the gentry of the village were dedicating an ancestral hall. Would it not be interesting to know the future career of this child? Let us hope it may be one of the chosen vessels of God to preach the gospel to many.

VOL. XV. JUNE, 1885. No. 6.

INDIA.

WOMAN'S WORK IN THE MADURA MISSION.

BOARDING-SCHOOLS.

[From the Annual Report of the Mission.]

THERE are at present five boys' and four girls' boarding-schools, and one for both boys and girls. Those at Battalagundu are for the stations of Periakulum and Pulani, as well as Battalagundu. As a rule, no pupils are taken into the boys' schools without having passed the government second-standard examinations. This rule is more flexible in regard to girls' schools, except the Madura Boarding-School, which is an advanced institution, taking pupils to the middle school examination.

. . . Miss Chandler mentions items of interest in regard to the girls' boarding-school at Battalagundu. "With few exceptions the pupils have shown diligence in their studies, and as a result passed a most satisfactory examination at the end of the year. The teachers' staff has been well filled by the head-master and two graduates of the Madura Girls' Boarding-School. As the principal building was too crowded for comfort, a small thatched building has been put up outside the inclosure, to accommodate ten or twelve of the youngest pupils. We put one of our oldest girls in charge of the cooking department, promising her slight wages if she did well. This has proved an excellent arrangement, and we are thus enabled to reap from her faithfulness what has been sown in the years past. At the communion in October three girls were admitted to the church on profession of faith. Six others who had also shown a desire to be received were formed into an inquirers' class, and met with me weekly for the study of the Bible on subjects relating to their souls' salvation. At the last communion four more were admitted to the church. A class of three girls goes from us to the Madura Girls' Normal School.''

Of the Madura Girls' Boarding-School, Mrs. Jones reports:—

In some respects it has been a year of trials and changes. Miss Rendall left at the beginning of the year, and since then no one has been able to devote as much time and attention to the school as we felt it needed. In May, Mr. Thomas Rowland, the efficient and beloved head-master, died, after a long and painful illness, and it was some time before his place could be filled. Miss Swift has been now for some months studying the language, and will ere long be able to take charge of the school.

The year closed with the government examination, which showed the classes in good order and training. There have been seventy-three pupils connected with the school this year. One, a day scholar, a little Hindu girl, died recently of cholera. Eleven of the older girls have united with the churches in the city, and others leave with the desire of uniting with the churches in their own stations. We expect to establish a normal department in the school the coming year, in order to prepare our girls more efficiently for teachers. This special course will begin with the fifth standard, and extend through the middle school. We look upon the work of the school as very important in its influence upon our educated Christian women, and hope the changes in prospect will add in every way to its usefulness.

HINDU GIRLS' SCHOOLS.

There are at the close of the year twelve Hindu girls' schools, with a total of five hundred and eighteen girls in attendance. Mr. Tracy mentions as a pleasant feature of the school at Tirumangalam, the readiness of the girls to attend regularly the Sabbath services. He reports, also, that, through the kindness of friends in America, a convenient and substantial building has been erected this year. That the children enjoy their school, and derive benefit as well as pleasure from being in it, we have many evidences. In times of sickness the Bible-woman is welcomed to their homes, and Bible-reading and prayer are not forbidden. Although there has been no resident missionary at Pulani, the Hindu girls' school has not only been kept up, but has done remarkably well. There has been an increasing amount of Bible instruction in the school at Dindigul. Dr. Chester adds, that there is no doubt that those who have studied in this school make better wives and mothers.

Mrs. Capron writes of the Hindu Girls' School in Madura City as follows:—

I have charge of four of these schools, with three masters and nine mistresses. The whole number in attendance during the year has been four hundred and twenty-two, and our number at present is two hundred and sixty-one girls. . . . The constant removals are a hindrance to substantial progress. In the North School an interesting little talk had been given on the words, "His name shall be called the Everlasting Father." A few weeks afterward a little girl who had seemed to be impressed with the words, died of small-pox. During her sickness she found pleasure in saying over those words. There have been two deaths among those connected with the South Gate School. One of the girls had passed the fourth standard, and had been prevailed upon to join the girls' boarding-school as a day-scholar. She had for a long time shown the effects of the truth by her changed conduct. She and her mother have, in the face of much opposition, long expressed their faith in the Lord Jesus Christ. The other case was that of a little girl in the second standard. When I went to see her, I asked what the blessed Saviour said to dear little girls like herself. Though burning hot with fever she promptly replied: "He says, 'I am the bright and morning star. They that seek me early shall find me.'" The next day she begged her grandmother to take her to school, that she might see the teacher once more. We have much comfort in remembering how her heart seemed to open to all holy influences.

VILLAGE SCHOOLS.

Outside the larger towns the village schools are usually small and irregular. The fact that the children of the Christians have to work during the busy season, often breaks up a school for months at a time. In the larger towns anglo-vernacular schools are kept up more easily, the pupils consisting of high-caste Hindu children. While the majority have more or less Christian pupils in attendance, there are quite a number who do not have a single Christian pupil. The Bible, however, is taught in all the schools. Mr. Chandler speaks of the examination in Bible of a village school where there is not a Christian pupil, as very creditable. He mentions, also, another heathen school where the boys hold a meeting by themselves to study the Bible, and who always begin their meeting with prayer. Pastor Seymour speaks of a similar instance. Owing to the new and increased fees called for by the Government for schools which have fifth-standard pupils, some schools have decreased in size by the discontinuance of the fifth-standard classes.

A native pastor writes: —

I have eight Christian schools in my village. I visited one of them on a Sunday, when the teacher was away. I found, to my surprise, all the boys and girls assembled, and asked them why they had come together on Sunday. They said they had been having a prayer-meeting. When asked how they conducted it, they said one of them read the forty-sixth Psalm, and then they all prayed. When I asked them for what they prayed, they said they asked God to bless their teacher and pastor, and to move the hearts of their parents to give up their idols, and become Christians, and that they might build a large church for the worship of the true God. The parents of these children are heathen, and the boy who conducted the meeting is the son of the head man of the village.

TURKEY.

LETTER FROM MISS WEST.

AINTAB, TURKEY, Dec. 27, 1884.

MY DEAR FRIENDS IN AMERICA: It is with a joyful heart that I write you at last of my safe arrival at Aintab. This first week in my new home has been full of varied experiences, but all have caused me to give a hearty response to the *Khosh gel den* (welcome) that I hear everywhere. As I look at the bright, interesting faces of the girls assembled in the schoolroom, and think of the influence they will exert in their homes here and in adjoining towns, my heart rejoices in the new field of labor to which the Lord has called me.

Eleven weeks ago to-day I was sitting on the stern of the Cephalonia, watching the lights along the western horizon that marked the place where I had had such an affectionate farewell. Many thousand miles intervene now, but God has heard the prayers following our missionary party. The journey has been a very pleasant one; it seems as if the sunshine had followed us all the way from America. The voyage was considered an unusually fine one. From Liverpool our route was a most interesting panorama,—the cultivated lands of England; Holland, with its dikes and windmills; the picturesque scenery of the Rhine; and Vienna, with its broad streets, handsome buildings, and beautiful gardens. In order to escape the quarantine we should have met had we gone down the Danube, all our party took the five days' carriage ride across the Balkan Mountains, from Nissa to Philippopolis (thus accompanying the Marsh family all the way to their home), and thence on to Constantinople by rail.

At Samokov we spent the Sabbath. It was a privilege to meet the missionaries there, especially Miss Graves, with whom I talked as with an adopted sister, for our interests in the Essex South Branch are one. The older girls of the school speak English very readily, and I was asked to take their Sunday-school class. I believe I never enjoyed teaching God's Word more. The church is small, but was well filled, the preaching services being conducted by one of the native preachers. Though the language was strange to me, yet it was beautiful to think that the language of our hearts was the same, as I joined with those native people in worshiping the one Lord and Saviour. Does it pay to preach his gospel in foreign lands? Oh, I wish the thoughtless and doubtful ones at home could have felt the influence of that meeting, and seen how the Lord had blessed his work in Samokov!

A hearty welcome was awaiting us at Philippopolis. Miss Stone met us with a face full of the same enthusiasm which brightened it as we listened to her words in America. Here we left Mr. Marsh's family, which had formed such a pleasant part of our party, and in two days were in Constantinople, where Mr. Barnum's family is to be located. It was my privilege to spend a few days with Mrs. Schneider, a description of whose work is to be found in the November number of LIFE AND LIGHT. I trust every one will read it, and pray more earnestly for this valuable work under her direction. With grateful feelings for this opportunity of seeing Constantinople friends, and receiving their warm words of welcome to Turkey, I accompanied Miss Bartlett to her home in Smyrna, where I was necessarily delayed for three weeks, waiting for company. Though impatient over the delay, I felt I was learning valuable lessons in missionary life, by seeing what the Lord could do with hearts and hands consecrated to his service.

The work among the Greeks in Smyrna seems specially encouraging; about sixty remained after one meeting for special prayer and personal talk. How I wish you could visit the girls' school in charge of the Misses Page and Lord! Do you ask how it is progressing? Go with me at the noon hour through that front hall to the teachers' room, and, opening the door gently, you will find the missionaries, the native teachers, and pastors in prayer. Sometimes the prayers are in three different languages; but they are to him who knows the language of all hearts, and says, "Ask and ye shall receive." Is not this daily noon meeting a main wheel of all the machinery of that school?

· Once more on the steamer — this time on the calm, blue waters of the Mediterranean Sea. How often the twenty-first chapter of Acts came to mind as I stood upon the deck and viewed the places that had been familiar to the Apostle Paul. I did not land at Tyre, but early on the fourth morning we reached Alexandretta, where Mr. Saunders was waiting to accompany me to Aintab. As I received the message he brought me from Miss Pierce, and saw the many things she had sent to make my ride into the interior comfortable, I began to feel that I was approaching my journey's end. How my heart rejoiced over my American mail that she had thoughtfully sent to me! For nearly ten weeks I had heard no word from those of whom I had thought daily.

It had been such a wonder to me how I was to get from Alexandretta to Aintab, that I will give some details of the overland journey for those of my friends who have been also wondering.

You would have been amused could you have seen our caravan as we set forth. Mr. Saunders led off, on his horse named "Gipsy," and I followed, on Miss Pierce's little gray pony. Bédros, the servant, appeared next, on a third horse, on which were the saddle-bags, packed with various dishes, eatables, bedding, etc.; and fourthly came the *kastiji* (driver), riding his donkey, and leading two horses with our boxes and trunks strapped to their backs.

So much had been said to me about the probable discomfort of the last part of my journey, especially because it would come in winter, that I had prepared myself for an unpleasant time. But the day was so bright, "Kate" was such a gentle horse, and, above all, my nice, new saddle was so comfortable, speaking continually to me of the dear sisters at home, that our first stopping-place was reached about two hours after sunset with little or no fatigue. Dismounting, I entered the curious little *khan*, and looked about the one room, wondering what accommodation it would afford for me, as it seemed filled with men, who were smoking and talking. But Mr. Saunders had provided for such an emergency, and a curtain was hung across one corner, behind which I retired, and had a nice time all to myself, reading over my precious letters. Made comfortable by a good supper from the saddle-bags, and with plenty of warm wraps for the night, I forgot my surroundings as soon as the voices on the other side of the curtain were exchanged for the silence of the stars, which peeped in through the little windows at the top of the low mud-wall of the *khan*.

As "one by one night's candles went out, and jocund day stood tiptoe on the misty mountain-top," we were again on our way. I need not tell you that the lunch at noon, in the bright sunshine and near a well by the wayside, was eaten with great relish. Once more in the saddle, five hours' ride brought us to another *khan* similar to the one where we had spent the preceding night.

We continued our journey the next day through broad plains, over steep hills, fording streams, going through places that sometimes in December are quite impassable. We had reason to be very thankful for the fine weather that favored us. Occasionally we met a train of camels going to the coast, sometimes a shepherd with a flock of sheep near a village. At one place we saw a "Rebecca at the well," drawing water — not with an "old oaken bucket," but with the Oriental bottles made of skin. It was a delight to pick the crocuses and pass the olive groves after going through sections that seemed nothing but heaps of stones. Early in the afternoon we came in sight of Killis, with its flat-roofed houses and pointed minarets. As we entered the city many Moslems were standing at prayer in an open square before a mosque. The sight caused a prayer to go from my heart that the gospel light might reach their darkened minds. The children laughed, and called after us, as we made our way to the homes of the native Protestant friends. What a hearty welcome the pastor gave us! Turfanda, the Bible-reader, came in with a face so bright and happy that one could not but get sunshine from it.

A school of about thirty young children, kept by graduates of Aintab Seminary, had not yet closed its afternoon session. I visited it with great interest, and was more than ever convinced of the far-reaching influence of the school with which I was to be connected.

The next morning clouds threatened rain, and gave us only a brisk shower, which moistened our bread as we took our dinner in the usual manner, when we again mounted. The horses needed no urging, for they knew well that only the hills ahead of us separated them from their final stopping-place. Soon Mr. Saunders reined his horse near mine, saying, "Beyond that turn in the road you can distinctly see your new home." The sun came out of the clouds as if to make ready a welcome, and in a few moments we saw approaching the missionary friends who had received our dispatch from Killis, and had come out to meet us.

I must leave you to become missionaries yourselves before you can know what it is to be met in such a way, and escorted to a new home in a strange Eastern city.

It was a happy family that sat down to tea that night — Miss Pierce and I at the table in one end of the dining-room, the schoolgirls seated on the floor around their trays, now and then giving shy glances from their bright eyes at the new-comers.

JAN. 10, 1885.

I have delayed sending the above that I might add a few things about the days which have occupied the thoughts of so many in the dear home-land, and have not passed unnoticed here.

Early on Christmas morning I accompanied the school to a union service of the three Protestant churches of Aintab, held at the First Church. So many things are just the opposite in Turkey from what they are with us — as one instance, prayer-meetings are before light instead of after dark. The large church was filled — the women sitting on the floor on one side of the church, the men on the opposite side. I was told that about one thousand persons were present. Though it was so very early in the day, I saw no one returning to the land of dreams from which they had just come. The long sermon, however, conveyed no ideas to me; but as the light of the morning dawned, displacing the dim light of the lamps, do you not think I was led to wonder in how many hearts around me the Sun of righteousness was shining?

New-Year's Day was a busy day with us; over one hundred called. I found use for every Turkish word I knew in helping Miss Pierce entertain so many.

And this is the Week of Prayer! Dear sisters, God's children here, though of different language and customs, are bowing at the same mercy-seat with you, and making the same petitions. There is power in united prayer, and surely a blessing will follow these. Services have been held here at the First Church every morning before sunrise, and at the Second Church at four in the afternoon. Many of the pupils of the Seminary are very thoughtful, and some are earnestly seeking the Saviour. While very busy about my work the other day I heard the voices of some of the girls in prayer. They had retired to a room near mine, for the purpose of talking with Him whom they had learned to love. While I was dwelling on the thoughts these sounds suggested, the *muezzin's* cry rang out from the minaret, calling Moslems to the worship of the false prophet. Are you not glad that you are helping, by your prayers, your Christian sympathy, your money, to support this school, which is such a power for good among the young girls of this land, and in time must also influence the Moslem community?

Do you ask me if I am happy here? How can I be otherwise? I never before realized how Christ can make up to us what we resign for his sake.

There is work in learning a language; it requires wisdom and knowledge to train these dear girls to a higher, better life; all about me there is so much to be done; but in Heb. iv. 15, 16 there is a precious promise which includes the smaller, every-day cares, as well as the greater burdens of life. Yes, dear sisters, with my whole heart I sing now, as when I stood upon the deck of the Cephalonia and sang with you, —

> " My faith looks up to Thee,
> Thou Lamb of Calvary."

GLEANINGS FROM RECENT LETTERS.
FROM MISS EMILY HARTWELL, OF FOOCHOW.

. . . CHINA New-Year's time is here again; and as this is the great time of the year among the natives, — the time for settling all debts, and making a clean page for the next year's beginning, — and as it was about this time that I arrived last year, I feel very much like taking a review of the year.

I am very glad that I can say that I think things have been growing better all the time; and when I contrast the present with a year since, I feel very thankful for the present, notwithstanding all the war and trouble with which we are surrounded. A year ago I was the only foreign woman in all this great city; now there are three just across the way, and one a doctor.

The war-cloud does not seem to lift. The officials have been very much afraid the French would return, and during the last few days the river has been closed to steamers by torpedoes; and instead of being allowed to come up to Pagoda Anchorage, they must anchor at Sarp's Peak. This will be a great hindrance to the business of the port, and we hope it will not last long; but it may continue until the war ends — which at present seems a far distant time, unless something more decisive is done. We often wonder what good can come from this very tedious delay; but we remember that the Chinese move very slowly as a mass, and it may be that the subject of foreign power and its source must be held before the people for a long time, in order to really awaken them from their proud indifference.

You may think it strange, but I think this year is better than last, because the war was approaching then; now we are in it, and must be nearer the end, although we cannot see it. It is good to live here now, because we are experiencing the kind providence of God in allowing us to stay here and work in the midst of excitement and trouble, and to see that the war is doing our work more good than harm. My father has just been to Changloh, and he says he sees that this is more than ever a good time to work, for the people are more attentive.

It seems to me that I can understand the Old Testament much better since I see how manifestation of power is needed to awaken these Chinese. God wrought signs and wonders then, and now the heathen seem to need to see the wonder of his power — the physical force nations have gained from Christian civilization — before the foreigner's God is made real to them, or worthy of their thought and attention. Surely God does cause the wrath of man to praise him in thus bringing good out of this unrighteous war.

It happened that just a year after I came was the day of the woman's prayer-meeting, and I led it for the first time. I took the subject of the crucifixion, and read most of the nineteenth chapter of John. It was a chapter that moved my woman teacher very much. As we read it together, she said it was something to weep over. This woman is an inquirer, and she says she is gradually letting out her feet, and I hope she will continue until they are quite natural size. We have had considerable discussion on the subject of foot-binding, of late, and the teacher of the day-school which Mrs. Walker has had at her house decided to let out her feet. She began in earnest, taking off all her bandages; but this is not the best way to do, as the feet are so weak that they cannot be used at all if they are unbound, and the blood rushes into them so fast that they become inflamed. The best way is to loosen the bandages, and sometimes it is months before the feet are as useful in walking as when they are bound; but in time they are, of course, far superior.

This delicate Chinese lady knew that her family, especially her mother-in-law, would bitterly oppose her, but she thought her husband would uphold her after it was done. We were afraid to urge her to do it, but she seemed to become convinced herself, and did it of her own free will. We were all very much disappointed, therefore, when her husband called and told her that, while she might lengthen out her feet, it would never do to let them out wholly. She now has feet about twice as large as before, and is waiting and hoping to let them out fully, in time. Pray for her, especially, that her light may enlighten her whole house.

FROM MRS. WINSOR, OF SIRUR, INDIA.

We are here in the Sirur Mission home, on the rough hillside, in sight of those villages in regard to which some of you in America are greatly interested. Glad are we to be at rest from traveling, and at home at work again; thankful, too, to the kind heavenly Father, who hath brought us through all the seen and unseen dangers to our desired haven.

We had a welcome which, in its brightness and heartiness, was a real surprise to us. We were within ten miles of Sirur, when Sawalyoram, one of our native pastors, came rushing toward us, riding on a native pony. It seemed but yesterday that we had bade this Christian brother a sad farewell; and now we met with smiles and joy. In about three-quarters of an hour we met others, who had brought out garlands of flowers, with which they covered us; they begged us to walk our ponies, so they could walk by our sides.

When we reached the industrial school building we were met by a group of Christians with a (native) band of music, and were escorted by them to our house. Just beyond the girls' school-building we were met by the children of the station school, each one bearing a tall bamboo, on the top of which was a small, bright flag of welcome. As we approached the carriage-road leading to our bungalow, we discovered that it was lined with a row of bamboos with the bright flags such as the children carried. Just before the steps of the house was an arch, which was crowned with the words in Marathi, "How beautiful are the feet of them that preach the gospel of peace, and bring glad tidings of good things!"

As we ascended the steps of the house, the pastor, Sudaba, opened a bottle of perfume, and in true Eastern style poured it upon the travelers. So, amid sweet perfume and flowers we entered our home again. We found the veranda filled with people, Hindus and Christians, but the best of all was the pleasure of uniting with the dear Christians in prayer and praise to the heavenly Father, thanking him that we had been brought safely over the great waters, and that the dear people in America had sent us back again to our work. After an hour of prayer and praise, our native friends suggested that we should continue the same the next day, and proposed that on New-Year's day we all meet together in the chapel. The next day we had a precious season of thanksgiving in the chapel, during which original hymns and addresses of welcome were given. We could not be too grateful for the very delightful way everything was done for us, and for the thoughtfulness of our dear native friends. It seems good to be among these women once more.

I wish you could have gone with me yesterday to the sewing-school; could have seen those who could not cut out the garments, being taught by those who could; could have heard the song of Jesus' love sung by those who love Jesus, to those who could not sing it because they did not love him. I feel much relieved to have such a good supply of material from friends in America, and the school-children are greatly encouraged by the gifts of books, cards, puzzles, pictures, and other articles. One of the girls, an especially lovely child, has united with the church during our absence. She says she is determined hereafter to "love Jesus all the time." While we are doing what we can for the station school and for the people about us, the call comes from the outside villages, "Come and see us, and tell us of Christ." "Come! we want to see our missionaries." We must soon march away with our tents, and from the villages far away from Sirur we shall hope to write to the Christian friends at home.

On Monday of the Week of Prayer, Mr. Winsor begged the people to see what each could do for his or her neighbor. "Let each one during the year lead at least one to Jesus." In two days one of the women came to the bungalow with a friend, saying, "This is my neighbor, who has decided to leave all for Christ." I was so rejoiced to see this woman, who had formerly been a member of my sewing-school, coming out on the Lord's side! Oh, pray for us, that this year of 1885 may be one of special blessing to us in these stations and in these villages!

FROM MISS M. J. GLEASON, OF CONSTANTINOPLE.

. . . I must tell you about Dr. Somerville's visit to us. He is a Scotch clergyman, who has been pastor of a church in Glasgow for forty years. For some time he has been traveling as an evangelist, and has been all over the world. He is doing what has never before been thought possible, — speaking to crowds of Armenians, Greeks, Jews, and others. We have no large churches, and no hall; but he has done the best he could. Some of his meetings for Greeks were in a large German hall in Pera, and crowded full. He has been four times to the Bible House, where he has had an audience of from four hundred and fifty to five hundred; and such an audience of fine-looking men — many of them young men — has never been seen here before. He speaks through an interpreter, but with such power that he holds the people spellbound for two or three hours. His illustrations are wonderfully beautiful and forcible, and he makes the Bible truths so plain that no one can forget what he has said. I cannot begin to tell you how anxious we are to have so many in whom we are personally interested decide now for Christ. We sit and listen with our whole hearts, so thankful that this one and that one is there to hear his earnest words. We thought we must have him at our house, for the sake of some of our young men and women who would not go to a church, and he kindly consented to come. The people came till the house was full, and many had to go away. There were two hundred and fifty present, and I think he gave us one of his best sermons. It was about Zaccheus, and he made it so plain, filling out the outlines given in Luke with his wonderful imagination, making it seem as if we were there, to see and hear it all. He brought out the plan of salvation most forcibly, and his invitations to all to come and be saved, was just what we have been longing to have said to the people. Many heard these things for the first time, and at times there was an intense stillness. They sat with their mouths open, and just drank it in. I think I never enjoyed anything so much as to see them.

Young People's Department.

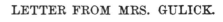

SPAIN.

LETTER FROM MRS. GULICK.

WE begin the Week of Prayer with very thankful hearts.

The First Evangelical Church of San Sebastian has been formally organized recently, with some twenty members.

Next Sabbath, at the communion service, four will unite with us for the first time, after making a public profession of their faith in their crucified and risen Saviour. Three of these are our own girls, and we hope and pray that the occasion may be one of such solemnity and power, that a great blessing may come upon the school.

We have had reason these last months to bless the Lord for preserving this family intact, when pestilence and plague have been all about us. The cholera, which has made such sad havoc in the south of France, and has appeared in several places in Spain, has not broken out in this exposed city. There has been an epidemic of small-pox twice during the year in San Sebastian, but it has not been allowed to come near this dwelling.

You will have heard of the terrible inundations in the Province of Valencia, on account of which hundreds have been rendered homeless, and their rice-fields and orange groves utterly destroyed.

While we were enjoying our Christmas-tree, December 25th, the Provinces of Granada and Malaga were visited by a devastating earthquake. Some villages have disappeared; others are nearly destroyed, and hundreds of bodies lie buried beneath the ruins. Those who have escaped the earthquake are encamped in the fields, without sufficient clothing, without food, and with terror in their hearts.

The more ignorant believe that the end of the world is at hand, and they wildly cry to God and the saints to protect them. A mountain has been cleft in two, and the continued shocks, up to January 1st, prove that the volcanic force has not yet expended itself. The shocks have been felt as far north as Madrid, but we have dwelt in safety. Have we not, then, abundant reason to believe that God's protecting love is about us, who are no more worthy than others to be thus cared for?

Perhaps the most notable event lately, in this quiet household, has been the wedding.

One of our first graduates who has been teaching for two years, during the last few months became engaged to a young man, a member of the church in Santander, a student in Mr. Thomas Gulick's theological class in Zaragoza — also a teacher.

The civil marriage in Spain is a matter of much red tape, many papers, and of some expense. All that the Protestant pastor can do is to have a religious ceremony in which God's blessing is asked upon those about to be married.

About a month ago we supposed all the necessary forms had been gone through with: the judge had also promised to perform the ceremony on the following day. The girls brought greens and flowers and decorated the rooms. All was ready, when Mr. Gulick received word that owing to a technical mistake of the Secretary the banns would have to be republished, and the wedding must be postponed. The green leaves withered, the flowers faded, we ate the cake, and time passed slowly by.

Mr. Gulick was called to Zaragoza, and to Pradejon to attend the dedication of a church. He was to leave on the 27th of December; when we received word that on *that* day the judge would perform the marriage ceremony. What should be done?

Neither the journey nor the marriage could be postponed, and the worthy couple would not go unblessed. So we compromised the matter by appointing the religious service at 6.30 o'clock in the morning, so as to allow Mr. Gulick to take the 8 o'clock train for Zaragoza.

I awoke at 3 o'clock; and shortly after the household machinery was in motion, the breakfast was prepared, and at 6.30 the invited guests and schoolgirls were assembled in the double parlor, already warmed and lighted.

The ceremony concluded (which, by the way, was much more impressive than the real marriage service afterward), we went to the breakfast-table, where we gratefully partook of coffee, bread and butter, and a large "bride's cake." In the meantime Mr. Gulick said "Good-bye," and we remained talking until the sunbeams forced their way through the closed shutters, revealing the fact that it was already day.

In the afternoon we went to the Judge's office with the young couple, where they were asked to sit upon a bench used by criminals or others brought there to be tried.

The judge walked in with his hat planted upon his head, which he removed only when he was ready to seat himself in his chair. He was evidently nervous, as this was his first "case" of marriage,—and possibly with him it was a case of conscience as well, for he is of known Carlist sentiments; consequently, believing only in marriage by the Church of Rome.

Spanish law is rather strict, we find, in regard to the position of the wife. One clause amused us much, as the wife is thereby prohibited from publishing any literary or scientific work without the consent of her other — shall I say *better* — half?

The new year begins with promise, and we hope that good will be done in the coming months. Will you especially ask for a spiritual blessing for us?

<hr>

MILK AND MISSIONS.

BY K. CONWAY.

"You see, Melissy, the other day when I was down to the city with some butter, an' eggs, an' chickens, — them last ones was proper plump, an' tender, too — Mis' Dean, she that used to live up by the schoolhouse, you know, but they moved into town, 'cause Tudy must go to the Young Ladies' Sem'nary, an' take music lessons, an' I don't know what all, an' they call her Gertrude, now — well, Mis' Dean, she says, 'Now, Mis' Slocum, can't you jest take off your things an' stay over night? You kin turn the horse and buggy right into the barn, an' there's goin' to be a meetin' to our church to-night, an' a lady from Turkey's goin' to speak, an' 'taint often you have a chance to hear a missionary.' An' I says to her, 'I don't have no faith in them foreign missions, Mis' Dean, there's sech misery an' heathenish doin's in our own land, what with 'them uneducated, shiftless things down South an' them folks out to the West, — that they actooally do say worships Mormon, or somethin' like; anyway they have no end of wives, — and the poor at our own doors; but I don't mind if I do stay over, bein' as I didn't get time to buy me a new gingham I'm wantin', an' I won't hender you from goin'·to the meetin'.' But after supper she said I must go with her, so's to keep her comp'ny; an' I didn't want to seem hateful, for Mis' Dean she was always real kind an' neighbor-like when she lived here, so I went along.

Well, there was a lot of folks there, an' the missionary she talked for quite a spell, an' 'twas real int'restin' to hear her tell how they built the house they live in, an' a schoolhouse, carryin' stones on their backs, an' gettin' the windows in crooked, an' havin' to do 'em over again; an' when she told about a revival they had, I declare for't, 'twas jest like people to this country, 'stead of them heathen, that I couldn't never make myself believe had many brains. But I thought, after all, I wasn't goin' to send none of my money 'way out there, the land knows where; so when they come around to take up a c'lection for to help build a road for the missionaries, I jest hardened my heart, an' set back. An' then, first I knew, I heard her say 'milk;' an' thinks I to myself, for the land's sakes, what's milk got to do with foreign missions ? an' this is what she was sayin': 'We found a woman who was willin' to sell us milk; but you know, dear friends, the people are very superstitious, an' we always had to put some salt in the pail that we sent, or else she would have bad luck come to her; an' she must always put in a coal, to keep off 'the evil eye;' an' then she couldn't think of sellin' milk that wa'n't cooked, so 'twas always boiled; an' they're not very careful or very clean, an' the milk would be burned, an' the dish they cooked it in wasn't washed, an' they was always very generous to water it, an' by the time we got it — well, somehow, 'twasn't very good.' Well, Melissy, I just set there a-thinkin' of all the nice, comf'table brown and buff creatures out to our barn, an' how the pails was filled all white, an' clean, an' foamy every night, an' how partic'lar I was to always scald them pails an' pans, an' strain every drop o' milk, so's not even an eyelash should get into the pitcher; an' even then how Darius'd set down his glass sometimes, an' speak of two or three little specks that like as not was in the glass, an' not.in the milk, after all; an' then I thought of them women goin' out there, workin' with all their might, an' tryin' to live on sech stuff as that to cook with an' drink, an' it seemed to me as if I couldn't stan'.it, an' I was wishin' I could jest send one of our cows out to 'em, only I couldn't seem to see how I could manage it; an' then the minister he up and says, 'I think we want to help buy a cow, so they kin have one of their own; an' a man jumps up an' says,

'Cows is pretty good stock, an' I'll take five dollars' worth;' an' another one he put in for a share, an' a mission Sunday-school took a five-dollar share, an' I was wishin' I was a man for a minnit, so's I could say I'd do somethin', an' jest then around come that man with the hat agen; an' I — well, I didn't buy no gingham next day, an' I no need to, really, you know, for the one I had two years ago is lastin' well, what with puttin' new unders to the sleeves. An' thinkin' things over after we went home, it kind o' struck me that Turkey wan't no further off than Utah, so far as any chance of my gettin' to either place was concerned; an' so, after all, distance not bein' counted, 'twas sort of home missions, an' I rather allowed I'd better take hold an' help 'em a little.

An' next day when I was comin' home, Mis' Dean she gave me a little tract, only 'twas a story like, about a woman that put by some butter out of every pound, an' some eggs out of every dozen, an' so on, to give to missions; an' 'twas consid'able my case, only her husband was close-fisted, which Dari' he ain't, an' I told him some 'bout the meetin', an' how I didn't buy my gingham; an' then I left that little tract where I knew he'd pick it up an read it, bein' cur'us like, as most men are. But I didn't say nothin' till he come in from the barn one night, an' says he, 'Nancy, that new cow gives a powerful sight of milk; you'll have to be makin' butter oftener. An' I've be'n thinkin', Nancy, p'raps you'd better call that cow yours, an' then what you make off of butter an' milk you could have to give away like that woman did in the story;' an' do you know, Melissy, I was that pleased that I couldn't hardly say a word; but I think Dari' he understood. An' in the evenin' I was fixin' the sleeves to my dress, an' he picked up a piece of it, lookin' at it kind o' smiley, an' says, 'I'm rather pleased you didn't get a new gown, wife; this one always looked so neat an' pretty on you, an' I like to see you wear it.' An', Melissy, he ain't no great for sentiment, you know, an' it jest did me good to find out that he noticed what I'd been wearin', for I always used to try to please him when I was a young thing, an' so I got into the way of buyin' what I thought he'd like; but I don't know as that belongs to my story 'special. An' now you know how I come to believe in foreign missions; for if men an women is willin' to go out 'mongst them heathen, an' if, with the help of the Lord, they kin bring 'em to be decent folks, lovin' an' servin him, we'd ought to help 'em, an' not let 'em want for the necessities of life, which I count milk one!"

Our Work at Home.

"IT IS THE HAND OF CHRIST;"
OR, A CONTRIBUTION-BOX TRANSFORMED.

IT was the Sabbath for the semi-annual contribution to the missionary society, of which announcement had been made a week previous. According to her usual custom, Mrs. Whitcomb expected to put fifty cents into the box. If the amount seemed small to others, her conscience was quieted by a thought of two dollars paid annually to the Ladies' Missionary Society, which was auxiliary to the other.

"There are so many objects for benevolence, so many calls nowadays, one must plan justly for all, and not 'rob Peter to pay Paul,'" was a favorite saying of Mrs. Whitcomb. One habit of this lady was to look over a collector's book before pledging a first subscription to any cause. If the amount credited to most subscribers was fifty cents or a dollar, she accepted this as the limit of payment for herself, without any comparison of her ability with the majority of supporters. No special pleas, no suggestions to "double contributions," or presentations of present needs, moved her to increased and occasional large-hearted giving. "One must never be governed by impulse in these matters," was often urged in explanation; "in charity, as in everything else, I am controlled by judgment and experience."

It was most fortunate that the "regular fee" paid by his wife was not infrequently supplemented by Judge Whitcomb with sub stantial donations. These were always signed "From a friend," to escape the imputation of prodigality and unsound judgment from his better half. To prevent unwarrantable liberality, the judge's wife often took the precaution to sound her husband upon his intentions shortly before a stated collection, and advised as to the amount to be given. Knowing his special leaning toward missions, the prudent lady felt some misgivings upon the Sabbath in question; so, as they were about starting for church, she casually reminded her husband of the collection, — as if there were any need, — adding, "I have some change in my purse if you have none."

The judge had, on the previous evening, taken special care to empty his pocket of all coin, in anticipation of the coming collection; for how could he drop change into the box if he hadn't any! The good man had been reprimanded upon several occasions for depositing a bill. "It is as well to give dollars where your name is signed, and there is some accountability; but small coin will do for the box," had been the instruction.

In deep chagrin the would-be-generous man turned to his wife, unequal to the emergency. She guessed the secret, but purposely misinterpreted his silence, and bantered him upon forgetting his favorite collection, adding, "Never mind; I have enough for us both. How much do you want?"

"Oh, I have money enough with me, but you can let me have a half-dollar, if you like," was the reply, made with such apparent sincerity that the schemer was puzzled. The silver piece was handed over with much self-querying: "Does anybody suppose he'll really give only half a dollar? There is hope of reformation in the most stubborn, if John is at last become prudent."

The choir usually rendered some incomprehensible "voluntary," but the opening of service that day was very unusual. A simple gospel hymn was sung. From a sweet voice the words directly fell upon Mrs. Whitcomb's ear:—

> "I gave, I gave my life for thee,
>   My precious blood I shed;
> I gave, I gave my life for thee,
>   What hast thou given for me?"

The prayers which followed were embodiments of two petitions : that the people might be able and ready to make large and grateful return for the blessings of salvation, and be enabled to regard the Lord's work with a spirit purified from selfishness and avarice. After the reading of the notices the pastor said : "The collection to-day will be taken after the sermon. Let us, my dear people, consider together our duty and privilege in the matter of giving to the Lord. Let us look at the urgent need for increased liberality in every part of the vineyard, and then make unto the Master a free-will offering, both sweet and acceptable."

Thinking of her husband's unaccountable conduct, of the opening hymn, with its refrain still echoing through her mind, and of the unusual postponement of the collection till the close of the service, Mrs. Whitcomb did not pay much heed to the discourse. Meditation during the sermon is ever a potent soporific; and such· it proved.

It was most natural that her waking thoughts should follow Mrs. Whitcomb in sleep, and that she should, in dreams, see good old Deacon Beman come down the aisle to gather the tithes into the storehouse. The dreamer very vividly went through the form of taking a half-dollar from her pocket and lifting it to the extended box — when lo! it was a box no longer! With chilled heart the lady saw the hard, lifeless wood assume the appearance of living flesh. It was a hand, now, and from its pierced veins flowed drops of blood. Looking up, she beheld a form like unto the Son of God, with a face which betokened a knowledge of grief and acquaintance with sorrows. Almost paralyzed with remorse the sleeper cried, "Have mercy upon me, O Lord! I am not worthy to put aught into my Saviour's hand."

With pained and pleading look these words were spoken:—

> "I gave my life for thee;
> Wilt thou give naught to me?"

Quickly the half-dollar was thrown away by the trembling listener, and a coin of gold was laid instead upon the bleeding palm. As the shining bit touched the wound the flow of blood was lessened. In the attitude of divine benediction the Lord Christ thus spoke: "Disciple, thou hast wrought a good work upon me. The tears of my people must be wiped away; the nations must be purged from sin; the gospel of good tidings must sound in every ear before this bleeding wound can be wholly healed. Blessed be they who hasten on the day!"

Deep organ tones wakened the sleeper when the collection was about to be taken. Clutching at her husband's arm, Mrs. Whitcomb whispered eagerly, "John, you won't put in that fifty cents, will you? Why, dear, it is the hand of the Lord!" In bewilderment the judge looked at his bewildered wife, who pleaded again: "I mean the contribution box, John; it is the hand of Christ, our Lord! Could you lay a few cents upon it?" "No, wife," was the joyous reply; "I will give fifteen dollars." "Very well; and I'll give as much more."

Was it his wife who thus spoke — the same who had outwitted him in the morning? Yes, the very same woman, renewed. She had seen the Lord, and heard his words; she had learned the deep meaning of the Saviour's "inasmuch." Never again would "good judgment" keep her from ministering to her crucified Redeemer through the poor, the sorrowing, and the benighted. The contribution-box had been transformed; but still more wonderful and blessed was the transformation that had taken place in one of the King's daughters! — *Congregationalist.*

A HELPFUL BOOK.

OUR EASTERN SISTERS, AND THEIR MISSIONARY HELPERS. BY HARRIET WARNER ELLIS; PP. 184. ANSON D. F. RANDOLPH & CO., NEW YORK.

THIS book gives a rapid survey of the work done by women in educating and Christianizing their Eastern sisters. Beginning with the English and American missionaries who went out in the early part of this century, the story comes down to our own time. English women now have twelve societies, and Americans have twenty, at work in India, China, Burmah, Singapore, Egypt, Syria, Turkey, and Persia. One chapter is given to medical work, and another to the zenanas. We are already familiar with the prison to which every Hindu wife is consigned, with her mother-in-law for her guardian. One poor creature said: "The life we lead is just like that of a frog in a well. Everywhere there is beauty, but we cannot see it." But if Hindu wives are wretched, widows are far more miserable. One missionary noticed a pale, woe-begone child of thirteen, who always sat in a corner and wept. Asking the reason, she said: "I am hated, scorned; no one cares for me. I was a widow at three years old." Truly, such a life is a living martyrdom. A tiny widow of six would sit in a corner and cry, "I know I am a widow, and despised by all."

From "Burmah" we are glad to quote the opening sentence: "To American ladies belongs the honor of commencing female education in the East." This chapter is devoted to the work of Dr. and Mrs. Judson; and Persia to Miss Fisk and Miss Rice.

From "Persia" we quote an incident showing Miss Fisk's difficulties: "You can have no idea of their filth; they all lie and steal. Nothing is safe except under lock and key. I cannot keep a pin in my pincushion." One day, being much discouraged, she had recourse to the following expedient: Just before they all passed through her room to the flat roof above, where they slept, she put six black pins in her cushion, and stepped out till they had passed. As soon as they had gone, she looked, and found the pins were gone, too. She then called the girls all back, and told them of her loss; but, no — not one had seen or taken them. Six pairs of little hands were lifted up as they said, "God knows we have not got them." "I think God knows you have," was her reply; and she then searched each one, but found nothing. She then said, "All kneel down, and we will ask God to show who took them;" adding, "He may not see fit to show me now, but he will sometime." She prayed, and as they rose from their knees remembered she had not examined their caps. In the first cap were the six pins, carefully concealed. The children looked on the discovery as an answer to prayer, and began to be afraid to steal, when God so exposed their thefts. The girl in whose cap the pins were found became a converted and useful woman.

The book abounds in interesting incidents, and we can recommend to all the "home talent" which has topics to prepare for auxiliary meetings.

WOMAN'S BOARD OF MISSIONS.

RECEIPTS FROM MARCH 18 TO APRIL 18, 1885.

MAINE.

Maine Branch.—Mrs. Woodbury S. Dana, Treas. Boothbay, Aux., $7; Auburn, High St. Ch., Y. L. M. B., $25; Gorham, Helping Hands, $5, Little Neighbors,$2; Bethel,Second Ch., Est. Sarah J. Chapman, $30; Skowhegan, M. C., $6.50; Lewiston, Pine St. Ch., Aux., $36; Rockland, Aux., $50; Milltown, Aux., of wh. $25 const. L. M. Mrs. E. L. McAllister, $29.22; Portland, Aux., Second Parish Ch., Young People's Aid Soc'y, $37; Greenville, Aux., $30, | $257 72
Castine.—Desert Palm Soc'y, | 20 00
Centre Lebanon.—Mrs. Noah B. Lord, $5, A Friend, $5, | 10 00
Kittery Point. — Mrs. J. S. Brown, | 2 00
Machias.—Cheerful Workers, | 5 00

Total, | $294 72

NEW HAMPSHIRE.

New Hampshire Branch.—Miss Abby E. McIntire, Treas. Amherst, Miss M. C. Boylston, $15; Dunbarton, Hillside Laborers, $12; Keene, Second Ch., Aux., of wh. $50 const. L. M's Mrs. S. P. Livermore, Mrs. J. Page Whitcomb, $61; Nashua, Aux., $33.90, Y. L. M. C., $53; No. Groton, A Friend, $5; West Concord, Aux., $6.50; Wilton, Aux., $3, Forget-me-nots, $5; Wolfboro, Newell's Circle, $75, | $269 40
New Boston.—A Friend, | 1 00

Total, | $270 40

VERMONT.

Vermont Branch.— Mrs. T. M. Howard,Treas. Barnet,Aux., $16; Castleton, Aux., $15; Colchester, Aux., $5.35; Newport, Cheerful Workers, $11.22, Banyan Seeds, $12.78; Richmond, Aux., $12; Rutland, Aux., of wh. $75 const. L. M's Mrs. Mary Burgess Johnson, Mrs. Abbie L. Barrett, Miss Julia E. Twichell, $87.43; Woodstock, Aux., of wh. $25 const. L. M. Mrs. Sarah A. Jewett, $32, | $191 78
Peacham.—A Friend, Thank-Off., | 2 00

Total, | $193 78

LEGACY.

Vermont Branch.— Legacy of Mrs. Lucy Spaulding, Brandon, | $240 00

MASSACHUSETTS.

Andover and Woburn Branch. — Miss E. F. Wilder, Treas. Malden, Aux., $40; Lexington, Aux., $7.20; Andover, Aux., $18.20 | $65 40
Barnstable Co. Branch. — Miss Amelia Snow, Treas. So. Wellfleet, Aux., $13; Yarmouth, Aux., $7; Truro, Aux., $6; So. Dennis, Aux., const. L. M. Mrs. Mary S. Nickerson, $25, | 51 00
Berkshire Branch—Mrs. S. N. Russell, Treas. Curtisville, Aux., $10; Dalton, Jun. Aux., $49; So. Egremont, Aux., $35; Lee, Willing Workers, $30; Pittsfield, First Ch., Aux., $9.57; Stockbridge, Loving Helpers, $15, | 148 57
Essex South Conf. Branch.— Miss Sarah W. Clark, Treas. Gloucester, Cong. Ch., Children's M. C., $5; Boxford, Aux., $10; Peabody, Aux., by Mr. Charles A. Haskell, const. L. M. Mrs. Mary R. Haskell, $25, | 40 00
Everett.—Ladies' Miss'y Soc'y, | 5 00
Fall River.—T. T. T. Club, | 1 00
Fitchburg.—Cong. S. S., | 3 00
Franklin Co. Branch. — Miss L. A. Sparhawk, Treas. Greenfield, Aux., $2.06, Daisies, $14.35, | 16 41
Hampshire Co. Branch.—Miss Isabella G. Clarke, Treas. Northampton, Edwards Ch., Jun. Aux., of wh. $100 const. L. M. Miss Hattie J. Kneeland, $113; So. Hadley, Aux., prev. contri. const. L. M. Mrs. H. W. Smith, $72; Easthampton, Emily M, C., $79.20, | 264 20
Ipswich.— First Parish Little M. C., | 3 00
Lawrence.—Ladies' Miss'y Asso., | 14 00
Medfield.—Aux., | 34 22
Middlesex Branch.—Mrs. E. H. Warren, Treas. Wellesley, Aux., $5; So. Sudbury, Ladies' Miss'y Soc'y, $11, | 16 00
Norfolk and Pilgrim Branch. —Mrs. Franklin Shaw, Treas. Cohasset, Seaside Workers, $15; Brockton, Mission Sunbeams, of wh. $75 const. L.

M's Miss Ellie Porter, Miss Jennie Howland, Miss Mabel Holmes, $125, Coral Workers, $5;Weymouth and Braintree, Aux., $8.50; Hanover, Aux., $2; Holbrook, Torch-bearers, $40, $195 50

Norfolk.—Mrs. Levi Mann,   4 40

Old Colony Branch. — Miss F. J. Runnels, Treas. New Bedford, Wide-Awake Workers, const. L. M. Miss Hattie Almy, $100; Fall River, Aux., $330, Willing Helpers, $60,   490 00

Princeton.—S. S. Cl.,   1 25

Reading.—A Friend,   5 00

South Abington. — Cong. Ch., Ladies,   10 00

Springfield Branch.—Miss H. T. Buckingham, Treas. Chicopee, Third Ch., Aux., $25; Ludlow, Aux., $11.05; Palmer, Second Ch., Aux., $20; So. Hadley Falls, M. C., $22; Springfield, First Ch., Aux., $38.28,   116 33

Suffolk Branch.—Miss Myra B. Child, Treas. Boston, Old South Ch., Aux., of wh. $25 by Mrs. Charles Stoddard, const. L. M. Mrs. A. K. Washburn, Lyndonville, Vt., $388, Central Ch., Young People's Soc'y, $241, Union Ch., Jun. M. C., $90; South Boston, Phillips Ch., Aux., Miss M. E. Simonds, const. L. M. Miss Etta D. Morse, $25; East Boston, Maverick Rill, $21; Roxbury, Eliot Ch., Anderson Circle, $6; Dorchester, Second Ch., Aux., $120.55; Jamaica Plain, Wide-Awakes, $30; Chelsea, First Ch., Aux., $100, Third Ch., M. C., $5; Somerville, Franklin St. Ch., $67.43, S. S., $10; Cambridgeport, A Friend, $25; Allston, Cheerful Workers, $20;Brighton, Aux., $30; Watertown, Aux., $30; Newton, Eliot Ch., Aux., $275, Y. L. M. S., $80; Newton Centre, First Ch., Aux., $70; West Newton, Mrs. Luther Hall, $2; Dedham, Asylum Dime Soc'y, $4,   1,639 98

Wellesley, College Miss'y Soc'y,   295 00

Worcester Co. Branch.—Mrs. G. W. Russell, Treas. No. Brookfield, Aux., $62; Blackstone, Aux.,$7; Worcester,Woman's Miss'y Asso., Salem St. Ch., $30, Piedmont Ch., $45, Union Ch., $83.39,   227 39

Worcester.—In mem. Miss Ellen M. Whitcomb,   500 00

    Total, $4,146 65

LEGACY.

Legacy of Mrs. Mary A. Bertram, Townsend, $80 00

RHODE ISLAND

Rhode Island Branch.—Miss Anna T. White, Treas. Providence, Central Ch., Mrs. A. D. Lockwood, const. L. M's Mrs. John T. Blodgett, Miss Mary E. Hall, $50, Plymouth Ch. Aux., $16.50; Barrington, Bayside Gleaners, $25, $91 50

Providence.—Mary A. Marvin,   5 00

    Total, $96 50

CONNECTICUT.

Eastern Conn. Branch.—Miss M. I. Lockwood, Treas. Offering at quarterly meeting, $55.43; Jewett City, Aux., of wh. $25 const. L. M. Mrs. Jane C. Brewster, $35.79; Preston, Aux., $8; No. Stonington, M. C. $30; Taftville, Aux., $7.11, M. C., 7.51; Groton, Fireflies, $55; New London, First Ch., Faithful Workers, $5; Colchester, Aux., $75, Est. of Mrs. Joshua Clark, by her children, $50; Bozrah, two Friends, $4; Norwich, Broadway Ch., $75, Park Ch., A Friend,$5; Plainfield, Aux., $10.50; Thompson, Aux., $7, $430 34

Hartford Branch. — Miss Anna Morris, Treas. Collinsville, Aux.,$32.50; Coventry, Aux., of wh. $25 const. L. M. Mrs. Jane B. Porter, $41.40; Enfield, Aux., $85.25, Helping Hands, $40; Ellington, Aux., of wh. $25 const. L. M. Julia Reynolds, $45; Hartford, Centre Ch., Aux., $5, M. C., $50, Windsor Ave. Ch., Aux., $75.60, M. C., $30; Plainville, Aux., of wh. $25 by Mrs. L. P. Buell, const. L. M. Miss Ella W. Corban, $101, Windsor Locks, Aux., $50,   555 75

New Canaan.—Cong. S. S.   80 00

New Haven Branch.—Miss Julia Twining, Treas. Hadlime, Friends, $1.30; Ansonia, Aux., $43; Bridgeport, South Ch., M. C., $28; Cheshire, Aux., $40; East Haddam, Aux., $11.20; Greenwich, Aux., $93.50; Fairhaven, Second Ch., Aux., $59.40; Higganum, Aux., of wh. $50 const. L. M's Mrs. D. M.Pratt, Mrs. R. J. Gladwin, $57.63; Kent, Aux., of wh. $25 const.

L. M. Mrs. Levi Stone, $31; Killingworth, Aux., prev. contri. const. L. M. Miss Mary A. Lane, $4; Madison, Willing Hearts, $30; Meriden, First Ch., Aux., of wh. $100 const. L. M. Mrs. E. T. Merriman, $125; Mount Carmel, Aux., $50; New Britain, Centre Ch., Aux., $39.15; New Haven, Centre Ch., Aux., $5; Church of the Redeemer, Aux., $57.50, College St. Ch., Aux., $35.70, Dwight Place Ch., Aux., $64.50; Fairhaven, First Ch., Y. L. M. C., $30, Howard Ave. Ch., $26, United Ch., Aux., of wh. $25 by Mrs. Pierce M. Welch, const. self L. M., $100.50, Y. L. M. C., $60; New Milford, Excelsior, $50, Golden Links, $14; New Preston, Aux., $30; No. Cornwall, Mission Bank, $5.20; Portland, Aux., $37.50; Reading, Aux., of wh. $25 const. L. M. Mrs. F. M. Abbott, $31; Salisbury, Aux., $38; So. Canaan, Aux., $3.50; Stamford, Tiny Helpers, $35; Westport, Aux., $40; Whitneyville, Aux., $50, M. C.,$40; Winsted, Aux., $68, A Friend, $50. Friends, 30 cts., ... $1,484 88
Southington —Zulu Band, ... 4 00
Windsor Locks.—A Friend, ... 5 00

Total, ... $2,559 97

NEW YORK.

New York State Branch.—Mrs. G. H. Norton, Treas. Binghamton, Aux., $20 50; Rodman, Willing Workers, $30; Brooklyn, Puritan Ch., M. B., $16; Gloversville, Mrs. N. M. Place, $50; Jamestown, Aux., $25; Rochester, Mount Hor Miss'y Friends, $10, ... $151 50
Claverack.—M. R. Zabriskie, ... 1 00
Denmark.—Mrs. J. T. Kitts, ... 2 40

Total, ... $154 90

PHILADELPHIA BRANCH.

Mrs. Samuel Wilde, Treas. NEW JERSEY: Orange Valley, Cong. S. S., 25 cts.; Jersey City, Aux., $29.14; Plainfield, Aux., $10; Bound Brook, Aux., $20. MARYLAND: Baltimore, Aux., $47 27. D. C.: Washington. Aux., $68.03, Cong. Ch.; Y. L. M. S., $170. Ex., $56.67, ... $288 02

Total, ... $288 02

OHIO.

Lorain.—Cong. S. S., ... $2 50

Total, ... $2 50

ILLINOIS.

Turner Junction. — Look Up Soc'y, ... $4 00

Total, ... $4 00

MINNESOTA.

Minneapolis.—E S. Jones, $100, D. P. Jones, $10, F. H. Carleton, $5, W. O. Jones, $1, ... $116 00

Total, ... $116 00

IOWA.

Anamosa.—Cong. Ch. S. S., ... $8 18

Total, ... $8 18

COLORADO.

Leadville.—First Pres. S. S., ... $12 50
Alexandria.—Mrs. Amy Downs, ... 1 00

Total, ... $13 50

KANSAS

Dunlap.—Ladies' Co-operative Miss'y Soc'y, ... $2 20

Total, ... $2 20

FLORIDA.

Jacksonville.—Sunbeams, ... $50 00
Orange City.—Aux., ... 6 20

Total, ... $56 20

CANADA.

W. B. M., ... $167 50

Total, ... $167 50

NOVA SCOTIA.

Horton Landing.—A Friend, ... $3 30

Total, ... $3 30

General Funds, ... $8,378 32
Leaflets, ... 42 48
Morning Star, ... 11 09
Legacies, ... 320 00

Total, ... $8,751 89

Miss EMMA CARRUTH, Treasurer.

Board of the Interior.

AFRICA.
SCHOOL-WORK AT AMANZIMTOTE.

We have received some examination-papers from the school in which our missionary, Miss Day, is teaching, which compare well with those that are brought to us from our own grammar schools. A letter from one of the boys tells us how they work and play there, and gives an account of a little literary society they carry on among themselves.

AMANZIMTOTE, SOUTH AFRICA, Dec. 16, 1884.

I AM glad to answer your letter, and to tell you what you asked of our secretary. There have been great changes in our secretaries. The one we now have has gone home in the middle of this term. Henry Lutuli was the name of the first secretary, and he studies no more. In consequence of these changes your letter was lost. I saw the letter, yet I did not read it carefully,—that is, to answer every question that was asked,—because I did not know that I should be secretary at any time. I think you asked about the games we have. We have just a few games. In our game of ball we make a circle, and let one strike the ball, and others catch it. We also play at cricket, sometimes, and we march; but I do not think that you call that a game. Another game is to have a number of the boys have pins, and strike them with a flat stone. Then we draw lines on the ground crossing each other, and have a little piece of a broken plate, and we throw this into these spaces between the lines, and throw one by one. We have been having this term much sickness, and many boys are out of the school. Now I am going to tell you about our school — that is, what we study. We are studying very hard. We study History of England, and physics. The latter one is great use, and general knowledge, too. We study Bible, and grammar. The latter one is of great use; that is, it helps us in writing and speaking the English language. We study arithmetic, too. We do little work this term. Every Friday we have meetings, and the boys speak, read essays, and criticise each other. I shall be very glad to have a letter from you. Yours respectfully,

POSSELT J. KUZWAYO.

TURKEY.

CENTRAL TURKEY GIRLS' COLLEGE.

MARASH, TURKEY, Feb. 16, 1885.

A GREAT pile of more than fifty letters, waiting answers, compels me to group you, and tell you all that you must be very patient with me, as I have come to the point where I must choose between "*doing my work* and *writing about it.*" You will all be glad to know that I continue well and strong, able to do the "half-work" for which I came, and am growing more and more "happy" in it, as I become accustomed to multitudinous blessings showered upon my pathway. Miss Childs has been with us since November, and quite makes us feel that she has always been here, by her loving interest in every department of our work. I am sure we could never get along without her, now we have learned the joy of having her. The busy wheels have stopped, to-day, seemingly — the first time since early in October, when they were set rolling; for, though we did have one week of vacation during the Holidays, the dread diphtheria in our circle interfered with plans for use of our time, while it gave us fresh cause for praise and thanksgiving in merciful deliverance from affliction such as has come to the homes of our Aintab missionaries. Our household here at the college has been unusually blessed with health this term, and *entirely free* from our local trouble — fever and ague. Of course we ought not to expect it among such as constantly remain in our pure hill atmosphere and dry rooms; but vacations often fill the systems with disease that continues for months.

Our girls are beginning to enjoy the regular exercise required daily in the open air; also the gymnastic exercises recently introduced; and we see the forms changing, and a quick, elastic step taking the place of the heavy, shuffling gait so universal in this land. After discontinuing, at different times since the opening of the term, six of those admitted to the preparatory department, we have left a fine class of sixteen taking the prescribed course of study for this one year, and fourteen in the three college classes — in all a school of thirty pupils. This number requires, of course, the same routine of lessons that would be needed for three or four times the number. Our semi-annual examination of Friday last was very much an everyday order of exercises — lessons being conducted in the different recitation-rooms simultaneously, our guests passing from one to another at their own inclination, seeming to enjoy the arrangement. Our pupils, as a whole, have made a good degree of advancement in all their studies; and while we have not been free from anxiety in regard to some, we do see the sweet Christian spirit dominating in their hearts. We hope all have begun the Christian life, and we love to see them gaining in self-control; such, for instance, as eating their regular noon lunch, because it is right and proper to do so, whether or not their last lesson has passed satisfactorily and pleasantly.

Perhaps in no one matter are we more tried than in this desire to yield to the *feelings of the hour*, instead of *acting from principle*. We not long since made a requirement of them that English only be used at table. Now there is almost entire freedom, with laughter and joking; so to-morrow, with the opening of our new term, we shall require English entirely in their conversation among themselves while in the house, except at table, the language then being pure Armenian. We wish to wholly discontinue their corrupt use of Armenian, which is a localism — believing in a pure, good language as a great aid to clear, strong thought. In various ways they are earning their "missionary money," and the meetings grow more and more interesting as more join the society, and take part in the reporting of countries, and in prayer for God's blessing upon the world. At the last meeting one said, "When can we, too, go to Japan, China, or Africa?" I asked if they remembered what was done in our land by the first asking this question, and they gave back the story of the students under the haystack, and organization of the American Board of Commissioners for Foreign Missions.

Surely the time must come when from Turkey missionaries will go to other lands. I long to write to each who has kindly sent me money for special expenditures in view of the poverty from the fires here and in Zeitoon. In time I shall try so to do; till then, accept please, the general statement that a careful account is being kept, and an effort being made to render it a blessing to many. Some have been helped to extra bedding, through comfortables made; some to text-books, on which only a low rate of rental is required; a garment here and there, or a pair of shoes, has helped a struggling student; while umbrellas to loan our girls in going to and from church, have, doubtless, been one of the means that, under God's blessing, have given us our healthy household. Scarcely a "cold" among them thus far. It is considered a disgrace to indulge in the useless ailment; I put it thus before them in the early winter.

Be assured your every effort is appreciated by us in the part you are doing on the other side of the ocean. Without you, *we* could do nothing here. How precious the thought that we are all *co-laborers with the Lord.* All of our girls would like me to send their salaams. Soon they will freely write for themselves.

Most sincerely yours,

C. SHATTUCK.

CHINA.

LETTER FROM VIRGINIA C. MURDOCK, M.D.

KALGAN, Jan. 15, 1885.

MY DEAR FRIEND,— I have intended to write you for some months past, but have been detained by sickness among the children of our station, and by my studies and general work. I have been reading Chinese medical books with my teacher, and have enjoyed them very much. I think it imperative to learn something of this branch from a Chinese point of view, so that I may possess the intelligence they think a doctor ought to have, and understand maltreated cases better. My teacher has made copies of the drawings illustrating the heart, lungs, etc. He is a very intelligent Chinese gentleman. I wish he were not an opium-smoker and a Mahommedan, and I should have hope of him; but as it is, I fear he cannot be much influenced. It is said a half truth is worse than none, and that may explain the fact that Mahommedans are so hard to convert to Christianity.

During this Week of Prayer we have had unusual interest. Twelve rose for prayers, and the first *Mongol* has been baptized.

Dr. Murdock sends some notes on Chinese medical books that may interest our readers. We can give only a few extracts:—

I send a copy of a drawing of the heart. It has seven eyes, or openings. The heart is the seat of the intellect, and its eyes are indicative of that power. Seven eyes would indicate great brightness; or, rather, since they never examine the heart, they would infer that a very intelligent person had seven eyes in his heart. A dull person has fewer; while a very stupid person may possess but one — or, unhappily, none at all. From the heart proceed vessels of exceeding fineness, resembling silk threads — one controlling the liver, another the pancreas, and one the lungs.

The Chinese doctors have but little knowledge of anatomy. They have no books upon that subject; and though there may be great desire and curiosity to learn the mysteries of the human frame, no physician has yet overcome his fear of spirits sufficiently to use the dissecting-knife — nor would the superstition of the people allow it. Since surgery is left to another class of people, they think they have little to do with this branch of study; so they

are contented with superficial observations, and theories of old
authentic authors. The butchers could tell something of the
structure of the animals they kill; but any analogy to the human
frame would never be thought of, and comparative anatomy is an
unheard-of study. The observations made by different authors
have been upon beheaded criminals or murderers, who have been
cut to pieces for their crimes; or upon children who have been
thrown away, and whose bodies have been torn to pieces by dogs
or wolves, thus exposing the internal organs. The observer could
get but imperfect ideas of the form, position, or size of the organs,
especially as they would not use the knife, and minutely examine,
the parts.

Home Department.

STUDIES IN MISSIONARY HISTORY.

Miss SARAH E. POLLOCK, who has charge of our "Studies,"
is herself learning tearful lessons — prepared for her by an all-wise
Father. Two of her family, a sister and her mother, have recently
closed their eyes on all earthly things, to open them where they
"see the King in his beauty." Her mother, Mrs. Robert Pollock,
of Cambridge, Wis., entered into rest on the 16th of April.

Miss Pollock is shut out from us for a time by this pillar of
cloud; but to her it is, we trust, only a pillar of light and of fire,
leading her safely on toward the heavenly Canaan.

The usual lesson will be given next month.— ED.

ANNUAL MEETINGS OF BRANCHES.

ILLINOIS.

EVERYBODY went to Quincy, Tuesday, April 7th; but the efficient committee of gentlemen who waited at the depot till half-
past ten at night, had a place for everybody, and in an hour's time
everybody in her place. The meeting opened at ten o'clock, April
8th, with a prayer-hour of great interest. Every prayer-hour of
the two days was memorable, whether we prayed for workers at
home or abroad, for the Bulgarian Christians persecuted for righteousness' sake, or for the little Chinese schoolgirls who ask the
Lord to convert the French, and keep them from doing such
harm.

The secretary, Mrs. Montgomery, reported 45 new auxiliaries — 25 senior, 14 junior, and 6 juvenile. She urged the holding of an annual meeting of young ladies' societies in each association, in accordance with the Chicago custom, and the adoption of such annual estimates of work by each association as would make sure the $18,000 asked from Illinois. She stated that while in churches where auxiliaries are already organized we have 12,000 women, only 5,000 of these are enlisted as members. "Where are the 7,000?" was the question laid upon the heart of each woman. And there are 3,000 more in churches where there are no auxiliaries: who will awaken them to their privileges?

The Treasurer, Mrs. Talcott, reported $15,876.89, with enough money sent too late to make $16,000. In the discussion that followed, Mrs. Montgomery showed how small an advance assumed by each association would bring the needed $18,000 next year.

The vice-presidents' reports showed efficiency and watchfulness. Bureau Association has given an average of two dollars for every woman in the churches.

Elgin Association has two churches that realize the State motto, "Every female member enlisted in the missionary auxiliary." One of these has 34 members, and 35 in the auxiliary.

The papers, "Am I My Brother's Keeper?" by Mrs. Arnold, of Stillman Valley, and "God's Handwriting on the Wall for Woman," by Mrs. Lloyd, of Ravenswood, were powerful appeals and will be printed. Miss Chapin of China and Mrs. Jenney of Monastir moved all hearts with pity for their poor people. In the Children's Hour, led by Mrs. Skeel, a mite of a girl, hardly out of babyhood, read a written report that brought alternate smiles and tears.

Dr. Humphrey, who believes that this is "The Golden Age," and Miss Bissell, always graphic and quaint in her Hindu costume, made Wednesday evening memorable.

The map exercise was a new and excellent feature of the Young Ladies' Hour. Miss Wingate gave greetings, tender and very suggestive, from the Woman's Board of Missions of the Interior. Our treasurer was wise, witty, and instructive at various points. The treasury and the treasurer always grow together.

The Question Box, led by Miss West, of Galesburg, brought out flashes of thought in quick succession. The parting words of the president, Mrs. Case, linger as a benediction.

And so, after a social evening, in which the pastor, Rev. Mr. Dana, and others speeded the parting guest with kindly words, we left Quincy, feeling that the two days' visit had taught us many a lesson, and made the Quincy people to seem like dear old friends.

MICHIGAN.

The twelfth annual meeting of the Michigan Branch of the Woman's Board of Missions of the Interior convened at East Saginaw, April 8th and 9th. We were favored with the brightest weather we have thus far enjoyed this spring, and every session was largely attended. Rare flowers and fine music added greatly to our enjoyment.

The meetings were most ably conducted by Mrs. J. B. Angell, of Ann Arbor, president of this branch. After the usual opening exercises we were pleasantly greeted by Mrs. Franklin Noble, of Saginaw, with kind and earnest words of welcome. The reports of the Secretary and Treasurer were very full and carefully prepared, and contained much cheering information. Our total receipts for the past year were $6,661.29, which is several hundreds of dollars in advance of last year; and before the close of the meeting we pledged $8,000, to be raised by the Michigan Branch the coming year. The reports showed the interest in missionary work to be steadily increasing throughout the State. The necessity of an ample contingent fund was well presented by Mrs. J. Estabrook, of Olivet, and elicited much discussion.

The greatest interest was sustained during the entire meeting by a full and varied programme. A most excellent paper by Mrs. J. L. Patton, of Greenville, upon "Home or Foreign Missions: Which, or Both?" was highly appreciated, and requested for circulation; and a story by Miss Baker, of Detroit, will be printed as a leaflet.

We were greatly favored in having with us three able and earnest missionaries: Mrs. Bertha Stover, of Bailunda, Africa, Miss Charlotte Spencer, of Hadjin, Turkey, and Rev. J. K. Greene, D.D., of Constantinople, Turkey. Their thrilling experiences were listened to with deepest attention, and their touching, stirring words will long be remembered.

The last afternoon of the session was mainly devoted to reports of Young Ladies' Societies and Children's Bands, introduced by an interesting paper on "Young Ladies' Work," by Mrs. M. L. D'Ooge, of Ann Arbor. The deep interest felt in this department of missionary work was evinced by the hearty appreciation of every report, not only of the young ladies' societies, but also of the smaller juvenile societies, such as Saginaw's little "Wide-Awakes;" and it was a timely thought, well expressed by Mrs. Angell, that the future missionary societies would be prepared to do better work than those of to-day, because of this early training in missionary work. A few earnest words by Mrs. W. H. Russell, in behalf of Mrs. Walker's Home for Missionary Children, at Auburn-dale, and a short, heartfelt talk upon "Consecration," by Mrs. Field, of Jackson, was followed by an inspiring and eloquent address by Mrs. Moses Smith, President of the Board of the Interior.

Between the afternoon and evening sessions of the last day a collation was served in the church parlors, affording opportunity for social enjoyment, and a better acquaintance, after which, we again heard earnest, parting words from each of the missionaries, who will soon be far away in their respective fields of labor. Their most urgent request was not only for "more money," but for more earnest prayers from all who remain at home, that their labors may be crowned with success through the abundant outpouring of the Holy Spirit upon the people for whom they spend their lives.

MRS. A. C. SATTERLEE.

MISSOURI.

The fourteenth annual meeting of the Missouri Branch of the Woman's Board of Missions of the Interior, was held in the parlors of Pilgrim Church, St. Louis, April 3d. The president, Mrs. S. B. Kellogg, led the devotional exercises, bringing to us a message from God's Word, and quoting from some of the "Wise Men of the East," who are of the opinion that the next ten years are to be very marked ones in the world's history, and who consider the outlook very hopeful and encouraging. Reports from auxiliaries throughout the State show a growing interest in mission work. The treasurer reported $2,263.78 for the year, and though this is less than the appropriation recommended to us, we are not discouraged, for there is a gain over last year.

Mrs. Goodell gave vivid pictures of mission life and work as she saw them in Egypt and Turkey during the past year. She told of missionary ladies and their many duties, their piety, their courage, their hospitality, and their testimony to God's faithfulness in caring for their children. She described a meeting of native women in Constantinople, whom she addressed through an interpreter. An Egyptian woman in full dress was introduced. Mrs. Goodell described visits made with missionary ladies to homes in Egypt, and told of many customs peculiar to that land. She read an account of the wonderful conversion of a Turkish officer, and his persecutions.

Dr. Goodell gave an hour packed full of choice thoughts brought back from the East. It was encouraging to hear of the great work being done by other Boards on all the shores of the Mediterranean. Medical work was heartily commended. The high type of piety said to be necessary to good results in mission work abroad, suggested that it would also be well in home work.

Memorials of a former State Secretary, Mrs. D. C. Young, and of the dear young missionary, Minnie Brown, were read. Resolutions were presented expressing appreciation of Mrs. Kellogg's long and faithful service as President of the State Branch, and regret that she should feel it necessary tò decline a re-election. Mrs. Rev. J. G. Merrill was elected to take her place. Much is expected from the meeting of the Woman's Board of Missions of the Interior with us next November.

THE TEMPLE WINDOW.

[THERE is a story of an artist who designed a window for a temple; and after he had selected the choicest pieces of glass, a workman gathered the fragments, and out of them made a window which so far exceeded in beauty the pattern designed by the artist, that, in a fit of jealous disappointment, the latter killed himself.]

Once, for a lofty temple,
　Whose walls rose stately and grand,
An artist designed a window,
　The masterpiece of his hand.

And for this wondrous window
　He gathered the choicest store;
And from the brilliant glasses
　He selected the rarest — no more.

Slowly the beautiful pattern
　Grew, like a glowing flame;
And the artist thought, while working,
　"This window shall bring me fame."

At last the work was finished,
　And the sunlight was sifted down
In many a dainty color
　Over the fretted stone.

But a workman had gathered the fragments,—
　Each glowing bit so rare;
Even the smallest and dullest
　Were used with peculiar care.

And out of these castaway pieces,
  With patient and tireless will,
He, also, fashioned a window
  Which surpassed the artist's skill.

The pieces were deftly fitted,
  And the delicate pattern shone
With an exquisite blending of colors,
  And a beauty all its own.

So, I think, for that heavenly Temple,
  Whose walls shine with jewels rare,
God is making a wonderful window,
  Each piece set with tenderest care.

Out of earth's lowly by-ways,
  From poverty, sin, and pain,
He gather *souls* for his setting,
  And washes them free from stain.

Shaped by the Master-Artist,
  Touched by that hand divine,
These souls, resplendent in beauty,
  With redemption's love-light shine.

                                          M. P. F.

CHEBOYGAN, March 15th.

--------◆------

RECEIPTS OF THE WOMAN'S BOARD OF MISSIONS OF THE INTERIOR.

MRS. J. B. LEAKE, TREASURER.

FROM MARCH 18, 1885, TO APRIL 18, 1885.

ILLINOIS.

ILLINOIS BRANCH.— Mrs. W. A. Talcott, of Rockford, Treas. *Alton*, 7; *Ashkum*, 2.70; *Beecher*, 10, Central East Asso., 6.52; *Champaign*, 11.50; *Chebanse*, 6; *Chesterfield*, 3; *Chicago*, M. A. R., 5, First Ch., 273, Mrs. A. Dow, thank-offering, 50, Union Park Ch., 150, Western Ave. 22, New Eng. Ch., of wh. 25 fr. Mrs. N. H. Blatchford, to const. self L. M., and 25 fr. Mrs. W. A. Montgomery, to const. self L. M., 97.20, Leavitt St. Ch.. 5, South Ch.. 28.78; *Clifton*, 2.30; *Danvers*, 12; *De-* *Kalb*, 3.16; *Delaware*, 10; *Evanston*, 201.12; *Forrest*, 4; *Galesburg*,1st Ch.,37.50, Brick Ch., 14.65; *Garden Prairie*, 3.15; *Geneva*, 7; *Granville*, 7; *Greenville*, 11; *Hamilton*, 5; *Hinsdale*, 16; *Kewanee*, 15; *Lanark*, 7; *Loda*, 4.50; *Malden*, 8; *Marseilles*, 13; *Maywood*, 10; *Mendon*, Aux., 11 60, Mrs. J. K. Fowler, 50; *Minooka*, 5; *Moline*, 25; *Naperville*, 9 50; *Neponset*, 5; *Oak Park*, 82; *Onarga*, 7.50; *Oneida*, 7; *Ontario*, 15; *Ottawa*, 33.85; *Payson* of wh 25 fr. Mrs. J. H. Scarborough, to const. L. M. Miss Mary

F. Leach, 42; *Pecatonica,*
5.20; *Pittsfield,* 10.50; *Peru,*
6; *Plainfield,* thank-offering,
5; *Polo,* Ind. Pres. Ch., 10;
Quincy, 30, thank-offering,
2; *Rio,* 5.70; *Rockford,* First
Ch., 52.69, 2d Ch., 50.50; *Roseville,* Mrs. L. C. Axtell, 3.75;
Shabbona, 1.93; *Sheffield,*
7.90; *Stillman Valley,* 16 95;
Sterling, 10; *Summer Hill,*
5; *Thauvville,* 2.50; *Toulon,*
12; *Undina,* 10.10; *Wayne,*
3; *Wataga,* 10; *Wauponsie
Grove,* 15; *Willmette,* 16.01;
Winnetka 12; *Woodburn,* 6;
Woodstock, 23, Delegates to
annual Branch meeting, to
const. L. M. Mrs. S. H. Dana,
of Quincy, 25, $1,720 26
JUNIORS: *A b i n g d o n ,* 31.69;
Bartlett, Lit. and Miss. Soc.,
2; *Canton,* Y. L. Soc., 10;
Chicago, 1st Ch., Y. L. Soc.,
65.80, South Ch., Y. L. Soc.,
25; *Evanston,* Y. L. Soc., 29;
Galesburg, Philergians, 10,
Knox Sem. Mission Circle,
30; *M a r s e i l l e s,* Helping
Hands, 30; *Rockford,* 1st Ch.,
Y. L. Soc., 24.65, 2d Ch., Y.
L. Soc., 18.70; *Turner Junc-
tion,* Look Up Soc , 10,   286 84
JUVENILES: *Cable,* Gospel Mes-
sengers, 2; *Chicago,* South
Ch. Mission Band, 10; *Elgin,*
Acorn Band, 5, Prim. Cl. S.
S., 1.55; *Galesburg,* Mission
Band, 10; *Maywood,* Busy
Builders, 5; *Moline,* 3; *Ne-
ponset,* 12.90; *Pecatonica,* S.
S., 3.28; *Rockford,* 1st Ch.,
Mission Band 25; *Turner
Junction,* Mission Band, $4;
Wheaton, 1; *Woodstock,* 1.75.   84 48

    Total, $2,091 58

IOWA.

IOWA BRANCH. — Mrs. E. R.
Potter, of Grinnell, Treas.
Ames, 5; *Atlantic,* Aux., 8;
"A memorial of David Press-
ley Findley," 6; *Cherokee,*
Abbie A. Strong, 5; *Denmark,*
25; *Des Moines,* 27; *Grinnell,*
28 35; *Genoa Bluffs,* 3.25; *Gil-
man,* 1 06; *Glenwood,* 10;
Iowa City, 13.50; *Le Mars,*
22.75, $154 91
JUNIORS: *Chester Centre,* The
King's Daughters,   3 00
JUVENILES: *Manchester,* Rain-
bow Band, 15; *Reinbech,*
Morning Star Workers, 6.25,   21 25
SABBATH-SCHOOLS: *Des Moines,*
5.19; *Oskaloosa,* 5,   10 19

    Total, $189 35

KANSAS.

KANSAS BRANCH.—Mrs. A. L.
Slosson, of Leavenworth,
Treas. *Blue Rapids,* 3; *Dia-
mond Springs,* 5.60; *Exeter,*
Mt. Vernon Aux., 4; *Maple
Hill,* 5; *Mount Ayr,* 4.65;
Parsons, 1.20; *Sabetha,* 12;
Sterling, 5.04: *Wakefield,* Bi-
ble-School, 15, $55 49
JUNIOR: *Topeka,* Miss J. Ly-
man's S. S. Cl.,   10 75
Less expenses, 1.24,

    Total, $65 00

MICHIGAN.

MICHIGAN BRANCH.—Mrs. Geo.
H. Lathrop, of Jackson, Treas.
Almont, 3.50; *Armada,* 1; *Au-
gusta,* 5; *Detroit,* 1st Ch.,
Aux., 104.50, Woodward Ave.
Ch., Aux., 53, Trumbull Ave.
Ch. Aux., 10; *East Saginaw,*
88; *Flint,* 25; *Hancock,* 10;
Hudson, 20; *LeRoy,* 20; *Lud-
ington,* 15; *Marshall,* Mrs.
Gallup, 2; *Port Huron,* 15;
Pontiac, 9.15; *Sandstone,*
4.75; *Vermontville,* 10, $395 90
JUNIORS: *Detroit,* Woodward
Ave. Ch., King's Cup Bear-
ers, 30; *Eaton Rapids,* King's
Young Daughters, 6.25; *East
Saginaw,* Young Ladies, 50;
Manistee, Young Ladies,
12.50,   98 75
JUVENILES: *South Haven,* S.
S. Mission Bank,   5 78
FOR NEW MORNING STAR:
Shelby,   1 00
Whitecloud,   70— 1 70

    Total, $502 13

Auxiliary Societies of Michigan
will please report hereafter to Mis.
Charles E. Fox, of Detroit, Treasurer,
who succeeds Mrs. Lathrop.

MINNESOTA.

MINNESOTA BRANCH.— Mrs. E.
M. Williams, of Northfield,
Treas. *Austin,* 20.15; *Fergus
Falls,* 5; *Medford,* 94 cts.;
Minneapolis, First Ch , Mrs.
McMillan, 25, Mrs. Kittredge,
22, Plymouth Ch., 149.65, Sec-
ond Ch., 7.66: *Northfield,* 43.74;
Spring Valley, 5; *St Paul,*
Atlantic Ch., 10; *Winona,*
100; *Zumbrota,* 5 80, $394 94
JUNIORS: *Minneapolis,* First
Ch., Y. L. Soc., 64.63; *Ply-
mouth,* Y. L. Aux., 31 25;
Northfield, Carleton College
Aux., 32 85.   128 73
FOR MORNING STAR:
St. Paul, Evelyn Y. Stone,   25

   Branch total, $523 9 2

MISSOURI BRANCH.

Mrs. J. H. Drew, 3101 Washington Ave., St. Louis, Treas. *St. Louis,* 1st Cong. Ch. 102.50, Y. L. Soc., 15, Ready Hands, 94, Pilgrim Ch., 22, Y. L. Soc., 81. 25, Pilgrim Workers,132.58, 3d Cong. Ch., 25, S. S., for New Morning Star, 3.51, Inf. Cl., birthday gifts, 2.50, Plymouth Ch.,25. 5th Cong. Ch., 22.25; *Hyde Park,* Gleaners, 6; *Webster Groves,* for Miss Tucker, 35; *Springfield,* Aux., 40.70; *Neosho,* 13; *St. Joseph,* 8.40, $628 69

Total,	$628 69

NEBRASKA.

NEBRASKA BRANCH. — Mrs. Geo. W. Hall, of Omaha, Treas. *Genoa,* 1.50; *Greenwood,* 6.20; *Lincoln,* 11; *Norfolk,* 8, $26 70
JUNIOR: *Crete,* Doane College Soc., 25 00
JUVENILE: *West Point,* Willing Workers, 5 00

	$57 06
Less expenses,	5 80
Total,	$50 00

OHIO.

OHIO BRANCH.—Mrs. Geo. H. Ely, of Elyria, Treas. *Brooklyn,* 20.22; *Burton,* Miss Ann C. Hitchcock, to const. self L. M., 25; *Ceredo,* W. Va., 5; *Chardon,* 6.26; *Cleveland,* Euclid Ave. Ch, 55, 1st Ch., 28; *Hudson,* 10; *Huntington,* W. Va., 4.50; *Kinsman,* 7.50; *Lyme,* 20.70; *Rochester,* 10.25; *Springfield,* 16.65; *Steuben,* 8; *Toledo,* 1st Ch., 110; *Twinsburg,* 7; *Unionville,* 16 74; *Vermillion,* 5; *Wellington,* 25, $380 82
JUNIORS: *Chardon,* Y. L. B. S., 10; *Mt. Vernon,* M. B., 15, 25 00
JUVENILES: *Brooklyn,* Waste Not Soc., 2.97; *Cincinnati,* Central Ch., Willing Workers, 60; *Elyria,* Little Helpers, 3.54, Opportunity Club, 10; *Lyme,* M. B., 24.22, 100 73

Total,	$506 55

PENNSYLVANIA.

Allegheny, Plymouth Ch., Young People's Soc., $20 00

Total,	$20 00

ROCKY MOUNTAIN BRANCH.

Mrs. Hiram R. Jones, of So. Pueblo, Col., Treas.
JUNIORS: *Colorado Springs,* Young People's Miss. Soc., 35, Pike's Peak Miss. Band, 40, $75 00
For Morning Star: —
Colorado Springs, 10 50
Greeley, S. S., 6 50— 17 00
Denver, Colorado, First Ch., Aux., 100 100 00

Total,	$192 00

WISCONSIN.

WISCONSIN BRANCH. — Mrs. R. Coburn, of Whitewater,Treas. *Beloit,* 1st Ch., Aux., 33.05; *Broadhead,* 5; *Bloomer,* 2.85; *Beaver Dam,* Easter offering, 12.35; *Browntown.* A. M. Lathrop, 1; *East Troy,* Mrs. Josiah Beadsley, 1; *Eau Claire,* 25, *Friendship,* 1; *Grand Rapids,* 4; *Kilbourne City,* Mrs. M. M. Jenkins, 10; *Menasha,* 10 65; *New Lisbon,* 3.50; *Rosendale,* 3.69; *Ripon,* 20; *Stoughton,* 8; *Viroqua,* 10; *Waupun,* 5, $156 10
JUNIORS; *Brandon,* Young Ladies, 4.65; *New Lisbon,* Young Ladies, 6.50, 11 15
JUVENILES: *Mt. Sterling,* (Gay's Mill S. S.), 1; *Racine,* Pansy Soc., 2.75; *River Falls,* 15; *Ripon,* Do Good's, 14, 32 75
A Friend, per Mrs. J. Porter, 100 00

	$300 00
Less expenses,	14 00
Total,	$286 00

TEXAS.

Austin, two widows, upward of fourscore years, $10 50

MAINE.

LEGACY.—*West Newfield,* Miss Olive A. Towne, $10 00

MISCELLANEOUS.

Sale of "Coan's Life," 13; of leaflets, 67.23; of envelopes, 1.35; chart, 60 cts., $82 18

Total,	$82 18

Receipts for the month,	$5,157 90
Previously acknowledged,	10,517 40
Total since Oct. 22, 1884,	$15,675 30

Board of the Pacific.

SITTING by an inland fireside and holding a sea-shell to the ear, fancy tells us that an imprisoned echo of the ocean is murmuring there with perpetual unrest; and as we listen to the "faint undersong," our thoughts go out over the waters in swift flight to distant shores. The tumult of great cities, the silence of dreary wastes, the culture of high civilization, the stupid brutality of savage life, the worship of Christian multitudes, the senseless, cruel tortures inflicted and endured to propitiate the heathen gods — all these become real to us in quick succession, as in thought we follow the encircling ocean, whose tides are ceaselessly rising and falling upon the continents and islands of the world. With special force do these visions come to those who are linked by prayer and effort to the missionary cause. To them "the whole round world" seems "bound by gold chains about the feet of God."

The conflicts that shake the nations, activities of commerce, advancement in learning, wonders of geographical discovery — in short, whatever stirs the pulse of humanity, is seen and felt in its relation to that great prayer of the Church, "Thy kingdom come."

To us upon the hills of San Francisco no sea-shell whispering is needful, for the waters of the Pacific roll through the Golden Gate, surcharged with importunate pleading from benighted millions who are separated from us only by these heaving waters.

This thought makes heathenism very real to us, together with the vivid object-teaching which we may receive by turning only a step down from our great highways into a transplanted section of

(237)

Asia, where the moral darkness is profound, and where the clang-
ing tomtoms from the joss-houses proclaim the instinctive longing
of their poor souls for deliverance from the bondage of this Evil
One, which they feel only a supernatural power can bestow. We
try to focalize upon them the gospel light, and a few begin to reflect its glory; but the vast multitude are wrapped so closely in
national conceit, which is awakened to intensity upon these foreign shores, that they shut out the life-giving rays, and ask only to
be let alone.

With patient persistence, however, the Christian laborers among
them are sowing the seed, knowing that God, in his infinite love,
will, in some way, give the increase; "For God so loved the
world, that he gave his only begotten Son, that whosoever believ-
eth in him should not perish, but have everlasting life."

In the sweetness and strength of this belief lies the hope of
missions. It gives courage to us who plan and organize at home.
It sustains the missionaries who are going forth for the first time,
to whom we on this Western shore are the last links with country and friends, as they take our hands in parting. It supports
those who are stemming the tide of heathenism in foreign lands,
where the dark waves so often threaten to submerge them. The
light of it shines from the worn faces of those who greet us after
years of service, at whose feet we delight to sit and listen to what
God has wrought by them, in fulfillment of his Word.

During the past few months we have several times been permitted to greet such workers, and also those who were going out
for the first time. On one occasion we met nine, who were on the
eve of sailing, and had a delightful hour with them in the library
of the First Church. Far-away Siam was represented in that little
company by two young ladies of the Presbyterian Board, whom
we shall always remember with peculiar pleasure.

Another privilege which came to some of us is now a tender
and sacred recollection. Mrs. Pruyn, after years of missionary
life in Japan, returned to this country to spend the remainder of
her days; but when the Union Missionary Society needed her
wisdom and devotion in the Margaret Williamson Hospital, near
Shanghai. she accepted an appointment there.

A short time only the Lord had need of her for earthly service,
and, prostrated by disease, Mrs. Pruyn, a few months since, entered for the last time our Golden Gate, and some of us were permitted to meet her as she tarried for a brief time on the way to
her Eastern home.

Not long after, the softened splendor of the Gates of Pearl fell
upon her as she passed to her reward. We shall never forget the

inspiration of her grand and noble soul, which shone like an un-
dimmed star while her body was enfeebled by disease. God took
her life — "gently, not smiting it, as a harper lays his hand upon
his harp to deaden the vibration."

The workers who touch our lives in passing will never be forgotten. We receive those who are outward bound, with their
hearts and hands yet warm from the loving farewells of the East,
and of the Interior, while through them we are fused by the fire
of Christian love into a more complete and sacred fellowship with
those who have sent them forth.

We have recently been favored with the presence of Mrs. Arthur
H. Smith, of North China. How our hearts are quickened as we
remember those interviews with her! The graphic recitals of
scenes through which she passed during the twelve years of her
residence in the Celestial Empire, held us spellbound as we were
drawn into sympathy with her trials and her joys.

She spoke of the ten years of waiting in Tientsin before fruitage could be seen; of studying the language, "which seemed at
first like pricking at a mountain with a cambric needle;" of their
joy when at last they could begin to speak to the people of the
gospel; of the insults with which their message was received; of
the prayers that went up from their disappointed, almost discouraged hearts; and of the strange way through which the answer to
their petitions came.

A wasting famine afflicted a region about two hundred miles
from Tientsin, where the missionaries were soon permitted to distribute the relief sent by England to the sufferers, who were dying
by thousands. Dr. Smith looked into the face of his wife, and
said, "I must go." It was the hardest trial of her missionary life;
but she knew that the one so dear to her could not be withheld
from such a service, and he departed. After six weeks he was
brought home to her on a stretcher, prostrated by typhus fever,
which nearly took his life. But this dark shadow was the portal
to that success for which they had longed and prayed. The stolid,
unresponsive hearts were touched. Said Mrs. Smith: "A thousand years of preaching and teaching would not have given the
access to those Chinese people that the famine did. Their hearts
were full of gratitude; they wanted to make some return. Our
helpers told them that the best return they could make was to
listen to the new doctrine which we had come to teach; and so
they did, and the light of the gospel spread with great rapidity."

Dr. and Mrs. Smith removed from Tientsin, that they might
take advantage of this providential opening, and "the work was
blessed from the very first." Now there are church-members in

ninety villages of that region, and interest is constantly increasing.

As the health of Dr. Smith imperatively demanded a rest, he and his wife are spending a few months in this country and the Sandwich Islands.

Dr. and Mrs. Pease, of Micronesia, were in California, and have gone Eastward. We of the Woman's Board have spent some delightful hours with Mrs Pease, who has pictured to us the strange, savage life with which they are surrounded in their island home, and the victories which have already been wrought there by the gospel of peace. We have been trying to adjust ourselves to her way of looking at missionary life in that far-away place, where only once a year the longed-for news from home and friends can come to them, borne by the white sails of the Morning Star. Notwithstanding their isolation, and the many deprivations and discomforts which they must of necessity endure, the little black-eyed lady came before us saying, "Do not even think of the word sacrifice in connection with our life." Then, in her cheery way, she gathered up pleasant things to tell us of their home and work. She felt that the thought of *sacrifice* was inconsistent for those whose highest joy should be to do the Father's will. After a year in the United States, Dr. and Mrs. Pease hope to return to their field with a printed edition of the Testament in the language of the Marshall Islanders, and they are earnestly praying that helpers may go with them to aid in meeting the imperative needs of the Micronesian work. They rejoice that the facilities for carrying on missionary efforts there will be so much increased by the new Morning Star, which will speed along by steam-power when her wings droop helplessly in the calms of the Pacific.

California is now robed in the beauty of her early springtime. The emerald hillsides, the orchards pink with peach-blossoms, contrasting with the white bloom of other fruit-trees, the fields already becoming radiant with wild-flowers, the upspringing wheat on the vast levels, the waving grain, already drooping with its weight of fruitage in the southern borders, and the orange groves loaded with golden splendor — all these glories of nature teach us of the divine, vital touch of Him who is "the Resurrection and the life," and they contain an earnest of victory amid the conflicts of truth in the world. Even "*now* is come salvation and strength, and the power of His Christ."   L. M. F

San Francisco, March, 1885.

VOL. XV.　　　　JULY, 1885.　　　　No. 7.

JAPAN.

WORK IN THE JAPAN MISSION.

FROM MISS A. M. COLBY.

THIS year has been one of advance, although there has been much anxiety, sadness, and weariness. We had a great astonishment and bereavement in the death of one of our most eloquent and promising young preachers, Mr. Uyehara. Early in the year he was married to one of the girls in our school in Kioto, and very soon after made a missionary tour with Mr. DeForest, giving grand promise for work in the future. After his return we heard that he was ill, but had no thought of danger till the terrible news flashed around, "Uyehara sleeps." Our Japanese Christians always say sleeps; never, "He is dead." His funeral, held in his church exactly four weeks from his joyful marriage, was intensely solemn. His place is still unfilled.

Our school has suffered somewhat from the change of teachers. As has been often said, the only thing certain in Japan is change. The air is full of the seeds of progress, but many of the ideas advanced on this subject are puerile, and heavy with the refuse of heathenism. Sometimes it seems as if the nation were on the threshold of modern civilization; but when we go into the country, away from the seaports open to foreigners, it seems as if ages must pass before the people, as a people, can be clothed and become decent. I have a letter from one of our Osaka Christians preaching in a city not three hours' *Jinrikisha* ride away, where we have been urged to do missionary work, in which the gentleman says he cannot promise that any women will come to listen now, but he will try to get the husbands and fathers to consent to allow them. He hopes he may succeed before long, and adds, "This place is where Osaka was ten years ago."

Our school has been steadily advancing in character and increasing in numbers ever since the change of governors, until we are now sadly crowded both in the boarding and school department. The city is divided into four parts, for easier government; and the Mayor of our fourth part sends two daughters, the Governor of the Osaka Fu sends an adopted daughter, and about every office and condition of life under that is represented in the school. We have never sought the higher classes, but they have sent their daughters, after careful official inspection.

In another letter Miss Colby says of her summer sojourn in Mt. Heyei:—

It was a great privilege to hear the sermons in English; but I have especially enjoyed, and been encouraged, by the meetings of the single ladies, and I long to have you know of the love and sympathy that was expressed for the home-workers. One of the special objects of thought and prayer one evening was your work at home. One of the ladies expressed a thought something like this: that it was hard for you to have so much work without the joy that comes to us in it. While I heartily sympathized with the feeling that prompted the remark, still, I thought God probably did not leave you joyless. The more I know of Christian work, the more I believe in God's compensation to his true workers. My heart is still in America, and I believe, as Mr. Joseph Cook says, that "the eyes of the world are upon you," and that every victory over heathenism in the United States means a victory for Christ all over the world. Blessed are we, indeed, who may see with our own eyes a nation wakening into a true sunrise; but much more blessed are you who are privileged to work in the nation that was formed from the sunrise to illumine the whole globe. That you may have strength and wisdom to accomplish your great work, is the prayer to our heavenly Father, not only from the little meeting on the mountains, but from every land where your missionaries are at work.

To give you a little of our joy, I will copy one or two of the letters that rejoiced us in the summer:—

"MY DEAR TEACHERS AND PARENTS: I was waiting to write you ever since, but postponed from day to day, not having time to write. I heard Hiyei Zan is very cool, and the view is so very beautiful! I am *zannen* (sorry for one's self) that I cannot live in such a pleasant place this summer; but Osaka, too, is a little cooler than last year, I think. I guess you have heard all about the school from the girls that are in the school now, so I want to write something about my home.

"From the Saturday of one week before last week I came back, but I am very unhappy at home, for the whole family are not Christian; so they do not care anything about the soul, and their words are all for flesh only. As I see such *arisama* (condition) I am very sorry, and almost became sick therefore. I feel that you are my true, dear parents, and that the school is my beloved home, so I am longing for your come back. But I think it is good for me to stay at home for awhile, for if I see those things that my parents do, my heart becomes more earnest to pray for them. When I read some verses in the Bible at home, it comforts me more than I read in school. Bible is the gushing water; and as I drink of the refreshing draught, my heart melts in gratitude to God for his great goodness."

Another writes:—

"MY VERY DEAR TEACHERS : I am very glad to receive your kind letter. I thank you very much for your kind heart and your good care of my weakly body. I do not know why my body is so weak, but I think it is my lazy makes me weak, so I determined to study more next term than last. . . . I asked my parents, and they will permit me to stay in school a long time. So I want to ask you and dear Miss Gardner something — that I and my parents want me to improve in English, if you will please teach me even after graduating; and if you can, and no trouble, will you please stay in Japan and live with me in our loving school which God gave us?

"Are you all safe? I am very anxious. Three days ago, one night, the wind blew very strong, and house, yard, and everywhere were very wasted by the wind; so if the wind blew there, too, I think your weak tents all fell down, and you are all very troubled. But our dearest Lord Jesus Christ is near, and God is very merciful, so I believe God will bless you, and you are all safe.

"I will tell you about my brother : he is teaching a young man English. Since I came here he does not go to church. I am very sorry. Another thing that I am sorry for,—he reads every day some books called in Japan Ninjo books. These are very impure books, and readers' hearts or feelings become impure by reading. Oh, pray for him! My mother says she wants to study the Bible with me every night, so please pray for her."

We received a call from an official yesterday, to consult about putting a girl, whom the governor's wife has just adopted, into the school to be taught English and foreign ways, but she is specially anxious she shall not be taught Christianity. He said: "I am afraid there is no help for it, as there is no school in Osaka where she can learn these things without Christianity."

CEYLON.

LETTER FROM MISS LEITCH.

IF there was one thing in our work that used to discourage and sadden us, it was the large heathen school at Santillipay. When we came here, four years ago, we found it with one hundred and twenty children — a strong school, having existed for seven years, and receiving a large grant from Government.

The people were very strict Sivites, requiring all children to come to school with the sacred ashes — the mark of Siva — on their foreheads, and to learn heathen catechisms and poems. They were taught to make a mock of Christ, and learned speeches and plays to be performed in school in which Christ was ridiculed. They were punished for attending a Christian church or Sabbath-school, or moonlight meetings. No Christian was allowed to visit the school, or speak to the boys on the truths of Christianity. They taught always on the Sabbath.

The result on the village may be imagined — a strong public sentiment hostile to Christianity and the missionaries. Our moonlight meetings were sometimes disturbed, Sabbath-schools and church services thinly attended, and the catechists and Christians now and then subject to petty annoyances. We ourselves, when we came to the field as strangers, and attempted to visit the school, were shabbily treated. You may remember a letter we wrote about our visit to a blind teacher and his school, published in LIFE AND LIGHT some years ago.*

I used to think that if this strong heathen school should be broken up, and a Christian one be established in its place, it would be a miracle. I saw no way for this to be brought about. The public sentiment of the place would not allow us to establish an opposition school, and the Government would not give us a grant while a strong school was in existence receiving grants. Day by day, as I passed the school, my heart used to ache, and I could not keep back the tears — it seemed so sad a thing to see

---

* LIFE AND LIGHT for September 1881.

these children taught to despise Christ. We used to pray about it; and many a time I have said in my heart, "If the Lord will indeed hear my prayer, and break up this school, and give as large a Christian school in Santillipay, then I promise him that I will have no doubt that he hears and answers prayer."

For two years no answer came. There were some little breaks in the cloud, however: a small girls' school had been established, at our own expense, and was prospering well; our Sabbath-school and other Christian meetings were better attended; we were making friends in the village, and several girls had been induced to go to our Christian boarding-schools; but still the heathen school continued as strong as ever.

At last a change came. It was "not by might, nor by power," but by the Spirit. The council of the enemy were confounded. Many a time, while we had bought land and built a preaching bungalow and girls' school, they had boasted that not one in Santillipay would become a Christian. But they themselves became their own worst enemies. The teachers quarreled about the pay, and the school was divided into two parts. They went to court; the head teacher perjured himself, and the school was stricken off the Government lists. The old proverb says, "Whom the gods would destroy they first make mad"; and, like the Israelites of old, we had only to stand still and see the deliverance wrought out for us. What a lesson of trust we learned in the Hearer of prayer, who, in his own time, will send an answer. The Government inspector then said the field was open to us; and you may be sure we were not slow to occupy it.

There were teachers to pay, a new school-bungalow to be built, books, maps, and furniture to be bought. We did not know where the money was coming from; but we could not doubt that God would complete his own work, so we went on. For nine months we have had one hundred and twenty children in our school. They have all been taught regular Bible lessons and Christian songs; and they have been brought to church and Sabbath-school. On any Sabbath morning the sight of all their bright faces, as they learn for the first time of Christ, and sing his praises, would bring happy tears to your eyes.

In another letter Miss Leitch writes of this same village:—

You would have been pleased, I think, if you could have been present at our last Christmas at Santillipay. You remember that was the place where they showed such hostility to Christianity — not only to us when we first came, but to the former missionaries. Their feelings seem to have undergone quite a change.

At our Christmas festival the people turned out *en masse.* Without a hint from us, and even without our knowledge, they lined the whole of the inside of our Santillipay church-bungalow, which is quite a large one, with red and white cloth, and decorated it with red and white flowers, trimmed the tree, and made an arch · to be over where we should sit, decorating this also in the same way. They hired a band of music for the day, and formed a procession to escort us, and carried a canopy trimmed with red and white flowers over our heads. The children strewed flowers before us on the way, sprinkled us and the procession with rose-water, fired guns, and rung bells. Although it was a glad procession, I think it was also a serious one; for was not all this to celebrate the birthday of the Son of God? Was there not in their hearts a dawning feeling of love to him? I feel sure there was. When the procession came to a close, the head man of the village, who had led it, knelt down, and with eyes and arms turning toward heaven, said, "Henceforth I shall worship only the Christian's God." The school exercises of the day were prepared by themselves, and the principal pieces were intended as arguments to prove that Jesus is the Christ, the true Saviour. In one piece a boy opened the New Testament and read a considerable portion of the first chapter of the Sermon on the Mount, in order to show the truth and beauty of Christ's words, while the audience listened with rapt attention.

. . . I wonder if the people in America know what a sad hindrance to our work the drinking-habits of Christian nations are. The fact that drinking is common in Christian countries is well known in all heathen lands; for are not their hands filled with books in which reference is constantly made to the commonness of drunkenness? The Hindus are afraid of English customs, fearing their sons will learn them, and become drunkards. The Hindu religions forbid the use of intoxicating drinks. Mohammedans have told me that if they could have sold liquor they might have been rich men, but their religion forbids it, and they dare not touch it; they dare not touch even an empty bottle. But under English rule, and with English officers in every town of any importance, drinking-habits are fast gaining ground. The young Hindus aspiring to Government offices, seem to think that learning to drink is a necessary part of learning English. They naturally confuse our drinking-customs with Christianity. Is not this "crucifying the Son of God afresh, and putting him to open shame?" When will Christians wake up to see what they are doing? Must I not call out to them, in the name of the millions of heathen, to beware how they dishonor Christ? Was slavery a shame calling for our utmost energy that it should be blotted out, and put far from the face of our fair land? And does temperance call for less effort by every man, woman, and child?

AUSTRIA.

THE KRABSCHITZ SCHOOL.

We have received from Mrs. A. W. Clark, of Prague, Austria, the following, with regard to the Krabschitz School. Our readers who have been saddened by the news of the death of Pastor Schubert, the efficient head of the school, will be glad to learn that the work still continues under competent assistants, and deserves their continued interest.

OUR dear "Mount Holyoke" of Bohemia is already well known to most of the friends of the Woman's Board of Missions. This institution for girls, located at Krabschitz, is this year, as in past years, doing grand work for the Master. There are some sixty pupils, all of them enjoying a thoroughly Christian training; and it is most encouraging to us to whom this work is so dear, to know what a blessed influence many of the girls there educated are now exerting in their own families, or as teachers in various parts of Bohemia and Moravia.

Presuming that any facts regarding the institution will not be unwelcome, I take the liberty of forwarding the following free translation of a letter I received a few days ago from one of the former teachers in Krabschitz, now the wife of an evangelist at one of the out-stations:—

"It was my privilege to spend many happy years at Krabschitz. There, while ministering to the souls of others, my own was singularly refreshed and helped, so that the impression left on my mind of those by-gone years is a very blessed one — one for which I shall never cease to be grateful. Such work is by no means easy; many tears and prayers are often necessary; but oh, how glorious are the fruits!

"Many of the young girls on entering the institution know but little of the Bible; to some it is an entirely unknown book. In the school, however, much time is devoted to reading and studying the Word of God, and many are the blessed results which have arisen from those hours of study and meditation. I think my happiest hours were those spent in prayer with my scholars. I still seem to hear the childlike petitions as they ascended to the throne of grace, so simple, and yet so fervent. Every week we had a regular prayer-meeting together, but I do not believe that a day ever passed without one or other of the dear girls coming to me for counsel, and requesting me to pray with them. In this manner we were drawn very closely to one another. The life in the institution is like that of a large family. The girls love each other like sisters, and their grief is great when the time for their leaving comes.

"We correspond with quite a number of our former pupils, and in this way often receive very encouraging news. The other day I heard from one who tells me how she loves to look back on the happy days spent in Krabschitz, where she first learnt to know her Saviour, and how she has succeeded in commencing a little Sunday-school with four small children. Several of our former scholars have organized Sunday-schools in the different villages in which they happen to be, besides frequently being the means of bringing different members of their own family to the Saviour. Such congregations as have been most largely represented in our school are now those where one finds the most of active Christian life. Those of our girls who appear to be more talented are educated as teachers, and obtain situations as such in schools or families. I may here remark that all the teachers employed in the Krabschitz school received most of their education there."

I am sure that the dear sisters in America who in past years have taken so deep an interest in this institution, and who still aid us in maintaining quite a number of pupils, will be glad of this testimony from one who, until recently, was a successful teacher there. We trust you will ever manifest a prayerful interest in this our "Mount Holyoke," the only school of its kind for Bohemia and Moravia.

THE BRÜNN HOME.

Mrs. Clark also sends a translation of Mrs. Freytag's report of the "Brünn Home." She writes: —

To all the dear Christian friends who have already done so much in the past toward supporting the Brünn Home of the American Board, the following report has been specially written, in the hope that, seeing the results, they may feel encouraged to extend their valued assistance to us in the future.

The Brünn Home has been in existence since September, 1879. Most of the girls come to us direct from Krabschitz, where they receive ample instruction in the Word of God. The work thus begun in these young hearts requires to be continued, as there is always a fear of their spiritual welfare suffering from their contact with the world, and we are becoming ever more aware of the necessity of such young girls breathing the atmosphere of a Christian home while finishing their course of studies in this city, where they would otherwise be exposed to so many temptations. Allow me now to give you one or two sketches of a few of the girls who have been inmates of our Home.

E. was the first. She studied at the institution of Krabschitz, and then came to Brünn, with the purpose of there completing her studies as teacher. Her expenses were paid partly by Christian societies in Germany, and partly by the Woman's Board. She had a sweet disposition, loved God's Word, and led a consistent Christian life. She took an active part in the woman's prayer-meetings, and would often beg me to pray with her alone. She graduated in July, 1881, and obtained a situation as teacher in Moravia, where she continued to work with much blessing. She has there organized a Sunday-school, which she directs in spite of the greatest opposition.

One of our most promising Sabbath-school scholars while we were in B——, in 1874, came to us in Brünn in 1879, intending to become a kindergartnerin. Living with us she was of course obliged to be present at our morning and evening devotions, as well as the services of Sunday. Soon, however, she became very tired of this, and finally openly rebelled against it. On going to school every morning she always went into her own church, and there persisted in performing her devotions. We remonstrated lovingly with her, talking most faithfully to her, but with no effect. After some time we remarked that she seemed more sober, until at length one day she burst into tears, begging us to forgive her for her wickedness, and lamenting her corrupt nature. We bade her look to Jesus, the sinner's friend, and prayed with her. From that day a marked change took place. She prayed regularly, loved God's Word, and her walk could truly be said to be that of a child of God. She now felt that she could no longer consistently remain in her own Church, which she immediately left, joining the Free Reformed Church. As this latter is not recognized by the state, it was impossible for her to obtain a certificate as kindergartnerin. She is now teacher in a Jewish family, where she proves herself to be an earnest Christian. I may also add, that she has been the means of converting a godless brother, who is now studying to be an evangelical pastor.

R., a teacher's daughter in Bohemia, was also supported by the Woman's Board. She was a humble Christian, loving God's Word and prayer. After graduating, in July, 1880, she went to help for a short time as teacher in Krabschitz, and then found a situation as governess in a gentleman's family in Russia.

Only lately we had a letter from her telling us how she missed the sweet, Christian intercourse with friends, to which she had always been accustomed, but adding that she found a balm for all her sorrows in her Saviour's love, and in the reading of the Bible, which seems more precious to her now than ever before.

M. came to us as servant, in April, 1882. She was very strict in her religious ideas, and prayed before coming to us, that God would guide her to a praying family. Her prayer was heard, but differently from what she had expected. Finding a religion so different in many respects from her own, she was at first unwilling to believe that it was the right one. She had never seen a Bible until we gave her one, which she read constantly. Gradually, as her knowledge increased, the teachings of her own religion became more and more unsatisfactory to her, until finally she determined to give all up, and accept Christ as her Saviour. She could no longer conscientiously remain in her own church, which she has since bravely left, although threatened with all kinds of persecution by her parents, who now refuse to own her.

M., a pupil of the orphanage school of Countess La Tour, came to study in Brünn two years ago, with the expectation later of becoming a teacher in the school of the Countess. We had at first a great deal of trouble with her, her defiant nature and unchristian behavior causing us much grief. God has, however, heard our prayers in a wonderful way, and Marie is now quite a changed girl. Since coming here she has been led to feel the lack of true religion in her Church, which she left some time ago. She must still study three years before graduating as teacher.

Such is a brief sketch of a few of the girls who, at different times, have been inmates of our Brünn Home. I could add much more, but will not trespass on your time and patience, trusting you may already have some little idea of the work carried on here.

Mrs. Clark adds: —

I have thus freely translated parts of Mrs. Freytag's report, in the hope that it will encourage the sisters at home to continue their prayers and gifts for our Brünn Home, which has done such important work in the past, and is doing a similar work to-day, as there are now ten girls there continuing their studies. Some of them are entirely supported by the Woman's Board — all of them in part. We have recently received two more girls, both daughters of pastors. One of them pays nothing, the other but half price. One can hardly expect a poor country pastor, father of eleven children, with a yearly salary of less than four hundred dollars, to pay much for the education of his family.

If the dear sisters in America could but fully understand the needs of the Brünn Home, and the important work it is doing for Bohemia and Moravia, I am sure they would give it a warm place in their hearts.

Young People's Department.

CHINA.

LETTER FROM MISS HOLBROOK.

(Extracts from a letter written to Mt. Holyoke Seminary.)

One of the greatest needs of the Board at the present moment is an increase in workers. At least sixteen young ladies are needed in the foreign field; not for enlargement, but to fill the places of those who must drop out, for one cause or another, and to keep the work from actually going backward. We need, also, an increase in the home force, especially among the young ladies— an increase in the number and efficiency of the workers, in gifts and consecrated talent, and in earnest prayer. We trust Miss Holbrook's letter may inspire some young lady to follow in her footsteps, and that the other suggestions may be of worth to those already engaged in the work at home.

AND now, girls, you want to know what the matter-of-fact "hardpan" missionary life is as seen by my eyes: and you must remember they are my eyes — not yours. One looking upon the missionary work from the home-land, must necessarily have more or less of visual aberration. Not only will the form be distorted, but there will be a halo of light around everything — it may be the yellow and the green, or the red and violet rays.

Then, too, I find the "field of vision" and "length of focus" vary greatly in different eyes at the same mission station, according to their power of accommodation. So to help you get a distinct visual impression as I see it, I will take up two or three points suggested by a letter I received not long ago. First, the position of single ladies in the work. You who have seen *Woman's Work for Women*, published in China, have noticed articles contributed by single ladies taking up both sides of the question.

When I consider how people of entirely different tastes and

affinities are associated in the closest relationship, each with decided convictions and independent views of methods of work,— for it takes independent character, and one who has methods to do the work at all — when I consider this great variety of personality of idea with mutual dependence in execution, the unity of the work is to me remarkable. It reminds me very much of a crazy quilt. The pieces may all be silk, each beautiful in itself; but unless they fit to each other, and combine harmoniously, it cannot last as a thing of beauty.

These missionary pieces are of every size, and shape, and hue — each a decided, independent character by himself. It is only that great law of harmony, that blessed gospel of love, that can combine this great variety of individual effort into a unity of force.

But is there a place for single ladies, and a work for them to do, that cannot be just as well done by the married ladies already on the field? Yes, indeed. ·The educating of her children must ever be the mother's first duty; and though she can share in much of the work for women at the station, yet there are lines of work that they cannot enter upon, and usually more than enough to fill the time of one wholly devoted to it. But they cannot work independently of each other. Each requires the other, that the best interests of the work may be advanced.

For myself, personally, I could not have asked a snugger corner than is my happy lot. At no time have I needed help, or love, or sympathy, and made that want known, and gone away hungry; or if at times it seems too dead-alive, still, and lonesome over at my house, I have only to run across the court, when a little dumpling three years old climbs up into my lap, gives me a good hug, putting her soft cheeks to mine, with, "I do love you, Auntie Marion"; or the older ones come with cuts and bruises, or bring headless, armless dolls for my professional sympathy and skill to cure. How I pity the solitary, who go through the world without the love of somebody else's children! Yes; there is a place, a broad, grand place for single ladies, both in the work and in the hearts of the workers. At this late date of missionary enterprise this seems a needless assertion, and would be but for those articles referred to in the magazine.

The second point suggested by the letter was a comparison of opportunity presented in private home practice and medical mission-work in the foreign field.

Girls, are you ambitious — ambitious in that high and grand sense that impels you on to make the most and best of all God has given you? If you have a fitness for it, you can ask no field wider, or broader, or higher than this. In the midst of it your ambition will seem like a pebble cast into the sea; or, permeated with that all-conquering principle of faith, it will be rather like the grain of mustard seed of the parable.

The work is trying—head-trying, heart-trying, soul-trying, body-trying; but the very trying strengthens every fiber of one's being.

This is not simply a figure of speech, but I say to you honestly, that in all I have given, there has been given back to me more than the promised hundred-fold.

Reach out as far as I will, reach up as high as I may, there is no barrier to my making the most of all the material given me with which to build *myself.* Reach out as far, or down as deep, as I may, there is no limit to the need of this poor people in their sin, their poverty, and distress; neither is there limit to the good news of salvation we bring them. Whose ambition could desire greater opportunities than these?

TWO TIMES TWO.

BY MISS W. A. PRESTON.

"WELL!" exclaimed Tessie Manor, as she looked around the pleasant parlor and saw, instead of the half-dozen girls she had expected, only her friend Thena Howells. It was half-past three, a half-hour later than it had been appointed — this little missionary meeting.

"Well, what shall we do?" asked Thena, coming over and sitting down on the sofa by her friend. "I am president and you secretary of this society, so we have all the power in our hands. Shall we give it up — the meetings, I mean; the girls said they would rather give ten cents a month than to come every month."

"We will have our meeting as usual, to-day," said Tessie, earnestly; "then we can talk it over and decide."

The exercises were very short that day. A few earnest thoughts from both girls did much toward solving their difficulties. Thena had brought several back numbers of LIFE AND LIGHT.

"We can't do as everybody else does," said Tessie; "everything is beyond us. I had no idea things would be so bad when we started, one little year ago."

"'What is that in thine hand'?" quoted Thena. "We will not try great things; but — Tessie, have you forgotten Mr. Hale's 'Ten Times One'?"

"No, indeed — not the great result; but, Thena, we haven't even ten workers. We have sixteen members, but no interest."

"We will try it on a smaller scale, then. Two times two are four; twice four eight; twice eight sixteen. We will simply have a splendid meeting two weeks from to-day, and we will each bring some one else, and interest them. Then next time there will be four, to bring four others. What if the progression should go beyond sixteen. Thirty-two comes next.

"I see what you mean," replied Tessie, eagerly. "And next time we will meet at Mrs. Drew's, if she is willing, she will be such a help to us."

"Come by all means, and welcome," said that lady, cordially, from the doorway. "Your mother said I might come right in, Miss Tessie. I thought your missionary society was to meet here, and I wanted help."

"We want you to help us, Mrs. Drew," Tessie said, quickly. "We are not in a condition now to help any one."

"What did you want us to do?" asked Thena, quickly.

"We ladies are filling a box to go to a missionary's family. I thought perhaps you would help us, as there is some hurry about it."

"That is just the thing," said Thena, eagerly. Then the girls told Mrs. Drew of what they had resolved to do, and received her promise of assistance.

Thena and Tessie went over the next morning, and taking packages of work, called on all the other fourteen members. They were all willing to do anything of the kind, and some even offered to do more than they asked.

"That is encouraging," Mrs. Drew remarked, when the girls had told her their success. "I advise you to keep some work in hand, and make your meetings useful, as well as instructive.

The two weeks soon passed, and four girls spent a pleasant hour at Mrs. Drew's, sewing busily on children's aprons, and listening to their hostess as she told touching tales of the lives and work of missionaries. They willingly promised to bring some one else with them next time.

"We will meet once a fortnight, until we are in working order," Tessie said decisively. "Then we will let the others decide it."

The next time there were the eight girls, busily at work, and after the short devotional exercises they just talked. A careful programme had been arranged, but instead they wished to discuss matters, and decide upon some real work to do.

"If we have something to do," Lotta Denio said, "we will come every month. When we don't do anything but listen, we might as well stay at home and read."

Thus the point was gained, and the vexed question solved, just by giving the restless girls something to do.

It was an easy matter to win the others over. Then, when for the first time within the year all the members were present,

Thena told them of the progression, and asked if it was not possible to go on a step farther. "Twice sixteen will make thirty-two."

It proved to be very possible. Tessie's uncle in the city wrote, asking if an evening's entertainment with the stereopticon would be liked. So the matter was soon decided. Mr. Lonley had traveled extensively, and would give views and descriptions of China and Japan to the mission society free; then the evening in the church afterward.

The membership remained at thirty-two for some months, as that number included almost all the girls in the village. Much can be accomplished by such a number of girls, and all were thoroughly interested.

"It is only five months since you came in and found Tessie and I alone, just arranging our progression. Contrast that with to-day, laughed Thena. "I think we girls did the wisest thing we have ever done when we asked you to help us."

"I wish we could go a step farther," said Tessie, thoughtfully. "Twice thirty-two are sixty-four; but there aren't so many girls around here."

"Take boys, then," Mrs. Drew suggested. "You each have brothers and cousins."

"Could we make it pleasant for them?" asked Thena.

"We will try and see," said Tessie.

Thus the progression reached its present limit. The girls are trying to gain the next number, one hundred and twenty-eight, but are doubtful of success. Other societies have been started on the same plan in adjoining towns; and who shall say that the progression started with "two times two," may not in time reach to numbers worthy of comparison with Mr. Hale's "Ten Times One," which started it?

THE CHRIST FUND.

BY LOUISE C. PURINGTON.

THE other day the collector of the Young Ladies' Missionary Society in one of our colleges was making her rounds, and came to two earnest Christian girls who perhaps had never belonged to a missionary society before. Said one of them; "How much are you going to give, Belle? I am sure I do not know what I ought to give? Father sends me money when I ask him, but it all goes, some way." "I am as much in doubt as you," replied Belle. "I have often wished my father would give me an allowance; but when I ask him, he says, ' What is the use? Do you not have all the money you need?'" Is it any wonder that girls like these, without training in stewardship, are often troubled about meeting the obligation of stewards? I am sure no more difficult problem comes to our young workers, and so very many, perhaps the majority, give in a desultory way. The chances are, that they do not give one half of what they ought. The last remittances from home may be exhausted, and they have no conception of a fund set apart and consecrated to Christ. In spite of difficulties like these, I believe that it is in the power of every girl to have a Christ fund — a portion from all that comes into her hands sacredly reserved for the Master's use. O my girls, you would not think so much of self-denial, but more of joy — the joy of having something to answer to His call! No purse so thin and slender but that it will be the richer for this consecration. There is this wonderful thing about our God, that he repays a hundred-fold even in this life.

The question with Mary Lyon was not, "What shall I give to the Lord?" but, "How much may I take for myself?" and her tithe was oftener one half than one tenth of her income. She was a living illustration of such teaching as this: "Personal consecration is a strong evidence of interest in mission work; but the money contributed is also an index of the feeling of the heart. . . . . This contributing is the current money of the heart. It shows, to an extent, how much we love; and oh, what a privilege, by giving money, to show our love to Him who has redeemed us. . . . . Charity is a test of Christian character — a pledge of consecration. Christian charity may be so practiced as to make us feel what a price was paid for our redemption: 'Ye are bought with a price.' . . . . How true it is that Christians have but little faith in any object till they have made sacrifices for its sake." She says, "Young ladies as well as young men, while engaged in study, are in danger of excusing themselves from contributing liberally, because they are spending money to prepare themselves for usefulness: they fortify themselves with this excuse, and are in danger of forming a habit of thinking of self first."

The solution of the problem for girls who can have money for the asking, may be met to a degree in this way: Train yourselves in this matter of stewardship and accountability. Look carefully over the ground of your expenses, and estimate closely your needs. If you must ask for money, form the habit of regularly asking, that you may regularly give. Your father, doubtless, will not mind, and very likely will not notice your new departure. As your money comes, each time have your own plan, prayerfully considered, of devoting a portion to Christ. Put it in your Christ fund, appropriate it in Christ's name, and you will be ready when the missionary collectors call upon you; indeed, you may not wait for them in your eagerness to give. The solution may be the same for those who earn their money, or for those who have but little to give. The difference is, that the privilege is a little sweeter if we earn it; and if we have but a mite the sacrifice is greater, and may bring us nearer to him.

There are still higher lessons in the spirit of giving, but the truly loyal heart will reach forth the larger joy to find.

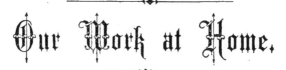

THE RELATION OF PRAYER TO THE MISSIONARY WORK.

BY MRS. A. C. THOMPSON.

WOULD we erect a building of solid masonry, one which shall be strong and enduring, we look well to the foundation. So in any business enterprise, we consider the principles on which it is based, no less than the object aimed at, before it receives our confidence. To insure a deep and abiding interest in the missionary work, we need to take an intelligent view of the great truths which form the motive for engaging in it, and furnish the promise of success.

At the very outset, therefore, we would recognize God's claim as the God of missions. "Ask of me, and I will give thee the heathen for thine inheritance, and the uttermost parts of the earth for thy possession," is his promise to his well-beloved Son, uttered centuries before the incarnation. The inspired psalmist, foretelling the blessedness of the universal reign of Messiah, when "he shall have dominion from sea to sea"; when all kings shall fall down before him, all nations serve him; when Tarshish and the isles, Sheba and Seba shall offer gifts, righteousness and peace everywhere prevail,—declares, "Prayer, also, shall be made for him continually, and daily shall he be praised."

It is, then, in fulfillment of God's purpose to bring back a lost world to himself; in obedience to the command of our risen Lord, "All power is given unto me in heaven and in earth; go ye, therefore, and teach all nations," — that the missionary enterprise has its origin. The missionary spirit is inspired by loyal devotion to our divine Leader, holy courage and faith in him, and finds all its strength in him. "Without me ye can do nothing;" "Power belongeth unto God," are its maxims. The great apostle could even glory in personal weakness, and "take pleasure in infirmities, in reproaches, in necessities, in persecutions, in distresses, for Christ's sake," saying, "When I am weak, then am I strong"; "I can do all things through Christ who strengtheneth me;" for he held fast to our Lord's promise, "Lo, I am with you alway, even to the end of the world."

Here we find the relation of prayer to all evangelistic effort. It is that which puts the individual soul, and every system of united Christian labor, into connection with the Divine Source of strength and life. Our little rills must be fed from the ever-living fountain, our personal and organized plans quickened by the Holy Spirit; and this will be only in answer to prayer. Men may speculate and disbelieve, but it remains the unchanging law of God's government, "I will be inquired of by the house of Israel to do it for them;" "Ask, and ye shall receive."

There is a liability that in these latter days, when science, and skill, and organized effort render such indirect aid in sending the gospel to the nations, we may look less directly to God. It is possible that we may glory in men and material resources, and rejoice in success, failing to maintain that attitude of dependence in which alone a blessing can be hoped for.

Missionary life no longer requires, in all cases, at least, that entire surrender of home ties, that heroic courage to face unknown perils by sea and land demanded in the pioneer stage of the work. Our steamships and frequent foreign mails, the respect and confidence secured by our missionaries in many lands, the knowledge acquired of foreign tongues and false systems of religion, the Bible and other Christian literature translated into many of those languages, and the blessed results of three fourths of a century of faithful labor—what a contrast do these present to the dark picture of that early day! An advance hardly less marked may be traced during this period in the sentiment of home churches in regard to missionary enterprise. It has become an accepted fact. Intelligence of the success of the gospel in all lands forms an important part of our Christian literature. In place of a few devout ones who hailed the first organized efforts in our country for the heathen with somewhat of the faith of Simeon and Anna of old, we have now hundreds and thousands of Christian men and women who have a share in these labors. That the religion of Christ is adapted to the needs of the world, and that its power will be felt wherever it is made known, is not now denied by intelligent Christians.

This increased acceptance of the missionary enterprise, and popular sympathy with it among Christian people, and all the secular resources which now contribute to its success, may form an element of weakness except as the purpose of our great Captain is kept constantly in mind. True loyalty to him will only be maintained by those who are in union with him. Many blessed results follow in the train of Christianity—civilization, better forms of government, reformed personal habits, mental culture, and higher social position. But not for these was our Saviour's mission to earth. Only those who know from personal experience the design of his mysterious incarnation, his atoning death, and glorious resurrection, and ascension, who know him as a Saviour from sin, can enter with full heart into the self-denying work of winning an alienated race back to him. Just in proportion as any are baptized with his Spirit, will they be faithful laborers at home or abroad. The spiritual character of the missionary work — its aim not so much to educate and elevate, as to convert, to make new creatures in Christ Jesus — will only be valued and maintained by those who are taught of God. That all our dear sisters at home and those in the foreign field may see eye to eye in this matter, should be our united prayer.

The American Board had its birth in prayer. The story of the prayer-meeting held by a few students by the haystack in Williamstown, followed by the personal consecration of those young men in the Society of Inquiry at Andover, is familiar to all. Other hearts were moved to unite their prayers toward the same end, and the society was organized. The monthly concert was early established from a felt need of continued divine guidance and blessing; and the records of the Board testify to more than one special season of prayer observed in a time of deep trial, which was shortly followed by songs of praise in view of God's interposition.

The origin and history of the Woman's Board are similar. There are some living who took part in those early gatherings in the private parlor or chapel, when a few godly women, whose hearts the Holy Spirit had stirred, asked, earnestly, "Lord, what wilt thou have us to do?" They received the guidance asked for, and during these succeeding years the Lord has not been slack concerning his promise. How many times has there been a striking connection between prayers offered in closets and circles in the home-land and the desired blessing in the foreign field? Each separate branch and auxiliary has its private memoranda to confirm the truth of God's promise. The records of answered prayer in missionary experience would furnish material to confound the doubts of the skeptic, and to encourage the faith of believing ones.

Miss Fidelia Fiske mentions in her journal that most of the revivals in Oroomiah commenced on the day of the Monthly Concert of Prayer, and several on or immediately after the first Monday in January. "But there was a special center of prayer for the female seminary in Oroomiah in the institution at South Hadley, and pious hearts loved to watch the connection between the two. While the two inquirers on that first Monday in 1846 were making closets for themselves with the sticks of wood in the cellar, some of Miss Lyon's pupils distinctly remember how she said to them that morning, 'We must pray more for Miss Fiske and her school.' They did so; and they remember, too, how the good news of the revival cheered them when it came."* Many mission stations and individual missionaries in recent years have borne like testimony to their experience of receiving marked answers to supplication offered by distant friends in their behalf.

While prayer is thus of vital importance in connection with missionary effort, we are not to forget that God's providence is universal; and we may ask that all political changes, that war, pestilence, famine, and even persecution, be overruled for his glory. To human view such events are great obstacles to the progress of the truth; but He who seeth the end from the beginning, often uses strange instruments to accomplish his purposes.

In view of God's gracious promises to prayer, confirmed by the experience of his people down to the present time, and in view of the fact that all spiritual efficiency is from God, is not the lack of prayer the weak point in our system? We acknowledge, gratefully, material prosperity — more money in our treasury, more missionaries in the field, many new doors opened, increased strength and confidence among our co-workers at home. Has there been similar progress in the exercise of prayer? Is there that boldness and freedom of access at the mercy-seat, that holy assurance in pleading God's promises, and patient waiting for results, which God's word authorizes and commands? Or, rather, may it not be our want of faith which stands in the way of those large displays of grace which God is ready to make? The stronghold of God's people in the campaign for the conquest of the world, is the mercy-seat. Fidelity there will insure success.

What is needed is not only more praying, but more acceptable prayer; offered in the name of Christ, and in deep sympathy with his desires and purposes. "Thy kingdom come," stands as the foremost petition in our Lord's prayer; and should it not hold the same place in ours? Our prayers should also be specific, intelligent, persevering, making large requests, and with hopeful expectation. There are devout women, the aged mother in Israel, the suffering invalid, the busy housekeeper, limited as they think

---

* "Woman and Her Saviour."

themselves in their sphere, whose closets bear witness to such daily intercession. These are praying missionaries, who will be openly rewarded, and permitted to share in the future triumphs of their Lord. Blessed are they who shall be thus acknowledged of him who "seeth in secret."

But special promises are made to united prayer, and we submit whether this service holds the place it should in our missionary meetings. Our beloved missionary sisters have often expressed pain in their visits home to find so little prayer at our stated gatherings, and so many gifted Christian women, whose voices are never heard at the throne of grace. How are we to explain this persistent silence, this plea of inability, when words so fitting and thoughts so fluently expressed often fall from the same lips ? Whatever cause we may assign, whatever excuse we may have made to others or to our own consciences, will we not make this the time for a re-consecration of all our powers ? If such silent lips were touched, as were those of Isaiah, with a coal from the altar, doubtless from many of them would be heard the ready response given by him to God's call, "Lord, here am I."

We live in the latter days of the Church, to which prophets and kings looked forward with longing eyes. We are under the dispensation of the Spirit,— God's last great gift. Pentecost was but the dawn of the blessed day foretold by the ancient lawgiver:. "As truly as I live, all the earth shall be filled with the glory of the Lord."

My sisters, have we received the spirit of prayer and supplications, in answer to which such large gifts are to be bestowed? If not, will we not, with the disciples of old, cry, "Lord, teach us to pray?"

"SOMEBODY ELSE."

I AM more and more struck with the duties and responsibilities thrown upon "Somebody Else." If she assumes them all, she must be awfully overworked. Is she more executive, more willing? Has she more leisure, more intelligence, more influence than others? She must be very obliging to undertake what others by good rights should have done themselves. She must be very conscientious to take up duties refused or neglected by those who are afraid of exertion, and hate self-denial. She must be very generous to stand in the lot and place of all the shirkers, or piteous, to minister when nobody else will.

Oh, the good, gifted, generous Somebody Else, who can do so much better than we can when God and opportunity are calling for our services!

Is it from modesty, from self-distrust, from a feeling sense of incapacity or ignorance, that so many wish to excuse themselves and secure her services, when Christian work is appealing to them for help, for *their* help and influence? This putting or even asking to put it on Somebody Else cannot be humility; for humility. gets *divine* help, and goes forward. It cannot be incapacity, for they were quite ready to fly in your face at any such imputation. Is it not selfishness? — for selfishness is very apt in self-disparagement when loth to quit its ease. Is it not spiritual idleness,— content with looking on, and nothing more?

Looking on is a pleasant exercise, but we must be doers of the Word, as well as spectators of the work. But suppose Somebody Else cannot be found — what then?

H. C. KNIGHT.

WOMAN'S BOARD OF MISSIONS.

RECEIPTS FROM APRIL 18 TO MAY 18, 1885.

MAINE.

Maine Branch. — Mrs. Woodbury S. Dana, Treas. Bangor, Aux., $64; Portland, Aux., High St. Ch., $219.85; Calais, Aux., $11; Eastport, Aux., $16.87; Bath, Aux., $19.25; Skowhegan, Aux., $5.50; East Machias, Aux., prev. contri. const. L. M. Miss Clara F. Harris, $10; Saco, First Cong. Ch ,$7; So. Berwick, Aux., of wh. $25 const. L. M. Mrs. Katherine B. Lewis, $35; Madison, Aux., $3; Wilton, Aux., $11; Winthrop, Aux., $25; Augusta, Aux., $55; Bucksport, Aux., $21.50; Camden, Aux., $13; Garland, ladies of Cong. Ch. and Soc'y, $13; Scarboro, Y. L. Aux., $10; Brockway's Mills, A Friend, 12 cts.; Machias, Cheerful Workers, $80; Wells, Second Cong. Ch., Aux., $41.25; Ellsworth, Aux., $5; Gorham, Aux., $6; Gilead, Mountain Rills, $10, $682 34

Total, $682 34

NEW HAMPSHIRE.

New Hampshire Branch.—Miss Abby E. McIntire, Treas. Amherst, Aux., $25; Bedford, Aux., $16 23; Brookline, Aux., $20; Candia, Willing Workers, $13; Hinsdale, Cong. Ch., S. S., $4.37; Keene, First Cong. Ch., S. S. M. B., $70; Manchester, First Cong. Ch., Aux., $95; Meredith Village, Aux., $17; Newmarket, Mrs. I. C. White, $2; Northwoods, Aux., $12; Raymond, Aux., $10.25, A Friend. $5; West Lebanon, Aux., $32.50, $322 35
East Jaffrey.—Aux.,   11 66

Total, $334 01

VERMONT.

Vermont Branch.— Mrs. T. M. Howard, Treas. Burlington, Aux., $20; Cambridge, Aux., $5.45, S. S., $3; East Corinth, Aux., $17.70; Gransboro, Aux., $9.60; Springfield, Aux., $27.60; Stowe, Aux., prev. contri. const. L. M. Mrs. W. L. Anderson, $9; St.

Johnsbury, So. Ch., Aux., of wh. Thank-Off., R. P. F., $15, $52, No. Ch., Aux., of wh. $5 Thank-Off., May 3, $29.42; Wilmington, Aux., p r e v. contri. const. L. M. Mrs. H. R. Titus, $10. Ex., $8, $175 77

Total, $175 77

MASSACHUSETTS.

Andover and Woburn Branch. — Miss E. F. Wilder, Treas. Dracut, Aux., $10; Ballard-vale, Aux., $10.52; Malden, Aux. (add'l), $1; Wakefield, Aux., $26, $47 52

Berkshire Branch. — Mrs. S. N. Russell, Treas. Dalton, Aux., $26.75; Hinsdale, Aux., $16; Lenox, Aux., $24; Pittsfield, First Ch., Aux., $4.15,   70 90

Essex North Branch. — Mrs. A. Hammond, Treas. Bradford Academy Foreign Miss'y, Soc'y, $25.04; Haverhill, No. Ch., Aux., of wh. $25 const. L. M. Mrs. M. A. Emerson, $70; Georgetown, First Ch., Happy Workers, $5, Rowley Aux., $25.65,   125 69

Essex South Co. Branch. — Miss Sarah W. Clark, Treas. Georgetown, Aux., $40; Lynn, Central Ch., Aux., of wh. $25 const. L. M. Mrs. Abbie M. Chesley, $26, North Ch., Young People's M. C., $5; Salem, Crombie St. Ch., Children's Miss'y Soc'y, $45,   116 00

Hampshire Co. Branch. — Miss Isabella G. Clarke, Treas. Northampton, Gordon Hall M. B., $23.25, First Ch., Aux. Div., prev. contri. const. L. M's Mrs. W. P. Strickland, Mrs. I. F. Pratt, $180, Edward Ch. Div., prev. contri. const. L. M. Mrs. Enos Parsons, $29.19,   232 44

Hubbardston. — Try To Do Good Soc'y,   2 00

Norfolk and Pilgrim Branch. — Mrs. Franklin Shaw, Treas. Brockton, Aux., $70; Cohasset, Aux., $20; Marshfield, Mayflowers, $26; Holbrook, Aux., of wh. $25 const. L. M. Miss Amy A. Learoyd, $127, Little Lights, $25,   268 00

New Bedford. — F i r s t C h ., Acushnet,   47 00

Old Colony Branch. — Miss Frances J. Runnels, Treas. New Bedford, Trinitarian Bible-School, $20.31; Lakeville Precinct, Aux., $60,   80 31

Royalston — M. B.,   18 25

Springfield Branch. — Miss H. T. Buckingham, Treas. Brim-field, Aux., $34; Holyoke, Aux., $100, Wide-Awakes, $40; Longmeadow, L i t t l e Helpers, $13; Ludlow Centre, Aux., $9.85; Wilbraham, Willing Workers, $20, $216 85

Suffolk Branch. — Miss Myra B. Child, Treas. Boston, A Friend, $10, A Friend, $5, New England Conservatory M. C., $6.50, Central Ch., Aux., $40, Berkeley St. Ch., Sunbeams, $12.50, Union Ch., Aux., $337.72; So. Boston, Phillips Ch., S. S., $100; Roxbury, Walnut Ave. Ch., M. B., $77.39, Immanuel Ch., Aux., $11.84; Dorchester, Pilgrim Ch., Gleaners, $45.50; Jamaica Plain, Central Ch., Aux., $38.11; Chelsea, Central Ch., Aux., $32; Cambridgeport, Prospect St. Ch., Aux., const. L. M. Miss Alice C. Baldwin, $25; Cambridge, First Ch., Young Ladies' Working Party, $30; West Somerville, Day St. Ch., Young People's M. B., $5; Dedham, Asylum Dime Soc'y, $1.92; Medfield, Morning Glories, $52, $30 48

Wellesley. — Aux.,   5 00

Worcester Co. Branch. — Mrs. G. W. Russell, Treas. Westboro, Aux., $35; Clinton, Aux., $23; Barre, Aux., $20.90; Westminster, Cheerful Givers, $5; Worcester, Woman's Miss'y Asso., Plymouth Ch., $50, Central Ch., $40,   173 90

Worcester. — Mrs. A. B. Smith,   50 00

Total, $2,284 34

CONNECTICUT.

Eastern Conn. Branch. — Miss Mary I. Lockwood, T r e a s. Norwich, Second Ch., Thistledown M. C., $80; Greenville, Aux., $31.25, Little Workers M. C., $56.25, $167 50

Hartford Branch — Miss Anna Morris, Treas. Bristol, M. C., $37; Canton Centre, Aux., $16; East Windsor, Aux., $25; Ellington, Earnest Workers M. C., $30; Hartford, Asylum Hill M. B., $40, Windsor Ave. Ch., Aux., $1 55; Poquonock, Cheerful Givers M. C., $15; Talcottville, Aux., $25,   189 55

New Haven Branch. — Miss Julia Twining, Treas. Bethlehem, Willing Hands, $6.40; Centrebrook, Aux., $65; Chester, Aux., of wh. $25 const. L. M. Mrs. S. W. Clark, $30; Clinton, Aux., of wh. $25 const. L. M. Mary Elliot Hull,

$45.43; Darien, Aux., $32.40, Busy Bees, $21; Derby, Aux., $36; East Hampton, First Ch., Aux, $38, Humming-Birds, $6.26, Union Ch., Aux., $10.15; East Haven, Aux., $39.60; Ellsworth, Aux., $25; Falls Village, Aux., $10, Y. L. M. C., $10; Georgetown, Aux., $11.50; Goshen, Aux., $31.50, Buds of Promise, $30; Guilford, Third Ch., Aux., $24.12; Haddam, Aux., prev. contri. const. L. M. Miss Martha E. Brainerd, $12 40; Harwinton, Aux., $27; Meriden, First Ch., Boys' Mission Band, $25, Cheerful Givers, $40; Meriden, Centre Ch., Aux., of wh. $25 const. L. M. Mrs. Ca ie L. Smith, $72; Middlebury, Aux., $17.75, Highland Gleaners, $5; Middlefield, Aux., $52; Middle Haddam, Aux., $8.29; Middletown, First Ch., Aux., $44.75, Gleaners, $10, Ten-Times-One, $15.85. So. Ch., Aux., $77; Milford, Aux., of wh. $25 const. L. M. Miss Katie S. Tibbals,$66; Millington, Aux., $10; Milton, Aux., $18; Naugatuck, Aux., $40; New Britain, So. Ch., Aux., $86, Little Helpers, $25.62; New Haven, Centre Ch., Aux., $37.14, Y. L. M. C., $5; Humphrey St. Ch., Y. L. M. C., $30, Temple St. Ch., Aux., $10.50, United Ch., Aux., $12.50: New Milford, Aux., $109.39; Newtown, Aux., $15; Norfolk, Aux., $50; Northfield, Aux., $35, Steadfast Workers, $3; North Stamford, Aux., $11; Ridgefield, Aux., $41; Roxbury, Aux., $38.50; Saybrook, Aux., $9, Seaside M. B., $20; Sharon, Aux., $20.50; Southbury, Aux., $16; South Norwalk, Aux., $65; Stamford, Aux., $60.20; Stanwich, M. C., $10; Thomaston, Aux., $25; Torringford, Aux., $21; Wallingford, Aux. $28.60; Washington, Aux., $45; Waterbury, Second Ch., Aux., $80; Westchester, Aux., prev. contri. const. L. M. Miss Sarah J. West, $19, Willing Workers, $5; West Haven, Aux., $43.38; Wilton, Aux., $50; Woodbury, First Ch., Aux., $10; North Ch., Aux., $25, $2,075 73
West Winsted.—Mountain Daisies,   5 00

      Total, $2,437 78

NEW YORK.

New York State Branch.—Mrs. G. H. Norton, Treas. Flushing, Faith M. C., $41.66; Newark Valley, Aux., $10; Napoli, Aux., $12, S. S., $2.72; Poughkeepsie, Aux., $45; Suspension Bridge, Aux., $5.71, Penny Gatherers, $50; Gloversville, Aux., $20; Homer, by Mrs. Coleman Hitchcock, to const. L. M. Marguerite Susan Hitchcock, $25, $212 09
East Bloomfield.—Aux.,   30 00
Paris.—Cong. Ch.,   7 56

      Total, $249 65

NEW JERSEY.

Roseville. — B. Mrs. John H. Tenney, to const. T. M's Miss J. B. Buck, Mrs. Harry W. Jaffers, $50 00

      Total, $50 00

PHILADELPHIA BRANCH.

Mrs. Samuel Wilde, Treas. NEW JERSEY: Orange, Trinity Cong Ch., Aux., $32, M. C., $20; Jersey City, Aux., $38.79; Montclair, Aux., $27.12, Collection at Neighborhood Meeting, $9.64. Ex., $5, $122·55

      Total, $122 55

ILLINOIS.

Sterling. — Mrs. Nathan Williams, $9 40

      Total, $9 40

MICHIGAN.

Saugatuck.—S. S., $8 00

      Total, $8 00

KANSAS

Stockton.—A Friend, $30 30

      Total, $30 30

CHINA.

Tung-cho.— Miss'y Soc'y, $18 00

      Total, $18 00

General Funds,	$6,402 14
Weekly Pledge,	1 45
Leaflets,	23 89
Morning Star,	12 50

      Total, $6,439 98

MISS EMMA CARRUTH, Treasurer.

Board of the Interior.

CHINA.

MRS. CHANG, OF MA YEN VILLAGE.

BY MISS MARY PORTER.

An old lady was baptized here last Sunday who has interested us all as few of those whom we meet ever do. We saw her first one day last winter, in a crowd which gathered to listen to, or rather to look at, the missionary lady who was visiting her village. The noisy, disorderly rabble was disagreeable to old Mrs. Chang, and after hanging about for awhile, trying to induce those about her to listen quietly, she gave up the effort, and went away without even speaking to us. A few weeks later, on a second visit to the village, the teacher was so attracted by her bright, interested face and winning manners, that she devoted much of an afternoon to direct personal conversation with her, urging her to improve the little time that could be left her of the earthly life, in making ready for a blessed home prepared for her by a loving heavenly Father, who had cared for her all these eighty-three years, although she had neither known nor loved him. She listened with an eagerness and receptivity such as we rarely meet, and the teacher came home with her own heart quickened with intense desire for that aged soul, although hardly hoping to see the sweet, bright face again.

It was not many weeks, however, before the old lady appeared at a meeting at a village two miles from her home, having walked that distance on a heavy, sandy road that she might hear more of this "new way." The old helper, a man of much fervor of spirit and simplicity of faith, whose home is in that district, has since then taken pains to see Mrs. Chang occasionally, and she has met the missionaries a few times. The instruction she has received has been most meager, and the hope that we have that she has indeed become a child of God, is largely due to the fact that, knowing so little, she seems to have laid such firm hold on the great truths of the forgiveness of sins and life through Jesus Christ.

Ten days ago we sent her an invitation to visit us, that she might hear more of the gospel, attend some of the church services, and become acquainted with its customs. No one had any thought of her being at once received to its communion; but when she came we found that her heart was quite set upon doing so.

The family consists of herself and two sons, but one of these has been adopted into another household; so, practically, she and a son of sixty, who has neither wife nor children, are alone in the world together. They are very poor, but there is nothing beggarly about the old lady. A quiet, self-respecting air marked everything she said, and touches of humor, here and there, gave piquancy and grace to the simple story which she gave us of her life. ' The son makes willow-baskets and dust-pans for sale; while the mother spins thread, which she carries to the village fairs, or does sewing for her neighbors. Let me give one scene from her story, as nearly as I can in her own words:—

"Before the famine time we had a few acres of land, and were very comfortably off, so that we not only had enough to eat and wear, but when I saw our blind neighbor, Mrs. Li, without fuel, I could say, 'Come over and steam your cakes at my fire'; or I could give her a bowl of millet-gruel from my kettle. I cannot do so any more. We sold all our land for food, and it brought so little in those bitter days, that it only fed us for a few months; and now we have only what we earn from day to day, and must sometimes go hungry ourselves. Still I can help Mrs. Li. I let her walk behind me to the fair, and tell her where the rough places are, or lead her around the holes. Sometimes I sell her thread for her, and she brings her wheel to my house, and we spin together."

Dear, bright-faced, sweet-hearted old lady! Are there not many such "little ones" not gathered into any "fold" which are Christ's, of whom he will say at the coming, "She hath done what she could"?

Both the pastors talked with Mrs. Chang, and it was decided that on Sunday she should be examined, and, if she seemed a suitable candidate, baptized. But for that, we should hardly have kept her here so long (four days) for the busy hands grew restless with nothing to do, and she longed for her spinning-wheel and reels of cotton.

Sunday morning she went to the chapel, her face, whose deep, deep wrinkles made more touchingly beautiful the sunny smile which lighted it up, all aglow. She answered the questions put her with most unembarrassed distinctness, saying, as simply and sincerely, "I do not know about that," when some unfamiliar point was touched upon, as she gave clearly her replies to those things of which she did feel sure. There was no hesitation or doubt as to why she desired to be a Christian: it was that she might be saved from the sins of all those eighty years, and find in Jesus, who died upon the cross, her Redeemer and Guide. As she was baptized "in the name of the Father, the Son, and the Holy Ghost," we felt a confidence, which we often lack in those far more fully instructed, that she had been taught of the Holy Spirit. Her assent to the Articles of Faith had in it the same gentle fervor which characterized all that we saw of her; and after entering into the solemn covenant of mutual watch and care, some of us longed for her benediction, as one of those "pure in heart" to whom it is given to "see God"—very dimly yet; but if by love and faith only united to him, so soon to "know as she is known." We could not bear to see our dear old Christian sister start on her five-mile homeward trudge alone, so proposed that the Bible-woman should accompany her; but she refused, protesting that there was no need of such trouble on her account. "Why!" she said, "I am not stupid; I can ask my way if in doubt about the path. My heart is full of joy and gratitude for God's goodness. I shall go on thinking of that, and before I know it I shall be at home; just one step at a time, and every step bringing me nearer." So she set out, the glow of gladness on her face, one of God's "little pilgrims;" and we let her go with the prayer that in the higher, deeper sense it might be just as she said — every step taken in the light of God's countenance, and every one bringing her nearer home.

TURKEY.
TOURING EXPERIENCES.
BY MISS MARY P. WRIGHT.

The often expressed desire to go with our missionaries into some of the native houses, may be largely realized by means of the following word-pictures taken from Miss Wright's account of her tours with Miss Bush the past winter. Our next letters from Miss Wright will be dated at Marsovan, where she has lately taken charge of the girls boarding-school.

HARPOOT, EASTERN TURKEY, Jan. 26, 1885.

As my thoughts glance backward over these months, I remember the picturesque old Roman walls, and towers, and gates of Diarbekir: its graceful minarets, where storks pose in stately ease; the narrow, filthy streets; and here and there some rude boys throwing stones, to emphasize yells and curses we do not understand; the sick old man slowly raising himself from his bed on the floor, and exclaiming, with uplifted hands and trembling voice, "It seems to me that angels from heaven have entered my room. Do read, do pray, and tell me how God's work prospers"; the many women there who promised to read the Bible every day; the *multitudes* who are not ashamed that they do not know how to read; and the sweet-faced Tonä, whom we established as Bible-reader, with nineteen married women learning to read. Then I think of the poor women in Aghau, whose husbands, according to the customs and necessity of that region, have nearly half of them gone to Constantinople, to seek a living there. How they listened to the consolation of the gospel — those poor women living in the same room with goats, calves, chickens, and donkeys! and how they overwhelmed me with blessings and pomegranates as I parted from them!

At Ainetsik, the preacher's wife, Hunazant (Obedient), told me how, two years ago, the women there had brought stones to build the chapel. She had brought twenty great stones, and another had brought eighteen, and so on. She seemed to be able to count the very stones of the house she loved so much. The women there used to come from their day's labor and work, often from sunset until midnight, singing together as they worked, until even Georgian women and girls used to come and help for the pleasure of it! This chapel is not whitened; and next spring these sisters will go to a place several miles away, where a certain white earth (porcelain clay, I suppose,) is found, which they will bring in great sacks on their shoulders to the village, mix with water, and mounting ladders where necessary (their work-trousers make this easy), will smear over the walls and ceiling with their rough, willing hands. Hunazant has done good work in teaching the women to read. She told of a bride in a village where she used to live, whose father sent word to her husband not to let her talk with the Protestants or learn to read. He seems to have "bettered the instruction," even beating her, if he found a Testament in her hands; but she was so anxious to learn that she would study her lesson at odd times, when sent for wood or water, and by a pre-arranged signal would call Hunazant to the shelter of a friendly stable to hear it when learned. In this way the poor woman read from Matthew to Hebrews. Then Hunazant moved away from the village, and does not know whether her pupil continues to read, but knows there is no one there to teach her.

At Arabkir I remember the young mother who burst into tears and sobbed a long time as I said, "How do you do?" because being too far away to hear the bell, and having no clock, she reached the chapel just at the close of the woman's meeting. "What was the text?" she asked, eagerly; and when I told her, "Our citizenship in heaven" (thanks to Dr. Rigg's scholarly care, the Armenian of Philippians iii. 20 has always been like the new version in English), she again asked, "Where is it?" as if determined to derive some profit from the meeting, at any rate. The tearful farewells of the Arabkir sisters still linger in my thoughts, and I shall not soon forget their entreaties that one or both of us remain "a few weeks" — "this winter" — "always."

LETTER FROM MISS MALTBIE.

THANKS FOR ENLARGEMENT.

SAMOKOV, Dec. 3, 1884.

How time speeds his flight! It is fourteen years since I came to this country; and though I often long unspeakably for my own dear native land, yet the ties that bind me to this dear people are becoming stronger and stronger as the years roll by. I have a deep interest in the several hundred girls scattered throughout this land who have been under my care as pupils of this school, and wherever I am they must live in my memory and prayer.

A few weeks ago the secretary of our mission was informed by Dr. Alden that an appropriation had been granted for the purpose of enlarging the accommodations for our school, and that the Board of the Interior had assumed the responsibility of raising the sum granted.

We wish to express our thanks to the ladies, through their officers, for the manifest interest and appreciation of our need which they make evident by their deeds. We accept this as the sign from our heavenly Father that he would have us " go forward " with renewed zeal and consecration, expecting *still greater things.* I would not enlarge the means for the education of mind, unless, at the same time, the spiritual power to direct this development in the right channel be more than proportionally increased. Pray for us, we beseech you, that our desire for more love and power may be granted. The present is a very critical time in the history of this nation, and we fear for her future.

Multitudes are enlightened, and understand the claims of the Gospel, but are ensnared by love of the world, and the honor they may receive from the world, and do not care to seek the honor that comes from God only. " The fear of God is not before their eyes," yet some earnest souls are praying, I trust, in faith. In one of our meetings with the girls, one of them spoke of the discouragement she felt because so few of her relatives and friends had received the truth into their hearts, although they acknowledged their obligation to do so.

She then read, from the eleventh chapter of Romans, Paul's argument to prove that the Jews had not been rejected of God, because a remnant should be saved; thus proving that all might receive the grace of God, if they would. From the study of this passage she said she had been greatly encouraged to pray for her people; for if God had not cast them away, there was great hope that the prayer of faith would have power before him who has shown his great love to the Bulgarian nation by sending the missionaries and the Bible. And thus, she urged, we may believe, if we are faithful, our friends will be saved.

CALLED HOME.

The Lord, in his providence, has spoken to many hearts in the death of one of our dear girls of the class of '83, Stepha G. Eleava. Last year she was connected with the Bible work as traveling

companion of Miss Stone; but in September she became teacher
in the Girls' School of the Methodist Mission, north of the Bal-
kans. She was the daughter of the oldest preacher and first
evangelical Christian in Bulgaria. He was called a Protestant
before the missionaries came, and gladly welcomed Dr. Long, the
first missionary. Stepha was with us five years, and stood high
as a scholar in her classes, although she was never strong, bodily.
She became a Christian in the second year of her course, and
when ready to enter special work for the Master, she entered it
with all her heart, and was very successful in interesting the
women where she went. Many will miss her words of cheer, and
we can but wonder why she was called away — so young, and so
full of hope for a life of usefulness. She quietly passed away at
midnight, awaking to spend the last Sabbath of November in
heaven. Blessed, happy spirit, forever free from sin and sorrow!
When a friend at her bedside said to her, "You will not be afraid,
for Jesus will go with you, will you?" she replied, "Oh, no!
I can *trust* him"; and he sweetly soothed her with the songs of
heaven, for her ear caught the beautiful strains, and she whispered, "I dreamed I heard music; but who knows? Perhaps it
was not a dream!" She was full of sympathy, and always ready
to help others. Her quick, skillful fingers often ministered lovingly to my needs, and the folded hands, many times, lightened
the heavy burdens of those about her. She loved life, and looked
forward to useful service; but she is introduced to higher service
above, and would not wish to return to her earthly house were she
permitted to do so. Every life leaves to us its lesson, but hers
was one of peculiar sweetness; still, the fruitage of the seed
sown in her heart must be realized in its fullness in heaven.

My great desire is, that through God's grace the dear child may
do more by means of her death than she could have done by her
life, and I think nothing has seemed to make a deeper impression
since I came here upon the whole school. There is much seri-
ousness, and three of the girls expressed their determination to
live for their Saviour henceforth.

STUDIES IN MISSIONARY HISTORY.
1885.

THE ARMENIAN MISSION — 1842–1846.

The Missionaries: Re-enforcements; Death of Mrs. Van Lennep;
Return of Missionaries to the United States; Mr. Temple — his
life, work, death.

Work of Translation and of the Press: What important work did Dr. Goodell complete in 1841? Sum up the other work done in the Armenian from the beginning until 1846; In the Greek. What periodicals were issued?

Education: First theological class. Seminary at Bebek. What was the fate of the rival Armenian College at Scutari?

Work Among Women: First Sermon to Women; Dr. Dwight's family visitation; Female Seminary opened in Constantinople, 1844; Arrival of Miss Lovell; Common schools for women.

Religious Death-Penalty Annulled: Causes; How brought about?

Native Missionary Work.

Death of Native Brethren: Baron Sarkis; Baron Mugurdich.

Persecution: When was Der Vertanes Imprisoned? Matteos made Patriarch. For what reason? His Treatment of the Evangelical Brethren; Fate of Bedros and Vertanes. The Bull of Anathema and Excommunication; Its pitiless execution.

Efforts to obtain Relief: Intervention of Sir Stratford Canning; Reschid Pasha to the Rescue.

Work at Nicomedia: Missionaries visit, 1840; Visit of Der Vertanes; Persecution; Haritûn's imprisonment.

Broosa: Indications of Spiritual Interest; Conversions.

Adabazar: How did the truth first reach this place? First visit of a missionary, 1841.

Locate and describe the stations, and thus make the surroundings *real*. Gather up incidents and anecdotes of the missionaries, and of the native converts. Enter into their struggles, their fears, their sufferings, and it will fill this meeting with interest and all hearts with overflowing thanks for the blessing of religious liberty. The early numbers of the *Missionary Herald*, Dr. Anderson's History, Dr. Goodell's "Forty Years in the Turkish Empire," and the Reports of the American Board, furnish abundant material. Those who cannot obtain these books may find some help in the chapter on "National Regeneration," in the Ely Volume. Dr. Bartlett's Historical Sketch is full of information. "Heroes of the Mission Field" numbers the lives of Dr. Goodell and Dr. Dwight among the series. American Tract Society. Price, 10 cts.

PLAN OF LESSONS.

THE lessons of the next two months will be devoted to the work among the Armenians. The attention will be directed chiefly to the great religious movements and great political events that brought about religious liberty in Turkey; and, while centering in Constantinople, affected more or less the whole empire. The study of station-work will be confined to the region north of the Taurus, which is now included in the Western Turkey Mission. The work in the interior, south of the Taurus, and in Eastern Turkey being of such magnitude and importance, will be separately considered. That we may not lose sight of the present in the study of the past, December will be taken up with a glance at the work of the present ear in the fields of the American Board, especially the work of the Woman's Boards. The lessons will then stand as follows : —

August, Work Among the Armenians, 1846–1860; September, Work Among the Armenians, 1860–1885; October, Central Turkey; November, Central Turkey; December, Review of the Present Year.

ANNUAL MEETING OF THE INDIANA BRANCH.

THE tenth annual meeting of the Indiana Branch was held Thursday, May 14th, in the lecture-room of the Congregational Church at Fort Wayne. Mrs. E. M. Elder, president, opened the meeting with a short devotional service. In the absence of the secretary, the annual report was read by Mrs. McCune, of Kokomo.

While deploring the little progress made the last year, she urged the auxiliaries to begin the new year's work with a sense of the responsibility resting upon Christian women, reminding them that women only can rescue our secluded sisters in heathen lands from their darkness and degradation. The Treasurer's report showed a slight falling off of the receipts — a fact accounted for by the great pressure that has been felt in some of the auxiliaries to work for their own church needs. These reports were placed in the hands of committees. Reports of auxiliaries followed. Six well established senior societies, three junior, and one juvenile were represented, while from two or three churches besides, contributions had been sent.

Greetings from the Woman's Board of Missions of the Interior were presented by Mrs. G. B. Willcox, who congratulated the Indiana Branch that never before had they retrograded ever so little in their contributions, and suggested methods by which the aim which had been set before them for the year might be reached. She encouraged their faith by the story of the "Lighters of Darkness," in Marash College, Turkey, who have just sent their pledge to the young ladies' fund, or the "Bridge." Four years ago the girls of the Interior laid the foundation of their Bridge by building Marash College. There these other girls found rescue from the tides of heathenism, and now they are helping to raise the topmost stones of this wonderful highway.

On Friday afternoon, at an adjourned meeting, after full and free discussion, it was voted to try to raise the $800 recommended by the Board. It was stated that there are more than twelve hundred women in the churches of Indiana, and those present were urged to seek out the weak churches and remind them of their privilege, that, if possible, no one of the twelve hundred might fail to give at least one dollar.

Mrs. Haddock declining re-election, Miss E. B. Warren, of Terre Haute, was chosen Secretary, and Mrs. N. A. Hyde, of Indianapolis, Treasurer.

With strengthened faith and new resolve, the Branch adjourned to meet next year at Elkhart.

TO THE YOUNG LADIES' SOCIETIES.

Three letters addressed to you in the Mission Studies for June, we would gladly copy entire, if we had space. The first is from a member of the young ladies' committee, who writes: —

I HOLD in my hands, dear girls of the Interior, a bit of cardboard not at all unfamiliar in its coloring and shape, somewhat ink-stained from dampness gathered in its two journeys over seas, and bearing this inscription: "The Young Ladies' Missionary Society of the Girls' College at Marash, Turkey, promise to raise $20 for the young ladies' work (Woman's Board of Missions of the Interior) for 1885."

Girls, I touch this pledge, I touch the letters which accompany it, and which are given below for your reading, with reverent hands. What are we, that our Lord should so quickly let us begin to gather in our harvest? In 1882 we built the college at Marash. Now, three years later, the Young Ladies' Missionary Society of this same college sends in its pledge for twenty dollars. Surely, we have found it wise to lend to the Lord.

Oh my girls, I wish I could speak face to face with every one of you, that I might implore you to do your full part in this work.

We live in a day of great opportunity. We cannot afford to let it go by. E. K. C.

The second is from the Secretary of the Young Ladies' Society in Marash College, a native girl. We give an extract: —

Our society having been organized April 1, 1884, we planned to observe our anniversary day; and while planning for the same, your letter was most providentially received. "The Bridge," and the work it represents, as explained by your letter and the printed articles sent, interested us exceedingly, and we voted to try to secure a share of the eighth degree ($20). We had considerable doubt, however, as to our ability to do this, but carried out our plan for the anniversary gathering.

While the last hymn was being sung, two of our smaller girls, each with a little plate in hand, began to gather the contributions. Our guests were generously disposed, and we received 470 piasters.* We shall now endeavor to make our entire contribution equal to the seventh share ($25).

The third letter is from Miss Shattuck, describing the annual meeting of these "Lighters of Darkness." We give an extract:—

One hundred and fifty were present, invited by the members — programmes and tickets being sent to such as we felt would appreciate the subject. The only gentlemen invited were the pastors, college teachers, missionaries, and theological students. We had a fine audience, as every missionary gathering I ever attended has been, here and elsewhere.

The feet of Chinese women were illustrated by a drawing. Our big missionary map, picture of the "Morning Star" (old one), and the "Mute Appeal" (greatly enlarged), all were helps to our girls' good reports on Japan, Africa, China, Sandwich Islands, India, and the Moslems. We sung familiar hymns to familiar tunes — "Ye Christian Heralds," "From Greenland's Icy Mountains,"—etc. for the audience's sake, and Miss Child drilled a choir of eight for two new tunes to familiar words, sung in different parts very nicely by our girls. Many said, "We ought to have brought more money with us. It is a shame to give so little." I rejoice exceedingly that the subject has been so studied by our girls during these months past, and that they become so impressed with it as to interest others.

Of course they did all the translating themselves, and were quite as self-helpful as girls at home, by way of preparation for such a meeting. They threw their soul into everything they tried to do, and then said, as did my Colorado little folks, "God did help us, didn't he?" Send us all the helps you do other girls, and we will be one of the great family.

CHILDREN'S WORK.

THE MORNING STAR MISSION FUND.

A NEW pink leaflet has just been issued by the Woman's Board of Missions of the Interior. The children who have read Miss Pollock's first pink parable, and "Another Message to the Coral-Workers," will have no doubt it is for them. It is to accompany and explain the new certificate which is now ready to be forwarded to every one who sends one dime to our treasurer, Mrs. J. B. Leake, 218 Cass Street, Chicago, or to the Secretary of the Woman's Board of Missions of the Interior, 75 Madison Street, Chicago. One dime will purchase a share in the "Children's Morn-

---

* One piaster equals three and four-sevenths cents.

ing Star Mission Fund;" and we hope every child in the Interior— which extends, you know, from Ohio to the Rocky Mountains, inclusive — will secure one or more shares. No child will be willing to be left out from this work for the children's ship and the children's schools.

The following paragraph from Mission Studies will show how the children's Morning Star Fund is to be expended:—

"We have this year, for the first time, I think, a concerted plan of work for our children. It is the raising of the sum of $2,500, which enables us to take a $250 share in Hadjin School (Turkey); a $300 share in Bridgman School (China); a $450 share in Umzumbi Home (Africa); and a $1,500 share in the work of the *Morning Star* (Micronesia)."

Do you see the beauty of the design?

The children of the Interior, with outstretched hands of faith and love, are going to band this great ball on which we live. Hand to hand with us in the ring, are our far-away sisters and brothers, little and big. In Turkey, Mrs. Coffing, Miss Spencer, and the children of Hadjin take hold; in China, Miss Haven, Miss Chapin, and the little flock at Bridgman; in Africa, our teacher there with her pupils; while to complete our circle we have the dear ones of Micronesia, who, because of our *Morning Star*, are come with us to worship Jesus. "It is he that sitteth upon the circle of the earth."

RECEIPTS OF THE WOMAN'S BOARD OF MISSIONS OF THE INTERIOR.

MRS. J. B. LEAKE, TREASURER.

FROM APRIL 18, 1885, TO MAY 18, 1885.

ILLINOIS.

ILLINOIS BRANCH.— Mrs. W. A. Talcott, of Rockford, Treas. *Crete,* Mrs. E. M. Porter, 1.25; *Chicago,* Mrs. N. B. Andruss, 2, Carrie Burnham, 25 cts., Bethany Ch., 4.80, First Ch., 100; *Farmington,* 26; *Tolono,* 10; *Winnebago,* 18, — $162 30
JUNIOR: *Chicago,* Y. L. Soc., Plymouth Ch., 100; Y. L. Soc., South Ch., 40; *Plano,* Y. L. Soc.,$3; *Waverly,*Y.L.Soc.,31, 174 00
JUVENILE: *Roseville,* Girls, Miss. Band, 1.50; *Wayne,* "Busy Builders," 14.97; *Wheaton,* 2.10, — 18 57

Total, $354 87

INDIANA.

INDIANA BRANCH.— Miss E. R. Warren, of Terre Haute, Treas. *Elkhart,* 13.75; *Indi-*

anapolis, Mayflower, 60.80; *Kokomo,*20.80:*Michigan City,* 21.60; *Terre Haute,* 56.55, $172 70

Total, $172 70

IOWA.

IOWA BRANCH. — Mrs. E. R. Potter, of Grinnell, Treas. *Anita,* 11.30; *Durant,* 6; *Davenport,* 8.10; *Denmark,* 25; *Des Moines,* 20; *Keokuk,* Mrs. M. A. S., 5; *McGregor,* 7.25; *Marshalltown,* 10; *Magnolia,* 3.75; *Oskaloosa,* 9.86; *Quaqueston,* 6; *Storm Lake,* 10; *Salem,* Mrs. S. F. Stevens, 1; *Tyrone,* Mrs. Mary A. Payne, 3.25; *Webster City,* 4; *Waucoma,* 10; *Waterloo,* 11.25; *West Burlington,* Mrs. J. B. Rarup, 1, $152 76
JUNIOR: *Des Moines,* Plymouth Rock Miss. Soc., 13.90; *Har-*

lan, Young People's Miss. Soc., 13, $26 90

JUVENILE: *Waucoma,* Miss. Soc., 25 00

SABBATH-SCHOOLS:*DesMoines,* 5.66; *Mount Pleasant,* 6.07, 11 73

Total, $216 39

KANSAS.

KANSAS BRANCH.— Mrs. A. L. Slosson, of Leavenworth, Treas. *Auburn,* 3.25; *Capioma,* Mrs. H. Job, 1; *Centralia,* 5; *Highland,* Mrs. W. Trevett, 6; *Kirwin,* 5.56; *Leavenworth,* 6; *Russell,* 8; *Stockton,* 2.80, $37 61

JUVENILE: *Topeka,* 25; *Hiawatha,* 60 cts., 25 60

Total, $63 21

MICHIGAN.

MICHIGAN BRANCH. — Mrs. Charles E. Fox, of Detroit, Treas. *Ann Arbor,* 25; *Dowagiac,* Aux., 5; *Grand Rapids,* Park Ch., Aux., 50; *Greenville,* 40; *Olivet,* 19.50; *Vernon,* 7, $146 50

JUNIOR SOCIETIES: Charlotte Y. L. Star Miss. Soc., 6.65; *Detroit,* Woodward Ave. Ch., Y. L. Miss. Soc., 50, 56 65

FOR NEW MORNING STAR:— *Vernon,* Aux., 3 10

Total, $206 25

MINNESOTA.

MINNESOTA BRANCH.— Mrs. E. M. Williams, of Northfield, Treas. *Aitkin,* 4.42; *Clearwater,* 6; *Dassel,* 3.70; *Excelsior,* 4.63; *Glyndon,* 10.50; *Hamilton,* 8; *Mantorville,* 1.66; *Northfield,* 9.85; *St. Charles,* 9.50; *Sauk Centre,* 30; *St. Paul,* C. G., 50, $138 26

JUNIORS: *Minneapolis,* Miss Hale, special for The Bridge, 20; *Northfield,* Carleton College Aux., 30, 50 00

JUVENILES: *Minneapolis,* 1st Ch., S. S, 59.75; *Northfield,* Cong. S. S., 60; *Owatonna,* S. S. Easter offering, 7.75, 127 50

Total, $315 76

OHIO.

OHIO BRANCH.— Mrs. Geo. H. Ely, of Elyria, Treas. *Alliance,* Mrs. J. M. Thomas, 10; *Austinburg,* 10; *Bellevue,* 22.25; *Cincinnati,* Walnut

Hills, 25; *Chagrin Falls,* 12; *Conneaut,* 17.50; *Elyria,* 72.40; *Geneva,* 16.50; *Hampden,* 6.21; *Kelley's Island,* 18; *Kelloggsville,* 4; *Mesopotamia,* 5; *Oberlin,* 56, Mrs. M. B. Hitchcock, 1; *Ravenna,* 15; *So. Newbury,* 11.67; *Thompson,* 2. Less expenses, 9, $295 53

Total, $295 53

PENNSYLVANIA.

Allegheny, Plymouth Ch., Y. People's Miss. Soc., 5, $5 00

Total, $5 00

SOUTH DAKOTA BRANCH.

Mrs. H. H. Smith, of Yankton, Treas. *Bon Homme,* 3; *Yankton,* 7.13, $10 13

JUVENILE: *Vermillion,* S. S., for Morning Star, 22.23; *Watertown,* Cheerful Workers, 10; *De Boe,* Harry L. Grover and Margery J. Davis, for Morning Star, 20cts., 32 43

Total, $42 56

WISCONSIN.

WISCONSIN BRANCH. — Mrs. R. Coburn, of Whitewater,Treas. *Appleton,* 20; *Beloit,* 2d Ch. 40.25; *Blake's Prairie,* 7; *Bloomington,* 2 of wh. is a birthday gift, 7; *Clinton,* 2.80; *Ft. Atkinson,* 6.25; *Lancaster,* 10; *Milwaukee,* Grand Ave. Aux., 35; *Madison,* 38.50; *Plymouth,* 6; *Racine,* 20.60; *Royalton,* 5; *West Salem,* Mrs. Faith H. Montague, 5; *Windsor,* const. Mrs. S. H. Sabin L. M., 25, $227 40

JUNIORS: *Evansville,* 8; *Milton,* 15, 23 00

JUVENILES: *La Crosse,* Little Helpers, 25 00

$275 40

Less expenses, 15 50

Total, $259 90

MISCELLANEOUS.

Sale of "Coan's Life," 6; of leaflets, 30.69; of envelopes, 30 cts.; chart, 50 cts.; cash, 65 cts., $38 14

Total, $38 14

Receipts for the month, $1,970 31
Previously acknowledged, 15,675 30

Total since Oct. 22, 1884, $17,645 61

LETTER FROM BROOSA.

BROOSA, Jan. 23, 1885.

. . . I THINK I have not written you since December 1st; and now, as my mind runs back over the period of nearly two months, I am amazed that they should have seemed such busy ones when so few events stand out as worthy of being recorded. Early in December I was far from well for several days; but I had to forget myself in helping to nurse and care for one of our older girls, who was taken with a severe attack of inflammatory rheumatism. When such cases occur I always wish I was under the same roof, for it takes many steps to run between the two houses and up the long stairs to the sick-room. . . . December 14th we had an interesting Sabbath, when our preacher's little baby was baptized, and two more of our girls made a public profession of their faith. One was Penelope, a Greek girl, whose home is on the island of Mitylene; the other, Rebecca, daughter of our preacher, who has been a day-scholar ever since I came to Broosa. Now, on account of her mother's ill-health, she is at home, and comes only for her music lesson through the week, but is regularly in her place in the Sunday-school.

A young man also joined the church, he, too, a Greek; and our hearts were rejoiced to see him take this stand, for he has been greatly persecuted by all the members of his family, and often turned out of the house without food or help of any kind, besides losing employment at his trade, so that at times he has been dependent on charity for his daily bread. Patiently he has borne it all for the Master's sake, and we know he will not lose his reward, for the promise is sure.

Lately another young Greek has become interested in the truth, and just as soon as it was known that he was attending the service at the chapel, and did not wish to work on Sunday, he lost his place — his employer a nominal Christian, however. He has been very firm, and his manly course has won our admiration; and now we hope that he may be not only intellectually convinced, but that he may be truly converted, and become as a little child, that so he may enter the kingdom of heaven. Calling at the preacher's house a few evenings since we met another inquirer, so that the leaven seems slowly working, and we want you to rejoice with us even over these few signs.

I have no record of the days immediately preceding Christmas; which fact in itself shows that we were unusually busy, for we did not want the preparations for that day to take time for our regular duties. We decided not to have a tree this time, but to get up some quieter entertainment; so, having made everything ready beforehand, we continued school up to Christmas noon, taking only the afternoon for our holiday. We invited all our pupils and one or two other little friends up into the school sitting-room, which was prettily decorated with ivy and flags, and there, with games, singing, distributing gifts and refreshments, we had a happy time, until the shadows warned us that even Christmas day must have its sunset. The contents of that beautiful California box, which had been but slightly disturbed through the year, were all distributed; and you can imagine how eyes sparkled as those nice boxes of stationery, fancy inkstands, bright pen-holders, and bottles of perfumery made their appearance. Then more useful, but not less appreciated, were the warm sacques, happily fitting as if made on purpose for the recipients, the stockings, brushes and combs, napkins, towels, needle-cases, and aprons. Maritza was a happy girl indeed as the soft, pink shawl made by Miss Dyer was bestowed on her; and there was no one who deserved it more, for she is a faithful, obedient, loving scholar. With donations from friends in the East besides, there was plenty to go all round, and make a merry Christmas for those in whom you are so interested. Our list, including the teachers, our preacher and bookseller, and their wives, numbered over forty; and this, with our personal presents to servants and others whom we wished to remember, gave us considerable thinking and planning,— but it was delightful work. I wish the echoes of the school's pretty Christmas song could have been wafted to your ears, when you were the ones to make such an occasion possible. The girls had prepared little gifts for each other and for us, showing that they, too, are learning the blessedness of giving. But I must not weary you with further details.

As our vacation must necessarily include the Greek and Armenian holidays, we continued school up to noon of January 2d, and then dismissed our little band, which had been kept steadily employed for fifteen full weeks. We had no public closing exercises, but reviewed before the school our several classes in their Bible and catechism lessons for the term,—Mrs. Newell the younger Greek pupils in Greek, I the younger Armenian girls in Armenian, and Miss Twichell those of both nationalities who were advanced enough at the beginning of this school-year to be united in an English class. Their subject had been the Life of Christ; and they did *well*, reflecting credit on themselves and their teacher. Some of their answers were so simply yet quaintly expressed that we could not repress a smile; but they showed that they understood what they had studied, even if there was an occasional slip in English.

Eight whose homes were too far away to allow them to visit them in the short interval, remained with us, and I was surprised to see how happy and contented they were. To be sure, many rules were suspended, and we tried to plan for their happiness as well as our own, but still I feel like commending them for the spirit they manifested. They sometimes say to me, "If you can be separated from your home for so many years, ought we to complain when we can see our parents every year?"

The few Europeans here keep up the habit of calling on New-Year's Day, and the native friends do the same at the beginning of their year, January 13th; and then with Greek Christmas and Armenian Christmas, the whole time seemed like a regular visiting-season. I was glad to be free to receive our friends, and I gave more time than usual to making calls myself, either with the other teachers, or my husband, or alone. I felt that I was leaving much undone at home in order to accomplish it; but there seemed to be no other alternative, as the weather was comparatively pleasant, and it was so much more difficult to go in school-time. An afternoon of calling here not only uses the time actually spent in visiting, but for me it means generally many hours of relaxation afterward; for the amount of sweets and Turkish coffee that I am obliged to dispose of usually produces a bad headache, if nothing more serious. For this reason, as well as on account of feeling that I can do more good by going in a quiet way, I never make more than a few calls at a time, if I can possibly arrange to do so.

There are certain claims of society that must be met even in a place like this, and which, being met, help us, at least indirectly, in our work. The English consul is very kind to us; so when on the day that our girls are gathering back, and parents are with them to be entertained, and numberless other things to be attended to, the consul's little five-year-old daughter arrives, accompanied by courier and nurse, they, too, must have their full share of attention, though you hardly know how to make it all come in.

I wish you could have spent this vacation with me! What with going to see the whirling dervishes, visiting Greek and Armenian houses, taking dinner with our preacher and his interesting family, lunching with our *taroohi*, who is expecting to be married very soon, taking a part in the betrothal of our Armenian teacher, receiving visits, and helping prepare for native company several times, sending off our girls, and welcoming them back again, I think you would have been entertained; for all these scenes, most of which are so familiar to me, would have had much in them novel, and of exceeding interest to you.

By Tuesday, the 20th, the girls were all in their places, with one or two exceptions; and on Wednesday morning the regular school exercises began. Our number is less by one, as family circumstances rendered it necessary for one of our Armenian girls to leave. She had been in the school just one year, and had only fairly learned *how* to *study*, so that it seemed as if the year and the money her father has paid were almost thrown away; but yet I don't want to look on the dark side. Who knows what influences may have been set to work that may change, or at least modify, her whole future? I shall try to keep a hold on her, though she is not by any means removed from Christian privileges.

. . . The lateness of the hour tells me I must not write more. With best wishes for the New Year to you and yours, and all the circle of California sisters,   Sincerely yours,

TILLIE J. BALDWIN.

--------------•◦•--------------

THE *Foreign Missionary* regards as orthodox the prayer of the little girl, "O Lord, bless the missionaries, and help them convert the heathen; and bless the heathenaries, and help them convert each other," and looks hopefully to its answer in the self-evangelization of the nations by their native ministry.

FOR WOMAN.

Vol. XV. AUGUST, 1885. No. 8.

MEXICO.

SEED–SOWING IN MEXICO.

BY MRS. JAMES D. EATON.

CHIHUAHUA, MEX.

THIS is, indeed, a " dry and thirsty land." Nothing could be more unpromising than the miles of barren waste that greet the eye of the traveler who follows the high table-land of Central Mexico, by the line of the Mexican Central Railroad.

From the border to the center of the republic there is but little variation — the hardy mezquit-bush and the varied cacti being almost the sole vegetation. And yet, even this desert land may be made to "blossom like the rose"; and where the few rivers have their courses, or the hand of man has been busy with the irrigating ditch, the fertility of the soil is surprising.

To the missionary who stands at these outposts and casts his eye abroad, this condition of the natural is but a figure of the spiritual state. The fruit which the "Lord of the harvest" looks for is but scant; the seed-sowing has been poorly done, or neglected altogether, and the careful after-tending, the irrigation, and the weeding, are utterly wanting. It is our privilege to be the first, in this part of Mexico, to break up the fallow ground, and to sow the seed of the Word of life. Among our recent experiences is one of peculiar interest, of which you may be glad to hear.

Parral is the second city of importance in the State of Chihuahua. A few days since a party of four — the two older missionaries from Chihuahua, with their well-beloved younger brother and sister, Mr. and Mrs. Case, of Parral — started from the latter point to visit Santa Barbara, a town distant about eighteen miles; formerly larger even than Parral, but now greatly reduced, by losses of mines and of population.

A drive of about three hours over a rough road, but through beautiful scenery, brought us to the town a little after dinner-time. In response to our eager inquiries, we were told that there was no such thing as a *fouda* (restaurant) or a *mesóu* (inn) in the place; but one of the bystanders (it does not take long for a crowd to collect in Mexico) offered to cook us some *frijoles* (beans) and eggs, in his chimney-corner. Although we declined his kind offer, hoping to find some place where a bed could be furnished as well, we marked the place as one where we should return, later. We finally obtained accommodations at a house in the center of the town, where the dinner of fried eggs, bread, *frijoles*, and coffee, that was prepared after some delay, seemed one of the best we had ever tasted.

A vacant house just opposite, belonging to an American, was put at our disposal for an evening meeting, and we sallied forth to advertise it.

Returning to the scene of our first entrance into the town, we were most cordially invited into the house — one of the humbler, though not the very poorest, it being furnished with a separate kitchen, a bedstead, a table, and a few chairs.

After a few moments of general conversation we produced our hymn-books, and asked if they would not like to have us sing a little. They eagerly assented, and we had not sung through one hymn before there were twenty-five or thirty people gathered in the room and about the door, listening. They were all squatted on the floor, in Mexican fashion, many of the women with babies, and two or three small children clinging to their skirts. After reading the well-known hymn, "Around the throne of God in Heaven, ten thousand children stand," and before singing, we asked how many of the women there had children in heaven. It was touching to hear the responses: "I have two;" "And I, three;" "And I, six;" "And I, eight;" until nearly every one present had given her testimony to the fact that the mortality among children of the poor in Mexico is very large.

Complete sympathy was established when it was made known that each of the missionary mothers present had a little one in that same holy state, and during the singing that followed, there was hardly a dry eye in the room. How easy and natural it was then to turn the thoughts of those mothers to the loving Jesus, who carries the lambs in his bosom! Then followed the reading of some passages of Scripture; and we rose to go, first telling them that there would be more singing and reading that evening at 7 o'clock, in a certain well-known house, and inviting all to come. We were not allowed to go, however, until we had first partaken of coffee and bread, prepared by our hospitable friend, and the hearty hand-shaking and embracing that followed testified to their hearty good-will.

On our way from this house to the plaza, we stopped at every open door and invited the people to come to the *free* meeting of the evening; and in one place we gathered another large company similar to the first, where we gained their hearts by singing of the birth of Jesus in Bethlehem, as we noticed that they had an altar erected in the room to St. Joseph.

The room which had been offered us was large, but unfurnished except for a table, which served to display the books and tracts Mr. Case had brought with him. The kind lady whose house we shared sent chairs enough for us, and we borrowed some candlesticks, to hold the candles we bought. At the appointed time a few had gathered in the room; but when we began to sing, many crowded about the door and windows, and soon we had about forty in the room, and as many more outside, listening eagerly. The singing of Christian hymns formed a large part of the exercises; the parable of the Prodigal Son was read; and then Mr. Eaton spoke briefly to them from the text, "God so loved the world, that he gave his only begotton Son," etc.

Their attention was perfect, and the interested way in which they looked at each other, and responded heartily to any question put by the speaker, showed that they clearly understood every word.

A number of books were sold after the service, and then we went to rest (!), on mattresses spread upon the floor of one room, that served as sleeping-room for six people.

When we came to leave, the next morning, it was with the most cordial feeling on both sides. The lady of the house assured us that she should be very sad after our departure, and that whenever we wished to return, even though it might be at midnight, we had only to knock at the door, and we should be admitted. Her hearty good-bye hug gave emphasis to her cordial words.

We were saddened, however, to think, as we drove away, that these poor people, so hungry for the Bread of Life, are yet so entirely under the power of their priest, that when he comes to know of our visit, and tells them that we are the hated "heretics," these same hospitable doors will be closed upon us; and instead of embraces, stones may be showered upon us. But the sword has entered, and even as in the time of Christ, it will divide, and some will be found on the side of the Lord.

Pray for Mexico.

CEYLON.

ANNUAL REPORT OF THE MANEPY AND PANDITERIPO FIELDS FOR 1884.

FROM MISS M. LEITCH.

THE past year has been one of much encouragement: 59 persons have united with-the three churches in the field; namely, 45 in Manepy, 11 in Navaly, and 3 in Panditeripo. Of these, 52 united on profession of faith, and 7 by letter. Besides these, quite a number from one field, former members of our day and Sabbath-schools and inquirers' classes, have been received, on profession of faith, in the Wesleyan and Church Mission churches, as they are now students in the boarding-schools of those missions. In all this we rejoice. Our native Christians, at the beginning of the year, during the Week of Prayer, united together to pray that fifty might be brought to Christ within the year. Some thought it was a very large request, but it was the prayer of faith from more than one heart. They feel that God has heard their prayer, and they take courage to ask for great things the coming year. We do not forget that dear friends in the home-land have been praying especially for this field and work, and we are glad that these prayers have been and are being answered, and we believe that we shall rejoice together at the last glad ingathering.

Another encouraging feature of the year has been the forming of several new inquirers' classes. There are now held weekly 17 inquirers' classes, with a total average attendance of about 150. In these meetings the portion of Scripture appointed to be read during the week is explained. Each one is expected to repeat a verse of Scripture and to offer prayer. The leader also inquires after and encourages each one in the class in regard to habits of daily prayer, Bible study, and church attendance. These classes are conducted by the native pastors, catechists, leading native Christians, and by ourselves. To join one of these classes helps the young people to take a step toward confessing Christ, puts them under the care of older Christians, and, by meeting together from week to week, they become a band of friends to encourage each other. They also become known in their villages as, inquirers. Such classes are rallying-points, to which any one showing signs of interest is at once invited. In countries where to leave idolatry and come over to Christianity is so great a change, such a class, as a stepping-stone, is a great help. It is our desire to see an inquirers' class, however small, in every day-school before the end of the coming year. For God's help in this, and for these 150 inquirers, we ask our home friends to pray. The way in which some of those who joined the church this year have been led to Christ, has seemed to us interesting. I will mention a few instances.

Chelappah, a man in Arnikotty, was led to Christ by the persistent efforts of a young Christian boy. He has shown so much earnestness in regard to bringing his family, as quite to put to shame many of our older Christians. He brought his wife and children to church. He did not make the common excuse of want of jewels and beautiful cloths; and though the heathen relatives persecuted and ridiculed him, he took no notice. He had his children baptized, bought a Bible, and began family prayers; sought the Bible-women, and invited them to teach his wife, though they are of a much lower caste than he. He brought his daughter often to the girls' inquirers' class, walking the mile both ways, and waiting patiently outside during the meeting. He had the joy of seeing his wife join the church at the close of the year. One of the inquirers, a young man of a high heathen family, has lately achieved a great success in being married without heathen ceremonies. The parents of both parties were strong Sivites, but the young man never for a moment wavered. The bride had formerly learned the Bible lessons in our day-school, and, again, when too old to go to day-school,— *i. e.*, after the age of twelve,— she had been taught in her home by one of our Bible-women; so she also favored a Christian marriage — one of the many good results of Bible-women's work.

Another, a young man of the pariah caste, who had studied in one of our day-schools, was threatened by the higher-caste heathen people, his former masters, with dreadful punishments if he should join the church; for the old system of master and serf, though under the English Government done away with in name, still exists in a greater or less degree, and the pariahs stand much in fear of, and are in subjection to, the higher castes. For three years he hid the light in his heart, living privately as a Christian, but fearing to confess Christ. At last the light would not stay hidden, and he joined the church. The next Sabbath he was stopped on his way to the morning service and ordered to work, and beaten because he refused. He still continued to attend church; and because of this, one day when on his way to town with a bundle of cloth to sell he was caught, his cloth, and earnings, and waist-chain taken from him, and he was compelled to walk sixteen miles in the hot sun, and left in a strange village, with threats that if he ever returned to his home he would be imprisoned. He stayed away some weeks, and then returned. This was done, it appears to intimidate other low-caste people from becoming Christians, lest they should become enlightened, and no longer submit to their control. The boy still continued to attend church. They then instituted a false case against him in court, but, by the efforts of our native Christians, it was abandoned; but both parties were fined 500 rupees for non-appearance. They were enraged that they had to pay this sum, and forthwith dragged the boy to their house, and made him stand for three hours in the midday sun, with his face turned toward the sun, and holding a stone on his forehead — a most cruel torture.

At this time we warned the people that if they committed another act of violence toward the boy they would be prosecuted. On the next Sabbath the boy, notwithstanding threats and punishments, was found in his place in church, both morning and evening. The lesson was about Paul being not only willing to be bound, but also to die, for the name of the Lord Jesus. I noticed while teaching it that the boy's face was shining. I little thought how soon another trial would come to him. The very next day those men took him to their house, and, tying his hands and feet, beat him in the most shameful manner, and left him tied in that way for some hours. I was called by his sister, and saw him in this state. The moment I had turned my back, fearing I should take a case against them, they dragged him for some distance on his back, which was unprotected by any clothing, over the dust and stones, and then marched him off to town; over fields and fences not the direct way, for fear others should see them, their haste being to get a false case into court before we could enter a true one. But their plan did not succeed. I saw the police inspector the next morning, and the magistrate at once ordered the men to be arrested and sent to jail, with the prospect before them, if the case was tried, of being sent to prison for a term of years. They begged for mercy, which, for the sake of peace in the village, we thought best to grant; but they had to pay fines, costs, etc., amounting to about 100 rupees, and they have promised in future to let the boy alone. The affair has proved for us a complete success; for if any low-caste wish in future to join the church, they will feel at perfect liberty to do so. The people of that village have learned several lessons. The self-control, firm-ness, and courage of the boy were admirable, and showed what Christianity could do even for a pariah.

In our three churches there are 303 communicants, and the total of church contributions this year has been 1351.30 rupees — making a better average than some American churches could show. Some of our leading men have given considerable in aid of the Jaffna College Endowment Fund, and the Training-School new building, and to several other objects, besides private charity to the poor. Christianity does not make its converts paupers. Many of these native Christians are well educated, and are highly respected and influential in the community.

Thirty-eight large moonlight meetings have been held during the past year in the tent and school bungalows in different parts of the field. These were attended by one or both of us. Besides these, many smaller meetings have been held by the helpers alone. The monthly moonlight preaching services held in the church for educated heathen, have been kept up. Various missionaries and native pastors have conducted the services, and good audiences have attended. Besides these, four special meetings have been held at the station during the year, at each of which the audiences have numbered between four and five hundred. One was addressed by the Rev. J. Philips, a missionary from Midnapore, India; another, by the Rev. M. Jenkins, one of the home secretaries of the English Wesleyan Mission; another, a good-bye sermon, by Rev. S. W. Howland, before his departure for America; and a fourth, a temperance meeting. Two union prayer-meetings for educated women have been held, with an attendance of about 100 at each. At the time of the large heathen festival held here at Manepy, con-tinuous singing and preaching services and tract distribution were carried on. Large audiences were present throughout the day.

The most encouraging thing in the line of day-schools is, that we have succeeded in building up a large Christian school in San-tillipay, in place of the heathen school. It will commence to re ceive Government grant about the middle of the year, and will then be self-supporting. This is "the Lord's doing, and it its mar-velous in our eyes." We now have 24 day-schools under our care, and there are three others which co-operate with us. In all of these there is a total of over 1,300 boys and 600 girls — altogether about 2,000 children who are brought under Christian influence. These schools are visited by our helpers, and their secular and re-ligious lessons are carefully supervised. They received aid the past year from Government. The extra expense to us has been 1;115 rupees — about $500. This we have given ourselves, but we believe the money to have been well spent. The Bible lessons taught uniformly in these schools, as well as by all the Bible-women to their village pupils, have been as follows : To be memorized, Psalms i., xxiii., ciii., li., xci., cxxxiii., xix., xxvii., xl. ; and Prov. xxiii. 29–35 ; also Eccles. xii. 1–13.

The International Sabbath-School Lessons have been studied, and the Golden Texts memorized, also twelve new hymns and lyrics. Part of Matthew's Gospel has been read. Quarterly examinations of these lessons have been held during the year, and the work done by each child carefully recorded, together with each child's day and Sabbath school attendance. Christmas gifts are given each year to all the children, but in accordance with this record.

TURKEY.

LETTER FROM MRS. SCHNEIDER.

. . . In the short time left me this morning, I would like to give you a hasty review of the year. Last autumn, when we resumed work after vacation it was with the feeling that if we, single-handed and alone, could only retain our hold till reinforcements came, it was all to which we were equal. We were then in eager expectancy that Mr. and Mrs. Fuller would soon come to take up this work. We said to each other, When they come the coffee-rooms will be visited, and seekers after the truth and cavilers will alike be counseled with by Mr. Fuller, with his good judgment and Turkish scholarship. But how will he, a stranger, reach the non-Protestant young Armenians who are not in the habit of calling here? So our "socials," or "receptions," were started, to draw in these young men weekly, by lectures or recreation. We did not once think of their becoming popular, but they soon came in such crowds we had to receive them by ticket. Art, law, and medical students, merchants and mechanics, seemed glad to come. Singing is always a part of the programme, and we close with prayer. We are richly repaid for any effort at entertainment by the gratitude shown, and now that prejudice is removed, the truth will find easier access.

Another blessing came to us in Dr. Somerville. Through an interpreter he preached in all these Eastern languages. We must have him in place of a "social," thought we, and he accepted our invitation to preach; and then to all his audiences in Pera, Scutari, and other places, he gave an invitation to everybody to come to "Mrs. Schneider's hall," not knowing ours was simply a dwelling-house. Numbers of these people had never been in a Protestant church, and to have the gospel truth presented to them that evening, and at the Bible-house at Vlanga,—and even in one of the largest theatres in Pera,—seemed a blessing of greatest im-portance. Although we as yet know of no conversions, still, inef-faceable impressions must have been made. A new class has been formed in our Sunday-school, including some of these young men who followed him from service to service, and they are all fre-quenters of our lower coffee-rooms.

Our six rooms and hall are occupied by the various classes on Sunday,— only my bedroom has been unoccupied,— and now, hav-ing curtained off my bed, I devote the remainder, with pleasure, to these interesting young men. A young translator in the Bible-house comes over from Scutari to teach them. Last Sunday they remained nearly an hour after school, discussing vital points with the teacher. Do not fail to pray for him. Our Sabbath-school has averaged more than any previous year, although two other Sabbath-schools within five minutes' walk have been started by other denominations. Another feature of the year is the interest in contributing for others. We joyfully contributed to the Morn-ing Star, and we are now doing for the Koords, in Koordistan.

After the removal of the pastor and his family here, a proposal for a mothers' meeting met with a cordial response. While the matrons have their meetings on alternate weeks, the young mar-ried women and girls have theirs meantime. A new life has been infused into these young women's meetings. Heretofore, in the presence of their elders, they had kept silence. Now there is not one who shrinks from prayer, and they are as much surprised at themselves as others are at their newly gained freedom. I feel deeply pained at being able to reach so few worldly women. Let us offer more urgent and persevering prayer for them.

The coffee-rooms are outwardly prosperous. At the lower room, there have been in the last three months 7,429 callers, averaging 110 a day. I cannot say how many of these callers have im-proved their opportunities for religious reading, yet I know that numbers have not only read portions of the truth, but have heard much religious discussion. Our coffee-maker says there was for-merly perfect apathy as to a future existence,— a heaven or a hell, —not enough interest to discuss the question. Now, everybody is more or less on the alert to discuss Bible questions, whether they accept them or not. The upper coffee-room has less patronage, but the frequenters are of a highly respectable character. The one great need in these coffee-rooms is for helpers or missionaries to meet seekers after truth and unbelievers.

𝕐𝕠𝕦𝕟𝕘 ℙ𝕖𝕠𝕡𝕝𝕖'𝕤 𝔻𝕖𝕡𝕒𝕣𝕥𝕞𝕖𝕟𝕥.

SOME CHINESE SUPERSTITIONS.

BY MRS. E. A. WALKER.

Two weeks ago a party of twenty, mostly missionaries, visited Kushan Monastery. Kushan Mountain rises directly from the Foochow plain to a height of 2,900 feet. The monastery is about

CHINESE SEDAN AND BEARERS.

half way up. We from the city went by sedan-chair, and those from Nantai (south suburbs) and Chong Seng Island went by boat to near the foot of the mountain. Some of us had planned to spend the night at the monastery, and on our return the next morning do some visiting at two villages on the route; but on reaching the monastery, we learned that a Chinese official was coming up early the next morning with a large retinue. We preferred to return that night, rather than take the chances of meet-

A CHINESE OFFICIAL.

ing a small army of Chinese soldiers, who would be unpleasantly curious, if not rude.

We are told that the object of his visit is this: Ten or fifteen years ago he was viceroy of this province, and as a work of merit he bought a cow and sent her up to Kushan Monastery, to be nourished there. Now, you must know that this is a Buddhist monastery, and the monks are strict vegetarians, never destroying life or eating animal food. Here is the home of cows, sheep, and swine, with domestic fowls, by the hundred, and a large fish-pond all alive with fish, mostly carp. These have mostly been brought and left there to enjoy a happy life, and die at a good old age. Even turtles and serpents are taken there and let loose. Of late years it has been reported that the monks sold the General's cow to a man who made beef of her. Last autumn he was sent here to defend this place against the French, and it had been reported to him that the monks had sold off his cow. He sent deputies to

KUSHAN MONASTERY.

investigate, and the monks assured them that the cow had died, and been buried, and the golden ear-rings which she had worn were shown as one proof. We saw a cock strutting about with ear-rings in his ears! But the general was still suspicious, so went himself to investigate. Whether he was satisfied, we did not learn. Perhaps the cow's bones were exhumed to satisfy the incredulous old man, who is over seventy years of age.

It is commonly said that the upper classes in China are Confucionists, and have no faith in the low superstitions of the common people; but this officer is, next to Li Hung Chang, the greatest man in China. He is said to have lost a son in the following manner: —

His wife was in feeble health, and the son had a piece of his flesh cut off for her to eat, as a strengthening medicine, and in consequence bled to death. According to Chinese ideas the son performed a most meritorious act, and secured great glory to his parents, who had trained up so filial a son.

We saw at this monastery a young man of less than thirty years who has been there for six years, and in all that time has preserved perpetual silence. He stays in his room much of the time, and sits cross-legged on a raised platform, which is curtained off from the rest of the room. We, of course, had our information from the other monks. We asked, "Why does he keep silent — what merit is there in it?" One answered that he was under a vow, and this vow of silence is said to be especially pleasing to the idols. One monk also told me that if he did not talk he would say neither good or bad, and in not talking he was also like the idols. "Yes," I said, "in that he doesn't speak, he is like them; but in that he *can* speak and doesn't, he is unlike them. He has a precious soul, and they have none." Some of our number gave the silent man a copy of the Sermon on the Mount.

Another young person we saw who seemed to have gone crazy. He spends much of his time sitting in the presence of and contemplating Buddha. He looked excited. His lips moved, and his body rocked to and fro. First he would look up to the idol with such a beseeching look, and then down to the floor, and talk to himself; one moment looking pleased and happy, and the next with such a sad expression it was painful to look upon. His dress was odd — patched in curious shapes, and of various colors.

If the time might only soon come when the ranks of these deluded and superstitious priests might be broken, and the entrance of God's truth might give them the light! He has said in his Word it shall.

But a thing quite as desirable and more to be prayed for is, that the *literati* and gentry should be reached, and more from among them be led to give up their pride of heart.

Miss Hartwell writes from Foochow, China: "We who are out here are only Christians sent on picket duty to the remote points of the great battle-field of the Lord. We miss the enthusiasm, the drum-beat, and the steady march of the great army; but the Great Captain knows our hearts need care as well as those of the main force. Pray for us.

Our Work at Home.

WITH BOTH HANDS EARNESTLY.

[Read at an Auxiliary Meeting in W——.]

WERE I called to preach a short sermon this afternoon, dear sisters, I would take for my text four words found in the prophecies of Micah; the words are these, "With both hands earnestly." But fortunately for us all, I propose to do no such thing. I only desire to bring these few words to bear upon our work of which we are talking.

We watch the infant of a few months catching at his rattle with one hand, not knowing that soon he will need both hands to retain his more weighty treasures. We see the older boy tossing the pebbles into the brook with one hand; but when wishing to create a great splash, he must empty both hands, and put their united strength upon the great stone that is to do his bidding.

Again why is it that the farmer holds his plow with both hands so steadily, but that his furrow may be dry and stright? And why, in felling the giants of the forest, does the woodman use all the strength in his brawny arms? but because his work demands it. The tree is big, and strong, and hard, and he must put all his bone and sinew into each stroke of his axe, until the tree falls at his feet.

So I would say in view of our work as a missionary society,—in view of all we know and have heard of the needs of the heathen world, and in full view of our Saviour's command, I would say, My sisters, let us put both hands to this work most earnestly. This we can do, I am sure, only by a more complete consecration to Christ, which includes his work. And this consecration must come by the full indwelling of the Holy Spirit; by the emptying of self, and the filling up with the better things that pertain to the kingdom of God.

We must pray for a holy ambition, and follow it up with a holy activity. We must pray for a spirit of self-denial, and then go from our knees to the practical ways of denying self. We must pray that our neighbors may be interested in missionary work in foreign lands, and follow up that prayer with visits, and with books telling of the wonderful success of preachers and teachers. We must pray that the Lord's treasury may be kept filled; and then we must see to it, "with both hands earnestly," that we save our pennies and our dollars, and give them a loving sacrifice to our Lord.

And, once more, we must pray that more laborers be sent into the field. And this prayer we ought to indorse by saying, "Here am I; send me;" or, as we lay our hand in blessing upon our sons and our daughters, say, "Here, Lord, take these; I only give thee what was thine before." Thus, dear sisters, it seems to me we may be working "with both hands earnestly." And I will leave the thought with you, asking God so to press the truth home to our hearts, that the year 1885 shall see more real earnest missionary work done than in any previous year of our lives. May we ever keep in mind the costliest gift ever borne to heaven — even the falling tear of the humble penitent; and may we be able to so tell of a Saviour's, love that many tears of repentance shall fall from the eyes of those now sitting in darkness, and who know nothing of the "Jesus way."

MAY MEETING.

The usual anniversary meeting of the Board in Anniversary Week was held in Mt. Vernon Church, Boston, on Thursday, May 28th, at 11 A. M. Bright skies and balmy air brought together a goodly number of interested listeners, and the blessed influence of the Holy Spirit inspiring the speakers to unusual power, and touching the hearts of all present with new love for the work, made the meeting one long to be remembered.

After the opening exercises the first speaker was Mrs. W. M. Stover, of the West Central Africa Mission, who told the thrilling story of the flight of the little missionary company to the coast, at the command of a hostile king. The vivid description of the suddenness of the command, coming like a thunderbolt out of a clear sky; of the vain attempts to change the heart of the king, bringing only the ultimatum, "Go in four days, or be shot;" of the fear that kept all the men and women, whether friendly or otherwise, from lifting a finger to help them; of the remarkable devotion of the children who followed them through all the long walk of two hundred miles to the coast, carrying the missionary children and provisions—sounded more like romance — all too serious though it was to the participants—than sober fact in the nineteenth century.

The next speaker was Mrs. S. W. Howland, of the Ceylon Mission. She spoke of her joy in the work, and the wonderful changes brought about by the gospel. During the twelve years she had been in the field, and specially interested in the school at Oodoopitty, twelve classes had graduated, and every member of them had been a Christian. These were many of them Christian wives, while others had gone as teachers to India or Southern Ceylon. Interesting incidents were given of the work done by these girls and the boys in the college in bringing others to Christ; also of the efforts of the natives to secure schools for their daughters, and of their generosity in giving.

Miss Henrietta Rendall, of the Madura Mission, then spoke of the educational work in the city of Madura. There were ten schools for boys and girls besides the girls' boarding-school, and they were a most important means in evangelizing the people. A new feature in the boarding-school was the coming of several heathen girls, the pupils having formerly been the children of Christian parents. An incident was given of the great pressure brought to bear on such girls by heathen parents, and the power of the Spirit that enabled them to stand firm under persecution.

Miss M. P. Root, M.D., under appointment to go to Madura, followed with a few words of farewell, expressing also the hope that more young ladies would take up the medical work in the various fields.

Miss Eliza Talcott, of the Japan Mission, spoke of the need of experienced teachers in Japan, asking prayers for parents, that they might be willing to consecrate their children to this service; for the young ladies, that they might give their lives to the work; and especially for the Japanese studying in this country, that they might withstand the great pressure of heathenism as they return to their native land, as well as the materialistic doctrines which they may not have heard of here, but which are rife in Japan.

Miss V. A. Clarkson, of the Japan Mission, who was to leave for Japan, gave a short farewell address, asking prayers for herself, and for those among whom she was to labor as she went back to her chosen field.

The next speaker was Mrs. C. R. Allen, of Harpoot, Eastern Turkey. As this was probably the last time Mrs. Allen will be present at any meeting of the Board before her return to Turkey, we give below her entire address, as we are sure many of her friends who were not able to be present will be glad to read her parting words.

The last address was by Miss E. M. Stone, of the Bulgarian Mission. She spoke of her sudden coming to America, to care for an invalid associate, and asked that this associate's place might be filled as soon as possible. She alluded to the political upheavals constantly going on in Bulgaria, the only hope for the country being in the quiet working of the gospel leaven hidden in the hearts of the people. Civilization is going fast, as may be seen in one instance, from the fact that in one of her tours she met a long procession of horses and mules which had on them "Boston Rum," in large black letters. The missionaries must go faster than civilization to save the country for Christ.

Prayer was offered by Mrs.. Allen, of Harpoot, and the meeting closed with the doxology.

MRS. ALLEN'S ADDRESS.

PAUL in writing to the Corinthians of his stay at Ephesus, says, "A great door and effectual is opened unto me;" adding, "and there are many adversaries." His experience is but that of most missionaries. The doors that are opened, and the opportunities that are offered for guiding souls to Christ, are so many, that it becomes a perplexing question how to meet them. My heart has often been burdened because so many calls for help must go unheeded. We cannot do as the disciples did, in telling Jesus all that they did and all that they taught.

We might give you an outline of our work, with its different departments and branches, with statistics of schools, scholars, numbers of churches and members of the same, but they would only seem as headings of the missionary record. No one would think she had any definite knowledge of any work by simply reading the table of contents. So no one interested in missions would presume to assert a thorough acquaintance with any field of labor from hearing now and then a missionary-talk of five or ten minutes' length. The pages of *Life and Light* and the *Missionary Herald*, into which so much intelligence is condensed from all parts of the world, will aid in this investigation. When I tell you that there are over a hundred girls in Armenia College, if you have had no previous knowledge of the condition of woman in that land, you can have no just conception of the far-reaching influence of so many young women who have not only secular education, but are rooted and grounded in the truths of Scripture. I may say that a small church and community in one of our cities contributed nearly $500 for the support of their pastor and schools; but if you have not known the extreme poverty of the land, the sum will seem too small to be mentioned. When I speak of the graduates of the College, and of those who have not yet finished their course, many of whom are teaching in remote towns and villages, do you know that this means a wonderful advance in intelligence and Christian experience, that permits the daughters to leave home and go forth unprotected? Hundreds of women have learned to read, some of them sixty and seventy years of age; but, my sisters, for many this means beatings, burning of primers, the lighting of the midnight lamp.

We learn something of the zeal of poor, tired women, when we see them still cling to their reading after toiling all day in the fields under a blazing sun, or in the cold, wet days of November picking cotton.

A few weeks before I left Harpoot, in company with a native sister, I visited more than a hundred families, in every one of which we read the Testament and offered prayer, men often being present. A few years ago, all these homes were closed against us.

But what or who are some of the adversaries? One of them is the Armenian hierarchy; another the poverty of the people. How can we talk of the duty of giving, when the masses are anxiously inquiring how they shall earn bread for their families? The Turkish Government is another adversary, which means the Mohammedan religion. The followers of the false prophet can never be said to be indifferent to the claims of their faith, and now that their eyes are opened to see what the Christian religion is destined to do, they have aroused themselves to oppose this enemy of the true Prophet; and unless He who guides the affairs of all nations sees fit to restrain the increasing hostility of the defenders of Islamism, we shall see yet greater demonstration of that spirit which seeks to destroy every remnant of the despised religion of the Cross.

I have traveled thousands of miles, visited scores of villages, have been at the homes of the wealthy, the poor, the wretched, and the sorrowing of the Turkish Koordish, as well as Armenian, and all alike, I declare, need the gospel of Christ.

The gospel has been preached in many cities and villages, and we can testify that the light is spreading. Would that I could tell you how much land remains to be possessed. I would like to take you for a few moments to a part of our field that is especially needy of evangelical work. In one of our tours we came, as we had planned to, to the town of Farkin, built upon and around the ruins of the ancient city of Marderopolis (City of Martyrs.) Maratha, an Armenian bishop in the fifth century, collected the bones of the martyrs slain by the cruel Sapor, and buried them there, building a splendid church to their memory. Every available spot within the ruins is literally paved with tombstones, so strong has been the desire of those dying in that region to be buried by the side of those who had given up their lives rather than their holy religion. You would naturally suppose that we should find a more than usual devotion to Christ, with such reminders before them; but instead of this, dwelling as they have for centuries among the barbarous Koords, they have lost their own tongue, and so have been debarred from the helps that would have come to them through their church service.

The women crowded about me, but I could speak with only one. They begged me to stay with them, pleading that they were ignorant: "Oh stay and teach us!" "We shall be lost!" My heart went out in earnest longings for them but I could only tell them I hoped that some one would come to instruct them.

As I stood by our tent at the close of day musing on the past, with its history unwritten, save by tradition, and in the architectural ruins which spoke of wealth, skill, glory, and power, the whole scene before me changed, as if by magic. Through the arched windows and sculptured gateways gleamed the rays of the setting sun. The church so chastely ornamented, the graceful minaret of the crumbling mosque, and broken fragments of polished stones, were bathed in a flood of light. "Type of the new Jerusalem!" I exclaimed, in the ecstasy of my delight; "the golden city that needs no light of the sun or the moon, for 'the glory of God doth lighten it, and the lamp thereof is the Lamb.'" To me it seemed a pledge of what the Lord was to do for those who had drifted away from the faith of this ancestor. "The blood of the martyrs is the seed of the Church." May it not prove so in this place, which we recently learned has planned, with help from the Board, to build a house of worship. Already the songs of Zion are sung there by those who have been redeemed by the blood of the Lamb.

Christian friends, can it be said of you, "Many daughters have done virtuously, but thou excellest them all?" I trust so; but surely you have not reached the goal of your ambition, duty, or privilege. You have as a body fulfilled your pledged work; but how is it in regard to individual responsibility? You to whom the Lord has intrusted small means — would it be true to say of your offerings, "She has done what she could?" And you whom the Lord has made stewards of larger wealth — are you satisfied, or do you think that the Master is pleased, with the offerings you bring to his treasury? Mothers of sons and daughters, what think you of the injunction of your Lord, "Pray ye the Lord of the harvest that he send forth more laborers into his harvest"? You certainly must pray that prayer if you love the Saviour. Are you willing that he answer your prayers by choosing your dear ones to gather in other lands the ripened harvest.

My heart pleads for Turkey, the cradle of the universe; the land where David sang his immortal songs, where prophets foretold the doom of empires long since passed away; where the angels first proclaimed the birth of him at whose name every knee was to bow — Jesus, the Saviour of the world, the light of whose love has fallen upon your homes, Christian sisters, making

them a prototype of the glorious mansions his cruel death procured for you.

I plead for China, with its perishing millions; for Japan, begging for the Bread of Life; for India, ripe for the gospel; last of
all I plead for the Dark Continent, where the greatest hero the
world has ever seen died pleading for its millions. Rather let
these "strings of captives of naked women and children" plead;
those *little* children hanging from the trees. Your missionaries,
weary and worn with the heat and burden of the day, plead. Shall
these all plead in vain? Gethsemane and Calvary plead. Our
glorified Lord pleads. Shall he plead in vain? Is any sacrifice
too great to make for Him who bore the cross to redeem a world?

> " Mētay Hesoos lōg hachu danē,
>   Yer martus azad ullar?
> Voeh, hach mu gar amen megoon,
>   Endze al hach mu gar."

> " Must Jesus bear the cross alone,
>   And all the world go free?
> No, there's a cross for every one,
>   And there's a cross for me."

ANNUAL MEETING OF THE NEW HAVEN BRANCH.

In response to a cordial invitation from the ladies of Middletown, the fourteenth annual meeting of the New Haven Branch
was held in the North Church of that city, May 12, 1885. The exercises of the day were preceded by a devotional meeting, the
leader giving as the key-note, *Love*; and indeed this seemed the
fundamental note of the entire day. "Blessed are ye that sow
beside all waters," was the appropriate motto that greeted us as
we entered the church.

Miss Daggett, who presided in the absence of Mrs. Hart, read
a short letter of greeting from her, in which she expressed the
wish that this might be "the best meeting ever held in this branch
of the Master's service." The responsive scripture-reading was
very impressive; and at the heart-searching question, "How much
owest thou unto my Lord?" with its answer, "All that thou hast;
even thine own self beside," was heard, I am sure the response
of all hearts must have been, "We will think on these things."
The report of Mrs. Cady, the Recording Secretary, was a brief
review of the specific branch-work and the monthly and special
meetings, including the union meeting of mission circles at New
Haven, where questions relative to interesting young people in
the mission-work were discussed. This was followed by the report of the corresponding secretary, who gave us glimpses of the
work in ten different countries, in all of which marked progress
was evident.

The treasurer's report showed the actual receipts for the year to be nearly eleven thousand dollars of which over two thousand dollars was from mission circles. Mrs. G. C. Knapp interested us with an account of her thirty years' work in Bitlis, Turkey. A faint idea of the gross ignorance of the people at the time her labors among them began, may be gained from the fact that in this city of thirty thousand inhabitants, only *one* man was found reading the Bible. In contrast to this there is at present a Protestant church, which has been self-supporting for several years, a girls' boarding-school, also a high-school for boys. These reforms have been accomplished by the gospel, and not by the Government. Her closing appeal, "Shall we not, as sons and daughters, take an interest in our Father's affairs," touched many hearts. Mrs. Whiting, of the Baptist Board, was present, and spoke with particular emphasis of the efficacy of prayer.

The condensed reports of the county vice-presidents proved that much good work was being done in the auxiliaries under their especial care, although of all it cannot be said "She hath done what she could." The basket collation proved a success, and seemingly did not in the least interfere with the usual social intercourse of the hour. Miss Stanwood, of the Boston Board, was present, and called particular attention to the fact that just now there was a loud call for more laborers. From Japan alone comes the call for twenty young women to engage in this work. Who will respond? Who will consecrate all to Him who gave his life for them, and thus have a share in this "woman's work for woman"? Oh ye idle, listless ones, living without seeming aim in life, will *you* not in this appeal see your *own* life work?

A glad surprise awaited us, which was fully appreciated, when Mrs. Titus Coan was announced as the next person who would address us; and as she advanced to the desk the audience could not refrain from cheering. Her countenance was a benediction, and her words abundant testimony of the entire consecration of her life as a sharer in early missionary work with the sainted pioneers who have passed on before. A spicy paper entitled "Patchwork," designed to stimulate home-workers, was next presented, showing the intermingling lights and shades of this work; also how even a faded life, if only once touched by the golden thread of missionary spirit, may be both adorned and beautified.

Mrs. S. W. Howland gave us a very pleasant view of the work. She said: "Among benevolent workers here, it is a very common thing as they meet to hear one and another saying, 'Oh, I am tired of this work!' or, 'I am so discouraged!' but never are such words uttered by the missionaries." Should not this be a reproof to us, who comparatively have so much to strengthen and encourage us in *our* field?

The spirit of the entire meeting was one of loving, earnest devotion to the cause, and betokened steady growth in all the various departments of this " beautiful work."

WOMAN'S BOARD OF MISSIONS.

RECEIPTS FROM MAY 18 TO JUNE 18, 1885.

MAINE.

Maine Branch.—Mrs. Woodbury S. Dana, Treas. Union, Rev. F. V. Norcross, $4; Blanchard, Rays of Light, $3.40, Ladies of Cong. Ch., $5; Cornish, Aux., $12.50, Hillside Gleaners M. C., $10.33; Gardner, Aux., $25.50; Greenville, Aux. (add'l), $5.50, Lakeside Helpers M. C., $3.60; Searsport, Aux., $18.34; Biddeford, Pavilion Ch., Aux., $15, Second Ch., Aux., of wh. $25 const. L. M. Mrs. Hannah A. Abbott, $42.30; Brewer, Aux., $11.40; New Gloucester, Aux., $25; Bath, Central Ch. and Soc'y, $45; Rockland, Aux. (add'l), $5, Golden Sands, $10, Armenian Aid Soc'y, $5, Mrs. Moffett's S. S. Cl., $5; Waterford, Aux., $17; Litchfield Corner, Aux., $23; Auburn, High St. Ch., Aux. (add'l), $5, Y. L. M. B., $5; Bethel, First Ch., Aux., $16, Second Ch., Aux., $12, Little Helpers, $4.50; Andover, Aux., $5.50; Hallowell, Aux., $10.50; Hampden, Aux., $20; South Paris, Aux., $19; Cape Elizabeth, Coral Workers M. C., $15; Gray, Aux., $9; South Freeport, Aux., $50; Harpswell Centre, Aux., $6, two ladies, $5; Foxcroft and Dover, Aux., $27.82; St. Albans, Aux., $5.48; Waterville, Aux., $16.50, Cong. Ch., S. S., $7.87; Norridgewock, Aux., $25; Gorham, Aux., $25, Little Neighbors, $5; Castine, Aux., $7.50; Yarmouth, Aux., $31.48; Farmington, Aux., of wh. $25 to const. L. M. Miss Carrie Titcomb, $31.75; Orono, Aux., $13; Belfast, Aux., $20; Dexter, Ladies of Cong. Ch., $2.50; Warren, Aux., $8; Bridgton, Aux., $16.50; Thomaston, Cong. Ch., $21; Washington Co. Conf., Aux., $5.06; Ellsworth, Aux. (add'l), $2, S. S., $5.43; Portland, Aux., $41.37, Y. L. M. B., $75, Young People's Aid Soc'y, Second Parish Ch., $12, State St. Ch., $80, West End Ch., $4.75,

High St. Ch. M. C., $108.28; Scarboro, Young Ladies' Aux., $27, $1,099 71
Castine. — Desert Palm Soc'y, with prev. contri. const. L. M. Mrs. Alfred D. F. Hamlin, 10 00

Total, $1,109 71

NEW HAMPSHIRE.

New Hampshire Branch.—Miss Abby E. McIntire, Treas. Candia, Aux., $16; Henniker, Aux., $17.75; Kensington, M. C., $5; Marlboro, Aux., $13.39; Newport, Newport Workers, $125; Pittsfield, Aux., $47.25, M. B., $26.18; Stratham, Lamplighters, $16.40; Swansey, Aux., $15, $281 97
Claremont. — Merry Workers, const. L. M. Mrs. Ellen A. Stone, 25 00
Raymond. — Mrs. James T. Dudley, 4 00

Total, $310 97

VERMONT.

Vermont Branch.— Mrs. T. M. Howard, Treas. Barnet, Busy Bees, $5; Brattleboro, Aux., $50; Chester, Young People's Miss'y Soc'y, $20.10; Danville, Aux., $13; Dorset, Aux., of wh. $25 const. L. M. Miss Janett Vance, $38; Fairhaven, Aux., $14.50; Hartford, Aux., $12; Westminster West, Aux., const. L. M. Mrs. O. F. Buxton, $25; Stanstead, P. Q., Mrs. Julia Benton, 40 cts., $178 00
Putney.—Mrs. A. S. Taft, 4 40

Total, $182 40

MASSACHUSETTS.

Andover and Woburn Branch. — Miss E. F. Wilder, Treas. Billerica, Willing Workers, $23 00
Barnstable Co. Branch. — Miss Amelia Snow, Treas. Yarmouth, Aux., $8.75, Y. L. M. C., $69.50; Wellfleet, Aux., 11.50; Falmouth, Aux., $9; East Falmouth, Aux., $12; Wauquoit, Aux., $1, 111 75
Berkshire Branch.—Mrs. S. N. Russell, Treas. Adams, Aux.,

$10; North Adams, Aux., $128.50; Peru, Aux., $32, Top Twig M. C., $10; West Stockbridge, Aux., $15.25; Richmond, Aux., $25; Mill River, Aux., $10; Pittsfield, First Ch., Aux., $17.14; Hachinosu, Aux., $100, Memorial Soc'y, $65, We Girls, $10, Coral Workers, $10, South Ch., Aux., $17.43, ... $490 32

Essex North Branch. — Mrs. Augustus Hammond, Treas. Collection at meeting, $25; Bradford Academy, Foreign Miss'y Soc'y, $24.84; Groveland, Aux., $30; Haverhill, North Ch. Industrial Soc'y, $60; Pentucket, M. B., $14.50; West Haverhill, Aux., $15, M. C., $17; Ipswich, Aux., $35; West Newbury, Aux., $21, ... 242 34

Franklin Co. Branch. — Miss L. A. Sparhawk, Treas. Deerfield, Aux., $12; South Deerfield, Aux., $15.55; Northfield, Mrs. A. M. D. Alexander, $100; Shelburne, Aux., $30; Shelburne Falls, Aux., $45.60, Little Women, $20; Sunderland, Aux., $16; Whately, Aux., $18.82, ... 257 97

Hampshire Co. Branch.—Miss Isabella G. Clarke, Treas. North Hadley, Aux., $15; South Amherst, Aux., $25; Hadley, Aux., $20, Mrs. P. $1, ... 61 00

Hamilton. — Thank-Off. from a mother, ... 5 00

Middlesex Branch.—Mrs. E. H. Warren, Treas. South Framingham, Willing Workers, $75, Aux., $35; South Sudbury, Ladies' Miss'y Soc'y, $1.50, Ashland Gleaners, $17.50, ... 129 00

Montague.—First Cong. Ch., ... 7 00

Norfolk and Pilgrim Branch. —Mrs. Franklin Shaw, Treas. Brockton, Coral Workers, $30; Hanover, Aux., $6; Braintree, Aux., $8, ... 44 00

New Bedford.—Union Workers, ... 10 00

Old Colony Branch. — Miss Frances J. Runnels, Treas. Rochester, M. C. and S. S., $3; New Bedford, Wide-Awake Workers, $5, Union Workers, $40; Taunton, Broadway Ch. M. B., $5; Winslow, S. S., $4.50; Attleboro, Boys' Branch of Lenses, $13.30; East Taunton, Aux., $32, ... 102 80

Peabody. — A Friend, const. L. M. Miss Susanna Mills, ... 25 00

Springfield Branch.—Miss H. T. Buckingham, Treas. Ludlow Centre, Aux., $6.15; Monson, Aux., $22; Springfield, First Ch., Aux., $1.16, ... 29 31

Suffolk Branch.—Miss Myra B. Child, Treas. Boston, Mrs. Charles A. Lord, $5, Park St. Ch., Aux., of wh. $25 by Mrs. M. J. Draper, const. self L.M., and $25 by Miss Abby Keith, const. self L. M., and $50 by Mrs. Jacob Fullarton, const. L. M's Miss Carrie F. Gibson, Mrs. James H. Work, $750, Echo Band, $70, Union Ch., Aux., $30; Roxbury, Eliot Ch., Aux., $33.50, Thompson Circle, $1.50, Ferguson Circle, $2.50, Mayflowers, $3, Eliot Star, $3, Walnut Ave. Ch., Aux., $7; Dorchester, Village Ch., Aux., $30; Charlestown, Winthrop Ch., Children's Winthrop Helpers, $66; Cambridgeport, Prospect St. Ch., Aux., $50, Bearers of Glad Tidings, $25; Jamaica Plain, Thank-Off., $10, Wide-Awake M. B., $30; Chelsea, Third Ch., Aux., $40, M. C., $10, Central Ch., Pilgrim Band, $15; Brighton, Young Ladies' Miss'y Soc'y, $10; Hyde Park, Aux., $31, Cong. S. S., $7.40; Dedham, Asylum Dime Soc'y, $2.51, B. C. M., $50; Newtonville, Aux., $125, Central Cong. Ch. M. B., $10; Newton Centre, Mite Mission Branch of the Maria B. Furber Miss'y Soc'y, $26; Newton Upper Falls, A Friend, $50; Walpole, Little Gleaners' M. C., $80.02; Waverly, Ladies' Miss'y Soc'y, const. L. M. Miss Sarah Blake, $25; Wayland, Young People's M. C., $6.80, ... $1,605 23

Topsfield.—Mrs. Ephraim Perkins, $4, In memory of Mrs. L. S. Crawford, $5, ... 9 00

West Brookfield.—Y. P. M. C., ... 5 00

Worcester Co. Branch.—Mrs. G. W. Russell, Treas. Whitinsville, Aux., Merry Gleaners' M. C., $50, collection at Quarterly Meeting, $37.13; Fitchburg, C. C. Ch., Aux., $36, Young Ladies' Circle, $15, Little Builders, $14.25; Leicester, M. C., $30; Athol, Aux., $25; Auburn, M. C., of wh. $25 const. L. M. Mrs. S. D. Hosmer, $35; Spencer, A Friend, $10; Worcester, Union Ch., Aux., $73.85, Piedmont Ch., Missionary Gleaners, $45, ... 371 23

Worcester.—Plymouth Ch., David Whitcomb, in memory of Mrs. David Whitcomb, ... 500 00

Wellesley. — College Christian Asso., ... 250 00

Total, ... $4,278 95

LEGACY.

Legacy of Mrs. Samuel Gardner, Wakefield, $500 00

RHODE ISLAND.

Rhode Island Branch. — Miss Anna T. White, Treas. Providence, Union Ch. Mission Helpers, $65, Beneficent Ch., Foreign M. C., $100, $165 00

Total, $165 00

CONNECTICUT.

Eastern Conn. Branch. — Miss Mary I. Lockwood, Treas. Groton, Aux., $22; Putnam, Aux., of wh. $25 const. L. M. Mrs. F. W. Perry, $48, Missionary Workers, $25; Colchester, M. C., $23.18; Pomfret, Aux., $33 70, M. C., $13.99; Danielsonville, Aux., $14; Montville, Aux., $3; Taftville, Aux., $11.51, M. C., $10.46; Hanover, Aux., $7.28, Willing Workers, $3; Waungan, Aux., of wh. $25 const. L. M. Mrs. Lydia C. Hunter, $30; Norwich, Park Ch., $108, Broadway Ch., Y. L. M. C., $110; East Woodstock, Aux., $10; New London, First Ch., $68; Second Ch.,$59.15; Brooklyn, Aux., $40, $640 27

Hartford Branch — Miss Anna Morris, Treas. Bristol, M. C., $16; East Hartford, Real Workers' M. C., $40; Poquonock, Cheerful Givers' M. C., $34; Tolland, Aux., $6, 96 00

New Haven Branch. — Miss Julia Twining, Treas. Bridgeport, North Ch., Cheerful Workers, $25; Cromwell, Aux., $9.26; Deep River, Aux., $20.50; Ellsworth, Golden Links, $20; Essex, Aux., $2.50; Meriden, Centre Ch., Y. L. M. C., $5; Middle Haddam, Aux., $2.50, Whatsoever Band, $20; Milford, Aux., $4; New Britain, South Ch., Y. L. M. B ,$52; New Haven, Centre Ch,, Aux., prev. contri. const. L. M's Mrs. Henry Farnam, Mrs. Dexter Alden, Miss Fannie B. Thomas, Miss Adele H. Baldwin, Miss Sarah A Clark, $50.25, Ch. of the Redeemer, Y. L. M. C., $30, Acorn Band, $5; Fair Haven, First Ch., Boys' M. C., $10.50, Second Ch., Quinnipiar Circle, $15, United Ch., Mrs. Cady's School, $11.61, Yale College Ch., Aux., $47, M. C., $10; Stratford, Alpha Band, $5; Trumbull, Aux., const. L. M.

Mrs. Nelson French, $25; Warren, Aux., prev. contri. const. L. M. Mrs. Lydia C. Calhoun, $16; Watertown, Aux., $50; Winsted, Aux., $86 59, Mountain Daisies, $30, $552 71

Total, $1,288 98

NEW YORK.

New York State Branch. — Mrs. G. H. Norton, Treas. Phœnix, Aux., $11.70; Brooklyn, So. Cong. Ch., Ladies' Benev. Soc'y, $100, Park Ch., Aux., const. L. M. Miss E. A. Cummins, $25, East Ch., Y. L. M. C., $17; Albany, Morning Star M. C., $100; Fairport, Aux., $55, Cong. S. S., $25; Buffalo, Aux., $100, M. B., $61; Canandaigua, Aux., $265; Morristown, Aux., $20; Crown Point, Aux., $20; Syracuse, Aux., $275; Lockport, Aux., $6, $1,080 70

New York City. — In memory of S. M. F.,   10 00

Total, $1,090 70

PHILADELPHIA BRANCH.

Mrs. Samuel Wilde, Treas. NEW JERSEY: Paterson, Aux., $6, Auburn St. Cong. Ch. S S., $5; Orange, Grove St. Cong. Ch., Aux., $38; Orange Valley, Cong. Ch., Children's M. B., 40 cts.; Jersey City, Aux., $38.18; Plainfield, Aux., $10. D. C.: Washington, Aux., of wh. $25 by Mrs. C. A. Weed, to const. self L. M., $43.44, $141 02

Total, $141 02

FLORIDA.

Interlacken. — Mrs. E. L. Camp, $1 40

Total, $1 40

OHIO.

Pomeroy. — Welsh Cong. Ch., $5 74

Total, $5 74

MICHIGAN.

Orion. — Cong. Ch., $0 56

Total, $0 56

General Funds,	$8,575 43
Weekly Pledge,	85
Leaflets,	23 57
Morning Star,	14 60
Legacies,	500 00
Total,	$9,114 45

MISS EMMA CARRUTH, Treasurer.

Board of the Interior.

CHINA.

OUR LITTLE SCHOOL AT KALGAN.

BY MRS. MARK WILLIAMS.

JANUARY 2, 1885.

I AM glad to write about the little day-school. It is mine only for this winter. I am just as happy as possible in working for it. What a pleasure and privilege it is to teach about Jesus! How quickening to one's self it is! With humility and shame one sees that one's living is a teaching that ought to match.

The girls are reciting only from the Bible and hymnbook at present. They some time since committed to memory two small Chinese schoolbooks, and reviewed, and re-reviewed. I hear the advance lesson of each one, and then the daily review lessons are recited together, each repeating one or two verses around. This last arrangement gives me time to talk about some one's lesson, and we sometimes have a beautiful time together. One day one of the girls recited, "Consider the lilies," etc.; "Wherefore, if God so clothe the grass of the field, shall he not much more clothe you?" We talked about the flowers, and the girls named those they knew. "If you plant aster seeds do nasturtiums come up?" I asked. Their eyes all grew very bright. "No, never," they said. "Who takes care of the seeds, and keeps them always true?" "God," they all answered. "Does God like the flowers, that he makes them so beautiful, and takes such care of them?" "I think he does." "Which does he care for most, a nasturtium or you, Er Nüza?" "He likes the flowers best." The others laughed. "He likes us best. We are the most important." "Why?" "Yinuri sz rên" (Because we are human). "If it was a baby, only so long, what then?" "It is human, too." "Yes; it has a soul, which may live with Jesus always. Now all remember how much God loves the flowers, but how much more he loves you. What did he do to show how much he loves you?" "He sent Jesus."

Mrs. Fêng, the teacher and matron, and I, are in great anxiety. One of the dear little girls has been taken away by her mother. The report is that she will sell her for a wicked purpose, for $20. I would gladly pay the $20, but the mother is one who would respect no agreement, written or otherwise. She would come and take the girl away whenever she pleased. I could require the child of her if I had a paper, but any appeal to law would ruin the school in its present condition. Five years hence I hope things will be different. I know God can overrule the mother's wicked plans, and have sent our cook to find the man to whose son the little girl is engaged. He is an opium-eater, and may not care what happens, but he ought to prevent such sin.

Evening. The cook came back without finding the man, but he did find the woman and her child. She told him she had no such plan as we had heard, but was going to get a husband for herself and one for her girl, at a village two miles out of Kalgan. The go-between, who was making the match, came and told the same story, so we hope it may be true. At the school the mother owned that she had had this other plan — the bad woman — to support both herself and her daughter; also that the daughter was to be paid for, as above.

The matron came for me, as Za meiza's mother and the go-between were at the school. After talking with them a few minutes I asked to see the little girl, to say good-bye. Her mother went home to bring her, she said, but did not come back. Lastly the go-between went, too, to bring them both, but she did not come back. They feared we might try to influence the child against the marriage — a mistake on their part. I wanted to say to her, " Don't forget to love Jesus. Don't forget that he loves you."

While we were waiting, Mrs. Fêng told the go-between about the time when she began to hear of the true God.

" I used to hear about the foreigners who were preaching a new religion, but never saw them. I was a young wife then, and could not go to the street-door to gaze. But I heard things sometimes which, though I did not understand them, started me thinking. My father was a doctor, and he had a nice tablet with gilt letters to the god of medicine. We burnt incense before it on the 1st and 15th of every month and on the god's birthday. After my father died, as my brothers did not keep on with the shop, they let the tablet be neglected, and finally threw it away.

" My uncle's family sold bean-curd, and they worshiped a *bai-fu-shên*; but when they stopped that business they no longer burned incense to their god. I saw that every body did the same. They worshiped only to forward their own interests. ' What kind of gods are these?' I said. ' Why are they not insulted when the people do so?'

" There was another thing. A man whom I knew used to talk against the gods: ' I do not worship the Horse God, but are my animals ever sick?' One day his horse was taken sick. The man was a carpenter, and he had a rather fair piece of wood which had been lying some time in an out-house. He got that out in great haste, and sawed, and planed, and put together a tablet to the Horse God. Then with all speed he prostrated himself, and burned incense. What kind of a god is that, thought I, who will allow his tablet to be made of such wood? So I had my doubts, but we always burned incense and *kow tówed* at the regular times. It could not do any harm, and we had always done it. The children's father had been at Kalgan; and the day he came home, as soon as he had washed the dust from his face, he took down the tablets and gods and burned them. I was not quite pleased, but I said nothing. The next day he left for Peking, to go to the training-school, and I thought, 'If the gods are angry, he will have misfortune on the way.' But he got there safely.

"That winter our daughter was very sick, and the neighbors said, 'This is because he burnt the gods; buy some more.' But I said, 'Then when my husband comes back, what shall I do?' They said, 'Take the gods down and hide them in a water-jar, and paste it up.' And I thought, '.Now, if I were pasted up in a water-jar I should die, and it would be an insult to the gods to put them in a place not fit for me.' It was surely the Lord who helped me to stand firm against them all. Afterward I was baptized. I knew very little about Jesus, but my husband wanted me to be baptized, so I said whatever he wanted me to say."

Here Mrs. Williams' story of her native friends suddenly ends. We hope to hear further from them.

QUESTIONINGS.

BY MISS ADA HAVEN.

PEKING, Feb. 13, 1885.

We are permitted to make extracts from a letter to a young society in Sioux Falls, Dak.:—

I DO not know whether you are young or old, dear girls, so I cannot tell exactly how to suit your tastes; but probably there is no one of you who could not, by a great stretch of memory, think back to the time when Bible truth was new and fresh to you, and the mind was just beginning to awaken to the mysteries and questionings of life. And what queer notions you had then. Even the wisest of you, looking back on the queryings of that wondering little soul, will feel tempted to smile at your own expense.

But did you ever ask yourself how it would be with your soul if, instead of the truth, you had been taught a lie, and all the while you had a kind of glimmering perception that it was a lie, until finally nothing seemed worth caring for but eating, and drinking, and playing?

Then fancy yourself getting some impression of the truth, and you can see how much more these little ones have to contend with than ever you had. Yet the same questions will come up as came to you. Here are some of their questions. You will see it is as hard for them to understand the spiritual nature of God as for any foreign child. "The catechism says that God is without form and substance. How is it then that you tell us Jesus is God, and yet show us pictures of him?" How can I find words to explain to them in Chinese the mystery of the Trinity, when I could not explain it even in English? One will say, pointing to the chapel, "That house has the name Jesus Chapel. If that is the place where Jesus lives, I don't understand how he can see in here."

Sometimes the little questioners puzzle themselves over the mysteries of life and death: "When was God born?" "Where were our souls before we were born?"

A scholar in the boarding-school had died, and the little Arabs came crowding into the funeral, anxious not to miss any affair that is going on, whether it be a "red affair" (a wedding) or a "white affair" (a funeral). They saw us all with sad faces and tearful eyes. The next Sunday there were more questions to answer. "Was not that scholar a good girl?" "Oh, yes; we hope she was a Christian?" "Well, couldn't she go to heaven, then?" "We hope she has gone to heaven." "I should think if heaven is such a very happy place, and all trouble is over, you would think it was something to be very glad about when some one has gone to heaven. How do you foreigners look at it? Is it a time to mourn or a time to rejoice?" Perhaps my little heathen scholar can teach me something. She can certainly ask questions hard to answer. If she had only asked how Christians ought to look on death, it would have been easier to answer. Again: The children seem to have trouble in putting the idols out of their minds. I ask them, "At New Year people paste up gate-gods on their gates; are those true or false gods?" "Oh," with a laugh, "those are false gods. Wait till it rains, and they will be hanging in tatters." "How is it with the kitchen gods?" "Oh, they are false, too — nothing but paper." "And how about the little Buddhas that people put up in their houses?" "Oh, they are nothing but mud; you can smash them all to pieces." "And the idols in the temples — are they false, too?" "Oh, no; those are real. They are brass all the way through." So you see though it is "virgin soil," there must be much rooting up of weeds before the good can take root.

MICRONESIA.

LETTER FROM MISS CATHCART.

PROGRESS IN SCHOOL.

KUSAIE, Oct. 9, 1884.

THANKS for your letter of January, 1884. It reached me on the twenty-second of August. You speak of your desire for late news from Micronesia. We might almost feel the same desire from the other end of the line, only we become so accustomed to old things that it does not make much difference. I do not see but letters of June, '83, were just as acceptable as those of June, '84, all coming together as they did. We think the Jennie Walker may be here any day. She has gone on to the West, with Mr. and Mrs. Logan, and will remain at Ruk till the walls and roof of their house are completed. It is October now, and I suppose you are preparing the report for the year. The past six months, since my last letter, school has moved forward steadily, but not rapidly. The scholars are attentive and studious, and are making satisfactory progress in English. The English is a hard language for them to learn, and we do not expect them to do more in it than to read understandingly easy books. We hope to be able to furnish each of the teachers, from year to year, some helpful books that they can read and explain in the native tongue to their scholars. Some of them can understand nearly all ordinary conversation. The natives of any of these islands are very quick in picking up the languages of the other groups. We have both Marshall Islanders and Kusaians in school, and they learn to converse with one another in either language in a short time.

Two of our boys who have been in school five or six years graduated last week, and will probably go to assist the teachers now at Jalny and Ailiulaplap. They seem to possess considerable missionary spirit. You can hardly imagine how great is our need of a family here to come by the next trip of the Star. Pray with great faith that the very right ones may be found — those who are full of the Spirit, longing to scatter the Word of God where it is not known. The call for teachers is great; and shall we let the people die without learning of Christ, because there are none to train up teachers? I will tell you of

THE CALL FROM ONE ISLAND.

It is probably the only one in Micronesia where the people have ever worshiped idols carved from wood or stone. On all the islands the natives worship stones, trees, animals, birds, and fish dressed and made sacred, but no carved images except on Nukuwor. There the natives are of Samoan descent, and idols have been common; but all were destroyed in 1883. One large idol in the form of a man was kept in their house of worship, and day and night the people congregated there, making such a noise that the trader could not sleep. So one day when the natives had all gone to the other side of the island, to make canoes, the trader set fire to the house and idol. The people, seeing the fire, rushed back to find out what was the matter; but they could not put it out. They were perfectly confident that after six days the idols would send a storm that would sweep the whole island away. They destroyed everything of value, and then came together on the fifth day, to wait for the final destruction of all. But after they had passed a sleepless night, the sixth day came in calm and bright. Then they said, "It is all a lie; our idol was good for nothing!"

In December of the same year some of the people visited Namerik, where we have a teacher. They greatly admired the people there for their knowledge, and earnestly requested a teacher. They had found out that their idol was false, and they also greatly desired to learn arithmetic, so that the trader could not deceive them in trade. Although of Samoan descent, they now speak the Marshall Island language. This is but one of many islands needing a teacher. How long shall they wait because there are so few workers and so little money? Then, when is our girls' school coming? Where are our teachers to find suitable wives? It is impossible till girls are trained. And the young men are growing quite particular in this matter. They wish for educated wives. * * * One request I make of you who meet every Friday morning: pray that strength and wisdom may be given for the added duties of this year, in the absence of Dr. and Mrs. Pease, and that the Holy Spirit may abide in the hearts of all our scholars.

By a chance vessel we get this later word:—

MARCH 11, 1885.

DEAR FRIENDS,—A vessel is near, and Mr. W. is going off to her. He may be able to send letters. I have not much time to write. You will be glad to hear, if you receive this, that I am well, also the other missionaries. Scholars well, and doing well. Of course I am working hard while there is no one else who can use native language, but God has wonderfully helped me beyond all I could have expected or hoped, for over four months now, and I am able to work every day. Very happy in the work.

Love to all, LILLIE.

God bless you all; and pray much for us!

Home Department.

STUDIES IN MISSIONARY HISTORY.
1885.

THE ARMENIAN MISSION, NO. 3 — 1846–1860.

First Results of the Persecution: The believers called Protestants. Letter from the Grand Vizier to the Pasha of Erzroom: Power of the Pasha reduced.

Organization of the Evangelical Armenian Church: First church in Constantinople. Pastor chosen. Number of churches formed during first two years. Number of members. How many in the Protestant community? Ordination of Baron Simon; Pastor Avedis. Third church. How many churches and pastors at the close of this period?

Progress of Religious Liberty: Protestant Charter of Rights obtained by Lord Cowley. Imperial Firman of 1850. When was Christian evidence accepted in the courts?

Crimean War. Aims of the Czar. Effects on Mission Work. Hatti Humaïoun, 1856. Causes.

Turkish Missions Aid Society.

The Missionaries. Re-enforcements. Fire of 1848. Tours. Removal of Dr. Smith to Aintab. Death of Mrs. Hamlin; of Mr. and Mrs. Everett; of Mr. Benjamin.

Printing and Book Distribution. The *Avedaper.* Editions of the Bible and Testament.

Education. Hostility of the Patriarch to the Seminary at Bebek. Effects of this persecution on the teaching of the Seminary. Growth and religious interest, 1848 and 1849.

Work for Women. The Female Seminary. Religious interest. Arrival of Miss West. Work of Miss Haynes.

Work at Nicomedia. Church organized; Pastor ordained. The Girls' School. Work at Broosa.

Work at Adabazar. Church organized: Pastor Hohannes Sahakian. Demirdesh. Persecution.

Marsovan. Beautiful situation. Interesting beginnings. Visit of Mr. Powers; of Mr. Bliss. Persecution.

Cesarea. Progress.

Finished Work of Pastor A. Kachadurian; of Bedros Kamaghielyan.

Heroes of the Mission Field. A series of bright little sketches published by the American Tract Society, at 10 cents each, contain the lives of Dr. Goodell, Dr. Dwight, and Julia Rappelye. Send for August number of Mission Studies.

"AM I MY BROTHER'S KEEPER?"

BY MRS. ARTHUR E. ARNOLD.

FAR down through the ages there has come to us the story of two brothers, the first the young world ever saw. Upon the broad plains of Asia,— outside, alas! the Garden of Eden,— "Abel tended his flocks, while Cain was a tiller of the ground." You all know the story — the two offerings; the one accepted, the other rejected; the tragic ending, when the angry Cain rose up against Abel, his brother, and slew him; and the voice of the Lord was heard calling unto Cain, "Where is thy brother?" And he said, "I know not. Am I my brother's keeper?" Nearly six thousand years have come and gone since that Divine Voice first determined the question of human responsibility in that terse sentence, "the voice of thy brother's blood crieth unto me from the ground"; but the lapse of ages has not lifted from humanity the weight of obligation toward its fellows. The destinies of the human race are inextricably interwoven. We are not a race of hermits. "No one of us liveth unto himself." God has established on the earth his kingdom of grace through his Son, our Saviour. He has intrusted the building up of that kingdom to us, his human instruments; and with the utterance of the command, "Go ye into all the world, and preach the gospel to every creature," the cause of misions was born on the earth. The very etymology of the word missions is full of the missionary spirit, coming to us from the Latin, meaning "to send." Every missionary society is a sending society, and the whole subject of missions means something or somebody sent somewhere. Our theme is responsibility toward Christian missions. Living as we do in the midst of nineteenth-century civilization, with all the privileges it gives to us, what is our duty as Christian women toward our less fortunate heathen sisters?

Our first duty is interest in missions. In the present stage of development of Christian missions, both at home and abroad, it is hard, indeed, to find any excuse for lack of interest in the work. It is too late in the day for any woman to say, "I do not believe in missions." Not believe in missions, when our ships ride the waves in ports where an anchor never would have been cast but for the civilizing power of Christianity? Not believe in missions, when every dollar expended in carrying the gospel to lands hitherto closed to commerce is returned fourfold to enrich the nation? Not believe in missions, when thousands have been brought from thick darkness into the marvelous light of the Son of righteousness? And yet there are those who are still asking, " *Cui bono ?* " What good is all this spending of time and treasure, this wear and tear of life and energy, this pouring out of precious ointment for such unworthy objects as heathen? Why not let them alone, to live and die worshiping their idols? God made them, and he will take care of them. Ah, dear, unbelieving friend, we are our sisters' keepers, and the voice of their blood crieth unto God from the ground!

There is a class of persons who sin through ignorance instead of prejudice. They know nothing about missions, and therefore do nothing. Theywhole subject is to them a sealed book. Many of these need but a word in season to awaken heart and conscience to the great need of the world for missionary work.

Others there are who have not discoverd that it is fashionable to work for missions. Many a woman who thinks she "might as well be out of the world as out of the fashion," would be astonished at the array of distinguished names on the rolls of our missionary societies, and would lose no time in joining a society so fashionable, if she only knew anything about it.

'Others do not realize the power of foreign missions as an agency in the civilization of the world. This we cannot longer ignore without confessing ourselves behind the times.

The way to civilize the world is to Christianize it. Go where you will, and the type of civilization of a country is indicated by the type of its religion. Not until we realize this fact to its fullest extent, shall we realize the extent of our responsibility as citizens of Christendom for the social, moral, and religious condition of Heathendom. *"Via crucis via lucis"* is as true to-day as in the days of the Fathers. The cross of Christ must be planted upon every shore before the kingdoms of darkness can become kingdoms of light. "The way of the cross is the way of light," and the only way.

But granted that we know all these things, and knowing them recognize our responsibility in the abstract, it is not enough. There must be a sense of personal obligation, a willingness to "do with our might what our hands find to do," before our whole duty is discharged. Knowledge of the work and acceptance of the responsibility it brings, will not fail to beget in our hearts an honest interest in it. But the qualification needed to make us thoroughly enjoy the work, is a fine enthusiasm that will lift us up and carry us over the hard places. It pays to be enthusiastic. Half-hearted service is never faithful service. Shall we work for missions simply because we ought? No; let us "do it heartily, as unto the Lord."

It is to the Christian religion we owe our proud position as queens in our own households. The preaching of the evangel of the Lord means honor and respect to womanhood; its withholding, means slavery and degradation to our sex. If these things are true, there rests upon us a weight of responsibility we may try in vain to shake off. Shall we sit in our homes, surrounded by tender, loving ministries, and render nothing to him who cast our lines in such pleasant places? Let us not hesitate because we cannot do some great thing. Though our circle be ever so circumscribed, there is still the "cup of cold water." Though we may not be able to "shine by great deeds" for Christ, there are still the corners. Have you seen that little hymn,

> "Jesus bids us shine
> With a clear, pure light,
> You in your little corner,
> And I in mine"?

Phillips Brooks, in a sermon on the text, "Prepare ye the way of the Lord," says these beautiful and encouraging things to those who can do but little in making straight the Lord's pathway: "Not one little brown and withered leaf falls to the ground on one of these November days, but the shape of the planet is changed: so there is not one little act of yours, one whispered prayer that his kingdom may come, but becomes a factor in the world's redemption. If I can only place one little golden brick in the pavement of the Lord's highway, I will place it there, that coming generations may walk thereon to the heavenly city." The times are ripe for work. We are our sisters' keepers; what to do for them, and how to do it, is the question of the hour.

An indispensable requisite to the discharge of our responsibility to Christian missions is the spirit of prayer. Dr. Alden once said

" there must be prayer somewhere, or foreign missions will go to the wall." Prayer has been called " the lever that moves the world." I say it reverently,— it moves the very throne of grace itself. The handle of the lever has been placed in our hands; with it, what may we not do for the field and the workers!

Again: after knowledge of the work, interest, enthusiasm, and prayer for it, comes that which is at once most helpful to ourselves and others — consecrated Christian giving.

The answer to the question "How much?" rests with each heart. As God has prospered us: a little if it must be a little; much if it may be much; something, at any rate. Things are worth to us what they cost us. If the evangelization of the world costs us nothing, we value. it accordingly. Give cheerfully, ungrudgingly, "freely as ye have received." It should be accounted a precious privilege to have a part in the eighteen thousand dollars apportioned to Illinois this year. It is not a burden grievous to be borne; it is the grateful offering of redeemed souls to Him who gave himself for us.

In conclusion, what I have tried to say may be summed up in one word: more knowledge, more enthusiasm, more prayer, more giving, are all included in that all-embracing term, *consecration.*

Upon the seal of one of the London missionary societies is the figure of an ox, standing with a plow on one side and an altar on the other, with this motto beneath, "Ready for either." This is the spirit that must pervade our hearts if we would see the Lord's work go forward in the earth. Ready for the altar of sacrifice — ready for the plow of toil! Has God blessed you in basket and store? It is that you may consecrate your substance to him. Has he given you the pen of a ready writer? Consecrate your gift to the Lord. Has he tipped your tongue with silver, whereby you may persuade many? Your path is plain before you. The noblest powers God has given to man or woman may well be consecrated to the cause of missions. The rapid culmination of events points with prophetic finger to the time when a nation shall be born in a day. Well for us if, in our selfishness, we do not let those glorious opportunities pass by, and miss of their equally glorious privileges.

————◄ ◆ ►————

OUR TREASURY.

GREAT needs develop great resources, we are told. Our needs are great. By our Treasurer's statement we are more than $2,000 behind our contributions at this time last year. We ask, and pray, and labor for $60,000. Last year we fell far short of this, and left much new and needy work undone, though we met all our actual obligations. This year the indications seem to be that we shall not meet them. Suppose a business company were confronted with this danger. Every member of it would immediately become a committee of one to secure means to meet these obligations. That is just what we must do. Our company is large. Reverently let us remember that our heavenly Father stands at the head of our work. One with God is a host; but we are many. The great need of the hour is, that every one should awake to this emergency, and make some special effort. Dear sister on the prairie or among the mountains, will you not join hands with us in the cities and give a special offering, according to your ability? Do not neglect to give the small things, if you have little. And do not forget the prayer that may make them as the five loaves and two fishes. But if you have means to gratify your taste in dress, and furniture, and books, give largely, *abundantly.* Let us see to it that our giving is in proportion to our style of living. And let us make the most of our other resources. Tithes of our talents, our time, and our influence must be freely given.

What has your talent for music or art returned to your Lord, dear sister? Remember how the children exercise their ingenuity to earn their pennies; and will you not gladly become as a little child?

Your influence is a great resource. If you can interest ten women to give one dollar each, you will do far more than if you give ten dollars yourself. Each dollar will be a seed-corn that will multiply itself in future harvests. There is no rest for the husbandman in these days before the autumn, and there should be no rest for us. Pray, labor, give, and pray again, that when we go up to our annual ingathering at St. Louis, in October, we may offer to the Lord of the harvest abundant sheaves.

RECEIPTS OF THE WOMAN'S BOARD OF MISSIONS OF THE INTERIOR.

MRS. J. B. LEAKE, TREASURER.

FROM MAY 18, 1885, TO JUNE 18, 1885.

ILLINOIS.

ILLINOIS BRANCH.— Mrs. W. A. Talcott, of Rockford, Treas. *Aurora,* New Eng. Ch., 18; *Canton,* of wh. 5 memorial offering, 15; *Chicago,* Mrs. C. W. Crocker, 5, Plymouth Ch., Mrs. J. A. S., 4, New Eng. Ch., 127.82, South Ch., of wh. 25 to const. L. M. Mrs. J. B. Smith, 26.25; *Dover,* of wh. 1.10 thank-off., 11.10; *Downers Grove,* 4; *Earlville,* 6.19; *Geneseo,* Zenana Soc., 25; *La Moille,* 20; *Lawn Ridge,* 10; *Lee Center,* 5; *Lyonsville,* 11; *Oak Park,* 118.15; *Port Byron,* 19; *Plainfield,* 25; *Rockford,* 1st Ch , 38.32, 2d Ch., 47.10; *Sterling,* 10; *Streator,* 5.57; *W a v e r l y,* "from a friend," 100, — $651 50

JUNIORS: *Chicago,* Lincoln Park Ch., Y. L. Soc., 25; *Quincy,* "Lend a Hand Club," 10; *Wyoming,* Light Bearers, 10, — 45 00

JUVENILES: *Chicago,* Union Park Ch. Mission Band, — 28 33

Total, — $724 83

INDIANA.

INDIANA BRANCH.— Mrs. L. F. Hyde, of I n d i a n a p o l i s, Treas. *Elkhart,* A u x., 8; *Fort Wayne,* 17.30, — $25 30

Total, — $25 30

IOWA.

IOWA BRANCH. — Mrs. E. R. Potter, of Grinnell, Treas. *Chester Centre,* 14; *Creston,* 16.28; *Clinton,* 10; *Des Moines,* 22; *Gilbert Station,* 13; *G r i n n e l l,* 55.15; *Holland,* "A Friend," 5; *Montour,* 10.50; *Mason City,* Mrs. Jennison, 1; *Oldfield,* 1.50; *Webster,* 5; *Wayne,* 10, — $163 43

JUNIORS: *Clay,* Y. L. M. Soc., for Bridge, — 10 00

JUVENILES: *Montour,* Willing Workers, — 5 00

Total, — $178 43

KANSAS.

KANSAS BRANCH.— Mrs. A. L. Slosson. of Leavenworth, Treas. *Dial,* 2.20; *Hiawatha,* Mrs. Frank Spaulding, 10;

Morril, 10; *Muscotah*, 1.75; *Osborne*, 3.53; *Wabaunsee*, 13; *Clay Centre*, A Friend, 3, $43 48

Total, $43 48

MICHIGAN.

MICHIGAN BRANCH. — M r s . Charles E. Fox, of Detroit, Treas. *Detroit*, Fort Wayne Ch., 5; *Grass Lake*, 15.50; *North Dorr*, 1st Ch., 10; *Ypsilanti*, 4, $34 50
JUVENILES: *East Saginaw*, Faithful Workers, 25; *Grass Lake*, S. S., 4.78, 29 78
For Morning Star Mission: — *Dowagiac*, Star Band, 3.20; *Grand Blanc*, Willing Workers, 2; *White Cloud*, S. S., 1.33, 6 53

Total, $70 81

MINNESOTA.

MINNESOTA BRANCH.— Mrs. E. M. Williams, of Northfield, Treas. *Douglas*, 3.85; *Elk River*, 8; *Lake City*, 15; *Minneapolis*, Second Ch., 8.66, Vine Ch., 10, First Ch., Mrs. Hastings, 12; *NewRichmond*, 2; *Northfield*, 8; *Rochester*, 15; *St. Paul*, Plymouth Ch., 30; *Sterling*, 3.50, $116 01
JUNIORS: *Clearwater*, "Gleaners," 10; *St. Paul*, Plymouth, Ch., Y. L. Soc., 25, 35 00
JUVENILES: *Hancock*, S. S. Miss. Soc., 5; *Minneapolis*, Pilgrim Gleaners, 9; *Brownton*, S. S., 2, 16 00

Total, $167 01

MISSOURI.

MISSOURI BRANCH.—Mrs. J. H. Drew, 3101 Washington Ave., St. Louis, Treas. *Hannibal*, Sunbeams, birthday offerings, 6; *Kidder*, Aux., 10; *St. Louis*, Pilgrim Ch., 5; *Windsor*, Mrs. Gorham and daughter, 20, Rogers Academy, Ind. Ter., 6, $27 20

Total, $27 20

NEBRASKA.

NEBRASKA BRANCH.—Mrs.Geo. W. Hall, of Omaha, Treas. *Clarke*, 2.50; *Fremont*, 10; *Hastings*, 15; *Nebraska City*, 10; *Sutton*, 2.25; *Syracuse*, 10; *Weeping Water*, 9; *Waco*, friends, 50 cts., $59 25
JUVENILE: *Hastings*, 5 00

Total, $64 25

NORTH DAKOTA DRANCH.

Mrs. R. C. Cooper, of Cooperstown, Treas. *Cooperstown*, 12.75; *Harwood*, 4.10, $16 85

Total, $16 85

OHIO.

OHIO BRANCH.— Mrs. Geo. H. Ely, of Elyria, Treas. *Collinwood*, 8; *Edinburg*; 30; *Huntsburg*, 3; *Kent*, 20; *Marietta*, 50; *Milan*, Mrs. M. S. T., 5; *Oberlin*, 50; *Saybrook*, 6; *Toledo*, 1st Ch., 110; *York*, 15, $297 00

Total, $297 00

PENNSYLVANIA.

G u y's M i l l s, Crawford Co., Woman's Miss. Soc. of Cong. Ch., $5 00

Total, $5 00

WISCONSIN.

WISCONSIN BRANCH. — Mrs. R. Coburn, of Whitewater,Treas. *Arena*, 3 85; *Berlin*, by Miss Bissell, 13; *Ithaca*, 4; *Koshkonong*, 5.25; *Ladoga*, 10; *Milwaukee*, a lady of Plymouth Ch., 1, Grand Ave. Ch., 26; *New London*, 2; *Pewaukee*, by Miss Bissell, 7; *Platteville*, const. Ella Marshall L. M., 25, from Mrs. M. P. Rindlaub and daughter, 4; *Racine*, 21.76; *Waukesha*, 36.61; *Whitewater*, 2, $162 47
JUVENILE: *Racine*, Pansy Soc., 3 00
FOR NEW MORNING STAR: — *Arena*, Willing Workers, 1 89; *Broadhead*, S. S., 4.10; *Ladoga*, 50 cts., 6 49

$171 96
Less expenses, 13 44

Total, $158 52

INDIAN TERRITORY.

Vinita, Worcester Academy, Indian girls, $5 50

Total, $5 50

MISCELLANEOUS.

Sale of "Coan's Life," 4; of leaflets, 36.97; of envelopes, 3.35, $44 32

Total, $44 32

Receipts for the month, $1,829 50
Previously acknowledged, 17,645 61

Total since Oct. 1884, $19,475 11

Board of the Pacific.

It may be of some interest to our friends in the East occasion ally to know something of our meetings on this side of the continent, which although they may lack the inspiration of large numbers, yet to those who attend are full of interest. An account of each meeting is published in the *Pacific*; but as this, our Congregational paper, has but a limited circulation at the East, many do not see our (to us) pleasant column.

As we have many inquiries from our auxiliaries for missionary intelligence, some steps were taken in regard to more effectual copying of letters which we receive from the East, and which are labeled, "Not to be printed." Our "electric pen" having proved a failure, for lack of a strong and skilled hand always "on hand" to run it, and our "tablets" somewhat difficult to use, it was suggested that the ordinary printing-press, always at our service in the city for a small compensation, was after all the most effectual method for multiplying copies of letters and tracts with which to supply our auxiliaries.

We are feeling that at last the missionary seed has taken root in our soil, and sprung up and brought forth fruit in the person of a dear young lady who has consecrated herself to the missionary work, to go wherever the Lord might direct.

This hope has often come into our hearts, that some of our young ladies might consecrate themselves to this service; and now we have the desire of our hearts in regard to this matter — Miss Effie Gunnison, a member of Bethany Church in this city,

(317)

who says, "Here am I; send me!" to Japan if I may, but any-where the Lord's leading hand may guide. Miss Gunnison is a teacher in the Irving Institute, has a capacity for acquiring languages, and has, it is felt by those who know her best, peculiar qualifications for the varied duties of a foreign missionary. She has received her commission from the American Board, which makes her destination North China. We had hoped she might take the place in the school at Kioto which has been left vacant by the return to this country of Miss Starkweather, the loss of whom we deplore.

In regard to the resignation of Miss Starkweather the following resolutions were adopted: —

Resolved, That in the resignation of Miss Alice J. Starkweather as our missionary in Japan, the Board of the Pacific has sustained a great loss.

Resolved, That we extend to her our Christian sympathy in the loss of health that has made necessary her return from the work she loved.

Resolved, That we recognize gratefully her patient, earnest toil for the Master during her residence of seven years in Japan as our missionary, the influence of which can never die.

Resolved, That we acknowledge with thankfulness the stimulus her labors in Japan have been to our efforts in California, in behalf of foreign missions. We feel assured that in the future, wherever her lot may be cast, her life, which is already consecrated to the work of saving souls, will still be a means of blessing to the world.

And the following resolution was heartily adopted in regard to Miss Gunnison: —

Resolved, That we adopt Miss Gunnison, member of Bethany Church, as our missionary, whatever her destination.

A very happy coincidence occurred in this connection. A member of Plymouth Church, an English gentleman, who is a convert from Judaism, has always taken a deep interest in foreign missionary work. To him, nothing exceeds in importance the work of bringing souls to Christ, whom he has long learned to love and honor as the true Messiah; especially has he followed with deep interest the work of "woman for woman" in heathen lands. And so, as he one day brought to one of our secretaries his gold-piece, he also brought a plain gold band wedding-ring, which had long been in his possession, and which, for some unexplained reason, had failed of its destined mission as the seal of a marriage vow. And so the ring was presented to us, and was placed, in its pretty velvet case, on our table. And now, "How shall we dispose of it?' was asked by one and another. Just at this time the thought of Miss Gunnison was uppermost, and by a natural transition of thought it was decided that the ring be given to her, as the seal of her union to us — her "engagement ring." Accordingly one of the ladies passed the box around among the not very large number in attendance that afternoon, and about eight dollars was raised for the treasury. The ring is engraved with name and date, and presented to Miss Gunnison. The following is her letter of acknowledgment: —

"SAN FRANCISCO, May 19th.

"MY DEAR MISS FAY, — My deep gratitude to the ladies of the Board for the token of their kindly feeling received a few days since, can be better understood by them than any words could express it. The thought that the ladies of my own native State will through my adoption feel a more earnest interest in work for the Master, must be a source, of joy to me. May the coming years prove me worthy of the love which the gift expresses!
Sincerely yours,
EFFIE B. GUNNISON."

It is a source of deep regret to us that Miss Fay must leave us for a time. This was her last meeting with us before leaving for the East. We will follow her with the benediction contained in the one hundred and twenty-first Psalm.

We were very glad to have with us one whose name has long been familiar to us in her work in Osaka. As she has come to this country on account of impaired health, we felt that it would not be right to allow her to speak long at a time, much as we would have enjoyed the privilege. Two years since she returned to this country, after continuous labor in Japan for eight years. And now it became again necessary that she should return. As she is somewhat improving in this bracing climate she may remain awhile longer.

Miss Gouldy said it was difficult to know just what to talk about, there was so much she would like to tell us. She spoke of a meeting that had been held in Osaka some time ago in the girls' school. Two large rooms, connected by sliding-doors, were filled with Japanese women. Some came from Kobe, a station on the bay, about thirty miles from Osaka, and some from Kioto. The most of these women were the wives of pastors of the churches. This was certainly a very wonderful meeting — wonderful in its significance. It was a meeting for prayer and conference. A Japanese woman presided over it, and only Japanese women

spoke. Nothing of this kind had ever occurred in Japan before.
The women from Kobe and Kioto were astonished, and wished
they could have such meetings. Miss Gouldy was not satisfied
even with *this* advance. She wanted to form a reading-circle, and
told them about Chautauqua. Soon after this the Japanese
women had a "sociable;" tea, cakes, and conversation were the
order of the evening. There were about sixty present, and they
had a delightful *shinbokan* party. Miss Gouldy's reading-circle
was on her mind, and at this meeting they talked it over.
She proposed the Bible. The women wanted something easy.
The result was they selected "Luke," reading six verses a day.
After awhile they read "Matthew," and then "Mark," and were
so interested in the reading that they talked about it to each other
in their homes and to their husbands. When they met to read
they took up contributions for missions. Women from other denominations came, and they, too, dropped in their money. The
women who first started the readings thought this wasn't exactly
right, as these Presbyterians and others were not especially interested in the objects to which they contributed, but they did not
see the way out. They talked the matter over, and it ended in
their having a time set apart especially for a missionary meeting.
Now the women have their "sociable," their reading-circle, and
their missionary meeting.

STEPHANOS.

Stephanos Rappelye, our bright little Greek boy in Mr. Moody's
school at Northfield, Mass., is an object of our love, and not a little solicitude. The school where he is now is not in all respects
adapted to his needs, and various plans are discussed for his future. He must not be neglected, and must have a thorough Christian education. This we feel to be a sacred duty. Is there not at
the East some Christian family of means who would esteem it a
privilege to adopt this little boy, and give him a thorough education and Christian training. To any who are situated so as to
make this possible, this will be a blessed service for the Master as
they may hear his voice, "Take this child and train it for me,"
and will bring abundant reward in the love of an affectionate
little boy and of the Master we serve.

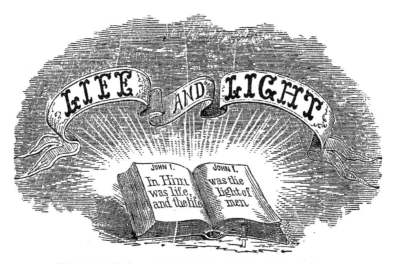

FOR WOMAN.

VOL. XV. SEPTEMBER, 1885. No. 9.

SURVEY OF FOREIGN WORK.

BY special request we give below a statement of our foreign work for the benefit of those who do not have access to our Annual Reports, or other means of information which include all the fields connected with our Board. While it must necessarily contain statistics that may prove uninteresting to the casual reader, we feel sure it will prove valuable for reference to those who wish to be intelligently informed as to our whole work. In order to do this, we are obliged to defer valuable articles to the next number.

ZULU MISSION, SOUTH AFRICA.

MISSIONARIES.— Mrs. Mary K. Edwards, Miss Martha E. Price, Miss Fidelia Phelps, at Lindley, formerly called Inanda (21 miles northwest from Natal); Mrs. Susan W. Tyler, at Umzunduzi (30 miles northwest from Natal); Miss Gertrude R. Hance, at Umvoti (40 miles northeast from Natal). SCHOOLS.—Lindley Female Seminary, in charge of Mrs. M. K. Edwards, Miss M. E. Price, and Miss F. Phelps, 46 pupils; boarding-school at Umzumbi, 28 pupils; Bible-women at Lindley and Umvoti.

Mrs. Edwards still remains at the head of the Lindley Semi-nary, as she has from its commencement, except when away on account of her health. Miss Price, who has been in the school since 1877, arrived in this country in June last, for a period of much-needed rest. Miss Phelps, who reached Lindley in Novem-ber last, has spent most of the winter and spring at Umvoti, in the study of the language, so as to be prepared for efficient assistance this autumn. The school-year began with forty-six boarders and a good number of day-scholars; but during the late winter and spring, several cases of meningitis — resulting in two deaths — so reduced the numbers (some being sent home because they showed signs of illness, and others going away from fright), it was thought best to close the school six weeks earlier than usual. Among the pleasant features early in the year, was the expressed desire of fourteen of the girls to deny themselves in their food — eating samp instead of rice — for the sake of giving to the Morning Star and other charitable objects. Early in the year, also, two of the older and more influential girls took a decided stand for Christ, which had a most favorable effect on the other pupils. The results of the school have their bright and their dark side; some who seem promising when in school, yielding to the temptations of their homes after leaving, while others prove most valuable Christian workers. The school for kraal girls at Umzumbi has had a prosperous year under the care of Miss Gilson and Miss Welch, who are neither of them missionaries of the Board, but who have ably supplied the emergency till some one could be secured from this country to take up part of the work. Mrs. Tyler, at Umzunduzi, assisted by her two daughters, continues her good work, fitting boys and girls for the seminaries at Amanzimtote and Lindley, making various tours among the Christian communities, holding meetings with the women, encouraging and advising them in the management of their families and in church-work. Miss Hance is still laboring in Umvoti and vicinity, superintending her krall schools, from which must come the future pupils in boarding-schools and seminaries. "The schoolhouses are preaching-places; and the native teaching, combined with the proclamation of the gospel, is slowly bringing light into the dark minds of the natives." A Government grant of one hundred pounds for these schools speaks well for their standing and efficiency. The two Bible-women are also doing good service in the kraals. The vexed question of polygamy (Shall a man with several wives who becomes a Christian, send away all his wives but one, to care for themselves as best they may? Shall a Christian woman continue to live with a polygamous husband?) still remains unsolved.

EUROPEAN TURKEY MISSION.

MISSIONARIES.— Mrs. Ellen R. Baird, Mrs. Fanny G. Bond, Miss Harriet L. Cole, Miss Emily L. Spooner, at Monastir (400 miles north of Constantinople, in Macedonia); Mrs. Isabella G. Clarke, Mrs. Mabel Sleeper, Miss Sara E. Graves, at Samokov (300 miles north northwest of Constantinople); Miss Ellen M. Stone, at Philippopolis (150 miles northwest of Constantinople); 7 Bible-women.

The school at Monastir (supported by the Woman's Board of Missions of the Interior) has been under the care of Miss Crawford and Miss Spooner, both of whom were obliged, by ill-health, to leave early in the year. Miss Crawford returned to this country in November, and has severed her connection with the Board. Miss Spooner went to Philippopolis for the winter, hoping to regain her health sufficiently to resume her work, but was obliged to return to this country, arriving in May.

At the request of the mission, Miss Cole went from Samokov to Monastir, as a temporary arrangement, and will probably remain permanently in charge of the school. She is in great need of an assistant. Miss Graves still continues as associate with Miss Maltbie in the boarding-school at Samokov (supported by the Woman's Board of Missions of the Interior), which is a most successful school. Mrs. Bond, Mrs. Clarke, and Mrs. Sleeper are doing efficient service in house-to-house visitation, Sabbath-school, and evangelistic work among the women. Mrs. Bond adds to these her medical work, which opens many hearts and homes to the gospel message. Mrs. Baird has returned to this country for needed rest. The department of special interest to our Board in this mission, is that of the seven Bible-women under the superintendence of Miss Stone. By their perseverance, and zeal, and great loving-kindness they are making their way into many houses, reading and teaching the Bible, and persuading the women to accept its blessed truths. Aside from this, Miss Stone has found time for many tender ministries to the sick and dying in her own home, and a flying trip to this country with an invalid associate, remaining less than a month.

WESTERN TURKEY MISSION.

MISSIONARIES. — Miss Clara Hamlin, Miss Isabel F. Dodd, Miss Flora A. Fensham, Miss Helen E. Melvin, Miss Ida W. Prime, Mrs. Kate P. Williams, of the Constantinople Home, Mrs. Susan M. Schneider, Miss Martha J. Gleason, Constantinople; Mrs. Fannie M. Newell, Miss Olive N. Twichell, Broosa (57 miles south to southeast of Constantinople); Mrs. Catharine Parsons, Miss Laura Farnham, Nicomedia (50 miles southwest of Constantinople); Miss Mary L. Page, Miss Agnes M. Lord, Miss Emily McCallum, Smyrna; Miss Phebe L. Cull, Manisa (6 miles from Smyrna); Mrs. Myra P. Tracey, Miss Eliza Fritcher, Marsovan (about 350 miles east of Constantinople); Miss Fannie E. Burrage, Miss Sarah A. Closson, Cesarea (370 miles southeast of Constantinople); Miss Laura B. Chamberlain, Sivas (400 miles southeast of Constantinople). SCHOOLS. — The Constantinople Home. Misses Hamlin and Patrick (Woman's Board of Missions of the Interior) associate principals; 50 boarding-pupils and 47 day-scholars. Boarding-School at Talas, Misses Closson and Burrage in charge; 40 boarders, 130 day-scholars. Boarding-school at Smyrna, Misses Page, Lord, and McCallum in charge; 27 boarders and 57 day-scholars. Nicomedia, Misses Farnham and Parsons (Woman's Board of Missions of the Interior) in charge; 34 boarders, 27 day-scholars. Boarding-school at Marsovan, Miss Fritcher in charge; 48 boarders, 28 day-scholars. Boarding-school at Sivas, Miss Chamberlain in charge; 18 boarders and 114 day-scholars. Forty day and village schools, and 14 Bible-women.

The educational work for girls in this mission is so extensive, it is impossible in our limited space to do much more than merely mention the different schools. The Constantinople Home still continues to be a "joy and delight" in missionary work. The perfect harmony in all its machinery, the strong religious atmosphere pervading it, the tender relations between teachers and pupils, all combine to make it that most lovely place on earth, a refined Christian home, and its influence extends far and wide through the regions roundabout. A class of seven, all Christian girls, were to graduate in June — four of them to teach in various places. In the prolonged absence of Mrs. Williams in this country, Misses Patrick and Hamlin continue as associate principals, while the others have their several departments. No one of the schools of our Board has achieved greater success in the same length of time than the one in Smyrna, which is only three years old, and numbers 84 scholars — 11 Greeks, 4 English, and the remainder Armenians. The boarders have increased from 16 to 27 the past year, which crowds the present building uncomfortably. Nine of the pupils united with the church the first Sabbath in March, and as many more are thought to have started in the Christian life, but, being quite young, need a longer test before being received to the church. On the return of Mrs. Bowen to this country, Miss Page was obliged to call to her aid Miss Lord, who was laboring with Mrs. Schneider, in Constantinople; and later they were reinforced by Miss McCallum, also from Constantinople. Mrs. and Miss Bartlett have also rendered great assistance. Miss Rebecca Jillson, who sailed July 30th, is also to go to Smyrna, so that the fall term will open with an efficient force. The school at Nicomedia (Bardesag) has had its usual prosperity during the year. "Too much," says the report, "cannot be said concerning the teachers in caring for the mental and physical, as well as the spiritual, necessities of these pupils." It is proposed this autumn to move the school to Adabazar, about thirty miles away. This is done at the urgent request of the Protestants there, who promise to meet all the expense of the school except the salaries of the American teachers — a most encouraging advance in the way of self-support. "The moving and starting a new school seems like a mountain to lift," writes Miss Farnham, "but I feel as if we ought to do all in our power to make these people independent of foreign aid." As these two lady teachers are located so far from all other missionaries, they will need special prayer and encouragement from the home-land. The school at Marsovan has again outgrown its accommodations, and a new dormitory and school-room have been added. More strenuous rules have been made as to the payment of tuition, which, it is thought, may lessen the number of pupils for the next year. Seven were received into the church in January, and others were specially interested. Miss Wright (supported by the Woman's Board of Missions of the Interior), who has been in Harpoot the past four years, has been transferred to Marsovan, to assist Miss Fritcher in the school. Miss Washburn, formerly at Marsovan, has severed her connection with the Board, and will remain in this country for the present. The school at Sivas has had a prosperous year, an advance being made in average attendance, though the total number of pupils has not increased. Miss Chamberlain writes: "As neither the civil nor religious rulers in this land personally know our Father, nor are friendly to his government, they do not recognize our right and title here, and wish to drive us from the country. As they are always in ambush against us, we are obliged to be on the alert, lest at some unexpected moment they seize our heritage, and hold it by possession — which in this land is ten-tenths of the law." Miss Blake, of this station, has found it necessary to return to this country, to remain here, which leaves Miss Chamberlain alone in the woman's work. At Cesarea (Talas) the school still sustains its high reputation. A class of sixteen graduated in the spring. A special effort at economy is very quietly told in a sentence in a letter from one of the teachers: "We are living in a very simple way, this winter. We have no cook. We teachers live with the girls, who do their own work." Under miscellaneous work we would mention Mrs. Schneider's wonderfully successful labors in Constantinople, of which a report is given in the August number, and the kindergartens that are so promising under Miss Bartlett's care in Smyrna, and in several other stations in connection with higher schools. The village-schools and Bible-women's work in this mission are eminently successful, but our space will not permit details. All over the mission-field are stationed the graduates of our boarding-schools, either gathering flocks of little ones around them, to teach them the beautiful gospel story as well as the rudiments of a Christian education, or going about from house to house, through summer's heat and winter's snow, fearlessly braving taunts and persecutions of many kinds, but withal gaining the interest and respect of many.

CENTRAL TURKEY MISSION.

MISSIONARIES.—Mrs. Emily R. Montgomery and Miss Harriet N. Childs, at Marash (90 miles northeast from Scanderoon); Miss Ellen M. Pierce, Miss Henrietta West, and Miss Myra A. Proctor at Aintab (90 miles northeast from Scanderoon). SCHOOLS.— Aintab Female Seminary; 22 boarders and 22 day-scholars; Misses Pierce and West in charge. Twenty-seven day and village schools; 5 Bible-women.

The old building of the Aintab Seminary has been sold, and new ones are in process of erection, on an admirable site just out of the city, about seven or eight minutes' walk from Central Turkey College. Various vicissitudes have been experienced in the progress of the building, but it is now expected it will be ready for occupancy this autumn. The school still maintains its high standing, and its graduates speak well for it in the village-school teachers and Bible-women all over the Central Turkey field. Miss West reached Aintab in December last, and is proving an efficient helper. Miss Childs, who was transferred from Constantinople to Marash a year ago, is busily at work with Miss Shattuck in the girls' seminary at Marash. Mrs. Montgomery and Miss Proctor are still in this country. Miss Ellen L. Blakely is about leaving this country, to join the ladies in Marash. A special feature in this mission are the village-schools, which are eminently successful.

EASTERN TURKEY MISSION.

MISSIONARIES. - Mrs. Caroline R. Allen, Miss Caroline E. Bush, Miss Harriet Seymour, Miss Emily C. Wheeler, at Harpoot (175 miles south from Trebizond); Mrs. Olive L. Andrus, Miss Clarissa H. Pratt, Mardin (150 miles southeast of Harpoot); Miss Charlotte E. Ely, Miss Mary A. C. Ely, Bitlis (near Lake Van, about 300 miles southeast of Trebizond); Mrs. Martha W. Raynolds, Miss Lauraette E. Johnson, Miss Grace N. Kimball, Van (east end of Lake Van); Miss Harriet G. Powers, at Erzroom (150 miles southeast of Trebizond). SCHOOLS.—Armenia College, Female Department, 128 pupils, Miss E. C. Wheeler in charge. Boarding-school at Mardin, Miss Pratt in charge. Boarding-school at Bitlis, the Misses Ely in charge. Boarding-school in Van; 15 boarders and 45 day scholars; Misses Johnson and Kimball in charge. Twenty-two day and village schools; 9 Bible-women.

The female department of Harpoot College has had a prosperous year, with more pupils than ever before. It is thought the numbers may be less the coming year, as a good many will go out to teach, and the pressure for larger payments may keep some away. In the absence of Miss Wright, Miss Seymour has rendered valuable assistance in the school. Miss Mary L. Daniels is now under appointment to Harpoot, and will probably sail some time in September. The touring in this field the last year has been done principally by Misses Bush and Wright, who were away from Harpoot six months in all, and reached thirty-three different places; eleven of them have been visited twice. Frequently their visits have been one long succession of meetings, neighbors and friends being called in, numbering from five to twenty. A full report of woman's work in the Harpoot field will be given in the October number. The boarding-school at Mardin is not so large as formerly, and at times has been suspended altogether, to give the missionaries opportunity to work elsewhere. The transfer of Miss Sears to Marsovan, as Mrs. J. F. Smith, and the absence of Miss Pratt, who is now in this country, leaves the woman's work in the hands of the married ladies in the station. Miss Ella T. Bray has been appointed to this station, and will be on the ground in the autumn, to do what she can while acquiring the language. In September, 1883, the school at Van was reopened on a tuition basis, and from very small beginnings, reached, in the spring of

1884, its former number of thirty, but of a much more desirable class of pupils, including eleven boarders. Another year having passed, there are sixty regular pupils, of whom fifteen are boarders. They are mostly Gregorians, but the study of the Bible is compulsory in the three upper classes, and there is very little opposition to a thorough instruction to every pupil. Mrs. Raynolds has resumed her work among the women, so far as her strength will allow. The school at Bitlis holds quietly on its way, and the Misses Ely find reason for gratitude for the abundant Divine blessing on their labors. Miss Powers is at Erzroom, doing efficient work among the women, "ploughing and sowing."*

MARATHA MISSION.

MISSIONARIES.—Mrs. Charlotte E. Hume, Bombay; Mrs. Mary E. Bissell, Miss Kate Fairbank, Miss Ruby E. Harding, Miss Sarah E. Hume, Ahmednagar (140 miles east of Bombay); Mrs. Mary C. Winsor, Sirur (30 miles southeast of Ahmednagar). SCHOOLS.—Boarding-school at Bombay, Mrs. Charlotte E. Hume in charge; 100 pupils. Boarding-school at Ahmednagar, Misses Harding and Fairbank in charge; 137 pupils. Two Hindu girls' schools in Ahmednagar, Mrs. Bissell in charge. Boarding-school at Sirur, Mrs. Winsor in charge. Twenty-six village and day schools, and 14 Bible-women.

In Bombay, the special object of interest to our Board is the school for Christian girls in Bombay, of which Mr. Hume writes: "This work has prospered more than anything to which we have put our hands. There is nothing except the church to which the Christians are so much attached, and for which they feel so grateful. Last year, in November, we sent up two girls for the university matriculation examination, and they both passed. They were the first native girls in this Presidency who have gone up in native costume and have passed this examination. There were nearly two thousand two hundred candidates, of whom only eight hundred and thirty-five passed. There were seventeen girls among the candidates, of whom eight were successful, one of our girls being the highest of them all." This girl is now a teacher in the school, having refused an offer in an English school, with much higher salary.. The school at Ahmednager continues prosperous. Recent trials have been the death of two of the native teachers, a man and a woman, which have had a softening, solemnizing effect on the pupils. As Miss Harding and Miss Fairbank are to be transferred to homes of their own in this mission some time during the coming year, two young ladies are needed to take the school. Miss Hume, who has been in Ahmednagar for several years in her brother's family, has now become a regular missionary of the Board. She has done good work among the women, one important item being the establishment of the "Chapin Home," in which women are taken to be taught industrial work, and trained for Bible-women.

---

* See page 334.

The ten Bible-women under Mrs. Bissell's care continue their efficient service. The death of one of the oldest of these women, Subabai, causes a great loss to the work. Mrs. Bissell says of her: "It was wonderful how she maintained her Christian character through more than thirty-five years. It seemed as if it were enough to compensate for all the labor and outlay of this mission thus far, to have been instrumental in securing just this one example to hold up before the women." Mrs. Winsor, with whom so many became pleasantly acquainted during her recent visit to this country, is at work again with new zeal and enthusiasm after her absence.

MADURA MISSION.

MISSIONARIES.—Mrs. Sarah B. Capron, at Madura (270 miles southwest of Madras); Mrs. Charlotte H. Chandler, Miss Gertrude A. Chandler, at Battalagundu (32 miles northwest of Madura). Five boarding-schools, 10 Hindu girls' schools, 21 village and day schools; 14 Bible-women.

The work in the girls' schools in this mission has been given in detail in the June number; that of the Bible-women will be found in the October number.

Miss Swift, who arrived in Madura in July, 1884, to take Miss Rendall's place in the Madura boarding-school, has spent a large part of her time in the study of the language, but was expected to assume full duties in the school the first of June last. At Mrs. Capron's special request, the Board are seeking some ladies to take up the work that she feels she must lay down during the coming year. One, a medical lady, Miss Mary P. Root, M.D., has already been secured, and is now on her way to Madura.

CEYLON MISSION (JAFFNA DISTRICT, NORTH CEYLON).

MISSIONARIES.—Miss Kate Hastings, at Batticotta; Mrs. Mary E. K. Howland, Miss Susan R. Howland, at Oodooville; Miss Mary Leitch, Miss Margaret W. Leitch, at Manepy. Boarding-school, 30 pupils, at Oodoopitty, Mr. and Mrs. Richard Hastings in charge. Twenty-three day and village schools; 17 Bible-women.

Although the Oodooville boarding-school is not now an expense to the Board, it is still under the care of the mission, and all are interested in its success. It has been regularly registered as a Training Institution for the education of teachers, and there are more candidates for admission than can be received. The position the school holds may be learned from the following incident: In a certain village when it was found that two girls were going to the school, relatives and friends came together, much excited, determined to prevent them from going. Money was subscribed to open a heathen school in the village, and great alarm manifested lest the "village should become Christian within ten years." In the absence of Miss Howland, who is now in this country for a period of rest, the school is taken care of by the Misses Leitch.

Of the work of these ladies in the Manepy and Panditeripo stations, an account is given in the July number. The school at Oodoopitty continues its good work, all but three of the present pupils being members of the church. The Bible-women also continue their important labors from house to house, teaching the women and girls in their homes. Mrs. M. E. K. Howland is also in this country, for rest and recuperation. Miss Hastings is doing efficient service among the women and village-schools in Batticotta and vicinity.

FOOCHOW MISSION.

MISSIONARIES.— Miss Elsie M. Garretson, Miss Emily S. Hartwell, Miss Kate C. Woodhull, M.D., Miss Hannah Woodhull, Foochow. Boarding-school at Foochow, 29 pupils, Misses Newton (Woman's Board of Missions of the Interior) and Garretson in charge. Day-schools at Foochow and Shawu.

The school at Foochow is in a prosperous condition, the pupils being mostly from Christian families. Miss Garretson writes of the incidental benefits of the school as seen in the homes of the girls, where cleanliness, and little touches of taste and refinement in the way of pretty cards and Scripture-texts on the walls and tables, distinguish their houses from those of the heathen around them. A Society for Christian Endeavor has been organized among the young people of the little church, which promises to be successful. The Misses Woodhull, though spending most of their time on the language, have found opportunities to gain many hearts among the people. Already plans are formed for their medical work on a larger scale than was anticipated; and although there is as yet no dispensary, they have begun to receive patients at the rate of about ten in a day. Miss Hartwell still continues her labors among the women and in the boys' schools.

NORTH CHINA MISSION.

MISSIONARIES.—Miss Mary E. Andrews, Miss Mary Anne Holbrook, M.D., Tung-cho (12 miles east of Peking). Boarding-school at Kalgan; day-schools at Tung-cho and Pao-ting-fu; 3 Bible-women.

Since the removal of Miss Garretson to the Foochow Mission, the school at Kalgan has been under the care of Miss Diament (Woman's Board of Missions of the Interior), assisted by other ladies in the mission, and is growing in numbers and favor with the people. Of the general work in Tung-cho, an account is given on page 331. Miss Holbrook's medical labor continues to be of absorbing interest. To provide suitably for the future, a larger lot of land than was first planned has been purchased for the new dispensary, and work on the building was to begin in March. Plans for the Training-School for Bible-women are also being matured.

JAPAN MISSION.

MISSIONARIES.—Miss Abby M. Colby, Miss Adelaide Doughaday, Mrs. S. E. De Forest, Miss Fanny A. Gardner, Miss Mary E. Gouldy, Mrs. Frances A.

Gulick, Osaka; Mrs. Agnes H. Gordon, Miss Anna Y. Davis, Miss Frances Hooper, Kioto; Miss Eliza Talcott, Miss Virginia Clarkson. Boarding-school at Kioto, 43 pupils, Misses Davis and Hooper in charge.

Progress in Japan still continues to be the wonder and delight of all interested in missions. As has been stated elsewhere, the favorable feeling toward Christianity amounts to a peril, lest Japan become a Christian nation in form and in name, without the vital change of heart that will make it permanently Christian. In the breathless effort to seize all the opportunities offered to our missionaries, we cannot wonder that many break down, and are obliged to flee to this country for rest. Miss Gouldy is now in this country, and others are expected soon. Miss Talcott and Miss Clarkson are now on their way back to Japan, their particular station and work to be assigned them on their arrival. The schools at Kioto and Osaka are holding quietly and steadily on their way; the one at Osaka (entirely supported by the natives) having become so crowded as to necessitate an enlargement of the building. The work among the women is more hopeful and more pressing than ever before, and the call for reinforcements is very earnest.

NORTHERN JAPAN MISSION.

MISSIONARY.— Miss Julia Gulick.

The work for women in this new mission opens most invitingly. Many women are already interested, and schools could be opened were there teachers to have charge of them.

MICRONESIAN MISSION.

MISSIONARY.— Mrs. Harriet A. Pease, at Kusaie.

Dr. and Mrs. Pease, of this mission, are now in this country for rest, and the work in the care of Mr. and Mrs. Walkup is going on steadily.

MISSION TO SPAIN.

MISSIONARIES.—Mrs. Alice Gordon Gulick, Miss Susan F. Richards, at San Sebastian Boarding-school, at San Sebastian, 64 pupils, Mrs. Gulick and Miss Richards in charge. Day-schools at Santander and Zaragoza; 2 Bible-women.

In San Sebastian the missionaries are specially grateful to the good Providence that has kept them from the perils of cholera and of earthquakes that have devastated some parts of Spain, and has enabled them to prosecute their work without interruption. The school at San Sebastian is constantly growing, and is in a most prosperous condition. The three graduates this year are already engaged as teachers in evangelistic schools. The day-schools and the Bible-women at Santander and Zaragoza continue as in former years. Signora Joaquina Martinez has married, and left the work.

MISSION TO AUSTRIA.
School at Krabschitz, Home at Brunn, Orphanage at Russitz.

A detailed report of the school at Krabschitz and of the Brünn Home may be found in the June number. The orphanage at Russitz is an exceedingly interesting work, under the care of the Countess La Tono; but as it has recently come under the care of the Board, we have received no special report of it. Aside from these, there are four devoted missionary Bible-women doing evangelistic work among the women, in as many different places.

We have thus been able to give the merest outline of our foreign work, but there are many of our friends who will read between the lines the amount of thought, labor, and anxiety that it represents. We trust, also, they will see the possibilities of this work in the future, and the absolute necessity that it shall be prosecuted with increasing vigor and earnestness as the years go on. May our heavenly Father grant to each one to whom he has intrusted any part in it, the needed wisdom, zeal, and grace for the great undertaking.

CHINA.

THE TUNG-CHO WOMAN'S MISSIONARY SOCIETY.

We give below, the third annual report of the Tung-cho Woman's Missionary Society. We have had occasion to mention this as a model auxiliary, since every member of the church is a member of the society, and a constant attendant of the monthly meetings, being drawn there by no tea-meetings or festivals of any kind, but by a real interest in the welfare of women in other lands. Miss Andrews sends the translation of the report, as follows: —

GREETINGS to our church friends (a term as common here as "the brethren" was in New Testament times) of the Woman's Board in America.

Our Tung-cho society has, as heretofore, held twelve meetings during the year. We have been studying the preaching of the gospel, and its success in all lands—the things which we ourselves cannot see nor hear. We have contributed this year 33,390 cash ($14.04, U. S. Gold), and we wish still to support our Bible-reader. We hear that the money we contributed last year lacked a little of enough for her full support. Now, we have promised, each of us, to add a little to our contributions from month to month, hoping that for the coming year we may be able to give enough for her full support. This is what, with willing hearts, we desire to do. Three new members have joined our society this year, making the whole number of women now nineteen. We ask you, our sisters there, to pray much for us here, that we may have warm hearts in working for the Lord.

And may you obtain God's grace, and be kept in peace, earnestly serving the Lord.

In behalf of the women of the Tung-cho Society, greeting.

In a letter accompanying the report, Miss Andrews says:—

There is one little word in the report which I think will please you, as it did us—that is, the determination of the women to make up the full amount this year. At their annual meeting J prepared a little Bible-reading for them on liberal giving to the Lord. It was not by any means the first time the subject had been brought to them, but it seemed to take a stronger hold of them than usual. Later in the meeting I told them the amount that was lacking for the full support of their Bible-reader, and asked if there was anything they could do about it. One of the women suggested that if each one of them would bear the matter in mind, and add just a few cash, though not more than five, to her regular contribution each month, it would make quite a difference in the amount at the end of the year. The plan seemed to meet the approval of all; they are acting on it, and seem very much in earnest about it, some of them having added more than a few cash each month, so that the contributions have very much increased. I have no doubt they will make up the full amount this year.

. . . . Our work for women has gone on quietly and pleasantly through the winter, and never seemed so promising and hopeful as now — hopeful of immediate results. Of course there is always the hope, or rather the certainty, that the Lord will fulfill his promises, and will use his own Word to accomplish his own work. But of late we do see tokens that he is working in some hearts among us. In the autumn we had fears lest the presence of so many soldiers in the city during the winter, and the wild rumors that were so prevalent in regard to the war and to foreigners, might seriously interfere with our work; but what we do in the homes of the people does not seem to have been particularly affected by the state of things.

Our two Bible-women, Mrs. Chang and Mrs. Wang, have had a few homes closed against them which were formerly open to them; but they still have work enough to fill their afternoons, and they seem very earnest and faithful, never willing to give up an afternoon's work, no matter what the weather may be. They have some forty women and girls under instruction, whom they visit two or three times a week for teaching, most of them seeming really anxious to be taught. Of course they visit other homes as they have opportunity, and talk with a great many who do not undertake to learn to read. In one neighborhood Mrs. Chang has a very interesting group of young women and girls, six or eight of them who are especially eager to learn, and would be glad to have her come to teach them, if she had time. I visit them once a week, and hold a little meeting with them. They are nearly all

Mohammedans (a very difficult and hopeless class of people to work for here), but their eager interest in Bible verses and Bible stories is very pleasant to see, and makes us quite hopeful for them.

From another neighborhood—one of Mrs. Chang's visiting-places—three women are coming quite regularly to our Sabbath services; rude, coarse, loud-voiced women (two of them, at least), but apparently sincere inquirers after the truth, intent not only on hearing and learning as much as they can, but also on living up to what they learn. I have seldom taught more disagreeable women, and yet there is real pleasure in it, remembering how precious their souls are in the Lord's sight, and thinking how beautiful they may be one day, in his image, if he chooses them for his own. I have them in my Sabbath-school class, and I try, also, to find an opportunity each Sabbath for a more quiet talk with them in my own room, so as to give them some teaching more especially adapted to their needs. One of them—a Mrs. Su—has a face which shows a very bad temper, and she told me on the occasion of her first visit that she had always been in the habit of railing a great deal, hardly opening her lips except to revile; but that since her first visit, since I had told her about God, and the things that displeased him, she had tried very hard to stop using such words. These women have taken up the habit of daily prayer and of Sabbath-keeping, and I am very hopeful for them.

Another one of my class in whom I am especially interested is a Mrs. Fay, the very opposite of these women in manner and appearance, in every way lady-like and gentle, apparently as eager to learn as they. Her husband and son are both members of the London mission church in Peking, but they have been very little at home for years, and the wife and mother seems to have been in no way benefited by their religion. Sorrow and trial in her home have been God's means of driving her to Christ for refuge. She has lately moved into the city and into our neighborhood, so as to be near enough to come to us for teaching.

I enjoy my part of the work in the woman's training-class very much. The hour that I spend with those women is one of the pleasantest hours of the day. We are studying the life of Christ, and my aim is to teach them how to use what they know in teaching others. Another pleasant work is the hour I spend with the two Bible-women each forenoon. Mrs. Tsua joins the other class, as she is far in advance of these two in ability to read and in knowledge of the truth. These two women give me first a report of the previous day, after which we give the hour to careful Bible-study, with the same object in view—that of teaching them how to teach.

Young People's Department.

PLOUGHING AND SOWING.

PLOUGHING; OR, A GLIMPSE AT TURNING UP NEW SOIL.

BY MISS H. G. POWERS.

P. KOHAR (Testament in hand) and I are seated on a piece of brown felt, spread on the clay floor of a large room, which is lighted only from the roof. Just before us is a hole, two feet in diameter at the top, and about three feet deep, from which warm air ascends, in place of the earlier flame and smoke. This is the family cook-stove. On its sides the bread is often baked, and in its ashes eggs and other things are cooked, or kept hot for hours. It has a flue under ground, for the purpose of draught, while the smoke goes out,— if it chooses,— when the light comes in. On one side of the room are arranged great clay bins, having small wooden doors fastened with padlocks. On another side are shelves containing rows of earthen jars and coarse dishes. Underneath is a row of big clay kettles, some of which, had we come earlier, we should have seen on the *toneer*, steaming and bubbling with the family dinner.

In one corner there is a huge pile of dingy bedding, partly covered by an old piece of carpet.

Close about us a dozen or so women and girls, some occupied with babies, some knitting coarse socks (with two threads and big steel needles, beginning at the toe); one embroidering an apron, which is now only an oblong piece of home-made, dark-blue woolen stuff, but after a few weeks or months will be one mass of embroidery, in brilliant colors and elaborate figures.

A fine-looking woman comes in and says, impressively, " Cast not your pearls before swine." Seating herself on a little wooden stool directly in front of us, she repeats her warning. After a little general conversation, P. Kohar begins to read:—

" There was a man of the Pharisees, named Nicodemus, a ruler —— "

" Are you both from the same village ?" breaks in a voice from behind.

P. Kohar. "No, I am from Egin; but this lady is from America, a country very far away."

Goes on reading:—   Two young women are whis-
" A ruler of the Jews: pering at one side.

                                1st. " Is she a woman or a girl?"

The same came to Jesus by night, and said unto him, Rabbi, we know —— "

2d. "A girl; and so is the other."

1st. "What! both unmarried?" Turns to P. Kohar: "Is it true that neither of you is married?"

P. K. "Yes." Reads.: "We know that thou art a teacher come from God; for no man can do these miracles —— "

"But do you never intend to marry?" persits No. 1, expressing in tone and face the utmost astonishment.

P. K. "Never mind about that now. We did not come to talk of such things, but to read to you God's holy Word." Reads: "Verily, verily, I say unto thee, Except a man be born again, he cannot see the kingdom of God."

A man standing one side picks up my umbrella, opens and shuts it; whereupon two girls drop my rubbers which they have been examining, and fix their attention upon the umbrella.

And so it goes, while P. Kohar is trying to put before them, clearly and effectively, one of the great truths of the Gospel. Have we been "casting our pearls before swine"?

SOWING.

About noon I walked over to the "Valley-fold" schoolhouse, sent some children off to call the women, and sat down with one or two, to wait for the others. Soon they began to drop in; one with a child on her back or at the breast, another with two or three hanging on to her skirts, besides a swarm of children quite independent of mothers. Then a sweet-faced, ladylike woman (whom I will hereafter indicate by the initial N.) came in and sat down close beside me, saying that she was deaf, and would I please speak loud, so that she might hear.

She was followed by a brazen-faced, loud-voiced woman, who entered sneering at those present. "It is a fine thing to come to hear when you don't practice, isn't it? Seating herself at a little distance in front of me, she continued to make her presence felt by administering a slap to a child who happened to crowd her a little, a verbal slap to a woman on the other side, treating another to a coarse joke, and so on, although I was trying to open the meeting. I found one or two girls who could read, and gave the Bible to one, indicating the passage, John iv. 46–54. Some one pulled my sleeve, and pointing to a large girl, said, "She reads nicely; let her take the book." I was pleased to find another reader, but thought best to let the little girl keep the Bible. There was so much noise and confusion as she read the first verse, that I finally stopped her, and turning to the children told them they must be still, and said to the other two or three garrulous women, "You can talk to each other any day. Now, I do not see you often, and have come a long distance on purpose to talk to you, so please keep quiet and listen."

"Listen!" broke out the loud voice; "ain't I listening? It is those others who make the disturbance."

I gave out a hymn, and was much pleased to find girls who could join in the singing, which had a quieting effect, so that at its close we once more began to read: "And there was a certain nobleman ——"

N. "Was this a man or a woman?" (The absence of gender in the Armenian makes such a question reasonable.)

"This was a man; but we read equally beautiful stories of Christ's quick sympathy with the woes of sorrowing women. When we finish this, I will tell you one."

As I went on with the story, showing how, in a few short minutes, the faith which was as a grain of mustard-seed became able to move mountains, most listened attentively, but the rapt expression of the delicate, wistful face nearest me was an inspiration.

Then I told them of the Syrophenician woman, and the blessed words of approbation with which Christ sent her away joyful — "O woman, great is thy faith."

"May I ask a question?" said a gentle voice. "If we now have faith like that, and pray for a child who is ill, will its life be spared?"

"Yes, N., if it be God's will."

"I have just buried a little one; I could not bear to have him die. I prayed so earnestly that he might be spared — being a mother, you know, I could not help it! If I had had faith like these ——" She paused for a moment. "Was it because my faith was weak that my prayer was not answered?"

"Dear sister, Jesus knew God's will, so he could always be sure. We do not know, so when we offer a petition it must be with faith in God as our Father, and not in the direct answer to our petitions."

N. "I do not quite understand."

"Suppose the death of your child will make you more humble, and lead you to think of eternity, and to seek God; may he not take your child away, disregarding your prayer, for the sake of the greater good of saving your soul?"

Then I told her of my father, and how his dying request was not granted. God does by us as we do by children, withholding the lesser to grant a greater blessing.

The children by this time had become rather noisy again, but the brazen-faced woman worst of all.

"Why do you devote yourself to one or two, when we all are waiting to hear you?" she demanded.

"If you will all keep quiet, you will hear everything I say ; but I cannot possibly talk loud enough to drown all this noise," was my answer; and then I gave out a hymn, with the usual quieting effect. At the close, N. asked, "What did the minister mean last Sabbath by the 'daughters of Jerusalem' ? He closed by saying, 'O my brothers and sisters, do not be like 'the daughters of Jerusalem.'"

I knew that Mr. Chambers had preached an eloquent and awakening sermon on the fifth chapter of Solomon's tender song, and I tried to explain it to her.

"The 'bride' has gone to bed, and is drowsing, when her Beloved's call comes. She cannot bear to get up again."

N. "Was she ill?"

"No; it was night, and she was dull with sleep. At last, however, love conquers lassitude, and she hastens to the door, to find, alas ! that she has tried her Beloved's patience too long, and he is gone. Then she is thoroughly aroused; no more sleep, no more rest for her, till she find him. Seeking him, she comes to the 'daughters of Jerusalem' — cold and backsliding Christians. They cannot understand her grief ; sin has dulled their consciences and deadened their feelings. They either never had that warm love for Christ of which he is worthy, or their hearts have grown cold; and instead of helping the unhappy bride,— the roused and repentant sinner,— they try to make her as indifferent as themselves. They are like the Pharisees to whom Christ said: 'Ye shut up the kingdom of heaven against men: for ye neither go in yourselves, neither suffer ye them that are entering to go in.' Now, do you see why the minister entreated his hearers not to be like the 'daughters of Jerusalem' ?"

N. "Yes; thank you so much."

We closed with prayer, and as I rose to go, N., with warm expressions of gratitude, seized my hand and kissed it.

Another woman (whom I will call Olive) told me eagerly that she would soon finish (reading) the Testament. "And what book will you send me then?" she asked. Another, who has expressed a wish to join the church, begged a Testament for her niece, who could read, but had no book. I promised to send her one if she would help Olive with her reading. She promised readily; but who knows? She may soon be married, and not free to use her time as she likes.

To have some, though it be only two or three, listen, because
they wished to,—rather than because I wished it,—was a treat;
and to have earnest questions asked, was a refreshment of whose
delight you can hardly conceive. There is a joy for those who
"sow in tears," — yes, even while sowing !

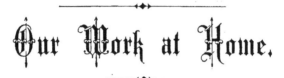

PRACTICAL CONSECRATION.

BY MRS. H. GRATTAN GUINNESS.

In view of the pressing demand for workers, we make the following extracts from an English leaflet, by Mrs. Guinness, hoping it may influence
some parents to dedicate their children to the great work of missions.

. . . I SOLEMNLY believe that one great cause of the low tone
of Christian life over which the Church mourns so often, is the
lack of missionary zeal, the non-cultivation of the missionary spirit
in Christian families, and that the first symptom of a really
"higher Christian life" will be a revival of this spirit. It has been
so in the past. The revival of spiritual religion in our land in the
last century was the birthday of missionary enterprise. Its growth
has kept pace with the extension of such enterprise, and its increase, if such is to come (and God grant it may), must be accompanied by a great increase of missionary efforts. In the nature of
things this must be so. In the physical world we have, first, life;
then food, thereby growth; and with growth, exercise. But given
life, food, growth, and no exercise, disease and decay must ensue.
If the Christian Church would thrive she must have exercise, and
her Christ-appointed exercise is the evangelization of the world.
The Church ought to be one great missionary society, and each of
her children, directly or indirectly, a missionary.

But what is the fact? A few individuals take a real interest
in this great work. They influence others to help; but the mass
of believers remain comparatively inert. Have we not thousands
and tens of thousands of Christian families, no one of which ever
contributed one single laborer to the heathen field? Have we not
parents who have reared six, eight, or it may be ten, sons and
daughters, and seen them by grace converted to God, and who yet
never trained, or attempted to train, one of them for a missionary
to the heathen? . . . Not only the heathen perish, but, O Christian parents! you and your children, those very children whom ye
would fain spare suffering, suffer — suffer most materially from this
very thing.

Father, what makes your heart heavy this day? "Ah," you sigh, "our precious boy, whom we thought to be converted years ago, has gone right into the world; we see no sign of grace in him now. We pray, and weep, and hope against hope, but we seem to have no influence over him." Ah, father, whose fault is that? What did you do with your boy when full of his first love? You sent him to a public school, perhaps; you sought great things for him in this life; you exposed him to temptation for the sake of mammon, it may be; you led him to seek first this world and its interests, instead of the kingdom of God and his righteousness; you never attempted to use your mighty parental influence to lead the ardent youth to consecrate his life to preaching Christ to the perishing heathen. You never gave him a Christian object worthy and likely to fill his heart, and mould his life, and engage his affections, and ennoble his aspirations, and extend his views out into eternity. Your son might have been a Brainerd, or a Livingstone, had you acted otherwise; but he is — well, you know what he is!

And you, mother — what saddens your eye, and sinks your heart? Your daughters — have they turned out as you would desire? "Alas, no!" you sigh. One of them is worldly, though perhaps saved; another is a confirmed invalid; another, who is a decided Christian, has gone over to the High Church, or perhaps even entered a Romish convent. You are disappointed in them — and, as a Christian, you ought to be. Ah, mother, whose fault is it? Those girls were Christians when young; they had talents, affections, health, leisure, ardor, spirits, zeal, knowledge of the truth, and a good education. What missionaries they would have made!

Had their compassions been drawn out, the self-sacrifice natural to every true disciple called into play; had they been prepared for, and early introduced to, the mission-field — what blessed helpers in the gospel they might have been! How many an Indian zenana they might have made happy and holy! How many a Japanese lady they might have taught to read the Word of life! How many a miserable Chinese mother might they have led into peace and joy in believing! What glorious results they might have secured for eternity! How every remembrance of each one might cause you to thank your God for the privilege of having been permitted to bear and rear such instruments for his glory! But you could not spare them; you could not expose them to hardships and suffering. It would never do to send your delicately reared girls among the degraded and ignorant heathen; and so they were doomed to the very uninteresting life of a Christian young woman, with little or nothing to do!

You would have been glad they should have served the Lord **at home, you say?** Yes; but they did not find occasional "amateur" work of this kind enough to engage heart and mind. Others were doing it abundantly. No important responsibility was laid on them to call out their energies, develop their abilities, and exercise their spiritual graces. They had not the stimulus of the urgent needs of others; they began, perhaps, to serve the Lord with one hand, daintily; but when difficulties arose, or novelty wore off, they gave it up, and no one was much the worse. That sort of work does not avail to save the young and energetic from worldliness, selfishness, or disgust with life. It is not a vocation.; it is not a life. It is all very well for those who have distinct and important secular duties devolving on them, to serve the Lord by the way, as it were, and fill up their odd moments of leisure by doing what they can. But your girls did not marry; they had not the natural and absorbing avocations of wife and mother; they were spared the sufferings, and cares, and self-denial, and responsibility involved in bringing up children; they had no claims of business; their time was their own; they wanted a life-work—hard, high, holy, life-work. Oh, had you laid before them the claims of the heathen, advised and assisted them to become missionaries, how differently your daughters might have turned out!

The young mind must have interests; the young heart must have objects on which to spend its ardor and its affections. Human nature must have difficulties with which to cope, hardships to endure, battles to fight, obstacles to overcome. What are cricket, and croquet, and chess, and all games of skill, but an artificial creation of these? Life, if natural and well-spent, is full of these; life without them is vapid and vain.

The lives of Christian young ladies are too often deprived of all interest by a false and foolish parental affection. I once knew a mother of two of the finest little girls I ever saw, who was insanely anxious about their health. The wind was never suffered to blow on their rosy cheeks; they were kept in bed for days if they chanced to sneeze; and the mother's life was one long misery, for fear they should be ill. She succeeded at last in making them ill, and soon after she died of over-anxiety. Then the girls, left to themselves, got well. Now, few mothers are so foolish as to the bodies of their children; but the characters of too many are developed under similarly unnatural shelter and protection. It is not natural for a woman grown to be an object of tender parental care. The fully fledged nestling leaves the nest and cares for itself, and soon for its young. If a young woman does not marry, and no special demand for her presence exists at home, she should be allowed, yea, encouraged to devote her life to some worthy object—not thwarted, and opposed, and restricted by petty conventionalities, perplexed by finding her Bible teach self-sacrifice, and her parents self-preservation; her Bible teach her to despise the world and earthly interest, and her parents teach her to put them in the first place!

Alas! friends, my heart aches when I think of the buried talents that exist in the shape of loving, well-educated, gifted daughters pining in Christian families for lack of an object worth living for; and then think of the miserable millions of their own sex pining elswhere, and perishing for lack, of the knowledge these could impart! Again I ask, whose is the fault? Dear fathers and mothers, does it not lie at your doors?

Train them for missionaries from their conversion onward, and it will be a wonder indeed if a large Christian family grows up without at least one missionary in it. And train those who are not fit for missionaries to support those that are. Put before them a holy object for money-making. Let the brother who stays at home labor for the brother that goes forth as a missionary; or yet, father, ere you die, render your missionary son or daughter independent, if you can. We want, the world wants, Christ wants, not a few hundred paid agents, but a whole host of voluntary missionaries — an army of volunteers to invade the realms. of heathendom. And say not, dear mother, " I cannot part with my daughter." Would you not give her up willingly if a suitable offer of marriage presented itself, even though it involved going to India or China? Will you give her to man and not give her to Christ? Say not, " We cannot expose her to a bad climate, and all the risks and hardships of mission-life." What! will you deprive your child of suffering with Christ, that she may reign with him? Will you rob her of the opportunity of learning practically to rely on God's all-sufficiency? Will you prevent her hearing the " Well done, good and faithful servant, " by and by? This were to act anything but a parent's part.

Far be it from me to say one word to grieve Christian parents who have done their best to train their children for God. Many such have nobly succeeded; and some who have failed have perhaps been more to be pitied than blamed. And far be it from me to disparage the urgent claim of home mission work. They lie before our very eyes, however, and can in a sense plead their own cause; and we have a hundred home missionaries, not to say a thousand, for every single laborer in heathen lands. And far be it from me to think lightly of the sacred demands of filial duty. But where parents have many children, can they not spare one for Christ's work? For mere worldly motives how many a worldly parent spares all! I only plead with Christian parents, that they may consider their ways in this thing. If in this year 1885, one **thousand Christian parents** of converted boys and girls now in the schoolroom resolved, before God, to devote one son or one daughter (if not more) to missionary work, to train them with a view to it, to endow them with money enough to provide them with food and raiment, and to send them forth as soon as they reach a suitable age, how glorious would be the result in ten years' time — a thousand well-educated, enthusiastic, and independent young missionaries going forth to preach Christ where he is not yet named! And in twenty years' time what fruit of their labor should gladden the heart of the great Husbandman! And in fifty years' time, when the laborers may all have gone in to the harvest home, what self-multiplying native churches in Africa, China, and Japan might be praising God for the lives and deaths of their founders! And in eternity, what multitudes might be added to the white-robed throng redeemed from the earth! and what bright crowns of rejoicing might forever grace the brows of the sons and daughters thus consecrated by their parents to missionary service!

And if one thousand fathers so acted, the result would soon be that ten thousand would follow their example — for a good example is contagious. Robert Raikes founded one Sabbath-school, and the world is full of them now. O may the day come when, universally and naturally, Christian parents shall regard it as one of their greatest privileges and most solemn duties to train one or more of their Christian children thus to serve Christ!

WOMAN'S BOARD OF MISSIONS.

RECEIPTS FROM JUNE 18 TO JULY 18, 1885.

MAINE.

Maine Branch. — Mrs. W. S. Dana, Treas. West Falmouth, Second Ch., Aux., $12.50; Andover, Aux.(add'l), 60 cts.; Bangor, Aux., of wh. $25 by Mrs. Walter Brown, const. L. M. Mrs. H. C. Goodenow, $30; Calais, Aux. (add'l), $7.32; Sacarappa, Aux., $25; Lebanon Centre, Aux., prev. contri. const. L. M. Mrs. Samuel Shapleigh, $24; Auburn, 6th St. Ch., Girls' M. C., $10; Moulton, Mrs. George B. Page, $8.20; New Castle, Aux., $12; Portland, Aux., Mrs. Edw. Baker, $2, St. Lawrence St. Ch. Missionary Gleaners, $30, $161 62
Castine. — Desert Palm Soc'y, 10 00

Total, $171 62

NEW HAMPSHIRE.

New Hampshire Branch. — Miss A.E. McIntire, Treas. Canterbury, Friends, $1.40; Charlestown, Aux., $5; Claremont, Aux., Merry Workers, $5; Hampstead, Aux., $15; Hanover, Rainbow Band, $30; Hopkinton, Aux., $12.90; Jaffrey, Aux., $11; Orford, Aux., const. L. M. Mrs. A. W. Blair, $25; Penacook, Aux., const. L. M. Mrs. A. W. Fiske, $25; Portsmouth, Roger's Circle, $33; Sanbornton, Hillside Gleaners, $18; Stratham, Aux., $20.75; Walpole, Aux., of wh. $25 const. L. M. Mrs. J. Barnett, $28, $230 05

Total, $230 05

LEGACY.

Legacy of Mr. Luther Melendy, Amherst, $2,000 00

VERMONT.

Vermont Branch. — Mrs. T. M. Howard, Treas. Granby, M.C., $1.20; Burlington, Aux., $25; Enosburgh, Aux., $18; Montgomery, Aux., $1.50;

Post Mills, Aux., $10; Sheldon, Aux., $4.40; St. Johnsbury, Y. L. M. Soc'y, const. L. M. Miss Abbie P. Brown, $25, South Ch.,Little Helpers, $3, Maids of Caledonia, $45, North Ch., Aux., $20.76; St. Johnsbury Centre (add'l), $1; Swanton, Aux., $10.63; West Brattleboro, Aux., $16; Westford, Cong. Ch., Aux., $9; Williston, Aux., $9; Windsor, Aux., const. L. M's Miss E. E. Damon, Miss Mary Smith, $50, $249 49

Total, $249 49

MASSACHUSETTS.

Andover and Woburn Branch. — Miss E. F. Wilder, Treas. Lawrence, Trinity Ch.,Happy Pilgrims, $14; Stoneham, Ladies of Cong. Ch., $6.25; Wakefield, Aux., $10; Woburn, Aux., of wh. $25 by Mrs. John Cummings, const. L. M. Miss Mary E. Alexander, $50, $80 25
Berkshire Branch.—Mrs. S. N. Russell, Treas. Adams, Parousia Circle, $50; Hinsdale, Aux., $18.84, M. C., $10; Mill River, Aux., $13; New Lebanon, Aux., $19.20; Pittsfield, First Ch., Aux., $20.85; Miss Salisbury's Scholars, $5.10, Coll. Annual Meeting, $46.34; South Egremont, Aux., $15; Stockbridge, Aux., $39; Williamstown, White Oaks Aux., $10,   247 33
Conway. — Mrs. Samuel Howland,   4 00
Clinton.—Aux.,   13 63
Essex North Branch. — Mrs. A. Hammond, Treas. Newburyport, Aux.,   23 00
Essex South Co. Branch.—Miss S. W. Clark, Treas. Peabody, Aux., $64; Beverly, Dane St. Ch., Ivy Leaves, $100; Gloucester, Cong. Ch. Children's M. C., $5; Danvers, Maple St. Ch., Aux., $40, M. C., $25; Salem, Crombie St. Ch., Aux., $63, Tabernacle Ch., Aux., of wh. $40 from Dr. Choate's class, $190, Y. L. M. C., $30; Lynn, First Ch., Young Ladies' Aux., $10, Central Ch. M. C., const. L. M. Miss L. Hortense Colby, $25; Middleton, Aux., $4,   556 00
Hampshire Co. Branch.—Miss I. G. Clarke, Treas. South Hadley Falls, Cong. Ch. and Parish, $16.50; Chesterfield, Aux., $10; Northampton,

Smith College Miss'y Soc'y, $33, $43 00
Lawrence.— Lawrence St. Ch. S. S. Mite Boxes,   10 00
Middlesex Branch.—Mrs. E. H. Warren, Treas. South Natick, John Eliot Ch., Cheerful Workers, $15; Framingham, Plymouth Ch., Aux., $160,   175 00
Old Colony Branch. — Miss F. J. Runnels, Treas. So. Attleboro, Cong. S. S., $12; Norton, Wheaton Seminary, $25,   37 00
Springfield Branch.—Miss H. T. Buckingham, Treas. Chicopee Falls, Aux., $31; Springfield, Hope Ch.,Hopeful Ones, $37.14, Memorial Ch., Aux., $27.50; West Springfield, Aux., Park Ch., of wh. $25 by Mrs. Lucy Ann Bagg, const. L. M. Mrs. E. H. Knight, $45.25, Helping Hands, $20,   160 89
Suffolk Branch. — Miss M. B. Child, Treas. Boston, Mrs. M. H. Baldwin, $5, Shawmut Ch. Y. L. M. C., $215; So. Boston, Phillips Ch., Aux., $140, S. S., $100; Roxbury, Walnut Ave. S. S., Boys' Mission Club, $19.28, Eliot Ch., Aux., $10, Anderson Circle, $6,Olive Branch, $10; Thompson Circle, 50 cts., Ferguson Circle, $1.50, Mayflowers, $4, Eliot Star, $4, Immanuel Ch., Aux., $31.70; Dorchester, Pilgrim Ch., Aux., $20.04, Second Ch., Aux., $344.93; Chelsea, First Ch., Aux., $103.07; Cambridgeport, Pilgrim Ch., Young Ladies Aux., $22; Brookline, C., Aux., $10, Ethel's Pennies, $1; Watertown, Phillips Ch., Aux., const. L. M. Mrs. Geo. K. Snow, $25; Newton, Aux., $330; West Newton, Mrs. Sarah B. Putnam, $10; Auburndale, Aux., $40; Dedham, Asylum Dime Soc'y, $3.15,   1,456 17
South Hadley. — Mt. Holyoke Seminary,   265 00
Worcester Co. Branch.—Mrs. G. W. Russell, Treas. Milford, Aux., $31; Ashburnham, Aux., $15.50; Wane, Aux., $7.75; Worcester, Union Ch., Aux., with prev. contri. const. L. M's Mrs. Roselle B. Curtis, Miss Abby W. Coes, $68.26, Willing Workers, $31,   153 51
Wakefield. — Rev. John W. Chickering, D.D., in memory of his deceased wife,   50 00

Total, $3,274 78

RHODE ISLAND

Rhode Island Branch. — Miss
A. T. White, Treas. New-
port, Aux., $8 80

Total, $8 80

CONNECTICUT.

Eastern Conn. Branch. — Miss
M. I. Lockwood, Treas.
Preston, Aux., $2; Norwich,
Park Ch., M. C., $20, First Ch.,
Aux., $60.85; Old Town, M.
C., $20, Broadway Ch., $105;
Woodstock, Aux., prev.
contri. const. L. M's Miss
Florence A. Child, Miss El-
len D. Chandler, $40, M. C.,
prev. contri. const. L. M.
Miss Flora Chase, $16; Wind-
ham, Aux., $19; Central Vil-
lage, $2; Griswold, Aux.,
$50.50, Pachaug, Acorns'
$14.38; Stonington, Second
Ch., Aux., $14 88; Lisbon,
Aux., $10. M. C., $14.34:
Wauregan, Aux., prev.
contri. const. L. M. Mrs. Alice
Wilson, $20, $408 95
Hartford Branch — Miss Anna
Morris, Treas. Buckingham,
Aux,. prev. contri. const. L.
M. Mrs. Harriet J. Blish, $10;
Hartford, Asylum Hill M. B.,
$12.60; East Hartford, Aux.,
$75; Plainville, Treasure
Seekers, $30; Poquonock,
Willing Workers, $22; Rock-
ville, Aux., $20; Southington,
Aux., $33; Windsor Locks,
Aux., const. L. M's Mrs. Wil-
liam Mather, Mrs. J. H. Coats,
$50; Wethersfield, Westward
M. C., $32.35,   284 95
Ivorytown. — Miss M. E. Nor-
ris,   5 00
New Haven.—College St. Cong.
S. S.,   20 00
Windsor Locks.—A Friend,   5 00
                            ————
                            $723 90

LEGACY.

Legacy of Mrs. Mary Ann Miller, New Haven, $2,000 00

NEW YORK.

New York State Branch.—Mrs.
G. H. Norton, Treas. Brook-
lyn, East Ch., Aux., $30, A.
L. M., $10; Sangerties, Sun-
beam M. B., $18; Madison,
Aux., $30; Massena, Aux.,
$7.50; Madrid, $1.75; New
York, Home Circle Aux.,
$31.34, Tabernacle Ch., Cheer-
ful Workers, $337; Albany,
Aux., of wh. $75 const. L. M's
Mrs. Oscar D. Robinson, Miss
Anna MacNaughton, Mrs.

Cyrus W. Pollars, $140.68,
Jessie Lyon Memorial, $12;
Junior Dept. S. S., $9, Lot-
tie Fletcher Memorial, $40,
Morning Star M. C., $16;
West Bloomfield, Aux., const.
L. M. Mrs. William A. Ayres,
$25, Ganundaak M. C., $20;
Gloversville, Little Coral
Workers, $30; Moravia, Aux.,
$10; Binghamton, Aux.,
$18.28, $786 55
Chateaugay.—Mrs. George
Whitehead,   5 00
Mt. Morris.—Mrs. A. Spinning, 1 00
                            ————
Total, $792 55

PENNSYLVANIA.

Phillipsburg.—Miss Jessie
Scott, $5 00
Guy's Mills. — Mrs. F. Maria
Guy,   1 00
                            ————
Total, $6 00

PHILADELPHIA BRANCH.

Mrs. S. Wilde, Treas. D. C.:
Washington, Y. L. M. S., First
Cong. Ch., $59.03; PENN.:
Philadelphia Central Cong.
Ch., Aux., $113.15, Y. L. Soc'y,
$30, Snowflakes, $15; MARY-
LAND: Baltimore, Aux.,
$16.05; NEW JERSEY: Bound
Brook, Aux., $20; East Orange,
Proctor M. C., $50; Westfield,
Cong. S. S., $21.12, Miss Wood,
$20, $344 35
                            ————
Total, $344 35

OHIO.

Rock Creek.—Mrs. H. W. Howard, $2 00
                            ————
Total, $2 00

DAKOTA.

Centreville.— A Friend, $ 40
Oakfield.—Miss Mary A. Susan, 7 40
                            ————
Total, $7 80

TURKEY.

Harpoot.—Woman's Board, $8 80
Koordistan—Mt. Holyoke Sem-
inary, Little Drops of Mercy, 4 40
                            ————
Total, $13 20

General Funds, $5,798 14
Leaflets,   15 84
Morning Star,   6 60
Legacies,   4,000 00
                            ————
Total, $9,820 58

MISS EMMA CARRUTH, Treasurer.

Board of the Interior.

MEXICO.

OUR SCHOOL AT GUADALAJARA—PERSECUTION.

BY MISS BELLE M. HASKINS.

Miss Haskins writes, under date of June 10th:—

WE have just had the rare privilege of entertaining our friends, Mr. and Mrs. Bissell and family, who came up from Tlajamulco to prepare to move to La Barca, a place of five or six thousand people, distant about one hundred miles. It was unusually pleasant when we were all here together; and after they went to Tlajamulco there was such frequent passing back and forth that they did not seem very far away. But now they will be quite isolated, though we hope there is to be a good work commenced at La Barca. Connected with their going to La Barca, there has been a sad case of bitter persecution. I think that in my letter written from Tlajamulco, last summer, I mentioned Feliz, who was so anxious to come to school, and whose mother treated her so unkindly because she would be friendly with Protestants. When I came back to Guadalajara she was only too glad to come with me. Her mother at first consented, thinking that Feliz was to receive wages; but as soon as she understood that she was to go to school, she was very angry, and said that Feliz should go to some distant pueblo first. It was finally arranged by Mrs. Bissell offering to take Feliz for nurse-girl. Then, when school opened, Mrs. Bissell sent her to school. When the Bissells moved to Tlajamulco, the parents expected that Feliz would go with them. She, however, had no thought of leaving school. They repeatedly sent word for her to go home, and during the five months she was with me the father came for her several times. But as she was twenty-two years old, we thought she had a right to decide for herself. When she finally went to help Mrs. Bissell, in Tlajamulco, they treated her more kindly. As soon, however, as it was known that Mr. Bissell was going to La Barca, they came after her, took her home, and after taking away all of her respectable clothing, shut her up in a filthy corral. The next morning they carried her to the *cura*, that he might reprove her. The two succeeding weeks they kept her tied, trying each day, by beating, to force her to abandon her belief, and thinking to frighten her by taking her frequently to the *cura*, and by forcing her to kneel before the images, and sprinkling her with holy water. Mr. Bissell tried to get the authorities to interfere; but they, of course, had no desire, their sympathies being with the parents, and, to

(345)

our surprise and indignation, the law giving complete control over an unmarried daughter to the parents until the age of thirty years.

Finally, however, after we had consulted the penal code and the authorities here in the city, one of the judges in Tlajamulco was persuaded to do his duty by reading to the parents the clauses which prohibit any person from persecuting another because of different religious views. Since then she has been better treated, and allowed to go to church and read her Bible. It has been such a joy and comfort to know that through it all Feliz has shown a really Christlike spirit, and has been given special strength and wisdom. We feel sure not only that she has gained in beauty and strength of character by this severe trial, but also that her steadfastness will honor the cause of the Master not a little. In the end we greatly hope it will be the means of bringing her parents and relatives to a true knowledge of the way of life.

Our present number in school is nineteen, and I am happy to tell you that three of these belong to my family of girls, two of them coming from Catholic families. These two do not, however, stay over night, but come at eight in the morning and leave at six in the evening. I hardly expected that they would be permitted to come to the house on Sunday, but, to my surprise and joy, they come to church and Sunday-school, and remain in the afternoon to study their Bible verses.

A few words from a letter of June 24th, from Mrs. Crawford, will give a little peep into the house of which Miss Haskins and her girls are an important part, and show how the missionary mothers are doing their part. She mentions the absence of her husband on a tour among the villages, and says:

Mabel and I are alone, but not lonely, for the Howlands live in the other side of the house. Miss Haskins's boarding-girls are here, and natives are coming and going all the time. Our Mabel and Bertha Howland are well,— only three days' difference in their ages,— and a great joy and comfort to us. Mrs. Howland and I visit among the women, and sometimes take the babies with us. Through them we find the way to the hearts of mothers who would otherwise scorn to speak to us. We go once a week to a *mezon*, or inn, where a number of families live. A dozen or so gather about us, to hear us read the Bible and talk to them. Poor things! not one can read, and till now few ever saw a Bible. Their husbands at first were quite opposed to their hearing us, but on the last two visits three of their husbands have come to listen, and to ask us to " come again."

We are always kindly received by all in their own homes, though they are afraid to come here to our house.

TURKEY.

A LETTER FROM MISS WRIGHT.

Monday morning, June 8th. — We (Mr. and Mrs. Smith, Henry Smith, and I) started out of Tocat about half-past six in the morning, *en route* for Marsovan. About three hours out of the city we were overtaken by four mounted Circassians (robbers), who took our money, watches, and everything of any value from our trunks and satchels, my horse, two horses from our drivers, and rode off, leaving us thankful that we were unharmed.

When they came up I was lying, with eyes closed, in the second wagon. I heard a sound of horses galloping by, a yell, felt the wagon stop, and looked up to see a man on each side of the front wagon, and one at the left of ours, all pointing revolvers toward us, and all perfectly silent, as were our party, also. The work was systematically done. Three dismounted, and gave their horses to the fourth, who kept watch of the road, and held their horses. At a signal, Mr. S. gave them his purse, then dismounted, and one took his watch, overcoat, and was taking coat, too, but Mr. S. said, "This is necessary to me," and he left it. After feeling about his pockets a little more, they let him go. Another opened Henry's coat, but dismissed him without much searching.

One signaled Mrs. S. to dismount, opened her dress, and took from the waist about forty-five dollars in money, and a gold watch that had been her mother's.

A dark, slender man, with cap of black lamb's wool, cloak of goat's hair, rows of cartridges across his breast, and pistol, revolver, and two-edged knife, or sword, about two feet long, came to our wagon and punched me two or three times with his sword. As he made no other motion I sat still. He quickly cut open the straps of my shawl-bag lying by, and took from it match-box, taper, knife, and such little things, then signed me to dismount. Perhaps I provoked him by my indifference, for I did not feel afraid, having always heard that Turkish robbers do not harm women. I said (as well as I could in Turkish), "I have a watch, but no money;" but he searched me very thoroughly, peering under my hat twice as I stood there by the wagon, with head turned away, unwilling to look at the ruffian, trying not to struggle. At last he motioned me to get into the wagon, and himself followed. Another man came up and began hauling out trunks and satchels, and I think called him. I called to our servant to bring my satchel, and tell them it had a little money in it. He gave the message, but showed me that his hands were tied behind him. My searcher motioned me to get the money, and I jumped from the wagon, glad to be farther from him, for by this time I was frightened, and handed him all the money I had, about four dollars. The man on horseback at once asked how much it was. They trust each other so little, that three separate men sent to Mr. S. to ask the amount taken from our whole party. Including clothing — all the wedding suits, for Mr. and Mrs. S. were on their wedding tour — it was about six hundred and forty dollars.

The worst was now over. I sat down on the ground beside Mrs. S. and Henry (he is about twelve years old), and thought, "Now I can pray." I quoted the text, "Call upon me in the day of trouble, and I will deliver thee;" and Henry said, "I have been doing it all the time." Perhaps his prayers saved him from being taken and held for ransom, as a little Turkish boy was last week, on another part of this road.

Now they overhauled trunks and satchels, cut open my beautiful leather trunk, as the key had been dropped from my shawl-bag, tumbled silk dresses, without folding, into great bags brought with them, sniffed at bottles of medicine, looked doubtfully at new shoes, but finally appropriated them, ripped open a writing-desk, and speculated over photographs of European scenes, in a way that was almost amusing. They took all our dresses but one each, and all our underclothing; but hose, gloves, laces, pictures, and ribbons were above their comprehension, except a black lace scarf.

Mrs. S. sat watching the havoc, saying, "Hope they won't take that silk scarf Mr. —— gave me. How it shines in the sun!" (They did take it.) And, again, "I am afraid I have thought too much of pretty things." One robber would open a silk work-bag and take out scissors and thimble; another would pick up and stow away the discarded bag; and so we watched the diversity of tastes.

But at last, after perhaps an hour, it was all over; the robbers rode slowly off with their three stolen horses, three watches, and all our valuables; and while they were still near we joined heartily in Mr. Smith's prayer (unconsciously offered in Armenian), while Henry, who had been perfectly quiet through the robbery, sobbed aloud. He thanked the Lord for our spared lives, and prayed that we might be better missionaries for this experience, asked a blessing on the robbers and all their race, prayed that they might be brought to justice, and, above all, that the Lord's will might be done.

THE MONASTIR BOARDING-SCHOOL.

In the Monastir school where there have been many changes of teachers, one native teacher holds on bravely, year after year, and has recently written the following account of her work to a society in Detroit who give largely for the support of the school. We give the letter as written by her in English, retaining her spelling. Our readers will excuse the few mistakes, and be glad to see how good an English scholar she is: —

MONASTIR, April 7, 1885.

DEAR FRIENDS, — It is very long since I have writen you about our school and the work among the women in this country. It is more than one year, and of course there are very many changes in our school. I am very sorry to tell you that one of our bourding-girls has fallen into temptation, and has gone very far from the Lord. She left the school and went back to stay with her mother, who is not a good woman. Three of the girls last year left our school and went to another Bulgarian school, because their parents and relatives did not want them to stay in our Protestant school. This year we have suffered very much without teachers. Last year, in July, one of our American teachers left here and went to America. In October, Miss E. L. Spooner became very weak, and went to Bulgaria; now she is going to America. Then another American teacher, Miss H. L. Cole, from Samokov School, came here to help in our school, but she does not know the Bulgarian language yet. Miss Cole and I have to take care for the day-scholars and bourders, and the all work of the school.

Beside this, I am glad to tell you that God has been with us this year, and has blessed us, and helped us in our duties. This year we have three new girls from Veles, Radovich, and Resen. The bourders are thirteen now, and three of them are little lovely girls about ten years old. Two of the older girls last summer became Christians, and two others are very near the kingdom.

Mrs. Baird has helped us in sewing, and Mrs. Bond, with her knowledge of medicine, is a great help to us. We have a great deal of anxiety for our pupils, that they may be rooted and grounded in the faith before they shall leave here. We have no Bible-woman to work among the women here. I am very busy in the school. Miss Cole does not know the language. Mrs. Baird has to take care of her four little children only Mrs. Bond sometimes has to leave her work and go to see some of the women; and I am glad to tell you that some of them are interested in the truth. Some of the women in my Bible class are very much interested to understand everything in the lesson. The work in Strumitza has been prospering under the earnest labors of Mr. Anastasoff. Two years ago I visited this place and found the brethren very faithful, but the ladies were to opposed their husbands because they did not want them to be Protestants. Only one of them disirde me to teach her to read. I tauaht her, and soon she began to read the Bible, and now she is a member of the church. There was another woman who listened attentively when I read the Bible, but she was a bad woman. Now, Mr. Anastasoff writes us that she is going to be a Christian, and the Protestant wives have changed their minds about their husbands. I am in good health.

Yours in love,

MARIKA B. RAICHEVA.

JAPAN.

AN INSTALLATION IN KOBE.

BY MISS KATIE SCUDDER.

It is a great pleasure to secure even a few words from our dear Plymouth Church missionary, who with her brother, Dr. Doremus Scudder, has been studying at Kobe for a few months, preparatory to going to their mission-field at Niigata: —

KOBE, May 5th.

YESTERDAY morning Doremus started for Niigata by the land route. He hoped to reach Tsuruga that evening, and Niigata before Sunday. He had made arrangements to go last week, but was induced to wait over and see the native pastors, who were coming here to attend the annual meeting of their Home Missionary Society. I was very glad he waited, as I think it wise to strengthen every bond between the missionaries and the native pastors. It gave us unalloyed pleasure to meet Mr. Ise, Mr. Furva, and Mr. Kozaki, whom we had not seen before, besides Kanamori and others whom we had already met. Mr. Harada was installed as pastor of the Kobe Church yesterday. It was a most solemn and impressive service, and many were deeply moved. Dr. Gordon assisted in the ordination, he and his native pastors gathering around Mr. Harada as he knelt. Mr. Ise delivered the charge to the pastor and Mr. Kanamori to the people. There was breathless interest among the people, and I enjoyed watching their faces. There were seventeen to be received to the church, and these came forward. Then mothers brought their children to be baptized, and formed a semicircle within the row of candidates. It was a memorable sight, and made me think that this was a fulfillment in part of that verse which speaks of those who are to be gathered out of every tribe and kingdom on the face of the earth. It carried me back to the native churches in India, too.

AFRICA.

THE UMZUMBI HOME.

We are permitted to copy a few words from a private letter telling of various improvements lately made in the Home. Miss Welch writes, March 5th: —

MISS GILSON and I get along very nicely together. She is a splendid teacher and manager, and I am sure if she is to stay on here I can very well be spared to go away for a year, at least, and give my eyes the rest they demand so constantly. I have not been in the school forenoons at all this term. Miss Gilson and Martha (a native teacher) take it half the day, and Martha and I the other half.

Mrs. Bridgman and the temperance people here got up a

meeting a few days ago; subject, " Temperance and Anti-native Customs." It passed off very nicely indeed, and our visitors (Mr. Ireland, Mr. Rood, and the Wilders) seemed both surprised and pleased with the stand the people here have taken, and their evident progress.

Mr. Rood was greatly pleased with our school, too. He remarked many times on the quietness of the girls, generally, at table and elsewhere — their respectfulness and absence of silliness in speaking in public. He said it far exceeded anything he had seen. In Mr. Wilder's opinion it is a model school. He recommended that the buildings be so enlarged as to accommodate fifty or fifty-five pupils, and that there be one or two more like it started in the mission, so as to accommodate the three or four hundred girls from the stations and out-stations ready to be taught, and needing the influence of such a home. The Bridgmans are expecting to leave for America about the middle of April. How we shall miss them! And yet, I hope nothing will happen to prevent their going.

20th, 9 A. M. Have just killed a snake over the spare-room door, and feel much inclined to go to work with axe and knife, and remove all the vines and plants so close up to the house. We've killed eight in one week just about the building here; and, judging from the continuous crying of the birds on the trees in the yard, we might kill as many more in a day, if we had only the time and patience to look for them. . . . While I was away, in the Holidays, Mr. Bridgman had Mr. Goldstone come and take down the dining-room ceiling and raise it higher, and put up new cloth; then had the dining-room papered with very light-colored paper, so it looked very fresh and nice when I arrived. He also had some air-holes made through the walls at the top. It seems much more comfortable and airy than before. We have twenty-nine girls this term with Yona. Yona Martha and Kut have an hour's instruction each day from Miss Gilson outside of school-hours, so they have little spare time.

I think in my last, I mentioned to you that two of our men had applied to the magistrate for exemption from native laws. It has been granted them, and they are now happy in the possession of certificates to that effect. They are so pleased that it will be impossible for their sons, or brothers, or any one to sell their daughters, even in all the generations to come, and that they are freed from the operation of native law, and amenable to the laws of the colony only! They are trying, also, to influence the rest of the church-members to follow their example, and I think they will before long.

Umzumbi Christians have a name that has sounded far and wide as lovers of temperance, and as having fenced themselves in with close rules of right. Some laugh at them, and some begin to envy them, for they find them a happy, industrious set, "clothed and in their right minds."

A CHINESE GIRL'S SPEECH.

MISS HU KING ENG, a young Chinese girl, made a rather unique speech at a recent meeting of the Ladies' Foreign Mission Society, in Cincinnati. Here is an almost verbatim report of it: —

"LADIES — I came to America last May. Don't learn much English, and hope excuse breaking their language. Last September came to Delaware (Ohio) School (Wesleyan University), and learn a few words. In America are many girls and boys going to school, very much studying books, but in my China I can't find one school for girls. Plenty schools for boys, so that boys may learn many things. Their mothers think boys study books hope some day make officers. Girls, their mothers think, study no use. In my China so many girls not like here. Here girls can go down street and buy many pretty things by themselves, but in my China always stay at home. Mothers teach their children to pray idols; here, in America, boys and girls pray one God. In my China are many idols, some very tall, some very little, some very not pretty; some made of silver, gold, stone, but many kinds. They think idols can help them, so pray to idols all time. If I want this, I pray this one; if I want that, I pray that one. This one (exhibiting a small image) is called a god of mercy, in my China. Mothers teach their children to pray to this idol until sixteen years old; then pray to others.

"In my China they don't know they have no spirit in this idol. I taught little school for little girls in my China, and talked to them about Jesus. After awhile I wanted to study medicine, so I came to Delaware College. I know God will help me. I can do without God nothing. I hope you all pray for me, so I may learn right fast, and then I go back to my China, to my dark land." — *Selected.*

STUDIES IN MISSIONARY HISTORY.
1885.

THE ARMENIAN MISSION, NO. 3 — 1860–1885.

Death of Mrs. Dwight: Dr. Dwight's tour; his death.
French Papal Influence: Mob at a burial.
Reaction among the Mohammedans, 1864: Mustapha and Ali banished, 1874.
Armenian Reform Movement, 1867.
Increase of Newspapers.
Scripture Translations: Death of Panayotes Constantinides; Circulation of the Turkish Scriptures in the Arabic character prohibited in 1874.

Work for Women: Girls' Seminary removed to Marsovan; Boarding-Schools at Cesarea; Manisa; Talas; Sivas; Bardesag; Broosa.

Work of Bible-Women: Miss West's work at Smyrna.

Famine: 1873–74.

War with Russia: Treaty of Berlin.

Missionaries: Dr. Goodell's last years and death; Mr. Parsons killed.

Station-Work in the Western Turkey Mission: Progress in Rhodosto; School; Death of " Prince of Colporters " at Baghchejuk, 1860; Interesting ordinations.

Revivals: Nicomedia, 1872; Sivas, 1873.

Education: Bebek Seminary removed; Seminary at Marsovan; Growth of common-schools.

Robert College.

The Constantinople Home.

Progress of Fifty Years.

Abundant material for the study of this lesson may be found in recent reports of the American Board, in the files of the *Missionary Herald,* and of *Life and Light* which are accessible to all. The Reports of the Woman's Boards will also be found rich in facts concerning schools and woman's work. See also Miss West's " Romance of Missions."

A MEETING FOR THANK-OFFERINGS.

A MEETING for thank-offerings will be held at the rooms of the Woman's Board of Missions of the Interior, 75 Madison Street, Chicago, Friday morning, August 21st. It is hoped that every auxiliary will hold a similar meeting before the third week in September, that all thank-offerings may reach the several Branch treasurers by the first of October, and be included in our report of this year's receipts.

DEAR AUXILIARIES:—Let us have a little plain talk about these thank-offerings. Times are hard, but that need not discourage anybody. If your offerings must be small, let them express your thanksgiving that you are not hungry or homeless in this season of pressure. And if "retrenchment" is already the fashion in your home, pinch a little more, that that dreaded word may not be heard in the borders of the missionaries. Take a lesson from the old Jews, who never omitted their "feast of ingathering" because of drought or scanty harvests. And remember, that when the remnant returned from captivity, this was one of the first ceremonials revived by Nehemiah.

Perhaps you ask, " Why is it that every year the pledges made in the outset have to be increased by special gifts?" Ah, my friend, the pledges are not large enough. We have adopted a system of tithing never heard of among the Jews. We tithe the church-members. Only a tenth of them, we are told, give regularly to the support of foreign missions. And then so many new doors are opening before us. O give thanks that "doors are opening on every side to immediate productive work; that the fields are ripening into a harvest beyond the power of the reapers to overtake it." Those pleading islanders of whom Miss Cathcart tells us in the August *Life and Light,* must not be left without a missionary because our pledges, made at the beginning of the year, are not sufficient to send one.

But some one asks, "What have our former offerings done? Have we made even a breach in the walls of heathenism?" Pretty large breaches have been made in Japan, if we may judge by that great "Fellowship Meeting" of nearly five hundred Japanese Christians held lately in Kioto. Give thanks for that, and for the promise that the "heathen shall be given to the Son for his inheritance." And give thanks that you may help to bring them in, and that some of their own number who have only recently had a new song put into their mouths, are also coming forward to help. Read the letters to our young ladies from Miss Shattuck's girls in Marash, printed in the June Mission Studies. A glance at the late numbers of the *Missionary Herald* and *Life and Light* will give abundant reason for thanksgiving. Pupils are crowding into schools where formerly only the promise of money or clothes could win their attendance. Missionaries are asked for where they once waited long for a welcome. As Dr. Humphrey says: "Some of the newer fields threaten to precipitate upon us an avalanche of success, which will make a demand for laborers and the means to sustain them beyond, it may be, anything in the history of the past." More new laborers are asked for than can possibly be sent. Twenty are needed at once in Japan alone; as many more could be employed in China. Everywhere the harvests are ripening faster than they can be gathered. "Pray ye therefore the Lord of the harvest, that he will send forth laborers into his harvest." And everywhere "let your requests be made known unto God with thanksgiving."

————————

At the meeting of the Executive Committee of the Woman's Board of Missions of the Interior held July 31st, it was unanimously voted that the auxiliaries be asked to give their thank-offerings as a special gift to the American Board at its approaching anniversary. Of this anniversary Dr. Humphrey writes : "Next October, at Boston, the American Board will celebrate its Diamond Wedding. Three quarters of a century ago, the Congregational body, the first in the sisterhood of the denominations, wedded itself to the cause of foreign missions." When we celebrate such events in our families, every one, down to the youngest child, brings some offering of love. And will not every auxiliary, older or younger, help to signalize this occasion by sending its thank-offering to our venerable Father of Missionary Boards.

————————

NOTICE.

The Annual Meeting of the Woman's Board of Missions of the Interior will be held in the First Congregational Church in St. Louis, on Wednesday and Thursday, Nov. 4th and 5th. Every auxiliary from Ohio to the Rocky Mountains is invited to send one or more delegates. See Article VIII. of the Constitution. . . And it is especially requested that, if possible, the President, Secretary, and Treasurer of every State Branch will be present.

The ladies of St. Louis hope for large delegations from the several States, and extend a general invitation to all who are interested. Railroad notices will be given in Mission Studies and *The Advance.*

RECEIPTS OF THE WOMAN'S BOARD OF MISSIONS OF THE INTERIOR.

Mrs. J. B. LEAKE, Treasurer.

From June 18, 1885, to July 18, 1885.

ILLINOIS.

ILLINOIS BRANCH.—Mrs. W. A. Talcott, of Rockford, Treas. *Ashkum,* 3 65; *Alton,* Ch. of the Redeemer, 6.75; *Buda,* 5; *Chicago,* M. Star certif., 30, First Ch., of wh. 50 const. L. M's Mrs. Calista Bigelow and Mrs. M. B. Norton, Plymouth Ch., 200, South Ch., to const. L. M's Mrs. Harriet N. Brooks and Mrs. Harriet P. Johnston, 50, Leavitt St. Ch., 10, Western Ave. Ch., 22; *Clifton,* 4.05; *Galesburg,* 1st Ch. of Christ, 37.50; *Garden Prairie,* 7.40; *Genoa Junction,* Wis., 6.49; *Granville,* 10; *Jacksonville,* 26.25; *Joy Prairie,* 10; *La Harpe,* 6.13; *La Grange,* 10; *Lee Center,* 12 95; *Moline,* 20; *Onarga,* 2d Ch., 3.35; *Payson,* 24; *Rockford,* 2d Ch., 81; *Roscoe,* 12.54; *Shabbona,* 18.51; *Sycamore,* 10; *Wauponsie Grove,* 15; *Wilmette,* 10 15, **$821 02**

JUNIORS: *Chicago,* 1st Ch., Y. W. M. Soc., 69.80, Plymouth Ch., Y.P. Soc., 13.50, South Ch , Y. L. Soc., 25, New Eng. Ch., Y. L. Soc., Miss Grant's Sem., 30; *Lake View,* Y. L. Soc., to const. L. M. Miss Florence Jewett, 25; *Sandwich,* "King's Daughters," 35, **198 30**

JUVENILE: *Ashkum,* Buds of Promise, 1.15; *Champaign,* "Coral Workers," 25; *Chebanse,* "Tiny Dewdrops," 1; *Chicago,* Western Ave. Ch., Star Soc., 17; *Farmington,* Mission Band, 1.60; *Geneva,* M. Star Band, 4; *Hinsdale,* "Earnest Workers," to const L. M. Miss Lieca Kennedy, 25; *Millburn,* Woodbine Band, 10; *Olney,* 2 Certif's Children's Mission, 50 cts.; *Stillman Valley,* Sunbeam Band, 3, **88 25**

Total, **$1,107 57**

IOWA.

IOWA BRANCH. — Mrs. E. R. Potter, of Grinnell, Treas. *Corning,* 5 25; *Corydon,* Mrs. C. E. R., 5; *Burlington,* 10; *Des Moines,* 16; *Farragut,* 15; *Grinnell,* 28 84; *Iowa City,* 12; *Midland,* 5; *Manson,* 10.33; *Stacyville,* 10, **$117 42**

JUNIOR: *Des Moines,* Plymouth Rock M. Soc., 12.55; *Storm Lake,* Y.L.M. Soc., 15, **$27 55**

JUVENILE: *Creston,* Pansy Band, 2.30; *Corydon,* Prairie Gleaners, 10, "six children," 60 cts.; *Des Moines,* S. S., 15.95; *Mt. Pleasant,* S. S., 60 cts., *Grinnell,* Busy Bees, 6.84, Miss Chafee's Cl., 60 cts., **36 92**

Total, **$181 89**

KANSAS.

KANSAS BRANCH.—Mrs. A. L. Slosson, of Leavenworth, Treas. *Lawrence,* 14.47; *Maple Hill,* 16.50; *White City,* 6.55. Less expressage, 35 cts., **$37 17**

JUNIOR, *Maple Hill,* Willing Workers, **3 75**

Branch total, **$40 92**

Junction City, Pres. S. S., per Miss Chapin, **70 00**

Total, **$110 92**

MICHIGAN.

MICHIGAN BRANCH. — Mrs. Charles E. Fox, of Detroit, Treas. *Detroit,* First Ch., 104.50, Woodward Ave. Ch., 80; *East Saginaw,* 136; *Edmore,* 2.60; *Jackson,* 150, of wh. 25 to const. Mrs. M. M. Wells L. M.; *Lansing,* Plymouth Ch., 50; *Memphis,* 5; *Morenci,* 7.35; *Port Huron,* 20; *St Joseph,* 17, **$572 45**

JUNIORS: *Detroit,* First Ch., Y. L. Circle, 94; *East Saginaw,* 25; *Eaton Rapids,* King's Young Daughters, 6.25; *Manistee,* Y. L. M. Circle, 12.50, **137 75**

JUVENILES: *Detroit,* Woodward Ave. Ch., King's Cup-Bearers, 37.25; *Flint,* Buds of Promise, 16; *South Haven,* Mission Bank of S. S., 5.72; *Stanton,* Hibbard Mission Band, 10, **68 97**

FOR MORNING STAR MISSION:— *Greenville,* Cheerful Toilers, 8.50, Morning Stars, 8.50, **17 00**

Branch total, **$796 17**

Detroit, Rev. and Mrs. Jeremiah Porter, thank-offering, **100 00**

Total, **$896 17**

MISSOURI.

MISSOURI BRANCH.—Mrs. J. H. Drew, 3101 Washington Ave., St. Louis, Treas. *Kansas City,* 55; *Meadville,* 11.93; *St. Louis,* Pilgrim Ch., 10, Fifth Ch., 8.76; *Springfield,* 10; *Windsor* 5, $100 69
JUNIOR: *St. Louis,* Pilgrim Ch., Y. L. Soc., 62.50; Hyde Park, Gleaners, 20.75,   83 25

Total, $183 94

MINNESOTA.

MINNESOTA BRANCH.—Mrs. E. M. Williams, of Northfield, Treas. *Austin,* 11.80; *Cannon Falls,* 16.18; *Glyndon,* 10.50; *Minneapolis,* First Ch., Aux., 34.50, Mrs. Swett. 5 50, Plymouth Ch., 128.05; *Northfield,* 81.10; *St. Paul,* Park Ch., 30, "D," 30; *Wabasha,* 13; *Stillwater,* 3; *Zumbrote,* 10 61, $374 24
JUNIORS: *Minneapolis,* Plymouth Ch., Y. L. Soc, 31.25; *Northfield,* Carleton College, Aux., 24.45,   55 70
JUVENILES: *Northfield,* Willing Workers,   11 35
SABBATH-SCHOOLS: *Fairmont,* 4.25; *Northfield,* 40; *Stillwater,* 1,   45 25

Total, $486 54

NEBRASKA.

WOMAN'S MISS. ASSO.—Mrs. Geo. W. Hall, of Omaha, Treas. *Exeter,* 25; *Fairfield,* 12; *Omaha,* 5; *South Bend,* 1, $43 00
JUNIOR: *Omaha,*   25 00
JUVENILE: *Exeter,* Children's Band, 2.50; *Omaha,* Steady Streams, 3.60, Mountain Rills, 4.25,   10 35

    $78 35
Less expenses,   7 85

Total, $70 50

OHIO.

OHIO BRANCH.—Mrs. Geo. H. Ely, of Elvria, Treas. *Atwater,* 18; *Cleveland Heights,* 25; *Hudson,* 18.90; *Lodi,* 5; *Lyme,* 10.26; *Meadville,* Park Ave. Ch., 26; *Sanduskg,* 34.50; *Springfield,* 21.50, $159 15
JUNIOR: *Oberlin,* Y. L. Soc.,   60 00
JUVENILE: *Elyria,* Little Helpers,   7 76

Total, $226 91

ROCKY MOUNTAIN BRANCH.

Mrs. Hiram R. Jones, of So. Pueblo, Col., Treas. *Denver,* First Ch., S. S., $50 00

Total, $50 00

SOUTH DAKOTA BRANCH.

Mrs. H. H. Smith, of Yankton, Treas. *Deadwood,* 15.30; *Huron,* 2; *Sioux Falls,* 25, $42 30
JUNIOR: *Yankton,* 1st Ch., Willing Workers,   108 24
JUVENILE: *Britton,* for two certificates,   20

Total, $150 74

WISCONSIN.

WISCONSIN BRANCH.—Mrs. R. Coburn, of Whitewater, Treas. *Appleton,* 16.25; *Boscobel,* 4.50; *Browntown,* 2; *Delavan,* 65.17; *Eau Claire,* by Miss Bissell, 7; *Fulton,* 8; *Milwaukee,* Gr. Ave., 25; *New Lisbon,* 8.40; *New Richmond,* by Miss Bissell, 20.25, Aux., 10.50; *Sparta,* by Miss Bissell, 11.59, Aux., 6; *Whitewater,* by Miss Bissell, 10.62; for Mrs. Goodrich, 3.04; Japan Miss., 2, $200 32
JUNIORS: *Fox Lake,* 12.10; *New Lisbon,* 97; *Racine,* King's Young Daughters, 50; *River Falls,* Earnest Workers, 20,   83 07
JUVENILES: *Beloit,* 1st S. S., 40; *Clinton,* Cong. S. S., 10; *Kilbourn City,* Methodist S. S., for Bible-woman in India, 10,   60 00
MORNING STAR: *British Hollow,* 1.10; *Mukwonago,* 5; *New Lisbon,* 3.18,   9 28
Branch total (less expenses, 17.05),   335 62
——, A Friend, 10; *Eau Claire,* Cheerful Givers, 10,   20 00

Total, $355 62

MISCELLANEOUS.

Sale of two gold rings, donated, 3; of sleeve-buttons, donated, 5; of "Coan's Life," 1; of leaflets, 13.90; of envelopes, 1.25, $24 15

Total, $24 15

Receipts for the month, $3,844 95
Previously acknowledged,   19,475 11

Total since Oct. 1884, $23,320 06

Board of the Pacific.

HOW WE TRIED TO ORGANIZE.

It was in a little country village, where mother and I were spending our summer vacation. The Congregational Church, though newly established, was in a flourishing condition, but the ladies had not yet organized an auxiliary to the Woman's Board. When we heard the notice for the sewing circle given out one Sunday, at once came the thought to both of us, What a good chance to start an auxiliary! After church, Mrs. B., at whose house the society was to meet, invited us so cordially to attend, that it seemed another "straw" Boardward. Under the impulse of the invitation, we asked the president of the society, Mrs. Merry, if she didn't think the church could sustain an auxiliary to the Woman's Board of the Pacific. "Why, yes; I think we could," was the reply. "Come to the sewing circle, and talk to us about it."

So Tuesday afternoon, at a little after two, we started, under the guidance of an ever-ready Woman's Board assistant, for Mrs. B.'s house, four miles. Half-way there we found quite a little procession *en route* for the sewing society. Ahead was the president (as was fitting), in a neat little buggy, driving the minister's niece, the minister's wife being in the East. Next came good old Deacon May, whose fifty years of Christian service the Master must have recorded in letters of gold, his fruit-wagon transformed into a carry-all,—no, a carry-nine,—three on a seat. I overheard his wife say, on Sunday, that they would be at the Hall in time to "pick up any who wanted to go." Two city girls boarding with them, members of our wide-awake "Bethany Gleaners" circle in San Francisco, were part of the cargo. On we all went, through a lovely valley covered with orchards and vineyards. Here and there small houses appear, "shut in by walls of living green," or else standing alone, unprotected, in the midst of acres of fruit-trees two or three feet high. Older orchards give forth the perfumes of apricots and figs. Many roofs are covered with the yellow apricots drying in the sun. In the distance are seen the foothills, up whose steep sides still climbs the undaunted orchard.

But we are not going that far to-day. The president's buggy takes a turn to the left, through a wide-open gate; more embryo fruit-trees, then the cordial welcome of our hostess, Mrs. B., and the sewing society begins — for us. The room is full; soon nearly twenty ladies are assembled. The senator's wife, the orchardist's wife, the real-estate dealer's wife, the two deacons' wives, are all here. The little church is well represented. What a good chance to talk "Woman's Board!"

Our ever-helpful escort has left us for a little turn farther up the valley, but he may be back at any time; so we wait rather impatiently for the business part of the meeting to begin. Neighbors, fancy-work, babies new and old, church matters, are all under review. We and our hostess discover some mutual Eastern friends, and are very happy. But the afternoon wears away. Five o'clock; mother's voice breaks in upon the wave of sound: "Mrs. President, is this a good time to talk about the matter in which we are interested?"

Mrs. President immediately calls the ladies to order, but she says: "Ladies, we have a very important matter to consider this afternoon. We wish to hear the report of the committee upon the church organ. We must decide what price we will pay for the new organ, and instruct the committee how to proceed."

Half-past five, and still the organ holds the attention of all, and gives forth most uncertain and varied sounds. There comes the deacon for his little company; and there — yes, there comes our "Dolly"— and Woman's Board not mentioned yet! A few words to Dolly's driver, as interested as we, and he remembers some vegetables to be had for the asking at the ranch of a friend near by, and off he goes. At sight of him the president remembers our burden, and calls upon mother to state it.

In a few words she says that most of the Congregational churches of our State contain auxiliaries to our Board; that we are pledged for $3,300 this year, and need all the help we can get to raise the amount. More than that, we need the sympathy and interest of all Christian people. "We believe in the watchword of the Woman's Board of the Interior,—'Every woman a church-member, and every church-member a worker for missions.' We are specially interested in three missionaries, Mrs. Baldwin in Turkey, Mrs. Gulick in Spain, Mrs. Holbrook in Africa, from whom we have letters regularly. We also expect to assume the support of Miss Effie Gunnison, one of our own 'Bethany Gleaners,' now under commission from the American Board. This work is in accordance with Christ's commands, and it really does seem as if such a flourishing church as yours should have a hand in it."

All the ladies listen quietly, some indifferently — all intent upon their fancy-work. The president seems interested. She says she is afraid the church is not in such a prosperous condition as appears to outsiders; inquires what the terms of membership are; thinks they could manage that, but doesn't see how they could hold regular meetings. "We have so much to do for our own church. The proceeds of every entertainment we can get up we shall need at home. We have our organ to pay for, and there are a great many other things we need."

Mrs. C. says she remembers very well how they used to send $25, $30, or even $40, from her home church to the Woman's Board, but that they never could sustain regular meetings. "It is almost impossible in the country."

Mother and I urge the monthly meeting as all-important in the way of awakening interest, and suggest our column in the *Pacific*, *Life and Light*, and the *Missionary Herald*, as helps. Dear old Mrs. May says that she and the Deacon have taken the *Herald* for twenty-five years.

Meantime, one little knot of ladies, too polite to openly oppose the matter, show their indifference by discussing the organ, bending their heads over the illustrated catalogue, and comparing the relative value of the $125 and $175 instruments. They are entirely dead to the Macedonian call freshly rung in their ears.

From another corner comes an earnest voice: "I tell you, a real live missionary meeting will do more for our church than anything."

The president takes mother's address as Home Secretary of the Woman's Board of the Pacific, and says that they will consider the matter, and let her know of their decision later. Mother urges that the names of those who will join, be handed in "this afternoon," and a committee be appointed to see those who are absent.

Mrs. C. thinks it would be a good time to organize, as there are so many of the ladies present. The "Bethany Gleaners," at mother's request, tell something of the work of their society — "how they made over $100 from the sale of candies last year," — "how they hold meetings every two weeks," etc.

The president's voice just here calls the ladies back again to the organ. Our chariot and charioteer appear in sight, and we turn to put on our wraps, and find an animated discussion as to the proposed society going on in the "cloak-room." Our hostess is saying, "No, Mrs. H., I don't believe we ought to have a missionary society here; we have too much to do for ourselves." "The very thing we need," Mrs. H. replies, in the same earnest voice that attracted our attention before. "The more people give, the more they *want* to give." "I remember very well how it was in our church in the East," Mrs. B. replies. "We had societies for everything, and a $30,000 debt on our church. Now, I think it would have been a great deal better if they had withheld all their charities till they had their debt paid." "They never would have done it, my dear Mrs. B.; the missionary money would not have gone into the debt. Besides, that is *selfishness*." "Not at all; only self-interest," interrupts Mrs. B. "Now, our church, too, had a large debt—a $60,000 debt; but they organized missionary societies, which are accomplishing a great deal of good, and they are paying off their debt at the same time."

Our amiable little hostess takes another tack: "Well, I'll tell you, Mrs. H., the men who are running this church feel the burdens pretty heavy now, and I don't see how they are going to support a missionary society." "Yes; but what is $1.25 a year to any of us," says gentle Mrs. G. (the discussion is quite general now); "we can any of us secure that by little economies." "We can," says Mrs. May, "I know, for I've been a member for years. I missed my home society; so when I found there was none in our church here . I joined the one in the Presbyterian Church." "I tell you," mother's voice breaks in again, "Christ will not bless a church wrapped up in its own little network, indifferent to everything else."

"To return to the organ again, Mrs. B., how was it, if you felt the finances such a burden, that you were the only one to vote for the highest-priced organ on the list — twenty-five dollars more than any one else wanted to give?"

"Oh! that was to make our church attractive; to draw out these people from the East who are used to churches elegant in all their appointments; who come here and find in our country towns such little bits of churches, and such little bits of organs, that they are disgusted, and won't go to church at all. I think we should spend all the money we can on our own church. We can't afford to run missionary societies."

Just here Mrs. May spoke again: "I think we can sustain an auxiliary easily enough, if we are willing to deny ourselves. I have paid my missionary dues, but I haven't had a new bonnet this year."

Mrs. H.'s reply was, "Neither have I; and yet I think we ought by all means to have a missionary society. It will help on our church spiritually, I am sure."

We said "Good-bye" after that. Mother's last words to Mrs. B. were, "I am going to send you 'Mrs. Pickett's Missionary Box.'"

On talking it over while driving home, we agreed that the world's attitude, even that of the Church, toward missions, was pretty well represented in the little sewing-circle: indifference on the part of most; a few directly opposed for various reasons; a few unable to look beyond the multitude of "things in sight" — church organs, carpets, upholstering, etc.; a few always loyal to the cause.

Oh for some missionary telephone to make audible in Christian lands the woes of heathendom!   A. D. J.

Hopkins Academy, Oakland.

FOR WOMAN.

VOL. XV.   OCTOBER, 1885.   No. 10.

MEETING OF THE AMERICAN BOARD.

SOON after this number of our magazine reaches its readers, the seventy-fifth annual meeting of the American Board will be in session.   Already we hear the sound of the coming of the feet of those who will gather at the homestead for the grand family feast. Hospitable homes and warm welcomes await them, and anticipations of an occasion of rare enjoyment are many.   The progress of the gospel in the earth during the last three-quarters of a century will be a theme of inexhaustible interest: mingled with this will be wise planning for future action and congratulations on the hard-earned success of this, the oldest foreign missionary society in the country.   As a Woman's Board, we rejoice that through our connection with it, though young in years, not quite eighteen, we may have the benefit of the dignity and wisdom of seventy-five, and that we may have a recognized share in the rejoicings and congratulations.   These will not be confined to those who are actually present, but will be shared by Christian hearts all over the land.   Of all these who may be connected with our Board, we ask that, in the quiet of their homes, there may be constant prayer for that alone which will make the meeting all that is to be desired — the presence of the Holy Spirit in manifest power, a power that shall stir all hearts with new zeal and love for the work of our Lord in heathen lands.

TURKEY.

WORK FOR WOMEN IN HARPOOT FIELD.

ANNUAL REPORT.

IT is with grateful hearts we acknowledge that He who at this season "causeth the grass to grow for the cattle, and herb for the service of man," who bringeth "seed time and harvest," has caused his work in our field to flourish and grow in its season, according to his will. The past year has been one of special blessing — not striking, but well worth observing by those who would understand "the loving kindness of the Lord."

The lady-tourers have been Misses Wright and Bush, the former having resigned her connection with the school and kindly consented to share in this arduous and trying work for the winter. Though a new work to her, she bravely endured its privations and weariness, until at the close of the village-work, in the spring, it seemed imperative that she should rest for the long journey to Marsovan. We are most grateful to her for the interest she has shown in this department of labor, and shall spare her to go to her new home with sincere regret, in which we believe that all her friends in the Eastern Turkey Mission will heartily share.

In all, we have been out in the field some six months, either together or separately, and reached thirty-three different places, eleven of which we have visited twice. The winter has been mild, and so unusually favorable for touring; yet we encountered severe storms of rain as well as serious danger from snow on our return from the Arabkir region, but we are grateful to a kind Providence which shielded us from harm.

GIRLS' SCHOOLS.

One of our first cares as we traverse this wide field, is that in each place we may have a suitable girls' school, which shall furnish material for our school at Harpoot. We spend many hours in examining classes, counseling teachers, and suggesting new methods to be used. There are now some twenty of these schools, with about nine hundred pupils — less than one third the number of those in the boys' school, the difficulties in the way of their education being greater than that of the boys. The teachers of these schools seem to love their work, and to have a good influence upon the mothers, as well as their pupils. Those who have gone out from our Harpoot school for a year or two of teaching, testify how great a benefit it is to them, broadening their ideas, giving confidence, impressing upon their memory what they have studied, and imparting new love for Christ's work. They are loved and respected by the people; and some of the older ones take an active part in Christian work, even leading the women's meetings. They also help to win other young girls to a desire for education, and often return to Harpoot bringing more than one pupil as fruit of their labors.

A regular institution of most churches is the women's meeting, attended by from fifteen to sixty faithful sisters; and when we are to lead, the number swells to one hundred and one hundred and fifty. I am sorry to say that I know of only two places where they hold a regular "mothers' meeting." These are all blessed gatherings, wherein souls often take their first start in the divine life. Think of the joy of speaking to such a crowd of women and girls, many of them bright and intelligent, and hungry for the truth! There are some sterling Christians among these; one of them, a dear saint of a hundred years of age, not long ago walked so briskly into the chapel, that she looked as if she was helping her staff, and not her staff her. She took a "front seat;" and when the proper time came arose and prayed in a clear, earnest voice. In one of our villages on the plain, only one woman dared to come to the chapel a year ago; this year from ten to fifteen are in regular attendance, and the two Sabbaths I was there, there were seventy, at least. The women of that village are just waking out of a deep sleep of ignorance and superstition; and a Bible-woman who now goes there every morning from a neighboring village, had fourteen scholars the first day, eighteen the second, and now twenty!

Frequently our visits all day long are one succession of meetings, neighbors and friends being called in from all sides to the number of from five to twenty. Often men are found at home, and stay right on through the reading, exhortation, singing, and prayer. I had the curiosity on one of my hardest days to see how many hours I had given to this kind of work. It was nine, followed by attendance at the general meeting at the chapel, and conversation all the evening. The mind must be on the alert all the time, and the voice pitched to a loud key, lest your unintellectual audience should find the squeaking of a door or the crying of a baby more attractive. But these conversations are holy seasons, and it touches our hearts to see how the women tell all their little confidences and greater griefs, look forward to our coming, and even lay the fault of their coldness on our shoulders if we have not been able to visit them. Perhaps you will excuse me if I gratefully add that many opportunities are also given to influence pastors and laymen, particularly when deprived of the presence of a missionary; so that this winter it was our privilege to reorganize a Sabbath-school and a young men's meeting.

WOMEN'S BENEVOLENT SOCIETIES.

Connected with the women's meeting is usually a society for doing good, the women pledging ten, twenty, or forty paras per month, as they feel able. (Ten paras is equal to one cent.) Some are so poor as to pay in cotton or wheat. In Hoolli, where in two years they have collected five hundred piasters (twenty dollars) and subscribed two hundred more, the proceeds will be used to help build a new chapel, or obtain maps for the girls' school. In Husenik they have put their money with that of the Young Women's Christian Association, who hope to raise enough for a grand school-building; and they even zealously beg of Gregorians and Protestants alike for this fund. In Egin they help a poor girl who has come to Harpoot to school. In Malatia they share the expenses of the girls' school, three of the women having been appointed by the brethren as trustees. In Hoh, Hoghi, and Keserik the chapels are to be better supplied with matting, the pulpits painted, and seat for preacher cushioned. The women of Oozoonoba have kept up a society for years, though having no preacher's wife to labor among them; and many a stray ornament of silver has gone to swell the proposed fund.

Often a very zealous care for God's house and the comfort of the pastor's family is evident. Wood and water are cheerfully brought for the latter. In Choonkoosh, one very rainy day, a trembling old woman, still brave of heart, came to the chapel and scanned it all over carefully, to see if it leaked, saying, " Let *my* house leak, but not the chapel." A woman in Keserik attended faithfully to the fall cleaning and white-washing of the chapel there; and now again this spring she peremptorily orders the sisters out on the hills for some white earth, saying, " Shall you whiten and clean your houses for Easter and not God's house? "

BIBLE-WOMEN.

A glance over the field reveals to us a new enthusiasm awakened in the matter of reading the Bible. This we believe is largely due to the earnest labors of twelve Bible-women. We hope to have at least twenty in the service the present year, with closer supervision, and in the end larger results. These Bible-readers are for the most part either preachers' wives, widows, or women who were formerly in our school and are now married to laymen. Some of these teach school half the day, as in Haboosie, where the former pastor's wife has a school of thirty-eight pupils, and also some thirty-five women under her care, a part of whom she herself reaches every day, sending boys or girls to give lessons to the rest. Quite a stir has been raised in this village by her efforts. Another pastor's wife, besides giving lessons to a few women, goes three times a week to different quarters of the village to hold meetings. The village being located in a valley, through which the wind sweeps unresisted, she is frequently obliged to wade through deep snowdrifts, and in the spring encounters a sticky, clayey kind of mud, which would dishearten any one less zealous in the good cause than is this bright-faced, hearty Christian woman, who, so far, has received no pay for her labors.

Most of our workers receive a small salary, varying from thirty to eighty piasters per month, according to the prices of food in different localities and the needs of the worker. In the majority of places the people assume from one fourth to one third of the salary. We endeavor to have each scholar pay ten, twenty, or forty paras a month for lessons, according to her ability. This is sometimes paid in money, sometimes in cotton, wheat, etc.

It has also been our special effort this winter to obtain pledges from those who have grown careless in reading the Bible; and I have a very precious little book by me in which I have recorded the names of those who have promised to read the Bible every day I, on my part, promising to remember them in prayer daily, asking for them the Holy Spirit to make them understand and love the Word of God; also to visit them some months later, to see how they progress. We often give them a pretty picture-card for a mark, and they really have seemed encouraged to make a new effort to love God's Word. We each carry a small satchel containing Testament, hymn-book, some tracts, and a couple of primers, to sell or give away. Now mine is new, with bright steel clasps, and no one is ever satisfied until the contents are revealed to her curious eyes; and the consequence is, that she has to part with her last precious piaster, or even runs behind the big earthern jars to cut off three still more precious ones from her head-dress for a much-coveted book or tract. They are hungry for tracts, which we often give away; but I confess that I feel as if I had "removed mountains" when I *sell* a book, and have strong hope for the woman who parts with her money for it. One Friday, Miss Wright and I were obliged to send from a near village to the city for twenty primers, as a good stock we had brought away with us two weeks before had failed; and in two days seven of the twenty were sold, and by the next week all were gone!

These are the bright spots of which I write. It is not profitable to dwell on those things which are discouraging, though, to tell the whole, of course such things exist. We mourn the lack of spirituality, neglect of the Bible, and work for Christ in many even who are church-members; but though coldness in some places, and especially differences among the brethren, have hindered work for women (as in one village where they stopped the women's meetings), still, as a general thing, even where the men have been quarreling, and backward in all duties toward the church, the women have taken no part in the discussions, and have retained much of their former faith and love for Christ's work. They show deep regret for the troubles in the church, and still love its pastor and services.

Miss Seymour expects to join me in the work of touring after July; and as we plan for our teachers and Bible-women the coming year, with sincerest gratitude for the past, it shall be our aim to form new plans for the advancement of the schools throughout our field, and find new means of influencing our sisters of this land, humbly recognizing that "neither is he that planteth anything, neither he that watereth, but God that giveth the increase."

CAROLINE E. BUSH.

TRAVELING EXPERIENCES IN TURKEY.

We have received the following extracts from letters describing a journey to the annual meeting of the Eastern Turkey Mission, which may give our readers some new ideas of this phase of missionary life.

Miss Bush writes:—

You, with us, would have been not a little amused in watching our caravan, noting the different styles of animals, dress, and baggage. Later, I counted and found that we were a company of forty persons and thirty-four animals. There was Dr. Thom on his spirited horse named Nebbie Eunice (the prophet Jonah), and his wife, and Miss Pratt, and Mr. Dewey, all mounted on horses; while Mr. Browne ambled along by his wife's *moffa*, on what he facetiously calls "Wilkins Micawber," or the "Ruins of a Fallen Tower"; and I, of course, was mounted on my brave "Pet," whose name, by the way, I must seriously think of changing, he is becoming such a wild, fighting character.

Do you ask, "What are *moffas?*" They are boxes, well curtained around, which hang on either side of a baggage-horse or mule, the animal being led by a man on foot. Mrs. Browne and baby Edith were in one side, and the nursemaid and little Edward in the other. In the same way Nellie and Minnie Thom occupied a pair of *moffas*, and Mrs. Dewey and her little daughter another pair. There was more or less competition between the Harpoot and Mardin *moffagies* (leaders), and many were the walking-races they had, to our great amusement. Another source of fun were three donkeys; one, a wee gray one, who, insignificant as he appeared, was called the " King," and two white Mosul donkeys, who were tied together and left to "gang their own gait," — which was rather an uncertain one, for each had a mind of his òwn, and a pretty firm conviction that it was his duty to act accordingly. Another amusing character was a black man who was rich, who has two homes, one in Mecca and one in Egypt. He sat in stately dignity on a loaded horse, often brandishing an umbrella like a gun, and occasionally taking an ignominious tumble into the mud, considerably ruffling his dignity. Then there were the little Browne girls, seated in a couple of baskets hung on either side of a mule, which persisted in following my horse. Their little heads went bobbing around, but what merry laughter went up from baskets and *moffas* as we wound our way over hill and valley! Our baggage for the road was in great leather bags hung on either side of horses and mules. These bags are called *hoorjies.* There were other boxes and trunks, all carried in the same way. The only amusing thing about them was their rolling off at unexpected and inconvenient seasons, causing, I fear, not a little hard language from the muleteers.

The first night, after a vain hunt for suitable ground in the village of Harboosie, five hours from Harpoot, we pitched our tents on the roofs of some houses. What a piece of work it was to get tents up, camp bedsteads arrànged, dinner ready and eaten, and all off to bed and settled for each night!

On Thursday there were two notable events during the day: one, the crossing of the Euphrates about noon under dark and threatening clouds; the other a violent storm of wind and hail and rain, just after getting safely over, frightening our horses and wetting us pretty thoroughly. We were three hours in getting our large company safely over the river. We could see the kindest Providence in the fact that no other traveler appeared on either side during this time to hinder us, but the old scow was as fully ours as if we had chartered it.. I love to see the hand of the kind Father above in just such things as these.

The next day we journeyed on, comparing notes, and chatting merrily of the scenery and many things. As the clouds threatened rain, three o'clock found us settling ourselves in tents on a hillside not far from a small village. Here occurred *the* experience of our journey.

No sooner had we comfortably laid ourselves down for the night, than over us burst a fierce gust of wind, which became a wild storm of wind and rain, with hailstones the size of walnuts, and awful thunder and lightning. It was the most frightful storm that any of us had ever experienced. Twice the lightning struck very near us; the hailstones caused the muleteers' horses to flee in terror, while mine tore round in a wild way, and I certainly thought he might come dashing into the tent at any moment. Mr. Browne stood up and held the tent until his fingers ached with the hailstones beating on them, while he was soon ankle-deep in a stream of muddy water which rushed down from the mountain right through our tent. This carried away shoes, bags, and every loose article, and we never should have seen them more had not the bottom of our tent been fastened tight to the ground, and held them. Mrs. Browne soon lay in a little pond of water in her bed, which she soaked up, thus managing to keep the baby dry. Soon my feet felt that a small lake was forming near them, which I should have been quite content to lie in had it not been that a stream commenced to pour down upon my head, making me jump up and stand on the edge of my bed the rest of the time, shivering from head to foot with fear and cold. I was holding on to one of the *moffas* in which Edward had been put to sleep, and which Mariam, the nursemaid held, pushing it on its very edge, to prevent his being soaked. The poor child was screaming with fear, while the other children quietly slept. I gathered up all the clothing I could reach, one shoe and my bag, and tried to cover them and my bedding with my rubber cloak; but they were far from protected, as we found later. Oh, how we waited for the severity of the storm to pass — with what anxiety lest the tent should fall, and we be struck by lightning or carried away by the torrent! What a relief when the storm became a calm!

Dr. Thom soon came over to see if we were alive. We talked of going to the village, but feared to venture in the mud and water. Finally the children were one by one conveyed to the Mardin tent, which had remained comparatively dry, and were snugly tucked away with the other dry and happy children, while Mr. Browne took his wife on his back and Mariam took me, and we, too, were carried to the same tent. What a welcome we received, and how good it was to get there! A big dish of coals was brought in; and while we dried our clothing over it, in spite of the fear and danger through which we had just passed, and the weariness that oppressed us, the jokes flew around as if we were seated in a parlor at home. By and by one and another quieted down, and found a half or a third of a bed to lie on. Sleep was not to be wooed by any devices, and soon the fumes of the charcoal began to tell on us, just as some had feared. Diantha Dewey started from her sleep with a cry that startled us all; this was followed by Edward Browne's almost going into a convulsion in my arms. By the time the children were quiet, some of us were complaining of a severe headache, which drove Mrs. Thom and Mrs. Dewey out into the open air, where the latter sank down in a faint in the mud. Mrs. Thom was very ill the rest of the night. Notwithstanding our misery, the funny people would be funny, and this sent Mrs. Browne and myself off into a slight attack of hysterics, which we tried in vain to hide. This, of course, afforded amusement for the whole party. But how shall I describe the desolation of the next morning? Mrs. Browne's shoes were found full of mud; skirts, stockings, a comb, etc., were imbeded in the soil, and with the greatest difficulty we found clothes to put on. We spent the time till noon drying clothing, then had to load and mount quickly, lest we should have another deluge before we reached our Sabbath resting-place in the village, five hours away.

Here Mr. Browne preached in the Gregorian Church, and Miss Bush held a meeting with the women. The road became very bad after this, and the *moffas* were often in great danger, one side touching the hillside while the other hung over a precipice — a frequent occurrence in Turkey.

As it rained every day but two of the ten traveling-days, cold food, mud, and misery were not lacking. Snow-covered mountains were crossed, but they often passed beautiful flowers, with which hats and horses, baskets and *moffas* were adorned. One steep descent was into the "Valley of Gehenna," which they thought rightly named.

Once they lost their way on the mountains, and were lost once more an hour before reaching their resting-place. Of this, Miss Bush writes: "We lost our way in a great marsh, where trunks and boxes were tumbled off, and Mrs. Dewey's *moffa* animal lay down, obliging her to take to the back of a man for conveyance. Mr. Browne struggled through to the village first, feeling himself to be in greater danger than ever before in his life. He sent out two guides to us, who at last brought us all safely upon solid land, to his great relief as he stood and watched our course. Two hours from the city of Erzroom a great company of friends met us, and there were warm and merry greetings. With what gratitude for God's mercies we rode into the city, and entered these hospitable homes!"

JAPAN.
A JAPANESE BIBLE-WOMAN.
BY MISS A. M. COLBY.

As I begin to write, words of contempt, of unbelief in and ridicule of, the work of missions and missionaries that I have heard crowd into my mind. Some of these words misled me when a child, some held me back when Christ's command, "Go ye therefore and teach all nations," had come to me in such a way that I felt that only two things were possible to me — either to go as a missionary, or to give up my Bible and all pretension to following Christ. I would that all who say that Christian missions are a failure, might live for five years with such a woman, to them, now, simply one of the heathen, as the Woman's Board has lost from among her ranks of workers on earth.

This woman, whose attractive face arrested the stranger's notice, who is mourned by hundreds of loving friends, and of whom it has been said that by her death she will be multiplied a hundred-fold in those who have been lifted into the light by her influence, was ten years ago a most unhappy heathen wife in the island of Shikoku, Japan, with black teeth and shaven eyebrows. I do not use the word unhappy in any cant way, simply because she bowed down to idols of wood and stone, instead of having been born in a so-called Christian land. She was unhappy. She belonged to a family of good rank, but while yet a child she lost her own mother, and spent many years simply as a little nurse-girl to her step-mother, who showed her no love; at fifteen she was married to a young *samurai*, seven years her senior, whom she had never seen before the day of marriage. Her husband had no faculty for saving money, and in a few years they were so poor that she became a dependent in the house of a miserly, though well-to-do relative, who begrudged her the necessary food; and her husband came to Osaka, seeking work. Misses Gouldy, Stevens, and Wheeler engaged him and his wife as house-servants, not knowing that in these "raw heathen" they would find a pearl of such value. The young man, on his side, felt deeply humiliated to be driven to this menial work with foreigners, and would not dishonor his own name, but gave an assumed one, which still clings to him, intending to terminate the engagement whenever he could do so with advantage. That was in November of 1876. The wife was simply known as O. Kane San. A Japanese friend has written me of her awakening into Christianity:—

"Two of the ladies went to Mino for the summer vacation, and O Kane San and I went with them, and were taught the Bible by Mr. Shimamura, who is now teaching in the Doshisha. Her husband sent her many letters urging her to return to Osaka, as he was too busy and lonely; but she as often returned answer that she did not wish to leave Mino, as she wanted to study the Bible with Mr. Shimamura. This is the cause why he began to hate O Kane San. She tried to study as much as she could, but she was too much excited to do much then, and wrote very unkindly to her husband. This was the reason that he hated Christianity so long; but after a few years she became a true Christian. Of course she believed the Bible, and became a Christian in a few months after that, but her husband would not permit her to be baptized until the January of 1879. She then became Miss Gouldy's Bible-woman, and went everywhere with her, teaching the women, until Miss Gouldy went to America." After Miss Gouldy left she became my Bible-woman. She was always frail, and suffered greatly from diseased lungs. Two or perhaps more years ago, her husband yielded to the quiet influence continually at his side, and became also a Christian — and more than that, one of the leaders in every Christian enterprise, even being one of our school committee. Although O Kane San had been taught all that a Japanese woman was supposed to need to know, she had never attended school until after she was thirty years of age, when she began the study of English in our school, where she also taught a Bible class. She was endowed by nature with wonderful tact, taste, and simple dignity of manner, that led all to seek her help in every direction. Her humble home was the resort of all classes and conditions of humanity, from the wife of the former chief-judge of Osaka, now promoted to senatorship, who sought her advice as a sister, to the lowliest beggar, who received equally kind attention. As a friend has said, "From her rank she might well have demanded to have been waited upon," but she served without any appearance of discontent in any way, however menial, that presented itself. I have heard that she has said that she had to continually fight against indolence and pride, but those sins were never shown to others.

Her final illness was short and acute. A few moments before the last, she said to her pastor, who was sitting near her, "I thought I should go to-day." Her husband inquired, "Do you mean to heaven?" She answered, "Yes." She soon asked to be lifted up, and a neighbor, a beautiful woman whom she had led into the light of Christianity, took her into her arms, when without a struggle she ended her earthly life. Mrs. Kane Yamaji passed from earth to heaven, April 4, 1885.

She left many words of remembrance for her friends. Respecting her father, who is not yet a Christian, she said: "I have always written about Christianity, but I cannot write any more, so please tell him to believe in Christ. I will wait for him in heaven." She left this message with her pastor for the church-members: "Please say for me to my brothers and sisters, that I want you to wash one another's feet (John, thirteenth chapter, fourteenth verse); fight the good fight, and come to my Father's house. I am going first, and will wait and pray for your coming." I was away, and in great perplexity, and she sent me these words, "I will watch over her and pray for her from heaven."

Mr. Sawayama said at her funeral, that he had heard many say, "She first led me to Christ." "So," he continued, "I say to my brothers and sisters, please work for Christ like this sister, and let it be said of you, ' He or she was my first leader into Christianity.' " Mr. Miyegawa, her pastor, made the thought very plain that, although her life had been bright and shining above and before them all, yet it was not beyond the attainment of the humblest. He has since said to me, "If she had died two years ago I should have been very much disheartened, but now she will be multiplied a hundred-fold. Several of the woman said to her before she left this world, to comfort her, "I will take up your work, and do it just as far as I am able." "Her virtue consisted in being filled with the love of Christ," and her chief characteristic was faithfulness in the small as well as the great things of life. Several asked for her old Bible (the New Testament only), which was full of marks and references — her helps in teaching. It was divided, her husband keeping one half, the other half being given to a young man to whom she had been a spiritual mother.

God grant that her life may be multiplied a hundred-fold, not only in "heathen Japan," but also in civilized America, and wherever her name may be told, as a memorial of the precious ointment of a loving life that she gave, without stint, to the cause of Christ.

INDIA.

WORK OF THE BIBLE-WOMEN IN THE MADURA MISSION.

FROM THE ANNUAL REPORT OF THE MISSION.

THERE are nineteen Bible-women employed by the mission at the various stations. This work for Hindu women is of comparatively recent commencement, yet it has grown into one of the most important departments of our evangelical work.

From Battalagundu, Mrs. Chandler writes: We have three Bible-women. One of these works at Pammanpatti and in the neighboring villages; she has four regular pupils, who are very anxious to learn to read. The other two women work in the town of Battalagundu, and are kindly received; they have been admitted to forty new houses the past year.

Of the work in Tirumangalam Mrs. Tracy, writes: It has

been interrupted to some extent by the death of the Bible-woman, Samiyadial, who was for many years a faithful, quiet worker in Tirumangalam. She had been in failing health for some time, and died a triumphant, happy death. The last words that were heard from her lips were those of the lyric, "Just as I am, without one plea, O lamb of God, I come, I come." During the later years of her life, in lonely widowhood, alone and childless, she was always cheerful and faithful in her service. She bore her cross with gentle patience, and at last has laid it down in exchange for a crown which an angel would envy.

Some mention should also be made of another worker who has this year gone from service to rest — the wife of the station catechist at Tirumangalam. She was a woman who seemed to gather into her life the graces and sweetnesses which are born of Christianity. In her home and among her neighbors she exemplified the best that Christianity has yet accomplished for woman. To say that she was a model for native women, is only to say what all who knew her felt. Her monument will yet be seen when time shall bring into the Lord's service the children whom she trained in Christian nurture, and consecrated to him in humble, fervent prayer. Many heathen women came to her stricken family with their testimony of sympathy, saying only between their sobs, "O mother, golden mother!" Such lives as hers are barbed arrows of conviction, finding lodgment in many a heart outwardly unmoved. They are the ripe fruitage of the gospel.

Of the work in Madura, Mrs. Capron reports: Seven Bible-women with their assistants, in all 10 workers, have been employed during the year. We have had under instruction 888 women, of whom 335 have been reading the Bible. Eight women have died, 143 have moved away, 72 have left for various causes, leaving 660 with us, of whom 255 are reading the Bible. Of the 143 who have moved away, 80 have carried their Bibles with them. There have been visited 851 houses where we have no learners, and 9,370 listeners have had the Bible read and explained to them. In the month of January we had a special mission. Eight verses on "What God thinks of sin" were selected, and the Bible-women read and explained them in every house where they could find entrance. In that month alone we had 2,359 listeners. In November we carried all over the city the sweetest and brightest verses on "God's love for us" that we could find. We found our way into 137 new houses; and if some smiled at us as if we were harmless enthusiasts, they were evidently impressed by the message. One woman followed the Bible-woman from one house to another, so eager was she to hear more. In a week she died of cholera.

We all had the feeling that we were the King's messengers, and that our main business was to proclaim his love for us. In the streets where we observed the most interest cholera has removed many. The two notable features of the year's work have been the opening among silk-weavers, of whom twelve are now studying with us, and the return to us of those who had left us because of their own indifference or the opposition of their relatives.

Mrs. Howland reports: The work of the Bible-woman in Arupakittai is more and more interesting. Thirty-four Hindu women and girls are now under instruction. It is interesting to notice that a number have purchased Bible portions, that they may read and study for themselves. What seems to affect them most deeply, is the story of Christ's sufferings and death. "Why did he suffer all these cruelties?" they will ask. When the reason is explained, they seem ready to receive him as their Saviour with their whole heart. Some show a desire to openly profess their faith, but the bondage of caste hinders them. The Bible-woman visits on an average thirty persons daily, and reads with them from the Gospels. It is encouraging that in many cases the men try to aid their wives and daughters, by removing the difficulties in the way of their study. The cordial greetings I receive from time to time, and their hearty response to the instruction given, assures me that there are here souls not far from the kingdom.

A woman who was badly burned sent at once for the Bible-woman. Without mentioning her suffering, she exclaimed, "The Lord Jesus loves me; I know it." When the Bible-woman read to her about the three men in the fiery furnace, her delight could not find expression. It has been interesting to notice an increasing disposition on the part of our more intelligent readers to read to others. Our former schoolgirls are helpful in this respect. A man stopped a Bible-woman, one day, to say to her that he had noticed her faithful work, going in and out of the houses, and added: "Your seed is bringing forth fruit. I hear these women reading aloud evenings." The work of the year has been unusually interesting, and more anxiously than ever have we tried to lead our dear friends to confess Christ openly. There is entire fearlessness in reading the Bible at home, and frank expression of conviction of the truth. May our duty be made plain to us all, both to teachers and taught.

Since we are so much interested in medical work, through Mrs. Capron, we add a few words on the general subject from Dr. Chester. To those who are watching the general influence of mission dispensary work in India, it is most interesting to notice that not only is the prejudice of the natives against European treatment diminishing, but that the people are beginning to learn the value of dispensaries. We still have to bear patiently with many of the inconveniences of ancient and Oriental custom. The patients who take six days' medicine in one, to get well the sooner; who chew up pills as if they were sugar-plums, instead of swallowing them direct; who are astonished if they are not ordered to observe all the strict diet of the native doctors, and so die of starvation, if not of disease,—are not all extinct.

But worse than all this is the evil habit too many of the natives have of trying all sorts and kinds of native doctors and native treatment, including city, town, and village doctors, Hindu and Mohammedan cow doctors, and old women, until there is very little left of them but skin and bones before coming to the dispensary; and then expect to be cured in a day! Among the many, however, are a few patients loyal to the dispensary and to European treatment, and it is a pleasure to see the improvement most of these make.

The total number of cases treated this year in the Madura and Dindigul mission dispensaries has been 58,406, of which 21,256 were new cases, or those coming for the first time to the dispensary.

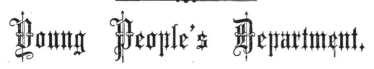

Young People's Department.

A CHRISTIAN TRAINING-SCHOOL FOR NURSES IN KIOTO, JAPAN.

BY JOHN C. BERRY, M.D.

In the March LIFE AND LIGHT we made a proposition to our young ladies to erect a building in Japan that should be at once a home for our lady missionaries, a center for Christian work and influence, and for the medical benefit of Japanese women. Plans that were then talked of did not mature quite as was expected, and it has been a source of regret to us that we have not been able to present the matter in a definite shape the past few months. We are now able to present the plan of the work to be established, kindly written out for us by Dr. Berry, whose medical experience in Japan enables him to write as one who knows whereof he affirms. We are sorry that valuable time, and, we fear, some enthusiasm, has been lost by the delay; but we hope our young ladies will take up the work during the remaining months of the year with a zest and energy that will insure its success. The whole expense will probably be about $5,500, of which the Japanese themselves will assume a portion. The sum which we ask is $4,000, to be raised in shares of ten dollars each. Of this we have recieved at the time of writing (Aug. 20th) $860, leaving a little more than $3,000 to be raised before the first of January. This will require real, persistent effort, but we believe it can be done. We have great faith in the ability of our young ladies to accomplish what they heartily undertake.

By few people is the value of hygiene more appreciated than by the Japanese; and yet, perhaps in no land is the art of nursing in a more primitive state. While it has been the writer's experience to witness his directions for the care of the sick listened to and noted down by friends with anxiety, lest something of importance be lost, yet he has not infrequently witnessed efforts for the relief of the sick frustrated, and life itself jeopardized, by the misguided attentions of well-meaning but ignorant friends. The fact, however, remains, that among few people are more conscientious efforts made to carry out the instructions of the physician in the sick-room than in Japan, affording proof that the value of nursing is fully appreciated there, though its art is poorly understood. Our missionary ladies are probably consulted upon nothing more frequently by the mothers of Japan, yea, and by the fathers, too, than upon points pertaining to the care of children and the nursing of the sick; and a Christian nurse with tact, and a thorough knowledge of her profession, would be one of the most welcome visitors that could enter a Japanese house.

If, as has been generously expressed by a prominent missionary brother, a missionary physician is a missionary and a half, a devoted and conscientious missionary nurse in Japan would be a double missionary; and if, as is contemplated, she is enabled, by the generosity of her sisters in America, to have a home and training-class where, from the churches of different regions, her native sisters may come and acquire a knowledge of those practical helps in the care of the sick which she has acquired here, her influence for good will be indefinitely multiplied.

At the General Missionary Conference, held in Osaka, in 1883, a resolution was unanimously adopted to the effect that the condition of Japan, and the character of Japanese women, combine to make that a field of rare promise for the work of competent and devoted Christian ladies in training Japanese women as nurses, there being many points in the Japanese character well suited to such work, but no knowledge whatever at present as to how to make use of them.

While ready, therefore, to educate all who may apply for admission to the school, and who shall subsequently be at liberty to engage in hospital or private work, as Providence may direct, yet the primary object of the proposed institution will be to train Christian women who shall, in Kioto and elsewhere, where churches exist, devote themselves to Christian work among the sick,— making use of their professional knowledge as the missionary physician makes use of his professional knowledge,— to relieve suffering, allay prejudice, win confidence, afford a practical illustration of Christian charity— all to give greater efficacy to personal efforts for Christ.

Its general conduct, therefore, may be outlined as follows:—

(1.) A competent missionary lady, who has a thorough knowledge of the language, and tact in personal work, to take charge of the Christian training of the women, giving them a comprehensive knowledge of the Scriptures, and a practical training (by visits, etc.) in the manner of conducting city missionary work. *

(2.) An experienced and thoroughly trained nurse, to have the immediate care of the more distinctly professional features of the school, listening to recitations, and, by personal attention to the sick in the Mission Hospital wards, and elsewhere, afford that practical instruction so essential to intelligent nursing.

(3.) That such didactic instruction as may be required in medical, surgical, ophthalmic, and obstetrical nursing, be given by the missionary physician of the station.

(4.) That the city and its suburbs be divided off into districts; and the women, after one year of training, be assigned, in suitable numbers, to those districts to work for a certain number of hours each day, visiting all known cases of want, co-operating, as far as practicable, with the native physicians, and imparting, upon all proper occasions, a knowledge of the truth and the consolations of the Christian religion : after two years of work and study, to graduate, and then return to the stations and churches whence they came, and there, as independent workers in their own neighborhoods, as Christian nurses supporting themselves in hospitals, or private families, or as missionary nurses encouraged, if necessary, by the churches, labor to Christianize the land.

The need for this work is urgent; its sphere of influence is wide; the ripened harvest waiting to be garnered is " the hundred-fold."

A WORD IN SEASON.

One pleasant June evening, as a company of young people met together for their weekly reading, one of the number

---

* The name of Miss Talcott, who is widely known as one of the most efficient workers on the foreign field, has been suggested in this connection, and she has expressed herself as prepared to regard such a relation with favor.

exclaimed, "O I'm so thankful I reached home safely from our fishing expedition this afternoon!"

"Why don't you put a cent in the mite-box, then?" was quickly suggested by another.

A missionary jug, devoted to the interests of a boys' missionary society, was close at hand, and a dime was soon transferred into it from the pocket of the thankful young man.

The others around the table would not be behind in this remembrance of mercies, so the little jug was heavier by many pennies before the close of that evening.

Nor was that all, for, through the interest aroused there, two young men asked that they each might have a missionary jug. So when the boys break their jugs in the fall, they will be happily surprised by the addition of two to their little army.

This was only a tiny seed sown, and it all came from a chance word, showing how we all may do much by using faithfully just such opportunities as come to us.　　　　　I.

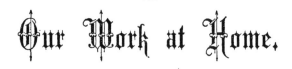

Our Work at Home.

LOOKING BEYOND THE HILLS.

BY ESTHER CONVERSE.

"Mrs. Brown," said the pastor's wife, "I wish you would come to our missionary meeting this week."

"Well, I don't know; I don't get out much," answered Mrs. Brown, evasively.

"I know you must be very busy with your large family and dairy, but perhaps it would *rest* you to come; we limit the exercises to an hour, so they are not tiresome."

"I didn't say I was too *tired* to go; I'm as strong as most folks, I guess. But, Miss Allen, I fail to see what earthly good it does,— your gettin' together and talkin' about Chiny, and Harpoot, and Koto. You get little enough money, and nobody seems to care much. Seems to me you might find plenty of work nearer home."

"My dear Mrs. Brown," said the pastor's wife, impulsively, "I thank you for your honesty and frankness. You have probably expressed the thoughts of many of our neighbors, for I am very unsuccessful in my attempts to awaken an interest in this work. May I tell you my reasons for deeming the work of great importance?"

"Certainly," replied Mrs. Brown. "I didn't mean any offense; I'm pretty free-spoken; I generally say what I think," she added, proudly.

"You gave no offense, and I am glad you have spoken; we cannot fight shadows. I am going to give you first a selfish view of the work. I need not remind you of the narrowness of a woman's life. The four walls of her home often limit her thoughts for days. I am sure you have sometimes felt the cramping, depressing influences of this."

"Yes;" interrupted Mrs. Brown; "only last night I stood at the sink washin' dishes and lookin' off onto the hills yonder, and it came over me like a surprise that there was something beyond; and then came a kind of bitter feelin' that I must go on washin' dishes, and mendin', and never know anything about it."

"Such thoughts are natural to most of us; and anything that sets in motion new currents of thought, broadens our sympathies, or rouses our intellect, cannot fail to be beneficial. Then, we revive our knowledge of geography; we learn of the manners and customs of other lands. I havn't time to speak of half the subjects in which I have become interested since my connection with this society. To the rich it is invaluable; it occupies much leisure time, and draws them from frivolity. Money that would, perhaps, be foolishly spent, is turned into useful channels. It helps to take us out of ourselves; it furnishes themes worthy of thought and speech, and in our prayers for others, we ourselves may, and do, receive a blessing."

"There's another thing," again interrupted Mrs. Brown: "prayin', I must say, is quite beyond me. I was all of a tremble the last time I went, for fear I'd be called on. I believe my words would have raised no higher'n the ceilin', and settled down on us all again like a chill."

"I'm sorry you feel so; if you will come again you need not fear that. You say we get little money; that is true, but even a little helps. A little money goes a great way in China or India, in clothing and educating the children, or feeding the hungry; and kind words of sympathy are fully appreciated by those faithful teachers. Why should they spend their lives in those far-away lands more than we?

"I know that the recollection of our interest and sympathy strengthens them for their work. I leave it to your own loving heart to tell you of the cup of cold water given in His name, and to remind you that —

> ' Whate'er we do for thine, O Lord,
> We do it unto thee.' "

"Well, Miss Allen, I'll come. What you say about geography is true. I used to be real good in that; but last night, when father says, 'Where's Boocharest?' it came upon me suddenly, like a glow out of the dark; I hadn't an idea — but, land! Annie spoke right up, and says, 'I'll show you, father!' *She* knew!"

Mrs. Brown was present at the next meeting, and listened to the exercises with apparent interest. Returning home, the Sunday dress seemed to give a feeling of Sunday leisure, and instead of resuming at once her usual sewing or mending, she opened a geography left on the table by the children.

"Annie," said she, "where is Ezeroon? I heard a letter read to-day from a missionary there, and I don't know where under the canopy it is." "I'll show you, mother," said Annie, kneeling by her side; "we've been studying about it lately, and our teacher has a brother, not far away, who is a missionary. She tells us wonderful things about the country. Mother," she asked, earnestly, "do you suppose I can ever see any of these places I study about?"

Mrs. Brown gave a startled glance at the flushed face so near her own, and carelessly answered, "O, may be you will."

"Is it wrong for me to say I *will* go there sometime?"

"I don't know, child; you'd better not talk about it." Mrs. Brown had resumed her sewing, and her needle flew through her work as she thought, "What if she should go to foreign lands! What if *I* should give a child to the work! Could I? And may be her letters would be read in missionary meetings, and *her* name come out in print in the *Life and Light!* I guess I should be mighty proud of that! After all, what better could come to the child? I won't say anything to her, but I believe I'll put down a few steppin'-stones."

She arose and went to the bureau-drawer, where, under a pile of handkerchiefs, lay the old portmonnaie containing the few dollars saved in those wonderful ways known only to prudent housewives. "I'll subscribe for the *Life and Light* and *Missionary Herald!* Miss Allen called for names, and I'll send Annie right over."

Before night the "stepping-stones" were laid that aided the daughter in after years to climb to the height of unselfishness and self-abnegation that enables one to leave father and mother, home, friends, and native land for labor in the vineyard where the abundant harvest awaits its reapers.

Mrs. Brown was induced to take a "field," in which, through the influence of enthusiastic Annie, she became interested. Day after day as she stood at her dish-washing her thoughts wandered away to the wonderful country she located before the hills that bound her vision; and while her hands were employed in their monotonous labor, she often thought of the occupation of her people — their dress, homes, food, amusements; and her questions in regard to these subjects greatly aided Mrs. Allen in maintaining the interest of the meetings. Her interest in the Sunday-school lessons increased, and often led to more extended research and thought. Can any one doubt that her own happiness also increased, and that husband, home, and children gained by the change?

When, unasked, her voice was raised in prayer with an earnestness that carried all hearts to that throne of grace from whence such prayers descend in gentle dews of divine blessing, Mrs. Allen was greatly moved. "Truly," she said, "in laboring for, in thinking of others, we ourselves are blessed; the two are one. We labor for foreign lands, but the larger blessing falls in our midst, even on our own hearts. Foreign work is home work, after all."

When in after years letters were read at missionary gatherings from the zealous teacher who was so untiring in her devotion to her work, no one guessed the pride and joy of that white-haired mother who once found no pleasure in missionary words and work. Her life had been broadened, her soul enriched. Home walls and surrounding hills had no power to shut in a spirit that had broken its fetters, and claimed, in its unselfishness, kinship with the ignorant and oppressed of every nation and clime.

MISSIONARY MEETING IN PROVIDENCE, R. I.

A MEETING was held Sabbath evening, August 5th, in the Beneficent Church, Providence, which marks an era in the history of the churches of Rhode Island in regard to the work of foreign missions. It has been known for some time that two young ladies, members of prominent churches in this city, had made application, and had been accepted, to the Woman's Board in Boston, and were soon to leave for their destined fields. As they were to sail from New York, it seemed desirable that the meeting of recognition and farewell should be held in the circle of their friends, before leaving home. The Secretaries in Boston heartily concurred in the arrangement, and deputed Secretary Alden to represent them on the occasion. Other services were omitted in the different churches, in order that pastors and people might participate in this one.

In the opening statement the pastor of the church, Rev. Dr. Vose, made brief mention of the ladies who had consecrated themselves to the service of Christ in foreign lands, and added, what was a surprise to many, that the parties in question were the first to represent the churches of the state in so important an undertaking.

Such an introduction seemed at once to invest them with additional honor as the first representatives of the churches on such a high and holy service. Several of the other pastors made addresses, one of whom took up the thought of self-denial, so prominent in the minds of many in connection with work in the foreign fields; and while admitting that in certain places there must needs.be trials and hardships, yet claiming that in any just estimate of affairs, the joys of the service far overbalanced its discomforts. No happier persons can be found than those enlisted in the work of foreign missions, as shown in the lives and testimony of the missionaries themselves. It was added by another speaker that persons would be happy in proportion as they became divested of selfish ends and aims, and devoted themselves to doing good to others, and hence, where consecration to Christ was entire, there would be experienced the supreme of earthly bliss. Whole-hearted, earnest missionaries were not, therefore, to be pitied, but to be congratulated, for the secret of bliss was theirs.

Dr. Alden, as the representative of the American Board, in accepting the missionaries, gave interesting details in regard to the fields of labor to which they were respectively assigned and the persons with whom they were to be associated, dwelling impressively on the thought which was always recognized in the Rooms of the Executive Committee,— that it is God who selects the missionaries, and appoints them their places of work; and in concluding, while referring to the important labors done by Christian women in extending the kingdom of Christ, he said the New Version had happily caught the true meaning of the eleventh verse of Psalm sixty-eight. " The Lord giveth the word: the women that published the tidings are a great host."

The meeting throughout was pervaded by a spirit of solemnity and power; and when Thomas Laurie, D.D., whose early consecration had been to mission-work in the Orient, and which he laid down, with such regret, in broken health, led the great congregation in prayer, and sought for those so soon to depart such vigor of health that they might never be constrained to return, the impression had probably reached its height that none then and there were so blessed as those two, henceforth to be known as our first foreign missionaries.

During the few days that remained before their departure, Miss Root, of the Madura Mission, and Miss Jillson, destined to Smyrna, were the recipients of generous tokens from friends. Their names and characters will be cherished in loving remembrance; and fervent prayers ascend in the meetings of the churches for rich blessings to attend them always. They sailed from New York on the morning of July 30th.   J. T.

WOMAN'S BOARD OF MISSIONS.

RECEIPTS FROM JULY 18 TO AUGUST 18, 1885.

MAINE.

Maine Branch. — Mrs. W. S. Dana,Treas. Williston Cong. Ch., $20; Bethel, First Ch., Aux., prev. contri. const. L. M. Miss Lucretia B. Colburn, $9, Second Ch., S. S., $21; Mechanic Falls, Aux., $19; Lewiston, Pine St. Ch., Aux., $30; Madison,Aux.,$4; Portland, Miss M. M. Holt's S. S. Class, $3; So. Bridgton, S. S., $30, ... $136 00
Castine. — Desert Palm Soc'y, prev. contri. const. L.M. Miss Mary F. Duren, ... 10 00
Oldtown. — Little Children's M. C., ... 2 50

    Total, $148 50

NEW HAMPSHIRE.

New Hampshire Branch.—Miss A. E. McIntire,Treas. Atkinson, Aux., $14, Flowers of Hope, prev. contri. const. L. M. Miss Mary A. Dow, $11; Bath, Aux., $18.40; Brentwood, Cheerful Givers, $10; Claremont, Aux., of wh. $25 const. L. M. Mrs. Sarah C. Chapin, $30; Cornish, Aux., $9.50; Goffstown, Aux., $24; Great Falls,Aux.,$50; Keene, First Cong. Ch., Aux., $43; Kingston, Aux., $15.65; Milford, Aux., $50, const. L. M's Mrs. Nathan Jewett, Mrs. Oliver H. Foster; New Boston,Aux., $8; No. Hampton, Aux., $22; Pembroke, Aux., $12; Salem, Aux., $10; Tamworth, Mrs. F. Davis, $25; Troy, Aux., $15.50; Wilton, Mistletoe Band, $5; Winchester, Aux., prev. contri. const. L. M. Mrs. Charlotte A. Smith, $21; Laconia, Aux., $25, ... $419 05
Franklin. — A Friend, ... 2 00

    Total, $421 05

VERMONT.

Vermont Branch.— Mrs. T. M. Howard, Treas. Burlington, Aux., $25; East Berkshire, Aux.,prev. contri. const.L.M. Mrs. E. W. Hatch, $6.50;

Essex Centre, Aux., $13; Jamaica, Willing Workers, const. L. M. Mrs. Lucy R. Kellogg, $25; Woodstock, Aux., prev. contri. const. L. M. Mrs. Paulina R. Haskell, $18, ... $87 50
Barre. — Ladies of Cong. Ch., 10 00
Peacham. — A Friend, ... 2 00
St. Johnsbury. — Member of No. Cong. Ch., ... 1 00

    Total, $100 50

MASSACHUSETTS.

Andover and Woburn Branch.— Miss E. F.Wilder,Treas. Lexington,Aux., $5.90; Billerica, Aux., $9; Lawrence, So. St. Ch., Aux., $13; No. Woburn, Aux., $11.30, ... $39 20
Berkshire Branch. — Mrs. S. N. Russell, Treas. Hinsdale, Egeirometha Soc'y, ... 10 00
Essex So. Co. Branch. — Miss S. W. Clark, Treas. Boxford, Earnest Workers, $25; Essex, Helping Hands, $44, ... 69 00
Franklin Co. Branch. — Miss L. A. Sparhawk, Treas. Ashfield, Aux., $45; Greenfield, Aux., $3.35, ... 48 35
Hampshire Co. Branch. — Miss I. G. Clarke, Treas. Hatfield, Aux., $82, Wide-Awakes, $23.35; No. Hatfield, Merry Winners, $14.75; Westhampton, M. C., $30, ... 150 10
Lawrence. — Lawrence St. Ch., Aux., of wh. $50 const. L. M's Mrs. Wm. P. Anderson, Miss Hannah Cole, ... 104 00
Leicester. — Strawberry Hill Gleaners, ... 7 50
Middlesex Branch.—Mrs. E. H. Warren, Treas. Saxonville, June Blossoms, ... 30 00
Norfolk and Pilgrim Branch.— Mrs. F. Shaw, Treas. Quincy, Aux., Mrs. Ira French, $1.10; Plymouth, Pilgrim Stepping Stones, $145; Randolph, Memorial M. C. $60; Brockton, Aux., $50, ... 256 10
Needham. — Joanna E. Mills, 50 00
Old Colony Branch. — Miss F. J. Runnels, Treas. New Bedford,Aux.,$210, Union Workers, F. M. Soc'y, $30; Attleboro Falls, Aux., $3; Fall River, Willing Helpers, $3, 246 00

Suffolk Branch. — Miss M. B. Child, Treas. Boston, Berkeley St. Ch., Y. L. M. C., $12.70; East Boston, Maverick Ch., Madura Aux., of wh. $25 by Mrs. Albert Bowker, const. L. M. Miss Mary T. Caldwell, $201; Roxbury, Eliot Aux., prev. contri. const. L. M. Miss Mary E. Bell, $20; Jamaica Plain, Central Cong. Ch., $126; Chelsea, Central Ch., Aux., $28; East Somerville, Franklin St. Ch., Aux., $25; Malden, Aux., const. L. M. Miss Esther Lowry, $25; Dedham, Asylum Dime Soc'y, $1.20; Foxboro, Aux., $35, ... $473 90

Worcester Co. Branch. — Mrs. G. W. Russell, Treas. No. Brookfield, Aux., $17.21; Happy Workers, $40; Millbury, Second Ch., Aux., $60; Southbridge, Aux., $20; Westboro, Aux., $35; Lancaster, Aux., prev. contri. const. L. M. Miss Carrie Litchfield, $15; Worcester, Woman's Miss'y Soc'y of Old South Ch., $50.78; Piedmont Ch., $45; Salem St. Ch., $30, ... 312 99

Wrentham. — Aux., ... 67 00

Total, ... $1,864 14

CONNECTICUT.

New Haven Branch. — Miss J. Twining, Treas. Bridgeport, Aux., of wh. $25 by Mrs. Mary W. Hawley, const. self L. M., and $25 by Mrs. Henry Elliott, const. L. M. Miss Jennie E. Sanderson, and $25 by Mrs. Lizzie Lockwood, const. L. M. Miss Mary E. Andrews, $115.07; No. Ch. S. S., $30; Brookfield Centre, Aux., $6.50; East Haven, Y. L. M. C., $7.74; Easton, Aux., $10; Greenwich, Bearers of Light, $24.43; Little Neighbors, $15.40; Litchfield, Aux., $62.17; Meriden, Centre Ch., Willing Workers, $30; Middletown, First Ch., Aux., $80; Gleaners, $40; New Britain, South Ch., Standard Bearers, $10; New Haven, United Ch., Y. L. M. C., $20; North Madison, Aux., $7.35; Norwalk, Aux., $100, Sunbeams, $4.50, S. S., $10; Ridgebury, Aux., $5; Salisbury, Aux., $35; Stratford, Y. L. M. C, $27; Wallingford, Aux., $34.78, $674 94

Hartford Branch — Miss A. Morris, Treas. Hartford,

Park Ch., Aux., $10; Fourth Ch., Aux., $25; Unionville, Aux., $22; Tolland, Aux., $8, $65 00

Stratford. — Y. L. M. C., ... 5 00

Total, ... $744 94

NEW YORK.

New York State Branch. — Mrs. G. H. Norton, Treas. Poughkeepsie, Young People's Aux., $25; Elmira, Park Ch., Aux., $30; Baiting Hollow, Aux., $10; Oswego, Y. L. M. S., $10; Jamestown, M. C., $25; Rochester, Mt. Hor, Miss'y Friends, $10.50; Oxford, Aux., $40, Little Women, $16; Brooklyn, Mrs. L. G. H., $10; Copenhagen, Aux., $20, ... $196 50

Rochester. — Mrs. George W. Davison, ... 2 00

Total, ... $198 50

PENNSYLVANIA.

Spring Creek. — Cong. Ch., $10 00

Phila. — Mrs. Kate W. Buck, const. self L. M., ... 25 00

Total, ... $35 00

FLORIDA.

St. Augustine. — Colored Union Bible School, ... $15 00

Total, ... $15 00

INDIANA.

Lowell. — Mrs. E. N. Morey, ... $3 00

Total, ... $3 00

MICHIGAN.

Grand Ledge. — Elizabeth T. Halcomb, ... $2 00

Covert. — Ladies' Miss'y Soc'y, 10 00

Total, ... $12 00

SOUTH AFRICA.

Inanda Seminary. — $5 00

Total, ... $5 00

General Funds, ... $3,547 63
Weekly Pledge, ... 1 34
Leaflets, ... 8 62
Morning Star, ... 4 05

Total, ... $3,561 64

MISS EMMA CARRUTH, Treasurer.

Board of the Interior.

CHINA.

TIMES OF REFRESHING.

BY MISS ADA HAVEN.

Miss Haven wrote from Peking, April 24th:—

WE are expecting four China Inland missionaries. Three of them belong to a party of seven University men just out, who have been holding revival meetings in Shanghai. Among the converts there is the rector of the foreign cathedral, who says if this is conversion, he never was converted before. He has been preaching fourteen years.

Again, May 7th, she writes:—

We have had a visit from some of Hudson Taylor's new missionaries. Among his recent accessions are seven or eight from Cambridge University. The seven who lately arrived in Shanghai are not all college men. One is from the army, and one from the Royal Artillery. Of the college men, one, Mr. Studd, was the champion cricketer, hero of many a field. Another one, of whom you will hear much, is Stanley Smith. One thing that surprised me much to hear was the interest now existing in England for the missionary cause, especially among the Cambridge students. At their farewell meetings there, fifty arose and pledged themselves to the work. I heard one man say, that in England there were at least a thousand men and women whose hearts were burning with desire to come to China. Though some may be prevented, the outcome of this must be a noble army of English missionaries for China.

From another letter we take the following:—

To tell you just what we have received would be a long story; and what we hope still further to receive would be a longer story still — one that will last to all eternity. I say we, for the foreign community has been shaken to its foundations. We have had meetings with the new-comers of the Inland Mission every afternoon and evening for the last ten days. They are over, now. The carts are being packed that are to take the three brethren away. What we have been praying for is the descent of the Holy Spirit. We have been literally tarrying for it, waiting to be endued with power from on high. We have all received a very special blessing. As yet it has manifested itself only in our own hearts, but we are still tarrying and waiting, and it must and will show itself in our work before long.

May 19*th.*   Perhaps I can get as far to-day as to tell you about these men.   There were three of the new-comers, and Mr. Baller, of Che Foo.   Mr. Baller is a very attractive man, tall, handsome, and very winning in his manners.   He and his wife have charge of the missionaries' children at Che Foo.   He came up to escort the young men, who, having just arrived, were of course helpless.   The Chinese were very much moved and interested with a talk he gave them on Sunday.   He took almost no part in the meetings for foreigners, leaving that to the young men. But he has the same thing that I have always observed in every one of that society whom I have met — a certain depth and earnestness of Christian character, and a consecration to the service of the Lord.   I thought first that this came from giving up all that makes life attractive in a worldly point of view, and going into the interior to live among the Chinese, in Chinese dress, living on Chinese food — in short, giving up everything.   But I know now what gives the consecration to the members of the Taylor Mission.   It consists simply in giving up everything else held dear, and tarrying for the Spirit, waiting to be filled.   We have been waiting together, all the missionaries of Peking.   Never have I attended such meetings before. No one could go and come away the same as when he went.   It seemed as if we were in the very presence-chamber.   The whole thought of these afternoon meetings with the Christians was not the framing of new petitions, but a claiming of the promises that I never thought we had any right to claim, supposing they had either been fulfilled at the day of Pentecost, or would not be fulfilled until the end of the world.   "But no," said Mr. Smith, quoting from Mr. Taylor; "he who is filled with the Spirit may claim the millennial promises."   And he went on to tell how we were commanded to be filled with the Spirit: "Be ye filled with the Holy Ghost."   First be emptied, then filled. ┼

20*th.* Yesterday I started to introduce the three men to you, and spoke only of Mr. Baller.   The three are Mr. Cassels, Mr. Hoste, and Mr. Stanley Smith.   Mr. Cassels is a regularly ordained clergyman of the Church of England, and was already placed over a charge.   How he ever came to be persuaded to break loose from this, I can hardly understand.   He is thoroughly loyal still to his church.   If he had been the only one visiting the place he would have made a great impression, for he had a kind of burning intensity and earnestness in pleading with sinners to come to the Saviour.   There was something, partly in the distinctness and earnestness of his utterance, partly in the intensity of his eyes, seeming to read one's every thought, but more in the fact that what he said came from his very heart, that gave to his words great power.

Mr. Hoste was as different as possible from both Mr. Baller and Mr. Cassels. A tall man, but with a kind of feminine gentleness about him both in voice, manner, and feature, clad in the cap and petticoats of his order, the usual Chinese dress, one would hardly take him to be an extraordinary man. Yet he left a position as officer of the Royal Artillery to come and be a missionary. I was commenting once on his apparent unfitness of character for the profession of a soldier. " But I would not like to be before his cannon," remarked Dr. Blodget; which, certainly, I could say too. Not having the rare social qualities of Mr. Baller, or the eloquence of Mr. Cassels, he said little, but he taught us much. He seemed to know nothing else but a burning, intense thirst to be filled with the Holy Spirit. His days were spent almost entirely in prayer, with frequent fasts. He has been a Christian only two years, having been converted under Mr. Moody's preaching.

But Stanley Smith — how shall I describe him? His is a face that would strike you in a crowd as a wonderful union of strength and sweetness. A noble face, you would say, strong and manly, with an intellectual forehead, with a firm yet gentle mouth. There was nothing feminine about him. One glance at his hands, even if you did not see his face, would be enough. When he first began to speak I did not like to see him gesture. I kept thinking of his hands, and it seemed as if I could see an invisible oar in the great round space between his forefinger and thumb. But as he went on I forgot all about him as an athlete, and of his triumphs as stroke-oar of the Cambridge eight, first oarsman of England. That he was powerful at the oar one can well believe; but now he wields what is still more powerful, " the sword of the Spirit." By the way, I never knew what that meant till now — a simple verse of the Bible, heard a thousand times before, piercing one's very heart because brought home by the Spirit. Stanley Smith was beautiful, learned, eloquent; yet all these things were against the impression he wished to produce — to make you think of nothing but the eternal truth; and after awhile you forgot that he spoke with the tongues of men and angels, and it was as if you heard only the voice of the Spirit speaking in your own heart, urging you to give up sin, and give yourself wholly to Christ. If this is what it is to be filled with the power of the Holy Ghost, we all want it. And yet, in our afternoon meetings for Christians, held from house to house, he was the most earnest of any of us in praying for the Spirit. It was as if the receiving but increased the capacity to receive.

The evening meetings were all held in our chapel, and all were invited, a circular being sent to every English-speaking resident. At these meetings the three young men sat on the platform, and all took part in the exercises.

┬ I do not see how anything could be a more perfect counterpart of the meeting in Jerusalem, where they tarried praying for the enduement of the Spirit — a company of Christians already under commission to go and preach the gospel; the whole world around them lying in wickedness, they and they only having a knowledge of the truth, and not yet having it brought home to their own hearts, still less having the power to bring it home to others — they in the capital of Western Asia, we in the capital of Eastern Asia, tarrying and waiting for the one thing, the baptism of the Spirit. We put aside all thoughts of anything else — forgot politics, left newspapers unopened; we were living with that little company, waiting for the outpouring. If anything occurred to remind us that we were living in the nineteenth century, it seemed to come as a matter of surprise. We were of many lands,— English, Scotch, Welsh, Irish, German, Dutch, Americans,— but we knew only one kingdom, the kingdom of Heaven, and were determined to take it by violence. We forgot all distinctions of sect, Presbyterians and Congregationalists joining in "amens" with our Episcopal brethren as heartily as the Methodists themselves, and all men and women ready to testify of the Spirit as they were moved by the Holy Ghost. . . . I have had my eyes opened to so much light at once that I feel dazed. But I shall begin a study of the Bible such as I never had before. I never knew half that was meant by "clinging to the promises." I am quite convinced that this is the only way we can hope to win victories for Christ in China. In yesterday afternoon's meeting it was very plainly brought out, this conflict that is going on with "the heavenlies," this great battle that is being fought out with the princes of the air. We who have been fearing an actual warfare could realize it in its force. We have been trying to fight these powers, and have not prevailed. When we are endued with power from on high, the conflict must begin with ourselves. Then, when the Spirit has overcome in our own hearts, this same power will go forth as an overcoming force against the spiritual wickedness in high places. We have not won, yet we feel that the battle is ours. The Spirit of the living God must conquer. China must belong to Christ. China *will* belong to Christ. We will fight out the battle on our knees, and we shall prevail.

TURKEY AND INDIA.

SCHOOLS AND BIBLE-WOMEN.

One of our secretaries, an indefatigable explorer, who is determined to follow with her pen and her prayers all the dimes and pennies sent to minister to heathen women, has lately been making inquiries about Bible-readers and native teachers in Turkey and India. Some of the many items she has gathered we are privileged to give this month. We are greatly indebted to missionaries of other Boards for this information. Some of our smaller auxiliaries that support native schools and Bible-readers, if they study these items, will never have to ask again, "Where does my money go?" Of two schools supported by our Board near Broosa, Turkey, Rev. T. A. Baldwin writes:—

I CONGRATULATE you on being interested in the support of the schools at Soloz and Yenije, for they are the two best out-stations of the Brooza field. Though comparatively new, they have already progressed far beyond places much longer occupied. The former has its own church and school-building combined, recently built, the expense having been equally shared by the Board and the native community; and the latter has secured and walled in a site for church and school, and is waiting only for governmental permission to build.

At Soloz there is a mixed school of thirty or more pupils, who have been taught the past year by a young man, who was once a student for the ministry in one of our station-classes; but next year, beginning July 1st, they are to have a young lady teacher from the Bagchejuk boarding-school, taught by Miss Farnham (W. B. M.) and Miss Lella C. Parsons.

If I am not mistaken, you are interested in one or both of these young ladies, and will be glad to know that their influence extends beyond the limits of their own station, and is appreciated and valued by their neighbors.

The school at Yenije has about the same number of pupils as that at Soloz, and is also a mixed school. Up to the present time it has been taught by the preacher, assisted to some extent by his wife; but they expect to have a better organization of their school as soon as the new building is completed, and they will then employ a graduate of some of our girls' boarding-schools.

It is almost needless to repeat that great prominence is given to Bible study and to religious instruction in all our schools. We count them very valuable and necessary auxiliaries to our missionary-work, and are very grateful to the Woman's Boards and the societies who so nobly sustain them.

Mrs. Emily Fairbank Smith, of Tillipally, Ceylon, kindly sends the following letter describing the work of the Bible-women under her care, three of whom are supported by our Board.

The work for women is opening up on every side. Every month I hear of new pupils who are willing to be taught. I know of twenty-five in one village, twelve in another, and sixteen close by, so that I have simply to shut my ears to the calls. Even now I am greatly burdened, and I answer to all the calls, "When the Lord sends money I will send teachers." As you will see by the table I inclose, I am now teaching (with the help of eleven native

women) four hundred and fifty-six adult females, nearly all of them
mothers. The average age is twenty-three. The great majority
of girls are married young, but actual child-marriage is comparatively rare. You will also see, that three hundred and twelve are
farmers' wives and daughters, all women with dowries, and almost
without exception land-owners. There are twenty-two Brahmans.
There are now one hundred and twenty-six who can read the
Bible. Alas! they do not care enough to read it for themselves,
but if I send them teachers and fresh books, and keep up their
interest, they will read it. In time I hope the habit will be
formed, and a real love for the truth will take the place of indifference. "Home, Sweet Home" and "Jessica's First Prayer" are
such nice books for this class of women! "Tales of the Reformation" is now just out, and "Moody's Sermons" (six of them).
"Life of Miss Fiske" is much liked by many of the more thoughtful ones. The lives of "Sarah," "Mary," etc., in tract form, are
also attractive. There is quite a collection of books now. I am
very anxious to have help, and could then increase my staff of
teachers. I could also increase the number of pupils by a hundred or more in two months, had I the funds. "Who goeth a
warfare-anytime at his own charges," has often come to my mind
as the work has increased on my hands. Think of it — four hundred and fifty-six adult pupils; and to pay my teachers, I receive
less than $10 a month. Last year, Miss Hillis, formerly of our
mission, and the originator of this work at the station, sent me
$25 for the "Helping Hands," of whom more presently.

Now, my dear friends, I have felt heretofore that if the Lord
would have the work go on, he would incline the hearts of those
at home to send me help out of their abundance. Of late I have
thought, perhaps, it was not sufficiently understood how wide a
door was thrown open here, and that I ought to write and tell you
more about it. I am paying my teachers at the rate of one rupee
for every eight pupils. They all feel that this is not sufficient,
but I can afford no more at present.

All my teachers living within half a mile are required to come
every Tuesday afternoon at four o'clock to our church, to teach
the members of the "Helping Hands." These are very poor
women, mostly of the lower classes, though twenty-one belong
to the farmer, or Velalah caste. They come at four o'clock,
and are divided into eight classes, according to their proficiency —
one class using the Sabbath-school lessons (International), another
class, of old women, simply hearing the lessons read and explained, committing the Golden Texts to memory, etc. At five
o'clock all come together for singing and Scripture recitations.

Closing with the Lord's Prayer, they are dismissed, and usually pass out in single file.

The attendance has been large for the past year, averaging eighty-two for the year 1884. You will not be surprised that it took about six hundred yards of cloth to give each one a dress, the number of yards and the quality differing according to the attendance. This had been so remarkably good, that one hundred and eight women received cloths, to enable them to come to the class clean and whole. The cloth given is all unbleached muslin, about one and a half yards wide, costing about twenty cents a yard. Each receives from four to eight yards, according to the attendance registered. I wish I could give each of the teachers a cloth, too. They are all poor women, and do not receive a cent for this special work. It is very unpleasant work, and this will explain itself when I tell you that many of the women are so poor that they have no wells and no bathing privileges. What to do about the matter is a great question with us, for really they are not wholly to blame for their unwashed condition. Many of them, however, do keep clean, comb their hair very neatly, and look quite respectable.

Perhaps this glimpse of the well-to-do farmers' wives and daughters and the poor members of the "Helping Hand," may lead you to think of us, pray for us, and help some poor women to learn to read the Bible. This is our aim — Bible-reading. Who will come to "the help of the Lord against the mighty" in this battle with ignorance, superstition, and heathenism? Will you?

And Mr. Smith writes: —

One of your Bible-women is Mrs. Chinarchy Chinnapody. This name means in English, Mrs. Little-Mother Little-Boy. Its owner is one of our best Bible-women, though all of them are good and true. Chinarchy was educated in the village station-school. She has a remarkable memory and a wonderful knowledge of the Bible. She knows over twenty-five psalms and many chapters of the Bible by heart, and can tell Bible stories very effectively. The work of the Bible-women is twofold — teaching women and grown-up girls to read, or helping them keep up the habit, and telling the gospel message from house to house. All do the former, but only the more mature and experienced are allowed to devote their afternoons to the strictly evangelical work.

MICRONESIA.

CHRISTMAS GREETINGS.

If any reader should consider these Christmas greetings out of season, let her thoughts be tender and her prayers most earnest for our dear young lady teachers, whose news of the home-land is often just as much out of season. And when they read of Miss Cathcart's hope for a teacher to be sent by the Morning Star, and remember that it has been only a "hope deferred," let them hasten to send

"Around by the way of heaven
Their loving sympathies."

A "MERRY CHRISTMAS" and "Happy New Year" to you far over the sea. It may be it will reach you in time for '85 or '86. At any rate I will take the opportunity I have to send it as far as Ponape.

Yesterday, to give variety to Christmas, there came at early dawn the cry " Sail ho !" It proved to be a schooner run by one of the Captain Kiestels. She has been cruising about for four or five months, so there came no news of the outer world; but it is such a little while since the Jennie Walker came that we don't begin to feel the need of news. Well, I don't know that you would call it so very short a time, four months; but I did not think till after I wrote it how it might seem to you in the home-land.

The vessel came from the Gilbert Islands, via Namerik, and brought a letter from Joralik, our teacher there. He writes encouragingly of the work; over a hundred in the school, and all eager to learn. But there comes with it a plea that came by the other vessel from Jaluit and Ailinlaplap, " Cannot you send us books? We are poor for books;" yet months must pass before their needs can be supplied. When I see how greatly our people need the Testament that will come when Dr. and Mrs. Pease return*, I think nothing of the increased care, work, and responsibility that must come while they are absent, and am glad they are gone.

It is years since there has been such a scarcity of native food on the island as this fall — for over three months but little bread-fruit and but little taro. The Kusaians have gone to the mountains and hunted for wild yams, often requiring nearly the whole day to procure enough for their families. As a consequence, there has been but little that we could buy for our school; and as our usual supply of rice did not come, the outlook has not been very encouraging. We have been using our graham flour and beans for the scholars, and now bread-fruit is beginning to ripen, and we succeeded in buying a hundred pounds of rice of this vessel, and may secure a box of hard bread; so I think we shall, by careful planning, make both ends meet till June, when we hope our next year's supplies will come.

We omit an earnest plea for more money to educate native teachers, because it was published in the September *Missionary Herald*, but must not fail to give Miss Cathcart's requests for prayers. Her friends at home cannot read these too often.

You know this is the first time that I have had any real care and responsibility since I entered the work. One can't have very much until the language is learned, while at the same time new missionaries find plenty that they can do. The Lord has wonderfully helped and strengthened me, and with all my heart I thank him. I often think the strength for new duties comes in answer to prayers of Christian friends; and I rejoice in the thought that now, when you come to know our greater need of help from above for this year, you will exercise your prayers in our behalf.

Our prayers rise more tenderly and earnestly, if it can be, now, as the old year draws to a close and the " Week of Prayer" is at hand, that our land and friends may receive richer spiritual blessings; and that, in answer to prayer, thousands of souls may enter upon a new life at the beginning of the new year. And you who have not been on mission-ground cannot know how we long for an outpouring of the Holy Spirit here in our field. You who have

---

* The Morning Star carried out the Book of Genesis and an arithmetic prepared by Dr. Pease.

stood as we stand, in the midst of dawning light, know just how to feel.

The Kusaians, with both our schools, are to unite in prayer for the same subjects each day. We arranged the subjects, and I have written them in Kusaian, with Bible references, and sent them to Sela. It is surprising how rapidly I gain in using both Marshall and Kusaian, now that there is no one else to use them with the natives. I don't believe I should read or hear any English this year, except what I need for teaching, if it were not for Miss Palmer. I am too tired to read much in the evening, but she reads aloud for half an hour or so. She has read the life of Mrs. Prentiss, and we enjoyed and were helped by it. Now·we are visiting our brothers and sisters in other mission-fields, and sharing in feeling their joys and sorrows. Then almost every evening we hunt words for the next day's spelling lesson.

Two months have passed since Dr. and Mrs. Pease left, and we hope for only six more before some one comes in the Morning Star to strengthen our hands and take charge of this school. God only knows what is in waiting for us; pray that we may be prepared for all that he has prepared for us. And now a loving good-bye if this reaches you. LLLIE S. CATHCART.

Home Department.

STUDIES IN MISSIONARY HISTORY.

INSTEAD of the usual lesson this month, we offer some suggestions in regard to thank-offerings, in the hope that the first autumn meetings of auxiliaries will be "feasts of ingathering."

We hope to resume the lessons next month.

THANK-OFFERINGS.

WITH the mellow light of autumn days comes the happy work of harvest time, and the memory of our feasts of ingathering held one year ago. We are sure that all who have once joined in such an occasion will not let the season pass without repeating it; and to any of our auxiliaries who have this year to celebrate their first "thank-offering meeting," we reach the hand of congratulation that they have thus come to a new opportunity. Friday, August 21st, was our day at 75 Madison Street.

Only one basket stood on our table this year, and it bore the word "Self-denial." We are not sure but the reverse of the card was "Thank-offering." We know it well might be; for must we not hold any gift of thankfulness incomplete if it does not touch the point of self-denial? One gold-piece was enfolded with the words, "A thank-offering as well as a gift of sacrifice"; and most were accompanied with texts of praise.

Letters from far and near testified to the preciousness of the occasion, and made us resolve that this should be to us a regular annual feast.

One, referring to our treasury, gave this text as our incentive: "According to your faith be it unto you." Another, who has lately left us, and is now about returning to her work in China, said, "I give *myself* anew, a glad thank-offering to the Lord."

We commend to our auxiliaries as the theme for thank-offering meetings, " Causes for thankfulness in the history of the American Board," now completing its seventy-fifth year.   Let us remind ourselves, by some review of its history, how the work begun in the anxiety of untried seed-sowing seventy-five years ago, has grown into large harvests already gathered; while broadening and whitening fields call earnestly for more laborers.   The early workers, seeing the heathen world closed to them, prayed for open doors; now their abundantly answered prayer is seen in open doors in every part of the earth, inviting the Church of God to enter in.

It is a good time to seek the answers to prayer in which this history abounds; the casting away of idols in the Sandwich Islands; the large ingatherings of souls there, and, later, in Japan and Turkey; and to be reminded of Elijah as we read the story of answered prayer told by Mr. Logan in his "Work of God in Micronesia."

The lives of officers of the Board, as well as of its missionaries, have given us a rich legacy of prayer and faith of which the fruits are not all garnered.   We may well learn of them, and of the families born to missionary work as to an inheritance — the Gulicks, Scudders, Riggs, Schaufflers, Binghams, and others.   Shall we not give thanks for such a line of nobility in the kingdom of our Lord?

We were privileged in having at our meeting the presence of foreign workers, who are at home for rest.   We wish we could give to every auxiliary the inspiration of such presence — the contagion of their enthusiasm, the impulse of their words, and glowing faces. We *will* give you the thought we received from one who spoke to us: " O let every gift be winged with a spirit of thankfulness and praise, and sweetened and perfumed by loving and consecrating prayers.   Remember, it is an unblest offering which is given without prayer."

NOTICE.

THE Annual Meeting of the Woman's Board of Missions of the Interior will be held in the First Congregational Church in St. Louis, on Wednesday and Thursday, Nov. 4th and 5th.   Every auxiliary from Ohio to the Rocky Mountains is invited to send one or more delegates.   See Article VIII. of the Constitution. . . And it is especially requested that, if possible, the President, Secretary, and Treasurer of every State Branch will be present.

The ladies of St. Louis hope for large delegations from the several States, and extend a general invitation to all who are interested.   Railroad notices will be given in Mission Studies and *The Advance.*

CORRECTION.

IN a note in the July issue we inadvertently spoke of Miss Wright as in charge of the Marsovan Boarding-School.   She calls our attention to it, and asks us to state that she is only assisting Miss Fritcher in the care of that school.   We are glad to make the correction.

RECEIPTS OF THE WOMAN'S BOARD OF MISSIONS OF THE INTERIOR.

MRS. J. B. LEAKE, TREASURER.

FROM JULY 18, 1885, TO AUG. 18, 1885.

ILLINOIS BRANCH.— Mrs. W. A. Talcott, of Rockford, Treas. *Altona*, Mrs. P. F. M., 1; *Beecher*, 10; *Champaign*, 10; *Chandlerville*, 5.90; *Chicago*, Miss M. S. Taylor, 3, Union Park Ch., of wh. 25 from Mrs. S. H. Clark, const. L. M. Miss Emma A. Isham, 25 from Mrs. F. A. Noble, const. L. M. Mrs. Alice L. Williams, 150, New England Ch., 12, Mrs. W. A. M., certificates, 1, Lincoln Park Ch., 25; *Danville*, South Ch., 22; *De Kalb*, 4.50; *Elmwood*, 14; *Galesburg*, Brick Ch., 18.50; *Geneva*, 16; *Hamilton*, 8; *Huntley*, 9.25; *Marseilles*, of wh. 16 Thank-offering, 22.50; *Naperville*, 10; *Nunda*, Miss M. L. W., 1; *Oak Park*, 19; *Oneida*, Mrs. M. F. H., 13.75; *Princeton*, 10; *Quincy*, 15; *Rockford*, 1st Ch., 25.61; 2d Ch., of wh. 25 from W. A. T., const. L. M. Mrs. W. A. Talcott, 50.50; *Waverly*, 11.25; *Wheaton*, 5, $493 76

JUNIOR: *Aurora*, 1st Ch., Y. L. Soc., 15; New Eng. L. M., Helping Hands, 40; *Batavia*, Y. P. Soc., const. L. M. Mrs. Will Wolcott, 25; *Chicago*, Union Park Ch., Y. L. Soc., 61.99; *Elgin*, Y. L. Soc., 18.75; *Evanston*, Y. L. Soc., 29; *Huntley*, Harvesters, 5.38; *Paxton*, Girls' Miss. Soc., 10, 205 12

JUVENILE: *Aurora*, New Eng. Ch., Little Thumbs, 15.50; *Cary Station*, Ada Smith, 30 cts., *Chicago*, Union Park Ch., Emma's Pennies, 23 cts., Morning Star, certificate, 10 cts., *Galesburg*, Brick Ch., Mission Band, 8; *La Grange*, Cheerful Givers, 3; *Maywood*, certificate, 10 cts., *Providence*, Mission Band, 25; *Ravenswood*, Coral Workers, 14.58,   66 81

Total, $765 69

IOWA.

IOWA BRANCH. — Mrs. E. R. Potter, of Grinnell, Treas. *Atlantic*, 8.40; *Brush Creek*,

Mrs. D. Robbins, 1.05; *Creston*, 20; *Dunlap*, 27; *Grinnell*, 49.15; *Iowa City*, Mrs. J. L. Pickard, const. Mrs. Julia B. Clark, L. M., 25; *Magnolia*, 4.50; *Monticello*, 17.35; *McGregor*, 8.22; *Sioux City*, G. R. Smith, 5; *Toledo*, Mrs. E. N. Barker, 25.30; *Tabor*, 24; *Waverly*, 15, $229 95

JUNIOR: *Grinnell*, Iowa College, Miss. Soc., 70.07; *Tabor*, Y. L. M. Soc., 10,   80 07

JUVENILE: *Brush Creek*, A Little Boy, 25 cts.; *Cromwell*, Harvey Allen and Fanny Bacon, 30 cts.; *Durant*, S. S.; 3.00; *Grove Township*, Union S. S., 1.70; *Humboldt*, S. S., 2.30; *Iowa City*, Eva May Jones, Cora M. Hughes, Lizzie Davis, Cynthia Davis, Anna E. Roberts, and Hannah Kline Smith, 50 cts; *Marengo*, Bertha Pearce, 20 cts.; *Sibley*, Mission Band, 4.04,   12 29

Total, $322 31

KANSAS.

KANSAS BRANCH.— Mrs. A. L. Slosson, of Leavenworth, Treas. *Brookville*, 3; *Diamond Springs*, 4; *Fairview*, 15; *Leavenworth*, 5; *Sterling*, 5; *Stockton*, 5; *Topeka*, Mrs. Rippey, 25; *Wakefield*, Bible School, 10; *Waushara*, 1.25, $73 25

JUNIOR: *Sterling*, 4; *Topeka*, 25,   29 00

JUVENILE: For Morning Star, *Lawrence*, 20 cts.; *Topeka*, 10 cts.,   30

Total, $102 55

MICHIGAN.

MICHIGAN BRANCH. — Mrs. Charles E. Fox, of Detroit, Treas. *Alpena*, 25; *Alpine and Walker*, 10; *Ann Arbor*, 15.82; *Chelsea*, 10; *Clinton*, 9; *Detroit*, Woodward Ave. Ch., 30; *Dowagiac*, 5.50; *Grand Rapids*, 36; *Greenville*, 30; *Imlay City*, 10; *Ionia*, 4.55; *Middlville*, 2.50; *Pottersville*, Mrs. B. Sanders, 2.00; *Sand-*

stone, 6.00; *Union City,* of wh. 25 const. L. M. Mrs. H. A. Corbin, 45.35; *Vermontville,* 16.80; *Victor,* 13, — $271 52
JUNIOR: *St. John's,* Young Ladies, and Children's Soc., — 13 00
JUVENILE: *Memphis,* Cheerful Workers, 5.00; *Sandstone,* Children's Soc., 8.75, — 13 75

FOR MORNING STAR MISSION:—
Memphis, — 70

Total, — $298 97

MINNESOTA.

MINNESOTA BRANCH.—Mrs. E. M. Williams, of Northfield, Treas. *Excelsior,* 5.98; *Litchfield,* 5.70; Mrs. L. B. C., 40 cts.; *Minneapolis,* Plymouth Ch., Scandinavian Mission Soc., 32.28; *Northfield,* 10.25; *Spring Valley,* 3.75; *Worthington,* 6, — $64 36
JUVENILE: *Dodge Center,* Island Miss. Band, 3; *Litchfield,* Pres. S. S., 3, — 6 00

Total, — $70 36

OHIO.

OHIO BRANCH.—Mrs. Geo. H. Ely, of Elyria, Treas. *Akron,* 86.14; *Berea,* 14; *Cincinnati,* Central Ch., 86.50; *Cleveland,* 1st Ch., 15; *Cleveland,* Plymouth Ch., 37; *Columbus,* 1st Ch., 25; *Gambier,* Mrs. Sawer, 5; *Hudson,* 5; *Mantua,* 7.50; *Oberlin,* 66; *Painesville,* 65; *Steuben,* 8; *Tallmadge,* 24.70; *Toledo,* 1st Ch., 110, — $539 84
JUNIOR: *Hudson,* Y. L. S., 25; *Painesville,* Y. L. Soc., 20, — 45 00
JUVENILE: *Bellevue,* Happy Workers, 10; *Bristolville,* S. S., 1; *Conneaut,* M. B., 5; *Mantua,* S. S., 2.50; *Oberlin,* Cheerful Workers, 27.67, — $46 17

— $631 01
Less expenses, — 1 00

Total, — $630 01

PENNSYLVANIA.

Allegheny, Y. P. Soc., Morning Star Mission, — $2 60

Total, — $2 60

NORTH DAKOTA BRANCH.

Mrs. R. C. Cooper, of Cooperstown, Treas. *Fargo,* 25, — $25 00

Total, — $25 00

ROCKY MOUNTAIN BRANCH.

Mrs. H. R. Jones, of South Pueblo, Col., Treas. *Cheyenne,* 50; *Denver,* 2d Ch., 4.60; *Highlands,* 10; *Longmont,* 7; *Manitou,* Aux., 5; Mrs. Bickford, 2; *South Pueblo,* 10.75, — $89 35
JUNIOR: *South Pueblo,* Y. L. Soc., — 5 00
JUVENILE: *Longmont,* S. S., — 11 00

Total, — $105 35

TENNESSEE.

Chattanooga, Miss L. M. Lawson, const. self L. M., 25, — $25 00

Total, — $25 00

WISCONSIN.

WISCONSIN BRANCH. — Mrs. R. Coburn, of Whitewater, Treas. *Bloomer,* 2.08; *Brandon,* 2.85; *Fort Howard,* 1.05; *Fulton,* by Mrs. Copely, 1; *Janesville,* 46.24; *Kinnickinnick,* 3.10; *Lancaster,* 7.50; *Monroe, Conn.,* Mrs. F. A. and Miss H. L. Curtis, 20; *Ripon,* const. L. M. Mrs. E. A. Lockwood and Mrs. Anna M. Congdon, 50.60; *West Salem,* 14.87; *Whitewater,* 2, — $151 29
JUNIOR: *Lancaster,* 11; *Milwaukee,* Grand Ave., Young Ladies, 25, — 36 00
JUVENILE: *Gay's Mill,* 3; *La Crosse,* Little Helpers, 6; *Ripon,* Do Goods, 5; *Sparta,* 5.25, — 19 25
FOR MORNING STAR: *Milwaukee,* Grand Ave. Ch., Children's Mission Band, 50; *Ripon,* 1; *River Falls,* 6.90, — 57 90

— $264 44
Less expenses, — 15 28

Total, — $249 16

TURKEY.

Marash, by Miss C. Shattuck, Meuneoveri Mezzelet, or Miss'y Soc. of Girls' College, — $22 85

Total, — $22 85

MISCELLANEOUS.

Sale of "Coan's Life," 6; of articles donated, 1.50 — $7 50

Total, — $7 50

Receipts for the month, — $2,627 35
Previously acknowledged, — 23,320 06

Total since Oct. 22, 1884, — $25,947 41

Board of the Pacific.

EXTRACTS FROM LETTER FROM MRS. BALDWIN.

BROOSA, June 22, 1885.

. . . ON Sunday last our Sunday-school exercises were disturbed by a violent thunder-shower, preceded by a sudden wind, whirling the dust in clouds everywhere. Sitting out on our little balcony as it subsided, I heard the voice of one of the younger children saying, "Mrs. Baldwin, do you see the rainbow? God will bring no more flood on the earth." And looking up, I saw a beautiful bow spanning the sky, and rejoiced in its beauty; while a deeper joy came from the thought that little Narcisse connected so quickly the sign and the promise. Well for us if we always see the "bow in the clouds."

During the closing weeks of the spring term, just before Easter, we had great cause for solicitude on account of the prevalence of small-pox in the city, and especially in this quarter where our school is. We took every precaution possible to preserve the health of our large family, even suspending the day-scholars for a time, and omitting the usual public closing exercises. It seems almost a miracle that we escaped; but to us who prayed so earnestly during those days, it came like a direct answer to prayer, and our hearts are filled with thankfulness yet whenever we think of it. On account of our carefulness we lost two scholars for this term. One went home to her village in Semirdesh, for vacation; and though we warned her not to go to the house of her relatives, where the disease was, she disobeyed, and we felt we could not receive her when school opened. Another was a new applicant— a promising girl; but there had been a case of the worst kind in the family, and after allowing the full time for disinfecting, the remainder of the year seemed too short to make it worth while to change her from the school where she was.

The natives seem to us perfectly reckless about such things; they hardly ever isolate the sick ones — in fact, I knew of one case where the baby was put right into the bed of the patient, so that he might take it, and be free from it afterward. We told them some of the strict rules and regulations at home; and while some seemed to regard us with a sort of pity, that we should be so afraid, others took some useful hints. The wonder here is, that having once begun, the disease should ever find a place to stop; one would expect it to go on indefinitely. But the Lord is merciful. As we go out for our walks we see the badly-marked faces of those who recovered, and the sight makes us feel still more thankful for our deliverance.

Such a quiet school-closing we have seldom had; but scholars and friends all seemed to appreciate and respect our motives, and so accepted the disappointment very gracefully.

. . . The obstacles to be overcome here seem to us no greater than those in other parts of the field; perseverance, patience, and looking above for help, alone can win the victory.

Our beautiful natural position, with the nice buildings and grounds, and such an interesting set of girls to labor for, is to me an attractive place for missionary effort; and if the Lord continues to bless us as he has in the past, what more can we ask? . . .

One action of the mission touches our work here in this station pretty closely; namely, the removal of the ladies connected with the school (Miss Twitchell and Mrs. Newell) to a city missionary work in Constantinople, now under the care of Mrs. Schneider and Miss Gleason. We regret this breaking up, but we hope such successors may speedily be found that the school may begin its next year at the usual time. . . . Meanwhile I'll try to stand in the breach, though I have hardly the physical strength for it that I had five years ago. But my faith and hope are stronger, for the Lord has helped me most graciously, and accepted, I humbly believe, what I have tried to do for his little ones, though I wonder that he could do so. You have helped me more than you know by your sympathy and encouragement, and your share in the work is probably greater than mine.

. . . It is now Thursday evening, and almost time to take my little flock to prayer-meeting. I think I have told you that one week we have it in the schoolroom in Greek, and the alternate week at the chapel, in Turkish, when my husband has charge of it.

It is Ramazan now, the long fast of the Turks, and the cannon has just announced the hour of sunset — a joyful sound to those who have eaten nothing since dawn of day.

A pleasant incident of to-day was a call from an Armenian pastor from Constantinople, who gave us our first lessons in Armenian eighteen years ago. With his white beard he looked very patriarchal, and his face fairly shone he was so pleased with all he saw. He will be with us on the Sabbath, and take part in the exercises, as we gather once more round the table of the Master.

With much love,

T. J. BALDWIN.

An African trader said to a missionary, "There must have been a lot of heathen people joining your church, because they have been here buying dresses, shawls, etc." This is merely one illustration of how Christianity promotes commerce.

LETTER FROM AFRICA.

GROUTVILLE, NATAL, May 12, 1885.

To the Woman's Board of Missions of the Pacific : —

DEAR FRIENDS: In my last letter I told you a little of my work among the outside people, and now I will tell you more of this pleasant work for the Lord; for it is pleasant, though so beset with difficulties. Some seem ready to hear and heed, while others are totally deaf to "the old, old story." Sometimes we find these two extremes in one family. Umsikaba is a woman in whom we have felt much interest. She gave her heart to God when Mr. Wilcox was laboring at Mapumulo, before her arrival. We noticed her as one who seemed an attentive listener to the truth. On inquiry, she told me that she loved Jesus, and was trying to follow him; and when the subject of beer-drinking was placed before her, she was willing to leave it, and took the ribbon. Since then, whenever her poor health permitted, she has been a faithful attendant at our meetings, and earnest in her service of God. On being asked if she would join the church, she at first expressed her unwillingness, on account of her ignorance (for she does not know how to read); but Mr. Holbrook invited her into his class of inquirers, where she has since been under instruction. When again asked to unite with God's people, we found that she stood in fear of her heathen husband, though she was willing to obey God rather than him. As she did not wish to join the church till he returned from a journey, we consented; and when he came back, Mr. Holbrook gained his consent to her union with God's people. Umsikaba seemed very glad that she could at least be numbered among the followers of Christ, and the first Sabbath in this month she was to publicly confess her Saviour. The day arrived, but she was not there, and we found that her husband had forbidden her to come. Mr. Holbrook again talked with him, but he persisted in his refusal, and so Umsikaba is in deep trouble. We hope that she may be given strength to obey God rather than her wicked husband. Pray for her, dear friends, that "her faith fail not."

We have been deeply interested in another family who, when we came, were numbered among the heathen, though, through Mr. Wilcox's faithful labors, they had heard the Word, and the mother seems to have found the Saviour, even when she is so ignorant. Gradually, she, with her husband and children, have come into the light. They have gladly adopted civilized dress, and four children attend our station-school, walking a long distance. We hope that before long the husband may yield his will to that of God.

Our station-school has increased in numbers from twenty-five to fifty during the past year, and we hope it may, before long, number seventy-five. Many of the kraal people are sending their children, and you would enjoy seeing the interest with which they don their first civilized dress.

Some months ago I talked to the children about earning some money to give to Jesus, and tried to induce them to plant small gardens, the proceeds of which they should use for this purpose. I think the gardens were, for the most part, not a success, but two weeks ago I told the children to bring what they had on Saturday, and Sunday would be the time for their offering. There were quite a number who brought little baskets of corn, and Sunday more than twenty came to the table with their offerings. It was a pleasant sight, and enjoyed by all. Other children wanted to send their share, and so on Monday I think ten or twelve more came with their gifts. I believe more than five shillings ($1.25) were thus given by the children, which, in most cases, was their first offering to the Lord. The effort awakened so much interest that I think it will be repeated, and thus these dark little hearts may be brought to labor for others still more degraded.

There is so much to do among these people, that I am too apt to look upon the discouraging side. Heathenism is so heathenish, degradation is so degrading, that it clings with dreadful tenacity, even to those who are trying to do better. Pray for the Christians here, as well as the heathen, that they may be kept from the contagious influence of evil around them.

Sincerely, your sister-worker,

SARAH L. HOLBROOK.

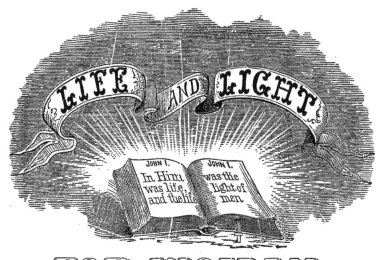

FOR WOMAN.

VOL. XV. NOVEMBER, 1885. No. 11.

MEXICO.

PERSECUTED FOR CHRIST'S SAKE.

BY MRS. H. M. BISSELL.

WE spent about seven months, lately, in Tlajomulco, a pueblo twenty miles from Guadalajara. It has the reputation of being unusually liberal. So it is, so far as any general and public molestation of Protestants is concerned; but occasionally cases come to our notice of persecution in the family. The latest of these was of a dear girl living in our own family.

For more than a year, ever since she began to show an interest in the gospel, she had been unable to live with her parents, who were bitterly opposed; her mother on one occasion having beaten her, and showing in every way her hatred of her daughter's choice.

Feliz was part of the year out at service, part of the time was in Miss Haskins' school, where she showed much interest in study. I believe she had begun during the year past to learn to read, that she might read the Bible. At the March communion she was baptized and received into the church, giving good evidence of a renewed heart. She has often surprised me by the care she still showed for her mother, going occasionally to see her, and giving her money from her slender earnings. I felt she was rightfully entitled to keep for her own needs all she could earn, as she had no longer any home.

She had gladly consented to go with us to our present home in La Barca, about a hundred miles away. One day, just before we left, her mother came to the door and requested her to come to the house at evening. I sent another girl to accompany her, who, after an hour, returned quite excited, saying they had forcibly detained Feliz, and declared with many threats that she should never return to us. We were much afraid she would be carried away, especially when neither that night nor the next day could any tidings be had of her. Mr. Bissell went repeatedly to the village authorities, to see if there was any help through them; but, although Liberals, their own interests would prevent their taking any active measures in her behalf. He found, also, that the law declares an unmarried woman subject to her parents until thirty years of age.

Sabbath morning, during Sabbath-school, she came hurrying into church, and took a seat by my side. They had brought her to our house to get her clothes, and she slipped across to the church. Her father was with her, and sat down in the door. Soon after her mother entered, and demanded that she go immediately out; she made quite a disturbance, but prudently restrained herself from violence or threats. We insisted that she be allowed to remain until the close, and the mother at last went out leaving her in charge of her father. The poor girl trembled and cried, in evident terror, and told me she knew the woman had a knife with her.

I was very glad of the chance I had to talk with her after service. She said that first (Friday) night she was taken to the house of the *cura*, and locked in a room otherwise occupied by hens and numerous vermin. In the morning they tried to make her take part in the mass, which she refused to do. The *cura* sought to persuade her; others have said she was quite able to answer him — that he even went to consult his Bible, to see if she quoted correctly!

It was very hard to advise her to return home quietly, but we felt that in the end her cause was much safer, if she could be declared free by the law, than if she escaped, and we would see what could be done through the higher officials in Guadalajara.

It seems from that time her mother was determined to stamp out her Protestantism — "to exorcise the Devil," as they say. She was taken to the *cura*, beaten in his presence, to compel her to perform the ceremonies, and placed in the *ejercicios*. These are seasons of retirement, fasting, and penance usually undertaken by the faithful, who shut themselves up in a room of the *cura's* house, each one alone. The candidate is sometimes treated to apparitions, supposed disputes between Christ and Satan over the proprietorship of his soul, clanking of chains, and explosions of gunpowder on the floor; all these in the dark. I hear of some who have lost their reason in these performances. One old lady died in the pueblo this year,—probably from the effects of fasting. Feliz had herself told me of these *ejercicios*, which I suppose are a kind of substitute for the monastic life, which is now prohibited by law. They are usually held after Holy Week.

From this time, when in her father's house, she was tied to a post if it became necessary to leave her a moment. She was taken daily to a house where was a shrine and image of the Virgin; cruelly beaten by her parents to compel her to count the beads, which she refused to do; made to kneel by force, her hands clasped around the crucifix, her mouth held open and filled with holy water. Her own clothing was hidden, and she was compelled, even in the street, to go barefoot and in indecent rags. This was no small mortification to one of her neat and modest tastes.

I did not see her again, as we went to the city; but she sends me messages: "Do not cease to pray for me; none of these things move me. I have even joy when I am beaten, thinking of the hymns and of the precious things of the gospel. If we never meet again here, we shall meet in the congregation of the saints."

While we have suffered much with her, we rejoice to know how firm she is, and how sweet spirited. She is wonderfully sustained. What gracious purposes the Master must have to fulfill in her!

After many trying delays in Guadalajara, we could find out nothing in her favor except the penalty provided for religious persecution. A messenger was sent out to the pueblo to secure its enforcement, if possible. Apparently nothing very decided was done; but we hear that no more physical torments were inflicted since that day, and that the next Sabbath she was allowed to attend church.

We cannot suppose she will have any earthly comfort while she remains in that place. Perhaps if they find they cannot prevent her being a Protestant, they will be very willing to let her go.

JAPAN.

A LETTER FROM MISS DAUGHERTY.

OUR Japanese friends, as perhaps you have already learned, have been greatly encouraged and strengthened by the blessing they received at the great Christian Convention held at Kioto, in May. There seems to be a spiritual uplifting among all the churches. One man said for years he had been endeavoring to serve the Lord, but it was all duty with him. Now, the deep and abiding joy he has day by day is dearer to him than life itself. Another, a young man, was asked by his heathen friends, "Have you received a gift of money, or has some very good fortune happened to you, that you always look so happy?" He replied, "Far better than that. I know that my sins are all forgiven, and the great God in heaven is my Father."

It is wonderful how the Holy Spirit can enlighten and spiritualize those who, but a short time ago, were living in dense ignorance and superstition. The father of one of our schoolgirls died recently. He had been an idol-maker. Often when at work upon his "graven images" the thought came to him, "How strange it is that the thing I am making is going to be an object of worship, — that people are going to ask this to help save them!" One Sunday, when returning from a place of amusement, he was attracted by the sound of preaching, and stood listening for awhile at the door of a native church. In that short time he gained his first idea of a Supreme Being, and his soul, that had been so long feeling after the light, eagerly welcomed and grasped it. He began to attend church regularly, and in different ways tried to learn about this glad news. In time he became a very earnest Christian. He was a manufacturer of ornamental stonework; but the fine particles of stone almost destroyed his sight, so that for years he could only push a little cart about, selling a few wares. Even this poor business was often interrupted by long attacks of illness. During the whole of his Christian life he seemed to be "under the rod," but he always maintained a hopeful, patient, loving spirit, and died a happy death. His daughter, who has been supported at our school by a missionary gentleman, and who graduated this summer, will soon be in a position to care for her mother and little brother.

Almost every one of our girls has a history. Now that school has closed for the summer, we know that some have returned to heathen homes, where they will be objects of ridicule, if not of persecution. Last year the father of one of our girls sent her, during vacation, to stay at the house of a Buddhist priest for special instruction, to counteract the Christian training she had been receiving; but she remained true to her faith. Another father, however, said he thought he must learn about the Jesus way; for if that were the cause of his daughter's wonderful improvement, it must be a very good thing. As our end and aim is to make them such women as "shall adorn the doctrine" they profess, when told of this we "thanked the Lord, and took courage."

The graduation exercises of the Raikwa Jo Yakko (Plum Blossom Girls' School) took place on the 16th of July. Six girls were graduated from the English, and three from the Japanese course. Our plain little building really looked very pretty, with its decorations of flowers and of American and Japanese flags. The exercises began with prayer by a pastor who is a member of the school committee. The monotony of the reading of nine compositions was broken by the singing of choruses by the school. These had been carefully prepared by a missionary gentleman, and the girls sang different parts. The president of the school, another pastor, presented the diplomas. Each graduate received her diploma with both hands, bowed profoundly, raised it to her forehead, retreated two steps, bowed again very low and deliberately, then returned to her seat. An address was delivered by a professor from the Doshisha of Kioto. At the close, after the doxology was sung, all remained in silent prayer for five minutes. Two of the graduates are soon to be married, — one to a pastor, the other to a Christian teacher, and she and her husband are to open a Japanese school of their own. The others are in great demand as teachers and Bible-women.

You will learn by the papers, probably before this reaches you, that we have been suffering from a disastrous flood in Osaka. Two thirds of the city and miles of the surrounding country have been inundated. The rainy season of the year was characterized by storms of exceptional severity; and the river embankments, yielding to the unusual pressure of water, gave way, converting the fertile Osaka Valley into a great lake. Five hundred villages were submerged, some being entirely swept out of existence. Thousands of people fled to the mountains, where they remained many days during the continuous rain, without shelter or food, until rescued by government boats. Others clung to the roofs of their houses in extreme suffering. Many became crazed by fright and exposure, and had to be taken by force into the boats of the Christian relief societies or government rescue parties. They said, "Our children are drowned, our farms ruined, everything we owned is swept away, and we don't want to be saved." Some of the houses were lifted up bodily, and carried down the stream by the current with the families clinging to them; but a very large number broke in pieces, and thousands, it is positively known, were drowned. It was a pleasant sound when again the rattle of jinrikishas on our streets took the place of the cries of boatmen and the splash of water. Our school being on somewhat higher ground than the surrounding streets, we were safe, and two missionary families took refuge with us. The government officers

deserve the warmest gratitude and praise for their untiring efforts
to assist both foreigners and their own people.

A MOHAMMEDAN APPEAL.

The following letter, which has been circulated in the zenanas in the
north of the Punjab, in India, is most significant as an evidence of the hold
the lady missionaries of various denominations have obtained upon the
homes in that country. It will be of great interest to all interested in the
woman's missionary work.

EDUCATION OF FEMALES.

In the name of God, the merciful and gracious! O believers,
save yourselves and your families from the fires of hell! O readers, a thing is taking place which deserves your attention, and
which you will not find it difficult to check. Females need such
education as is necessary to save them from hell. The Quran
and the traditions teach this necessity, and two great philoso-
phers say, "Home is the best school;" but to make it so, women
must be taught. We are doing nothing, but are trying to destroy
our children.

Although we are able to teach our own girls, yet wherever you
go you find zenana mission schools filled with our daughters.
There is no alley or house where the effect of these schools is not
felt.

There are few of our women who did not in their childhood
learn and sing, in the presence of their teachers, such hymns as
"We lo Isa Isa bol" ("Take the name of Jesus with you"), and
few of our girls who have not read the gospel. They whose
faith has not been shaken, know Christianity and the objections
to Islam. The freedom which Christian women possess is influencing all our women. They being ignorant of the excellencies of
their own religion, and being taught that those things in Islam
which are really good are not really good, will never esteem their
own religion.

Omar, one of Mahomet's four bosom friends, was fond of reading the books of Moses and the Gospel; but Mahomet forbade him, saying, "These may lead you in the wrong way." How much more danger, then, is there in our little daughters reading them! There are multitudes of missionaries in the land whose object is to destroy our religion. They see the condition of a country depends on the condition of women, and therefore they send women to teach ours to work and read, and at the same time to sow the seeds of hatred to Islam. Christian women teach Mohammedan women that they should have the liberty which *they* possess; and the Mohammedan teachers in these schools, who are only nominal Mohammedans, by pretending to teach the Quran,* draw our daughters into their schools, and then teach them the gospel and hymns. For a little while they may teach the Quran; but when the missionary lady comes in they hide it under a mat, or throw it into some unclean place, into which if a man had thrown it he might have been sent to prison; and as long as the lady is present they teach Christianity and expose Mohammedanism.

Can we be pleased with such instruction as this? O believers, why teach your children Christianity instead of your own religion?

How far has this religion influenced our women? So far has the love of liberty extended among our daughters and daughters-in-law, that they get into carriages with their teachers, go to Shalimar Gardens, bathe in the tank, sit at table and eat, and then make a quantity of tea to fly.†

At Ludhiana, Amritsar, Lahore, Sialkote, and other places how many converts have the missionaries made in the surrounding country! At Ludhiana two Afghan princesses have become Christians, and have been sent to Massouri. Sometimes we hear a daughter of a *lambidár* has become a Christian, and then that a Mohammedan woman has married a black Karain.‡ We certainly hear of such things, but they produce no effect on us. O believers! if you have any love for your religion, any respect for your ancestors, think how this thing may be stopped. Give your money, establish your own schools, where your daughters can be taught what is necessary for them to know.

---

* The Quran is not allowed in any mission school.
† This accusation is a mistake.
‡ A term of contempt for East Indian Christians.

Young People's Department.

A TRIP TO KALGAN.

BY MISS M. A. HOLBROOK.

N invitation from Mr. and Mrs. Sprague, of Kalgan, for Miss Andrews and myself to spend as much of the summer vacation as we can with them," I announced, holding up a letter.

"You must go," everybody exclaimed.

"Miss Andrews is really worn out, but I don't need it. I never was in better health in my life."

"Yes; but the real hot weather hasn't come yet, and you must remember last summer's experience, and the summer before that."

"Yes, and the summer before that," somebody else added.

"Shan't give you a mouthful to eat if you stay," the house-mother of us all exclaimed.

After that everybody seemed to begin everything by saying, "When you and Miss Andrews go to Kalgan." I had always looked forward to a trip to Kalgan as a treat in reserve, and it seemed to be decided for me that now was my opportunity. So we glady accepted, saying we would return with whoever came down to mission-meeting. . . .

Our party, Mr. and Mrs. Chapin and two children, Dr. Murdock, Miss Andrews, and myself, was made up a week in advance, and five litters and three pack-mules promised for a certain Tuesday. That next week was a good sample of expectations in China, from the buying of a wisp-broom to the conversion of souls (I say it with all reverence). And perhaps if I could give you an accurate account of what we planned to do, what we didn't do, and what we finally did do that week, you will not wonder that the climate of China is so trying. . . .

At light *Saturday* morning there were five litters, each with their two mules, three pack mules for our baggage, five donkeys for the drivers to ride, and our own little "Spotty" for Miss Andrews to use after reaching Kalgan,—nineteen animals in all, in the Beach's back-yard, waiting to bear us to Kalgan.

Do you know what a litter is like? Not like anything you ever saw, I know, so let me give you a pen-picture of it. It is

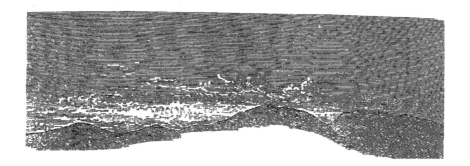

A BIT OF CHINESE SCENE

a lattice-work box with a wooden floor, the top made of close-woven basket material, the whole covered with blue jean, now faded to all degrees of blueness. There are doors in the front part of either side, and one also in the front end, so it can be quite open, or closed in rainy weather. Two long, strong poles are on either side, extending out forward and behind, to form the shafts in which the mules are harnessed, one in front and the other behind.

The packing of the litter is a very important matter, as not a little of the comfort or discomfort depends upon it. The steamer trunk goes in first, and bedding and smaller articles are stowed in the space left. Then a single mattress is spread, with its extra length doubled in at the back. This, with the large pillows, makes it comfortable either sitting or lounging. "What luxurious traveling," you exclaim. "Get in, and try it." "I'll wait till the mules are harnessed in." "No; for then you would have to have a step-ladder to climb in with. When you are in China do as the Chinese do; so get in as it stands there on the ground."

You sit there talking with your friends, when all of a sudden you are pitched forward at an angle of forty-five degrees, and you realize by the scuffling and noise behind that one of the mules is being harnessed in. Instinctively you hold on for dear life, and hold your breath as well, as three men now grasp each forward shaft and raise it even with their shoulders. The mule is backed in, rings from the shafts are hooked into great pins in the large wooden packs upon the mule's back, the litter swaying to and fro as the animals step uneasily with their load. They are always restive while standing, so a constant yelling and yanking goes on all the while. You can see what the head mule is up to, but that hind mule you always feel concern for.

At last you start — swing, swing, jerkity, jerk; swing, swing, kerchunk, kerchunk. What is this motion like? O yes; that's the cradle motion. That isn't so bad. Does it suggest to you that it would be a little more comfortable if you should lie down. Yes; that's better. But what is that jerkity jerk motion like? you ask, for your mind seems strangely analytical. That's the pepper-box motion, as you have heard travelers say. Yes; you certainly recognize it as such. But this kerchunk, kerchunk — that's the sieve motion. And is this thing going to keep up for five days? And without any volition on your part you go over the words, swing, swing, jerkity, jerk; swing, swing, kerchunk, kerchunk, till you feel yourself grow pale, and a saline taste in your mouth suggests to you former experiences on the briny deep.

Yes, I had to confess that, though I had crossed the Pacific without succumbing, I was not outside the city of Tung-cho before I had a genuine attack, and felt decidedly unhappy for several hours afterward.

We stopped an hour at noon for lunch. As we alighted, a man in official dress saluted Dr. Murdock very cordially, and talked with her, a little to our surprise; for it is quite contrary to Chinese etiquette for a man to publicly recognize a woman. This man, it seems, was an official of quite high rank in Kalgan, and Dr. Murdock had cured his mother of paralysis of one side of her body, so now she was able even to sew. This is the man who gave Dr. Murdock the two white horses, and otherwise showed his gratitude. He sent his respects to the rest of the party, and requested the favor of paying our inn bill, which we declined, with thanks.

Just as the sun was setting we found ourselves at the foot of the first range of mountains, but only forty miles from home. Before we reach the inn we have been announced by the bells on the litter mules, great cow-bells. Oh how tired we do get of them! We come first from the street through the big, double doors into a barnyard. Mules, horses, donkeys, pigs, dogs, hens, each trying with the others to see which could get up the biggest racket, — animate voices of nature, truly! With a plunge we stop, for the hind mule didn't know when the front mule was going to stop, — he never does, — and so kept on a few steps, trying to "telescope the train." The head mule doesn't like that, so he goes on a step or two after the hind mule has come to a stop, and then you have the sensation of being the worm between two chickens, and wonder where the break will come; when the driver, with a yell, as usual, yanks the head mule into place, and the hind mule sidles round to see what is expected of him next. Here come the men, to help us dismount. The front shafts are lifted up, and the mule goes off, with a shake, straight for the sheds, the shafts being set upon the ground. The same process is gone through behind, and you are set down with a thud, though you were sure they would tip you over this time. It seems good, after a long day's jouncing, to be allowed a little voluntary motion on one's own account; but, like the mule, we shake ourselves together and turn our thoughts toward supper.

What! eat in such a place as that? Walls black with smoke, every little ledge covered with dirt that is more than dust, a floor of broken brick, doors that won't shut, windows that won't open — what, eat here! Yes, not only one meal but five; for we spend Sunday here, and not only eat, but sleep as well. Why, the richest

Chinese merchant or the highest official has no better accommodations. But we are not dependent upon the inn for food. We have our own food-boxes, which are institutions in their way,—compartments for all-sized tin boxes full of goodies, which shut tight, and are themselves shut away from any possibility of dust. The owners of these inns are Mohammedans, who will not let us cook a particle of our food on their fire, for fear of defilement; but we have brought along our own braziers,—a large coffee-kettle, with a place below for charcoal, and a chimney running up through it,—so we are independent. The inn table washed off, we spread our own table-cloth. Agate-ware plates and cups and saucers are set out, and soon the supper comes on the table—Boston baked beans, (canned), a dish of boiled rice, canned tomatoes, lettuce and cucumbers bought at the door, bread, butter, canned peaches, cake, tea and coffee. Soon after tea we make ready for bed. Miss Andrews and I had brought cots, so we set them up side by side, with a mosquito-netting stretched like a tent above us, and lying there in that comfort and luxury, what cared we for anything beyond. Our little play-house was safe from everything that creeps, or crawls, or flies, and oh! so comfortable, so restful to aching limbs and tired heads.

Monday we went through the pass, at this season of the year a nearly dry river-bed, filled with huge boulders. The scenery here is magnificent. Often the winding, precipitous path seems dangerous, but great care is taken, and seldom does an accident occur. At sundown we passed through the gate in that portion of the Great Wall so familiar to you all in pictures, and spent a night at an inn just a little way beyond.

Tuesday we traveled all day over a dreary, sandy plain, upon which the sun beat down with fiery heat. At noon, as we stopped for lunch, one of our men said, "An official saw Mr. Chapin's New Testament in his litter, and reading a little has become interested in it, and wants to buy it." Mr. Chapin was invited to his room, and after general conversation was asked to explain what the book was about. He talked quite a little, till being called to dinner, he invited the official to eat with us. The Chinese do not like our food any better than we like theirs, so we set only cake, tea, and fruit before him. He had never seen foreigners before, nor any of their books. He seemed very pleasant, and had little of the haughty contempt so marked in most even of his class.

Wednesday we crossed another range of mountains, wild and grand beyond anything I had experienced since leaving our own beautiful Rocky and Sierra Nevadas; nor was this day's journey wholly without real danger, as my head mule was inclined to be obstreperous. At last we were down on another sandy plain, and passed through quite a large walled town. Just as we came out the other side, on the plain again, we heard cries of "Come back; come back." Looking back, none of the other litters were in sight, mine being ahead. We waited till one of the men of our party came up, riding his donkey at a gallop.

OUTSIDE OF A CHINESE INN.

"Where are you going?" he asked. "The rest have gone to the inn."

"We are not going to stop here," the driver said. "We have seven miles yet to go before we reach the place we agreed to stop at."

I listened quietly till the driver said, angrily, "Do you suppose I'm going to put up at that expensive inn, and eat their rich food and spend all that money?"

I turned to a little boy standing near, and asked the name of the place.

"Sandy City."

"Driver," I called, "what does the doctor want?"

"I want to go back where the rest of the party are."

"But we all agreed to go on to the next place; and if we don't go on farther to-night, we can never make to-morrow's stage. It's the hardest day of all."

"But we did not agree to go on; we agreed to stop at Sandy City."

"Well, that's seven miles farther on," and he started up the mules.

"This is Sandy City, and you know it, and you know we agreed to stop here."

Then looking him square in the eye with that "schoolma'am" look that is seldom disobeyed, I commanded him to stop. I then called the man to bring his donkey up for me to clamber down on, at the same time rising and tipping the litter to one side:

"Sit down, or you will have the litter over."

"Turn back," I said.

"Not if I stay here all night."

"I don't propose to stay here all night," I said.

"What are you going to do about it?"

"Walk back to the city; it's only a few steps;" and again I told the man to bring his donkey up — I, meanwhile, thinking I had my cot and bedding with me and money in my travelling-bag, if he should persist in carrying me on, and wondering what kind of Chinese food I should order for supper. As the donkey came up to the door and I rose to step out, the driver said, "Sit down," and turned the team back to the city, muttering that there wasn't a particle of the law of right in it, and it was all a mean trick, to which in my heart I said, Amen. As we came into the inn-yard the other drivers met him with a loud laugh, and said, "So she made you come back, did she;" and he looked sheepish enough, and laughed with the rest.

And this was that expensive inn, was it? There were two lines of mud-rooms facing each other, with just room enough between for carts to pass one another, the space now being filled with vehicles and animals. Just opposite our rooms was the inn kitchen; and oh, such odors and such noise! I was too tired for supper, and as soon as my cot was set up I retired, though not to sleep. The carters brought out their supper, and ate it sitting on the ground around our door. When they were nearly through they began to ask a schoolboy I had brought along to be my teacher during the summer, about us and our business in China. When he had answered all their curious questions he told them we were religious teachers. "What religion do they teach?" they asked. This gave him the opportunity he had been watching for,—to talk to them of our religion; and he explained it earnestly and well, for I could hear every word through the thin wall and paper windows.

The next morning saw our dishes packed for the last time, and we bade good-bye to inns, looking forward to the joy of meeting friends and home—somebody's home, even though it were not ours. Noon of Thursday, after four and a half long days to accomplish the one hundred and fifty miles, brought us in sight of Kalgan, and we espied up through the pass our first glimpse of Mongolia. We had no desire for a closer view, and glad were we, oh, how glad! to find ourselves in the warm welcome of our friends.

Our Work at Home.

REALITIES OF MISSIONARY LIFE.

At the request of one of our missionaries—who says the experiences described agree with her own, and, she is sure, with those of others also— we print the following article from *Woman's Work for Woman*, by Mrs. L. O. Van Hook. We regret that its length makes it necessary to abridge it to some extent.

THE seclusion of Oriental women is one of the greatest obstacles in the way of the missionary. The women must be reached in their own homes. The difficulty is to obtain an entrance there. All Orientals are excessively polite, and unwarrantable intrusion would be no more pardoned among them than in America. Some sort of an introduction must be the prelude to every visit, demanding unceasing watchfulness on the part of the missionary, lest some favorable opportunity for making an acquaintance be let slip. Not only must the door always be on the latch in the mission home, but invitations must be accepted that mean sitting on the floor for hours listening, with an aching head, possibly, to an excruciating din called music, or perhaps waiting far into the night for the bridegroom to come; then during the feasts making twenty calls a day, drinking as many cups of tea, and trying to make way with refreshments urged upon you in the shape of a heavy compound, shortened with mutton fat, smeared with saffron, and denominated *delicate cake*. Then, when out, the almost hidden faces must be closely scanned, that no acquaintance purchased thus be lost through lack of recognition.

It is often stated that the harems and zenanas of the East are open only to woman, and she is urged to enter and proclaim the gospel to her sisters who are held there, soul and body; but I think few realize how our American manners are regarded by those who consider it immodest to unveil their faces in the presence of a man, or hold conversation with any man outside the members of their own families; and so it happens oftentimes that the missionary, instead of being hailed as a messenger of glad tidings, is looked upon with suspicion, and her morals questioned. Almost every pioneer has the humiliation of being obliged to establish her own reputation. Right here let me beg of you never to send your first missionary to any station without an associate.

Women reared in the manner of the East usually have not the intelligence or information of an average American girl ten years of age, and are so unaccustomed to fix their minds upon any subject requiring attention or thought, that all instruction must be of the simplest character and with the most wearisome repetition, "line upon line and precept upon precept," over and over and over again; and even then much will be seed sown by the wayside. With the more intelligent, one is often at one's wit's end to know how to illustrate a truth or clinch an argument. Any appeal to common scientific truths, facts of history, of experience, of illustrious persons, is useless, for science, history, and biography are all unknown; while on their part they will offer tales more absurd than those of the Arabian Nights as facts not to be gainsaid. Their credulity leads them to believe and circulate the most ridiculous statement in regard to our motives and practices, — such as, that if intrigued within our walls, they will be obliged to perform acts most offensive to their own deity; that writing is connected with incantation; and that people are made Christians by machinery, for which Americans are famous. A missionary once told me an amusing anecdote of a woman who called upon her, and on being invited to sit down, chose a rocking-chair, but got into it feet and all; then attempting to sit down as if on the floor, of course the chair pitched forward, and she fell headlong. She bounded up with a terrific scream, thinking she had been thrown by a monster, and seeing it swaying back and forth, concluded it to be a machine for making Christians, and rushed from the room. Neither explanations nor persuasions would induce her to re-enter.

The lack of form in the Christian religion is something difficult to be understood by those who have such faint perceptions of spiritual things, who are without even an ideal of moral beauty,

and whose sensibilities are blunted by vicious habits and practices. Once a native, in describing a missionary lady, said, "She
does not lie, she does not steal, she does not use bad words, but,
poor thing, she has no religion." The firm belief of every illiter-
ate nation in witchcraft, the evil eye, influence of spirits, and kindred superstitions makes it difficult to dispel these illusions, and
superstitious beliefs and practices are the bulwarks of heathenism.
This superstition begets bondage to those in religious authority,
whose intolerance of all free action in religious matters directly
incites persecution. Confessing Christ involves Christian observances. These mark the convert, and persecution follows, varying
in degree, from loss of employment and ostracism to death. Is it
surprising that some have not the courage to take up such crosses?
It is not so difficult to take the heroic stand which defies death, as
it is to bear the daily anxiety and destitution arising from loss of
friends and employment; and when you see professedly Christian
men in *this* enlightened and prosperous land holding positions
involving Sabbath labor, and arguing their right to do so for the
sake of their families, do you wonder that where life is at the best
a struggle for mere subsistence, some will set their families over
against Christ? Human nature is much the same everywhere,
and it is no more true that all heathen rejoice in persecution, than
that all Christians live a life of consecration.

Then there is a fallacy in supposing that every convert becomes
in turn a missionary. The probabilities are against the supposition that one just rescued from heathenism will be an efficient
helper. She has heard and believed that Christ came into the
world to save sinners, but she may have yet to learn that it is
wicked to take God's name in vain, for a man to have more than
one wife, to work on the Sabbath-day, and many other things
which she has always done, and always supposed she had a right
to do. It is difficult to realize how many ideas of evil and good
we have inherited from pious, or at least moral ancestors, until we
see how faint is the perception of virtue in one of these converts.
A quickened conscience will warn of some sin; but so largely do
one's ideas of right and wrong depend upon education, that she
will not recognize others as opposed to God's will until her attention is called to the fact. If she cannot read, and so cannot study
her Bible, and lives at a distance from the missionary, from
whom she might receive enlightenment, though her life may be a
glimmer of light in a dark place, her advancement will be slow
unless she is exceptionally spiritual minded. Then there are
some who are not gifted even if they be instructed, and others, as
at home, who have not the disposition to rise and work for the

Master. The record is often given of converts who, by their devotion and labors, have been the means in their turn of converting large numbers of people or of evangelizing a nation; and I often meet with the supposition that all converts are remarkable in their zeal and desire for the spread of the gospel. But while there are some whose fruitful lives have been wonderful instances of what God is able and loves to accomplish through his servants, yet as a whole our mission churches are much like those of early times, and have to be tenderly nurtured,— the unruly warned, the feeble-minded comforted, the weak supported, and patience rendered to all. Our Saviour chose fishermen for his apostles, but he kept them under his personal divine tuition three years before he sent them forth to proclaim his Word. And our modern Peters and Johns and Timothys, most of them, need much and careful instruction, though here and there a man is raised up like Paul, jealous for the Lord, and providentially prepared for his service. And in the Church at large, abroad as at home, it is the few who gird on the harness of activity.

A lady recently said to me that she had been supporting a Bible-women abroad, but thought she would change, because she had heard she was not efficient. Now, my friends, there is no land deprived of the advantages of this our beloved home-land, whose natives are as efficient as Yankees; and that this inefficiency is the only assistance which can be procured in any department, is one of the burdens a missionary must bear. I hear ladies say they are worn out with a single incompetent servant girl. Supposing you had twenty-five such to manage, and the work to which you had devoted your life depended on managing them! Yet these are the ones on whom the future depends, and it depends on the many who may be frail and halting in their beginnings, rather than on the few prodigies. And then these are the ones who most need your pleadings and intercession with God; so if the one in whom you are specially interested is not promising, rejoice that the Lord has given you so large a share in the work, and just pray her up to where she can be used for, or at least live to, his glory. I was greatly impressed while in Nebraska, last year, as a dear one, now a saint in heaven, told me how she daily bore to the thrown of grace, in agony of prayer, a Persian woman she was supporting. Knowing how the Lord was using that woman, I felt that this dear mother in Israel was most truly a Persian missionary.

But is it all obstacles and difficulty, faith and patience? Nay, verily. There is one great advantage in working among those who are not gospel-hardened, to whom the story of the cross comes with the fascination of novelty. Added to this, the people of the East are universally religious. Their religion is a matter of their common, every-day life, and they exhibit no reluctance to discuss the matter, nor delicacy about making the conversation personal, while it is perfectly proper to introduce the subject anywhere and upon any occasion. In considering it they are occupied with vital truths rather than theological questions, which gives them a deeper hold upon divine things, while the danger of persecution to which they are subjected arouses the spirit, and helps develop heroic, consecrated lives. It also prevents those who are not ready to follow Christ everywhere, from joining themselves to his people, keeping the Church smaller, but purer. Above and beyond all else, the heralding of His gospel to every creature is the interest nearest the divine heart of the world's Redeemer, and his peculiar blessing rests upon it; so we see, as an actual fact, far greater results from the same outlay in the work of foreign missions than in any other department of Christian enterprise.

In the heart-life of missionaries there are some things that perhaps all do not realize. You who are sitting in the noonday privileges of this blessed land, do not know how it would try your very souls to be suddenly thrown into a sea of ignorance, degradation, and vice, obliged to breast the surging waves, while overhead the thick clouds of Mohammedanism, Brahmanism, or Confucianism cover the heavens as a black pall, making perpetual night, and a darkness that can be felt. It is one thing to sit in a pleasant parlor or stirring missionary convention and have one's heart yearn over the heathen, and quite another to sit down on the ground in a close, hot room, full of tobacco smoke and the sickening odor of unwashed bodies and unsavory food, with women whose clothes are full of fleas and other vermin, to tell the story of Jesus and his love. The missionary needs daily a renewed baptism of the Holy Spirit to enable her to take heathen women into her heart when she comes to see and live among them.

I used to think that in some magical way missionaries were lifted above the perplexities, and failures, and weakness of other Christians, and always kept on a high plane of spiritual life; but most of us find in going on missionary ground that we take ourselves along, and that "the world, the flesh, and the devil" are not peculiar to America. Where everything is crooked and wrong, and every one seems bent on exhibiting stupidity with a slowness of motion and awkwardness of manner utterly exasperating, trials of temper are increased a hundred-fold. Many climates induce nervousness; constant intercourse with ignorance and degradation is depressing; and the absence of any spiritual atmosphere or stimulus from without is wearing and exhausting.

I think there is much truth in the idea that the evils of life are due to the direct agency of Satan. It would follow from this that those who have devoted themselves to the interests of Christ's kingdom, are sure to receive especial attention from his arch enemy. So he takes the life of some of the most devoted, sends sickness to the most active, brings home the best beloved, and upon the heads of those he cannot force away he pours an avalanche of trials, perplexing mental and moral problems, weariness, sleeplessness, disappointment, and grieving that Christ is "wounded in the house of his friends."

Sometimes the avalanche is red-hot, and sometimes it is icy cold; but in the midst of it all the Saviour stands whispering in the ear of each one, "Lo, I am with you alway, even unto the end." "When thou passest through the waters I will be with thee, and through the rivers they shall not overflow thee: when thou walkest through the fires thou shalt not be burned; neither shall the flames kindle upon thee." To every one who is pressing on to follow where he leads, in many an unexpected moment he reveals himself, and the missionary in her isolation will in visions often catch a sight of his wondrous face, or in her own chamber hear the stately steppings of the King.

In this contest with sin and Satan which the Church has undertaken in allegiance to the Son, though difficulties be enormous, defeats frequent, and many fall in the midst of the fray, ultimate success is assured, for "the mouth of the Lord hath spoken it." Therefore, while it has seemed well at this time to spy out the enemy's camp, and the people that dwell therein, whether they be strong or weak, few or many, we do not return as did some of old, saying, "There are giants in the land," but rather, exulting in Emmanuel our King, we should shout with all our might, "Let us go up at once and possess the land, for we are well able to overcome it."

ANNUAL MEETING OF THE BERKSHIRE BRANCH.

We regret that the following account of the Berkshire Branch meeting did not reach us for earlier insertion in our magazine, but we trust our readers will be none the less interested in the doings of this wide-awake Branch.

THE eighth annual meeting of the Berkshire Branch was held at the First Church, Pittsfield, June 18, 1885.

The day was perfect, and the meeting largely attended and enthusiastic. Devotional exercises opened the morning session, and Mrs. Giddings, the president, announced as the text for the day, "According to your faith be it unto you." Then came the reports of the officers.

The recording secretary chronicled the last meeting held at Housatonic, in October, 1884. The home secretary reported two new auxiliaries and a new mission circle formed since the last meeting. She felt there was great reason for encouragement in the work, but urged the need of special work among the children. The treasurer has received two thousand six hundred and fifty-eight dollars and thirty-two cents [$2,658.32] during the year, besides a sum more than sufficient for branch expenses. The pledged work has been done, and there is a surplus for the general treasury.

The foreign secretary gave a report of the work abroad, containing much valuable information carefully gleaned. In summing up, she spoke earnestly of the grand openings for work and the great want of more workers — a pressing need now that the force is unusually small.

Reports of the auxiliaries and mission circles were next presented, and were for the most part cheering.

Mrs. Giddings then read an inspiring paper, dwelling on the great and earnest work to be done, the need of the active service of each member of the "Branch," and the inspiration of the work. Is there not demand for our efforts when there are 800,000,000 who have never heard God's name? Such "facts are the fingers of Providence." Our president emphasized her conviction that the hope of the Branch is in the mission circles, whence are to come the Fidelia Fiskes and Harriet Nerwells of the future.

The social hour at lunch was a pleasant feature of the occasion.

The afternoon session opened with singing, scripture-reading by two young ladies, and prayer.

The following officers were then chosen for the year:—

President, Mrs. E. J. Giddings, of Housatonic; Recording Secretary, Mrs. S. A. Warriner, of Hinsdale; Corresponding Secretary, Miss E. Morley, of Pittsfield; Home Secretary, Mrs. W. Plunkett, of Adams; Assistant Secretary, Miss M. E. Gibbs, of Lee; Treasurer, Mrs. Solomon Russel, of Pittsfield; Auditor, Mr. John Power, of Pittsfield.

Mrs. Howland, of Ceylon, then addressed the meeting. She gave us many interesting and thrilling details of her work in Jaffna, talked much of her joy in the work, touched lightly on its shadows, spoke of "sanctified common sense" as an essential to a missionary's success, and closed with a strong appeal for more helpers.

Miss Child, of Boston, brought kindly greetings from the parent society, and congratulations on the work done by the "Berkshire Branch."

The singing of the Doxology closed the meeting — one of the largest and best ever held by the "Branch."

M. E. G.

Miss P. L. CULL of Manisa and Miss C. H. Pratt of Mardin, Turkey, arrived in this country August 28th, for a period of rest.

Miss MARY L. DANIELS for Harpoot, Miss Ellen S. Blakely for Marash, and Miss Ella T. Bray for Adana, Turkey, in company with Mr. and Mrs. Allen for Harpoot, sailed from New York in the Servia, October 3d, for their various fields of labor.

Miss REBECCA G. JILLSON, who left New York July 30th, is now in Bardesag, where she will spend some time in the study of the language. Miss M. P. Root, M.D., who left America at the same time, has been detained in England, for want of steamer accommodations, but was to sail for Madras September 9th.

WOMAN'S BOARD OF MISSIONS.

Receipts from August 18 to September 18, 1885.

MISS EMMA CARRUTH, TREASURER.

NEW HAMPSHIRE.

New Hampshire Branch.—Miss A. E. McIntire,Treas. Mason, Aux., $10.15; Pelham, Mrs. E. W. Tyler, $5; Alton, Aux., $2; Amherst, Aux., $13; Bristol, Aux., $18; Chester, Aux., $30; Dover, Aux., $55; Durham, Aux., $41; East Wilton, Aux., $15 10; East Derry, Aux., $35.25; Brentwood, Mrs. E. B. Pike, $2; Exeter, Aux., of wh. $25 const. L. M. Miss Frances F. Perry, $60.60, Lily Band, $3.67; Fitzwilliam, Aux., $12.75; Greenfield, Aux., $20; Greenland, Aux., of wh. $25 by Mrs. Louisa P. Weeks, const. L. M. Mrs. Rufus W. Weeks, and $25 by Aux., const. L. M. Miss Mary Izette Holmes, $50.50, Claudia Circle, $1.50; Greenville, Aux., $7; Hampton, Aux.,

$30; Hanover,Aux., $15, Soc'y of Christian Endeavor, $5; Hillsboro Bridge, Aux., $7; Hollis, Aux., $23 50; Hudson, Aux., $12; Jaffrey, Lilies of the Field. prev. contri. const. L. M. Miss May Woodruff, $20; Lebanon, Aux., $42.70; Lisbon, Aux., $16; Manchester, First Cong. Ch., Aux., $100, Wallace Circle, $50, Franklin St. Ch., Aux., $134, Hon. F. Smythe, to const. L. M. Mrs. Lucretia Eaton, $25; Merrimac, Aux., $15.50; Mt. Vernon, Aux , $20.75, Buds of Promise,$4.75, Young Ladies' Band, $7; Peterboro, Aux., $21; Portsmouth, Aux., $100.29, Rogers Circle, $7; Raymond, Aux., $2; Salem, Raindrops, $10; Seabrook and Hampton Falls, Aux., $10; Tamworth, Aux., $6; Temple, Aux., $12, Laurels,

$20; Wolfboro, Aux., $25.84, Newell Circle, $5; So. Newmarket, Aux., $13.50, Forget-Me-Nots, $15; Northwood, Aux., prev. contri. const. L. M. Mrs. J. J. Cate, $17; Meriden, Aux.,'$19, $1,194 35

Total, $1,194 35

VERMONT.

Vermont Branch.— Mrs. T. M. Howard, Treas. St. Johnsbury, No. Cong. Ch, $10, No. Ch., Aux., of wh. $50 by Mrs. Horace Fairbanks, const. L. M's Mrs. Walter P. Smith, Mis. Robert McKimm, $25 by S. F. S., const. L. M. Mrs. H. B. Davis, $25 by Mrs. E. A. W., const. L. M. Miss Isabel A. Kinney, $140 83, Boys' Miss'y Soc'y, $20, So. Ch., Aux., of wh. $25 by Mrs. Henry Fairbanks, const. L. M. Miss Orris Paddock, $63.50; Barton Landing, Aux., $15; Burlington, Aux., $25; Cabot, Aux., $10; Charlotte, M. B., $10; Clarendon, Aux., $2; Essex Junction, Aux., $8.15, Mrs. M. H. Seaton, $2; Georgia, Aux., $18; Middletown, Aux., $6; Newport, Aux., $22.13; Norwich, Aux., $20; Rochester, Aux., const. L. M. Mrs. L. M. Wing, $25; Rutland, Aux., $22.07, Y. L. Miss'y League, $66; Springfield, Aux., $48.58; Pittsford, Aux., $44; Thetford, Mrs. A. H. Farr, $1; Westminster West, M. B., $20; West Brattleboro, M. C., $17; Wells River, Aux., $6, $622 26
Putney.— Cong. Ch.,   5 50

Total, $627 76

MASSACHUSETTS.

Andover and Woburn Branch.— Miss E. F. Wilder, Treas. Chelmsford, Aux., $5 00
Barnstable Branch. — Miss A. Snow, Treas. Sandwich, Aux., $10.10; Cotuit, Aux., $25; Yarmouth, Aux., $8, Postage Fund, $1.90,   45 00
Berkshire Branch. — Mrs. S. N. Russell, Treas. Enfield, Woman's Miss'y Soc'y, $25; South Egremont, Buds of Promise, $45; Dalton, Aux., $32.05; Hinsdale, Aux., $16.35, 118 40
Essex No. Co. Branch.— Mrs. A. Hammond, Treas. Amesbury and Salisbury, Union Ch., $10; West Box-

ford, Aux., $16; South Byfield, Aux., $15; Haverhill, No. Ch., Pentucket M. B., $31.50; West Newbury, First Ch., Aux., $12, $84 50
Essex South Co. Branch.— Miss S. W. Clark, Treas Gloucester, Aux., of wh. $25 is a Thank-offering, $55; Beverly, Aux., a S. S. Cl., Dane St. Ch., const. L. M. Miss Abby S. Whitehouse, $25,   80 00
Franklin Co. Branch. — Miss L. A. Sparhawk, Treas. Orange, Aux., of wh. $25 const. L. M. Mrs. F. D. Kellogg, $28, Y. L. M. C., $14,   42 00
Greenwich Village. — Miss L. A. Parker,   1 40
Hampshire Co. Branch. — Miss I. G. Clarke, Treas. Chesterfield, Aux., Thank-offering, $10; Granby, Aux., $5; Northampton, Aux., Edwards Ch. Div., $33; South Hadley, Aux., $36; Westhampton, Aux., $50,   134 00
Middlesex Branch.—Mrs. E. H. Warren, Treas. Maynard, from a Mother, in Mem. of Hattie, Mary, and little Vickie, $6; Natick, Aux., $12; Lincoln, M. C., $10, Aux., $50, const. L. M's Mrs. Martha E. Whitney and Mrs. Mary F. Smythe,   78 00
Old Colony Branch. — Miss F. J. Runnels, Treas. Wareham, Merry Gleaners, $25; Fall River, Miss Buck's S. S. Cl. of boys, 80 cts.,   25 80
Springfield Branch.—Miss H. T. Buckingham, Treas. Longmeadow, Aux., $22; Ludlow Centre, Precious Pearls, $7; Palmer, Second Ch., Aux., $10; Springfield, First Ch., Aux., $44.50, South Ch., Aux., $88 42, Y. L. M. C., $50.73,   222 65
Suffolk Branch. — Miss M. B. Child, Treas. Roxbury, Eliot Ch., Aux., $80; Hyde Park, Aux., $13; West Newton, Mrs. C. E. Frost, $1; Newton Centre, First Ch., Aux., of wh. $25 by Mrs. L. S. Ward, const. L. M. Mrs. Mary P. Bliss, $52; Dedham, Asylum Dime Soc'y, $2.20,   148 20
Worcester Co. Branch. — Mrs. G. W. Russell, Treas. Whitinsville, Aux., of wh. $50 by Mrs. J. Lasell, const. L. M's Miss Mabel Pa Delford, Miss Sarah Dawley, $25 by Mrs. M. A. Batchelor, const. L. M. Miss Lucy G. Pond, $148.50, Merry Gleaners, const. L. M.

Mrs. Augusta S. Thurston, $25: West Boylston, Aux., $8.25; Leominster, Aux., $25; Leicester, M. C., $7.65; Baldwinsville, Aux., $6.25; Winchendon, No. Cong. Ch., $23.70, S. S., $25; Worcester, Woman's Miss'y Asso., Plymouth Ch., $50, $319 35

Total, $1,304 30

LEGACIES.

Boston.—Legacy of Mrs. E. C. Foid, $3,000 00
Foxboro.—Legacy of Miss Susan Payson,   200 00

Total, $3,200 00

RHODE ISLAND

Rhode Island Branch. Miss A. T. White, Treas. Providence, Beneficent Ch., $393.07, Free Ch., $50, Elmwood Workers, $25, Friends, $8.80; Tiverton, Aux., $13.50; East Providence, Aux., $26; Pawtucket, Park Place, $12.25, $528 62

Total, $528 62

CONNECTICUT.

Eastern Conn. Branch. — Miss M. I. Lockwood, Treas. Jewett City, Aux., $3.50; East Lyme, Aux., $7; North Woodstock, Aux., $16.25; Pomfret, Aux., $18, M. C., $8.35; Willimantic, Aux., $15; Taftville, M. C., $7.50; New London, Second Ch., of wh. $25 by Mrs. J. N. Harris, const. L. M. Miss Nettie Woodworth, $51.90, First Ch., Aux., $48, $175 50
Hartford Branch.— Miss A. Morris, Treas. East Granby, Aux., $10, M. C., $16; Ellington, Aux., $35; Glastonbury, Y. L. M. C., $70, Cheerful Givers, $30; Kensington, Aux., $40, Simsbury, Aux., $48; Tolland, Aux., $8,   257 00
Marlborough.—A Friend,   40

Total, $432 90

NEW YORK.

New York State Branch.—Mrs. G. H. Norton, Treas. Spencerport, Aux., $30, Cong. S. S., $30; Antwerp, Aux., $25; Copenhagen, Aux., of wh. $25 const. L. M.

Mrs. Elmira M. Cuthbertson, $50; Seneca Falls, Aux., $6.70; Kiantone, Aux., $8.90; Paris, Judd M. B., $2.76; Homer, Aux., of wh. $25 by eigh ladies, const. L. M. Mrst Walter Jones, $75; Danby, Aux., $25, Y. L. M. C., $39; Lysander, Aux., $30; Honeoye, S. S. Cl. No. 4, $30; Pitcher, Mrs. W. W. Warner, $2; Flushing, Miss'y Class, $1 15; Morristown, Aux., $12; Warsaw, Star Band, $20; Sandy Creek, Aux., $17; Binghamton, Faithful Workers, $15; Lockport, Aux., $10; Buffalo, Aux., $10; Syracuse, Mrs. Mary D. C. Gane, $10; Candor, Ladies' Miss'y Soc'y, Cong. Ch., $5, $454 51
Deansville.—Ladies' Aid Soc'y, Cong. Ch.,   17 67
Spuyten Duyvil.—A Friend,   1 00

Total, $473 18

LEGACY.

Walton —Legacy of Elizabeth Bassett, $517 44

Total, $517 44

OHIO.

North Monroeville. — Mrs. H. M. St. John, $2 00

Total, $2 00

IOWA.

Nugent.—Cong. Ch., $10 00

Total, $10 00

CANADA.

Canadian W. B. M., $167 50
Montreal.—Mrs. Ruth M. Fraser,   5 00

Total, $172 50

ENGLAND.

London.—Miss S. L. Ropes, $20 00

Total, $20 00

General Funds, $4,765 61
Morning Star,   4 25
Weekly Pledge,   15
Leaflets,   7 14
Legacies,   3,717 44

Total, $8,494 59

MISS HARRIET W. MAY,
Ass't Treas.

Board of the Interior.

TURKEY.

REPORT OF WOMEN'S WORK ON THE CILICIAN PLAIN FOR 1884 AND 1885.

BY LAURA TUCKER.

WE were in Adana on the 18th of September, ready to gather together the threads of our winter's web of work.

But the weather being still very hot, and the people not yet having returned from their vineyards and summer resorts, we were able to do little more, for a couple of weeks, than settle our house, and prepare for nine months of housekeeping.

At last, October 11th, enough had come in from vineyards and cotton-gathering to warrant the opening of three girls' schools in the city. There were thirty children in the primary, twenty boys and thirty girls in the second grade, and forty girls in the intermediate department, on the first Monday morning — a good beginning. According to the previous station plans, doors stood open, and the teacher sat ready in one room of the Mission-house to receive candidates for the grammar school. Two only came. Disappointed indeed we were after all the cries for girls' higher education in Adana. The teacher stayed by her two, ready to receive more; while Baron Avedis and I set out to visit all the families where there were eligible daughters. During the week we called at sixty houses, enlarging at each upon the value of female education, and inviting pupils to the new school. We found, to our disgust, that girls whom we thought eligible for the school were also upon the matrimonial market. They had, many of them, been at our school the previous year, and learned to read and write and add a little, and had memorized a few Bible stories, and learned how to sew a little, or do fancy work. So they thought themselves quite learned. Their mothers, utterly ignorant of books, thought them quite oracular, and inquired if we wished to make priests of their children. Some were "too large to be seen in the street"; some were "engaged," or just going to be — that is to say, the doting father was negotiating with some unprincipled youth, offering various sums of money as dowry, to get him to take his dear daughter, already too old, having spent fifteen or sixteen tedious years in this weary world, to be sought in marriage. Perhaps at that very moment the tender mother was expressing her attachment to her beloved offspring by conferring with some neighboring woman anxious to get a young bride into the house to do her washing, scrubbing, and other drudgery. The relation of the young bride to her mother-in-law is that of a menial to an exacting mistress. However, at the beginning of the second week we had eight, and on the third Monday morning we had nineteen, promising girls, though not all in the regular classes, which were, physiology, practical arithmetic, English grammar, and Bible lessons, beginning with Samuel. We formed a second class, taking mental arithmetic from fractions, English and Armenian second readers, Osmanleji primer, and reciting Bible and physiology with the higher class, which, by the way, was composed of younger girls. Friday afternoons were devoted to sewing. Complaints were rife that there was not enough sewing. "What will our girls do with so much book-learning? We want them to learn just sewing and writing." We refused to devote another day to sewing, but as soon as the pupils could handle their needles, we introduced cutting and fitting children's clothes as a part of Friday afternoon's work.

Meanwhile the primary school had increased in number to eighty-five. They had oral lessons in numbers, object lessons, singing, and primer. Yester's room, the one above the primary, was so full that it was thought best to remove all the boys to the boys' school, leaving her with an average of fifty girls, to whom she gave oral lessons in numbers and arithmetic, second Turkish reader, Armenian primer, first lessons in geography, writing, and Bible lessons in Genesis.

In the intermediate, under Jibinly Merurh, a warm-hearted, efficient woman, there were forty-five pupils, arranged in two classes, and pursuing the studies that naturally fall into the intermediate department. The three latter schools were supported entirely by the native brethren; so we felt obliged to comply with the request of the committee to have two afternoons each week devoted to sewing. Many of these had never learned the use of the sewing or crocheting needles. So when, at the close of the term, fifteen pretty fairy zephyr shawls, looking like the product of fairy fingers, and sixty clean, neatly finished pieces of work, consisting of children's dresses, jackets, hoods, sofa-pillows, and tidies were ready for sale, it was thought a great success.

Before the private grammar school had been long in progress, the Moslem neighbors opened their eyes to their neglected duty —

persecution. Boys from twelve to fifteen years of age would hide behind street-corners and snatch the girls' shawls off their heads, and stone them, often with harmless pebbles. Only two of the girls were beaten so as to bear the marks. The girls, none too enthusiastic, began to drop out of the school. Mr. Montgomery appealed to the Government, and a few weeks' quiet followed. ·At last we sent our servant, Moses, to escort them each way — an efficient plan, at last. But our girls were only twelve besides the bright little fourteen-year-old bride, who came in to learn to read.

In February our leaky roof had to be re-covered. The yard was crowded with noisy workmen, lumber, and tiles. The small room used for school was sunless, damp, dark, and cold — no place for study or recreation. So it was decided to be best for us to go down to one of the rooms under the church-building.

Here we decided to transfer the five most advanced pupils of Merurh's school to the grammar department, making eighteen, almost the original number, many of whom are in training for teachers. The lessons were so combined as to reduce Yeghsa Varshubi's recitations to five; viz., Armenian Grammar, mental and practical arithmetic, Osmanleji, and writing. Dr. Ohan gave the physiology. I gave the Bible lessons, which, during the year, passed over I. and II. Samuel and Luke, the English, English grammar alternating the latter with the higher arithmetic, in order to train our young teacher in teaching the arithmetic. The examination took place the last of April, and gave general satisfaction to both parents and committee. The schools continued on until June, of course.

Marashli Anna, Bulgarian, acted as Bible-woman, visiting daily from house to house, talking, reading, and often having little prayer-meetings where a few happened to be together. Among those who could read, we distributed lists of Bible verses upon certain subjects. These they repeated at our monthly meetings. It proved an interesting and helpful exercise, and promoted a more systematic study of the Bible. Twenty of the more earnest Christian women devoted one day each week to visiting their Armenian and Greek neighbors, and talking with them of Christ. The verses that they had memorized were a great help in the efforts to do good. Hundreds of families were in this way visited, and influenced to attend public worship. The work done in this way was always reported at "our woman's own meetings" or the monthly meetings. My Sunday-school class, a company of twelve brides and earnest women, proposed prayer-meetings at their homes, in the hope of getting some there who would not come to church. Accordingly the city was divided into eight *mahals,* at each of which a little band of twenty or thirty women met two Sunday noons of each month, and by the aid of the teachers, who usually led the meetings, this also added many to the congregation.

It is useless to try to estimate the number of calls one makes in a year; and who can estimate the good resulting from them ?

Weddings and engagements stepped in between the Tarsus work and workers, depriving them of a Bible-woman. There were forty pupils in the one girls' school. Being alone at Adana, I had no time to spend there; indeed, I had but two meetings there during the whole year.

ADANA, May 1, 1885.

LIFE IN HADJIN.

Translation of a letter written by the pastor of the Second Church in Hadjin, Turkey, to Miss Spencer.

PRAISE be to God, we are all well. As a church our work is prospering, and, according as you know, we are at work, and await your prayers.

During the last three months four men have joined our little congregation. Mrs. Coffing is working with us as before, Sabbath morning giving the Sabbath-school lesson to the class of men, and on Thursday the lecture to the women. Miss Hollister continues in the school. She has also opened a new society among the women of the two congregations, and is laboring in the young men's league. She is well and strong, and not weak at all. November 23d, on Sabbath day, one hour before divine service, the monthly concert of the women's missionary society was publicly celebrated in the presence of the congregation. It was conducted in a very pleasant manner. There were addresses and reports showing the number of houses without the Holy Book; the number of families without family prayers; the number of houses visited; the number of persons talked and prayed with; the number of women reading; and many other things. It was most delightful and profitable, only Miss Spencer, with the "Home" girls, was not there to sing the song of the bells, "with the lingering echoes of its chimes." If so it had been pleasanter.

I pray that the divine influence of the Holy Spirit may fill and guide, the presence of Christ and blessing of God the Father rest upon, our every plan used — our preaching, Sabbath-school lessons, and committee meetings.

Our committee for the relief of fire sufferers has built more than ninety houses for the poor people. The rest are still to be built, but, because of the winter, there will be a rest of three months. As soon as the spring opens, the work will be continued.

The Armenians' Relief Committee have not given one para from the relief fund in their hands. Armenian men, widows, and priests have received aid from the Protestants for building their houses, and for this cause have shown, and still continue to show, their gratitude and thankfulness. They are not pleased with the strange, unmerciful actions of the Armenian committee, but are making great complaints, and most justly. On the evening of the 10th they talked with the honorable Mrs. Coffing, and made known their intentions, saying that a good number had decided to become Protestants, and had enrolled themselves as such. I, also, being present for a time, talked with them of the need of leading a Christian life. Dec. 14th more than seventy men, fifteen women, and a number of children came to church, and are still continuing to do so. These are coming because of their anger to the Armenians; but some, being enlightened by the Word, are hopeful persons.

Again we wait your prayers, your special prayers. Kootsi* and I send special *salaams* to you. One who desires your peace.

A teacher in the Hadjin school writes also a pleasant letter, from which we make extracts: —

I reached here (after vacation) about three weeks after school had begun. All the teachers and girls came up the mountain-side to meet us, with great fun and rejoicing.

Reaching the house, I saw many changes. In the sitting-room the boxes of plants had been painted walnut color, and on the side toward Mrs. Coffing's room the vines had climbed up to the bookcase. Your large plant (calla) has a little one, and is very beautiful.

Parsek began work in the kitchen the first of November. Mrs. Coffing is much of the time in the kitchen, teaching him. She must look after the city schools, prepare the lectures for the women's meetings, give the Sabbath-school lesson to teachers of the Sabbath-school, take charge of family prayers (also a Bible lesson), and look after the work among the women and the young men's league. How can she keep well through it all?

As soon as I came the girls began to say, " Teacher must go to her room." They could not rest, so I arose and went up. Opening the door, what did I see? Such a beautiful room! I

---

* His wife.

was astonished. It was adorned with a number of pictures, a new bed, a lounge, rag carpet, stove, curtains at the windows, etc. It was so clean and pretty I turned to Mrs. Coffing and said, "Did you think I was coming from Europe, that you prepared so beautiful a room for me?"

Miss Spencer, you should see our girls! Sweet as they were when you left us, they are now still sweeter, and their faces are full of light, of love, and obedience to their teachers. You know that last year they began to read the Holy Book. When I came, I asked if they had continued, and each one said, "Yes; we read every day." And upon my asking who remembered the verses Miss Spencer left with us, most of them showed me the places in their Bibles, saying they had read them at home.

The new desks have been set up, at last, in the schoolroom, and are very tasteful and convenient; but you should see the Hadjin girls try to sit in them! It is real funny. The carpenters worked very slowly, setting up only four desks a day. I thought then if all parts of them had been made here, it would have been like the old story of the forty-six years building of the Temple. The hillside in front of the schoolhouse has been leveled for a play-ground. Yours and Miss Tucker's flower-beds have been filled with good earth. All is well, and going on nicely, but there is everywhere a great lack, which to do without is very hard. It is Miss Spencer; and when she comes all will be more beautiful and perfect.

Yours, with much love,

TURFANDA.

Home Department.

STUDIES IN MISSIONARY HISTORY.
1885.

CENTRAL TURKEY MISSION, 1845-1870.

Beginnings of the Work by the exiled Bedros at Aleppo and Aintab.

Early Work of Messrs. Thomson, Ford, and Benton.

Aintab: What was accomplished by Messrs. Johnston, Van Lennep, and Smith? Death of Mrs. Nutting.

Aintab: Dedication of First Church Edifice; Death of Mrs. Schneider; Training-school for young men; Formation of the Second Church; Girls' school; Revivals.

Labors of Native Helpers.
Life and Labors of Dr. Azariah Smith.
Marash : Organization of First Church; Revivals, 1859, 1869.
Kessab and Oorfa.
Expulsion from Hadjin : Murder of Mr. Coffing.
Mrs. Coffing's Work in Marash : Girls' boarding-school; Revivals
in the school; Growth of schools in the city; Work in the villages.

The back numbers of *Life and Light* and of the *Missionary
Herald* furnish material of great interest for this lesson. The
next lesson will complete the study of the Central Turkey Mission; the lesson for December will be given to a glance at the
work of the present year.

LADY DUFFERIN AND MEDICAL WORK IN INDIA.

The following letter, recently sent to our rooms by Dean Bodley, of the
Woman's Medical College of Pennsylvania, has great significance to those
who, about the time Lady Dufferin went to India, united in special prayer
and effort in behalf of the women of that great empire. In the assurance that
the Queen first suggested to Lady Dufferin the great enterprise in which she
is engaged, we gratefully recognize the answer to the many prayers that accompanied our memorial to her Majesty. Dr. Anna J. Thoburn, of Calcutta,
writes to her *Alma Mater:* —

I WENT yesterday, at the request of Lady Dufferin, the wife of
our new viceroy, to talk over plans for establishing dispensaries
and training-schools for native women all over India.

The idea was suggested to her first by the Queen, before she
left England, and now she is making an effort to carry the idea
out. Her plan is to raise a fund in India, from whatever sources
she can, and from this support the work.

I am not able to say what salary could be guaranteed, but it
would probably be equal, all things considered, to what an ordinary doctor would make at home; and then it would be an assured
income, which, of course, is an advantage. Lady Dufferin says
that she herself would prefer those who would come as missionaries, but that some object to such. I told her what persons of
more experience than myself also say is true —.that the natives will
choose the missionary physicians in preference to the others.

A new hospital has just been opened in this place (Simla), and
the surgeon in charge is anxious to get a lady doctor to take charge
of the woman's ward, and one who can train classes of native
women for midwives. He is willing to give $80 per month, and a
house; and as living in India is cheaper than at home, this sum is
equal to a little more than $1,000 per year.

What can the Woman's Medical College of Pennsylvania do for India? There will be little trouble, I think, in raising the money needed, for the natives of India are anxious to have their women treated by women. If people at home had a better idea of what India is like, I am sure they would be much more willing to come. I must say that I prefer this land, in many respects, to my own native Ohio, and believe that the work of a doctor is, on the whole, easier here than there, for those suited to this climate, as I seem to be. . . .

In this connection I would say, that only those alumnæ who are especially well fitted to be doctors should be sent to India, as the English doctors here scrutinize them most closely. To begin with, they think our system of medical education superficial — that we turn out doctors too rapidly. Whenever I have an opportunity I make as good a defense as possible, but, at the same time, I do think we Americans are in too much of a hurry. I believe, however, that our doctors, as a class, do their work more conscientiously than the majority of those one finds in India.

A recent number of the *Indian Witness* has the following, which is interesting in this connection: —

While maternity is held in honor, and the mother of sons derives a special dignity from her position, the treatment of all women on the occasion of the birth of children is unimaginably cruel and stupid. The education and civilization of which some classes of native society can justly boast stop short of any attempt to ameliorate this evil, and an English speaking, and, to some extent, thinking, Hindu gentleman still considers that all the assistance which his wife needs in the supremest trial of her life can be sufficiently rendered by a woman of the lowest caste, whose ignorance is her greatest recommendation, since all that she has learned of the art she professes, tends only to make her help more dangerous than neglect. The wretched mother whose husband beats her with a stick because her new-born babe is a daughter instead of a son, is really little more to be pitied than the woman of higher caste, whose life is imperiled and whose health is destroyed by the barbarous customs of the country. The remedy for a state of things which it is unnecessary here to do more than hint at, lies in the proper training of native nurses, and in affording facilities for medical and surgical attendance to those willing to avail themselves of it, by the establishment of lying-in wards wherever hospital accommodation makes this possible.

Lady Dufferin, in interesting herself in a work which commends itself to the hearts and minds of all thoughtful Englishwomen, has, given an impetus to such a movement here, and the Ripon Hospital is to have a lying-in ward. The ladies of Simla are contributing toward the object in view, and Lady Dufferin also has kindly given permission for a popular *fête* to be held in the grounds of the Viceregal Lodge, toward the end of the month, of which she is patroness.

A LADY of our Board says: "I am sometimes wakeful at night, and the thought always comes to me that I am awakened on purpose to pray for China — that vast nation where all is life and activity while we sleep."

A STATE Secretary writes: "Two dollars came to me to-night, which I took up reverently, knowing the heart that prompted the sending. These words accompanied the gift: 'I send it because I am so anxious about that $60,000.' She has a husband who is a helpless invalid, is full of home cares, yet burdened in heart for our treasury." Would that each of the 75,000 women of the Interior had the same spirit.

THE Woman's Board of Missions of the Interior was represented in the farewell meeting on Thursday, Oct. 8th, by Miss Ella T. Bray, of Kenosha, Wis., who goes as our missionary to Adana, Turkey, to assist Miss Laura Tucker. Miss Tucker's letter in this issue shows how bravely she has held on alone, there, and how great is the need of more laborers.

TO AUXILIARIES.

WHEN this number reaches our readers our Treasurer's books will have been closed for the year. That phrase recalls the terror with which, as a child, I used to think of the closing of the book of record of my life, to be opened only at the judgment. How I used to wish there might be a possibility of changing that record, if it should be against me. This year's record can no more be changed than that. If we have not kept our pledges, they stand forever as witnesses against us. But the

ANNUAL MEETING

opens new books for us here. Let us begin aright. And, first, let nobody who can possibly be at St. Louis, fail to go in time to attend the mass meeting Tuesday evening, November 3d, or, at least, to be present at the opening session, Wednesday morning, November 4th. The missionaries from China, Turkey, and India, the reports and discussions on Senior, Junior, and Juvenile work, will surely interest all. Four classes especially, need the meeting:

(1.) State secretaries, that they may know the aims and methods of the Board. (2.) Leaders of auxiliaries, for they will find hints and suggestions given there by both example and precept. (3.) Leaders of young ladies' societies, for they will give and receive so much enthusiasm that they will gain new consciousness of their power to help. (4.) Leaders of mission bands, for they need to catch some of the electric power of the meeting to keep them charged through the year with all the purpose, and system, and faithfulness they hope to communicate to the children. Children's work will be presented by earnest, practical workers.

We need everybody who is interested to help bind our Board as by strong cables to its duty of courage, energy, vigilance, and prayer unceasing. Let no one say she is not needed. The little strands of hemp that make the great cable are easily broken, and of little use alone, but bound together what power can destroy them!

And we especially want a representative from every church in the Interior that is not interested. Such a representative would go back to be the entering wedge that would open a way for missionary enthusiasm and purpose enough to revive the Church in all its departments.

RECEIPTS OF THE WOMAN'S BOARD OF MISSIONS OF THE INTERIOR.

Mrs. J. B. LEAKE, Treasurer.

From August 18, 1885, to September 18, 1885.

ILLINOIS.

ILLINOIS BRANCH.—Mrs. W. A. Talcott, of Rockford, Treas. *Buda,* 8.60; *Canton,* 38.15; *Chicago,* Union Park Ch., 50, First Ch., 30, New Eng. Ch., 20, Western Ave. Ch., 22, South Ch., of wh. 25 from H. M. B., to const. L. M. Mrs. C. W. Brown, and 25 to const. L. M. Mrs. E. O. Hills, 50; *Chebanse,* 7.76; *Englewood,* M. S. Taylor, 3; *Granville,* 10; *Harvard,* 6; *Kewanee,* 15; *La Harpe,* 4.78; *Lombard,* 10.50; *Oak Park,* 40; *Princeton,* 36.15; *Providence,* to const. L. M. Mrs. E. A. Paddock, 25; *Prospect Park,* 9; *Rantoul,* J. S. Renner, 2; *Rockford,* 2d Ch., 49.55; *Roseville,* 4.50; *Ross Grove,* 19.36; *Springfield,* 66.35; *Sycamore,* 10; *Thawville,* 7.50; *Toulon,* 7.95; *Udina,* 10; *Washington Heights,* Mrs. Mary E. B.

Howe, 5; *Wheaton,* Mrs. W. R. Guild, 5; *Wythe,* 10, $583 15

JUNIOR: *Hinsdale,* Earnest Workers, 50; *Illini,* Y. L. S., 26; *Rockford,* Y. L. S. Rockford Fem. Sem., 10; *Sandwich,* King's Daughters, 30; *Springfield,* Jennie Chapin Helpers, to const. L. M. Electa W. Sutton, 26.50, 142 50

JUVENILE: *Chicago,* New Eng. Ch., M. Star certif's, 2; *Evanston,* Children's Asso., 9; *Lombard,* S. S., 13; *Wyoming,* S. S., 1.55, 25 55

THANK-OFFERINGS: *Chebanse,* 7.30; *Evanston,* Children's Asso., 1.80; *La Harpe,* 2; *Marseilles,* Helping Hands Diamond off., 30; *Rockford,* 2d Ch., 47.50; *Roseville,* 4.35; *Sycamore,* 10.25; *Toulon,* 13.80; *Wilmette,* Agnes Smith, 5, 122 00

LEGACY: *Toulon,* Mrs. Rhoda E. George, 50 00

Total, $923 20

IOWA.

IOWA BRANCH.— Mrs. E. R. Potter, of Grinnell, Treas. *Anamosa*, 17.36; *Algona*, 3.80; *Blairstown*, Mrs. J. H. French, 2; *Burlington*, 67; *Bell Plain*, A few friends, 3; *Clinton*, 10; *Cedar Rapids*, Mrs. L. B. Stephens, 40; *Cedar Falls*, Mrs. C. Townsend, 5, Mrs. A. G. Thompson, 2, Mrs. L. C. Gibbs, 2; *Chester Centre*, 35.38; *Durant*, 5; *Davenport*, 16.25; *Eldora*, 10; *Fairfield*, 10; *Fayette*, 10; *Green Mountain*, 27.60; *Gilbert Station*, 6; *Grinnell*, 83; *Genoa Bluffs*, 5.25; *Glenwood*, 19; *Independence*, 10; *Iowa Falls*, from sale of gold chain bequeathed by the late Mrs. Mary Wright, 50; *Keokuk*, 24; *Lyons*, 23.08; *Miles*, 12; *Marion*, 12.50; *Mt. Pleasant*, 31.50; *Mason City*, 3.30; *New Hampton*, 5.46; *Postville*, 10; *Shenandoah*, 6; *Sabula*, 5; *Salem*, 10; *Traer*, 50; *Toledo*, 6; *Wilton*, 4; *Waucoma*, 10; *West Mitchell*, Mrs. Elmer Butler, 5, $657 48

THANK-OFFERINGS: *Grinnell*, 63.73; *Glenwood*, 25; *Lyons*, 26.12; *Marshalltown*, 3, 117 85

JUNIOR: *Des Moines*, Plymouth Rock Soc., 9.40; *McGregor*, Y. L. M. Band, 20; *Mason City*, Soc. of Christian Endeavor, 3; *Marengo*, O. B. M. Soc., 30 cts.; *Chester Centre*, King's Daughters, 16, 48 70

JUVENILE: *Davenport*, Sunbeams, 5.35; *Durant*, S. S., 7; *Lyons*, Children's Soc., 13; *Mt. Pleasant*, S. S., 4.50, 29 85

Total, $853 88

KANSAS.

KANSAS BRANCH. — Mrs. A. L. Slosson, of Leavenworth, Treas. *Carbondale*, 5; *Eureka*, 10; *Leavenworth*, 5; *Stockton*, 3, $23 00

THANK-OFFERING: *Sabetha*, 13 50

Total, $36 50

MICHIGAN.

MICHIGAN BRANCH. — Mrs. Charles E. Fox, of Detroit, Treas. *Alamo*, 5; *Bridgeport*, 3.25; *Detroit*, Woodward Ave. Ch., 32; *Eaton Rapids*, 10; *Portland*, 15; *Romeo*, 25, $90 25

JUNIOR: *Detroit*, Woodward Ave. Y. L. M. Soc., 9; *Jackson*, Y. L. M. Circle, 35; *Litchfield*, Y. P. M. Circle, 5, $49 00

JUVENILE: *Detroit*, Trumbull Ave. S. S. Infant Class, 12; *Eaton Rapids*, Cheerful Workers, 1.31, 13 31

MORNING STAR MISSION: *Bridgeport*, Morning Star Mission Band, 1 50

THANK-OFFERINGS: *AnnArbor*, 82.86; *Detroit*, Woodward Ave. Young Ladies' Miss. Soc., 9.10; *Eaton Rapids*, 3.35; *Grass Lake*, 12.10; *Summit*, 7.85; *Union City*, 12.50. 127 76

Branch total, $281 82
——. A Friend, per Mrs. J. Porter, 75 00

·Total, $356 82

MINNESOTA.

MINNESOTA BRANCH.— Mrs. E. M. Williams, of Northfield, Treas. *Austin*, 33.10; *Clearwater*, 3; *Cottage Grove*, 12; *Duluth*, 13; *Elk River*, 7; *Excelsior*, 6.13; *Fairmont*, 3.50; *Faribault*, 65; *Fergus Falls*, 5; *Glyndon*, 21; *Hamilton*, 3; *Litchfield*, 1.35; *Little Falls*, 3.05; *Mankato*, 11.88; *Mantorville*, 1; *Mazeppa*, 6; *Medford*, 4.88; *Minneapolis*, First Ch., Aux., 43.50, Mrs. Pratt, 11, Mayflower Ch., 5.27, Pilgrim Ch., 26.48, Plymouth Ch., 221.52, Union Ch., 13.63; *Northfield*, 49.27; *Ortonville*, 5; *Owatonna*, 18.81; *Plainview*, 6; *Rochester*, 15; *Rushford*, 9; *St. Charles*, 15.50; *St. Cloud*, 11; *St. Paul*, Park Ch., 25, Plymouth Ch., 74.27; *Sauk Centre*, 30.58; *Wabasha*, 7; *Waseca*, 14.61, $802 33

JUNIOR: *Austin*, Jr. Miss. Soc., 29.21; *Excelsior*, Y. L. M. Soc., 20; *Faribault*, Helping Hands, 30; *Glyndon*, Gleaners, 10; *Minneapolis*, First Ch., Y. L. Soc., 16, Earnest Workers, 30; *St. Paul*, Atlantic Ch., Y. L. M. Soc., 25, Plymouth Ch., Y. L. Soc., 40, 200 21

JUVENILE: *Elk River*, M. Band, 5.68; *Litchfield*, Friends, 35; *Minneapolis*, Plymouth Ch., Y. P. Soc., 20; *Owatonna*, Merry Hearts, 27; *St. Paul*, Plymouth Ch., Mrs. Fanning's S. S. Cl.. 7.24; *Wabasha*, Young Folks' Band, 7, 67 27

Total, $1,069 81

MISSOURI.

MISSOURI BRANCH.—Mrs. J. H. Drew, 3101 Washington Ave., St. Louis, Treas. *Amity,* 10; *Carthage,* 25; *Kansas City,* Clyde Ch., 18.48; *Hannibal,* 12; *St. Louis,* Pilgrim Ch., 5.60; *Breckenridge,* 20, which with 5 from Juveniles, const. Mrs. Josie Read L. M.; *St. Joseph,* 8.55; *Cameron,* 9; *Sharon,* 1.50, ... $110 13
THANK-OFFERING: *Hannibal,* 2 30
JUVENILE: *Breckenridge,* 5; *Bevier,* Busy Bees, 7; *St. Louis,* 3d Cong. Ch., Coral Workers, 10, ... 22 00
MORNING STAR MISSION FUND: *St. Louis,* 3d Cong. Ch., 4; *Kansas City,* Clyde Ch., Cheerful Givers, 3.50, ... 7 50

Total, ... $141 93

NORTH DAKOTA BRANCH.

Mrs. R. C. Cooper, of Cooperstown, Treas. *Cooperstown,* 12.50; *Jamestown,* Mrs. M. S. Wells, 5, ... $17 50

Total, ... $17 50

SOUTH DAKOTA BRANCH.

Mrs. H. H. Smith, of Yankton, Treas. *De Smet,* 3; *Sioux Falls,* 25; *Yankton,* 14.35, ... $42 35

Total, ... $42 35

NEBRASKA.

WOMAN'S MISSIONARY ASSOCIATION.—Mrs. Geo. W. Hall, of Omaha, Treas. *Albion,* A Friend, 2; *Columbus,* 10; *Camp Creek,* 6; *Genoa,* 5; *Harvard,* 3; *Irvington,* 15; *Milford,* 5; *Steele City,* 10; *Springfield,* 7.50; *Weeping Water,* 11.50; *York,* 5; *Lincoln,* certificates, 25 cents, ... $84 25

Total, ... $84 25

OHIO.

OHIO BRANCH.—Mrs. Geo. H. Ely, of Elyria, Treas. *Andover,* 16.64; *West Andover,* 6.83; *Clarksfield,* 2; *Conneaut,* 19.50; *Cuyahoga Falls,* 4.57; *Randolph,* 5; *Wakeman,* 42.88, of wh. 30.38 thank-offering, ... $97 42
JUVENILE: *Elyria,* Opportunity Club, 10; *Unionville,* S. S., 2.62; *Wakeman,* Reliance Band, 2, ... 14 62

Total, ... $112 04

WISCONSIN.

WISCONSIN BRANCH. — Mrs. R. Coburn, of Whitewater, Treas. *Arena,* 6.83; *Antigo,* 8.25; *Baraboo,* 10; *Beloit,* 2d Ch., 10; *Brandon,* 2.75; *Big Spring,* Mrs. H. Hatch and J. Keith, 1.25; *Bloomer,* 2.20; *Bloomington,* 5, thank-offering, 5.85; *Darlington,* 5; *Evansville,* 4.30; *Eau Claire,* 25; *Fon du Lac,* 15; *Ft. Howard,* 8; *Ft. Atkinson,* 3.72; *Green Bay,* 35; *Hammond,* 4; *Hartland,* 20; *Kaukauna,* 1.50; *Lancaster,* 20, thank-offering, 10; *La Cross,* 45.25; *Madison,* 6.53; *West Salem,* 3.50; *Prairie du Chien,* 2.35; *Platteville,* 30.25; *Racine,* 79.79; *Stoughton,* 6; A. B. S. (14) and State of Wis. (11), to const. Miss Emily Bissell L. M., 25; *Sharon,* 10.50; *Sparta,* 22.40; *Shopiere,* Hadjin Home, 7; *Virogua,* 5; *Wauwatosa,* 43.47; *Windsor,* 36.65; *Whitewater,* 22.25; *Watertown,* 27.18, ... $586 72
JUNIOR: *Arena,* Bridge, 7.05; *Eau Claire,* 50; *Fon du Lac,* 10; *Green Bay,* 4.50; *Madison,* 50; *New Lisbon,* 30 cts ; *Wauwatosa,* 30, ... 151 85
JUVENILE: *Eau Claire,* thank-offering, 15; *Lancaster,* Shining Lights, 2.25, ... 17 25
MORNING STAR: *Arena,* Willing Workers, 10; *Evansville,* Little Gleaners, 7.50; *Eau Claire,* S. S., 10; *Hartland,* Miss. Band, 2.50; *New Lisbon,* 20 cts.; *Stoughton,* 20 cts., ... 30 40

..... $786 22
Less expenses, ... 25 72

Total, ... $760 50

MISCELLANEOUS.

Sale of leaflets, etc., 64.49; of mittens donated, 1.25; of "Life of Coan," 3, ... $68 74

Total, ... $68 74

THANK-OFFERINGS.

At Mission Rooms, Chicago, Aug. 21, 153.80. Later, from Mass., three friends, 15. From Iowa, a friend, 10; an old friend, 2; a "shut-in," 1. From Beloit, 1. From Ill., H. M. B., 2; S. B. B., 2, ... $186 80

Total, ... $186 80

Receipts for month, ... $4,654 32
Previously acknowledged, ... 25,947 41

Total since Oct., 1884 ..... $30,601 73

Board of the Pacific.

MRS. CLERICUS' WISDOM.

BY LUCY MOOAR, OF OAKLAND, CAL.

MRS. CLERICUS was the minister's wife, and lived in the manufacturing town of Pine Brook, and I don't want you to begin her acquaintance under the impression that she had the wisdom of Solomon: indeed, her neighbor, across the street, Mrs. Peterson, even went so far as to splutter out one day in a fit òf desperation, "Of all women livin', Mrs. Clericus is the foolishest. There's no head nor tail to her."

I was visiting with Mrs. Clericus when the above remark was imparted to her by one of those kindly intentioned neighbors as common in Pine Brook as elsewhere. Mrs. Clericus winced a little, but got along with her sympathetic neighbor without giving her any more unpleasant remarks to carry back to Mrs. Peterson, which I thought was quite a triumph of grace.

When the door was shut, and we were left alone together, she turned to me and said, with a curl to her lip but with a tear in her voice, " Pleasant, isn't it, Kate, to hear what your neighbors think of you ? I don't know that I regret the want of tact, but to be without a head in this intellectual nineteenth century is to be without everything; and do you know, Kate, sometimes I believe myself that I haven't any head — at least, not any level head. You and I were talking foreign missions just before Mrs. Tellall came in. Do you know what a twist-head I am about foreign missions ? Some days I read some interesting intelligence from the field, or an inspiring story or biography, and my eyes are full of tears and my heart full of prayers, and my fingers tingle to their tips to be at work for so divine a cause. And then perhaps I will take up something else, — Rose Terry Cooke's story in the *Congregationalist*, that was the last thing, — and I will really get to wondering if foreign missions are any use, and whether it would not be better to devote our time and money to the bettering of the crying evils at home. Why, I even go so far as almost to think that we are making things harder for the poor heathen by bringing them to the light, and giving them the chance to refuse it. It's a curse, isn't it, Kate, to have a head like mine, which sees so many sides of so many questions ? Give me the woman of one idea, who sees it plainly, and goes after it without a doubt that

(437)

she is after the idea best worth having in the world! She accomplishes something!"

So Mrs. Clericus had her little say, and you see, perhaps, the foolishness of it, and do not have much sympathy for so wavering-minded a person, "driven of the winds and tossed." But I give you this scene because I happen to know that my friend Rebecca Clericus, with her unstable mind, has considerable of the wisdom of the heart, and I want to tell you about it.

It was five years ago that Mrs. Clericus first went to Pine Brook, and she was appointed to try to collect some money for the Woman's Board. I was there when collecting-time came around, and so she took me with her as a kind of "moral support."

We first went up Broad Street, and turned down the lane to call at Mrs. Goodsy's. I remember there were some chairs and a melodeon in the parlor, but I remember Mrs. Goodsy herself better — a tallish, "fat as a match" kind of a woman, all of a width, with pale cheeks, straggling hair, and a shabby gown. Becky was hurried, so she sailed boldly in.

"I have come to see if you wouldn't like to contribute something to the Woman's Board, Mrs. Goodsy. I see that the former collector has your name down on her list. The Board is a little behind, this year, and needs all the help we can give it."

Mrs. Goodsy gave a thin, watery smile, tried to look equal to the occasion, coughed a little, and said mildly: "Mr. Goodsy, he says he hain't got no money to throw away on them foreners. There's Vévy—since we got the melodeon she takes music lessons, and Maudy and Claudy has to have new aprons all the time, and all the money that comes in seems to be swallered up as fast as we git it. I'm makin' some dresses now for Maudy and Claudy, all tucked and fixed up fine. Wait a minute," for we had risen to go, "and I'll fetch 'em;" and off she ran.

"Maudy, and Claudy, and Vevy, indeed!" fumed I; "I hope, Becky," ——

"Hush!" said Becky; and in came Mrs. Goodsy with the "fine" dresses, fifteen tucks in each, and ten-cent lace in cascades everywhere.

"Ain't the lace waterfalls pretty? an' there's goin' to be pink bows on 'em," said the proud mother. Becky looked at the dresses and replied: "It's real pleasant to make pretty things for the children, isn't it, Mrs. Goodsy? I am so glad Genevieve can take some music lessons. Let her come round to my house; I have some easy duets which I think she would like to play over with me."

We moved toward the door, and as we said our good-byes, Mrs.

Goodsy, hesitating a little, turned to Becky, saying, "I'm real sorry there wasn't anything for the missions, Mrs. Clericus. When does the money have to go? Perhaps I might save some egg-money, if I tried real hard."

"I think I will wait about a month before sending it down," returned Becky. "We shall be ever so glad to get even a little help from you. I'd like two dozen eggs myself on Saturday; if the twins will bring them, I will send you that apron pattern you wanted."

"Now we'll go to Mrs. Smith's; she lives right across the street;" and Becky pulled me along before I had a chance to relieve my mind concerning the feminine follies of Mrs. Goodsy.

Mrs. Smith met us with a somewhat sour look, and took us all in from head to foot. I was so glad we had on our gingham dresses and thread gloves.

"You have not been here very long, Mrs. Smith, but I thought perhaps you would like to join our auxiliary to the Woman's Board."

"What's it for?" briefly asked Mrs. Smith.

"Why, to support lady missionaries in foreign lands, and to help build schools, and do Christian work for the heathen."

"Heathen enough round here. Such a whiskey-saloon, gadabout, scandal-mongering place I never seen in all my life!" snapped Mrs. Smith. "Begin at home, and stay there till you've done something; that's my rule. If I have any money I guess I kin find use for it here, without going to Feejee, or any of them outlandish places."

"Yes, there's always plenty to do everywhere; and those who don't like to go abroad can fill their hands at home easily enough," said Becky. "It's just come to me, Mrs. Smith; but I wonder if you aren't just the woman my husband and I are looking for. We have found some poor girls among the factory hands who want to learn sewing and plain housework, and perhaps you could help them. You are praised all about as such a good housekeeper."

"Yes, I reckon I know a thing or two about housekeeping. Them premiums on the wall I got for my bread and pies at a fair last year;" and Mrs. Smith began to look somewhat less vinegary, and said she'd think about "them gals;" perhaps she could "give 'em a lift." "I ain't nowise averse to helping them that needs it, but I hain't got no call to them that's way off across the ocean."

As we went out of the gate I said to Becky: "Well, what have you gained by going there? I don't see why women are so narrow as not to be able to see outside of their own dooryards."

"Oh, she'll come around, Kate; never fear. If I can only get them started a little! Now we will go to Mrs. Jessup's."

Mrs. Jessup was a young bride, in her little, fresh, new home — a pleasant, roly-poly little woman, full of smiles and blushes. She would ask "Will;" he never liked to have her spend any money without asking him. "Will," explained Becky, on our way down the street, "is as close as two Jews, but that soft little woman thinks he's perfection. We shall not get any Board money there."

The next person we called on was Mrs. Holt. She seemed sur. prised when our errand was made known. "Why, I gave to that last year!" cried she (as if "that" were able to convert the whole world in one year). "I don't like to belong to societies which are always coming around. One can never feel settled and easy."

"Well, it isn't such a very easy thing to convert the world, you know. The societies have to keep working and working away, and we want to help them along as much as we can, don't we?"

"I suppose so," admitted Mrs. Holt, perceiving that this was the proper thing to say. "I don't know anything about those things, and I don't like to think about them; however, if Mr. Holt will give you the money I don't know as I object. But I don't want to ask him; you know he is always ready to give to everything, so you call at the office and ask him."

"Becky," cried I, as I saw her heading for the office, "you surely are not going to collect that money from Mr. Holt, flung at you that way!"

"Yes, indeed," smiled she. "Mr. Holt is generous; I have only to ask for it. It will pay for just as much as yours or mine."

"But the spirit, Becky, the spirit!"

"She has no begrudging spirit, Kate. It is only that she does not know, as she says. She needs help. Who knows but the money which Mr. Holt pays for her will be one of the drawing-strings?"

"Do these women attend the missionary meeting, Becky?"

"Missionary meeting!" I wonder if you know what you are talking about, Kate! There's never been a missionary meeting in this town. I keep urging Mr. Clericus to start a missionary concert, and he's going to, but he hasn't quite spurred up his courage yet. I shall not let him rest: I am determined that before another year we shall have a missionary concert and a ladies' meeting; yes, and a young folks' band, too. A day like this is a fire in my bones!"

[*Concluded in next number.*]

VOL. XV. DECEMBER, 1885. No. 12.

TURKEY.

LETTER FROM MISS MARIA A. WEST.

THE following letter was sent to be read at the Woman's Meeting held in connection with the Annual Meeting of the American Board of Foreign Missions in Boston, but, owing to the full programme, it was impossible to secure a place for it.

BELOVED FRIENDS OF THE WOMAN'S BOARD AT HOME, — GREETING : —

Allow me to break the silence of years past by a brief epistle on this rare occasion. Although not permitted to be present in person at any of your blessed convocations since that in Chicago, ten years ago, my spirit has been with you, and I have rejoiced, yea, I do rejoice with great joy, over your unequaled growth, in your marvelous prosperity in awakening and sustaining a deep and practical interest in the cause of foreign missions among the mothers and daughters of our dear native land, and in your more important work of training the children of our churches for this co-operation with Christ, that future generations of men and women may spontaneously carry on this work till the earth shall be filled with the knowledge of God according to his promise. . , .

Many of you are doubtless aware that, since the early part of the year 1880, my labors here have been more especially confined to the Constantinople "Rest," or Gospel Coffee-Room for all nationalities. Last November I was enabled to transfer this enterprise into other hands. It is now linked with the Smyrna Rest, according to my original plan, while I am thus set free to return to my original calling — my "first love" — in direct spiritual labor for the Armenian mothers, daughters, and children of this land. . . .

Last March I was again permitted to visit Smyrna, and resume my work among Armenian families there, so suddenly dropped, and with so much sorrow, five or six years ago. To my great joy, I found that doors then open for my entrance were not closed; on the contrary, new ones were unclosed and admittance gained with the gospel of Christ.

In this family visitation I was greatly helped by a comparatively new-comer into the household of faith, in whom I had become much interested before leaving Smyrna.

E—— then told me her story, which I will briefly relate for your encouragement. Her eldest sister was my next-door neighbor when I lived in Smyrna,— a widow with two sons and four lovely daughters,— and my relations with the family were very pleasant. They belonged to the better class of Armenians, and the home and its surroundings all bespoke wealth and position. The eldest son had received part of his education in England, and was quite superior in point of intelligence. With him, especially, I often had long and earnest discussions on the vital principles of Christianity, while his mother and sisters usually sat by in silence, but manifesting interest. The mother, a woman of perhaps forty-two or three, with a mind of more than ordinary strength, could not read, but wished her children to have every advantage. One evening E—— joined the family party. I had never seen nor heard of this sister of my good neighbor, but was struck with her pleasant countenance. She also listened in silence while the difference between a living and dead Christianity was plainly set forth, with illustrations in accordance with our Saviour's word, " By their fruits ye shall know them."

It appeared that the elder sister, in visiting her house, had often related these conversations, and E—— acknowledged that these were good words. She could read, and, possessing herself of a copy of the New Testament in modern Armenian, began to study God's Word and life. After months of this study she became convinced that this was the true way; but, at the same time, she decided in her own mind not to leave her church or people, or come out as a Protestant. That she could never do!

During this period I had opened a day-school for Armenian

children, and E——'s three were among the first to attend. They, in all the simplicity of childhood, carried home to their parents many precious seeds of truth, and the work deepened in the mother's heart. 'One Sunday her little boy was distressed because he had forgotten the place for his Sunday-school lesson. Finally his mother sent him to the teacher to inquire about it. The answer was,—

" Tell your mother to select some verses for you to-day."

"At this," said the mother, "I was greatly perplexed. How could I, who knew so little, tell what was suitable? and where should I look to find the verses? But I had learned to ask God for help, and so I lifted up my heart to him, and told him I did not know what to select, and would he please to show me; and the first words to which I opened were like his voice to my soul! I cannot describe to you how they took hold of my conscience: 'No man having put his hand to the plow and looking back, is fit for the kingdom of God,' and 'Follow me; let the dead bury their dead!' I saw that, whatever it cost, I must come out of the old church. If I had found life in Christ, how could I any longer live among the dead?"

Social ostracism was, for some time, the result of this step; but at the time of my visit most of her family and friends were again in pleasant relations with her. Day after day she accompanied me with great delight to houses never before entered by a missionary.

Let me give you somewhat in detail an account of a visit which was to me deeply interesting. It was with an aunt of E——'s husband — a charming old lady, with delicate complexion and fair hands, showing a life of exemption from toil. There were rich carpets on the floors of her house by the seaside, lace curtains draped the windows, and the furniture was in modern fashion, as also the daughter's attire. Two married daughters came in, and we were in the midst of a truly spiritual conversation, with the Bible open as our standard of appeal, when an elegant Armenian lady was announced for a fashionable call. She came in, card-case in hand, with much style and society polish, and my heart sank, for I thought our visit spoiled. But it was not Satan's device, after all; or, if so, God overruled it for good. We were speaking of the weather, and it was remarked that the climate had changed of late years, and that the old inhabitants of Constantinople said the same. I spoke of the change in climate elsewhere, and that in England many people believed that Christ was coming, and the end of the present state of things was at hand. This at once arrested attention, and caused the eager inquiries as to what changes were anticipated, and what preparation was to be made. Again the Bible was opened, and passages read by E—— at my request, while her apt remarks and convincing arguments greatly helped to deepen impressions made. The new-comer seemed to be seriously interested, and an hour or two was spent in this way, our last words being about the need for preparation for death and for heaven, and how we may be ready for the call that may come any moment. It was a solemn ending of the visit that all seemed to feel. There were seven of us grouped around that Bible as the center; and as the visitor rose to go, she expressed her "gratification at the profitable interview" in terms which I felt were more than polite phrases of society usage. This lady was educated at the school of the Smyrna Deaconesses, and, as the wife of one of the young and leading Armenians of Smyrna, occupies a position of influence. Will you not pray over this seed dropped by the wayside?

In bringing this lengthy and rather wandering narrative to a close, I must mention a work which E—— was induced to take up in her own home. Her husband had lost much of his business the last few years, and the work of the household devolved upon the labor of her own hands, besides aiding in its support. Yet she was glad to do what she could for the love of Christ. I spoke to her about calling in her neighbors for a Bible-reading. This she at first thought impossible. "On this street," she said, "we do not know our neighbors; it is not the custom; I have lived here two years, and have not spoken with one of them." But I urged her to try it,—to make some advances, at least,—and appointed a day for the meeting when I could be present. She shook her head rather doubtfully, but promised to see what could be done.

In the meantime she had told me of a "bad woman" who had contended for a few feet of land that really belonged to their lot, and that this woman gained her cause by appealing to the "rulers of the nation" (Armenian), and then built a room right up against their premises, and proved herself in every way such a torment, that they called her a "Satan." When I went to the house at the time appointed, seven women were present, and we had a very pleasant Bible-reading, E——, at my invitation, taking the lead. When all were gone, I asked how she had managed to succeed so well; and her answer was a lesson to those similarly situated:—

"I was standing at the door, and I saw my neighbor across the way at her window, and I said, 'Good-morning.' She replied very pleasantly, and before we knew it we were conversing. She said: 'You are different from the rest of us, and your children are different. We have watched your family these two years, and there is love and peace in your house. What makes the difference? Is it because you are readers?' This opened the way to invite her to the meeting. So of others."

"Did you notice the old woman at your right hand?" asked E——; "well, that was our enemy!"

"What!" I exclaimed—"the Satan that you told me about?"

"Yes; the very one," she assured me, with a smiling face. "When I was asking the others, I could not help remembering what our Lord said about loving our enemies, and so I asked her also; and she came."

Of schools visited, and other families where sickness or death had entered, time fails me to tell. I returned to Constantinople in April, hoping to make a similar visit to Smyrna another winter, and meanwhile to carry on the same work in and around this great city. But I was soon prostrated with an attack of pneumonia, which left me too weak for labor during the summer. I am now beginning to use my voice again, and took part in the quarterly meeting of our Protestant women at the Bible House yesterday. A goodly number were present, and one of the graduates of the Home School presided with modest dignity. Her husband was the former teacher of the boys' school in Smyrna. Another of the Home graduates played the organ, and made some interesting remarks. This young lady is a grandchild of the first mission school in Constantinople, her mother being the first pupil. She was also present, having hobbled from the bridge to the Bible-house with a sprained foot rather than to be absent. Scattered here and there were some of my own early pupils; also one from Harpoot.

A new generation is now coming to the front, and much depends on the stand they take. The children of those who have received a gospel education should be burning and shining lights in this land, but many are the snares and allurements to draw them aside into worldly conformity. Pray much for them — for me, also, that I may yet gather some sheaves in this field ere I am called hence.

REPORT FROM THE CONSTANTINOPLE HOME.

BY MRS. C. H. HAMLIN.

CONSTANTINOPLE HOME, Aug. 12, 1885.

ANOTHER school-year is done, and our family is scattered far and wide to enjoy a refreshing rest and change till the 15th of September. It has been a good year. Our little school-world has gone on its way smoothly and happily, bringing no greater difficulties and anxieties (excepting two cases of serious illness in the winter) than must necessarily come with the daily routine of so responsible a work. Our numbers have been about the same as the year before. We have had 57 boarders and 40 day-scholars, the usual number of nationalities being represented — Armenians, Bulgarians, Turks, English, and Americans. Our Bulgarian force had decreased a little, owing, partly, at least, to the quarantine of last summer, that made it so difficult to get into this city from outside. We thought the girls who did come, and braved the five days' quarantine, were deserving of much praise. We have had only three Turks, but more Armenians than have come for several years. The girls came back more promptly than usual, and in a very few days we were well started on our year's work. One new girl objected to the religious services, and her parents took her home in a few days, saying that they had been misinformed about the school; their daughter should not attend Protestant services. Aside from her, all seemed happy and contented. We have enjoyed our sewing-classes very much this year. They were a new feature, and we feel much pleased with the attempt. We had never felt satisfied with the instruction in plain sewing; so this year we divided up all the boarders among ourselves, and met our classes in our own rooms in the evening after dinner. They made very pretty, cozy-looking groups, gathered around a table, free to talk and laugh, provided they kept their needles going. Each girl was required to make a garment for herself, every stitch to be taken by hand. Some became very ambitious, and we were proud to show their handiwork at the close of the year. The girls were very enthusiastic about it, and we all enjoyed those home-like hours with them; sometimes reading them an interesting book, sometimes letting the conversation go as it would. As winter came on our hearts were stirred with pity for the miserable poor around us, and we resolved to try to interest the girls in work for the poor. We had quite a bundle of warm clothing which had been made the year before ; a request for old clothes brought another pile. We took the girls, two or three at a time, with us to distribute these garments, and I think the misery and destitution they saw was a revelation to them. They made a good many more garments for the poor in the course of the year, some sewing-classes working for them one day in each week, some completing their own garments first, and then working entirely for the poor. My class organized themselves into a little charitable society, electing a treasurer, and agreeing to pay one piastre (five cents) each every week. I cannot tell how much was contributed altogether through the year, for we kept no account of the whole. It was not very much, but it was at least a beginning, and we hope to enlarge this work next year. The girls have always contributed more or less for the poor, but this was the first time that we took them with us to come in contact with them. There are many, many needy ones in Scutari, and the poverty is of such a hopeless kind that our hearts ache in thinking of it. I know widows who work all day long painting head-handkerchiefs, and can get only eight or ten cents a day to support themselves and their children. The whole family occupies one miserable, shaky room, through whose leaky roof the wind and snow come down on their beds. They cannot read; they know almost nothing of Bible truth. There are no charitable institutions to offer help to those who deserve it. Some of our seniors have taken great pleasure this year in going regularly once a week to read the Bible to these women. Their minds are very dark, and it is almost impossible to induce them to make any mental effort to learn to read, or even to commit a verse to memory. Yet perhaps the good seed may find a place in some sad hearts, and spring up and bear fruit.

Our monthly concerts have been sustained with interest all the year. The girls take part in these meetings, and are always glad when the evening comes round once a month. The contributions this year amounted to about $50. Some of this was devoted to work among the Koords, some was given for Africa, and some went to buy a Seamen's Library. I think the interest has been specially for Africa, this year. I read the whole of "Blaikie's Life of Livingstone" to the juniors, and they always came eagerly to the reading. At our June meeting we got Dr. Hannington to speak to us,— a gentleman who was sent out by the Scotch Mission to Lake Nyassa, but who nearly died of the African fever, and was obliged to leave. We had a very good senior class this year of seven girls. They were good scholars, and earnest Christian girls, and we felt very sorry to lose them when the year ended. But we hope they are going forth to do good work in the world. Three or four of them expect to teach, and though their work is not yet quite decided on, they seem ready to go wherever they can be useful; and we hope to send one to Marash, one to Smyrna, and the others will, perhaps, be nearer to Constantinople. It seems to me we have reason to be pleased with the lives of most of our graduates. Many of them have been good, faithful teachers. Some are letting their light shine bright in homes, where they have no helps and many hindrances in their Christian life. One died in faith, and another has for three years been a bed-ridden sufferer, longing to "depart and be with Christ."

We had hoped for a more strongly marked religious interest than we have seen in the school this year; yet it has been a year of steady growth to many of our girls, and we have been specially pleased to see a more earnest spirit of Christian activity and readiness for self-sacrifice than before, and several have, we believe, been awakened to a new life during the year.

Young People's Department.

LETTER FROM MISS RUBY HARDING, OF AHMEDNAGAR, INDIA.

HALL I tell you about a little society the younger girls of the school have formed among themselves this term?

It began something in this way. The pastor's daughter, with three other little girls, decided to go by themselves each day to pray. They chose as their meeting-place the back veranda of a small house which stands unoccupied in one corner of our compound. For a time no one knew anything about their going there; but after a few weeks, when a teacher found out about it, she said, "Why do you not form a society among the little girls, and in this way do more good?" They liked the idea, and soon about fifteen girls met together each morning, at recess, on the back veranda.

All this time it had been kept so very quiet, just among themselves, that we knew nothing about it. We only noticed that the little girls, a certain number of them, went very regularly in the direction of that veranda. One day I said to Miss Fairbank, "It must be they have built a playhouse or something of that sort back there, and before we know it they may do some harm to the house." Not long after, I saw some girls as they started for the place; so, with as much reproof in my tone as possible, I asked them what they were doing back of the house, and started to see for myself if there were any mischief on foot. Of course there was nothing to be seen; and when, in a timid voice, one girl spoke up and said, "We come here to pray," I felt I was the one who needed reproof rather than they. I told them how glad I was to know this, and if there was any way in which we could help them, we would be glad to do so.

About a month ago a petition was sent us asking if there was a room anywhere that we could give them in which they could meet. They said some wasps had built some nests near there, and people said snakes had been seen near the veranda, so they were afraid to meet there any longer. When a room was found and given to them, the joy of the little praying circle knew no bounds, and they became more earnest than ever before. This last week Miss Fairbank and I were invited to meet with them one afternoon. No such occasion is considered properly carried out without some present and flowers; so we were presented with a white handkerchief and a bit of betel-nut, and for our wrists a garland of white flowers. On our inquiring a little into their experiences, one girl said: —

"Two or three girls have tried to trouble us all they could, but when they came on the veranda the wasps stung them, so they do not trouble us any more. When we used to pray on the veranda the wasps came right on us sometimes, but they never stung us once, because we were praying."

"Do you have a leader?" we asked.

"O yes; we choose one every fourth day. She has to read a few verses and pray; and then, after others have prayed, a hymn is given out, and while we pray a plate is passed around for contributions."

During the mission meetings in October, when special offerings are made, they hope to have a sum gathered in that way to hand in. The members of this praying circle are only girls from eight to twelve years of age, so all their proceedings are very simple and childlike. This, however, makes them none the less earnest, and their simple faith has been a real lesson to me.

Just now we are all saddened by the illness of one of our girls. She has never been a strong, healthy girl, and now quick consumption has set in, and the doctor gives us no hope that she can recover. All that is left for us to do is to smooth for her these last days of pain and weakness that await her. She and her younger sister are orphans, and have been in the school for several years. Both are members of the church, and are quiet, faithful girls. Do pray with us that this experience may lead the girls to be more serious and earnest, and more faithful in their work while the day lasts.

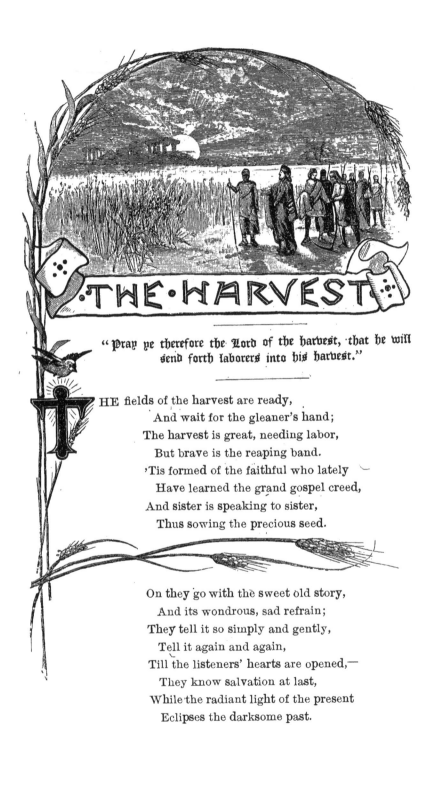

THE·HARVEST·

"Pray ye therefore the Lord of the harvest, that he will
send forth laborers into his harvest."

HE fields of the harvest are ready,
　　And wait for the gleaner's hand;
The harvest is great, needing labor,
　　But brave is the reaping band.
'Tis formed of the faithful who lately
　　Have learned the grand gospel creed,
And sister is speaking to sister,
　　Thus sowing the precious seed.

On they go with the sweet old story,
　　And its wondrous, sad refrain;
They tell it so simply and gently,
　　Tell it again and again,
Till the listeners' hearts are opened,—
　　They know salvation at last,
While the radiant light of the present
　　Eclipses the darksome past.

And those who believe in its promise
  Are never content to rest
Till the dear ones around have heard it,
  And they, too, join with the blest.
With faith for a shield to protect them,
  They go forth in God's own strength:
From afar men flock to their standard,
  And the ranks are swelled at length.

And that host, with Christ for its Captain,
  Each day is growing more strong:
This strain is caught up and repeated
  As the army wends along.
The legend traced on their banner
  Is the blest one, "God is Love,"
And the hymn they sing finds an echo
  In the angel choir above.

                  G. E. M., *in "Indian Jewels."*

Our Work at Home.

HOW SHALL WE MAKE MISSION-CIRCLES INTERESTING?

BY MISS S. E. DOWD.

[Read at the Annual Meeting of the New York State Branch, Oct. 21st.]

I FACE a company of anxious questioners, perhaps,— those whose hearts are truly in the work we have in hand; who desire that the children of our church shall be trained to systematic and conscientious giving, and to the proper sense of their share in the redemption of the world. Our hearts die within us, almost, as we look at the magnitude of our task, and then at the multitudes of obstacles that come up as we labor. This is such a busy world, and the care of it tells even upon child-life. It is a selfish world, and we have selfishness to combat. We cast the seed with liberal hand, with all carefulness, all watching, all prayer, and now, as in the times of Him who taught in parables, much of it seems lost. We need to see, as did Elisha's servant, that "they that be with us are more than they that be with them." We need to stay our timid souls upon the sure promises of God.

> "No word he hath spoken
> Was ever yet broken."

Therefore we may safely assure ourselves that "no blight, nor mildew, nor scorching sun, nor rain-deluge can turn that harvest into failure."

The Master is sure to give, somewhere, the hundred-fold, the sixty, and the thirty.

Robertson says, "On earth we have nothing to do with success or with results, but only with being true to God, and for God; for it is sincerity, and not success, which is the sweet savor before God." Another comforting thought of the same author is, "It is not talent, nor power, nor gifts that do God's work, but it is that which lies within the power of the humblest: it is the simple, earnest life led with Christ."

First of all, then, I would say that we need great faith, great singleness of heart, great perseverance, if we mean to succeed. We must not allow ourselves to think of failure even as a remote possibility.

I still hear the question, "How make the meetings interesting?" That is easily and briefly answered: be interesting. In other words, be so full of your work, so interested in every detail of it, so familiar with every turn of it, that your feeling shall be contagious. Enthusiasm in you, dear leader, will create enthusiasm in the children. If you are really and heartily interested in any special field, you cannot fail to impart your own feeling to them. Be certain about everything you try to talk to them about, and you will carry conviction into their young minds. I might describe an ideal leader, and an ideal circle, but I shall be surer of my ground if I tell you about the doings of our own particular organization, now in its ninth year.

From the first, we have tried to give the children just as many offices to fill as possible. There has always been some one who could take the position of Secretary, and discharge its duties in a perfectly satisfactory manner. Two girls serve as librarians, and are exceedingly zealous, while very little ones are trusted with the important matter of passing the plates for collection. Sometimes we have a "Music Committee," whose duty it is to select the hymns for singing, and perhaps secure something extra, either in the way of vocal or instrumental music. The Literary Committee do the work of distributing any material we give them among the members. The chairman of the Entertainment Committee take all that work off our hands, although she is only a girl of fifteen; and the task of giving supper to fifty or sixty mites of humanity used to make us tired to think of, for a fortnight ahead. Our President and Treasurer have been teachers of the Primary and Intermediate departments of the Sabbath-school for some years, and so have had nearly all these children in their classes at some time or other. They are thoroughly acquainted with them, and endeavor to keep whatever influence they may have gained. Doubtless much of the interest in our circle is due to Sunday work — to the word in season that it is easy to speak in one's own class.

We have tried to awaken an intelligent interest in our children. Once we attempted to make the matter of organization clear, by drawing a tree upon the board: its trunk bore that familiar inscription, A. B. C. F. M. ; its branches were labeled with the names of different States ; conspicuous among them was New York, divided into as many limbs as we have Associations. Then the Associations each had their Woman's Society, and on the tip end of our Woman's Society were spread the green leaves of our own Mission Circle. We began with the leaves, and traced them up to the great trunk. Then we explained the mystic letters by comparing the Board to our village school-board, with the workings of which the older members were familiar. We went on, by the help of a map, to learn and locate our different mission-fields, and to learn the names of some of the missionaries in each place.

We like very much to make studies of the different countries, and that involves a little, or perhaps a great deal, of preparation. We like to have some sort of plan run through our exercises, so we often make out scores of questions; for I have yet to find anything readymade that will just fit the requirements of the case. We have used some of the exercises published by our own Board as partial helps in such meetings. Then from our stores we interspersed recitations, music, anecdotes, map-work, explanations, and, if possible, some curiosities from the country in question. It is a great pity that there cannot be a well-stocked museum for every mission circle to consult, for we all know how an object will hold the attention of children. Let Fannie be ever so uneasy, hold up a Chinese shoe, and she will forget to twirl her handkerchief as she looks at the curious thing, and her small brain is set into a state of wonder and curiosity about it. Call up some mite, and compare her shoe with that of the Celestials, and then tell them how the cruel process of foot-binding is begun and carried on. Freddie is given to punching his neighbor on the sly, and Willie's shoe-tips are sad wanderers; but take a stick of wood and show how the Pacific Islanders dig out their canoes and rig them, and the eyes of those boys will give you all the inspiration you will need, while at the same time there will be peace in your borders. Next to objects are really good pictures. There are plenty of them in our various publications. Yet it is difficult to do much with them, on account of their diminutive size. But you can buy a roll of cheap wall-paper, the kind that has a light gray or yellow back, and with a generous brush you can make for yourself idols of noble proportions, temples, Turkish houses, African kraals, etc. A more delightful way still is to have a number of these large blank sheets of paper of perhaps a yard square. Upon them have exceedingly faint outlines of what you mean to draw, done with a hard lead pencil; then, before your circle, with a handful of soft crayons, talk, and dash on the color. A little practice will give one a great deal of boldness in this kind of rapid, effective work, and the delight of the children will be unbounded as they watch the pictures grow with magical swiftness. If you can't do this work yourself, perhaps you can enlist the cunning hand of some one whose "one talent" that gift may be.

Once we made a missionary scrap-book. The children enjoyed cutting and classifying the pictures, and they like to look at the book. In time we hope to have a stereoscope, with a goodly number of views, and we even aspire to a missionary album. Our library is still drawn upon at every meeting, and much interest evinced in the books read.

The circle is so large that we meet in the chapel of the church. One of the older girls presides at the piano. Our devotional exercises are brief, and as varied as we know how to make them. Instead of hearing a chapter, we sometimes repeat one together, or responsively. Sometimes the children repeat the prayer after the leader, and always we use the Lord's Prayer in concert. As to our supper, we have reduced the labor incident to that interesting exercise to about the minimum. The hour for it is early, and our older girls do not think it necessary to have a great variety every time. Sometimes they give us sandwiches, sometimes only cake; sometimes they are more indulgent, and we have quite a feast. We have disposed of the bulk of the dish-washing in a very neat way. Our ladies brought some dozens of wooden plates for picnics, and we use them, on account of their lightness. We have no breaking of crockery, therefore, and we have dozens of little tin cups, and they are very convenient for small people to drink from.

We have gone through the discipline of special efforts. We have had fairs, a paper festival, a loan exhibition, public exercises, etc. The children are always immensely enthusiastic, and ready to do anything and everything; but these things involve days of solid labor, and midnight oil, too. They are good, perhaps, to interest the elders and to stimulate the youngers. But, above everything, we try to teach systematic giving, and conscientious giving. Many of the children are glad to take mite-boxes, and the little sums thus brought into the treasury are often the fruit of self-denials and sacrifices of no mean order.

Once we suggested that everybody try to secure honorary members to our circle at a fee of twenty-five cents, which should entitle the person to come into our meetings at any time. This brought quite a hearty response. At the yearly meeting we mean to give these members special invitations to our festivities; and we mean to be so very interesting that we shall win them to a lasting interest in us, in our purposes and work. We have alternate meetings for work, and those mean wear and tear of body and brain — probably because we haven't yet discovered the royal road to success. We confine our work mostly to the making of useful objects. We hem towels, make holders, sweeping-caps, teapot-holders, and bibs. Some of our girls can do Kensington outlining, and they work on splashers, etc. The stand-by for general employment is patch-work. Everybody aches to work, but, in these days of school-cramming, there is zeal without knowledge so far as finger-craft is concerned, and the patience of Job is needed for the engineering of even one small quilt. There isn't much that boys can do, unhappily, but we try to make them useful in some capacity.

As to material for our literary programmes, we have in our possession a very capacious box. Into its depths goes whatever we think may, by any possibility, be made available for use. Stories of life in fore'gn lands, bright little stories, scraps of missionary intelligence, the *Mission Dayspring, Children's Work for Children,* and all the leaflets of all the different societies — all these are hoarded up for time of need, and thus are at hand when wanted.

I doubt not that many mission-circle leaders are in the habit of preparing original matter for the use of their own societies, or of adapting the material of others. Is it not possible to set up an exchange bureau, and so let these good things be used again and again? The young are the hope of the world. Its burdens will soon shift from our shoulders to theirs, and no painstaking effort made to give proper bent to their minds will be lost.

Dear mission-circle laborers, go on with fresh zeal and courage. Your own earnestness and interest will be met by an equal measure in your children, and the future will show the result; for

"Others shall
Take patience, labor, to their heart and hand
From thy heart, and thy hand, and thy brave cheer,
And God's grace fructify through thee to all.
The least flower, with a brimming cup, may stand
And share its dewdrop with another near."

MEETING IN CONNECTION WITH THE AMERICAN BOARD IN BOSTON.

BY MRS. S. BRAINARD PRATT.

" WE will arrange for an overflow meeting, but I do not think it will be needed. Women's meetings are no novelty in Boston."

So said one on whose judgment it is usually safe to rely, but for once she was mistaken.

Up through the pleasant autumn sunshine, on the morning of October 15th, came women by twos, women by threes, women by scores, women in unbroken procession; till, before the hour appointed, there was neither sitting nor standing room in the large church in Ashburton Place. An overflow meeting in the vestry below, at which Mrs. Lemuel Guliver presided, was soon crowded to discomfort, also. A third in Park Street vestry was led by Mrs. Judson Smith. This, also, was more than filled, some unable to gain admittance there, taking refuge in the church above.

The missionary ladies kindly consented to speak in all three places, and the interest in the overflow meetings was quite as great as in the main audience-room.

At Mt. Vernon Church the meeting was called to order by Mrs.

Albert Bowker, and after the great congregation had united in the grand old doxology, the forty-first chapter of Isaiah was read and commented upon, and Mrs. Moses Smith, President of the Board of the Interior, led in prayer.

Mrs. Bowker gave a warm welcome to those who were present, saying, "We are all daughters of mothers who helped to lay the foundation for this American Board.

Mrs. Moses Smith brought loving greetings from the Board of the Interior. The Woman's Boards, she said, formed a chain of three links, welded together by the love of Christ and joy in the Holy Ghost; but a meeting like this tended to bind them still more closely, and fulfill Christ's last prayer for his own, "That they all may be one." A letter of greeting came from the Pacific Board, and was read by Miss Child; also, a loving written word from the venerable Mrs. Schauffler, now in her eighty-fourth year.

Mrs. S. W. Howland, of Ceylon, was introduced, and said she was enjoying so much, that her body did not feel large enough to hold her heart. She spoke of the power of littles, and referred to the promise for him who was "faithful over a few things." She told a story of a little lame girl living in a dark alley, who was like sunshine there, and when one asked her for her secret, she said she "only asked the Lord to make her eyes clear to see what she could do for him." We want to offer the same prayer. The Christian women of Ceylon are trying to be faithful in little things. In the morning when measuring out the supply of rice for the day, they take out a double handful and put it in a bag by itself: that is for the Lord's work. No native Christian ever refuses to take part in the prayer-meeting.

Mrs. Pease, of Micronesia, said Christians at home have no idea how much the Morning Star means to missionaries on the Islands. The natives, too, always remember her in their prayers, asking that she may come safely. Three young ladies and seven families are needed immediately in Micronesia, to carry on the work; and Mrs. Pease had wondered, in looking at these immense audiences, whether it was possible that all these Christians had settled it on their knees whether they should go or stay. Jeremiah, one of their devoted natives, had sent his love to all Christians in America; but if he could see these throngs he would say, "Is it possible there are so many of them, and so few willing to come and help us. Allusion was made to Mrs. Snow, of Micronesia, who was apparently near her end, and Mrs. Horton, of Wellesley, led in special prayer in her behalf.

Mrs. Bowen, of Smyrna, took the audience back from these islands of the sea to the cradle of the human race, where her missionary life had been cast. She referred to a full chorus in process of training — discords and failures abound; but wait a little, till the training is ended, and the harmony will be complete. So it is on missionary ground — many jarring notes, many failures; but when the training is ended, and they all sing together with us in the grand hallelujah chorus, there shall be nothing wanting.

Miss Childs read a historical paper, giving some of the causes which led to woman's work for woman.

Mrs. Montgomery, from Turkey, who has been at home for a year and a half, said the missionary work never looked so grand to her as when seen from this side of the globe. She looked upon a meeting like this against a dark background of dusky faces, and she appealed to Christians at home to pray for them.

Mrs. Goodrich, of North China, said we had only begun to work upon the rim of China, but we expect wonderful things of that land, and we shall see them; for China is stirring, and she is to become one of the great powers of the world. Do we not all want to help in her redemption?

Mrs. Palmer, of Springfield, led in a prayer of consecration, and the meeting, which in common with all the sessions of the American Board, was one long to be remembered, closed with the old but ever new doxology, "Praise God, from whom all blessings flow."

ANNUAL MEETING OF THE NEW YORK STATE BRANCH.

BY A. F. EASTMAN.

THE annual meeting of the New York Branch, held at Pulaski, October 21st, was one of special interest, being the tenth anniversary of its formation. Notwithstanding leaden skies and frequent showers, both of its sessions were attended by a goodly number of delegates and friends, and much interest and enthusiasm was shown.

An address of welcome from one of the Pulaski ladies was fittingly responded to by our president, Mrs. Bradley, who wished for all a birthday blessing — a tenfold blessing in the work — from this day's meeting.

The secretary's report was full of encouragement. Six new auxiliaries have been formed, most of these in the Welch churches, in which there seems to be a growing interest in missions. She reported nine hundred and seventy-five subscribers to LIFE AND LIGHT, but among these two hundred and sixty-three, whose subscriptions are unpaid. Do these dead-heads represent dead hearts? The resignation of one vice-president was reported,—

Miss Taft, of the Ontario Branch. Mrs. Fitch, of Buffalo, was elected to fill her place. The treasurer reported our receipts to have been $6,434.71, which is $176 less than last year.

The Secretary of Mission Circles then made her first report. She divided the circles, as heard from, into three classes — active, less active, and dead. She urged co-operation in this work on the part of parents. The forty-seven mission circles connected with our Branch represent fifteen hundred children working for missions. Miss Ames closed her interesting report by a reference to the fact that sailors often have to guide their vessels into harbor by means of the lower lights along the shore, because the lighthouses are too high to be of use to them. The children are our lower lights.

The foreign secretary reported progress in all directions, yet abundant room for more work and more workers.

After singing, Miss Price, who is at home for rest after eight years' labor in Inanda, Africa, told us much of her life and work in that dark country. This is a Jubilee year in Africa, being the fiftieth anniversary of the beginning of work there. There is much to discourage, in the superstition of the people and the tenacity of their hold on some heathen customs, even after their conversion. Temperance work at Inanda has received a great impulse recently. Three years ago there was but one man at the station who did not drink beer daily. Now, there are one hundred and fifty men members of the Total Abstinence Society. At one of the smaller stations every man has given up his beer. This temperance work began in a day of fasting and prayer held by six women at a time of great discouragement in the church. The English colonists are taking a new interest in the work of the mission. Some of the English ladies sent for Mrs. Edwards to come and speak to them of the work being done. Mrs. Edwards being unable to go, sent one of their pupils to plead the cause of her people before these English women.

Miss Price showed a number of interesting articles from Africa, and answered several questions asked by persons in the audience.

A paper by Miss Halsey on the best way to raise money,— whether by entertainments or otherwise,— was listened to with marked attention: the interest it excited showed that this is a vexed question in many minds. After presenting all that could be said in favor of entertainments, the writer urged a more excellent way — a way which should be more worthy of the spirit that animates us in this work. She urged individual effort, founded on earnest prayer, the use of the highest motives in appealing to ourselves or to others.

After this paper—on which we wish there might have been time for discussion—Miss Fry, of Syracuse, favored us with an exquisite solo.

In the afternoon we listened to a greeting from the Woman's Board in Boston, by Miss Child, who thrilled all hearts by her array of the present needs of the Board.

The Conference of Mission Circles, led by Miss Ames, was a new feature of the meeting, and called out much enthusiasm. The important question seemed to be, "How shall we interest the boys, and get them to work as the girls do?"

A paper by Miss Cummins, entitled "Some Phases of the Work Among Young Women," was read by Mrs. Pond, which vividly presented the problem of our over-taxed girls, with the demands of study and society upon them—versus the missionary work, in which we long to see them bearing their part.

Then followed ten-year reminiscences; those of the first five years written by Mrs. Holbrook, who is now in California, and the last five by Mrs. Hough, of Antwerp, former home secretary of the Branch. Mrs. Holbrook spoke of the peculiar pleasure of beginning, of watching, and tending the early growth of the work. The third year the Branch had twenty-seven auxiliaries and nine mission circles. The first year the receipts were $1,000, the fifth year four times as much.

Mrs. Hough added items of interest in the last five years' work, among them growth of mission circles and increase of contributions. The sum received and expended by the Board during the ten years is $56,423.56. Mrs. Hough closed with the message of the past to the future of David to Solomon,—"And thou mayest add thereto."

Mrs. Butler, the former president, spoke a few warm words of greeting and encouragement; after which Mrs. Bradley read a brief anniversary paper, emphasizing the advantages of organization, the need of the world, and the privilege of the worker.

Mrs. Montgomery, of Turkey, then gave a missionary address, urging the need there and here, which aroused in all hearts a desire for more entire consecration to the Master's work.

The thank-offering fund, which amounted to $368, was voted to be sent as a seventy-fifth birthday gift to the American Board, from the New York Branch, on its tenth birthday. The meeting closed with the singing of one verse of "Blest be the tie that binds,"—all the audience joining hands during the singing.

Thus closed one of the most inspiring meetings it has been our privilege to enjoy.

ANNUAL MEETING.

THE Annual Meeting of the Woman's Board of Missions will be held in Beneficent Church, Providence, Rhode Island, on Wednesday and Thursday, January 13 and 14, 1886. All ladies interested are cordially invited to be present. The ladies of Providence will be happy to entertain in their homes all regularly accredited delegates, or their substitutes: all such desiring entertainment are requested to send their names, before December 15, 1885, to Mrs. Harriet N. Lathrop, 17 Angell Street, Providence. To any besides delegates who may desire to secure board, suitable places, at reasonable rates, will be recommended, on application to the same address.

WOMAN'S BOARD OF MISSIONS.

Receipts from Sept. 18 to Oct. 18, 1885.

MISS EMMA CARRUTH, TREASURER.

MAINE.

Maine Branch. — Mrs. W. S. Dana, Treas. Bangor, Aux., $22; Calais, Aux., $10; Searsport, Aux. (add'l), $1.50; Bucksport, Aux., $5; Bingham, Aux., $4.65; Madison, Aux., $4, $47 15

Total, $47 15

NEW HAMPSHIRE.

New Hampshire Branch.—Miss A. E. McIntire, Treas. Bennington, Aux., $5.85; Dover, Busy Bees, $50; Dunbarton, Mayflowers, $14; Fitzwilliam, Aux., prev. contri. const. L. M. Miss Eliza W. Jenkins, $8; Hanover, Aux., $42.95; Hinsdale, Aux., $16.50; Hollis, Aux., $3; Lake Village, A Friend, 40 cts.; Nashua, A Friend, $1; Nelson, Mrs. G. H. Dunlap, $10; Piermont, Aux., $3.30; Rochester, Aux., $30; Tilton, Aux., $4.50; Wilton, Aux., $5.50, Sale of E. S. Morris's Palm Oil Soap, at Annual Meeting, $45.55, Mrs. E. S. Goddard, const. L. M. Elizabeth Goddard, $25, Ladies in

Dublin, $5.26, Scattering, fr. Friends, $1.75 $272 56
Atkinson.—A widow,   1 00

Total, $273 56

VERMONT.

Vermont Branch.—Mrs. T. M. Howard, Treas. Barnet, Aux., prev. contri. const. L. M. Mrs. Caroline Holmes, $17, Busy Bees, $5; Barton, Aux., $6; Bellows Falls, Aux., $12.50; Bennington, Aux., $25; No. Bennington, Aux., prev. contri. const. L. M. Mrs. H. D. Hall, $8; Bradford, Aux., $21.15; Brandon, Aux., $17.50; West Brattleboro, Aux., prev. contri. const. L. M. Mrs. Sophia E. Smith, $9; Brookfield, First Ch., Aux., prev. contri. const. L. M. Mrs. Gilbert Bigelow, $20, Mayflowers, $1.30, Second Ch., Aux., $17; Burlington, Aux., of wh. $25 const. L. M. Mrs. Sarah P. Torrey, $55; Brownington and Barton Landing, Aux., $5; Castleton, Aux., $10; Charlotte, Aux., const. L. M. Mrs. Henry McNeil, $25; Chester, Aux., $20; Colchester, Aux., $10.12; Cornwall, Aux., of wh. $25 const. L. M. Mrs. M. M. Peck, $32.15; Danville, Aux., $27.90; Derby, Aux., $9; Dorset, Aux., $2.50, Willing Workers, $15; East Dorset, Aux., $15.65; Dummerston, Aux., $20; East Burke, Aux., $7.15; East Berkshire, Aux., $8; East Poultney, Aux., $14.14; East Hardwick, Aux., $9.50, Y. L. S., $5, Miss F. M. Delano, $5; Enosburg, Y.P. M.C., $40; Greensboro, Aux., $20.40; Guildhall, Aux., $17.60; Jericho, Aux., $15; Lower Waterford, Aux., $7; Lyndon, Aux., of wh. $25 const. L. M. Mrs. R. M. McKoy, $30, Buds of Promise, prev. contri. const. L. M. Miss Minnie Clowe, $10; Lyndonville, Aux., $32.85, M. C., $4; Ludlow, Aux., const. L. M. Mrs. Myra A. Wheldon, $25, M. C., $18; Manchester, Aux., $49.75, Miss'y Workers, $15; Montpelier, Aux., $26.25, Miss Amy B. Fisk, $5; Morrisville, Aux., $10.70; Newbury, Aux., of wh. $50 const. L. M's Mrs. Sydney Johnson, Miss Mattie Atkinson, $61.30, Beacon Lights, of wh. $25 const. L. M. Miss Maggie Laurie, $34, S. S., $12.60; Newport, Aux., prev. contri. const. L. M. Mrs. Mary J. Blanchard, $3; Northfield, Aux., prev. contri. const. L. M. Mrs. Lizzie Whittemore, $19, Y. L. S., $6; Norwich, Aux., $32.30; Peru, Aux., $7, M. C., $3; Peacham, Aux., $25; Post Mills, Aux., $10; Putney, We Gifts, $30; Quicker, Aux., $20; Randolph, Aux. and S. S., $11; Richmond, Aux., $8; Rutland, Aux., $21.40; West Rutland, Aux., $8; Sharon, Aux., $13; Shoreham, Aux., $25; South Hero, Aux., $43; Springfield, Aux., $11.20; Stowe, Aux., $20; St. Albans, Aux., $42.05; East St. Johnsbury, Aux., $8; St. Johnsbury, So. Ch., Aux., of wh. $25 by Mrs. Wm. P. Fairbanks, const. L. M. Mrs. Henry French, $41, B.M.Y.S., $10, No. Ch., Aux., of wh. $25 is a Thank-Off., $36; Strafford, Aux., $14; Thetford, Aux., $10; Vergennes, Aux., $34, S. S., $40; Wallingford, Aux., $14.50; Waterbury, Aux., $13.50; Williston, Aux., $5; Woodstock, Aux., of wh. $25 const. L. M. Mrs. Harriet T. Rice, $33.02, We Girls, $10,

Wide-Awakes, $10; Cambridge, Aux., $14.50, Gift at Annual Meeting, $2; McIndoes Falls, Aux., $18.39, $1,561 87

Total, $1,561 87

MASSACHUSETTS.

Athol—Busy Bees, $5 00
Andover and Woburn Branch.— Miss E. F. Wilder, Treas. Melrose, Aux., $11, Light-Bearers, $3,   14 00
Berkshire Branch.— Mrs. S. N. Russell, Treas. Adams, Memorial Band, $25; Lee, Senior Aux., $310.60; Lenox, Aux., $21.80; Stockbridge, Aux., $21; First Pittsfield, Aux., $11.05,   389 45
Essex South Co. Branch.— Miss S. W. Clark, Treas. Swampscott, Aux., of wh. $25 const. L. M. Mrs. Barnet W. Redfern, $38.25; Lynn, Central Ch., Aux., const. L. M. Mrs. Lucy T. Wheeler, $25; Marblehead, Junior Aux., $15.40; Topsfield, Aux., $40; Essex, Helping Hands, $10; Middleton, Aux., $12,   140 65
Franklin Co. Branch.— Miss L. A. Sparhawk, Treas. Bernardston, Aux., $9.75; Conway, Aux., $22,   31 75
Hampshire Co. Branch.— Miss I. G. Clarke, Treas. Belchertown, Aux., $36.50, M. C. Rally at Easthampton, $25,   61 50
Middlesex Branch.—Mrs. M. W. Warren, Treas. Natick, Aux., $126.40, Y. L. M. C., const. L. M. Mrs. Mary Balcom, $25; Saxonville, June Blossoms, $30; Southville, Aux., $14; Holliston, Open Hands' Soc'y, $25; South Framingham, Aux., $77,   297 40
Middlesex Union Conf. Asso.— Mrs. E. D. Sawin, Treas. Ayre, Aux., $15; Dunstable, Aux., $28; Harvard, Aux., $38; Littleton, Aux., $10; Groton, Aux., $17; Westford, Aux., $19.25; Townsend, Aux., $44.15; Lunenburg, Aux., $3,   174 40
Norfolk and Pilgrim Branch.— Mrs. F. Shaw, Treas. Plymouth, Mary Allerton, Y. L. C., $60; Rockland, M. B., $35; Halifax, Aux., $14.50; Braintree, Aux., $4; Hanover, Aux., $4; Marshfield, Mayflowers, $7.50; So. Abington, Ladies of Cong. Ch., $6, Thank-Off. for 75th Anniversary of the A. B. C. F. M., $90,   221 00
Springfield Branch.— Miss H.

T. Buckingham, T r e a s. Chicopee, First Ch., $22.50; Feeding Hills, of wh. $25 const. L. M. Mrs. T. M. Price, $26; East Longmeadow, Aux., $36.66, Young Disciples, $4.15; Ludlow Centre, Aux., $14.92; L u d l o w Mills, Aux., $4; Springfield, First Ch., Aux., $42.97, Cheerful Workers, $100, South Ch. Wide-Awakes, $45; West Springfield, First Ch., Aux., $46.25, Park St., Aux., $80.75, Young People's Soc'y, $40, $463 20
Suffolk Branch. — Miss M. B. Child, Treas. Boston, Mrs. J. N. Fiske, $10, Berkeley St. Ch., $5, A few little girls, $5; South Boston, Phillips Ch. S. S., $100; Roxbury, Eliot Ch., Anderson Circle, $4; Dorchester, S e c o n d Ch., Aux., $163.70, Village Ch., Aux., $57; Newtonville, Mrs. S. J. Parker, const. self L. M., $25; A u b u r n d a l e, Aux., Thank-Off. for 75th Anniversary of the A. B. C. F. M., $27.65; Dedham, A s y l u m Dime Soc'y, $2.55; Medway, Aux., $15.50,   415 40
Worcester Co. Branch. — Mrs. G. W. Russell, Treas. Millbury, Aux., Second Cong. Ch., const. L. M. Mrs. Alice Davis Annesby, $25; Princeton, S. S. Cl., $5; Clinton, Aux., $32.80; Upton, Aux., $68; Blackstone, Aux., $10; Southbridge, Aux., $10; Worcester, Woman's Miss'y Asso., Piedmont Ch., $45, Salem St. Ch., $30, Union Ch., Aux., $95.23,   321 03
Westhampton. — M i s s M a r y Edwards, in Mem. of Mrs. Catharine Edwards,   5 00

Total, $2,539 78

RHODE ISLAND.

Rhode Island Branch. Miss A. T. White, Treas. Barrington, Aux., $50; Central Falls, A u x., $73.50; Pawcatuck, Aux., $27; Little Compton, Aux., $21.18; Woonsocket, Aux., $15; Bristol, Aux., $53; Kingston, Aux., $28; Pawtucket, Aux., $272.43, Y. L. M. C., $44.45, Happy Workers, $8.12; Providence, Pilgrim Ch., Aux., $57.78, Plymouth Ch., Aux., with prev. contri. const. L. M. Mrs. Lewis Wiswall, $19, Children's M. C., $6, Union Ch., Aux., $460, Central Ch., Aux., of wh. $25, by Mrs. Lockwood,

const. L. M. Miss Mary Pauline Root, M.D., and $25 by Miss A. De F. Lockwood, const. L.M. Miss MaryAmelia Salisbury, $520, The Wilkinsons, $5, Mrs. Wilkinson, $4, North Ch., of wh. $25 const. L. M. Mrs. Wm. Corp, and $25 const. L. M. Miss Mary E. Eastwood, $93.05, $1,757 51

Total, $1,757 51

CONNECTICUT.

Columbia. — Annual Members, $21 00
Eastern Conn. Branch. — Miss M. I. Lockwood, T r e a s. Old Lyme, Cong. Ch.,   3 54
Goshen. — Mrs. Moses Lyman,   5 00
Hartford Branch. — M i s s A. T. White, Treas. Bristol, M. C., $20; Canton Centre, Aux., $22.59; Collinsville, A u x., $37.50, Hearers and Doers, $30; East Windsor, Aux., $20; Enfield, The Gleaners, $40, King St. M. C., $8; Granby, Aux., $24.45, M. B. $5.50; Hampton, Aux., $20.85; Hartford, Asylum Hill M. B., $34.90; Newington, A u x., $109.75, Shining Lights and Seed-Sowers, $12.03; North Manchester, M. C., $46; Poquonock, Cheerful Givers, $16, Willing Workers, $12; Rocky Hill, Aux., $20.25; Rockville, Aux., of wh. $25 const. L. M. Mrs. L. M. Beckwith, $71, Earnest Seed-Sowers, $21, Little Helpers, $5; Simsbury, Pearl-Gatherers, $28.02; Somerville, M. B., of wh. $25 const. L. M. Mrs. Hattie B. Bell, $28; South Windsor, Aux., $12; Suffield, Aux., $78.10; Talcottville, A u x., $70; Terryville, Aux., $4 30; Tolland, Aux., $10; Vernon, Aux., of wh. $25 const. L. M. Miss Mary Kellogg, $30; Wethersfield, Aux., of wh. $50 const. L. M's Mrs. Mary D. McLean, Mrs. Marietta Sunbury, $120; W i n d s o r Locks, Aux., const. L. M's Mrs. Wm. Ashley, Miss Mary Smith, $50, Miss'y Rill, $57.76; Windsor, Aux., of wh. $25 by Mrs. Wm. Pierson, const. L. M. Miss Julia Filley, $25 by Miss Olivia Pierson, const. L. M. Miss Emma D. Wilson, $63, Splinters of the Board, $50,   1,178 00
New Haven Branch. — Miss J. Twining, Treas. Bridgeport, Aux., $263.02; Danbury, Aux., $121.94; Deep River, Aux., $10; East Haddam, Aux., of wh.

$25 const. L. M. Mrs. Anne A. Butler, $77.75, Phœnix Band, $12; Litchfield, Aux., $17.95; Monroe, Aux., $18; New Britain, South Ch., Aux., of wh. $25 by Miss Jennie E. Case, const. L. M. Miss Mary L. Stanley, $50, Y. L. M. B., $25, const. L. M. Miss Anna L. Smith; New Canaan, Aux., $39.55, Prospect Gleaners, $40; Salisbury, Aux., $40; Saybrook, Aux., $42.30; Sharon, Busy Bees, $50; Sound Beach, Aux., $25; South Canaan, Aux., $7; Torringford, Highland Workers, $40; Westbrook, Aux., $22; Wilton, Morning Star, $5, ... $906 51
Sharon.—Mrs. Mary L. Peck, ... 10 00

Total, ... $2,124 05

NEW YORK.

New York State Branch.—Mrs. G. W. Norton, Treas. Norwich, Aux., of wh. $25 const. L. M. Mrs. Lucy H. M. Upton, $39.25; Walton, Aux., $19.75; Agavnie, Aux., $21; New Haven, Aux., $25; Sidney Plains, Aux., $11, Suspension Bridge, Aux., $8, Penny Gatherers, $10.35; Little Valley, Aux., $5; Sherburne, Aux., $25; Sing Sing, Ossining Inst. M. C., $50; Franklin, Aux., $46, Happy Workers, $20; North Walton, Aux., $21; West Groton, Aux., $20, Penny Gatherers, $2.25; Berkshire, Aux., $23; Chenango Forks, Aux., $4.25; Coventryville, M. C., $7; Norwood, Aux., $26.50; Lisle, Aux., $10; Randolph, Aux., $20; Warsaw, Aux., $50; Brooklyn, Central Ch., Aux., of wh. $100 by Mrs. C. H. Pond, const. L. M's Miss Louise C. Pond, Miss Carrie Angell, Miss Jennie E. Pond, Mrs. Lucretia Hale, $400, Boys and Girls M. B., of wh. $11 prev. contri. const. L. M. Miss Maggie Anderson, $55, Tompkins Ave. Ch. Aux., $370, S. S. Cl., $5.04, Puritan Ch., M. B., $23, Park Ch., Aux., $37; New York, fr. Benefit Jug on Miss Halsey's Desk, Bible House, $4.20; Buffalo, W. G. Bancroft M. B., $20; Fairport, Aux., of wh. $25 const. L. M. Mrs. M. A. Davies, $92.26, Pine-Needles, $50; Napoli, Aux., $10, Cong. S. S., $3.09; Flushing, Aux., $36.25, Faith M. C., $13.93; Gaines, Aux., $6.55; Owego,

Aux., $20; Poughkeepsie, Aux., $20, Opportunity M. C., $30; Millville, Aux., prev. contri. const. L. M. Mrs. Zenas M. Colburn, $11; Canandaigua, Aux., $25, M. B., $10; Nelson, Aux., $6; Saratoga Springs, Aux., $10; Binghamton, Aux., $27.22, Doers of the Word, $25; West Bloomfield, Aux., const. L. M. Miss Sarah Sheldon, $25; Gloversville, Aux., $15; Black Creek, M. C., $3.50, Maine Gleaners, $36; Albany, Aux., $3; New Lebanon, Cheerful Workers, $5; Strykersville, Aux., $5, $1,867 39

Total, ... $1,867 39

NEW JERSEY.

Jersey City Heights.—Mrs. C. L. Ames, ... $5 00
Montclair.—A Friend, ... 50

Total, ... $5 50

PENNSYLVANIA.

Guy's Mills. — Mrs. F. Maria Guy, ... $1 00

Total, ... $1 00

PHILADELPHIA BRANCH.

Mrs. S. Wilde, Treas. N. J.: Newark, Belleville Ave. Cong. Ch., Aux., $31, M. B., $45; Orange Valley, Cong. Ch., Aux., $100, Y. L. M. B., $100; East Orange, Cong. Ch., Proctor M. C., $30; Montclair, Cong. Ch., Aux., $33, .. $339 00

Total, ... $339 00

OHIO.

Toledo.—Washington St. Cong. S. S., ... $25 00

Total, ... $25 00

CHINA.

Foochow.—Mrs. A. C. Walker, const. L. M. Mrs. Lucia M. Frost, ... $25 00

Total, ... $25 00

General Funds, ... $10,566 81
Morning Star, ... 2 00
Weekly Pledge, ... 1 80
Leaflets, ... 24 42

Total, ... $10,595 03

MISS HARRIET W. MAY,
Ass't Treas.

Board of the Interior.

MESSAGES FROM ABROAD.

We regret that the various delays of type-setting, proof-reading, and mail-carrying necessarily postpone any report of our annual meeting till another month, but we are allowed to give one little message received during its progress from one of our workers in Turkey.

WILL you please give to the ladies gathered in their annual meeting this Armenian proverb from me: "Grape looks at grape and reddens." Of all the fine grapes of this land of grapes, none seem to me so beautiful as the red ones, with their shapely clusters of full, juicy globules.

The proverb reminds us that they ripen, not independently, but by mutual influence of each on the other. This may be only poetry when applied to grapes, but for mankind it is a deep truth. One looks at another's progress, her growth in the beauty and maturity of Christian life, and an inward prompting bids the looker grow, too, into the loveliness and ripeness of goodness.

Dear sisters, let your example in missionary zeal, in loving and helping souls near and far (for Christ loves all), be a constant incitement to others to grow into this grace of holiness. So as "grape looks at grape and reddens," soul may follow soul in glowing with the joy of love given — the joy of doing good.

Mrs. Wood writes from Scutari, September 18th: —

We have had heartaches over the parting with our dear father and mother, Dr. and Mrs. Riggs, who left us in August for the home of their daughter in Aintab, Syria. We learn by telegram of their safe arrival at their future home.

Our Home ladies, except Miss Dodd, who is very ill at her home in America, have returned, and school has reopened this week. The numbers hold good, and our ladies are full of bright hopes for the coming year. I cannot but feel anxiety for them, for their hands were over-full when all their number were here, and of course their duties are increased with one of their number missing. Her sister writes that it will be months before she can resume teaching.

FROM CHINA.

Miss Diament has been with Miss Haven in the Bridgman School during the absence of Miss Chapin, who has been taking her first season of rest in this country, after thirteen years of missionary work. Miss Chapin sailed from San Francisco, on her return voyage, Sept. 20th. Miss Diament writes from Pekin, Aug. 18th:—

I had dreaded the warm weather, especially the long month of August; but now I am wishing there were more of its long days. By keeping very quiet I have kept well through the great heat. I spent one week at the hills, which braced me up for the hot days.

My time for leaving Pekin draws near; only two months remain. I want to see Miss Chapin, and the new friends who came with her; then I shall gladly turn homeward. I have found the society of the missionaries of other missions very helpful and pleasant. The work in the school, and the little I have been able to do for women, have been enjoyable. Mrs. Blodgett makes a home for the single ladies here, and has been very kind, making me feel much at home.

We are very quiet here now — Miss Haven and I alone in the compound, except as Mr. Noble and Dr. Blodgett come and go. We keep house in a small way, but it occasionally develops into a large way very suddenly, as we keep open house for those coming and going: this is necessary, as the other houses are mostly closed for the summer. This is where we have the advantage in Kalgan. The summers there are very comfortable, and we take no vacation, making our tours serve for health-changes. We miss very much those who are in the home-land, and long for some to come and fill the places.

Every breeze which comes to us from mission-fields bears the same cry, More helpers! Here is a word from Miss Evans, dated from Tung-cho, Aug. 13th:—

Do you know, I sometimes wish I could stand again before such an audience as the one I had in Milwaukee, in 1883. I should plead for helpers as I never did while at home. Why, *we just must have them.*

Do you know, when Miss Andrews returns from Kalgan, she is to go from us to Shantung, to take Miss Porter's place. What are we ever to do? It is supplying one great need at the expense of another.

JAPAN.

PICTURES OF REAL LIFE.

BY MRS. ANNIE L. GULICK.

WE reached Maki in our jinrikishas in the middle of the afternoon, and were whirled up in fine style to the door of a hotel. We stepped out into the earth floor passage-way, which generally runs the whole length of the hotel on one side. Here the wooden clogs are left as the guests step out on the clean mats of the entering-room of the hotel. We, of course, take off our boots and put on slippers, always carried with us in traveling. In this hotel the bathroom was back of the entering-room, all open to the passage-way, and we were glad to escape to the quiet room assigned us in the back part of the hotel. Supper-time came, and our supper was brought in on four square trays with short legs. (For Mr. and Mrs. Gulick and the two helpers.) On each tray there are always five dishes, one on each corner and one in the middle, and the servant always places each tray before the guest so that the rice-bowl is at the left hand in front. At the right hand is a smaller bowl, containing a little bit of soup made from a dried fish, and very disagreeable to the uninitiated. At the back of the tray, at the right, is the plate of fish, and at the left a bowl of stew made with fish, vegetables, etc., sometimes quite palatable, sometimes not so much so. The little plate in the middle contains pickles, or greens, or something else for a relish. The bowls are usually of lacquer, and are more or less nice. Chop-sticks complete the furnishing. The servant-girl or the lady of the house brings in a covered wooden tub of rice, and takes her seat by it, to replenish the bowls of the guests. All are, of course, seated upon the floor. We always take some bread and some other provisions of our own on our tours, but as we become more accustomed to the Japanese dishes, we depend more upon them and less upon our own food.

AN IMPROVISED BIBLE-MEETING.

At our last stopping-place, after finding a room at the hotel, we called to see a doctor and his wife, who are Christians. I was glad to see that the woman so far departed from Japanese etiquette as to sit quietly and listen to the conversation, instead of spending the time of our call in providing us with tea and cakes, though they apologized for their impoliteness in not offering us anything. A meeting in the evening at our hotel had been arranged for by the doctor and his wife, and a notice of it was hung outside the door. The lower rooms of the hotel were thrown open, and were soon filled. All the sitting-space was crowded, and numbers stood in the passage-ways. Mr. Gulick and Manabe San preached, and the audience listened, for the most part, quietly and respectfully. A few young men came up stairs to our room after meeting to ask questions, and we soon found out that it was no desire to know the truth that prompted them, but only a desire to show off their own smartness, and turn a laugh upon Christianity, if possible. We do not feel that it is of much use to talk with people of that spirit, but Manabe San and the doctor argued with them for awhile, and gave them some plain talk.

CHINA.

A PEEP INTO MY DISPENSARY.

BY VIRGINIA MURDOCK, M.D.

To-day I am listening for patients,—as it is Chinese day,—and at the same time teaching my dispensary gate-keeper to read. Mr. Gold is not my regular gate-keeper. He is acting as substitute for his son, who has served in that capacity for three years. During that time I have taught him to read, drilling him lately on the Gospel of John. And I have also taught him about a number of diseases, and the medicines that are especially useful in them. He is hardly capable of becoming a regular medical student, but I hope to make a Bible-reader of him, and to have him so combine the explanations of portions of Scripture with his knowledge of common diseases that he may get access to the people in the villages. He has gone out on his first tour. A month before he left I thought he was ready; but his lamentable deficiency in the explanation of certain passages of Scripture almost discouraged me. In spite of the fame the Chinese have acquired on account of their retentive memories, it is only by constantly studying and repeating their books that they keep them in mind.

They have little reasoning power, and have no studies to bring out that faculty. It is hard to learn to read Chinese. One must recognize a character, then learn its name and meaning in the abstract, then collectively in phrases and sentences, and then learn to draw this character or picture. But my assistant was finally allowed to go. He will spend one day in each village, and we shall see how much he can accomplish. His father, my present gate-keeper, is an old man of fifty-nine years, and has been a church-member two years. Two days ago he was asked to pray in morning prayers. He hesitated, sighed, then said, "Our heavenly Father," then stopped, then repeated the same phrase, then a long pause—so long I thought he was not going on; but after a sigh, he said, "We are sinners"; then another long pause; but a neighbor suggested that he should repeat the Lord's Prayer, which he did, others joining in. In reading, though I tell him what a character is over and over again, and have him write it ten times, he is still so unfortunate as not to remember. Not long ago he left his books, and I thought he was tired of study; but when I asked him if he really wanted to learn to read, he said he did, and that he only left to pray. "It is hard work learning," he said, and tears stood in his eyes.

Now I must give you a few notes on medical study and practice here. Most of the Chinese books are taken up with an elaborate system of astrology, and the medical student spends his time un-ravelling that. There are no colleges. A person wishing to be a physician buys the Chinese medical books, and reads. They have quite a number of authors. Mr. Wang is a modern observer and writer who dares to differ in many respects from the ancient standard works. His book is not considered first-class by the profession, though it is much read. It is less voluminous on the mysteries of astrology, and that is an important subject in the study of medicine. The ancients say that the heart is the birth-place of the blood; but this author that the heart receives and expels the air. The air enters the heart by two passages, and after circulating through it, it is carried by the surface of the lungs to the back-bone to the lumbar region, and is collected in a large vessel, which has eleven branches; the air passes through these to all parts of the body.

The body is divided into two parts by the diaphragm. The old author said it was divided into three portions. The upper portion contains lungs, heart, and a portion of the great air-tube. In the back portion of the diaphragm is to be found a pool of blood, and from this the body is supplied. Patients often say that the blood rushes to different parts of the body, and charms and strings are worn to prevent it.

The stomach receives the food. The omentum has air in it, and is full of steam, which heats the stomach and digests the food. This passes from the stomach through a large tube about an inch long, which divides into three tubes; one goes to the brain and makes that substance; one to the spinal column, to the tank or pool of blood, and is converted into blood; and the third passes to the liver and other organs.

The liver has four lobes, and is situated on the right side : in this he triumphs over the old authorities, who said the liver was on the left side.

For the Young Ladies.

SAN SEBASTIAN.

THE young ladies of the Interior who have helped to sustain the girls' school at San Sebastian, will be interested in this report of its progress. Those who have appreciated in any just degree the influence on American womanhood of schools like Mt. Holyoke, and others of its class, will rejoice in the founding of a school of similar purpose for the daughters of Spain. We wish we could show to each one of "our girls" the photograph of the bright-faced, brave-hearted and loving woman who, in addition to the cares of a missionary's wife and the mother of a large family, finds time and strength to be the ruling spirit of this school. Also, we would like to show you the pretty sheet which accompanied this report, bearing the title, "Programa de los Examens del Colegio Norte-Americano de San Sebastian;" among the exercises we notice not only "Geografia, Nociones de Algebra y Geometria, Aritmetica, Botanica, Teoria y practica del Sistema Kindergarten," etc., but a goodly space devoted to "Evidenceas del Cristianesmo," and "Historia Sagrada." May the "Bendicion" which closes the list rest most abundantly on all those who are thus striving to hasten the dawning of a brighter day for the women of Spain.

An interesting letter from Miss Richards, teacher in the same school, may be found on page 70 in February LIFE AND LIGHT.

REPORTS.

The whole number of scholars connected with the school during the past year was sixty-four. Of these, thirty-seven were boarders; six were students of English and French.

These latter were from San Sebastian. Three of them were from families of high standing, which proves in itself that prejudice against the school is not so strong as formerly.

Among the scholars are representatives of the following cities and provinces: Malaga and Puerto Santa Maria in Andalusia; Gibraltar, Salamanca, Madrid, Asturias, and Barcelona. There are two German children, two French, and one English girl.

The year of study has been uneventful. An advance in scholarship is, however, noticeable. The conduct of the scholars has been very good, when the past education of most has been taken into account. Three have united with the church. The older ones are all Christians, and we see the signs of the beginning of true Christian life in many of these little ones.

God has been very good to us in preserving this large family from illness. There has never been a case of serious illness in the school. This we attribute to the loving care of our heavenly Father, and to the healthful location and general sanitary arrangements of this good house. Three girls will graduate this year who are already engaged as teachers of evangelical schools for the coming year.

The five who have previously graduated are all engaged in successful work as teachers. We receive many requests for teachers that we are not able to supply. During the past year two of our former pupils have been married; one to a colporteur in the Asturian Provinces, and the other to an evangelist. These last named are doing real missionary work among the Spaniards who live near Pau, France. Their influence will be felt all through the North of Spain, wherever the people return to their native villages, carrying the truth they have heard in the little Hispano-French village of Jurançon.

Our present needs are great. There is no apparatus for advanced study,—not even a microscope. There are but few books in the library, which as yet has neither place nor name. Laundry conveniences are imperatively needed.

We have been obliged to limit our furnishing to the necessary beds, tables, chairs, etc., for the growing school.

We believe if it is God's will, Christian friends will be led to see the need of such a school in Spain, and to help place it on a permanent foundation, so that it may continue to be, as we hope, a blessing to many young girls who shall here be fitted to become Christian wives, mothers, and teachers.

In behalf of the school,

ALICE GORDON GULICK.

JUNE 20, 1885.

STUDIES IN MISSIONARY HISTORY.
1885.
THE CENTRAL TURKEY MISSION.
NO. 2. 1865–1885.

THIS lesson brings us to a period of rapid development in the woman's work in the Central Turkey Mission. As there is such an ample fund of information by which to trace this progress in the pages of our own LIFE AND LIGHT, we devote this lesson mostly to a study of this phase of the work.

Description of the Field. See LIFE AND LIGHT, 1874, pp. 257, 290.

Removal of Theological School to Marash.

Revival at Marash. Anderson's History, Vol. II. p. 401.

Schools at Marash. Mrs. Coffing's Work. See LIFE AND LIGHT, 1871, p. 130; 1872, p. 204; 1873, p. 69; Revivals, LIFE AND LIGHT, 1874, pp. 83, 277; 1876, p. 245; Revival of 1877, pp. 218, 245; Revival of 1878, pp. 217, 119.

The Women of Marash. Mothers' meeting. LIFE AND LIGHT, 1875, p. 261; 1876, p. 181.

War of 1877. Influence in Central Turkey. LIFE AND LIGHT, 1877, p. 343; 1878, p. 183.

Village Work Connected with the Marash Station. LIFE AND LIGHT, 1873, pp. 116, 369; 1875, p. 274; 1786, p. 341; 1877, pp. 183, 311; Zeitoon, 1882, pp. 389, 425.

Girls' Seminary at Aintab. LIFE AND LIGHT, 1872, pp. 203, 253; 1878, p. 161; 1879, p. 311; 1880, p. 7; 1881, p. 129.

Work in the City of Aintab. Cholera Incidents. LIFE AND LIGHT, 1876, pp. 100, 277, 311; 1877, p. 181; 1880, p. 167.

Work of Translation. LIFE AND LIGHT, 1879, p. 97.

Village Work Connected with the Aintab Station. LIFE AND LIGHT, 1871, p. 62; 1873, p. 1; 1874, p. 33; 1877, pp. 7, 116; 1878, pp. 245, 181; 1879, pp. 171, 289, 348, 371; Baghchegaz, 1882, p. 125; Kessab, 1881, p. 167; Revival, 1883, p. 450.

Work and School at Hadjin. See Leaflet published by W. B. M. I. LIFE AND LIGHT, 1876, p. 37; 1879, pp. 293, 331; Removal of Mrs. Coffing and Miss Spencer, 1880, pp. 105, 225; Arrival of Miss Brown and Miss Tucker, 1881, pp. 69, 192; Revival, 1881, pp. 194, 307; Persecution, 1881, p. 347; Revival, 1883, p. 347.

New Work in Adana. Removal of Miss Brown and Miss Tucker, 1883, p. 265; Revival, 1883, p. 185.

Marash College. LIFE AND LIGHT, 1882, p. 347; 1883, p. 305; Revival Work, 1884, p. 185; Examinations, 1884, p. 427.

We commend this lesson to the young ladies as one of the most delightful and stimulating in the whole series. It shows what honor God has put upon woman in this our day, in that her work has become so large a factor in the crowning work of redemption.

RECEIPTS OF THE WOMAN'S BOARD OF MISSIONS OF THE INTERIOR.

MRS. J. B. LEAKE, TREASURER.

FROM SEPTEMBER 18, 1885, TO OCTOBER 18, 1885.

ILLINOIS.

ILLINOIS BRANCH.—Mrs.W. A. Talcott, of Rockford, Treas. *Ashkum,* Aux., 2.45, certif. M. Star Mission, 10 cts.; *Alton,* Ch. of the Redeemer, 5.50; *Amboy,* to const. L. M's Mrs. W. B. Andruss and Mrs. H. T. Ford, 50; *Atkinson,* 10; *Aurora,* 1st Ch., 100, New Eng. Ch., 30.60; *Batavia,* 55; *Blue Island,* 11.50; *Bowensburg,* 7; *Champaign,* 10; *Chebanse,* 2; *Chesterfield,* 8.50; *Clifton,* 2; *Chicago,* A Friend, 5, Certif s M. Star Mission fund, 60 cts., 1st Ch., to const. L. M's Mrs. Mary Farwell, Miss Jessie P. Smith, Miss Sarah Elizabeth Mead, 80.25, Lincoln Pk. Ch., 50, Union Pk. Ch., 100, a mother, in memoriam, 25 cts., New Eng. Ch., 35, Plymouth Ch., 148.75, South Ch., of wh. 25 to const.

L. M. Mrs. L. Green, 46.13, Bethany Ch., 7 82, Millard Ave. Ch., 31.28; *Danvers,* 19; *Downer'sGrove,* 4; *Earlville,*10; *Elgin,* 127.65; *Englewood,* 50; *Evanston,* 131.69; *Farmington,* 32.40; *Galesburg.* Brick Ch., 50.50, 1st Ch., 37.50; *Geneva,* 11; *Glencoe,* 35; *Granville,* 7; *Griggsville,* 50; *Geneseo,* 74.57; *Greenville,* 11; *Hinsdale,* Mrs. J, H. Phillips, to const. L. M's Miss Mary B. Adams of Hinsdale, Miss Mary L. Marsh, Oberlin, Ohio, 50; *Ivanhoe,* 30; *Jacksonville,* 15.75; *Joy Prairie,* 45; *Kewanee,* 10; *La Moille,* 26; *Lee Center,* 3.05; *Lyonsville,* 35.70; *Macomb,* 15; *Marseilles,* 6.50; *Moline,* 20; *Naperville,* 22.41; *New Windsor,* 20; *Oak Park,* 89.92; *Onarga,* 2d Ch., 4.58; *Ontario,* 15; *Ottawa,* 130.50; *Paxton,* 50.15; *Payson,* of wh. 25 from

Mrs. J. K. Scarboro, to const. L. M. Miss Carrie L. Kay, 25 to const. L. M. Mrs. Anna T. Robbins, 52.25; *Pecatonica,* 5.15; *Pittsfield,* 10.90; *Polo,* Ind. Pres. Ch., 11.35; *Princeton,* 18.45; *Ravenswood,* 31.96; *Rockford,* 1st Ch., 57.83, 2d Ch., 58 60; *Roscoe,* 15.62; *Sandwich,* 83.63; *Springfield,* 11.65; *Sterling,* 1st Ch., 10; *Stillman Valley,* 27.17; *Thawville,* 3; *Wataga,* 6; *Waukegan,* 16; *Wauponsie Grove,* 17.50; *Waverly,* 24.50; *Wilmette,* 9,50; *Wheaton,* 8, $2,519 66
JUNIORS: *Aurora,* Y. L. Soc., 35; *Canton,* Y. L. Soc., 22; *Chicago,* 1st Ch., Y. W. Soc., 58.89, Lincoln Pk. Ch., Y. L. Soc., 34, Union Pk. Ch., 16.15, New Eng. Ch., 30, Western Ave. Ch., 50, Plymouth Ch., 40.56; *Elgin,* 45; *Geneva,* 10; *La Grange,* 15; *Lockport,* Mrs. Palmer's S. S. Class and others, 2; *Mendon,* 25; *Oak Park,* 75; *Ottawa,* Y. L. Soc., to const. L. M. Emma Caroline Cole, 66.15; *Payson,* Cheerful Workers, 10; *Peoria,* 100; *Princeton,* Whatsoever Band, 10 47; *Ravenswood,* Y. Peo. Soc., 10; *Rockford,* 1st Ch., 55 61; *Sandwich,* King's Daughters, 10; *Springfield,* Jennie Chapin Helpers, 25; *Wilmette,* 2.36; *Wyoming,* Light-Bearers, 10, From one who earned it, 2.50,   760 69
JUVENILE: *Ashkum,* Buds of Promise, 3.70; *Cable,* S. S., 70 cts., Gospel Messengers, 1; *Chicago,* Lincoln Pk. Ch., Lamplighters, 12.57, Union Pk. Ch., 7.84; *Danvers,* Busy Bees, 11.98; *Farmington,* 1; *Galesburg,* 1st Ch., 20; *Griggsville,* Wm. Starr Memorial Band, 15; *Maywood,* Busy Builders, 3.46; *Oak Park,* Torchbearers, 50; *Peoria,* S. S. ch., of wh. 1.50 Primary Class, 11.50; *Princeton,* Samaritan Band, 7; *Sandwich,* Lamplighters, 32.30; *Waverly,* Light-Bearers, 3.22,   181 27
THANK-OFFERINGS: *Ashkum,* 1.85; *Aurora,* New Eng. Ch., 29 25; *Champaign,* 14; *Chicago,* 1st Ch., 100, Lincoln Pk. Ch., Aux., Jun. Juv., 28, Union Pk. Ch., Aux., to const. L. M. Miss Aurelia Mabel Crosette, 25, Y. L. Soc., 17.62, New Eng. Ch., 22, Western Ave. Ch., Aux., 7.32, Star Soc., 1.51, Plymouth Ch., Mrs. S., 5, South Ch., Y. L. Soc., 15.82, Oakley Ave. Miss. Ch., 10.01;

Danvers, 5.05; *Downer's Grove,* 9.18; *Danville,* 1; *Evanston,* 38.50; *Galesburg,* Brick Ch., 29.50, 1st Ch., of wh. 25 to const. L. M. Mrs. J. D. Wykoff, 40; *Galva,* 2.35; *Granville,* 24; *Geneseo,* 35.25; *Joy Prairie,* 16; *Kewanee,* 21; *Lyonsville,* 19.30; *Marseilles,* 9; *Neponset,* 8; *Oak Park,* 32.20; *Oneida,* 4.25; *Payson,* 18.75; *Peoria,* Aux. and Y. L. Soc., 45.75; *Providence,* 13; *Rockford,* 1st Ch. Aux., 27.40, Y. L. Soc., 18 05; *Roscoe,* 3.38; *Springfield,* 20; *Stillman Valley,* 20.45; *Waverly,* Aux., 28.50, Earnest Workers, 13 40; *Wilmette,* 11.50; *Winnetka,* 15; *Winnebago,* 1.70, $808 84

Branch total, $4,270 46

INDIANA BRANCH.

Mrs. N. A. Hyde, of Indianapolis, Treas. *Elkhart,* const. L. M. Mrs. Darling, 25; *Michigan City,* 17.93; *Terre Haute,* 28.18, $71 11
JUNIOR: *Terre Haute,* Opportunity Club,   23 63
JUVENILE: *Michigan City,* Little Grains of Sand, 2, Wall-Builders, 2.75,   4.75

Total, $99 49

IOWA.

IOWA BRANCH. — Mrs. E. R. Potter, of Grinnell, Treas. *Anamosa,* 22.16; *Ames,* 15; *Atlantic,* 1.75; *Burlington,* 18; *Big Rock,* 10; *Creston,* 15.70; *Cass,* 3; *Cedar Rapids,* 25; *Corning,* 2.28; *Cresco,* offering of four ladies, 3.25; *Cherokee,* a few ladies, 12; *Dubuque,* 85; *Des Moines,* 77.77; *Decorah,* 30; *Farragut,* 10; *Garden Prairie,* 3; *Grinnell,* 24.72; *Humboldt,* 7; *Iowa City,* Aux., 8, Mrs. Borland and Mrs. Irwin, 20; *Kelly,* 1; *Keokuk,* 1.60; *Keosauqua,* 26.60; *Lansing,* 4; *Magnolia,* 7.35; *Muscatine,* Mrs. Belendda Kirby, 1; *McGregor,* 23.40; *Oskaloosa,* 50.14; *Ogden,* 20; *Ottumwa,* 15.50; *Odebolt,* Mrs. Emeline Bogwill, 2; *Polk City,* 4 50; *Quaqueston,* 7; *Stuart,* 10; *Tabor,* 15; *Warren,* 5. $587 72
THANK-OFFERINGS: *Big Rock,* 5; *Corning,* 7.72; *Des Moines,* 36; *Farragut,* 21; *Le Mars,* 11,   80.72
JUNIORS: *Big Rock,* 5; *Cresco,* Willing Workers, 33; *Clay,* 5; *Dubuque,* Y. L. B. Soc., 15;

Des Moines, Plymouth Rock Soc., 36.10; *Grinnell*, Y. L. M-S. of Cong. Ch., 37 40; *Iowa City*, Busy Ring, 18.50; *Kellogg*, Miss Kate E. Lyman, 2; *Stacyville*, 25, $177 00
JUVENILES: *Algona*, Miss. Band, 3; *Anamosa*, Acorn Band, 10; *Creston*, Coral Workers, 3; *Denmark*, Busy Bees, 5; *Des Moines*, S. S., 13.46; *Iowa City*, Gleaners, 3, S. S., 3.25; *Muscatine*, Seeds of Mercy, 25, 65 71
Branch total, 911 15
——, A friend of the cause, an offering of consecration, 25 00

Total, $936 15

KANSAS BRANCH.

Mrs. A. L. Slosson, of Leavenworth, Treas. *Auburn*, 20; *Atchison*, 12; *Boston Mills*, 6.50; *Delmore*, 1.50; *Detroit*, 4; *Emporia*, 27.50; *Hiawatha*, 4; *Jetmore*, 1.54; *Kinsley*, 8; *Lawrence*, thank-offering, 23; *Leavenworth*, 14.25; *Manhattan*, 52; *Maple Hill*, 7.75; *Ottawa*, 25; *Parsons*, 1.80; *Reading*, 4; *Spearville*, 26 cts.; *Sabetha*, 8.50; *Seneca*, 6; *Salem*, N. J., Miss Margaret R. Warner, 7.50; *Topeka*, 50; *Twelve Mile*, 6; *Wyandotte*, 46.37; *Valley Falls*, 1; *Wabaunsee*, 11, $349 47
JUNIOR: *Sabetha*, Y. L. Useful Hour Club, 10 00
JUVENILE: *Maple Hill*, Willing Workers, 3 25

Total, $362 72

MICHIGAN.

MICHIGAN BRANCH. — Mrs. Charles E. Fox, of Detroit, Treas. *Allendale*, 1; *Ann Arbor*, 33.56; *Armada*, 37; *Augusta*, 10; *Bedford*, 5; *Bridgeport*, 1; *Ceresco*, 11; *Coloma*, 13.47; *Dexter*, 18.20; *Detroit*, Trumbull Ave. Ch., 20, Woodward Ave., 258, of wh. 75 to const. L. M's Mrs. Alice B. Davis, Mrs. H. D. Taylor, and Mrs. M. Currie, and 50 from Mrs. D. M. Ferry, to const. L. M's Mrs. Sherman R. Miller and Mrs. C. C. Miller, First Ch., 104.50; *Edmore*, 2.50; *E. Saginaw*, 100; *Flint*, 32.65 *Galesburg*, 10.20; *Greenville*, 80; *Grandville*, Mrs. Nearpass, 50 cts.; *Grand Rapids*, Second Ch., 50 cts., Mrs. Pollard, So. Ch., 1; *Highland Station*, 5; *Jackson*, 115; *Kala-*

mazo, 51.65; *Lansing*, 20.30; *Lexington*, 5; *Ludington*, 13; *Manistee*, 40.70; *North Adams*, 21.60; *North Dorr*, 3.25; *Owasso*, 28.55; *Port Huron*, 48.50; *Portland*, 8; *Pontiac*, 7; *Raisinville*, 3; *Richmond*, 17; *Salem*, 5; *St. Johns*, 10.65; *St. Joseph*, 15; *S. Haven*, 7; *Somerset*, 1.50; *Stanton*, 44; *Three Oaks*, 21; *Vermontville*, 33; *Wheatland*, 27; *White Cloud*, 1; *Ypsilanti*, 10.35, $1,303 13
JUNIOR: *Alpena*, Mission Band, 18.28; *Bridgeport*, Y. L. S., 3.75; *Detroit*, Woodward Ave., Y. L. M. S, for The Bridge, 35; *Eaton Rapids*, King's Young Daughters, 12.50; *Manistee*, Y. L. M. C., 12.50; *Muskegon*, Dorcas Soc., 9; *St. Johns*, Y. P. M. C., 10; *So. Haven*, Mission Bank, 6.97; *Stanton*, Hibbard Mission Band, 5; *Wheatland*, Y. L. M. C., 40, 153 00
JUVENILE: *Bedford*, of wh. 2.19 from C. M. S., and 50 cts. from S. S. Class, 2.69; *Detroit*, Woodward Ave. King's Cup-Bearers, 10; *Owasso*, Ready Helpers, 10, 22 69
FOR MORNING STAR MISSION: *Bridgeport*, M. S. M. B., 1.25; *Edmore*, Pine-Tree Mission Band, 5; *Muskegon*, Coral Workers, 5; *Port Huron*, Earnest Workers, 24.80, 36.05
THANK-OFFERING: *Ann Arbor*, 2.14; *Bridgeport*, 50 cts.; *Dowagiac*, 8.65; *Eaton Rapids*, 5; *Hancock*, 12; *Lake Linden*, 19; *Ludington*, 20; *Olivet*, 31.05; *Owasso*, 16; *Port Huron*, 10; *Raisinville*, 3.50; *Romeo*, 14; *St. Joseph*, 25; *Stanton*, 8.60; *Somerset*, 11.50; *Three Oaks*, 13; *Wheatland*, 10; *Ypsilanti*, 8.65, 218 59

Total, $1,733 46

MINNESOTA.

MINNESOTA BRANCH.—Mrs. E. M. Williams, of Northfield, Treas. *Brownton*, 3.25; *Douglas*, 5; *Excelsior*, thank-offering, 10.90; *Luverne*, 5; *Minneapolis*, Lyndale Ave. Ch., 10, Open Door Ch., 4.28, Second Ch., 8, J. T. E , 5; *Northfield*, 14.08; *Winona*, 100, $165 51
JUNIOR: *Minneapolis*, Plymouth Ch., Y. L. M. S., 31.25; *St. Paul*, Park Ch., Y. L. M Soc., 14.15, 45 40
JUVENILE: *Austin*, Scatter Good Soc., 4.50; *Minneapolis*, Plymouth Ch., S. S., 50;

Northfield, Willing Workers, 11.62; *Plainview*, Primary Cl., Cong. S. S., 6, $72 12

Total, $283 03

MISSOURI.

MISSOURI BRANCH.—Mrs. J. H. Drew, 3101 Washington Ave., St. Louis, Treas. *Brookfield*, 20; *St. Louis*, 1st Cong. Ch., 12, Pilgrim Ch., 5, 5th Cong. Ch., 13.25; *Kansas City*, Clyde Ch., 2.98; *Kidder*, 10; $63 23
THANK-OFFERING: *St. Louis*, 1st Cong. Ch., 9.56, Y. L. Soc., 1.40, Pilgrim Ch., 41.50; *Meadville*, 2.45; *Breckenridge*, 4.92; *Kansas City*, Clyde Ch., 12.55,   72 38

Total, $135 61

NEBRASKA.

NEBRASKA W. M. ASSOCIATION.—Mrs. Geo. H. Hall, of Omaha, Treas. *Ashland*, 19; *Aurora*, 7; *Blair*, 26; *Crete*, 26; *Columbus*, 25; *Clarks*, 15; *Camp Creek*, 8; *Exeter*, 9.44; *Franklin*, 3.80; *Fairfield*, 15.11; *Hastings*, 10; *Harvard*, 5; *Lincoln*, 31; *Norfolk*, 5; *Omaha*, 1st Ch , 86.50, St. Mary's Ave. Ch., 59.30; *Plymouth*, 5; *Red Cloud*, 5; *Steele City*, 1; *Syracuse*, 10; *South Bend*, 2.50; *Waco*, 50 cts.; *Waverly*, 5; *Wahoo*, 3; *Weeping Water*, 16.25; *York*, 6 85, $406 25
JUNIOR: *Blair*, 25; *Omaha*, 3.50; *Wahoo*, 5; *South Bend*, 2,   35 50
JUVENILE: *Blair*, 8; *Exeter*, 35; *West Point*, 5.10; *Omaha*, Prairie Lights, 5,   58 10
THANK-OFFERING: *Exeter*, Juv., 5; *Omaha*, 41.25; *Plymouth*, 1; *South Bend*, 1.50; *Greenwood*, 5,   53 75
                              $548 60
Less expenses,   27 81

Association total, $520 79
Blair, thank-offering, 6; *Lincoln*, Y. L. Soc., 20,   26 00

Total, $546 79

OHIO.

OHIO BRANCH.—Mrs. Geo. H. Ely, of Elyria, Treas. *Atwater*, 16; *Austinburg*, 10; *Belpre*, 33; *Bristolville*, 10.10; *Cambridgeboro*, Pa., 5; *Cincinnati*, Columbia Ch., of wh. 13 thank-offering, 33; *Chardon*, 6.11;

Charlestown, 10; *Clariden*, 14; *Clarksfield*, 14.25; *Cleveland*, 1st Ch., thank-offering, 15.50; *Columbus*, Eastwood, 10; *Columbus*, High St., 23; *Conneaut*, thank-offering, 8.65; *Coolville*, 477; *Cortland*, 14.99; *Elyria*, 154.05; *Geneva*, 26.50; *Harmar*, of wh. 25 to const. L. M. Miss Lydia N. Hart, 61.25; *Hudson*, of wh. 5 thank-offering, 18.85; *Jefferson*, 19; *Johnsonville*, 3.75; *Kinsman*, 35.07; *Kelloggsville*, 6 25; *Lindenville*, 20; *Locke*, 3; *Lyme*, thank-offering, 5; *Madison*, 44.30; *Mansfield*, 43.68; *Marietta*, 65; *Medina*, thank-offering, 5; *Mt. Vernon*, of wh. 10 thank-offering, 36; *Newark*, Plymouth, 8; *No. Bloomfield*, 10; *No. Monroeville*, 13.40; *Norwalk*, 10; *Oberlin*, of wh. 5.50 thank-offering, 86.50; *Paddy's Run*, of wh. 14 thank-offering, 28; *Pittsfield*, 17; *Rochester*, 5; *Rock Creek*, 6 50; *Ruggles*, 10.55; *Saybrook*, 10; *Springfield*, of wh. 2.50 thank-offering, 23.85; *Steuben*, of wh. 10 thank-offering, 18; *Twinsburgh*, of wh. 25 to const. L. M. Mrs. Oscar Kelsey, 30; *Unionville*, of wh. 8.35 thank-offering, 22; *Wauseon*, 15; *Wellington*, 50.59, M E., thank-offering, 25, $1,164 46
JUNIOR: *Akron*, Y. P. Asso , 10; *Cleveland*, 1st Ch., Y. P. Soc., 20; *Marietta*, Y. L. Soc., 35; *Springfield*, Y. L. Soc., 20;   85 00
JUVENILE: *Atwater*, Willing Workers, 23; *Conneaut*, M. B., 5; *Harmar*, Wide-Awakes, 12; *Norwalk*, S. S., 12 51; *Ruggles*, M. C., of wh. 1 thank-offering, 11; *Tallmadge*, Cheerful Workers, 28,   91 51

Total, $1,340 97

PENNSYLVANIA.

Allegheny, Plymouth Ch., Aux. Soc., 10; *Conneaut*, Aux. Soc., 6.50, $16 50

Total, $16 50

NORTH DAKOTA BRANCH.

Mrs. R. C. Cooper, of Cooperstown, Treas. *Fargo*, 10.68; *Grand Forks*, 10; *Harwood*, 4; *Wahpeton*, 10, $34 68
JUVENILE: *Fargo*, Gleaners,   10 00
THANK-OFFERING: *Fargo*, 4; *Cooperstown*, 7.75,   11 75

Total, $56 43

SOUTH DAKOTA BRANCH.

Per Mrs. H. H. Smith, of Yankton, Treas. *Howard*, 4.50; *Huron*, 7; *Sioux Falls*, 25; *Valley Springs*, 4; *Yankton*, 26.66, $67 16
JUNIOR: *Yankton*, Y. L., 27 65
JUVENILE: *Deadwood*, Earnest Workers, 6; *Enemy Creek*, Busy Bees, 10, 16 00
THANK-OFFERING: *Valley Springs*, 3 00

Total, $113 81

Per Mrs. F. D. Wilder, of Huron, Treas. *Faulkton*, 6; *Lake Preston*, 5, $11 00
THANK-OFFERING: *Sioux Falls*, 16 55

Total, $27 55
Pierre, 7.75; *Vermillion*, 10, 17 75

Grand total, $159 11

ROCKY MOUNTAIN BRANCH.

Mrs. Hiram R. Jones, of So. Pueblo, Colorado, Treas. *Boulder*, 45; *Cheyenne*, 50; *Colorado Springs*, 79; *Denver*, 2d Ch., 9.25, West Ch., 22.50; *Greeley*, 20; *Longmont*, 19.01; *Manitou*, 8; *So. Pueblo*, 1st Ch., 22 05, 2d Ch., 4; Collection at annual meeting, 10 53, $289 34
THANK-OFFERING: *Denver*, West Ch., 19; *Highland Lake*, 7; *Greeley*, 13, 39 00
JUNIOR: *Colorado Springs*, Y. P. M. Soc., 15 00
JUVENILE: *Cheyenne*, S. S., 25; *Colorado Springs*, Pike's Peak Band, 60; *Denver*, 2d Ch. S. S., 11.45; *Highland Lake*, S. S., 16.55; *Longmont*, S. S., 4.84, 117 84
FOR MORNING STAR: *Cheyenne*, S. S., 10; *Denver*, West Ch., S. S., 10; *Greeley*, S. S., 4.60, M. Band, 2; *Highland*, M. Band, 10; *Highland Lake*, S. S., 16.45; *So. Pueblo*, S. S., 1.70, 54 75

Branch total, $515 93
Denver, 1st Ch., Aux., 100 00

Total, $615 93

WISCONSIN.

WISCONSIN BRANCH —Mrs. R. Coburn, of Whitewater, Treas. *Appleton*, 42.28; *Alderly*, 2; *Baraboo*, 4; *Boscobel*, 2; *Beloit*, 1st Ch., thank-offering, 16; *Clinton*, 10, thank-offering, 17 35; *Columbus*, 14; *Delavan*, 22.70; *Eau Claire*, 10, thank-offering, 18.20; *Elkhorn*, const. Mrs. G. F. Hunter L. M., 31; *Friendship*, 2; *Grand Rapids*, 9; *Genesee*, 9 30; *Janesville*, 14; *Kenosha*, 30; *Koshkonong*, 2.85; *Kilbourn City*, M. M. Jenkins, 10; *Lake Geneva*, 30; *Milwaukee*, Grand Ave. Ch , 35 67, Hanover St. Ch., 17.17; *Menasha*, 40.11; *Milton*, 15; *Oconomowoc*, 14; *Plymouth*, 8; *Royalton*, 5; *River Falls*, 20; *Ripon*, 25; *Rosendale*, 17; *Racine*, Mrs. H. S. Durand, 10; *Springvale*, 8.50; *Waukesha*, 40.20; *Whitewater*, 51.04, $603 37
JUNIOR: *Brandon*, Y. L., 8 50; *Geneva*, Y. People, 10, 18 50
JUVENILE: *Appleton*, 35; *Genesee*, Buds of Promise, 2; *Kilbourn City*, Meth. E. S. S., 10; *Rosendale*, Flower Band, 7, 54 00
FOR MORNING STAR: *Clinton*, S. S., 5 00

Total, $680 87
Expenses, 13 61

Total, less expenses, $667 26

Of the above, 51.55 is thank-offering.

TENNESSEE.

Memphis, Second Ch., Aux. Soc., $19 55

Total, $19 55

TEXAS.

Jefferson, A Friend, thank-offering, $5 00

Total, $5 00

CHINA.

Peking, Mission Band of the Bridgman School, $10 00

Total, $10 00

MISCELLANEOUS.

Sale of leaflets, 30.72; of envelopes, 2; of " Life of Coan," 2; of mittens, 1.50, $36 22

Total, $36 22

Receipts for the month, $11,294 68
Previously acknowledged, 30,601 73

Total, $41,896 41

Board of the Pacific.

MRS. CLERICUS' WISDOM.

BY LUCY MOOAR, OF OAKLAND, CAL.

(Concluded.)

AT Mrs. Stout's we found her sister, Mrs. Drumm, from the city. They were jolly, hearty, comfortable-looking women, both of them, and I breathed a sigh of relief, for I knew Mrs. Clericus was tried and excited, and was not able to be much more tried.

"Well, Mrs. Stout, I've come. You know I told you last Sunday I was coming around for your missionary money."

"Yes, and I said you should have it; but Sarah has been telling me the way they have of doing things: how much money it takes to carry on the business of the Board, and how the missionaries come home for a vacation every few years, and have silk dresses and stylish bonnets, and everything in the best style, and she thinks it is a sin to support so much extravagance, and I have about decided not to give any more money."

"Yes," said Mrs. Drumm, "my brother was traveling in Japan, and he told me all about these things — how the parlors in missionary houses are full of Japanese bric-a-brac, and how the missionaries travel off to the mountains in the summer just like everybody else, and he says the Secretaries at home get big salaries, and only a little of the money gets to the heathen."

I was just boiling over with rage at such bare-faced lying and contraction of spirit. "Just like any body!" Why shouldn't they be "just like any body!" But Becky sat quietly in her chair and spoke in her usual gentle way. (People called her "undemonstrative, and without enthusiasm.")

"I suppose it does take a great deal of money to administer for the Boards, but I have often seen very complete statistics showing that a far less percentage goes to the administration of the Board's business affairs than to that of most business corporations." Then turning to Mrs. Drumm: "I believe you go to Dr. Rostrum's church! He has a very handsome church, and is a very eloquent preacher. Is he at home this summer?"

"O no; he is off on his vacation. He has two months' vacation every year."

"Is he in poor health?"

"O no, he's as healthy as can be; but then he likes a rest, you know. All the other ministers go, and city life is very trying to ministers. We give him a fine salary, and he has only his wife and two children. They have life very pleasant."

"Don't you think the missionaries need vacations just as much as the home workers do? I should like to tell you something about one missionary's life, if you will listen." So she told them what I knew it was most painful for her to speak of — of the life and work of her only brother, in Africa. It was but two years before that he had been called higher, and those who know what a loving, laborious, self-sacrificing work he did, will know what a story Becky Clericus had to tell; and she told it with heart on her lips,

as those speak who have felt the close touch of a life bound in
with the Master's. When she got through there were tears in the
eyes of us all, and I trembled a little lest Becky had not done the
fitting thing.

They said very little, and we took our departure without mentioning the money; but I may tell you that when the money came
in from the auxiliary of Dr. Rostrum's church, twenty-five dollars
was set against Mrs. Drumm's name as a "thank-offering;" and a
friend told me that Mrs. Drumm said she gave it because she had
been "touched of God at Pine Brook." And when Mrs. Stout
sent in her money, there were five dollars instead of her usual two,
and she wrote in the note that she wished it were more.

In a postscript was added: "My sister wishes you to accept five
dollars from her, also, and we are both so glad you told us about
your brother. We have made up our minds that if the Board send
out but one faithful missionary in a year, it is well worth our
while to help its work."

'Twas getting late, and Becky must go home, for there was
supper to get. But as we passed a little cottage whose garden
was gay with posies, she said, "There's Mrs. Bennison in the
garden;" and at that moment Mrs. Bennison looked up — a little
dried up bit of a woman, but looking as if much sweetness had
remained in the drying — and cried, "O, it's you, is it? Come in
and see my pansies." As we stooped over the bed to admire the
bright little flowers, arrayed in robes of purple royalty, but knowing no toiling, she reached up to kiss Becky. "You need not tell
me what you've been doing, my dear; but never mind; these
things move slowly, but they do move. Pine Brook never started
down that mountain but it found company before it got to the
bottom." And we went away with a bunch of heartsease in our
hands and a sense of it in our hearts, to the little parsonage on
the slope of the hill.

Five years ago, dear friends, and this summer, I went to Pine
Brook again, and there were some changes. The ladies' missionary meeting comes every fourth Friday afternoon; and if you
should go in there you would find the *Missionary Herald* and
the *Life and Light*, and you would see a band of ladies who
have learned, little by little, to love the Lord's harvest, wherever
in the world they find the white fields.

One of them said to me, one who a year or two ago would not
have been found in any religious meeting: "It's ignorance, Miss
Kate, that makes people so ugly about givin' to missions; they
don't *know* anything, nor did I. But Mrs. Clericus kept a-comin'
and lendin' me papers: of course I was 'shamed not to read 'em,
and I kept gettin' interested, and now I wouldn't miss a meetin'
for anything, and I lend my own magazines."

And there is a Young Ladies' Circle, too, working along, and,
in its own way, finding out the secret of the giver's joy.

I mustn't forget the missionary concert, must I? where the
young folks read papers, and help the pastor in a way which
makes his heart burn within him. As I write this, I think of
quiet Mrs. Clericus, and I say to myself: "No; it is not always
the woman of one idea that the world needs. There is a place
for her of many ideas who consecrates herself, and every one of
them to the service of Him 'in whom are hid all the treasures of

wisdom and knowledge.'" And I pray that there may be found in my own heart, more and more abounding, "the wisdom that cometh down from above, pure, peaceable, gentle, full of mercy and good fruits."

A NEW DEPARTURE.

A YOUNG LADIES' BRANCH.

At three o'clock P. M. there was an enthusiastic meeting of young ladies, for the purpose of completing the organization of a young ladies' branch of the Board of the Pacific. Miss Ladd, Chairman of the Committee on Constitution, etc., presided. Miss Harriet Mooar was elected Secretary *pro tem.* About fifty young ladies were present.

The constitution recommended by the committee was adopted, article by article, and the following officers were elected to serve one year; President, Miss Lucy Mooar; First Vice-President, Miss Fannie Kellogg; Treasurer, Miss Grace Goodhue; Recording Secretary, Miss Harriet Mooar; Foreign Secretary, Miss Carrie Pond.

The going of Miss Effie Gunnison, of San Francisco, to mission work in Japan, in September, gave an impetus to this new movement, and her salary is assumed by this Young Ladies' Branch.

EVENING EXERCISES.

A large and enthusiastic meeting greeted the representatives of the Woman's Board on the evening of October 8th. Rev. I. E. Dwinell presided. The following programme was carried out: Reading of Scripture and prayer, by Rev. H. W. Jones; report of Recording Secretary, Mrs. S. S. Smith, read by Miss Grace Goodhue; report of the Treasurer, Mrs. R. E. Cole, showing total receipts, $3,203.92, with about one hundred and twenty-three dollars deficit; reports of the foreign and home work by the respective Secretaries, Mrs. Jewett and Mrs. Dwinell, were read by Mrs. Jewett. A very interesting address was delivered by Rev. W. W. Scudder, of Alameda. Just then came the collection, and a feature not mentioned in the programme. Judge Haven came forward, and said he had been called to assist the ladies of the Board in the disposal of a gold chain which had been given them. They would like to have it bought and presented to Mrs. Thoburn, of Rio Vista,— 85 years of age,— the oldest member of the Board, and one of those who helped at its organization. Upon her death it is to go to the then oldest member of the Board, and so pass from oldest to oldest through the coming years. Such was his eloquence, and so great the enthusiasm of the General Association, that before its adjournment, the sum of $103 was realized on the chain. This amount, with the collection of $55.70, enables our Board to start the year about thirty dollars ahead. Such encouragement gives us great cheer in our work.

TWELFTH ANNIVERSARY OF THE WOMAN'S BOARD OF MISSIONS FOR THE PACIFIC.

"There's no enthusiasm about foreign missions in California," said an Eastern lady to me one day.

"Have you ever been to any of the Woman's Board meetings?" was my interrogative reply.

"Well, no; I haven't. I didn't suppose you had much of a Board out here." ·

"Next week comes our anniversary, and I want you to be sure and go. It comes on Thursday. You'll have to leave San Fran-cisco on the 8.30 boat, so as to be in Berkeley by 9.30. I do hope you will plan to be there, for you can't possibly form an opinion on foreign missions in California till you have been to a Board meeting."

BERKELEY, 9.30 A. M., Oct. 8, 1885.

The ladies "are gathering from near and from far," and here, too, comes our Eastern friend. I do hope we'll have one of our best meetings. "Good-morning, Mrs. Observant; I am so glad you could come! Sit right down here. There are not many seats vacant, you see; there are fully one hundred and fifty ladies out, although so early in the morning. That is Mrs. Noble who is presiding. Her husband is pastor of one of our largest San Francisco churches. Miss Fay, our President, is traveling in Europe. At the left of Mrs. Noble sit Mrs. Smith and Mrs. Cole, each of whom has been an offi-cer of the Board from the beginning. That lady next, with the lovely white hair, is Mrs. Warren, whose husband is Home Mission-ary Superintendent. But I can't name them all; besides, it is time for the meeting to begin. . . . Now we are going to have the re-ports from our auxiliaries. We begin with the A's and go through to Z's — seventy-one societies there are, altogether. You don't do that way in the East, I know; you have reports from the secretaries of your branches. We do enjoy this part of our programme, for we find we all have about the same measure of success and failure. We rejoice with those who rejoice, and weep with those who weep (figuratively speaking), and realize, once a year, at least, that we are one sisterhood, from Siskiyon to San Diego. . . .

"A vial of gold-dust in our treasury, 'panned out' by a home missionary's wife. Who bids? It is valued at $8.00." That is the Treasurer who is speaking. "Can it not be bought in shares of $1.00 each?" How quickly those shares were taken — eleven in all, I think! . . . Now we are to have a talk from Miss Berry, who served as a missionary in China two years, under the Presbyterian Board. How every one seems to be enjoying it! No interest here in foreign missions?

Here are some of the reports from auxiliaries:—

Berkeley, First. — Miss Carter reported the Ladies' Society as in a flourishing condition. The report of the Theodora Society was read by Miss Dibble. Much regret was expressed at the long ill-ness of the President, Miss Mardin.

Cloverdale. — The church at Cloverdale sent a written report: "We bring our offerings with thankful hearts, and can report more interest in missions than hitherto. Believing, as we do, that this is an index of spiritual growth, we thank God and take cour-age. We have been able to send $40 to your treasury this year.

D. R. WHEELOCK, *Sec.*"

Nordhoff. — Four towns in the neighborhood unite, holding quarterly foreign missionary meetings.

[*Concluded in next number.*]

Lightning Source UK Ltd.
Milton Keynes UK
UKHW021531090219
336936UK00007B/676/P